A History of the London Stock Market
1945–2009

George G. Blakey

HARRIMAN HOUSE LTD

3A Penns Road
Petersfield
Hampshire
GU32 2EW
GREAT BRITAIN

Tel: +44 (0)1730 233870
Fax: +44 (0)1730 233880
Email: enquiries@harriman-house.com
Website: www.harriman-house.com

First published 1993, second edition published 1994, third edition published 1997.

Fourth edition published in 2000 by Management Books 2000 Ltd, as 'Bulls v. Bears'

The fifth edition published in Great Britain in 2008 by Harriman House Ltd
This edition published in 2010
Copyright © Harriman House Ltd

The right of George G. Blakey to be identified as the author has been asserted
in accordance with the Copyright, Design and Patents Act 1988.

978-1-906659-62-2

British Library Cataloguing in Publication Data
A CIP catalogue record for this book can be obtained from the British Library.

Printed and bound in Great Britain by CPI, Antony Rowe, Chippenham.

CONTENTS

FOREWORD, 2007

I am delighted to introduce this latest edition of George G. Blakey's long-running labour of love.

For investors who lack a crystal ball, history is the next best thing and *A History of the London Stock Market* is my historical reference book of choice. I frequently turn to it when seeking to understand why the financial markets of past years behaved like they did.

A leading broadcaster recently invited me to discuss major bear markets of the twentieth century. They included the 1937-1940 downturn when shares fell by 57 per cent and our worst-ever 73 per cent drop in 1972-1974.

Thanks to George G. Blakey, I quickly established that British investors were hurt by a combination of recession and rising taxes to pay for rearmament from 1937 through to the first few months of 1940. Shares fell 33 per cent during this period.

The trigger for the final sell-off in May and June 1940 was a series of serious military reversals. Many investors feared an invasion by Germany was imminent. Shares slipped an additional 24 per cent during this period. If not for the military threat, the bear market of the late 1930s would have been of normal duration and intensity.

Research into the 1972 to 1974 downturn found another set of surprises. A serious world-wide bout of recession and inflation, what pundits now term stagflation, caused our stock market to lose about half of its value by the end of the summer of 1974. This decline was comparable to falls on Wall Street and Tokyo.

Selling finally ran out of steam at the beginning of October 1974 in New York and Toyko but the UK stock market continued to fall until year-end, eventually losing almost three-quarters of its value. Why did UK investors suffer so much additional pain? Blakey helps to place those depressing times into perspective. He reminds us of the animosity that existed between the Labour party and investors. Their October 1974 election manifesto called for "a fundamental and irreversible shift in the balance of wealth and power in favour of working people".

Shares also reacted negatively to the government's unwillingness to reign back excessive union power and wage demands. On the economic front, November 1974 saw the largest-ever trade gap and a government unable to produce a credible anti-inflation policy. *A History of the London Stock Market* reminds us there was very real fear among investors that Britain was on the verge of complete social and political chaos.

Other lessons emerge if you study the periods surrounding major bull market peaks. The corporate names change from peak to peak but the underlying story remains the same. Greedy investors become captivated by speculative tales spun by glib, persuasive financial salesmen. Shares get bid up to foolish levels. Once prices peak, these same investors learn the hard way of the importance of traditional values like earnings, cash flow and management expertise.

The bull market peak in 2000 featured giants like Enron and Global Crossing, as well as hundreds of lesser names. Shares in many of these over-valued companies eventually declined by 90 per cent or more. Back in 1987, investors clamoured to invest in tiny "shell" companies, operated by entrepreneurs no one had previously heard of. 1974 saw the demise of many second-line financial institutions who borrowed short and lent long, a dangerous strategy to follow during a period of rising interest rates.

Each story was a bit different but the thread linking each peak is strikingly familiar. Just look at the so-called 'credit crunch' of 2007 and reflect on the rueful comment of the Bank of International Settlements back in 1989 on 'the apparent propensity of the banking system to make repeated mistakes on a rather grand scale'. Some things never change!

A famous promoter who lived more than 100 years ago, P.T. Barnum, claimed a sucker is born every minute. Hopefully, a careful reading of Blakey's fine book will help you to avoid this trap.

David Schwartz, stock market historian

December 2007

FOREWORD, 2000

I thoroughly recommend George G. Blakey's book to investors. Reading it offers a painless way of understanding bear markets and of seeing how easy it is to miss opportunities to buy great growth stocks.

The story of the growing divide post-1945 between the first Labour administration's ambitions for a just society and their realisation underlines the inevitable contrast between idealistic politics and practical economics. It also more than justifies the author's contention that the growth of the economy and the stock market owed more to the skill and adaptability of British businessmen than to the plans of politicians. The relative freedom for business conceded by the Conservatives on their return to power in 1951 sparked the first post-War bull market and prompts the reader to wonder why another thirty years had to elapse before the economics of the marketplace were released from their political straitjacket.

From 1965 onwards, there is a chapter devoted to each year. The highlights and important news items of companies like Hanson, Slater Walker, BTR, Polly Peck, Racal, Tomkins, Williams and Cavenham are followed from infancy through to the present day, or to the moment they faded from the scene.

It is interesting to see year by year how the great growth stocks of today appeared to investors then. For example, in 1973 Sainsbury offer for sale of 27% of its equity at 145p a share gave the company an overall market valuation of £117 million. There was no forecast and the P/E ratio based on the 1972/73 figures was a lofty 20.6 against 17 for Tesco. But housewives knew a thing or two, so the issue was 14.5 times oversubscribed and the shares opened at a 17p premium. Anyone who acquired the minimum subscription of 100 shares for £145 would have a holding today worth £5,000.

In 1974, although BTR's share price was depressed by the raging bear market, pre-tax profits for 1973/74 were up by 38% to £6 million, and the target for the following year was £10 million pre-tax; the P/E ratio was only 3.7 with a dividend yield of 9.1%. Although there are bound to be many future bear markets, you may never see such a bargain again.

At the bottom of the bear market on 6th January 1975, the FT 30 share index was selling on an average P/E ratio of 3.8 with a dividend yield of 13.4%; ICI yielded 14.0%, Trust House Forte 26.4% and British Oxygen 19.5%. As George G. Blakey says: "There was no doubt that the market was discounting every possible disaster." Easy to see now, but at the time fear had the upper hand.

The author's comments on the more speculative counters in 1987, following the crash, are also pertinent today: "The October crash was a watershed for these speculative favourites as investors clamoured to sell in an unwilling market where the size had contracted and the spread had widened alarmingly." If a bear market develops today, these kinds of shares, many in the now fashionable bio-tech and computer software fields, are likely to be among the main casualties.

The important point for active private investors is that a bell does not ring at the bottom of a bear market or the top of a bull market. In both cases there are tell-tale signs for an experienced investor that a familiar pattern is developing. This book gives the backcloth and the highlights of the last fifty years. Inexperienced investors will obtain a basis for comparison and experienced investors will have their memories refreshed.

There is also another reason to read this book. Great growth companies can sometimes emerge after being almost unnoticed for many years. There is no way of knowing for sure if a small growth company you select is going to make it all the way. However, this book will give you the highlights of the history of other growth companies as well as those that fell by the wayside. You will obtain a better insight into the characteristics to look for and those to avoid.

Since the first edition, political developments year by year have been fleshed out. The interplay between changes of Government and the stockmarket makes fascinating reading. I recommend this book as an enjoyable and instructive read that captures the spirit of the times. In the absence of a crystal ball, a history book is the next best thing.

Jim Slater

2000

PREFACE

The inspiration for the original edition of *The Post-War History of the London Stock Market* was the work of the same name covering the period 1945-1980 written by the late Alec Ellinger and the late Harvey Stewart of Investment Research, Cambridge. It was much more compact and written from a chartist's point of view, but it still provided practically the only background to the stock market for a newcomer to the investment business. That this has remained the case despite the huge expansion of market size and activity was always a matter of surprise to me and I planned in due time to write a more comprehensive and detailed version of their book. However, an unexpected turn of events leading to the premature interruption of my career in the City, gave me the opportunity to do so rather earlier than intended.

My aim has been to do no more than present the facts together with the comment of the day, and to this end I have used the *Financial Times* – the acknowledged authority in financial reporting – as my principal source material. Wherever possible I have still checked the corporate histories with the companies concerned, and with one notable exception have received their broad approval. Where certain controversial issues are involved, if comment might be interpreted more as criticism, this is likely to be in cases where the objective reporting of the *Financial Times* has been supplemented by personal experience which may have given rise to a measure of prejudice on my part.

The sheer volume of information revealed by a study of over fifty years of stock market history has led inevitably to a considerable degree of editing, and although many more companies and personalities merited inclusion, it was not possible to feature more than a representative selection within the confines of a single volume. However, in this latest edition I have supplemented the political background with a view to making the book as useful to students of politics as it is, I hope, to students of the stock market.

ACKNOWLEDGEMENTS

I am indebted to my agent J.A.Associates for their diligence in seeking out a publisher, and to Nicholas Dale-Harris and James Alexander of Management Books 2000 and to Stephen Eckett of Harriman House for recognising that there could be a place on a business book list for a work about the stock market which was neither academic and full of mathematical formulae, nor 'popular' in the sense that it was a parody of City life portraying all the market professionals as knaves and the investing public as fools.

My thanks too to Martin Hall, John Aarons and Brian Bartholomew at the Stock Exchange, and to Chris Davis, former Chairman of the Institute of Investment Management and Research, for their support, and to Bill Jamieson of *The Scotsman*, John Percival of *Currency Bulletin*, the late David Sawyer and Raymond Salami, for their invaluable help and advice.

I am grateful also to the *Financial Times* for providing me with the raw material to work on, and to Thomson Reuters Datastream for supplying the charts and to Ken Miller for secretarial services.

Last, but by no means least, I wish to express my appreciation for the help and encouragement provided by my wife, Kristin, during the two years it took to research and write the original book.

INTRODUCTION

The history of the UK stock market since 1945 has reflected not only the struggle between the competing economic philosophies of the two main political parties, but also the relative success of the economy in spite of it. The fact that the economy and the stock market have managed to grow and prosper against such a background is a tribute more to the skill and adaptability of British businessmen than to the actions of a succession of Chancellors of the Exchequer, well-intentioned but still governed by political timetables, or often simply overwhelmed by events. Steady and sustainable economic growth accompanied by an improvement in the standard of living, all without too much inflation and unemployment are admirable goals, but the means employed in trying to achieve them have been so diverse and haphazard that the casual observer might be forgiven for thinking that the occasional brief successes have occurred more by luck than judgment. Nationalisation, denationalisation, and renationalisation of the commanding heights of the economy with all the uncertainty thrust upon key industries, could never be interpreted as the reasoned implementation of long-term economic policy in the national interest.

To go back to 1945, it is difficult not to admire the idealism of the first post-War Labour government that gave rise to the conviction that it must 'arm itself with anti-slump powers so that never again as in past years shall prices and productivity and employment all fall away through the failure of private enterprise'. Idealism, however, was not enough. After an initial burst of enthusiasm, the market relapsed when the vision faded thanks to a plethora of bureaucratic controls and the failure of organised labour to respond to the exhortations of its political representatives. At the same time, the creative destruction of the War years had killed off the militaristic traditions in Germany and Japan and led to the emergence of a new professional business class in both countries which was soon to make them formidable competitors in Britain's traditional markets. Indeed, the first sterling devaluation in 1949 coincided with the introduction of the German currency reform, which involved a massive revaluation and laid the foundation of that country's economic miracle.

For Britain, devaluation did little more than mark the first of a series of soft options. In such a climate it was not surprising that the FT 30 remained locked in the 100-150 range for nearly a decade. It broke out only in 1954, after the first post-War Conservative administration had been in office for three years and its moves towards decontrol had at last begun to work through. Unfortunately, the transition from a regime of strict control to one of relative freedom was not the key to economic success. The trade unions had never accepted controls under 'their' government in the first place, while the corporate sector which had done so to a great degree, was now eager to make up lost ground.

It was doubly unfortunate that these first steps towards a market economy coincided with the outbreak of the Korean War in June 1950. Coming so soon after the 1949 devaluation, it provided a major inflationary boost as commodity prices rose worldwide. The cost of imports shot up 50% over the next two years, affecting final output prices directly and also indirectly through wage bargains revised in line with the cost of living. By the end of 1952 prices were up nearly 25%, and by 1958 the cost of living had risen 50% on immediate pre-devaluation levels. Inflation was here to stay. The stock market responded, practically doubling to 338 by the end of the decade, reversing the yield gap in the process in August 1959 as the urge to get out of fixed interest stocks and into equities gathered pace. No longer would equities have to yield more than gilts in order to compensate for a supposedly higher risk. They had proved themselves to be much more exciting and profitable. Capital gain as well as dividend growth was now factored into the income calculation and 'total return' had become the name of the game.

The first half of the sixties saw little progress for the stock market at the tail end of a tired Conservative administration, but the break through the 400 level of the FT 30 in October 1967 owed less to hopes for the success of Labour's National Plan than to expectations of its certain failure. Devaluation three weeks later, accompanied by undertakings to a supranational body, the International Monetary Fund, were an acknowledgement by the Labour government of its inability to manage affairs, sabotaged as it was at every turn by its natural supporters, the trade unions. Their attitude to negotiations remained dominated by the folk memories of Tolpuddle and Tonypandy, and without their cooperation all attempts at planning the economy were doomed as surely as those of the Attlee administration in 1945-51.

By the end of the sixties, the motor industry had provided the classic illustration of what was going wrong with much of British industry. In the late fifties, Japanese car manufacturers stopped making the Austin Cambridge under licence and began to produce their own models for both home and export markets. In 1958 they produced 50,000 cars. In 1961 the figure had risen to 250,000, and in 1970 to 3 million, making Japan the second largest manufacturer in the world outside the US. Similarly, even as early as 1956, the once war-devastated German motor industry had toppled the UK from first place in Europe, and by 1968, at the time of British Motor Corporation's £400 million merger with Leyland, Volkswagen had become the biggest carmaker in the world outside the US. Production in the UK reached a peak of 1.9 million in 1972 and since then it has been downhill all the way, a performance symbolised by the fate of British Leyland, once the country's biggest exporter. Plagued by bad management, shifts in government policy and constant industrial disputes, and in spite of being propped up with over £3 billion of taxpayers' money, twenty years later British Aerospace was paid, quite literally, to take away what was left of the group.

But during this same period, fortunately for the economy, another side of British industry began to emerge. Entrepreneurs like Arnold Weinstock at GEC (1961), Raymond Brown and Ernest Harrison at Racal (1961), James Hanson and Gordon White at Hanson Trust (1964), James Goldsmith at Cavenham Foods (1965) and Owen Green at BTR (1969), laid the foundations of industrial empires and had no difficulty in raising through the stock market the capital they needed to expand.

There was no reason for the next Conservative government to congratulate itself.

Not only did it have to contend with the same obstructive trade unions but also with its own undisciplined supporters, the banks and the other lending institutions, as Chancellor Barber embarked upon his 'dash for growth'. To complicate matters further, the good years of economic management in the US were coming to an end. Vietnam War spending had taken its toll on the economy, the mighty dollar crumbled and in 1971 the system of parities established at Bretton Woods in 1944 finally broke down. America's failure now became the world's failure. The absence of a level playing field in economic management has to be taken for granted, but the fact that neither party of government could rely upon the cooperation and self-discipline of its own supporters left no alternative for Britain but to elevate the policy of 'muddling through' to the appearance of a virtue in a climate of national and international free-for-all.

The late sixties and most of the seventies witnessed an extraordinary boom in real assets, helping to form attitudes and set trends that persist to this day. During this long period of broadly rising inflation, interest rates lagged and it rapidly became obvious that it paid to borrow in order to invest in assets, whether in the form of a private house or an office block. In 1970, for example, when borrowing costs were around 8%, the yields on residential and office properties were of the order of 14% and 9% respectively. As property prices rose in acknowledgment of what was perceived as an anomalous situation, this yield gap also went into reverse, and the new order managed to survive the 1973/74 collapse that followed over-speculation fuelled by excessive lending. The shakeout was inevitable as the Barber Boom peaked, but the oil crisis in the autumn of 1973, which saw the price of oil quadruple in a matter of weeks, made it a worldwide one and intensified the impact on the UK economy. In one sense, OPEC did the industrialised world a favour by pointing out the folly of relying upon the cheap and plentiful supply of a commodity, the production of which it no longer controlled, to subsidise its prodigality in other areas. It was another milestone along the road towards learning to live in a competitive market economy.

The trade unions were not prepared to cooperate with the Heath administration's brand of interventionism designed to face up to this new reality and inflation took off. Ironically, it was left to a Labour government to try to deal with the aftermath of the Barber Boom, and to preside over the collapse of financial confidence in 1973/74 that saw the FT 30 back to below 150 amid talk of industrial breakdown and even rumours of a coup d'état. Under the tutelage of the International Monetary Fund, Chancellor Healey tried to pursue economically responsible policies, cutting back on public spending and restraining monetary growth, but he was unable to win the backing of the trade unions for anything but the shortest-term implementation of such unsocialist measures. Extravagant wage demands accompanied by strike threats had become standard operating procedure in industrial negotiations and there were no signs in the late seventies that any change was forthcoming in an environment where inflation had become practically a way of life. Reaction against this attitude paved the way for the return of the Conservatives under Mrs Thatcher in 1979, and the first practical efforts to get a grip on an economy that had given up the competitive struggle and was close to descending into anarchy. The event coincided with a very similar hard-line approach by the US authorities.

The Iranian revolution and then the war between Iran and Iraq had resulted in drastic cuts in oil production, driving up oil prices yet again and boosting inflation into double digit figures. President Carter appointed Paul Volcker as chairman of the Federal Reserve with the task of 'slaying the inflationary dragon'. Instead of tinkering with short-term interest rates, he decided to target the monetary base, and real interest rates soared in response to a restrictive monetary policy designed to squeeze inflation out of the system but at the risk of the economy enduring a brutal period of recession. If President Carter's political will faltered, that of his successor did not and President Reagan backed Paul Volcker to the hilt.

In the UK, by happy coincidence, Chancellor Howe's 'Medium Term Financial Strategy' very largely mirrored the policy being employed in the US with its emphasis on restraining monetary growth and reducing public expenditure allied with corporate and personal tax cuts. Just as in the US, industry was hard hit, especially the manufacturing side, but a growing flow of North Sea oil took the strain on the current and capital accounts. Two years later, critics of these 'tough love' policies were proved wrong as the inflationary momentum of the sixties and seventies was clearly seen to have been broken, a view that quickly became current in practically every capitalist economy around the world as equities and bonds moved strongly and consistently upwards. The Dow topped 1000 for the first time and kept going, while in London the FT 30 sailed through the 600 level. The continuing boom owed much to the collapse of the oil price as well as that of other basic commodities as the laws of supply and demand reasserted themselves after three recession-hit years, to the benefits of enforced reorganisation and rationalisation showing up in a dramatic increase in corporate profits, and to the attractive pricing of privatisation issues.

The final seal of approval to the Thatcher government's "there is no alternative" policies was conferred by the crushing defeat of the politically-inspired miners' strike of 1984/85 and then the print workers' rebellion against the introduction of new technology at Wapping. Coupled with the introduction of legal curbs on trade union freedoms, these events not only effectively ended half a century of industrial strife but they also put the unions out of the regulatory business. No longer were they 'combinations in restraint of trade'. But once again, the financial establishment still had lessons to learn. A new wave of disruption and loss was soon to follow from the irresponsible lending in the new climate of deregulation, by banks and financial institutions, ever-eager to fuel the consumer booms and corporate hyperactivity on which they battened. The process was aggravated by the continuing obsession with asset appreciation, this time driven not by inflation, but by competition and the apparently unlimited willingness of the banks to fund property development and investment.

The October 1987 Crash provided no more than a brief interruption to such excesses, which were not to burn themselves out for another two years. But while these areas had acquired a 'haven' status for institutional funds to the detriment of what was seen as dull and unreliable manufacturing industry, the market still managed to provide the backing for a new generation of entrepreneurs like Nigel Rudd and Brian McGowan at Williams Holdings (1981) and Greg Hutchings at Tomkins (1983), enabling them to launch their ambitious plans for transforming key sections of manufacturing industry.

Arguably the confluence of policies in London and Washington when politicians and economists got together to elevate economic necessity over political expediency, served to lay the foundations for the low inflation, low interest rate environment that has led to their extraordinary growth in economic prosperity in the US and the UK and among the developing nations over the next 25 years. The accompanying worldwide bull market has had a few hair raising blips along the way, but it is in the nature of stock markets not just to mirror but also to exaggerate the trends of their underlying economies, and fortunately the in-built resilience and flexibility of those economies has enabled markets to tolerate such extremes. Thus, stock markets have dipped, recovered and moved ahead again in response to the October 1987 Crash, the 'Asian Contagion' crisis of 1997, the Russian Default and the LTCM failure of 1998, 9/11, and then the DotCom collapse of 2000/2003, a process aided by the strenuous efforts of the world's central bankers led by the US Federal Reserve, who like sea captains in a storm have learned to keep their ships on course and all our heads above water.

As far as the London stock market is concerned, the most ground-breaking change of the post-War years was the so-called Big Bang of the late eighties, when most of the stockbrokers, jobbers, merchant banks, commercial banks and fund managers ceased to be separate entities and came together under one roof and often under a foreign flag. The City has since been described as the financial equivalent of Wimbledon, where we provide the playing area and the foreigners walk away with the prizes. This development also raised the game to a new level of sophistication. The Dickensian offices disappeared along with the marble floor of the Stock Exchange in Throgmorton Street with its jobbers' pitches set up like those of bookmakers at a race meeting. Banks of screens now dominated shiny new offices, often far away from the famous Square Mile of the City of London. Where once simply shares and bonds were traded, all sorts of new products began to make an appearance. Traded options were the first, soon to be followed by a whole range of exchange-traded derivatives. Clearly the City had come a long way from the days when visitors to the Public Gallery of the London Stock Exchange would be treated to a film show demonstrating that it existed for the primary purpose of raising capital for industry and providing liquidity for investors. Wall Street went through much the same transition following the advent of the Financial Services Modernisation Act that did away with the Glass-Steagall Act, the Depression-era law limiting the ability of banks, investment firms and insurance companies to trespass on each other's markets.

That this new era of deregulation should be followed by the collapse of the USSR thanks to the evident failure of its economic system based on state control and central planning and by the dawn of the information technology revolution as a defence-related communications back-up system evolved into the worldwide web, was to create a unique combination of circumstances seemingly designed to inspire the unprecedented economic growth of the last decade. It was now obvious to China, to India and to Russia's new leaders that central planning was not the way to go and their embrace of free market capitalism has led their extraordinary resurgence to become giants in the world economy of today. Such developments have been reflected in stock markets across the world. The London stock market was quick to recognise and adapt to the new world order and many companies that began their lives as relative minnows in London have been transformed into global leaders. Vodafone, for example, was originally part of Racal from which it was partially demerged in 1988 with a market capitalisation of £1.7 billion. Today it is the world's top mobile phone operator with a market capitalisation of £100 billion, although to demonstrate the uncertainty that accompanies any stock market investment it is worth noting that Vodafone's share price today is a little under half its peak attained ten years ago.

The big domestic banks were also eager to seize the opportunities presented by globalisation and as prime beneficiaries of the IT revolution were ideally positioned to do so, even if it meant that the question, 'when did you last see you bank manager?' was meaningless to anyone under fifty. However, their headlong rush to expand their market share and to exploit the new financial instruments has been criticised for being inspired more by interbank rivalry than by sound economic logic. Hence their dramatic fall from grace over the past three years, a fate shared by their American and European counterparts, as markets realised that the banks themselves were becoming the first victims of the 'credit crunch' for which they were primarily responsible.

It seems that many of our bankers and businessmen were no more altruistic and skilled in the direction of the economic, monetary and industrial policies than our politicians. Indeed, they often had their own agendas for building corporate empires and personal fortunes, derived from a cynical and ruthless transformation of stock and bond markets from their primary role as servants of industry into casinos rigged to rival anything to be found in Las Vegas or Macao. As a result, governments have had to return to centre stage, pick up the pieces and take control of banks and financial institutions and even major industrial enterprises. The rapid implementation by governments across the globe of the greatest financial stimulus in history appears to have avoided systemic failure in the banking system, and stock markets everywhere have rebounded dramatically in the confident expectation that the worst is over and the foundations of economic recovery have been laid. However, in solving one problem by bailing out the private sector with largesse from the public purse, governments have created another by elevating the risk of default to a national level. Sovereign states are now the leveraged institutions in need of rescue.

This presents a major problem for the Western democracies since their political process involves giving the electorate what it wants and necessary but unpopular policies all too often will be watered down for political considerations. On the other hand, authoritarian states like China and Russia have no such hindrance, a distinction that can only hasten to shift the power and prestige from America and the West to China and other emerging giants. Furthermore, the shift is going to be accelerated by the formers' self-imposed and costly climate change legislation at a time when China, now leading the developing nations' G77 organisation, has no intention of rolling back its industrialisation programme by adopting any such measures. After all, the bulk of their billion plus population is too accustomed to living from hand to mouth to worry about climate continuing to do what it has done since time began.

As for the future, how to avoid the recurrence of another financial crisis of such magnitude is the big question but one with no obvious answer to suit everyone. FDR's proposed solution in 1933 of 'a strict supervision of all banking and credits... and an end to speculation with other people's money' led to the passing of the Glass-Steagal Act separating commercial from investment banking. Now Paul Volcker's plan to split off proprietary trading and involvement in hedge funds and private equity from commercial banking does not find favour with the all-powerful banking lobby but if it gets through Congress, it should serve to take much of the risk element out of the day-to-day business of banking. Taken in conjunction with Basel's more demanding capital requirements, the tendency to future booms and busts should be diminished, but it should not be forgotten that in a fast developing world there is another banking system out there to which the Volcker Rule does not apply and where the Basel writ does not run. Clearly, management of such issues is going to require international cooperation and political skills of the highest order ,but considering that it was the lack of skill and judgement on the part of our political and business leaders that got us where we are today, the investor would be well advised not to bet too early on a successful outcome.

The Moving Finger remains firmly attached to the Invisible Hand.

George G. Blakey

January 2010

The History

"All these clever men were prophesying with every variety of ingenuity what would happen soon, and they all did it in the same way, by taking something they saw 'going strong', as the saying is, and carrying it as far as ever their imagination could stretch. This, they said, was the true and simple way of anticipating the future."

G.K. Chesterton
'The Napoleon of Notting Hill'

PRELUDE 1939-45

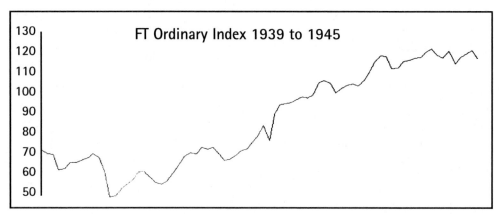

FT Ordinary Index 1939 to 1945

130
120
110
100
90
80
70
60
50

Source: Thomson Reuters Datastream

A review of the war years

"Buy when blood is running in the streets" is the most reliable, if the most difficult to follow, of time-honoured market maxims. It was true, quite literally, in June 1940, a month which witnessed the evacuation from Dunkirk, the entry of Italy into the War, and the fall of France. German forces appeared poised to cross the Channel and the *Financial Times* Ordinary index plunged to a low of 49.4.

Fears of the coming war in Europe had depressed both gilts and equities in the two years leading up to the outbreak of war and the actual event came as not so much of a shock as it had in 1914. The Stock Exchange bowed to the dislocations of war and closed from 1st to 6th September 1939. When it reopened gilts and equities were only fractionally lower with their indices at around the 100 and 80 marks, respectively.

Strict control of the capital markets was the cornerstone of the government's war financing policy. Bank Rate was cut from 4% to 2%, minimum prices were set for gilts, and interest rates were simply not permitted to rise as the war went on. In addition, a whole package of emergency financial measures was introduced. It included large increases in taxation, both personal and corporate, higher duties on tobacco, beer and spirits, and the levying of purchase tax on a wide range of consumer goods, the prices of which were in most cases strictly regulated. At the same time, in order to avoid a sharp rise in the cost of living and its unsettling effects on the working population, the prices of essential foodstuffs were heavily subsidised. In combination, all of these measures gave a degree of artificial stability to markets.

At this stage, the principal beneficiary from war prospects was Home Rails, and in anticipation of greatly increased activity their index, which had begun in 1939 at close to 40, reached 47.4 by the beginning of 1940. There was, however, no rush for gold or gold shares. Gold was a fixed-price commodity in 1939 and had been since 1934. The price was raised marginally to 168/- an ounce, but government restrictions on the distribution of profits and the prospect of disruption of production, meant that gold shares failed to benefit.

Wall Street at War

Wall Street's performance during the War years paralleled very closely that of London. The Dow Jones Industrial Average had reached a post-1929/32 recovery high of 194.4 in 1937 but declined sharply in the wake of the recurrent clashes between the Administration and business. Political factors continued to block any sustained recovery as did anxieties over the course of the War in Europe. The attack by the Japanese on Pearl Harbour and their initial successes in the Far East pushed the Dow to a low point of 92.92 in early 1942, but thereafter it was recovery all the way. The 1937 peak was matched by VJ Day under the influence of post-War prospects judged to be very promising in the light of the huge increase in productivity in the war era, the large rise in national income, and the political commitment to full employment. All these factors were expected to sustain both income and profits at levels well above pre-War peaks, and by the close of 1945 the Dow had crossed the 200 mark.

The military disasters of June 1940 proved a major test of the stability of financial markets. Gilts, sustained by the official cheap money policy and encouraged by the Churchill leadership, maintained their levels even in the country's "darkest hour". Industrials and Home Rails, on the other hand, both slumped dramatically but from that point on, recovery was practically continuous. There were minor reactions on the news of the German invasion of Russia in June 1941 and when the Japanese attacked Pearl Harbour in December, but the industrial index still managed to end the year at 85. Anxieties over the fall of Singapore and then Rommel's push into Egypt caused industrials to slip below 80 in February and again in June 1942 but the recovery was swift and subsequently aided by the Allied landings in North Africa in November, leaving the index at 93 at the year end. The turn of the tide in 1943, marked by Russian successes on the Eastern Front and then confirmed by the German and Italian surrenders in Tunisia in May, led to all- round gains. By the end of the year the gilts index stood at 112.8, the FT 30 at 100.6 and Home Rails at 67.6.

"Awaiting the sunrise"

Markets could now begin to set their sights on post-War prospects and the advance gathered pace after the Normandy landings in June 1944. A combination of low returns in investment quality stocks and high taxation prompted a search for more remunerative, if more speculative, holdings. Investors remained cautious, however, balancing the potential trials and tribulations of the post-War economy with consideration of the new and exciting commercial opportunities created by changes in habits and taste acquired during the War years coupled with the benefits of accelerated research.

Prosperity in Store

Stores edged up slowly during the later War years. Their dividend yields were modest but it was widely forecast that they would benefit in peace time from a renewed wave of consumer spending after five years of enforced restraint. At the same time, investor enthusiasm was tempered by consideration of the difficulties stores would have in obtaining stock, increasing floor space and finding enough counter staff. The investment statistics of three principal stores in March 1945 were as follows:

Company	Shares in issue (m)	Price	Earned %	Paid %	Dividend Yield %
Woolworths	5/- Ord. 30.0	78/6	68	45	3.0
Marks & Spencer	5/- Ord.& A 8.45	73/6	70	35	2.0
Debenhams	1/- Ord. 10.0	12/-	100	25	2.0

The worries were well-founded. Britain was now heavily in debt to the rest of the world. Invisible earnings, always a big component in British calculations, had halved and the country's ability to rebuild its export trade had greatly diminished thanks to a 30% reduction in its merchant fleet and the dislocation, destruction and rundown of so much productive capacity at home. At the same time, government expenditure abroad, mainly for maintenance of the armed forces, was five times as great as it had been pre-War. A contemporary US survey estimated that Britain would have to double its exports to regain pre-War living standards.

Neither was it going to be a simple matter to devote physical resources to building up the export trade. The civilian population and returning service personnel had endured great hardship and deprivation during the War and their needs, especially in terms of housing and clothing, had to be met. There was no alternative but for the government to make a virtue of necessity and create a strong domestic market upon which to build the export trade. Certainly the demand existed and, fortunately, so did the ability to pay. As a whole the population was much better off. The cost of living in 1944 was 50% higher than in 1939 but weekly earnings were 81.5% higher and spread among an employed population that had grown by 3 million during the War years.

The Coming Motoring Revival

Motoring was obviously going to resume and increase its popularity in peacetime and from early 1945 investors intensified their search for bargains in the industry. During the War private motoring had virtually come to a standstill. Many cars had been requisitioned and all available production went on military and official use. Furthermore, there was no petrol. Garage companies suffered greatly and their share prices all languished well below pre-War levels. **Lex Garages**, with its many depots in and around London, began to attract buyers and rose from 3/- in January 1945 to 5/3 in May. Midlands-based **Kennings** also became a target and over the same period advanced from 20/- to 26/6, with prospects further enhanced by its involvement in hire purchase, property development and agricultural and commercial vehicle distribution. Interestingly, even at the higher prices, Lex was capitalised at just £145,000 and Kennings at £1.58 million. Among motor manufacturers, **Jaguar Cars** also found buyers. Originally SS Cars – the name had been changed at the outbreak of war for obvious reasons – the marque had always had an enthusiastic following, but at 16/6 in 1945 the price was still a long way from its pre-War peak of 25/6. Jaguar's equity market capitalisation in October 1945 was just £400,000.

Moreover, the War had stimulated technological breakthroughs which had created new industries. This was in sharp contrast to the period after the end of the 1914-18 War when the emphasis had been more on reviving the old staple industries of the nineteenth century. Now there were new developing industries like electricals and electronics, radio and television, synthetic textiles, chemicals, pharmaceuticals and plastics, automobiles and jet engines, all of which would come into their own in peace time. Industrially, Britain had taken the decisive leap into the twentieth century. The whole country was looking forward and no longer back.

"War Babies"

"War Babies" was a term used affectionately by investors to describe companies whose development had been greatly aided by wartime orders and where the potential for further growth post-1945 was reflected in their share prices. Two leading high fliers in this category were **Decca** and **De La Rue**. Neither had been very successful pre-War but electronic expertise transformed the prospects of the former, and plastic technology those of the latter during the War. Decca invented a navigational system which was widely employed by the Allied forces and is still in operational use today, and then developed a revolutionary gramophone and record system ready for the peacetime market. De La Rue, although best known as a security printer, set up a plastics subsidiary in 1941. It developed Formica, a brand name which became practically a generic term for plastic, and with no timber being imported at all, demand for plastic substitutes soared. By the end of 1945, Decca's share price had risen from 16/6 to almost 70/-, and De La Rue's from 25/- to over £11.

1945–50

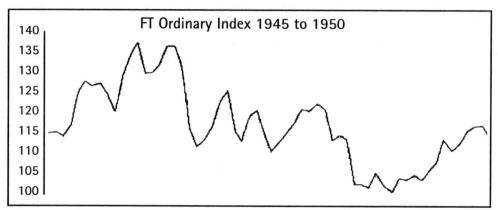

FT Ordinary Index 1945 to 1950

Source: Thomson Reuters Datastream

Labour takes charge

It was this spirit of change which led to one of the most dramatic political upsets of all time. Against the most pessimistic computation in House circles of a majority of as low as 30 seats for Churchill and the Conservatives, the Labour Party under Clement Attlee swept into power on 26th July 1945 with a 146-seat lead. "Never has so much been forgotten so quickly by so many," wrote Julian Amery to Winston Churchill. The FT Industrial index, which had risen to 118 on the eve of the declaration of the poll, confident of the maintenance of the political status quo, slumped to 115 the next day. The selling continued and at the beginning of August the index touched a post-election low of 105.9. Gilts largely held their prices on the prospect of a continuing cheap money policy under Hugh Dalton, the new Chancellor, while gold shares and dollar securities moved up on hedge buying. A measure of the shock to the City can be gauged from the *Financial Times* editorial on 7th August. It referred to Labour's victory as "the most serious reverse since the dark days of 1940", adding that the market's reaction was "a commentary on the hopes and fears engendered throughout the world of investment by the advent of a Socialist government whose clearest intentions seem to be embodied in the one word 'nationalisation'." And the King's Speech, announcing the proposed nationalisation of the coal industry and the Bank of England, did nothing to allay these fears. Even Wall Street juddered on the view that "if it can happen there, it can happen here".

> ### Properties out of favour
>
> Property companies remained the Cinderellas of the stock market after the War, right up to the early 'fifties. Their investment standing was impaired by a combination of factors, namely: (1) war damage, particularly for those companies with large holdings in the City of London; (2) the difficulty of getting licences to repair or rebuild; (3) rent restrictions; and (4) the unsympathetic attitude of the Labour government which was in power from July 1945 until October 1951. **City of London Real Property** (CLRP), with nine acres of freehold properties in the City and seven acres of leasehold, did not begin to pick up until the Conservative election victory of 1951, when controls began to be relaxed. Priced at 19/- in 1939, six years later the shares were 14/6 to provide a market capitalisation of around £6 million against a 1944 asset value of £12.1 million. **London & County Freehold & Leasehold**, the proprietor of Key Flats, was the largest operator in the private rented sector. Its properties were in the balance sheet at their 1928 valuation of £10.25 million and, in 1945, at 23/-, the company was capitalised at £5.7 million.

But just as Dunkirk presented the investor with a buying opportunity, so did the Labour victory. Less than three months later, on the eve of Chancellor Dalton's first budget, the industrial index had managed to recover practically all the ground lost since the election. The budget itself was hailed by the *Financial Times* as a "tonic for both industry and labour". Income tax was cut by 1/- to 9/- in the pound, Excess Profits Tax (EPT) was slashed from 100% to 60%, personal allowances were increased, and many consumer items were freed from purchase tax. The stock market responded by having its most active week on record and industrials moved into new high ground at 119.6, just topping the previous peak of 118.5 achieved on 30th April.

> ### £sd
>
> The pre-decimalisation currency in everyday use until 1971 was complicated in the extreme and a mystery to all foreigners. There were 240 pence or 20 shillings to the pound. Decimalisation retained the pound by consolidating every 2.4 pence into one new penny. Thus a shilling made up of 12 old pence became one containing 5 new pence.
> Terms relatively commonly used until 1971 were 'guinea' for 21/-, 'crown' for 5/-, 'half a crown' for 2/6 and 'florin' for 2/-.

Clearly markets, too, were becoming imbued with the spirit of change and were prepared to give untried Socialist policies the benefit of the doubt. Even nationalisation had lost its terrors. Investors now welcomed the prospect of receiving compensation for old and rather dull holdings and the ability to reinvest the proceeds in new and more exciting ventures. Consequently, when on 21st December the government announced its plans for the nationalisation of the 850 undertakings that made up the coal industry, colliery shares rose and other equities rose with them.

The Dalton "cheap money" era

Even the Investment Control Bill, introduced in January 1946, was greeted as a bull point for equities in that by restricting the supply of new issues, it would prolong the bull market by leaving investors' demand for stock unsatisfied. There is little doubt that a year earlier such legislation would have been regarded by the City as part of the socialist apparatus for the control and direction of industry to its certain detriment.

Industrials had moved broadly sideways since the ending of the War in May 1945, albeit staying at the upper end of the range, and it was only after Chancellor Dalton's first full budget on 9th April 1946 that investor enthusiasm really began to take hold. Chief among the measures was the scrapping of Excess Profits Tax by the end of the year, and there was no mention of limitation or onerous taxation of dividends. Investors were both surprised and relieved and the industrial index topped 120 by the end of the month on record turnover. The market clearly had warmed to a Chancellor who believed it was the aim of the government "to cheapen money and to lower rates of interest to the greatest extent that economic and financial conditions permit". Of course, the cheap money policy had not been a creation of the new Labour government. It was one which had been determinedly pursued by successive administrations since 1932, the year 5% War Loan had been converted to a 3.5% coupon. Low interest rates had been designed as a key feature of the full employment policy between the wars, then became a cornerstone of financing during the Second World War, and post-1945 they were regarded as an absolute necessity to see the economy through the vital period of reconstruction and rehabilitation.

Sentiment was further aided in July when US Congress voted its approval for a $3.75 billion loan to help the UK "over the hump" in restoring its economy and covering its adverse balance of payments. This was a great relief to the market. Approval had by no means been a fait accompli. Initial negotiations had been undertaken with the Churchill administration and there were real doubts that Congress would vote through a loan to a socialist government.

Chinese or Japanese Bonds?

Immediately after the ending of the War in the Pacific, there was no doubt among investment commentators that Chinese bonds were the ones to buy, not Japanese. Their reasoning was that the US would pour millions of dollars into China to help rebuild its war-devastated economy and that the Chiang Kai-Shek government would thus inevitably triumph over its Communist opponents. Japan, on the other hand, was considered likely to be crippled by reparation payments for the foreseeable future, quite apart from the wide-spread conviction that it was morally repugnant to invest in that country. As a result, in 1946 Chinese bonds were selling at around £70-80 as against £17-25 for the principal Japanese loans. However, it soon became clear that investors preferred the "speculative" attractions of Japanese bonds to the "investment" merits of the Chinese, an approach which was soon seen to be fully justified when the Communists seized power in 1949 and the Chiang Kai-Shek administration decamped to Taiwan. By now Chinese bonds were back to £12-16 while those of Japan had crept up into the £35-55 range. The Korean War put the finishing touches to this role reversal as the US turned its attention to bolstering Japan's position in South-East Asia as a bulwark against the spread of Communism. By mid-1951 Chinese bonds were practically a nominal market at £8-12, while Japanese loans were actively trading in the £50-80 range.

Inflationary pressures build up

However, it was at about this time that some commentators began to point to inflationary dangers ahead. All the signs were there, they argued. Crowding in shops, queues, waiting lists and a flourishing black market, all indicated a physical inability of current production to satisfy the pent-up demand for goods and services by a public that had gone without for five years. Prices began to rise and the inflation hedge argument for buying equities made its appearance. As an *FT* editorial pointed out at the beginning of May, industrial equities were practically the only example of pre-War prices remaining in a world where real values had appreciated by 50% or more. As if to confirm this view, a 16.66% rise in rail charges at the end of May was greeted with a surge of buying leading equities under conditions of acute stock shortage, taking the index to 126.2.

The Chancellor's cheap money policy now began to come in for criticism. While the provision of cheap capital to government and industry at a time when high expenditure was required to rebuild the country's infrastructure was clearly desirable, it was not without its dangers. After all, critics pointed out, the whole policy rested upon interference with the normal functioning of supply and demand in the capital markets. The increasing unimportance of the debt burden could encourage wasteful spending by government and industry, and also act as a disincentive to reduce debt. On the other side of the coin, cheap money could discourage saving to a point where the holders of capital might prefer to spend it on consumer goods and services rather than invest it for the benefit of industry. Such considerations did not appear to worry the Chancellor or investors. Later in the year he issued an irredeemable stock with a 2.5% coupon at par, and it was snapped up.

The *Financial Times* Industrial Ordinary 30 Share Index (FT 30)

On January 1st 1947, the *Financial Times* decided to discontinue using its broader Industrial index, and to establish its index of 30 leading industrial ordinary shares as the new market barometer. The FT 30 had been compiled first in 1935 with a base value of 100.

The 30 constituents on 1st January were:

Guest Keen	Watney Coombe Reid
Vickers	Imperial Tobacco
United Steel	Tate & Lyle
Murex	London Brick
EMI	Associated Portland Cement
General Electric	Pinchin Johnson
Rolls Royce	Imperial Chemical
Hawker Siddeley	Dunlop
Courtaulds	Turner & Newall
J&P Coats	William Cory
Lancashire Cotton	Swan Hunter
Patons & Baldwins	Morris Motors
Harrods	Leyland Motors
Woolworths	P & O
Distillers	Spillers

In this text, for the sake of ease of comparison year by year, we have quoted the FT 30 throughout to record the movement of equities even though they may be referred to as "industrials" and "ordinaries". Following its introduction in 1962, the FT Actuaries series is also quoted, and from 1984, the new FTSE100 share index tends to become the principal yardstick.

There were two developments in the autumn of 1946 which could have had serious repercussions on London equities. In the event, they caused nothing more than a relatively minor and short-lived reaction in the indices. One was a severe shake-out on Wall Street, pulling the Dow back from over 200 in mid-July to 163 in mid-October. The other was the prospect of an acute coal shortage threatening industry with shutdown. But at the time investors were far more concerned with seeking a better return on their capital than that available on government stocks, and in pursuit of this aim they competed for a limited supply of good quality industrial debentures and preferences and for leading equities. In July a £6 million offering of a 3.5% Debenture from Dunlop was seven times oversubscribed, and a general shortage of prospectuses for new issues led to a Stock Exchange ruling that investors could make their applications on ordinary notepaper. The attraction of equities was further enhanced during the second half of the year by a great number of high percentage dividend increases and even though the FT 30 had risen from 112 to 134 since the beginning of the year, the average dividend yield was still 3.54% whereas that on Consols had fallen from 2.74% to 2.54%.

Equities were given yet another boost in November when compensation terms for the nationalisation of the railways were announced. Stockholders who had been enjoying yields of about 4.5% were to be bought out at market value with government stock carrying the rate of interest found to be ruling on 2nd January 1948, a figure widely assumed to be 2.5%. These terms were condemned as confiscatory, and started a scramble for good class industrial equities which were yielding a full point more on average. Not surprisingly, the year ended in fine form with both the gilt and equity indices at new peaks.

The Fuel Crisis

As is so often the case in the markets, a strong move up in the face of what appear to be serious and obvious problems, does not necessarily mean that these problems have been adequately discounted. On 2nd January 1947, ironically the vesting date for the nationalisation of the coal industry and in the middle of one of the severest winters of the century, Electrical & Musical Industries (EMI) announced that it was on the verge of a total shutdown as a result of the lack of fuel supplies. The next day the FT 30 hit a new peak. It continued to rise until 18th January when it touched 140.6, but reality reasserted itself in February and the index crashed to 126 as industry after industry was forced to curtail production. By March industry was practically at a standstill.

The government's honeymoon period with the markets was nearing its end. The curbing of private enterprise was coming to be seen not only as a political act offering no compensating advantages, but also as one which had created an economic void nationalisation was incapable of filling. There were plenty of departmental plans and targets but a lack of planning and control to cover the whole economy. Hence the coal crisis and the acute shortage of practically every essential commodity accompanied by swingeing price rises.

Much of the blame for this state of affairs now began to be laid at the door of organised labour. While politicians on both sides of the House stressed the need for greater productivity to overcome the shortfalls in production, the TUC was demanding a 40-hour week and "closed shop" agreements, and absenteeism in the coal mines was recognised as a major cause of the fuel crisis. Because of its historic links, the Labour government was able neither to control the demands of the TUC nor to disassociate itself from them.

More austerity measures

A better than expected budget in April followed by a bumper crop of dividend announcements prompted a strong rally in mid-May which almost reached the January peak, but that was the market's swansong. Gilts also failed to regain their best levels of November. The first post-War bull market had run its course. The three props of cheap money, scarcity of investments and weight of funds looking for a home, had been around for so long that they had lulled markets into a false sense of security. It was soon to be dispelled as the economic background deteriorated. In July the Chancellor introduced the first of a new series of austerity plans, cutting dollar imports of tobacco, petrol, newsprint and films. Investors sensed that the government was losing control. Heavy selling hit gilts, pushing yields up to 2.75% and undermining the relationship with equities, which also fell away sharply.

There was one bright spot on the horizon. It was the Marshall Aid proposal to help reconstruct the European economies by channelling in £6 billion a year for the next three to four years. Unfortunately the complexities of the deal meant that the negotiations were unduly prolonged, and news that they had been adjourned until the following January led to an all-round fall in markets. The last week of July saw 4.5 points knocked off gilts and nearly 10 points off the FT 30, taking it to 120. An appeal to the nation from Sir Stafford Cripps, a leading left-wing socialist and wartime Minister of Aircraft Production, warning that the country's economic survival was at stake, did not help matters and there were calls from all quarters for the government to come up with a plan of action to deal with the crisis.

A Star is born

1947 saw the public launch of *Glaxo* when the subsidiary of that name took over the parent, Joseph Nathan & Co., in a share exchange deal. Originally a New Zealand-based produce merchant founded by East London emigré Joseph Nathan in 1873, the company pioneered the development of dried-milk babyfood in the early 1900s, and graduated to pharmaceutical production in the inter-War years. Glaxo Laboratories was formed in 1932 and rapidly grew in importance to the group. It became a major provider of medical products during the Second World War, including the newly-discovered substance, penicillin, for which it developed mass-production methods. At the time of the reconstruction, all the former operations of Joseph Nathan were disposed of and 100,000 Ordinary 10/- shares in Glaxo were issued to the original shareholders. The move attracted buyers, and with the share price at £29 the new group was capitalised at just under £3 million as compared with today's figure of close to £70 billion following the takeover of Wellcome and the merger with America's SmithKline Beecham.

The "plan" when it came on 6th August did nothing to reassure markets. The measures comprised further powers to cut imports and direct exports, and with the agreement of the TUC the government also acquired control over labour with the power to direct it for the benefit of the country's basic industries. Later in the month additional measures were enacted, including a ban on pleasure travel outside the sterling area, the scrapping of the basic petrol ration, and a reduction in the meat ration. Only essential motor cars were to be manufactured for domestic consumption and all others were to be for export. And sterling, which had become convertible in mid-July in accordance with the terms of the Anglo-American Loan agreement, was promptly made inconvertible again.

The government's actions were widely criticised as panic measures that would do little to solve the underlying problem of the economy, which was lack of production. Much was made of the fact that, despite the huge shortfall in coal production, earlier in the year the miners had been permitted to move from a six-day working week to one of five days, and had then refused to honour agreements to change their working practices to boost productivity. The country was 'hanging by a thread' said Minister of Fuel and Power, Emmanuel Shinwell, and the miners should "play the game by the nation", but such exhortations fell on deaf ears and indeed were counterproductive – quite literally – in that they resulted in a wave of pit strikes. By the end of the first week in September, gilt yields were well in excess of 3% and the FT 30 had fallen to 104.2.

The remainder of the year saw a slow but steady recovery in equities. They had taken heart from a speeding up of the Marshall Aid plans for Europe and from what was seen as a more realistic approach to the country's economic problems by Sir Stafford Cripps, who had become Minister for Economic Affairs at the end of September. His drastic measures to reduce the dollar outflow by more import cuts and by a reduction in domestic capital spending in order to leave more materials available for export, were viewed as unpleasant but necessary, and did not hinder the market's recovery.

Chancellor Dalton resigns

There was some nervousness about what action Chancellor Dalton might take in an autumn budget, and it was widely feared that a large increase in distributed profits tax was likely in order to strike a political balance against a further reduction in the huge bill for subsidies. In the event equities remained firm ahead of the budget and even the doubling of profits tax and further increases in purchase tax failed to stem the advance. Gilts, on the other hand, took a sharp knock the day after the budget, when Mr Dalton resigned after admitting to having inadvertently disclosed details of the budget to a journalist minutes before his speech. He was replaced by Sir Stafford Cripps. While the former's commitment to an ultra-cheap monetary policy was never in doubt it was thought the new Chancellor might adopt a more flexible approach and be tougher on inflation.

Vesting date for the nationalisation of the railways was rapidly approaching and the prospect of the pending reinvestment of the compensation proceeds was a major factor behind the burst of strength in equities towards the end of December which left the FT 30 at 128.3, up 23% from the September low. Gilts, meanwhile, had settled around a 3% yield basis on the assumption that the Transport stock to be issued to former Home Rails stockholders would be given a realistic 3% coupon on 1st January 1948 and not an untenable 2.5% one.

Marshall Plan to the rescue

Speculation towards the end of 1947 that the summer collapse had perhaps constituted the shortest bear market on record did not last long into 1948. Despite an improving domestic situation characterised by rising production and sharply higher coal stocks, February saw a deterioration in the external situation. The US loan was down to the last $100 million and more gold sales had to be made to counter the drain on the country's dollar reserves. There were fears, too, that the post-War US boom was collapsing and already the Dow was testing its 1946 low point. The scene was set for another round of austerity measures from the new Chancellor. His wages and prices policy was seen as a threat to equities in that as well as turning the screw on inflation, limitation on profits and dividends had to be a political quid pro quo for the restriction on incomes. The FT 30 slipped back to 111.3 in March on rumours of a dividend freeze, but when it became a reality in the budget a month later, the index, which was already back to 118.1 ahead of the news, went better again.

The passing of the Marshall Plan by Congress helped sentiment further. The austerity measures had met with a degree of success and now US aid was giving the country a breathing space to put its house in order. This period of relative calm was abruptly shattered in July when the Russians sealed off Berlin. The index touched its low point of the year at 109.2 but then began a slow recovery as the airlift proved a resounding success and the situation stabilised. President of the Board of Trade, Harold Wilson, gave the upward movement a further boost with his "bonfire of controls" on 5th November.

In December, the Chancellor detailed his Four-Year Plan for the UK, to be ready for the ending of Marshall Aid in mid-1952. As might have been expected, it called for a greater proportion of imports to be raw materials and essential foodstuffs and for the export drive to continue unabated. With industrial production recovering to a new post-War peak and the gold and dollar drain stemmed following the coming into operation of the Marshall Plan, equities were not unduly depressed by the restraint on profits and dividends, and closed the year at 121, a fall of 6%. Gilts held steady throughout the year and the Government Securities Index, which had been 112.88 at the end of December 1947, stood at 113.66 precisely a year later. Golds were the year's worst performer as ever rising production costs set against a fixed selling price, inevitably took their toll of profits, and the index closed the year down 22.7% at 94.67, its lowest since 1932. All in all, 1948 was a year in limbo for the stock market with the low level of investor interest resulting in the smallest turnover to date in any post-War year.

The first devaluation

If 1948 was the year in which the government faced up to the realities of the economic situation and began to take steps to deal with it with some apparent success, 1949 demonstrated that problems of such magnitude were not easily solved. Exports were rising, the balance of payments was moving towards equilibrium with the large dollar deficit offset by US aid, thus taking the pressure off the country's gold and dollar reserves, but the recovery was still fragile and susceptible to external shocks. The shock, when it came, was from the US in the shape of a business recession causing a substantial reduction in purchases of UK goods in the context of an export market where the criterion had changed from one of availability to one of price. There was a renewed decline in the country's gold and dollar reserves and its cost structure was exposed as excessively inflated. Drastic measures were called for and on 18th September the pound was devalued against the dollar from $4.03 to $2.80.

The event meant that the Government had been forced to acknowledge that it was trying to do too much with the resources available. Attempts to modernise and expand UK industry and to increase exports, at the same time as extending the social security system, were simply unrealistic and overambitious. As a result, growing inflationary pressures undermined the international status of sterling, and demonstrated the fragility of the foundations of an economy based on a policy of full employment and a welfare state.

The size of the devaluation – or the "change in the rate of exchange" as Sir Stafford Cripps preferred to call it – was greater than had been expected. Equities, nevertheless, responded positively to the news and the FT 30 gained 1.9 to 110.1 but losses in gilts ranged up to £2. The real beneficiaries were gold shares. They had been edging up since the summer when rumours of a coming devaluation were rife, and on the now certain prospect of at least doubled mine profits, their index jumped 20% to 129.63. However, the absence of any significant supplementary action by the government suggested that perhaps too much reliance was being placed on devaluation as a cure for all the country's economic ills. In particular, doubts were expressed that the reduced dollar yield on exports could be outweighed by a proportionately greater increase in volume, and equities failed to hold their initial gains. In mid-November, the index slipped to a new post-War low of 99.8, recovering to 106.4 at year end for an overall loss on the year of 12.25%. Over the same period the Government Securities Index recorded a loss of 7%.

The Korean War and rearmament

The failures of 1949 made 1950 a critical year. The coming election in February meant that the government had to tread warily, and after winning with only a 17-seat margin, the prospect of any economic crisis rapidly turning into a political one dictated that the more controversial contents of the manifesto had to take a back seat. As one of the Opposition members put it, there could be no more "frogmarching of doctrinaire legislation through the House". Fortunately for the government, a boom in the US, a better flow of raw materials and the coming on stream of much of the capital investment undertaken since the end of the War, were good for production and for exports and equities began to respond. The FT 30, which had fallen 2.4 to 105.6 on news of the election result, was already up to 110 ahead of a tax-cutting budget and the announcement at the end of May that petrol rationing was to end.

The outbreak of war in Korea towards the end of June was a shock, but recovery was rapid as the demand for sterling area commodities increased and the balance of payments strengthened. Rearmament to meet what was perceived as a worldwide Communist threat now became an industrial priority but, inevitably, inflationary pressures began to increase as this new burden was imposed upon an already overstretched economy. This meant trouble ahead, but fired by the prospect of steel nationalisation funds looking for a new home following vesting date early in 1951, equities ended the year on a strong note at 115.7, up 8%, with a momentum which carried on well into the New Year. Wall Street also provided an encouraging background. The long bull phase that began in the spring of 1949 had passed the Dow's May 1946 peak of 212 in April 1950 and was not set to run out of steam until September 1951.

The way we were...
Sterling Exchange Rates
Currency Units per £
31 December 1950

France (Franc)	9.80
Germany (DMark)	11.76
Italy (Lira)	1750.00
Japan (Yen)	1012.00
USA (Dollar)	2.80

1951–55

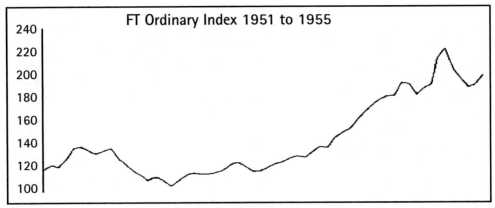

FT Ordinary Index 1951 to 1955

Source: Thomson Reuters Datastream

Conservatives back in power

The first half of 1951 witnessed a gradually gathering economic crisis. The devaluation of September 1949 had bought time for the Labour government but policies based on the assumption that public expenditure could not and indeed should not be reduced, that wage and dividend restraints could continue indefinitely, and that exhortation and patriotism would look after the export drive, could only lead to disaster. By the middle of the year imports were rising sharply, and exports lagging as a recession in the prices of dollar-earning commodities from the sterling area, combined with higher dollar purchases, reopened the dollar gap. The balance of payments was weakening again and a deficit of £500 million in the first half threatened to grow to £1.2 billion by the end of the year. The new Chancellor, Hugh Gaitskell, felt compelled to reverse the tax cuts of the previous year. He also imposed NHS dental and optical charges for the first time. These were to help pay for defence commitments but they prompted the resignation from the cabinet of Aneurin Bevan and the young Harold Wilson, seriously dividing the Labour Party in the process.

In order to back up its calls for wage restraint, the government, noting that even a 50% distributed profits tax was not keeping dividends in check, imposed statutory dividend limitation in late July. This was hardly effective in dealing with what was rapidly becoming a major crisis, and feeling that his administration needed a new mandate, Mr Attlee called a general election for 27th October. Labour's victory in 1945 owed much to the fact that it had broadened its appeal to win over a large section of the middle classes, but over the next five years it did little or nothing to retain their allegiance. Not only were they more heavily taxed but they also lagged behind in pay awards and were subject to the verbal onslaught of ministers like Aneurin Bevan and Emmanuel Shinwell. The former's "two nations" speech, in which he called the Tories "lower than vermin", and the latter's assertion that the working class was all that mattered and he "didn't give a tinker's cuss" about the rest, were reckoned by Professor Laski to have cost Labour two million votes in the February 1950 election. The Conservatives, led by Mr Churchill, won with only an 18-seat majority, and Mr R.A. Butler became Chancellor. The FT 30, which had risen 3.3 to 138.6 a month earlier when the date of the election was announced, began to fall away as soon as the Chancellor revealed his emergency measures, reaching 121.9 by the end of December.

Chancellor Butler's measures

His actions were conventional enough in that they included a £350 million cut in imports together with sharp restrictions on domestic capital spending, but the monetary measures marked an important change of principle in the way the new government would exercise control of the economy. Bank Rate was raised from 2% to 2.5%, the foreign exchange market was reopened, and a number of commodities were decontrolled and left to the workings of the price mechanism. Markets continued to take a cautious view, and at year end the FT 30 was back to 122, with the Government Securities Index depressed at 96.03 on higher interest rate fears. Few doubted that these drastic measures were necessary to deal with a crisis situation but investors preferred to wait until the first Conservative budget before celebrating. Perhaps they had become cynical after seeing the early promise of the Labour government dissolve in crisis after crisis, and were simply not prepared to take the new Conservative administration on trust.

The budget, when it came in March, was shaped by two overriding factors. One was the defence requirement and the other was the need to improve the balance of payments. Chancellor Butler called it an "incentive budget", but while it did bring longer-term benefits to industry, the raising of the Bank Rate to 4%, the introduction of the Excess Profits Levy, and further restrictions on capital investment, were not well received by the markets. Funds fell by up to 3.5 points, pulling the Government Securities Index back to 92.73, and the immediate reaction of the FT 30 was a 3.9 fall to 109.3. Confidence did not return until the beginning of the second half of the year when it became clear that the gold and dollar drain had been stemmed and that the balance of payments was moving back into surplus. Certainly, Butler had proved to be a very effective Chancellor, implementing all the major pledges in the Conservatives' 1951 election programme "Set the People Free". Rationing had been eliminated, taxes reduced, living standards raised, full employment maintained, and the Welfare State left intact. Furthermore, Harold Macmillan as Minister of Housing had fulfilled the election promise to build 300,000 houses in the Conservatives' first year of office. At the end of the year, the FT 30 had recovered to 115.8 to show a loss of 8%, while Government Securities at 94.41 was down just 2%.

The bull market gets under way

The improving trend of the economy carried on into 1953, and the confidence that it engendered in investors was now, slowly but surely, beginning to be reflected in the stock market. The first major post-War "popular" bull market was getting under way. It was popular in the sense that investors were making money, not out of shares in exotic companies from "far away places with strange-sounding names" like Mexican Eagle or Wiluna Gold, but from shares in stores, breweries and motor car manufacturers they came into contact with every day. Everybody knew Marks & Spencer in the High Street and it was comforting to know that by buying their shares as well as their merchandise, a capital gain and an ever increasing dividend were assured. In fact, 1953 could almost be pinpointed as the foundation year for the cult of the equity and the share-owning democracy. Stores were very much the darling of the developing boom, and every new set of results from Marks & Spencer, Great Universal Stores (widely known as Gussies) or Woolworths, was eagerly awaited to see, not only how many new bonus shares were to be issued, but also whether the dividend was going to be maintained on the last increase of capital. Investors were rarely disappointed more than momentarily in the wake of the liquidation after a pre-results surge of speculative buying. This air of optimism was reinforced by the coronation of Elizabeth the Second, an event widely hailed as marking the dawn of a new Elizabethan Age.

Savoy under Siege

The opening shots in the long-running battle for control of the Savoy Hotel came in the autumn of 1953. Charles Clore and Harold Samuel of Land Securities were both interested in what they saw as the underdeveloped property potential of the group, and both had quietly accumulated shares. In order to foil a suspected takeover attempt, the Savoy board, led by Hugh Wontner, formed a special subsidiary company to hold the group's properties and keep them separate from the hotel operating side. Charles Clore then sold his stake to Harold Samuel, who promptly tried to use his resulting 37% holding to block this defensive move through the courts. However, after talks Harold Samuel agreed to sell his stake to the Savoy board and "friends" at 62/6 a share, a price which gave him a £1.3 million profit on the deal. This is probably the first reported case of "greenmail".

Considerable additional excitement was brought to the party by bid activity. In the early 'fifties few companies had bothered to embark upon a revaluation of assets – even ICI had been taken to task by the *Financial Times* for complaining that to do so would be too costly and time-consuming – and most had their land and buildings in the balance sheet at often absurdly low pre-War cost prices. Furthermore, conservative boardroom practice, reinforced by Labour's dividend restraint policy, meant that dividends were often covered four or more times by earnings. The British industrial scene thus represented a happy hunting ground for entrepreneurs like Hugh Fraser, Charles Forte and Charles Clore, all of whom were to lay the foundations of their business empires during this era.

The budget in April was welcomed by the *Financial Times* as "good for the public, good for industry and good for the market". Its principal provisions were 6d off income tax, a 25% cut in purchase tax, and the ending of the Excess Profits Levy on 1st January next. After some initial hesitation, equities resumed their steady rise aided by a stream of good economic news in the shape of a post-War peak in new car registrations, record aircraft exports and a sharp recovery in textiles output. It was now clear that the trend in profits was changing quite dramatically. Reported profits had been disappointing earlier in the year, but they were reflecting conditions in 1952. It was now possible to look at the production figures and the obvious signs of prosperity all around and anticipate a sharp improvement later in 1953 carrying on well into 1954.

This sort of intelligent speculation was good for the equity market; confidence was further boosted in September by a cut in Bank Rate to 3.5% and the following month by the announcement of the terms for the offer to the public of denationalised **United Steel**. Even Wall Street, which had been depressed all year, now weighed in with a sharp recovery, casting doubts on the validity of earlier fears of a recession. As a result, 1953 ended on a strong note with the FT 30 up 14.9% to 130.7, Government Securities up 5.8% at 100.21 and only Golds disappointed, down 5.17%. Since industrial profits had fallen by 8% during the year, the auguries for 1954 were good.

Into new high ground

At the beginning of 1954 there was much talk of, not whether, but when the index would surpass its January 1947 peak of 140.6. The big event took place on 3rd April, just ahead of the budget which was well received, confirming the breakthrough. It was widely noted that the peak prices of April 1954 looked far more sustainable than those of January 1947, in that industrial dividend yields were now geared to a more realistic level of interest rates than that ruling in the Dalton cheap money era. A period of rising dividends also meant that with equities yielding around 5% on average, the yield gap was much wider than in 1947, providing them with what could be regarded as a greater margin of safety. It should be remembered that this was the time of the "yield gap", long before the advent of the "reverse yield gap", when equities yielded more than gilts in order to compensate for the higher risk attached to them.

There was no stopping the market in 1954. Company profits and dividends appeared set on a permanently rising trend and every key announcement sparked a new round of buying. The stores continued to reveal brilliant results as did the motor car manufacturers, with Ford reporting doubled profits in April. In May Bank Rate was again reduced, this time to 3%, a move interpreted as a sign of the government's confidence in continuing industrial recovery and its belief that production and exports could continue to rise without risk of inflationary pressures building up again. In November, British Motor Corporation (formed in 1952 by the merger of Austin and Morris) reported profits up from £14.3 million to £20 million along with a £4 million rights issue to fund an increase in output of 25% over the next eighteen months. The following month Vauxhall announced a £36 million plan to double output over the next five years. And Jaguar shares rose strongly on rumours of an American bid. Furthermore, the underlying balance between the dollar and sterling areas was moving strongly in favour of the UK, and trade with the OECD countries was yielding a substantial monthly surplus. Also powering the upward drive in stock prices was the simple fact of too much money chasing too little stock. The performance of equities vis-à-vis gilts was not lost on the institutions and the composition of their portfolios was undergoing a sea change in favour of ordinary shares.

There had to be a spectre at such a feast and it turned out to be the familiar one that had haunted the last days of the Labour administration in 1951. A combination of acute labour shortages, big wage claims and awards, rising personal consumption, heavy capital investment by industry and increasing government expenditure, served to put an intolerable strain on productive capacity which in turn led to lengthening delivery dates and a deterioration in the balance of payments as imports rose and exports fell. The most quoted economist of the day, Roy Harrod, warned of a "drift towards inflation". The shape of things to come was evident in the fact that German car output had risen by 38% in 1954 to 675,000 vehicles of which 300,000 were exported. None of this seemed to worry investors very much during the last days of 1954 and equities entered the New Year on a rising trend. Gilts, however, had a better nose for dearer money and failed to share their enthusiasm, ending the year with just a 3% gain against one of 53% for equities.

The brakes go on

The opening days of 1955 saw increasing activity in equities and the latest of the denationalised steels, **Colvilles**, received applications totalling £169 million for the £13 million of stock on offer. Then at the end of January, Bank Rate was raised by 0.5% to 3.5%, not, it was stressed, to remedy a critical situation but to ensure that one did not arise. It did not work. Gilts continued to fall and the Government Securities Index, which was 103.94 on 1st January, had slipped below the 100 mark by the end of the month. Sterling also failed to respond and the drain on the gold and dollar reserves persisted. It was now time for the government to show that it really meant business in its anti-inflationary drive. Accordingly, at the end of February, Bank Rate was raised a full point to 4.5%, and hire purchase restrictions were introduced for a wide range of consumer goods, cars included, specifying a minimum 15% deposit and a maximum two-year repayment period. Gilts promptly fell by up to four points, the FT 30 lost seven points to 177, and sterling steadied.

The markets quickly recovered their poise, for the consensus was that the country was flourishing and that some degree of inflation was inevitable in a full employment economy where unfilled vacancies actually exceeded the number of unemployed. Thus the Chancellor's measures were regarded as necessary to nip inflation in the bud, to protect the balance of payments and to remove uncertainty in markets as to the government's intentions. In the budget in mid-April, the Chancellor seemed to confirm this sanguine view of the state of the economy by cutting the standard rate of income tax from 9/- to 8/6, and halving purchase tax on some consumer goods. By May there were some signs that the original credit squeeze was working. Furniture sales were down by over 30% in March compared with a year earlier. This sort of restraint on domestic consumption was precisely what was intended and, coupled with evidence of an improvement in the gold and dollar reserves and in the balance of payments, the market lost its nervousness ahead of the election, reaching 196 on the eve of the poll. Churchill had resigned in April, and his successor, Anthony Eden, wanted to obtain a fresh mandate at the earliest opportunity.

Fortunately for the Conservatives, Labour had learned nothing from its defeat in 1951. Its election manifesto, "Challenge to Britain", appeared to be out of touch with a new and more optimistic mood. Steel and road transport were to be renationalised, and heavy chemicals, machine tools and water were to come under the umbrella of the state. Inheritance taxes were to be increased and capital gains tax introduced.

The Conservatives win again

A Conservative victory with a majority of 60 seats against the 17 of 1951 was exactly what investors wanted and the result was greeted with a surge of buying which carried the FT 30 through the 200 level for the first time. US buyers now came in for such international stocks as Unilever, Bowater, ICI, Ford and BP (formerly Anglo-Iranian Oil). Gilts, on the other hand, paid more attention to the domestic background, where large pay claims were often accompanied by the threat of strikes, and the strikes, when they occurred, were followed by large pay awards, and then in rapid succession by large price rises. Equities, nevertheless, pressed on regardless, touching a high of 223.9 in late July, despite the announcement of a sharply widening trade gap in June which indicated that the credit squeeze was failing to reduce the excessive demand for imports. A few days later the new Chancellor, Harold Macmillan, countered with a tightening of hire purchase controls by increasing the minimum deposit from 15% to 33.33% and by requesting the banks to reduce advances to private customers.

The June trade figures, showing imports up by 14% on those for the first half of 1954, seemed to confirm the need for this new wave of restrictive measures. After all, as an *FT* editorial argued, the benefits of the last devaluation had been exhausted, and if the value of the pound was to be maintained, the reserves strengthened and provision made for investment, then credit had to be restrained. Despite consideration of the probability that the credit squeeze would lead to caution on the dividend front, equities took the restrictions very much in their stride. Forced selling in a thin market in the wake of the banks cutting back on overdrafts, pushed the FT 30 into the 180/190 range in August but even further increases in purchase tax (including that on motor cars from 50% to 60%) failed to do any more harm and the index ended the year back at the 200 level. Meanwhile gilts were in broad retreat, victims of what was now realised to be a worldwide trend towards dearer money on the emergence of inflationary pressures everywhere. Increasingly, the Dalton era of cheap money was seen as nothing more than a brief and temporary interruption of this trend, to which markets were having to make a belated adjustment. On the political front, December saw the elevation of Hugh Gaitskell to the Labour leadership on the retirement of Clement Attlee with the Garter, a peerage and the OM. The Government Securities index was down by 12.8% over the year to 90.

1956-60

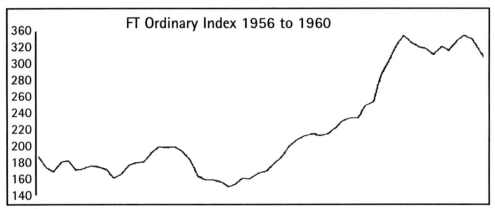

FT Ordinary Index 1956 to 1960

360
320
300
280
260
240
220
200
180
160
140

Source: Thomson Reuters Datastream

The squeeze begins to hurt

In the first few days of 1956, it was clear that the new Chancellor was not going to be able to preside over any relaxation of the restraints imposed by his predecessor. There was a sharp decline in the gold and dollar reserves in December, leaving them at their lowest level for three years, and the December balance of payments figures showed imports up by 15%. There were already signs that the impact of the credit squeeze was being felt in the motor industry, where some factories had already begun short-time working. Nevertheless, Mr Macmillan was not convinced that enough had been done to damp down home demand and in mid-February he raised Bank Rate to 5.5% and brought in a new package of restrictive measures. The motor industry once again was singled out for particularly harsh treatment and hire purchase deposits were lifted from 33.33% to 50%. In addition, the investment allowances introduced in the April 1954 budget were suspended, the capital spending programmes of the nationalised industries were to be cut in 1956/57, and the Capital Issues Committee was directed to take a more "critical" look at prospective new issues.

The ordinary share and Government Securities indices were already trending downwards from the beginning of the year and these latest moves depressed them further in early March to 170 and 85 respectively. Such falls appeared more than justified by a rapid succession of announcements from industry detailing the drastic effect the squeeze was having. Huge stocks of new cars were building up and more and more companies were forced to lay off production workers. The same situation applied to the domestic appliance manufacturers, and the radio and television makers were reporting production cuts of up to 40%. Not surprisingly, investors became more interested in putting their money overseas and there was a run on dollar stocks, particularly those of Canadian natural resource companies. The fact that both equities and gilts rallied strongly to 196 and 88 by the end of April suggests that markets sensed a degree of overkill in the Chancellor's measures, pointing to a rapid reversal of policy in the not too distant future. Support for this view was drawn from a progressively narrowing trade gap in February and March, accompanied by a sharp recovery in the gold and dollar reserves. With the crisis in the motor industry aggravated by import restrictions operating in two of its largest overseas markets, Australia and New Zealand, this theory had a lot to recommend it on the reasoning that the abrupt change from expansion to contraction would cause alarm in government circles.

Nasser seizes the Suez Canal

Then in July, Colonel Nasser seized control of the Suez Canal and created a more serious crisis which was to dominate the economic and political scene for the rest of the year. The initial reaction to the news was a relatively minor fall in the ordinary share index to 183.2, with the largest declines being registered by shares in oil and shipping companies on the prospect of having to pay higher dues to the new owners of the Canal. However, the lack of any real progress towards achieving a settlement and the growing shortage of oil supplies soon began to erode investor confidence and the index was back to 175 when the shooting war started at the end of October. There had been an outbreak of fighting between the Egyptians and the Israelis, and Anglo-French forces intervened ostensibly to "separate the combatants" and to safeguard the Canal. The incident was widely believed to have been stage-managed. The political embarrassment caused by the withdrawal of the Anglo-French forces under pressure from America and the United Nations was matched by the economic damage resulting from the closure of the Canal. The UK was now faced with the double problem, first of all, of getting enough oil to keep industry going, and then of paying for it without depleting the gold and dollar reserves. By the end of November, the FT 30 had reached its low point of the year at 161.5 with the Government Securities index similarly depressed at 82.38. The introduction of petrol rationing in December was a further blow to the motor industry, where one fifth of the workforce was already on short-time, and it prompted the first selective reflationary move, which was a reduction in the minimum hire purchase deposit from 50% to 20%. December witnessed a modest recovery in the markets despite news of the Russian crushing of the Hungarian uprising, and the FT 30 closed the year at 178.8.

Bank Rate to 7%

The political legacy of Suez was shaken off in January 1957 with the resignation of Anthony Eden and his replacement by Harold Macmillan, with Peter Thorneycroft taking over at the Treasury. The economic legacy, however, persisted with restricted oil supplies which were much more costly and thus a severe drain on the country's gold and dollar reserves. Although alarmed by their decline, less than a month after taking office the new Chancellor lowered Bank Rate by half a point to 5%. Such anxieties failed to dent the rally in equities which had begun in the previous December, and by the end of April the index had breached the 200 level once more. Mr Thorneycroft's first budget had been anything but restrictive, and a number of wage disputes had been settled on generous terms, both of which factors served to encourage further pay claims, many of which led to serious strikes. All this provided an ideal background for the wave of currency speculation against the pound in the second half of the year in the wake of the devaluation of the French franc. The cost of defending the pound led to another sharp fall in the gold and dollar reserves, and the Chancellor decided to act.

> ### The Bank Rate Tribunal
>
> The shock 2% hike in Bank Rate to 7% caught some jobbers napping, and since some of the biggest sellers of gilts ahead of the announcement were institutions where certain directors with Government links were privy to the impending rise, rumours of a 'leak' swirled around the City. The newspapers picked up the story, questions were asked in the House and the Government felt compelled to hold a public inquiry to clear the air.
>
> The inquiry was a wide-ranging one and its dissection of the way business is conducted in merchant banking circles was described by one contemporary commentator as "a window and a shaft of daylight into the City". The fact that some of the merchant bankers questioned had been in Scotland shooting grouse at the time was a gift to Labour MPs who for years had maintained that, when the Tories are in office, key financial decisions are made on the grouse moors.
>
> In the event, after twelve days of detailed examination of all the evidence, the Tribunal decided that there was no justification for allegations that any of the parties involved had improperly disclosed information or used it for the purpose of private gain.

The two-point rise in Bank Rate in September to 7% stunned the City. The move was accompanied by a brake on investment spending by government departments, local authorities and nationalised industries, and by instructions to banks to limit loans to the private sector. The immediate reaction in the markets was an 8.7 point fall in the FT 30 to 183.5 and one of 3.99 in Government Securities to 77.52. The decline continued and by the end of November the ordinary index was down to 162, and while gilts had steadied, their prospect of recovery was not helped by a report from the Church Commissioners that they had just trimmed their gilts portfolio by £11 million to £35.8 million. The feeling of apprehension among investors was heightened when the government announced its intention to take a firm stand against exorbitant wage claims regardless of strike threats, and confirmed its resolve by vetoing a 3% pay award to Health Service workers. However, Chancellor Thorneycroft felt that the Prime Minister's firmness was more apparent than real, and believing that the will to curb actual government spending was lacking, he resigned in January. Whether or not the event marked a turning point in the battle for fiscal probity is arguable, but it is probably true that Macmillan feared unemployment more than inflation. He had first entered Parliament as member for the North East constituency of Stockton-on-Tees and knew first-hand the misery that unemployment could cause.

The recovery begins

The year had ended on a quiet but more hopeful note after a sharp improvement in the November trade gap and a marked revival in the motor and steel industries. There was now a widespread feeling among investors that markets had discounted a great deal and that in 1958 things could only get better. They were right. The disinflationary measures of 1957 were to prove more successful than the government had hoped, and served to provide a period of rest and recuperation for the economy in 1958 which paved the way for the boom year of 1959. January saw a sharp improvement in the gold and dollar reserves, and a significant reduction in the December trade gap to the lowest monthly level for seven years. This set the pattern for the rest of the year and encouraged the new Chancellor, Mr Heathcote Amory, to embark upon a series of Bank Rate reductions beginning with a 1% cut in March. The figure of 154 touched by the FT 30 in February proved to be the low point of the year, and from then on the advance was practically continuous, boosted by a mildly reflationary budget in April, and by each successive cut in Bank Rate. The last one, which brought the rate down to 4% in November, saw the index within just a few points of the 1955 high of 223.9, and on the last day of the year it broke through. Investors had good reason to believe that they "had never had it so good".

Equities had gained 36% and gilts 6.7%, providing a fair reflection of the recovery in the economy during 1958. That recovery had been greatly assisted by two factors. One was a much milder recession in the US than had been expected, which meant that the UK was able to take full advantage of the opportunity offered by a favourable change in the terms of trade. Of course, Wall Street's performance was no drawback either with the Dow Jones adding nearly 150 points to reach a new record high of 583.65. The other was the government's drive towards financial liberalisation with the elimination of a great many of the controls that had hampered the free working of the economy ever since the war years. Industry was confident that it was entering the New Year in good shape, and secure in the knowledge that it had a large enough margin of spare capacity to meet home and export demand without running into production bottlenecks and stirring up new inflationary pressures.

The Great Aluminium War

One of the major corporate events of 1958 was the battle for control of **British Aluminium**, which was a milestone on the road towards the formulation of the City Takeover Code. BA supplied about one third of aluminium demand in the UK and appeared an attractive target to two American aluminium producers, both looking for a stepping-stone into the fast-growing European markets. One was **Reynolds Aluminium** and the other was **Alcoa**, the Aluminium Company of America. In order to make its planned takeover of such a key industrial company more acceptable to Britain, in September 1958 Reynolds went into partnership with Tube Investments, and both began buying BA shares in the market using nominees. In November, Reynolds and Tubes, advised by Warburgs, a relative newcomer on the merchant banking scene, met with the BA board, advised by Lazards and Hambros, to try to reach agreement on the terms of a bid. The meeting broke up with BA flatly rejecting the approach.

In December BA announced that it had agreed a deal with Alcoa, justifying it on the grounds that only a one-third stake would pass into American hands whereas in the case of the Reynolds-TI bid, all the BA stock would be held by a joint company with a dominant American partner. By the end of the year, neither offer had received sufficient acceptances, a stalemate which sparked an independent offer by a consortium of institutions. This new offer, supposedly, was not on behalf of BA but since the accompanying letter to BA shareholders was signed by the chairmen of Lazards and Hambros and called for the Reynolds-TI offer to be rejected "in the national interest", there was little doubt whose side they were on. This manoeuvre turned out to be ill-judged on two counts. One was that it gave the impression that the City establishment was trying to slam the door in the face of newcomers, especially those who did not instantly accede to its wishes. The financial press was not happy with this and neither were many of the other financial institutions, some of which were holders of BA stock. The other was that Reynolds and TI were goaded into instant action and Warburgs promptly began buying BA stock in the market, much of it from those same disgruntled institutions. Within ten days, it was all over. The Reynolds-TI camp had amassed 80% of the issued capital of BA and some of the oldest and most revered institutions in the City had suffered an embarrassing defeat.

The yield gap goes into reverse

The year 1959 was an "annus mirabilis" for the equity investor. If the bull market of 1952/55 had laid the foundations of the cult of the equity, then the first real construction work on those foundations was done in 1959. It was also the year the yield gap finally went into reverse, just twelve months after the move had been pioneered in the US. There were still many household names among the top performing shares of 1959 just as in 1955, and Steels and Motors were up by 160% and 100% respectively, but the stars were two of the new acquisitive industrial holding companies, and two of the many new issues that had flocked to the market during the year. Two headline making bids had also served to prove to the enthusiastic investor and speculator that no company, however exalted, was safe from the attentions of the new breed of entrepreneurs.

The year opened in a mood of cautious optimism but sentiment soon became adversely affected by the start in January of another strike in the motor industry involving both British Motor and Standard. The suspension of the Capital Issues Committee in February prompted a revival of interest in that it was seen as another important step along the road to financial decontrol, giving companies freedom to raise capital for the first time since the outbreak of war in 1939. It was the budget in April that finally convinced investors that the government, if not exactly throwing caution to the wind, at last believed that it was safe to put the economy back on an unashamedly expansionist path. There was a 9d cut in the standard rate of income tax to 7/9 in the £, further reductions in purchase tax, 2d off a pint of beer (supposedly a great psychological boost for the working man), and investment allowances were restored following their suspension two years earlier. The next day, the FT 30 finally recovered all the ground it had lost since the beginning of the year and edged to a new high of 226.1, with Government Securities reaching 86.3, up nearly two points over the same period.

Car exports boom

From that point on, it was good news all the way. Production rose rapidly, and the recovery spread from consumer goods to capital goods. Productivity gained dramatically too, with the increase in employment lagging well behind the rise in production. Exports soared, particularly of cars. These were the days when British sports cars were conquering America, and over 50% of UK car exports in 1959 went to North America, which had taken over from Australia, New Zealand and South Africa as the most important market for British cars. In May, BMC announced that it was planning to step up production in the face of "overwhelming demand", and after unveiling the new Mini (priced at £497 including purchase tax) in August, it reported that its home market order book stood at three times the level of the year before.

British aircraft, too, were very popular with overseas buyers, and the Vickers Viscount became the staple of airlines in many parts of the world. And all this was against a background where the new upsurge in profits was seen as certain to bring a delayed benefit to shares, the current rating of which in terms of earnings and dividends still reflected the near-stagnation of the years 1957/58. Not surprisingly, on 28th August, the yield gap at last went into reverse with the FT 30 at 256 yielding 4.76%, or 0.01% less than Government Securities at 85.09. The equity revolution was now complete. Fixed interest stocks no longer figured in the calculations of the average private investor constructing a portfolio. Equities were much more exciting and profitable.

The bids for Harrods and Watney Mann

The two bids that aroused the most interest during the year and made a significant contribution to the cult of the equity, was the one for **Harrods**, London's best known department store with its internationally famous flagship building in Knightsbridge, and that for **Watney Mann,** one of the biggest brewing groups in the UK. After a hard fought, three-cornered battle, Harrods eventually fell to the fast-growing Glasgow-based stores group, **House of Fraser,** for £37 million, but Charles Clore's £20 million bid for the property-rich brewer was withdrawn after a vigorous defence by Watney and the bidder's unwillingness to raise his offer. Unsuccessful though it was, the bid for Watney served to highlight the hidden property potential in all sorts of companies well beyond the circle of the breweries. There were also a number of mergers in the insurance world, and towards the end of the year the big aircraft manufacturers embarked upon the amalgamations necessary to make sure they had the clout to compete successfully in world markets.

As for the two best performing shares of the year, these were **Harper Engineering & Electronics**, up 450%, and **Arusha Industries**, up 400%. Both had been "shell" companies, in the sense that they had disposed of their original businesses and used the proceeds to go on the acquisition trail aided by the provision of further funds from shareholders. They were thus the forerunners of the fast-growing industrial holding companies that were such a feature in 1986/87 leading up to the October crash.

Among the many new issues floated during the year, **Berry's Magicoal**, with its electric imitation log and coal fires, was an instant success and recorded a 355% gain. **Shannon**, which made innovative business systems, also caught the imagination of the investing public and rose 360% over the year. Other newcomers to be welcomed by the stags were **Showerings**, the makers of Babycham, **Daintifyt Brassieres, Roy King Properties**, and **Frank G. Gates**, the car dealers. The year also witnessed the original flotation by Raymond and Sybil Zelker of **Polly Peck**, who offered 250,000 of the one million 2/- ordinary shares at 6/- each.

The Conservatives re-elected

Everyone had money and seemed willing to spend it. Unemployment was low at around 1.5% and wages were rising, providing a degree of spending power to the working classes they had never before possessed. Everyone wanted a car and the rise of the hire purchase industry meant they could buy it on the 'never never'. Companies like **Bowmaker, Mercantile Credit, Lombard Banking** and **United Dominions Trust** all thrived during this period. If there was one element lacking in this booming market, it was confirmation of the political stability of the Conservative government. It was duly supplied by the October election when the Macmillan administration was returned with a majority of a hundred seats. The result was regarded as a personal triumph for the Prime Minister, who was portrayed henceforth as "Supermac" by the cartoonist Vicki. The market had been rising strongly ahead of the poll and on news of the Conservative victory, the FT 30 leapt an unprecedented 16.1 points to 284.7 and kept going day after day to reach 338.4 by year end. There were few doubters during the boom, and optimism was reinforced by the fact that the bull market was a worldwide phenomenon and that dividend yields in the US and in Germany, for example, at 3% and 3.3% on average, were much lower than those ruling in the UK. Towards the end of the year, an editorial in the *Financial Times* wisely if cynically observed that "the surest sign of future trouble is present prosperity", and pointed prophetically to rising world interest rates, fast-growing imports, and a pick-up in extravagant wage demands, as all signs of possible trouble ahead. Another indication of a peaking market was a fine arts boom culminating in the record price of £275,000 paid for Rubens' 'Adoration of the Magi', although it should be noted that it was bought by a college and not by a tycoon.

The Trustee boomlet

The performance of the equity index in 1960 demonstrated very clearly the truth of the market adage that it is better to travel hopefully than to arrive. The rise in profits, earnings and dividends so firmly established in 1959, accelerated dramatically in 1960, but it had been well discounted. After a rise of no less than 50% in the FT 30, most of it in the last three months of the year, investors had turned cautious. Past experience had taught them that it was time for a touch of the brakes. A wave of New Year enthusiasm carried the index to a new record high of 342.9 in the first week of January, but there was no follow-through. By the end of the month, it had lost more than twenty points in the wake of a BBC Panorama programme warning of the unstable nature of stock exchange booms and dearer money fears which were soon realised by a 1% hike in Bank Rate to 5%. This was the first increase since November 1958, but it was well received, being regarded as a "stitch in time" necessary to trim the marginal excesses from the boom and keep it healthy. After touching 321.5 on the Bank Rate news, equities rebounded smartly on institutional buying. At least part of this buying was in anticipation of the implementation a year hence of the government's proposal to widen the investment powers of trustees to permit them to hold up to 50% of their funds in equities. The LCC (London County Council) had already obtained powers to invest up to 25% of its superannuation and provident funds in equities and announced that it had been "active" in the equity market. Unit trusts were increasing in popularity and in numbers, and their policy was to invest on setbacks.

Curbing the boom

However, it soon became clear that the rise in production was being constrained by difficulties in the supply of labour and other resources rather than deficiencies of demand, especially on the home front. In consequence, imports began to rise faster than exports. Wage claims and strike threats became very much a daily routine, and the April budget was appropriately restrictive in an effort to strengthen sterling and bring the expansion back within bounds without reviving dangers of inflation and balance of payment problems. One of the provisions was a requirement for the banks to deposit with the Bank of England 1% of their reserves of liquid assets, thereby reducing their ability to expand advances. The FT 30 reacted by slipping below 300 in early May to 295.8, close to its lowest point of the year, but by the end of the month it had recovered to 320. The rally was dented only briefly in June when the Chancellor tightened the screw once more by lifting Bank Rate another point to 6% and by upping the banks' Special Deposits from 1% to 2% in order to restrict their lending powers even more. By September, the rally was a spent force and after peaking at 340, the broad index declined to reach the year's low point of 293.4 in early December before staging a recovery to 305.5 at year end after a second half-point cut in Bank Rate had brought it down to 5% again.

Still, this apparently lacklustre performance by equities, as evidenced by an FT 30 down almost 10% on the year, masked a great deal of activity as institutions switched from sector to sector, causing a new pattern to emerge rather than a new level. The Financials, Properties, Stores, Plastics and Foods all moved up, while Consumer Durables, especially Motors, Household Appliances and Radio and TV, took a back seat as it became clear that their profit margins were being squeezed by a combination of flat demand, rising wages and constant final prices. Attractive new issues were often substantially oversubscribed, and in January the House of Fraser-related offering of 3.6 million shares in **SUITs** (Scottish Universal Investment Trust) for £2 million, received applications for £50 million. Indeed, but for the fact that the FT 30 was predominantly an industrial index with no Financials represented at all, it is more than likely that a decline from the January 1960 peak would not have registered at all. This was also a year of consolidation for Wall Street after a near hundred point rise in 1959 to 680. By the middle of March, the Dow had slipped below 600 again, and had great difficulty in holding the line until a year end rally carried it up to 614 as investors began to share in the popular enthusiasm for the charismatic new Kennedy administration.

If equities had an uneventful year, Gilts and Golds had a rotten one. The Government Securities index fell almost six full points from 85.09 to 79.12 in response to a double blow. One was from institutions rejigging their portfolios in anticipation of the changes in the Trustee Act, and the other from the banks which were heavy sellers of gilts to fund a rising level of advances following the ending of the credit squeeze in mid-1958. The effect of all this was to push up the gilts yield to 5.68% from 5.04% at the end of 1959, but thanks to dividend rises the reverse yield gap actually narrowed, with equities yielding 4.82% against 3.74% a year earlier. Golds fared even worse. Reports of the Sharpeville shootings in March, followed by the declaration of a State of Emergency, prompted panic selling of Kaffirs which knocked the index back to 70.2 at its lowest point against a figure of 88.8 at the start of the year.

1961-65

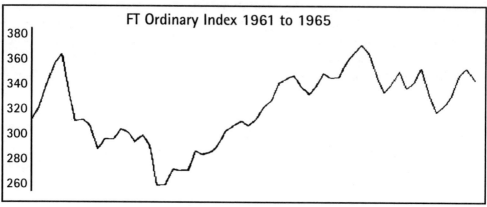

FT Ordinary Index 1961 to 1965

Source: Thomson Reuters Datastream

Bids and mergers dominate

The New Year opened strongly, continuing the recovery from 1960's low point of 293.4 touched in early December. There was a good two-way business in the market with sentiment helped by a rash of bids and mergers featuring many well known names. **Thompson Newspapers** announced in January that it was planning a merger with **Odhams** to form the UK's largest press group, and was then promptly outbid by the **Daily Mirror Group**. January also saw the merger of Charles Clore's property flagship, **City & Central** with Jack Cotton's **City Centre**, and in February they launched a joint bid – ultimately unsuccessful – for the capital's top property company, **City of London Real Property**. And in March, **Ind Coope** merged with **Tetley** and **Ansells** to form the biggest brewery group in the country. Another bid in March, the significance of which was not widely appreciated at the time, was **GEC**'s agreed offer for **Radio & Allied Industries**, the makers of MacMichael and Sobell radios. The managing director of Radio & Allied was Arnold Weinstock and he retained this position in relation to the new combined undertaking. Without doubt the bid of the year was that of **ICI** for **Courtaulds**, which at £200 million was the largest ever mounted in the UK. It was a hard fought battle with Courtaulds pulling out all the stops to escape ICI's clutches, and when the offer closed ICI had failed narrowly after receiving acceptances from holders of 38.5% of Courtaulds' stock. There was also a new issue boom, with many of the new flotations instantly establishing huge premiums thanks to enthusiastic public participation.

A new all-time peak of 365.7 was attained in May, but those early months of the year had witnessed a dangerously large and growing excess of imports over exports, together with a new surge of wage claims in the wake of a sharp fall in unemployment. Mr Selwyn Lloyd, the new Chancellor, was keen to put his stamp on the economy by ensuring that the expansion would not be pursued in such a way as to endanger the position of sterling, the balance of payments or the stability of prices. It was not going to be an easy task. International competition was increasing apace and traditional export markets were no longer the exclusive preserve of UK industry. Neither was the domestic market safe, following the abolition of import controls. Two straws in the wind, with very significant longer-term implications for the UK motor industry, were the fact that Nissan had stopped making the Austin Cambridge under licence and had begun producing its own models both for the Japanese domestic market and for export, and that Renault was beginning to export its Dauphine model to Britain in considerable numbers. Clearly, continuing economic success was going to depend on a very real effort to be competitive in international terms, and in this context there was much discussion of the merits of joining the EEC. General de Gaulle remained opposed to Britain's entry but negotiations continued with the stock market broadly in favour, seeing membership as providing a wider target for UK exports, greater stability for the economy and better management, as well as providing increased US interest and investment in the UK as an operating base within the EEC.

Bank Rate to 7% again

In anticipation of a new round of restrictive measures, the ordinary share index had retreated from its May peak well before the Chancellor unveiled his formidable July package. Bank Rate was hoisted to 7%, indirect taxes were subjected to a 10% surcharge, there were to be cuts in government and local authority spending including a 'pay pause' to put a brake on public sector wages, and restraints on building. Special Deposits were raised to 3%, and worst of all, for market operators, was the announcement of the long feared and long awaited plan to tax capital profits. At the same time, he announced the setting up of the National Economic Development Council ("Neddy"), drawn from the ranks of the trade unions, management and government, to co-operate in planning the future of the economy. The initial reaction of equities was a fall to 305, but a strong rally developed in August as the new Trustee Act came into operation.

However, the rally soon petered out and the index relapsed to 285 before recovering to end the year practically unchanged at 304.8 after two half-point falls had reduced Bank Rate to 6%. Gilts did not fare so well and the effect of sales by trustees switching to equities pushed the Government Securities index to 72.01 in the first week of August, its lowest level since the compilation of the index forty years earlier.

Just as in 1960, fairly narrow fluctuations in the index concealed a good deal of switching between sectors as investors became more sophisticated. Capital Goods shares were out of favour as it became clear that increased foreign competition had eroded profit margins, causing large and unsettling swings in profits and dividends. Steel plant suppliers like **Davy United** and **Wellman Smith**, whose share prices had risen more than fourfold between 1955 and 1960 as orders and profits boomed, now began to fall back, as investors turned their attention to companies benefiting from more reliable consumer expenditure and rental income. Low-yielding shares were also greatly sought after on the assumption that they offered superior growth potential, and buyers were rarely disappointed in 1961 by their investments in Stores, Insurances, Merchant Banks, Properties and Electronics.

The year also witnessed the fall from grace of **Harper Engineering & Electronics**, the industrial holding company that had topped the best performing share table in 1959. Just like its successors in 1986/87, it had expanded too fast and neither wisely nor well. In July, the interim dividend was passed and lower profits were forecast for the year just ended, the chairman citing the familiar litany of provisions for losses and overvaluation of stocks and work in progress among its recently acquired subsidiaries, all resulting in a severe strain on the group's financial resources and necessitating an operational and financial reorganisation. Its fellow star performer in 1959, **Arusha Industries**, followed much the same pattern and had declined by some 80% by early 1961. Among new issues, the most notable without doubt was **Racal.** Described by the *FT* as "one of the most interesting newcomers in recent months despite its short history", the placing of 25% of the shares at 20/3 capitalised the whole group at £1.3 million. Despite caveats about heavy dependency on government orders, the shares topped the most active stocks list on the first day of dealing, establishing a premium of 64% on the issue price.

Trading places

The pay pause had not been popular with the trade unions and the autumn of 1961 witnessed an outbreak of major industrial disputes. At Rootes' Acton plant a thousand unofficial strikers were holding up car production in Coventry and putting thousands more out of work. In South Wales, 15,000 were idle as a result of a dispute concerning the wages of just 300 furnace bricklayers. 1962 opened with 160,000 postal workers operating a "go-slow" after the rejection of their 4% wage claim, and union after union was queueing to present demands well in excess of the Chancellor's 2.5% "guiding light", a figure calculated by the Treasury to keep earnings in line with their estimate of the probable rise in productivity.

Not surprisingly, equities continued to drift for the first six months of 1962 despite three half-point reductions in Bank Rate, taking it down to 4.5% by April, and a broadly neutral budget, apart from the introduction of short-term Capital Gains Tax. To use a phrase of the 'eighties, the economy seemed to be "dead in the water". Earlier assumptions of a rise in consumer spending fuelled by a rise in personal incomes, appeared to be wide of the mark regardless of the Bank Rate cuts, the easing of restrictions on bank lending and the lowering of minimum HP deposits.

Industry, too, seemed to have pulled in its horns. Stocks were being run down and capital expenditure reduced as company profits fell back and confidence waned.

FT Actuaries Indices

Introduced in June 1962, the FT Actuaries Indices (so-called because they were devised by the *Financial Times* in cooperation with the Institute of Actuaries), provided a much more representative and thus more accurate picture of what was happening in the UK stock market. The broad indices like the All Share and the 500 Industrials break down into main groups of Capital Goods, Consumer Durables etc., and then into individual sectors, i.e. Electricals, Stores, Properties. It was now possible to look at the performance of a single share in relation to its sector as well as to the market as a whole. The indices are based on an arithmetical mean and weighted for market capitalisation to reflect the growing – or declining – importance of companies and sectors.

In May, this mood of depression deepened when Wall Street took fright at what it saw as President Kennedy's anti-business stance after he had forced the US steel industry to withdraw its price rises. The Dow Jones index was already well down from its January peak of 726, but on 29th May a shock 35-point drop to 563.4 panicked London into an 18-point slump to 261.3, its largest one-day fall since Hitler's ultimatum to Czechoslovakia in September 1938. Although the lows in both centres were not touched until the following month (535 and 252.8), the violence of the falls served to clear the air and a base was established for a new primary rise. The advice of Lord Ritchie, Chairman of the Stock Exchange, given at the height of the May panic, that "small investors should put their heads down and let the wind blow over them", was particularly appropriate at the time.

Selwyn Lloyd resigns

Political factors now began to assert themselves. A run of disappointing by-election results had persuaded the Prime Minister that his Chancellor was not presenting the right "image" to the electorate, and in July Selwyn Lloyd was invited to resign. This was part of a drastic Cabinet reshuffle in which no fewer than seven out of 21 ministers were replaced on the evening of 13th July, henceforth to be called The Night of the Long Knives. 'Supermac' became 'Mac the Knife'. Selwyn Lloyd's successor was Reginald Maudling, at 45 one of the younger members of the Tory hierarchy, described by the *Financial Times* as "a gregarious man, with experience of economic matters, an acquaintance with businessmen and a mind of his own". With retail sales stuck on a plateau, unemployment rising, and an encouraging surge in exports leaving room for expansion at home, the new Chancellor might have been expected to provide some new stimulus for the economy. In the event, he stood pat on the measures of his predecessor, influenced by evidence that expansionary forces were already well underway. There were sound political reasons for adopting this "steady as she goes" approach. The forced departure of Selwyn Lloyd had been interpreted in many quarters as a panic measure presaging a switch to more expansionist policies, and the Prime Minister was eager to demonstrate that it was simply part of a carefully-planned strategy. The former Chancellor had won a respite for the economy with his "pay pause", and what was needed now was a slide into permanent "wage restraint", the transition to be marked by the setting up of the National Incomes Commission. The TUC immediately declared it would have nothing to do with any sort of incomes policy, but the body operated with varying degrees of success until March 1965, when the Labour government replaced it with the Prices and Incomes Board.

At 275 in October, the equity index had staged a modest recovery from its June low, but there was little to encourage further progress. Gilt-edged stocks, on the other hand, were enjoying a revival as anxiety over the prospects for industrial equities, coupled with the reductions in Bank Rate, brought in new buyers. Already well up from the August 1961 low point, the Government Securities index was back to 85 again in October. Both gilts and equities, however, had a surprise in store when the Cuban missile crisis blew up at the end of that month. Irrefutable US aerial photographic intelligence had shown that the Soviet Union was engaged in the building of surface-to-surface, medium-range missile sites in Cuba. President Kennedy insisted that Soviet ships already on their way to Cuba with missiles turn back and that the nuclear threat to the US be withdrawn immediately. After a few tense days, Khruschev backed down, the ships turned around and he agreed to dismantle the sites and remove all the missiles. Although the world teetered on the brink of nuclear war, markets reacted with relative calm. In the wake of the Dow losing 10.5 to 558, the FT 30 dropped 7.8 to 264.4 and just over two points were knocked off Government Securities. The rapid resolution of the crisis prompted an instant rebound and, by the end of December, equities at 281.6 had recorded a loss of just 7.5% while gilts were up by no less than 14%. The revival in equities had been helped in November by a package from the new Chancellor designed to restore business confidence and provide a moderate stimulus for the economy, consistent with a 4% growth target. The measures were targeted at the weak spots in the economy, namely the motor industry and industrial investment generally. They included a reduction in purchase tax on private cars from 45% to 25% (which brought down the price of a new Mini from £509 to £448), more generous investment allowances and a quicker write-off for outlay on heavy capital goods.

Rebirth of Rolls Razor

One event in May 1962 was to occupy the attention of investors and the financial press for the next couple of years. This was the return to the market of **Rolls Razor**, a "shell" company whose shares had been suspended in January 1960 pending details of the reorganisation following "an agreement for the manufacture and distribution of Electromatic washing machines". Approximately 10% of the capital was made available to the public by way of a tender offer at 23/- a share. The issue was only modestly oversubscribed, but before long Rolls Razor was regularly featured on the list of active stocks. Its managing director was John Bloom, 28, son of an East End tailor, determined to challenge the domination of the domestic appliance market by the big manufacturers. His chosen method was direct selling using newspaper advertising backed up by a highly motivated sales team. The shares rose rapidly following a production deal with Pressed Steel, and then a £10 million HP financing arrangement with Sir Isaac Wolfson's Drages. However, after touching 36/3 in September, they fell back to 27/6 in October when John Bloom was served with a writ for enticement by a husband who had already been charged with the murder of his wife, the subject of the enticement. In November, there was also a spate of adverse rumours about the company, concerning its methods of trading, the quality of its products, and its general solvency. A vigorous denial, authorised by its eminent trading partners, settled any doubts investors may have had and the shares ended the year at 36/9.

De Gaulle says "Non"!

Shares entered the New Year on a high note, continuing the post-Cuban crisis recovery and helped on their way by a cut in Bank Rate to 4% in the first week of January. Thereafter progress was slow, particularly during the first half of the year. The worst winter since 1947 provided no encouragement to the market or to the government. Its effect was to hit production in all areas of activity and to inflate the unemployment figures. Misery was piled on misery as the power workers seized the perfect opportunity to further their pay claim and embarked upon a "go-slow" with the inevitable power cuts and black-outs. A number of political shocks also had to be absorbed. The first came later in January when General de Gaulle, at a press conference, effectively vetoed Britain's entry into the Common Market and ensured the failure of the Brussels talks two weeks later. The market dropped from 292 to just under 280 on the press conference statement, but rallied strongly on the final decision not to enter, relieved that a period of uncertainty had come to an end.

The FT 30 was soon above 300 again and, following an "expansion without inflation" budget giving widespread tax reliefs and encouraging share buyers by halving Stamp Duty to 1%, looked set to continue its advance. Then in June, the Profumo scandal broke, casting doubts over the future of the government and of Mr

Macmillan in particular. Despite pressure from many in the Conservative party to hand over the reins, Mr Macmillan stayed on until October when he became seriously ill and was replaced by Sir Alec Douglas Home. The index had just managed to hold above 300 at the height of the Profumo revelations in June and July, and had recovered to the 330/340 range by October in anticipation of a change of leadership putting an end to the whole dreary episode. The week of Sir Alec's appointment duly saw a 5.8 rise to 344.1. By November it was clear that the economy was responding to the expansionary measures of late 1962 and of the budget. The Chancellor had no wish to apply the brakes after such a long period of stagnation, and given that a useful margin of spare capacity remained, his wish appeared justified on more than simply grounds of political expediency.

President Kennedy assassinated

The final shock of the year was the assassination of President Kennedy on 23rd November. The Dow had been falling in the four days ahead of the event – it would be interesting to know if the Warren Commission looked at the short interest opened during that week – and on news of the shooting the Dow fell 20 points to 711.59 before trading was suspended at 2.20 pm. The news broke on a Friday after the London close, leaving a whole weekend for the implications of the event to be absorbed. On Monday the FT 30 opened 6.7 lower but closed only 3.9 down at 334.8 as Wall Street came in with a strong rally, eventually closing up 32.03.

The FT 30 ended December at 348.3 in "very active" trade to record a gain of 23% on the year and one of 37% on the June 1962 low point of 252.8. Gilts had a relatively uneventful year and the Government Securities index ended down 1.4% at 84.78. It seemed that the market had shown itself to be much more resilient to major political upsets and changes than might have been expected, and that the state of the business recovery had been the overriding factor to influence investors. And on these grounds, the prospects in 1964 were encouraging. There was no doubt that the economy was expanding. Car production had reached new peak levels, machine tool orders were picking up, and bank advances were increasing. A high level of pay settlements, however, showed that the Chancellor's efforts to continue his predecessor's plans for an incomes policy were not having much success. This failure, inevitable though it may have been, was to haunt him in the latter part of 1964.

On the corporate side, 1963 was an active year. John Bloom's **Rolls Razor** went from strength to strength in share price terms after announcing a succession of new ventures, including the sale of his own holding to **English & Overseas Investments**. **Shell** and **BP** made a £290 million bid for **Burmah** and **English Sewing Cotton** tried to buy **Tootal** for £5.6 million. Both bids failed.

Harold Wilson becomes Labour leader

For many market commentators the apparently excellent prospects for 1964 were marred by the likelihood of a change of government. This anxiety had been heightened by the elevation of Harold Wilson to the leadership of the Labour party following the death of Hugh Gaitskell. Others were less worried. Despite his pro-left reputation, they saw Mr Wilson, variously described as "enigmatic", "pragmatic" and "empirical", as perhaps not such a damaging alternative to a Conservative administration that was looking tired after thirteen years in power that had culminated in the Profumo affair and then led to an unseemly leadership tussle. Mr Wilson's plans for a harsher capital gains tax and for the introduction of corporation tax in place of income tax and profits tax had been well aired, and it may have been the prospect of their implementation that kept market activity at a low level throughout the year. Nevertheless, 1964 was not without its moments. Belief that Mr Maudling would be forced to take a more restrictive line early in the year, evidenced by a 1% rise in Bank Rate to 5% and a record January trade gap, depressed the share index to 322 in February, but when it became clear that he was committed to his 4% growth target, shares began to rise again. A rise in imports, it was argued, was inevitable as manufacturers adjusted their stocks to the higher levels of output, and exports would rise in due course. In the meantime, any deficit could be accommodated by drawing on the IMF. The budget was not at all restrictive in any broad sense, save for increased duties on tobacco, beer and spirits, and the FT 30 rose by 6.5 to 352.5 on relief at its unexpected mildness. The advance of the index continued, despite an obviously deteriorating trade balance, and in early October a new record high of 377.8 was reached against a background of public opinion polls indicating a Conservative victory in the election scheduled for the middle of the month.

Labour inherits a bed of nails

Two factors then contributed to a sharp reaction. One was a sudden change in the message from the polls, which now indicated a strong swing to Labour. The other was increasing evidence that the deterioration in the balance of payments was not going to be a temporary affair. It was now clear that exports were actually falling, and that imports had begun to include a large element of finished capital and consumer goods, both manifestations of the deficiencies of production at home. The September trade gap at £111 million was the third largest on record, and in the same week that it was announced Labour won the election, albeit with only a five-seat majority. Asked what was his greatest shock on taking over the reins of government, Harold Wilson, echoing President Kennedy's words in 1962, replied: "It was to discover that everything we had said about our opponents was true." The index dropped another 5.4 points to 359.4 and then paused to see what the new Chancellor, James Callaghan, would do to combat a trade deficit for the year that looked like approaching £800 million.

The option of devaluation had been discussed but decisively rejected by the Prime Minister, despite the advice of some of Labour's most influential economic advisers, who considered it essential if the new administration was to achieve its domestic objectives of rapid growth, full employment and greater public spending. Wilson's decision was perhaps more a political than an economic one. He did not want Labour to become the party of devaluation. With devaluation ruled out, it fell to the Chancellor to devise an alternative strategy. His task was not made easier by an almost immediate post-election run on the pound, sending it to a seven-year low against the dollar. Foreign confidence was not helped by Chancellor Callaghan's failure to consult with his trading partners before imposing a 15% import surcharge in his first emergency package at the end of October. The autumn budget two weeks later, in which he raised petrol duty by 6d a gallon and gave early warning that income tax would go up by 6d the following April when the new capital gains tax and a 40% rate of corporation tax would become effective, was also seen as unnecessarily anti-capitalist in a crisis situation. The pound continued to slide amid talk of another devaluation and even a shock 2% rise in Bank Rate to 7% failed to stop it. What did turn the tide was the announcement two days later that the Bank of England had arranged with the Bank of International Settlements (BIS) and other central banks a $3 billion support operation for sterling. The situation remained fragile, however, since it was clear that Labour's 4% growth target for 1965 was no longer viable. Priority would have to be given to the defence of the pound and the boosting of exports, aims which must necessarily involve a major check to home consumption and cuts in public spending. The "hundred days" of action promised by Mr Wilson had begun so badly that the inevitable comparisons were being made with Napoleon's road to Waterloo.

Ordinary shares had not taken too kindly to this succession of post-election impositions nor to the sterling crisis, but after dipping below 330 on the rise in Bank Rate, they rallied to 335 by year end on expectations that the worst was over. Gilts were less resilient with Bank Rate at 7% and the Government Securities index showed a loss of 6.7% on the year at 79.07.

Hanson makes his debut

The corporate news in 1964 was a striking mixture of the good, the bad and the positively ugly. In the first category, March saw the launch of **Wiles Group**, a Yorkshire-based fertiliser manufacturer and sack hirer, with the offer for sale of 41% of the equity or 350,000 shares at 11/- each, valuing the whole company at £370,000. Three months later, Wiles made a double bid for Oswald Tillotson, motor engineers, owned by Yorkshiremen James Hanson and Gordon White, and for Commercial Motors (Hull). The shares gained 4/6 on news of the bids, closing at 18/-. The following year, George Wiles resigned, Hanson became chairman and White joined the board. The Hanson family accountant, Derek Rosling, took over the finances and acted as company secretary. He was to remain in a key position in the Hanson empire until his retirement in 1994. Thereafter, the new board began to carry out the aim laid down in the March prospectus "to consider the acquisition of further businesses, to be run in addition to present activities".

Among the flood of new issues in 1963 and 1964 notable newcomers were fresh produce distributor **Albert Fisher**, valued at £350,000; Robert Maxwell's **Pergamon Press**, in a £962,500 offer of 29% of the equity; and two companies whose lives were much shorter and less spectacular namely the 177 times oversubscribed **Headquarters & General Supplies**, and **Vehicle & General Insurance**.

Beginning of the end for Rolls Razor

The corporate scandal of the year was provided by **Rolls Razor**. The shares had peaked at 47/9 in November 1963 but were still 39/6 at the beginning of 1964, boosted by a flurry of new ventures including the acquisition of businesses overseas and the launch of a gift stamp scheme with 12,000 outlets, 35 redemption shops and a fleet of 20 mobile showrooms. Then in March the first clear danger sign appeared when Pressed Steel announced the closure of its Swansea plant and its intention to terminate the production agreement with Rolls Razor because of "overcapacity in the refrigerator market". The shares fell to 33/- on the news. They continued to fall, dropping to 23/6 on the results in May despite a doubled dividend providing an 8.8% yield. Talks with rival Duomatic failed to stem the slide and by the time of the Annual Report in June forecasting "considerably lower" profits in the current year, the shares were down to 14/-. There had also been reference to an improvement in the second half following "vigorous action" and the coming on stream of "new ventures", but by the time of the AGM in the first week of July, the price was down to 10/3. The meeting opened with the announcement of the resignation of five directors, including the Chairman, Mr Reader Harris, MP, and shareholders were told that trading was not very satisfactory and that there would have to be a rights issue to improve liquidity. Despite the well-attended meeting, there were no questions.

Two weeks later, while John Bloom was in Bulgaria arranging a travel deal for the tourist arm of English & Overseas, the rest of the board of Rolls Razor petitioned for the company to be voluntarily wound up. There were "wild scenes" on the floor of the Stock Exchange as the price crashed to 1/-. The next few days were taken up with frantic talks to implement a last-minute rescue but no one was prepared to come up with the money and on 31st August, the quotation was cancelled, the final price having been ¾d. The failure of any rescue operation was understandable in the light of the liquidators' report that "in the latter stages of the company's business, documents were not properly kept, minutes not followed up, and a state of complete confusion existed".

Given that the decision to liquidate had been taken just two months after the publication of the annual results, the Stock Exchange almost immediately issued an ordinance requiring quoted companies to announce interim reports to show "early warning" of profits trends.

Chancellor Callaghan gets tough

The year 1965 opened with the announcement that "a strict review" of all government expenditure was to take place. In the first stages, defence spending was the principal casualty, but when duty increases in the April budget and curbs on bank lending and hire purchase in May failed to boost overseas confidence as reflected in sterling, in July the Chancellor brought in a new package of spending cuts. This time, capital projects by government and local authorities were to be cut back and building licences were reintroduced into the private sector. Delighted at the sight of a Labour government doing what "a Labour government is not supposed to do", the Conservatives were quick to counter-attack. "The budget soaks the rich; it also soaks the poor", said Edward Heath in the Commons. On the plus side, the import surcharge had been reduced to 10% in April, and Bank Rate to 6% in June, but sterling obstinately failed to respond. The problem, argued the pro-devaluationists, was that the budget was simply not deflationary enough. Even so, the National Institute opined that the measures should correct the balance of payments, albeit "at the cost of slowing down the rise in national output nearly to a stop."

The stock market reacted by going to ground. Activity fell by 25% to its lowest level since 1958, but despite the general air of uncertainty the market was buoyed to some extent by consideration of the supposedly much more professional approach that the Labour administration of Harold Wilson was taking to the country's problems. The new Department of Economic Affairs (DEA) under George Brown with its National Economic Development Councils (Neddies) and its National Plan, was an attempt to remedy the deficiencies of overall planning that had bedeviled the first post-War Labour government. Although the aim of a 25% growth in output in the period 1964-70 was doomed to failure by the restrictive policies that the Chancellor was forced to pursue, large sections of business responded positively by continuing to invest, to hoard labour and hold down prices. The idea that the DEA would prevent the Treasury from thwarting a Labour government's plans for a new socialist Britain seemed to have quietly faded away. Sentiment was also aided by the government's apparent eschewing of doctrinaire socialism in favour of a more "pragmatic" attitude towards the economy, although the cynical pointed out that with such a tiny majority – it was down to just two in the summer – this was more a matter of necessity than of choice. Certainly there was no chance of steel being renationalised during the life of this Parliament, and mention of it was omitted from the Queen's Speech. Meanwhile on the other side of the political fence, Sir Alec Douglas Home had resigned the leadership of the Conservative party in July, and was succeeded by Mr Edward Heath after a democratic election.

The ordinary share index ended the year up just 4.7 points at 339.7 after reaching a high of 359.1 in May and a low of 313.8 in July. Gilts were practically unchanged at 78.74.

Cavenham comes to market

Among the more significant corporate events of 1965, although its importance was not realised at the time, was the flotation of **Cavenham Foods**. During the two preceding years, James Goldsmith, then 30, described as "a French businessman", had acquired controlling interests in Procea, the specialist bread manufacturer, Carson's, a maker of chocolate and cocoa products, and Carr & Holland, a confectionery company, all through the medium of Lanord, his private French food company. In the summer of 1965 all these holdings were put into a new group called Cavenham Foods, which now had a turnover of £27.5 million and negligible profits. There were 5 million Cavenham 5/- ordinary shares in issue, but there were another 5.6 million in Deferred shares, all owned by Cavenham Trust controlled by James Goldsmith and his French associate, Baron de Gunsberg. It was announced that a quotation would be sought and in July the ordinary shares were floated at 6/- on the basis of a profits forecast of "not less than" £215,000 in 1964/65 and one of "substantially more" the year after, a level which was judged by the *FT* to be "looking some way ahead for a group with a lot of problems to be put right". On the first day of trading, the shares opened at a small discount.

1966

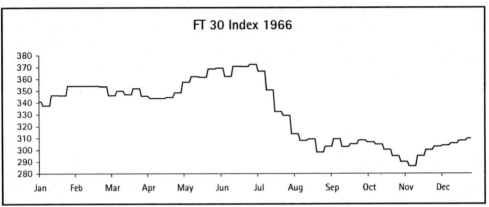

FT 30 Index 1966

Source: Thomson Reuters Datastream

Labour increases its majority

At the beginning of 1966 the Prime Minister had forecast that it would be a "make or break" year. In the event, it was neither but simply a continuation of 1965 with government policy still dictated by concerns over sterling and the balance of payments. At least the second Wilson administration could feel that it had a freer hand in dealing with the economy. By-election results in January showing a 4% swing to Labour, had prompted Mr Wilson to go for a snap election in March, and as a result a majority of three was increased to one of 97. Steel renationalisation was back on the agenda. The equity market took the event calmly enough. With the polls giving Labour an 11% lead at the end of March, a Labour victory had been well discounted. So too had the likelihood of further consumer restraints in the wake of the February trade figures revealing that imports were continuing to rise, and already down from a mid-February high of 358.6, the FT 30 was practically unmoved at 345 on the election result.

Mr Wilson had asked for a clear mandate from the country to "get on with the job". Having got it, the onus then fell on his two chief economic ministers, James Callaghan at the Treasury and George Brown at the Department of Economic Affairs, to tackle the problems embodied in the disparity between wage rises running at 9%, price increases at 5%, and productivity gains at 1%. Shadow Chancellor Iain Macleod coined the word "stagflation" to describe this situation, where inflation coincides with stagnant output and employment. Certainly numbers like these were not conducive to achieving any sort of growth target, and in an attempt to find an answer to the problem by keeping wages in step with production, a voluntary early warning system for the notification of proposed price increases and wage claims was introduced.

The IRC is born

Another of the methods chosen to achieve the country's necessary economic transformation was by the creation of the Industrial Reorganisation Corporation (IRC) with a pool of £150 million of public money to be used to devise and promote mergers aimed at improving the UK's competitive position in world markets. Mergers would provide the size vital to meet the challenge to industry on an international scale and rationalisation would produce the necessary degree of efficiency. The application of the 'white heat' of the technological revolution would do the rest. That such a body was the creation of a Labour government may seem strange today, but to a very large extent the IRC was an agent of government directing the fate of large sections of industry which otherwise would have been left to the interplay of market forces. The ICI bid for Courtaulds and the joint Shell and BP bid for Burmah had caused great consternation in the ranks of the opposition and they made it very clear that in their view, contests involving such key industrial groupings had to be subject to the test of national interest. The creation of the IRC was therefore an inevitable consequence of the next Labour government. It was also part of the devaluation alternative in that one of the arguments against devaluing in 1964 had been that the country's economic problems originated not so much from an overvalued exchange rate but from a structurally deficient industrial sector.

Selective Employment Tax introduced

The budget in April saw the introduction of the controversial Selective Employment Tax (SET), designed to give teeth to the socialist conviction that it is more virtuous to make things than to provide services. This tax on employment in the service industries had an immediate deflationary impact by adding something like a 3 to 4% imposition on services, with the benefit of premium repayments to manufacturers not scheduled to begin until February of the following year. Taken in conjunction with Corporation Tax at 40% and one side of a prices and incomes policy, the implications for company profits and dividends were not favourable, but once again the market was prepared to give the government the benefit of the doubt, and by mid-June the FT 30 had reached 374.2, just three points short of its all-time peak of October 1964. This enthusiastic response turned out to be premature, however, when hopes and expectations of renewed stability for sterling and further progress towards eliminating the balance of payments deficit had to be deferred as a result of a lengthy seamen's strike and the Rhodesia crisis. Chancellor Callaghan saw no alternative but to introduce a new deflationary package in July. First of all he raised Bank Rate to the familiar crisis level of 7% and a week later brought in a twofold series of measures to reduce the balance of payments deficit, one by direct action on government expenditure abroad, and the other by indirect action aimed at deflating home demand. The latter was especially onerous and included measures tightening hire purchase terms and building controls, the postponement of many public expenditure projects, further restrictions on bank lending, a 10% increase in all direct taxes, a 10% surcharge on surtax payers, and a six-month standstill on all wages, salaries, prices and dividends. The measures were not popular with the Chancellor's cabinet colleagues, who criticised them on the grounds that the function of a Labour government was to protect public spending, not slash it. The alternative of devaluation was again considered but once more rejected by the Prime Minister. One interesting by-product of this dispute was that, three weeks later, George Brown agreed to move from the DEA to the Foreign Office. Chancellor Callaghan was now firmly in control of economic policy-making.

The market slumps

Already weakening ahead of the Chancellor's moves, by mid-August, the index had fallen 20% from its June peak. September saw a brief rally to just above the 300 level, but it failed to hold and by early November the index was back to 284.2, closing the yield gap and touching its lowest point since 1962. To a great extent the market slump was a reflection of a serious loss of business confidence. The deflationary impact of the Chancellor's measures on home demand had been very great, resulting in a four-point fall in the industrial production index for October. This was the largest decline in a single month since that of January 1963 when snow and ice had brought the construction industry to a virtual standstill.

However, by the end of the year, hopes were rising that the balance of payments would now begin to improve. It was also perceived that if the cost of this improvement had been a long period of stagnation and a relatively high level of unemployment, then the pressure on the government – especially a Labour government – to reflate demand was bound to grow. There had already been some mild reflationary moves in the autumn in the form of a temporary increase in investment grants, and an easing of the credit squeeze on house-builders. Confidence had also been boosted by a series of currency swap agreements with the US and other central banks coupled with the Chancellor's vigorous assertion that another devaluation was neither necessary nor desirable. Buyers began to reappear and by the end of December, the FT 30 had recovered by 9% from the November low to 310.3, but still showed a loss on the year as a whole of 8.6%. Gilts were practically unchanged, despite a 7% Bank Rate, at 78.20 against 78.74 at the beginning of January. It is also worth noting that Wall Street failed to set a bullish example in 1966. The Dow had begun the year by hitting a new record high of 970.82, but with fears of a recession becoming a reality during the subsequent months, it was down below 800 again by the end of December.

Australian nickel boom gets underway

Almost unnoticed behind the meanderings of the London equity market in 1966, were the first stirrings of one of the most remarkable speculative booms of all time. This was the Australian Nickel Boom in which fortunes were made and lost, and mostly the latter as far as the small speculator was concerned. The first hint of excitement came with an announcement in early April of a strike by **Western Mining** at Kambalda to the south of Kalgoorlie, the principal mining town in Western Australia, revealing a "high grade nickel sulphide orebody". The shares of Western Mining rose 2/9 to 26/9, a new high, on the news, and tiny **Hampton Gold Mining Areas**, with land adjoining the location of the find, doubled to 6d. At this stage there was no popular appreciation of the significance of the discovery and it remained the province of the mining columns. Nevertheless, Western Mining ended the year at 55/3, while Hampton Gold soared to 4/- for a 1500% gain on the year. There was more excitement to come in 1967.

1967

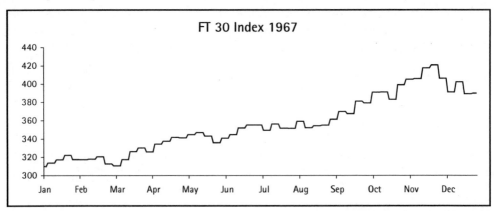

FT 30 Index 1967

Source: Thomson Reuters Datastream

Countdown to devaluation

Speculation about an imminent cut in Bank Rate provided equities and gilts with a firm start to 1967, and sentiment was helped by a sixty-point gain in the Dow Jones to 850 during January. The expected cut to 6.5% duly came, but the index marked time in the 300/320 range until mid-March when it suddenly came to life on news of three by-election results showing a strong swing to the Conservatives. The breakout was encouraged by a further reduction in Bank Rate to 6% and by early April the index had moved above 330. The budget was broadly neutral given that the economic recovery was expected to gain momentum as the year progressed, and also because the delicate state of the balance of payments appeared to rule out any early expansionist moves. Nevertheless Bank Rate was taken down another half point to 5.5% at the beginning of May. Equities also drew some encouragement from the government's formal application to join the EEC, and investment interest began to focus on those companies likely to benefit from access to a wider market. Significantly, it also called into question the level of the pound in its role as a reserve currency.

The outbreak of the Arab-Israeli War and the closure of the Suez Canal in early June led to a 7.5 point fall in the FT 30 to 332.1 on fears that a potential oil shortage could adversely affect the trade balance and restrict even further the Chancellor's room for manoeuvre. In the event the early resolution of the conflict, coupled with a mild reflationary move in the shape of a relaxation of the severe hire purchase controls introduced in the previous July, prompted a rapid rebound and by the end of the month the index stood at a new peak for the year of 356.8, thereby demonstrating at least some confidence in the achievement in due course of the Chancellor's projected 3% growth rate.

July provided a very clear illustration of the government's dilemma. The unemployment figures had topped half a million in June to reach the highest monthly total for twenty-seven years, the trade gap for that month had deteriorated sharply, and profits and dividends were at their lowest point for twenty years. Yet while any new expansionary measures looked bound to lead to another sterling crisis, Mr Callaghan denied categorically that he had any intention of resorting to devaluation. Later in the month, the government managed to defeat a 'no confidence' motion, and subsequently announced plans to more than halve the rate of growth of state spending to 3% over the next three years. The Chancellor's policies were not popular with the trade unions or with his own back benchers, and it seemed politically inevitable that further reflationary measures had to be undertaken almost regardless of the risk. In a "hands on" gesture designed to bolster confidence, the Prime Minister took over at the Department of Economic Affairs, sharing responsibility with the Chancellor for the conduct of the economy, and at the end of August hire purchase controls were further relaxed with special concessions to the hard-pressed motor industry for the second time that year. The FT 30 responded by adding 4.6 on the news to 361.2.

New peak for the FT 30

The sharp contrast between the buoyancy of the stock market and the parlous state of the economy was not lost on the editorial writers. In mid-September the index rose above 380 to surpass its June 1966 peak of 374.2 and its all-time high of 377.8 achieved in October 1964. In the same month, the country's gold and dollar reserves fell to their lowest level for two years, the Bank of England warned of a setback in world trade delaying the UK's return to an external surplus, and company profits and dividends were still trending downwards. The explanation for this apparent contradiction was that long-term institutional buyers were convinced that the worst of the recession had been seen and were prepared to wait for a recovery in profits and dividends in the wake of the inevitable reflationary measures. Furthermore, while the personal sector was still a net seller of equities, rising savings meant that more funds were going into pensions, life policies and unit trusts and thus back into the market. There was also a stock shortage factor at work in that the advent of corporation tax had tended to dry up the supply of new shares, capital gains tax had inhibited selling to some extent, and continuing merger activity was taking equity out of the market. And in the wings was the prospect of steel renationalisation creating substantial reinvestment demand just as it had under the first Labour administration's programme for public ownership.

Biting the bullet

The autumn of 1967 was marked by a further widening of the trade gap, growing industrial unrest, persistent weakness of sterling – and new highs for ordinary shares. Even the lifting of Bank Rate to 6% in response to rising US interest rates failed to hinder the advance and in the last week of October the FT 30 crossed the 400 barrier for the first time in its thirty-two year history.

By early November, the pound had fallen to its lowest level against the dollar since the late 'fifties, and even though well-publicised discussions were being carried on with the Bank of International Settlements over refinancing credits to bolster sterling, talk of another devaluation intensified. A further rise in Bank Rate on 11th November to 6.5% came just days ahead of the announcement of the October trade deficit, which at £107 million was the worst on record. Then on 20th November, the pound was devalued by 14.3% to $2.40. The act was accompanied by a Letter of Intent to the International Monetary Fund (IMF) undertaking that home demand would be reduced by £750/800 million almost immediately, but the aim, said Chancellor Callaghan, was not to deflate total demand and create more unemployment, but to curb consumption and investment at home in order to make room for additional exports that devaluation should make it possible to sell. To this end, Bank Rate was hoisted to the record level of 8%, bank advances were to be strictly limited, hire purchase deposits on cars were raised and repayment periods shortened. In addition, 2.5% was added to corporation tax, SET premium payments were withdrawn together with export rebates and dividends were to be subject to a "strict watch".

Ten days later James Callaghan resigned on the grounds that having broken so many pledges about not devaluing, he could no longer continue as Chancellor of the Exchequer. For three years he had pursued unpopular and damaging policies as an alternative to a course of action that was ultimately inevitable. These deflationary policies ensured the failure of George Brown's National Plan which, imperfect though it was, offered some hope of reversing the country's industrial decline. The inability of future Labour governments to make any progress at all with industrial relations legislation suggests that the National Plan could never have worked, but it is more than likely that the decision not to devalue in 1964 sealed its fate. The process of industrial restructuring would have to wait until the early 'eighties. Callaghan was succeeded by Roy Jenkins.

The market's reaction to the devaluation package was one of extreme volatility. The index touched a new peak of 420.7 on the eve of the event, lost 5.2 on the day of the announcement, another 11.9 the following day, and promptly rebounded to 420.6 over the next two days. It then lost 17.5 in a single session on fears that severe restraint in the home market would be necessary to enable the shift of resources into export production to take place, and that a tough budget had to be in prospect for 1968. This view was apparently confirmed by the November trade deficit, which at £153 million was the highest monthly figure ever, and the FT 30 closed the year at 389.2, down 7.5% from its November peak but up 20.2% on the year. The

Government Securities index lost 2% to 76.56, depressed by an 8% Bank Rate, but gold shares once again benefited from devaluation and revaluation hopes, their index gaining 26% to 65.6. Given all the excitement in November, General de Gaulle's further veto on Britain's entry into the EEC, already well signposted, passed almost unnoticed.

Nickels continue to shine

1967 was an eventful year for Australian nickels, which continued their apparently inexorable rise with **Western Mining** topping the £10 mark while **Hampton Gold** did even better, moving above 60/- against a starting price for the year of just 4/-. **Great Boulder** now joined in the fun and became the year's best performing share with an advance of 1370%. It is interesting to note that none of these companies had actually produced any nickel as yet, and more cautious investors had started to buy the larger diversified groups like **RTZ** and **BHP**.

Slater Walker wins a following

The soon-to-be-famous **Slater Walker** now began to make its mark. The company had begun life in 1963 as a partnership between Jim Slater, a 35-year-old accountant and protégé of Lord Stokes at Leyland Motors, and rising young Conservative politician Peter Walker. In mid-1964 they took control of a tiny quoted "shell" company called H. Lotery and began to make some minor acquisitions.

Greengate & Irwell Rubber, bought in January 1967 for £2.3 million, became their most important acquisition to date. It was a typical Slater deal, adding 46% to profits and only 29% to equity. Four more acquisitions during the course of the year led to the forecast profits for 1966/67 of "not less than £750,000" being revised to an indicated £1.3 million for a P/E of 18 at 27/6. (The practice of expressing share prices as a multiple of earnings had been long established in America, but did not come to the UK until March 1966 with the introduction of a flat rate Corporation Tax in place of income tax and profits tax). The share price had practically doubled and Jim Slater was attracting growing support from both private and institutional investors. Meanwhile in February, James Hanson and Gordon White made their first major bid, acquiring Scottish Land Development for £655,000, a deal which enabled them to forecast profits of "at least" £550,000 for 1966/67 after just £200,000 had been realised in the first half. James Hanson was also building up a following and **Wiles Group** featured among the year's top performers with a gain of 152%.

Among new issues during the year, perhaps the most interesting was **Ladbroke** which, in September, made an offer for sale of 1.35 million shares, 35% of its equity capital, at 10/- a share. The issue attracted applications for no less than 120 million shares, and opened at a premium of 2/6.

GEC buys AEI

There was no doubt that the bid of the year was by **GEC** for **AEI** (Associated Electrical Industries). The initial offer was worth £120 million, but after a spirited defence by AEI this was raised to £151 million and in November AEI conceded when GEC's acceptances topped 50%. At the time, this was the largest successful contested bid on record, and marked the crowning achievement in the career to date of Arnold Weinstock. The IRC was active in promoting the bid, much to the annoyance of the board of AEI. Their defence was to lead to a new ruling by the Takeover Panel to the effect that profits forecasts in such circumstances should not be made unless the current year was well-advanced, and certainly not for the following year. Already with ten months of the current year under its belt, AEI had forecast profits of £10 million, a figure which under GEC's bookkeeping was to turn into a loss of £4.5 million!

1968

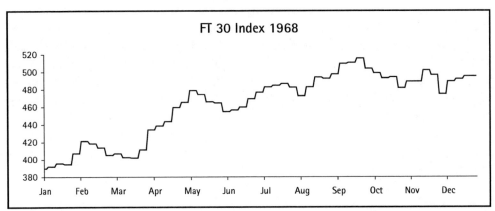

FT 30 Index 1968

Source: Thomson Reuters Datastream

A year of bids and mergers

There were two key questions at the start of 1968. One was about where the promised cuts in public expenditure would fall and to what extent they would need to be reinforced by further restrictions on consumer demand. The other was whether the government would be able to combat the inflationary effects of devaluation by means of an incomes policy which relied solely upon voluntary restraint. Both questions presented the new Chancellor with a major political problem which went to the root of Labour's philosophy in that he was forced to acknowledge the practical impossibility, when actually in office, of reconciling a policy of full employment and expansion with a payments surplus. His position was further aggravated by the fact that the reflationary measures of the previous August had sparked a retail sales boom that had led to increasing pressure on wages and prices, and that any countermoves would have to be made against a background of high and rising unemployment.

Equities began the year hesitantly under the influence of US measures to reduce their own balance of payments deficit, which were calculated to affect the UK balance of payments to the tune of about £100 million in a full year. Even evidence from industry of sharply higher export orders since devaluation and a December trade gap halving that of November, failed to enthuse the market, and it was not until the public spending cuts were announced in mid-January that the FT 30 came to life and crossed the 400 level again. That it did so in one bound of nearly 20 points owed a great deal to the absence of any simultaneous action against consumer spending, but sentiment was also greatly helped by a rash of major bids in January, more indeed than in any month since 1945. **RTZ** bid £55 million for **Borax**, **Schweppes** £44 million for **Typhoo**, **BMC** and **Leyland**, with the blessing of the IRC, had agreed to merge to create Britain's fifth largest company with a market capitalisation of £400 million, and **Westminster Bank** announced that it was linking with **National Provincial Bank**, to produce the largest ever bank-merger in the UK.

The last day of the month saw **Thorn** make a £155 million bid for **Radio Rentals**, and the index surpassed its post-devaluation peak to reach a new record high of 422.9 with heavy private and institutional buying – the unit trusts in particular were very active – further encouraged by a continuation of the upward trend in profits that had emerged during the final quarter of 1967.

George Brown resigns

Despite another sharp reduction in the trade deficit for January and more mammoth mergers, including a proposed £530 million alliance between **Barclays, Lloyds** and **Martins** to create the fourth largest bank in the world (instantly referred to the Monopolies Commission), equities were nervous ahead of the budget and reacted to 400 by the end of February. They were further unsettled in March by a doubling of the trade deficit to £70 million, a runaway gold price leading to the establishment of the two-tier market, and the resignation of George Brown from his posts of Foreign Secretary and Deputy Prime Minister because "of the way the government is run and the way we reach our decisions". In the event the budget took £550 million off demand, mainly by raising indirect taxation, and imposed a 3.5% limit on wages, salaries and dividends. It was widely regarded as tough but fair and was described in an *FT* editorial as "a budget admirably suited to the present situation and one which the sternest observers will find it hard to criticise". The index responded by rising nearly forty points or 10% in the week following the budget to top 440 by the end of March helped by a half-point cut in Bank Rate to 7.5%.

The rise continued with the FT 30 eventually crossing the 500 mark for the first time in the last week of August, a month which had seen another sharp increase in the trade gap, the Russian invasion of Czechoslovakia and more dire warnings from the National Institute for Economic and Social Research (NIESR) about the state of the economy. It was clear that devaluation had made more and more investors conscious of the advantages of equity investment and that they now regarded them as an each-way bet. If government policy succeeded, they were bound to rise, and if it failed and another devaluation was seen to be on the cards, then equities would win again. As a result, after a day or so bad news was brushed aside and the scramble for stock continued unabated. Obviously investors were not impressed by Mr Wilson's argument that "the pound in their pocket" would be unaffected by devaluation. There were more rumours of bids than actual bids – although there were plenty of them. **Brooke Bond** announced a £37.5 million merger with **Liebig**, the **Royal Bank of Scotland** got together with the **National Commercial Bank of Scotland** to create a £112 million group, and **Commercial Union** bought **Northern and Employers** for

£113 million. However, **Unilever** was unsuccessful with a £60 million bid for **Smith & Nephew**, the Independent Television Authority vetoed **EMI**'s £38 million bid for **Associated British Pictures**, and **Trafalgar House** failed to win **City of London Real Property**. New issues were hugely oversubscribed. A notable feature was the offer for sale of 720,000 shares in **H. Cox & Sons Plant Hire** at 8/9, which attracted applications for no less than 102 million shares to the value of £44.5 million.

FT 30 reaches another new peak

At the same time there was one fundamental prop for equities in the dramatic improvement in company profits since devaluation. Much of this rise was attributable to productivity gains, but to the extent that they stemmed from post-merger rationalisation and the ensuing redundancies – the GEC/AEI merger almost immediately led to 5000 job losses following the cessation of telecommunications equipment production at Woolwich – they proved a major source of embarrassment to a Labour government supposedly dedicated to a policy of full employment. As a result the Wilson administration found itself attacked as much, if not more, by its own side than by the opposition, a situation which induced a degree of paranoia in government circles. The "Wilson must go" campaign waged by the *Daily Mirror* had led to the sacking of the editor, Cecil King, and not that of Mr Wilson, but the pressure remained unrelenting. In July, John Gunter, the Minister of Power, had resigned on the stated grounds that he "no longer desired to be a member of a government led by Mr Wilson". This obvious political instability, coupled with an apparent lack of progress towards achieving a balance of payments surplus, did not help the pound during a period of worldwide currency disturbances, and in September, Mr Jenkins obtained a $2 billion stand-by credit facility from the BIS to help quash devaluation fears arising out of the pound's role as a reserve currency. This did not stop Mr Wilson from fulminating against the "gnomes at home" as well as the "gnomes of Zurich" for conducting a campaign to undermine sterling, and Labour left-winger, Eric Heffer, demanded that the former should be arrested. Encouraged by this evidence of international support and by sharply improved August trade figures, the Chancellor cut Bank Rate by 0.5% to 7% on 20th September. The index promptly added 6.6 to 521.9, a new peak which was to remain a record until 1972. Within a week, the FT 30 fell below 500 again in anticipation of a further round of HP and consumer credit controls in the wake of indications of a continuing boom in consumer spending to a degree which could jeopardise the balance of payments objective.

A touch on the brakes

The first of these restrictions duly came in early November, and principally involved an increase in the minimum deposit for car purchase and a shortening of the repayment period. Mr Jenkins was quick to point out that his actions should not be regarded as a sign that anything had gone wrong, but simply as a move to ensure that an incipient boom was channelled towards exports and industrial investment rather than towards domestic consumption. The index staged a recovery to over 500 again, but relapsed into the 480/490 range when a new set of deflationary measures was introduced at the end of the month. Purchase tax was upped by 10%, bank lending to the private sector was further restricted, and an import deposit scheme was introduced. The object was to cut home demand by 0.5% and private consumption by 1%, but by adding 1.5% to the cost of living an additional strain was imposed on the incomes policy at great political cost to the government. Engineering union leader Hugh Scanlon warned that "all hell would break loose" unless the government abandoned its wages legislation.

In the autumn, **GEC** announced that it had agreed merger terms with **English Electric**, having pushed **Plessey** off the scene, again with the help of the IRC. There was another flurry of bids in December. **Consolidated Goldfields** won **Amalgamated Roadstone** with a £37 million bid, **Rank Hovis** bought **Cerebos**, **City Centre** accepted a £65 million offer from **Land Securities, Beechams** bid £14 million for **Horlicks** – a figure boosted by **Boots'** intervention to £19.3 million – and **Unilever** proposed a merger with **Allied Breweries**. All this frantic bid activity, coupled with the reporting of a November trade deficit of only £17 million, helped industrials to end the year at 506.4 for a gain of 30%. Wall Street was no hindrance either. It had begun the year badly, influenced by the intensification of the war in Vietnam following the Tet offensive, but perked up decisively on the announcement that President Johnson would not run for a second term. Subsequent peace moves and then the Nixon victory in November saw the Dow by 31st December at 943.7, up over a hundred points on the year. Gilts, on the other hand, were down 6% at 71.75, a new low, affected by continuing currency uncertainties, high interest rates, and a growing disillusionment among investors about the investment merits of fixed interest stocks in an inflationary environment that was obviously here to stay. Golds continued to move ahead as the bullion price topped $40 and the index closed the year at 79.3, up 21%. The highlight of the Kaffir market was the flooding of the West Driefontein mine which caused the price to halve to 83/9 on the day the news broke.

Hanson begins to expand

1968 was an important foundation-building year for James Hanson and the **Wiles Group**. A modest rights issue in January raised £705,000 net "to finance continuing growth in existing activities and to provide cash for future acquisitions". Part of the sum was also earmarked "to reduce bank indebtedness", a policy demonstrating an early aversion to high gearing. At the same time, a profits forecast for 1967/68 was made of £675,000 along with the promise of a raised dividend to leave the shares at 28/- yielding 4% and with a P/E of 15. In April, a successful £2.9 million bid was made for **West of England Sack**, a deal which added 18.5% to equity and no less than 50% to earnings. The immense benefits of the West of England Sack deal soon became apparent and in September profits for 1968/69 were widely estimated to top £1.2 million. Wiles' share price was now over 50/-, and on a prospective P/E of 27.5, the market was clearly expecting more acquisitions. **Butterley Brick** was the next target at £3.7 million in cash and loan stock.

Hanson and Slater join forces

Now came the much lauded link with **Slater Walker** via a share exchange deal which resulted in Slater Walker taking a 14.4% stake in Wiles. Slater Walker had a market capitalisation of £120 million at the time, compared with one of just £20 million for Wiles, and the rationale for the link was that the latter would undertake acquisitions which, though attractive, were too small for the larger group. James Hanson and Jim Slater had become acquainted when Slater was a director of AEC, the commercial vehicle maker for which Tillotson, the original Hanson transport company, had been a distributor. In an interview for the Men and Matters column of the *Financial Times*, James Hanson recalled that in those early years, Slater was telling him what companies he ought to be buying when at the time Hanson wanted simply to consolidate. "We were slow starters," he added.

Slater Walker goes from strength to strength

Meanwhile **Slater Walker** was also having an active year. April saw the hugely successful launch of its first unit trust, **Invan**, as well as its biggest bid yet in the form of an £18 million offer for the UK's leading window maker, **Crittall Hope**. On the assumption that profits from Invan and earlier acquisitions would take Slater Walker's pretax total for 1968 up from £1.16 million to nearer £2 million, Crittall Hope was estimated to add 37% to equity and an immediate 40% to earnings with the further benefit of a high asset value and a low return on capital providing scope for a quick turnaround. By early August the forecast profits cum Crittall Hope were raised to £3 million for a P/E of 41 on a share price which had now reached 73/-. A week later, when the purchase of a small Bahamian bank was announced, the forecast was raised yet again to £3.25 million. Then in September an agreed £33 million bid was made for **Drages**, part of Sir Isaac Wolfson's empire, which with its large hire purchase interests and its Ralli Bros. merchant banking subsidiary, brought Slater Walker closer to achieving what was widely perceived to be its ultimate goal of becoming a major force in the investment banking world.

Devaluation favourites

Among the likely gainers from devaluation to find favour with investors in 1968 was **Racal**. By the end of the year, the shares had risen to 146/- for a prospective P/E of 33.5 on forecast profits of £950,000 pre-tax for 1968/69 against £855,000, and analysts took the view that with R & D expenditure almost on a par with this figure, then it would produce more profits post-devaluation than it had before.

Another was **Lesney Products**, the maker of die-cast toys, about 70% of which were exported. So popular were the toys that despite annual increases in capacity, overseas buyers were actually "rationed". The company had enjoyed an apparently unassailable competitive position throughout the 'sixties, and investors who had been lucky in the offer for sale when the company came to the market at 20/- in 1960, had seen a £100 investment grow to something like £10,000 in the wake of an original prospectus forecast of pretax profits of £300,000 turning into an actual figure of £3.64 million in 1967/68.

Pass the parcel

The year's big disappointment, especially for the small investor, was the demise of **Headquarters and General Supplies**, a speciality stores and mail order group. It was launched in July 1963 with an offer for sale at 9/3, and was oversubscribed a record 177 times. On the first day of trading it opened at 15/9 and eventually touched a peak of 37/- in 1964 on expectations that the prospectus profits forecast of £160,000 would be exceeded by at least £100,000, and that a raised interim dividend indicated a 40% payment for the year against the original 27.5% forecast. Chairman and owner of 57% of the shares, Major Collins, enthused shareholders at the company's first AGM by saying, "I can see nothing but going forward, the sky is the limit" – a view which seemed to be confirmed by the report of a rapid sell-out of a stock of 25,000 Beatle wigs! The actual profit figure for the first year turned out to be £273,000 but it marked both the peak for profits and for the share price. After a mediocre performance over the next three years, in July 1967 Major Collins resigned from all his positions on the board of Headquarters and General and sold the bulk of his shares at around the current price of 10/9 to the new Chairman, Jack Harrison. In March 1968 he sold the rest at 8/-, at a time when the new management had just forecast a profit of around £90,000 for the year to 31st March 1968 after a first half profit of £43,000. Then in July the company announced that "a substantial loss" was now in prospect for the year just ended instead of a profit of £90,000, and the following month the company was declared insolvent after the auditors had restated the first half profit figure as a loss of £125,000. Fortunately, Jack Harrison had managed to pass on his holding to Ionian Bank at 8/- a share, and hopes that the bank would stage a rescue kept the shares at around the 2/6 mark for a time. In late September, however, they were declared valueless and subsequently the quotation was cancelled.

Cyril Lord's empire collapses

One of the best known names in retailing in the 'sixties was Cyril Lord, who tried to do for household textiles what John Bloom had done for washing machines. He lasted longer but still failed for much the same reason. Vertical integration combining the role of manufacturer and retailer in a wide range of products left him with the necessity of maintaining a consistently high throughput in order to be profitable. Despite heavy and costly TV advertising, his range of products proved too wide to be economic and there was too much competition both from manufacturers and from specialist retailers. Launched at 10/- in 1964, the shares peaked at 18/6 two years later, and collapsed in a wave of rumours in November 1968 after reporting a £766,000 loss and exceeding bankers' limits. When a bailout by Courtaulds at 1/- a share had to be abandoned, a receiver was appointed.

Australians boil over

Australian mining stocks peaked in early 1968 but though down, they were by no means out and as some of the early favourites faded, there were plenty of newcomers to take their places. Dealing was often frenzied and the case of **Metals Exploration** in January was not at all unique. Reuters had mistakenly added a nought on to the estimated tonnage of nickel ore at the company's Greenvale site, and as a result the share price rocketed from 37/- to 85/- only to relapse to its starting point when the mistake was corrected!

    Western Mining also helped to restore some sanity to the market by coming out with a large rights issue and at the same time detailing its production plans. Analysts now had some facts and figures to work with and once the shares could be judged on solid investment merits, they lost much of their speculative "blue sky" appeal, practically halving by the end of the year. **Hampton Gold** followed a similar pattern, closing the year at 40/9 against an all-time high of 130/- in March. A new name began to appear in the mining columns in May. It was that of a tiny Adelaide-based company called **Poseidon**, reporting that nickel values had been found at its Bindi Bindi prospect, 100 miles north of Perth. In order to raise additional exploration funds it had placed A$157,000 of shares at A$1.30 with a London institution. Less than two years later, it was to be called the "share of the century".

Sir Billy Butlin retires

Sir William Butlin, better-known to the public as simply Billy Butlin, retired at the age of 69 as chairman and joint managing director of the holiday camp and restaurant chain he had founded in 1935. His was a classic rags-to-riches story. He worked his passage from Canada to Liverpool on a cattle boat in 1921, and with £5 in his pocket walked to Bristol to save the cost of the rail journey. There he joined an uncle who owned a travelling fair, and his first business success came from buying a hoop-la stall for 30/- and expanding it. The idea for the holiday camps came from seeing holidaymakers sitting in the rain with nothing to do, and he set up his first camp at Skegness in 1935. By 1939 he had three camps, all of which were requisitioned on the outbreak of war. Business boomed after 1945, when everyone wanted cheap holidays and Continental Europe had no facilities to offer. The move into the restaurant business was instigated by Sir William's son, Robert, and their flagship establishment was the Top of the Tower, a revolving restaurant at the top of the Post Office Tower, commanding a panoramic view of London. Butlins was taken over by the Rank Organisation in 1972 for £43 million.

1969

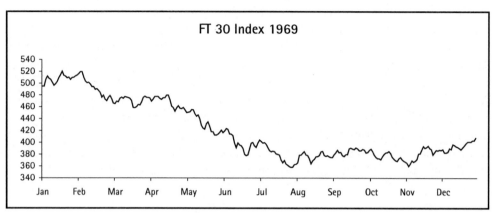

FT 30 Index 1969

Source: Thomson Reuters Datastream

The bear market begins

Equities began the New Year in fine form, managing on two occasions in January to get within a couple of points of the September 1968 high of 521.9 on turnover topping the £1 billion mark for the first time ever. Sentiment was helped by a sharply improving trend in the balance of payments in the final quarter, a continuing merger boom and evidence that the strong rise in industrial investment and consumption in 1968 was paying off in terms of productivity gains and corporate profitability. Contrary to earlier expectations, a high rate of growth had been achieved at the same time as an improvement in the balance of payments.

None of this meant that the rest of the year was going to be plain sailing for the equity market. For one thing, at 520 the FT 30 was selling on a P/E of 22 and yielding 3.5% with a reverse yield gap at a new record level of 4.78%, which meant that a great deal had already been well discounted. For another, the Chancellor had no intention of throwing away the advantage he had gained, and was determined that the economy should not grow faster in the months ahead than was compatible with his planned balance of payments surplus. Now, faced with evidence that a scramble for labour was developing and that a shortage was the factor most likely to limit further growth in output, in early February he began to intensify the domestic squeeze instituted the previous November. The banks were reminded that their lending restriction requirement was behind target and that they had to trim another £150 million by the end of March, and then to underline the message, at the end of the month Bank Rate was raised from 7% to 8%.

The FT 30 had topped out at 519.2 on the last day of January and was practically in freefall throughout February, declining another 7.7 points to 465.7 when the Bank

Rate increase was announced. Gilts suffered too, dropping to a new all-time low of 69.38 on the Bank Rate decision. The declines continued ahead of the budget, with sentiment adversely affected by signs of a worldwide trend towards higher interest rates and more restrictive credit policies, and also by a sharply higher February trade deficit. The gloom was alleviated briefly by a 16% swing to the Conservatives at the Walthamstow by-election, which sparked a 20-point rally, but the budget in mid-April knocked that very firmly on the head. A combination of measures which included a rise in Corporation Tax from 42.5% to 45%, a 28% boost to SET, the disallowing of interest on bank borrowing as a set-off against income, and the exemption of gilts from long-term capital gains tax, at a stroke hit company earnings, reduced the buying power of the private client, and altered the balance of attraction between gilts and equities. From 479.6 on the eve of the budget, the index was down to 452.3 within a week, and gilts also fell to yet another new low of 68.47.

IMF to the rescue

The decline gathered pace as the background continued to deteriorate. There was considerable turmoil in the currency markets with the French Franc in the front line following the departure of de Gaulle, ultimately leading to a 12.5% devaluation in August. There was also much speculation on the prospects of a revaluation of the DMark, which duly occurred in October. Inevitably the pound came under severe pressure after the first event, with foreign sentiment not helped by the strident opposition both from the trade unions and from within the Labour party, the Cabinet included, to Barbara Castle's proposed industrial relations legislation, "In Place of Strife".

"In Place of Strife"

Harold Wilson had become thoroughly disillusioned with the trade unions, seeing their unrestricted pursuit of self-interest as damaging both to Labour's programme for growth, redistribution and investment and the party's broad electoral appeal. He had blamed the seamen's strike of 1966 for "blowing the government off-course", and firmly believed that the high-profile dispute in the Liverpool docks in November 1967 had contributed to the loss of international confidence and to devaluation. Trade union reform was now high on his agenda, and Barbara Castle was appointed Employment Secretary with the task of restoring order to industrial relations and at the same time pre-empting the Tories who were already preparing their own plans. In retrospect, the main provisions contained in the White Paper seem no more than commonsense; but at the time they were a bombshell to trade unions accustomed to "their" government giving them anything and everything they wanted. In the event, the legislation had to be abandoned and the TUC's face-saving formula "Programme for Action" was adopted in a "solemn and binding" fashion by all parties.

An International Monetary Fund (IMF) report actually referred to "a tinge of anarchy" in Britain's industrial relations but, if it did not stop them providing a $1 billion standby credit facility in May, it caused them to impose strict conditions in the accompanying Letter of Intent. The two principal conditions were for a target to be set for a £300 million balance of payments surplus by the following March, and for a £400 million ceiling on domestic credit expansion in 1969/70, or one third of that which had taken place in 1968/69. The fact that the latter provision was aimed mainly at the public sector created more political unrest within the Labour party.

The squeeze stays on

With no prospect of a let-up in the credit squeeze, given the terms of the Letter of Intent and fears that it would soon begin to affect the corporate sector and its investment intentions, by mid-June the FT 30 had slipped below 400 and gilts were at a new low. America was showing a parallel decline. The squeeze there and fears of a recession had pulled the Dow back from a high of 963 in early May to 806 at the end of July, by which time the FT 30 had reached 357.4. Wall Street had closed on 21st July, the day of the moon landing, but failed to celebrate this remarkable achievement when it reopened. Instead, the Dow fell 11.9 on worries about government spending cuts and falling profits at Chrysler. These dismal performances prompted a number of commentators to speculate that the post-War period of adjustment of equities to inflation had come to an end, and some to suggest that the cult of the equity was dead. Even the optimists who argued that in percentage terms the market had now matched the declines recorded by earlier bear markets, had to admit that there was nothing very attractive or at all comparable with previous lows about a dividend yield of under 5% and an earnings yield of less than 6.5%, especially in the context of a much higher interest rate structure.

In the autumn, there were occasional rallies towards the 400 level with buyers encouraged by clear signs of improvement in the trade figures but just as in America, they faded on even clearer signs that there was going to be no softening of the government's hard line on inflation. Even though the Dow had fallen below 800 in early December, the London market managed to stage a year-end rally which carried it just above 400, largely on the suspicion that the Chancellor was unlikely to intensify the squeeze in the run-up to an election. The announcement of the proposed ending of dividend restraint was also a help. On the last day of the year, the FT 30 stood at 407.4, down 22% from the September 1968 high, and the Government Securities index at 69.04 was down 3.8% on the year but well up on the all-time low of 64.28 touched in June, when the US prime rate had risen to a record 8.5% and there were fears of another rise in Bank Rate. The Dow was 800.36, having begun the year at 943.75.

Hanson and Slater pull in their horns

Neither **Wiles** nor **Slater Walker** got through the year with their share prices and ratings unscathed. James Hanson bought **Provincial Traction** for £1.5 million in January but pulled out of a £3.6 million agreed bid for **Ibstock Brick** the following month over difficulties in agreeing sales and profit forecasts. Thereafter he did nothing save for making a few minor disposals and profits for 1968/69 came out at £1.96 million, leaving the shares at 18/3 in December, down from a high of 42/-, on a P/E of 13.5. By contrast Jim Slater was much more active on the takeover front, adding **Forestal Land** and boosting his stake in **Ralli Bros**. to 75%, acquisitions which raised his 1968/69 profits forecast from £4 million to £8.9 million. At the same time he acknowledged the fact of the bear market by making a number of strategic disposals. His African interests were sold to **Lonrho** for £3.9 million, albeit in Lonrho shares, and satellites **Barclay & Sons** and **Ralli International** were floated off. His share price ended the year at 47/- for a P/E of 8.6.

Goldsmith begins to make his mark

1969 was the year when Goldsmith's master plan for **Cavenham Foods** began to pay off. In September he announced that the reorganisation begun in 1965 had been completed and that he was now looking to expand both by internal growth and by acquisition, adding that the prospectus £650,000 forecast would be exceeded. By December he was able to announce that interim pretax profits were £458,000 against £161,000 and that on turnover up by 12%, trading profits had risen by 64%. The shares were now 8/9 and standing on a P/E of 21.5 on the basis of the original forecast, a rating judged by the *FT* to "leave scope for optimism".

Two "fringe banks" make their debut

Two new issues that were enthusiastically received, even in the middle of a bear market, were City banking newcomers **London and County Bank** run by Gerald Kaplan, and **Dalton Barton** run by Jack Dellal. Both had a five-year record of strongly rising profits with forecasts of doubled profits for 1969/70, and were hailed as filling a gap in the banking system by providing a more personal service for the smaller commercial customer. London and County came to the market by way of an introduction at 20/- and promptly attracted buyers at over 30/-, while Dalton Barton's offer for sale at 42/- saw a 13/- premium in the first dealings.

Meanwhile, in a similar line of business, Pat Matthews's **First National Finance Corporation** (FNFC) was attracting favourable investment comment as "one of the most dynamic shares in the market over the past five years with Tesco-style growth but without a Tesco-style rating". The company's lack of influential City connections was widely seen as the reason for the failure of its surprise bid for Bowmaker earlier in the year, but now with Hambros, the Crown Agents and Flemings as major shareholders, FNFC was regarded as having achieved respectability in the City. Its latest acquisition, **Financings**, a financial services company which specialised in guaranteeing second mortgages, was hailed as another clever financial operation of the kind it had exploited so profitably in the past. It was reckoned to complement neatly one of FNFC's other main businesses, which was the purchase and break-up of blocks of flats by sales to tenants. This activity was judged by one commentator to provide FNFC with "a very important element of flexibility" in that although it was vulnerable to sharp changes in the credit background, it could smooth out the bumps by phasing in its sales of flats! At 36/-, the shares were on a P/E of 17.

Lesney goes ex-growth

Even though Lesney beat its 1968/69 profits forecast of £5.5 million, it did so by only a narrow margin, which contrasted sharply with the previous year's £3.78 million against a £3 million forecast. The shares tumbled on the implication of a slowdown in growth, and six months later, in October, the market's worst fears were confirmed by lower first half profits. Inevitably, the company had not been able to maintain its monopoly position in the lucrative die-cast model market and Mattel was now providing stiff competition. Down from a high of 94/6, the shares ended the year at 34/6.

The Poseidon adventure

There is no doubt at all that the chief excitement of the year was provided by "the share of the century", **Poseidon**, whose discovery of high nickel values at Windarra, 160 miles to the north east of Kalgoorlie, sparked a renewed and far more intensive bout of nickel fever. The importance of the discovery for the whole of the Australian mining industry was that it indicated a possible major new mineral-bearing zone a long way from the known areas of proven reserves at Kambalda and Carr Boyd Rocks. And from the point of view of the market, it was important in that most shares had topped out in early 1968 and were still in a convalescent phase. Poseidon provided them with just the tonic they needed.

With only 2.04 million shares in issue, many of them in the hands of the directors and institutions, Poseidon was obviously going to be a thin and highly volatile market in response to any real volume of buying or selling. After a run-up in the early days of the nickel boom, the shares had relapsed to around the 13/- mark when a small placing was arranged in London in May 1968 to raise exploration funds. It then fell back again and on 3rd September a bargain was marked in London at 7/10½. In the last week of the month, a sudden flurry of buying saw the price up to 20/-, prompting a statement from the company that it knew of no reason to justify the rise. Then on 29th September it suddenly added 38/7½ to 59/4½ following overnight support in Melbourne and Sydney on reports that "nickel and copper sulphides had been encountered in a percussion drill at the company's Windarra prospect". No nickel values were available but Poseidon promised to publish assays of samples as soon as possible. On 2nd October the shares hit 130/- on publication of a bore hole result indicating continuous mineralisation in the core from surface to 185 ft, with the lowest 40 ft showing values of 3.56% nickel and 0.5% copper. The instant conclusion of the market on this evidence of a single borehole was that here was a massive orebody increasing in value with depth, which could support a cheap and quickly mounted open pit mining operation. Poseidon was now valued at £16 million compared with £20 million for **Great Boulder** and £400 million for **Western Mining**.

The next day the shares touched 170/- on reports from Australia putting Windarra into the Kambalda class and suggesting the existence of an orebody of 15 million tons grading 3.5% nickel compared with Western Mining's reserves of 15.5 million tons grading 3.7%. The fact that all this could not possibly be deduced from a single borehole was explained away by the belief that buying was coming from "those most intimately associated with the venture". By the middle of the month, the shares were 290/- ahead of the next set of assay results but their apparently disappointing values knocked them back to 170/-. They then quickly recovered on the basis of the assertion that the figures were "not representative", and on the last day of October reached 340/- on rumours from Australia that the next borehole result was going to be "a beaut"! The share price advanced to over 500/- in November but fell back on profit-taking at the end of the month on news that after 20 drill holes it was clear that the company had 20 million tons of good grade nickel ore capable of supporting a mining operation of 0.5 million tons a year.

Then in December the real rise began with much of the persistent buying being in anticipation of exciting revelations at the company's AGM in Australia on 19th December. The price crossed the £50 level on the day of the meeting and surged to £64 in hectic dealings after Chairman Tom Hutton had reported, to "prolonged applause and cheering" from the 500 shareholders attending, that "a major mining operation would be possible at Windarra" and that the Board "would try to begin operations as soon as possible", but he could not say what size of operation it would be, how soon it would start or upon what ore reserves it would be based! Another surge took the price to over £80 on Christmas Eve and the mania intensified for other nickel stocks. North Flinders, which had taken 100,000 shares in Poseidon out of a 500,000 placing earlier in the month, actually doubled from £5 to £10 in the morning's trading, and Western Mining added over £1 to top its June 1968 peak at 159/- on rumours of a big nickel strike at its Mount Clifford property. Not suprisingly, Colin Forsythe's **Pan Australian** turned out to be the year's best performing unit trust.

Maxwell v. Steinberg

Takeover activity was at a much reduced level in 1969 compared with 1968, but it had its moments. Perhaps the most interesting contest, with implications and complications which continue to this day, arose from US computer services group **Leasco**'s £25 million bid for Robert Maxwell's **Pergamon Press**. Clashes between Maxwell and Saul Steinberg, head of Leasco, caused the first approach to be abandoned but when Leasco's second offer was rejected once again by Maxwell, the outside shareholders controlling 36% of the equity compared with Maxwell's 26%, complained of lack of consultation and representation and a Board of Trade enquiry was launched. At the same time, in the US, Steinberg was not without his critics. He had recently made an audacious bid for Chemical Bank, an attempt which drew the Chairman of the SEC to express concern about the ambitions of "big game hunters" using debt instruments to finance takeovers and thereby producing artificial inflation of earnings. Clearly, 'junk bonds' were a subject of controversy long before the eighties.

1970

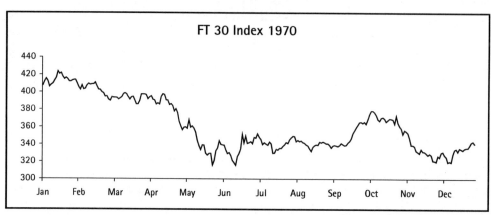

FT 30 Index 1970

Source: Thomson Reuters Datastream

The year began well, with many investors and market commentators convinced that the apparently decisive break above 400 had signalled the end of the bear market. Sentiment was also aided in no small part by the speculative euphoria engendered by the runaway nickel boom, and perhaps by the thought of having said goodbye to the 'sixties. 1970 also looked very likely to be an election year and some relaxation of the credit squeeze had to be on the cards. The sudden and unexpected abolition of the £50 travel allowance limit in the first week of the New Year seemed to confirm this view, which was given a further boost by the break-even December trade figures showing that the balance of payments was entering 1970 in strong surplus. On the news the index added 7.3 to 423.4, its best level since the previous May, but already the danger signs were appearing.

The great pay rush

After four years of wage restraint, a tremendous backlog of pay claims had accumulated. Barbara Castle and the Prime Minister found this "quite serious" and "disturbing" but the TUC President, Vic Feather, thought demands for higher pay were "understandable in the circumstances". December wage rate increases turned out to be at a level of 7.1%, the highest figure in fifteen years, but in an effort to placate trade union demands, the government elected to abandon the wage freeze and concentrate on maintaining some price controls in the hope that demands would be moderated. It soon became clear that no such moderation was going to occur and with more and more claims accompanied by strike threats, the index began to crumble, slipping below 390 by the end of February. Wall Street was no help. The US economy was faltering under the impact of continuing monetary restraint, and lower earnings reports were taking their toll of the Dow. Having begun the year at 800, by the end of January the Dow was down to 748 and reckoned by many commentators to be heading for below 700.

Despite urgings by the NIESR and from the TUC to reflate, the Chancellor was well aware of the tendency of both bodies to be over-pessimistic about the home economy, leading to a resultant bias towards excessive inflationary recommendations, and contented himself with a half per cent cut in Bank Rate to 7.5% in early March. The move helped gilts more than equities but the news that the balance of payments surplus had reached £450 million over nine months, comfortably exceeding the target figure in the IMF Letter of Intent, pushed the index towards 400 again. Further consideration of the implications for industrial costs of the wages explosion prompted a reaction to 385 but a recovery quickly set in ahead of the budget in mid-April. Another half a per cent off Bank Rate and an increase in tax allowances across the board was neatly balanced by a half per cent increase in Special Deposits in order to try to maintain restraints on bank lending. The market greeted the budget with a three point rise to 397.6, but that was the nearest it got to 400 for a very long time. A week later, it was back to 385 and then a succession of adverse developments pushed it decisively through the bottom of its trading range.

Conservatives return to power

A continuing decline in the Dow was a major influence on the London market as shock earnings reports, the Lockheed crisis, the collapse of Penn Central and the invasion of Cambodia saw the rapid approach of the downside target level of 700 and then its breach in mid-May. At the same time, there was a lot to worry about on the home front which was to have a direct impact on the stock market. Reports in April of large lines of blue chip stock on offer were widely suspected to come from the funds managed by **IOS** (Investors Overseas Services), an international fund management group rumoured to be experiencing liquidity problems. Since the group had no less than $2.3 billion under management and was a major force in markets around the world, forced selling from such a source was bound to have a serious destabilising effect on markets and on investor confidence.

A further factor affecting sentiment during the second quarter of the year was a serious dip in the Australian mining market, resulting in heavy losses for the many UK participants. And uncertainty was compounded by the pending election which Mr Wilson had called for 18th June, following a series of opinion polls which had given Labour a convincing lead. Unfortunately for Mr Wilson, the late publication of unemployment figures revealed an unexpectedly high total and the May trade figures released just two days before the election showed an unexpectedly sharp swing into deficit. Less quantifiable was the effect of Enoch Powell's well-publicised personal manifesto, in which he once again focused on the immigration issue. No one had forgotten his "rivers of blood" speech two years earlier and although it had led to his sacking from the Shadow Cabinet, it still served to confirm the voters' perception that the Conservatives took a tougher line on immigration than Labour. In any case, the Conservatives' emphasis on lower direct taxation, reduction of trade union power, law and order, and minimal state intervention in industry had greater appeal after a winter of constant industrial disruption.

In the event, and contrary to all expectations, the Conservatives won with a 30-seat majority and Edward Heath became Prime Minister with Iain Macleod as Chancellor. Mr Wilson's "100 days" had lengthened to over 1,500, but thanks to a remarkable coincidence, or perhaps to his well-known sense of history, they too ended on 18th June, the anniversary of the Battle of Waterloo. Having touched a low of 315.6 two days before the election, a week later the index was back to 350, despite the inherited problems of stagnant production, sagging capital investment and high unemployment, all accompanied by a rapid increase in earnings and prices. The plan of the Heath government for dealing with what was rapidly approaching a crisis situation, was not to impose a statutory incomes policy, but to try to break the wage/price spiral by acting primarily on public sector prices and by cutting taxes affecting costs, like SET. With this in mind, a review of government spending was promised by the autumn – but this did not avoid a State of Emergency being declared on 17th July in response to another dock strike.

Barber becomes Chancellor

Unfortunately for the Chancellor, with a growing number of wage awards fuelling cost inflation, any relaxation by cutting taxes or easing of the credit squeeze would risk adding a further element of demand inflation. Mr Macleod was prepared to hold the line by postponing tax cuts until the following spring, a policy decision which seemed more than justified by the June trade figures. The gap had jumped to £51 million as imports leapt ahead of exports, which were growing much more slowly in the wake of the recession in the US and also because of the drop in car deliveries from the strike-torn motor industry. Then at the end of July, Mr Macleod unexpectedly died after less than a month in office and his mantle passed to Anthony Barber.

The new Chancellor inherited a dock strike and a string of high percentage wage claims, all accompanied by strike threats. Unwilling to risk further disruption in such a key sector, he settled the dockers' claim on not especially onerous terms, but with unemployment topping 600,000 for the first time, and the production index falling for the third month in succession, he came under increasing pressure to reflate. Given that the money supply was increasing at over three times the official guideline rate envisaged in the April budget, and in the absence of a statutory wages policy, the Chancellor had no scope for administering any additional stimulus to the economy, but rather the reverse. Despite this obvious impasse, the market broke through the 350 level in late September into the 370/380 range ahead of the autumn mini-budget. A 2.5% cut in corporation tax, 6d off income tax and generous depreciation allowances, balanced by a wide range of public expenditure cuts and increased social services and welfare charges, were measures enthusiastically greeted by the market as evidence of government determination to check inflation. However, a reaction set in almost immediately when Special Deposits were raised by 1% to 3.5% in order to curb bank advances and within a week the index was back to 350 again with gilts losing over a point on fears of a rise in Bank Rate.

The decline now gathered pace with sentiment adversely affected by strike after strike as the TUC resolutely set its face against any moderation of wage demands as well as showing its unrelenting opposition to the proposed Industrial Relations Bill. But an even more serious worry for investors were signs of a growing number of companies suffering from a liquidity crisis, thereby further hindering the government's plan of checking inflation by intensifying the credit squeeze. In the first week of November, **British Leyland** warned that the financial position of Austin Morris was "serious" and the index slipped below 350. The following week, **Rolls-Royce** reported a shock loss of £48 million due to cost escalations on the RB211 engine, and was rescued by a £60 million cash injection. By then the FT 30 had fallen below 330 on rumours of problems at **Vickers** and **Alfred Herbert**, as well as at Australian brokerage houses, and it was only a meteoric rise in the Dow on US recovery hopes that helped the index to end the year at 340.6, down 16.7% on the year.

Australians on the move again

The first two months of 1970 witnessed increasingly frenetic activity in the Australian mining market. **Poseidon** had greeted the New Year with a £12.50 rise to £106.50, but after touching £120, it slipped below £100 by the end of January when it was given some competition – and a new lease of life – by **Tasminex**. This 2 million 25 cent share exploration company had started life in November 1969 at 60 cents (5/7) with a clutch of leases near Mount Venn in the Cosmo Newberry area about 55 miles to the north west of Windarra. Reports at the end of January that it had struck massive nickel sulphides while putting down an exploratory bore hole to look for water for its drilling crews, sent the shares rocketing from just under £3 to £40 in London before closing at £21 to value the company at £42 million. Chairman Bill Singline was quoted as saying that the find "could be better than Poseidon and bigger" but less attention was paid to his rider that he "thought it was there but didn't know because he hadn't got on to the geologists yet"! This was the highest price Tasminex ever reached and within six weeks it was back to where it started from as later reports made it increasingly clear that the "massive sulphides" were in fact "disseminated sulphides", including nickel and copper with "minor values". Both the Melbourne Stock Exchange and the Attorney General of Tasmania ordered a probe into Tasminex "in all its aspects", and the London Stock Exchange entered into urgent discussions with its Australian counterparts over the question of establishing a common policy on the release of information to shareholders. As matters stood at the time, the strict London rules were not enforceable on overseas companies.

Poseidon takes a dive

Poseidon was eclipsed only temporarily by the Tasminex affair and in early February it shot to a new peak of £123.50 in London on rumours that drilling was going well at Windarra and that chairman Tom Hutton, his chief geologist and his chief mining engineer had been observed at the site, "all three wearing smiles". Brokers, Panmure Gordon, also came out with a report that Poseidon was conservatively worth £140 and more optimistically £178 on a present value discounted basis. All eyes were now on the drilling report due towards the end of March, but by then a wave of selling had hit the Australian mining market, knocking Poseidon back to £88. The report, when it came, was good, but not good enough to sustain the price which instantly reacted to £67.50. A week later, it took another knock as mining expert Tom Nestel of Mineral Securities observed that it was impossible on the basis of the data so far released by Poseidon to obtain any idea of exactly how much ore was in the ground, adding that there were indications of a "far narrower width, lower grades and some lack of continuity" in the ore body. Down to £44 on this news, by the end of April the price had fallen below £30, only to rally to over £60 again in June ahead of director Norman Shierlaw's trip to London scheduled for early July and widely expected to herald good news preparatory to a fundraising operation.

The meeting was very much an anti-climax with the bulls disappointed at the lack of the expected massive upgrading of ore reserves. The shares fell back into the £30/£40 range as investors were forced to recognise that the company had moved into a less exciting preproduction phase devoted to raising working capital. Things were never the same again. By the time of the eagerly awaited quarterly report in December, the shares had fallen to £27 and on the unexciting news that ore reserves totalled 29 million tons averaging 1.5% nickel, they slipped again to end the year at £19.

Enter the "Nickel Queen"

Tasminex had stretched the credibility of the Australian mining market and the gullibility of investors, but there was still room for one more. In August a new "star" emerged in the shape of **International Mining Corporation**, chaired by Millie Phillips, reporting a near-surface strike of 2.2% nickel at Trough Wells, 135 miles to the west of Kalgoorlie in an area where Western Mining was exploring. The news doubled the price of the 5.57 million shares (with 5 million options) to 10/-. By the end of the week it had topped 20/- and then paused to await the first assays. Reports of nickel values of up to 3.74% sent the price soaring to over 90/- at one point in

October despite Mrs Phillips stating that it was "too early to tell" whether or not a major ore body existed. By the end of the month, the price was back to 30/- and with no exciting news forthcoming save for a temporary suspension following a breach of Stock Exchange rules, IMC ended the year at 8/9.

Mineral Securities feels the pressure

A new wave of selling hit the Australian mines in the closing weeks of the year, and even the highly regarded **Mineral Securities Australia** (MSA) began to come under pressure. The company had built up a portfolio of mining stocks for investment and for speculation and had prospered during the boom years under the administration of chairman, Ken McMahon, and thanks to the share trading skills of top mining expert, Tom Nestel. It had also taken stakes in a number of established and profitable mining operations and was widely recommended in the mining columns as a "safe" way to take a stake in the Australian mining market. It had also announced an "ebullient prospecting programme" spreading to the Philippines and the Sudan. The share price topped out at 91/- in line with the rest of the market, but by the time the Poseidon excitement came along, it was heading back towards its peak and soon surpassed it, reaching a high of 172/6 in 1970. In November 1970, while most of the supposedly more speculative stocks were collapsing, MSA announced a tenfold increase in profits and a one-for-one scrip issue "in recognition of its finest year to date", adding that profits were expected to improve "significantly" with share trading continuing to make its contribution. It was mentioned that no less than A$1 million had been made as a result of trading in Tasminex. The shares were then 120/-, but succumbing to the general weakness in late December, they had slipped below the £5 mark by the end of the year.

The rise and fall of IOS

Investors Overseas Services (IOS) was the financial phenomenon of the 'sixties and its creator, Bernie Cornfeld, tried to do for banking and investment what Hugh Hefner and his Playboy empire did for sex and style. The group had begun life in Paris in 1956 when the 29-year-old Bernie Cornfeld had conceived the idea of selling mutual funds to US servicemen. Early success had prompted him to build up a sales team selling funds to the many other expatriate Americans all over the world. IOS salesmen turned up everywhere, from drilling rigs in Alaska to mining sites in Brazil, selling the benefits of American-style capitalism on a save-as-you-earn basis. There were two vital driving forces behind this initial success. One was the great post-War bull market which provided the ideal background. The other was IOS's marketing technique whereby each salesman recruited his own sales team which then repeated the process almost ad infinitum, with everyone up the scale benefiting from the achievements of those below. While this sort of pyramid selling, or multilevel marketing, can have its place in the distribution of domestic appliances, there is clearly enormous scope for ethical problems to arise where financial products are concerned. As IOS expanded, growth went hand in hand with controversy, as regulatory authorities all over the world tried to curb the activities of this offshore colossus, which by 1969 had grown into the largest fund management group in the world handling funds totalling $2.3 billion. It was also building up a sizeable banking business as a result of sharing in brokerage commissions, in undertaking foreign exchange transactions for investors buying into dollar and sterling funds, and providing loans to clients to give them funds to invest.

There is no doubt that this degree of vertical financial integration sparked feelings of envy in many bankers, but it is also true to say that IOS carried within itself the seeds of its own destruction. Many of its sales operations involved breaching the exchange control laws of countries all over the world, and a great deal of investors' money was lodged in unmarketable shares and assets, the valuation of which was notional and highly vulnerable to any crack in confidence. Furthermore, the lavish lifestyle of Mr Cornfeld and his top aides meant that IOS figured in the gossip columns more often than in the business pages. In March 1970, the group reported that sales were up by 25% over 1968/69 and that it was planning to spend $44 million on expansion into new and potentially major market areas like Japan and South America. Yet a month later, in response to rumours of the dumping of large lines of stock to meet redemptions, and of sales, earnings and fund performance falling below target, top IOS executives were attending a two-day strategy meeting at the Geneva HQ to see what could be done to restore public confidence. A statement was issued to the effect that IOS was "sound" and that although 1969 earnings were substantial and still ahead of 1968, they were likely to fall short of projections. This did nothing to restore confidence, and the pessimists' fears were confirmed in the first week of May when break-even was reported for 1969 against a forecast of profits of $20 million, together with a loss of $5 million for the first quarter of 1970. Offers of help now became almost a daily event with the names of Rothschild (Paris) and King Resources particularly prominent. The latter company was run by John M. King who operated IOS's Natural Resources Account and had been responsible for "investing" $11 million of investors' cash in a half share of 22 million acres of highly speculative oil permits in the Arctic. The attraction for a rescuer was the fact that IOS still controlled perhaps the largest pool of fund money in the world. Rothschild were prepared to offer $1 a share for 51% control, but only on the condition that Bernie Cornfeld and all his top management team resign from the board. John King, on the other hand, was prepared to offer $4 and let them all stay. Even though the prestige of the Rothschild name would have saved the company, the vote was in favour of King. It soon became apparent that while Rothschild had the money, King had not and soon had no choice but to drop his bid, by which time Rothschild had walked away in disgust.

Out of the frying pan...

In May, Bernie Cornfeld was forced to give up his post as chairman and while talks were being carried on with an international banking consortium, former UK Treasury official Sir Eric Wyndham White took over. Negotiations were not helped by revelations in June of IOS's "unusual corporate generosity" to directors, officers, employees and friends in the form of loans totalling over $30 million, and then in September when it was announced that the first half loss for 1970 had swelled to $25.8 million. Salvation of a sort ultimately appeared in the unlikely form of Robert Vesco, the controversial 34-year-old head of International Control Communications, with a $15 million loan package. Bernie Cornfeld's initial opposition was overcome when he was allowed to remain on the board, but the deal was the end of IOS as he knew it. By the following May, he had disposed of his personal holding to ICC which transferred all IOS assets into a single holding controlled by ICC and its institutional backers. The outcome was not a happy one for IOS investors. In 1972 the SEC brought a civil suit against Vesco for allegedly looting $224 million from IOS funds, and in 1989 he was indicted by a federal grand jury on charges of smuggling cocaine into the US.

E.J. Austin and the "crock of gold"

Although operating on not quite such a global scale as IOS, another American-run company demonstrated once again that there are a lot of gullible investors out there. In 1967 and 1968, **E. J. Austin**, a small builders' supplies company, had been busy acquiring a number of similar businesses, but in May 1969 it abruptly changed direction when control passed to a Mr J.K. Howarth. He then began to make investments in chrome ore mines in Cyprus and in copper, gold, silver and platinum deposits in Nevada, and after suspension in August the company came back as E.J. Austin International, an international mining concern. The transformation benefited the share price, which rose from 15/6 to 18/9, at which level it was suspended yet again in January 1970 on the announcement that it was about to acquire the El Sobrante Mining Corporation of California for shares valued at £6.5 million. It was a complex deal in that El Sobrante, which was 51% owned by Mr Howarth, held the other half of the 40-acre ore body that E.J. Austin had already purchased, and the plan was to run the two properties as a single mining venture. Great excitement was generated by the deal when it was claimed that the mine was capable of producing annual profits of not less than £10 million when the plant was complete and in operation by the end of 1970. Since the earlier forecast for the current year had been no more than £500,000 pretax, the shares were soon changing hands at between 45/- and 50/- in unofficial dealings. At the AGM a week later it was further revealed that 300,000 tons of ore had already been stockpiled and that an assay report predicted a yield of $5,000 per ton, an extraordinarily high figure made possible by a revolutionary new extraction process patented by Mr Wayne Chambers, the owner of the other 49% of El Sobrante. Given that $35 a ton is reckoned to be a respectable yield for a gold mine, this claim was greeted with considerable scepticism as indeed was Mr Howarth's statement at the AGM that "there was literally a crock of gold at the end of the rainbow".

Some credence was given to these claims by brokers Spence Veitch having confirmed the accuracy of the profit forecast, but keen to convince his institutional shareholders, Mr Howarth announced that the Californian mining expert who had carried out the assays would be coming to London to hold a press conference and meet institutional investors. At this point the Stock Exchange stepped in and refused permission for the press conference on the grounds that information should not be given at such a meeting which was not immediately available to all shareholders, adding that no further announcements should be made ahead of the issue of the formal documents. To all intents and purposes, that was the end of the affair. On 10th March, it was announced that the El Sobrante deal had been called off, that Mr Howarth had resigned over the question of a conflict of interest, and that a completely independent assessment and valuation of the mining interests in Cyprus and the US had been commissioned. A week later, a receiver was appointed, and in due course a Board of Trade enquiry was ordered. Shareholders left nursing losses were principally the fast-growing fund management group, Surinvest, unit trust group Abacus, and a number of IOS funds managed by Surinvest.

Cavenham expands on the Continent

Two acquisitions in Holland in January sparked considerable interest in **Cavenham**, pushing the share price over the 10/- mark for the first time. Then in early February, the shares were suspended at 15/- pending details of a whole series of acquisitions in Europe at a cost of £5.5 million and judged to add between 40% and 50% to equity while doubling the £650,000 pretax profits forecast. James Goldsmith hailed the deal as creating a multinational company based in the strongest European countries with the greatest growth potential. When the offer documents eventually appeared in August, the forecast had been raised to £1.623 million, which meant that at the suspension price the shares were on a P/E of 18, or 23 with a full tax charge and allowing for the deferred capital. This was described by Lex in the *FT* as "a fancy rating" for a food company given a P/E of 15.3 for the sector, and the shares closed the year at around 13/6.

Hanson and Slater take a knock

The second quarter decline in the market took its toll of the conglomerates and May saw a precipitate drop in the shares of **Slater Walker** and **Hanson Trust** (the name was changed from Wiles Group at the end of 1969) as "bull market stocks" were downgraded to suit the new market conditions. At the time of its AGM in May, Slater Walker received favourable comment for having shed many of its industrial interests to concentrate on its banking and investment business, but this did not prevent the share price dropping from 61/- to 28/- at one point in the summer before recovering to 37/9 in September. In August, Jim Slater in a guest article in *The Director* had shared his intimations of problems ahead by opining that "the animals who learn to climb trees when the water is rising, they will be the ones to survive". Over the same period Hanson Trust fell from 24/6 to 12/6 before bouncing back to 19/6. Both companies had exceeded their profits forecasts for 1969/70, but while Slater Walker became more deeply involved in the financial world, Hanson Trust changed direction abruptly, dropping a £3.1 million bid for Steels Garages and selling its own vehicle interests to rival bidder Lex for £5 million cash. The motor side was worth £700,000 in pretax profits historically, but it was a cyclical business and the deal transformed the liquidity position of Hanson Trust which promptly launched an £800,000 bid in loan stock for **National Star Brick**.

BTR returns from the wilderness

For many years **BTR** had been regarded as the archetypal dull share in a dull industry. Making power transmission belting and industrial rubber products is not widely seen as a glamour activity, especially when the company loses money doing so. This was the case with BTR until 1968, when it reported a return to profits and forecast an "appreciably better" current year. Greeting a 59% rise in half-time profits to £526,000 in September 1969, the *FT* commented that the company "continues to pull itself up after long years in the wilderness" but noted that its return on capital was still only 8% and sales margins 5%. By now the shares had advanced from 7/- to 11/3 and on an indicated £1 million pretax total for the year, the prospective P/E was 14. But later that month it virtually doubled its size by making an agreed reverse bid for **Leyland and Birmingham Rubber**, at a stroke complementing its own product range and providing considerable scope for rationalisation. The move had been masterminded by the recently appointed 45-year-old Owen Green backed by the IRC. A year later he was able to report sales up 16% and profits up 33% to £1.3 million for an indicated total for the year of £2.8 million, giving a prospective P/E of 12.7 with the shares at 15/-.

1971

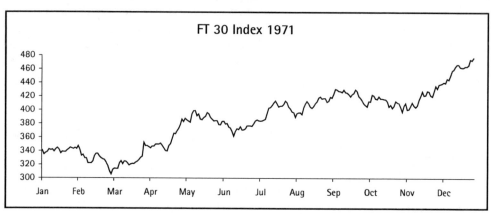

FT 30 Index 1971

Source: Thomson Reuters Datastream

Rolls-Royce goes under

The New Year opened on a note of continuing uncertainty. The government faced the choice of tightening the squeeze at the risk of more bankruptcies and higher unemployment or of not tightening it enough and letting inflation get out of control. News that average earnings in the twelve months to October 1970 had risen at a rate of 14% and that companies were evading domestic lending restraints by tapping the Eurodollar market, tended to favour the former course of action, but reports of unemployment figures heading towards 700,000 and then the appointment of receivers for **Rolls-Royce** in early February, argued for a degree of relaxation. The bringing in of an emergency Bill to nationalise the aero-engine division seemed to support this view, especially since it cast serious doubt on the new administration's pledge to abandon "lame ducks". The market, which had been holding in the 340/350 range, influenced by the Dow making new highs after a succession of interest rate cuts, took the Rolls-Royce news badly. It fell rapidly to 321.9 but then rallied briefly to 335 in the next couple of weeks, only to slip below 320 at the end of the month on growing fears about company liquidity aggravated by an announcement of 1,000 lay-offs at **Alfred Herbert** following a 30% reduction in orders for machine tools. Also adding to investors' fears had been the collapse in early February of **Mineral Securities Australia** (MSA) with its likely impact on Australian settlements.

The MSA debacle was totally unexpected, following literally within days of a fund-raising operation accompanied by a forecast profit of $3.5 million for the second half of calendar 1970. This was down on the previous half year's $4.77 million, but it was considered a good performance in the circumstances. The suspension of the shares and the revision of the $3.5 million profit to a $3.28 million loss sent a shudder through the whole Australian mining market – and through London. The Stock Exchange called for a list of outstanding Australian bargains from all its member firms, and dealings in all the shares of companies associated with MSA were suspended too. Ken McMahon and Tom Nestel both resigned and a $35 million funding operation was launched by a consortium of banks, all interested in seeing an orderly disposal of MSA's share portfolio. The problem appears to have been that MSA's long-term mining investments had been funded by short-term borrowings in the confident expectation that ever rising share prices and share dealing profits would take care of the interest payments.

Vehicle & General collapses

As if all this was not enough for the market to cope with, the first trading day of March witnessed the crash of **Vehicle & General Insurance**, leaving one in ten of the country's motorists uncovered. V&G was a relative newcomer to the motor insurance world but it had won a large slice of the market since 1960 by favouring "safe" drivers with a quickly achieved high rate no-claims bonus. It was also a member of the British Insurance Association, which the two previous insurance companies that had failed, Dr Emil Savundra's Fire, Auto & Marine in 1966, and London & Cheshire in 1967, were not. Furthermore, all this disastrous corporate news was being played out against a background of practically unparalleled industrial unrest. There was already a long-running postal strike creating considerable disruption in normal City business and the day the Vehicle & General collapse was announced coincided with a one-day strike called to protest against the Industrial Relations Bill in which 1.5 million workers were involved, making the action the biggest politically-inspired strike since the General Strike of 1926.

A new low for the FT 30

It was therefore hardly surprising that the index took another downward lurch, reaching 305.3 on 3rd March. In this instance, the FT 30 with its preponderance of traditional industrials, Rolls-Royce included, fared worse than the broader-based Actuaries indices which had bottomed in May 1970. Even though this dip turned out to mark the precise end of the 1969/71 bear market, there were few commentators prepared to recognise it as such since inflation was coming to be seen as just as much a threat to the corporate sector struggling with falling profits and stagnant output, as to the old age pensioner on a fixed income. Clearly, profits stated in money terms now bore little relationship to the replacement cost of fixed and working capital, and provided a poor outlook for investment. It was difficult to see any way out of this impasse, given the trade unions' resolute opposition to any form of cooperation over the question of wage restraint, and the government's determination to proceed with its industrial relations legislation.

In the event, the market turned up just as things looked to be at their worst, influenced to some degree by a continuing rise on Wall Street and also by the prospect that Chancellor Barber's budget at the end of March might offer some hope of salvation. This was precisely what it was regarded as doing and the FT 30, already on a rising trend, leapt a record 20.5 points after the budget announcement, to 352.2. Among its provisions were a 2.5% cut in Corporation Tax, a halving of the rate of SET, abolition of short-term Capital Gains Tax, and increased child allowances and pensions together with concessions to surtax payers, all timed to come into effect in July. The intention to introduce VAT, albeit at an unspecified rate and not until April 1973, was also announced. And very importantly, the ceiling on bank lending was raised significantly. The whole package was considered to be "a risk on the side of expansion" but there was no doubt that it came as a welcome relief, as indeed did the 1% reduction in Bank Rate two days later. By the end of April, the FT 30 stood at a new high for the year of 386.2, apparently undeterred by money earnings still rising at an annual rate of 14%, unemployment hitting a 31-year high, and a continuing stream of bad news from the corporate sector, with **Vickers** reporting a sharp profits fall and the passing of its final dividend. The Dow helped to redress the balance by simultaneously posting its own new high for the year of 950 despite warnings from the Federal Reserve Board about the effects of excessive monetary expansion and a very weak dollar.

The "Dollar Crisis" comes to a head

The following month the dollar crisis broke over Europe, and although it had little immediate apparent effect on equity markets, its implications were to have a profound influence over them for the rest of the decade and beyond. The origins of the crisis go back to the end of the Second World War when the European nations, devastated and poor, looked to America for aid and the financial stability provided by the dollar, ranking alongside gold, as the ultimate monetary standard. A system of parities was devised at Bretton Woods in 1944 and it worked well for a long period. Then there was a role reversal as the European nations became richer and the US, burdened by the huge cost of the war in Vietnam and its military presence elsewhere in the world, became a debtor nation. The country's gold reserves had dwindled, as had its surplus on foreign trade, and it was now forced to meet its overseas debts in its own paper currency.

During the 1960s, this meant that huge quantities of dollars were flowing out of America and into Europe, undermining the efforts of the European nations to control their own domestic inflation and threatening the system of parities. In early May 1971 the flow of dollars became a flood as US banks which had borrowed in the Eurodollar market to beat their domestic credit squeeze in 1969, repaid the loans in order to take advantage of the greater availability of cheaper money at home now that

President Nixon had taken the political decision to go for growth ahead of the election in 1972.

To the dismay of the other central banks accumulating large amounts of unwanted dollars, the US was not greatly concerned about the problems they generated. "Benign neglect" was the phrase coined to describe the US attitude formed by consideration of the facts that firstly the US economy was not heavily dependent upon external trade, and secondly the cost of US foreign policy was incurred largely in the interests of other nations.

The immediate effect of the influx of dollars in May was to force the Germans to allow the DMark to float, and of course it floated upwards. This was judged to be good for UK equities in that they gained the competitive advantages of a small devaluation without the penalty of higher raw material costs, and a strong advance took the FT 30 up to the 400 level. Gilts rose too on the expectation that a greater inflow of foreign money would lead to another cut in Bank Rate. The dollar price of gold also rose sharply, breaking the $40 barrier to reach its highest level in two years.

A monetary revolution

Two events on the domestic front in 1971 were to have a lasting impact on financial markets. One was the Crowther report on Consumer Credit, which concluded that all controls should cease and that the whole credit business be thrown open to competition. The other was the government's aim to introduce a competitive climate into the UK banking system by abandoning official ceilings to control liquidity for purposes of economic and monetary management in favour of the use of varying reserve and asset ratios. The members of the Finance Houses Association were quick to implement the recommendations of Lord Crowther, but the government's new methods for monetary control were not scheduled to take effect until September. These two measures, when allied with the Chancellor's reflation package in July, formed the foundations of what soon became known as the "Barber boom". Given the delayed effect of the March budget concessions, most serious commentators believed that no additional stimulus was required, and that the Chancellor had bowed to political pressure. Even the record level of unemployment which helped to influence his actions was seen by an *FT* editorial as paradoxically providing the best hope for the future in that it represented a once and for all labour shake-out which would have laid the foundations for productivity gains enabling the economy to accommodate a 4-4.5% growth rate without running into the usual problems of overheating and pressures on capacity. The danger was perceived that the coming recovery would be too consumer-based, leaving too little room for an adequate contribution from investment and exports.

End of an era for the dollar

Whatever the reservations about the wisdom of an expansionary budget, the stock market responded enthusiastically to measures which included the decontrolling of all HP transactions and drastic reductions in purchase tax. The FT 30 which had already crossed the 400 level again in anticipation of the package, rose to establish a new 1971 high of 413.2. Sensing unfinished business with the dollar, the Dow, however, was falling fast and its precipitate decline through the 900 mark pulled the FT 30 back to 400 again. Neither market remained depressed for long.

In mid-August, President Nixon made his move, marking the end of an era of dollar supremacy by taking it off the gold standard. This suspension of convertibility was accompanied by the levying of a 10% surcharge on all imports into the US, an action widely seen as an attempt to blackmail the rest of the world into accepting US demands for an effective devaluation of the dollar within a new and more flexible system of international payments and trading. At the same time, a 90-day wage and price freeze was imposed, offset by a formidable array of tax incentives. The Dow leapt 33 points on record volume, confident that the measures would bring the US economy back on course. When the foreign exchange markets reopened, the UK authorities had taken the decision to allow the pound to float, although at the same time reaffirming the $2.40 parity in the light of the existence of no obvious economic rationale for any significant degree of revaluation. The market greeted the news enthusiastically with the FT 30 surpassing its July peak.

Also buoying investor confidence was the acceptance in July of Britain's application to join the Common Market. After fourteen years of negotiation and three failures, this was regarded as something of a triumph, and one which would have long-term benefits for British industry. Its greatest immediate impact, however, was on the Labour Party, with Messrs. Healey, Crosland and Callaghan lining up with Harold Wilson in opposition to entry on the terms negotiated by the Prime Minister, while Roy Jenkins and Michael Stewart both agreed with George Brown (now Lord George Brown) that Labour would certainly have gone in on these terms. Labour had a three-line whip against in the entry debate while the Conservatives had a free vote. The latter prevailed with a majority of 112.

A new monetary agreement emerges

September saw a one per cent cut in Bank Rate to 5%, partly in a defensive move to stem the persistent inflow of hot money as the pound rose towards $2.50 but also in response to the chorus of calls for more reflation as the numbers of unemployed continued to climb. But if domestic developments argued for higher share prices, those on the other side of the Atlantic did not. President Nixon's August package had been well received by the market but Phase Two was a long time coming, as indeed was the new world monetary order expected to emerge from meeting after meeting of the Group of Ten. Wall Street soon began to have second thoughts and in October went into freefall, losing 70 points in three weeks with the decline assisted by prophet of doom, Eliot Janeway, forecasting a downside target of 500. The move pulled the FT 30 back to the 400 level again, but by the end of November both markets were rallying sharply on signs of progress in the latest round of monetary talks. Wall Street was further boosted by a cut in margin requirements, and London took heart from indications of yet another reflationary package with another half a point off Bank Rate. Then in Washington, just a few days before Christmas, President Nixon agreed to an official dollar devaluation in relation to gold from \$35 to \$38 and to all the major currencies, and lifted the import surcharge. The pound's new parity became \$2.6057 within the framework of the EEC currency 'snake' which provided flexibility of movement of 2.25% either side of that figure.

In the context of Britain's impending entry into the EEC, this joint relationship against the dollar established by the Smithsonian Agreement was an important step towards the professed goal of economic and monetary union in Europe. The news came as a great relief to financial markets with London's FT 30 ending the year at its best level at 476.5, up 40%, and the Dow continuing its recovery to within a fraction of the 900 level again. Gilts, which had advanced steadily throughout the year on the trend towards lower interest rates, were up 17% to 80.32. Only the FT Gold Mines Index disappointed with an 11.6% fall to 47.1 on fears that the new monetary agreement had diminished the role of gold.

Leopold finds nickel — and loses it

The Australian mining market was down but there was yet more excitement to come on the nickel front to show that it was by no means out. In March **Leopold Minerals** (6 million shares) leapt from 48p to 230p on news of a strike in Nullagine, near Pilbara, of 5.33% nickel over 25 ft at a depth of 665 ft. Three days later, the price touched 440p on talk that a second hole had come up with values as good as the first. Two days after that the shares were suspended following the resignation of one of the founder directors who had complained about "unauthorised statements" and the fact that the original drilling core could not be found. A new drill hole was put down in May at the same site, this time under the supervision of the Western Australian police, and came up with values of between 0.098% and 0.103%! The affair was widely judged to be more damaging to the Australian mining market than Tasminex, and effectively marked the end of what was probably the greatest speculative mining boom of the century.

Jimmy Goldsmith's masterstroke

Until June 1971, Jimmy Goldsmith's considerable achievements in building up **Cavenham** into an international food and pharmaceutical empire had been treated with a degree of scepticism. The event that changed all that and made the City columnists really sit up and take notice was his £9.5 million bid for **Bovril**. With Bovril's net assets two and a half times those of Cavenham, this was a bold bid by any standards, and remained so even though Rowntree's subsequent intervention led to Cavenham eventually having to pay £14.5 million to secure its prize. Given the scope for rationalisation and integration, this was a case where dilution paid, and three months later Cavenham managed to recover almost half the purchase price by selling Bovril's dairy interests to Grand Metropolitan for £6.3 million. By December, Moores Stores and Wrights Biscuit with combined net assets of £10.5 million had been acquired after an initial bid of £6.5 million, and the intention was announced of spending another £12.7 million on an unspecified European foods and pharmaceutical group. By this time the share price had begun to respond, and at 185p had more than doubled on the year to give a market capitalisation of £51 million.

Hanson and Slater Walker make further headway

Hanson eventually had to raise its bid for National Star Brick to £1.39 million after Ibstock had entered the fray, but the potential rationalisation benefits when put together with Butterley were considered great enough to overcome its well-known reluctance to pay up for acquisitions. That was practically Hanson's only major move in 1971, until November when he entered into talks with **Costain** with a view to a merger. Both companies were capitalised at around £25 million, but whereas the asset backing of Costain's shares was not far short of that figure, Hanson's represented barely 30% of it. On this simple comparison the Costain board was not happy with Hanson's proposed equal standing in the new group or with the idea of James Hanson at the helm. Ten days later the merger plan was dropped. By this time Hanson's pretax profits for 1970/71 had risen 21% to £2.87 million which, at 180p, meant the shares were selling on an earnings multiple of a modest 15.3.

Meanwhile, **Slater Walker** continued with its policy of cashing in its industrial chips and turning them into assets comprising mainly cash, investments and property. In March an £8 million bid was made for property-rich **Solicitors Law**, and then in October the last of the group's major industrial interests, Crittall Hope's metal window business, was sold for £9 million. The shares were now at a new high of 307p and, said Lex in the *FT*, a group "like any other to be judged on solid performance". However, in August the first serious rumblings of discontent with Slater Walker's aims and methods were heard. They originated in Singapore where the takeover of **Haw Par**, a leading local company and makers of the famous Tiger Balm, had angered Premier Lee Kuan Yew who did not want to see key economic interests falling into foreign hands. He also complained that Slater Walker's takeover practices bordered on the illegal, a charge vigorously defended by the local managing director, Dick Tarling.

The secondary banks had a busy year, and their often spectacular profit increases prompted equally spectacular rises in their share prices. **First National Finance** continued to find new supporters, adding ICI Pension Fund and Royal Insurance to its shareholder list following its acquisition of Spey Finance in a £9 million cash and share deal. It also boosted its property dealing potential by buying 114 blocks of flats from Metropolitan Estates for £33.5 million. Pretax profits had risen in 1970 to £5.36 million from £3.55 million, and then the first half figures for 1971 weighed in at £3.25 million indicating a total of at least £7.5 million for the full year. At 336p, the shares had practically doubled during the year and were selling on a prospective P/E of 20, very much in line with the market average. **Dalton Barton** recorded an even bigger profits rise, making £820,000 pretax in the first half of 1970/71, or more than the whole of the previous year, but even at 640p, up nearly threefold, the P/E was a modest 13.3 on the forecast total for the year of £1.7 million. Gerald Kaplan's **London & County** also did well but it had to swallow a disappointment early in the year when after acquiring a 25% stake in the newly floated merchant bank, **Leopold Joseph**, the target rejected any idea of a bid or indeed of any form of association. The shares ended the year at 180p.

Racal gains status

1970 was a bumper year for **Racal**. Interim profits were up by 68% to £769,000 against a modest 15% rise the year before, and the forecast for the full year was "in excess of £2 million". That forecast turned into an actual figure of £2.23 million, and at 141p, the P/E was a not very demanding 20 in the light of the recent acquisition of Amplivox which added 9% to equity and 11% to earnings. Racal, according to Lex, had become "one of the more reliable electronic growth stocks", and after its forecast for 1971/72 of £2.9 million, it was described as approaching "high-grade investment status".

Bids and deals

1971 was a very active year for bids and mergers, but one distinguished by the fact that so many of them failed. The biggest and the most acrimonious was **Allied Breweries**' £500 million proposed merger with **Trusthouse Forte**. It led to a split in the THF board, with the Trusthouse faction under Lord Crowther in favour of accepting, and Charles Forte resolutely opposed to the idea. The bid failed but Allied Breweries was left holding a 25% stake in THF as an "investment". Then in December, **Beecham** took advantage of **Glaxo**'s recent announcement of a dip in profits to launch a £290 million bid. It was instantly rejected and a month later Glaxo agreed a £346 million deal with Boots. Beecham quickly countered by upping its offer to £385 million, but fortunately for Glaxo shareholders over the next two decades, both offers lapsed following a reference to the Monopolies Commission. **Readymixed Concrete** failed in its £75 million bid for **Redland, Grand Metropolitan Hotels** lost **Truman Hanbury Buxton** to **Watney**, but **Trafalgar House** managed to win **Cunard**.

An early warning

The year also saw the result of the DTI's investigation into the affairs of **Pergamon Press** and the associated International Learning Systems. The report ended with the following words: "We regret having to conclude that, notwithstanding Mr Maxwell's acknowledged abilities and energy, he is not in our opinion a person who can be relied upon to exercise proper stewardship of a publicly-quoted company."

1972

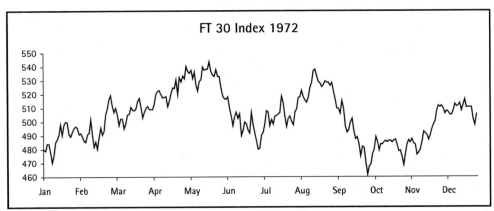

FT 30 Index 1972

Source: Thomson Reuters Datastream

The Chancellor's dilemma

In his New Year statement, the Chancellor referred to the economy having "a unique chance for expansion" and then added that "no government had ever before taken so much action in the space of one year to expand demand". It was a statement that was to haunt him forever after, but to be fair to Mr Barber many of the voices which had been critical of his reflationary moves in 1971 were now urging him "to take a risk on the side of expansion". Influencing this volte-face was the fact that there was remarkably little evidence that the economy was responding to earlier stimuli. Unemployment was still rising, crossing the million mark in January, and retail sales, after signs of a revival, were running out of steam. Industrial profits, on the other hand, were beginning to improve but again not enough to relieve worries about the eventual impact of soaring wage/price inflation. In late January even the usually cautious OECD urged the Chancellor to produce a new stimulus in his impending budget, while as usual the National Institute demanded tax cuts, in this case £2.5 billion. The latter insisted that Mr Barber had to exercise a value judgement in his budget and should give priority to the earliest possible reduction in unemployment over the risk of accelerating inflation "some years hence". Essentially, the problem was that if a 23% annual rate of growth in the money supply was necessary to accommodate a 5% growth rate, it was already accommodating a much faster rate of inflation.

Another reflationary budget

In the event, influenced by the unusual combination of a very high level of unemployment, a large balance of payments surplus and impending EEC entry, the Chancellor opted for an expansionary budget. If the tax cuts were less than the National Institute had called for, they were still substantial at £1.2 billion, taking 2.75 million people out of the tax net altogether and leaving the rest £1 a week better off. And as an incentive to investment, there was free depreciation on new investment and 40% allowances on industrial building, along with a range of help for the regions. If the Chancellor was later criticised for being too lax in the budget, in retrospect many of the economic numbers would have been distorted by the long-running labour disputes which dominated the first half of the year, causing the level of consumer demand to be underplayed. The year opened with a coal strike which ran for over five weeks leading to power cuts, the declaration of a State of Emergency and a three-day working week in mid-February. There was also a rail strike and a dock strike, and settlements were on terms which served to raise expectations in other industries.

Towards a new record high

The reaction of the markets to the economic situation at the beginning of 1972 was better than might have been expected. Gilts continued their advance in the New Year to reach a seven-year high of 81.86 in late January on expectations of a cut in Bank Rate, but perhaps sensing accelerating inflation and a reversal in the downward trend of interest rates, they topped out well in advance of equities. Fuelled by the growth in money supply, easier and cheaper credit, and encouraged by a high level of takeover activity, equities as represented by the FT 30 crossed the 500 level in early February. They reacted sharply on the three-day week and then rallied after the settlement of the miners' strike with the 30 per cent pay rise recommended by the Wilberforce Report, to end the month at 520.9, just one point short of the previous record of 521.9 in September 1968. The index dipped briefly below 500 on profit-taking but picked up again ahead of the budget and then surpassed the historic peak in intra-day trading the day after. It was not until April that it finally broke through decisively into new high ground. Then in late May, under the influence of apparently good economic news in the shape of a 31% rise in industrial profits in April, a CBI survey showing growing confidence in the industrial outlook, a sharp drop in the numbers out of work, and further encouraged by the Dow hitting a three-year high of 969, the FT 30 surged ahead to 543.6. That level was not to be matched for another seven years.

Thereafter, the implications of accelerating cost inflation began to dominate the market to the practical exclusion of all else. Even the National Institute urged tougher anti-inflation policies in the wake of the miners' pay settlement, believing that the government was relying too much on hopes of effective voluntary action emerging from the latest round of talks between the CBI and TUC. Within a fortnight, the FT 30 was back below 500 again and gilts were falling fast in anticipation of higher interest rates as Bank Rate was raised to 5% again. The deteriorating situation was not lost on the foreign exchange markets, where a strong run on the pound developed, despite concerted intervention by the other EEC member states. Given the background, the parity proved impossible to defend and although, as usual, "speculative forces" were blamed for the pressure, the Chancellor's own statement earlier in the month that he saw "no reason for the country to be frustrated in its determination to sustain sound economic growth in order to retain an unrealistic exchange rate", must have provided a clear signal to the markets.

The exchange rate, which had risen as high as $2.65 after the December 1971 dollar devaluation, was already back to $2.57 when in late June, Bank Rate was raised a full point to 6% and the decision was made to let the pound float freely for the first time, although it was stated to be a "temporary measure" ahead of EEC entry on 1st January next. The move provided a very short-term boost to the index on thoughts that the crisis had been very neatly defused by providing the opportunity of improving the trade balance at the same time as pushing up company profits. However, devaluation to an undetermined level soon came to be seen as no solution to a situation where money supply growth was approaching a 30% annual rate and wage awards were well into double figures, not to mention the possibility of other countries opting to follow the pound down and risking US retaliation on the trade front. All the post-flotation gains were quickly lost and by the first week in July, the FT 30 had slipped to 480 and the exchange rate to $2.42 as the inflation rate rose towards 10%.

The talking stops

Statutory action on wages and prices was now seen as inevitable, and initially equities rallied on the prospect, believing that if a wage freeze held down costs, the impact of a price freeze on profits would be offset to some degree by the higher volume trend promised by the continuing rapid rate of expansion. However, Mr Heath persisted in trying to get some sort of voluntary agreement out of tripartite talks with the CBI and TUC and the market crossed and recrossed the 500 level as the progress of the talks ebbed and flowed. Then in early November the talks finally broke down. The sticking point came when the CBI was prepared to accept a freeze on prices as well as on wages but would not have one without the other, and the TUC refused to accept a freeze on wages. Within days the government had brought in emergency legislation imposing a 90-day freeze on pay, prices, rents and dividends with the prospect of an extension for a further 60 days. The move was reinforced by the Bank of England making a 1% call on Special Deposits designed to mop up £220 million in the banking system, and preceded by a two-stage rise in Minimum Lending Rate (MLR) to 7½%. In October, Bank Rate had been dropped as the main signpost of Government policy towards interest rates in favour of Minimum Lending Rate, based directly on the average rate of interest ruling on Treasury bills. MLR was supposed to provide a more flexible instrument for influencing short-term interest rates, free from the drama associated with Bank Rate changes.

Managing the boom

Encouraged by this evidence that the government was at last taking a firm line on inflation, albeit at the cost of the complete reversal of the policies put forward during the 1970 election campaign, the market began to prepare for an end-year rally but its scope was limited by a continuing rise in interest rates and growing industrial unrest, factors which served to counterbalance the spirit of optimism which might otherwise have been engendered by the sight of the Dow Jones index soaring through the 1000 level to reach a new peak of 1036.37 in mid-December. Then three days before Christmas, the Bank of England, seeing another sharp drop in the numbers out of work as a clear indication that industrial growth was strongly established, added another 2% to Special Deposits, thereby taking a further £450 million out of the system, and lifted MLR by 1½%. The move came as a complete surprise to the market but the FT 30 still managed to end the year at 505.4, up 6%, while the Government Securities index at 71.11 was down 11%. Given that the reverse yield gap was now at a near record 6.6% and the average P/E around 19, both at a time when money was getting dearer and tighter, in retrospect it looks surprising that the market managed to hold its level during the second half of the year. The reason was that most commentators looked at a 5% growth rate and saw the Chancellor as managing the boom rather than strangling it, contrasting his actions with those of Roy Jenkins in 1969. It was also widely believed that although MLR had risen from 4.5% to 9% during the course of the year, interest rates were fast approaching a plateau from which they would fall in due course, thus enabling the government to fund its borrowing requirement.

This generous interpretation of events also owed a great deal to the fact that the system had been awash with liquidity in the first half of the year – London clearing bank advances had increased by 40% in the year following the abandonment of qualitative and quantitative monetary controls – and that inevitably there was a hangover effect into the second half. The remarkable performance of Wall Street was another major contributory factor, its rise fuelled by Vietnam peace hopes, the apparent success of Richard Nixon's anti-inflation policy and then his landslide re-election in November. Since the peaks of neither market were to be seen again until the end of the decade, the extraordinary performances of London and Wall Street in 1972 might be seen as a sort of "folie à deux".

Going for gold

Top marks for the year went to gold and to gold shares, both making up drastically for their dismal performances in 1971 in the wake of the dollar devaluation. It soon became apparent that when the dollar broke its links with gold it was not gold that had been cast adrift but the dollar. The gold price quickly recovered from an initial setback when the suspension of convertibility was announced, but the gold share index continued to languish on cost pressure fears until January 1972 when it suddenly began to move, adding more than 25% on the month to 50 with the gold price approaching $50. For the rest of the year the advance was practically unbroken, accelerating in the second half as anxieties grew over the stability of the new monetary order, to achieve a 101% overall gain at 95.3. Gold ended the year at $66.20, boosted by strong French demand. Gains of 100% were common among the big South African producing mines like **Western Holdings** and **East Driefontein** but the really spectacular rises were among the older, high cost mines, the so-called "marginals" like **Durban Deep** which went from 58p to 250p as profit projections soared.

Goldsmith buys Allied Suppliers

January was an active month for Jimmy Goldsmith. After strong rumours that he was about to make a reverse bid for **Spillers**, he surprised the market by offering £82.5 million for food stores group **Allied Suppliers**. Although **Cavenham's** market capitalisation was some £60 million, its net worth was no more than £10.5 million, a discrepancy which prompted Lex to refer to the proposed deal as "the reverse bid to end them all". Allied Suppliers accepted marginally improved terms and, having more than doubled the size of Cavenham at a stroke, Goldsmith wasted no time in reorganising and rationalising his new acquisitions. In July, the biscuit interests were sold to United Biscuits for £4 million cash, and in the same month the first property disposals were made from Allied Suppliers for £3.9 million to Argyle Securities, Slater Walker's property arm. In November, a 75% stake in a leading Swedish food company was bought for £6 million, and in December it was announced that Cavenham was making its first move into America by entering into negotiations to buy Squibb's baby food division for $30 million. The interim figures to November were announced a few days before Christmas, and did not disappoint. Pretax profits were £11.16 million against £5.2 million for the whole of 1971/72, leaving the shares at 200p on a P/E of 15 assuming a total for the year of £21.5 million.

Hanson goes for Costain again

The collapse of the planned merger with **Costain** did no harm to Hanson's share price, and in February, with the shares at 237p on the back of a "not less than" £3.6 million forecast for 1971/72, Hanson returned to the fray with a £28.5 million hostile bid. Costain put up a vigorous defence arguing that the bid undervalued the company. Hanson, however, was not prepared to raise its offer and walked away, answering critics who queried where the future success of his group now lay, by affirming that it was built on the fact of never having paid too much for any business and would remain so. Interim profits of £2 million were announced in June, accompanied by a raised forecast for the year of £4 million together with a 1 for 4 rights issue raising £8 million "to reduce gearing". The actual outcome for the year was £4.47 million.

Slater Walker approaches its zenith

1972 was a boom year for the financial sector and Slater Walker was very much the leader of the pack. Pretax profits for 1971 were up by a third to £16.3 million and with the shares at a new peak of 412p, the market capitalisation had grown to £225 million. Recently floated Ralli International, run by Malcolm Horsman, one of Jim Slater's original management team, reported profits up by 61% to £5.6 million as its move into overseas earnings situations began to pay off. Then in the autumn, Ralli acquired "instant blue chip status" by accepting a £200 million bid from Bowater in a planned marriage of assets and management. The move was not without its institutional critics, but it had enough going for it to defeat the intervention of Trafalgar House, which put in a bid of £126 million for Bowater on its own. Vavasseur, once an overseas trader but now transformed by the injection of foreign exchange dealers Harlow & Meyer into a fast-growing financial conglomerate, reported a 38% advance in profits for 1971 and forecast a 60% gain to £2 million for 1972.

Pat Matthews' **First National Finance** won bank status and in accordance with its new "image" sold the bulk of the flats bought the year before from Metropolitan Estates, netting a £26 million profit in the process. First half profits for 1972 weighed in at £5.63 million, up 73%, and in November there was no problem in raising £13 million with a rights issue in loan stock. Jack Dellal's **Dalton Barton** was not far behind and after reporting a 109% boost to 1971 profits at £2.61 million, an agreed merger with merchant bank Keyser Ullman left him running a group capitalised at £175 million with the potential for making £12 million in its first full year of operation. Once again, the property element was strong since earlier in the year Keyser had merged with the £70 million Central and District Properties. Gerald Kaplan's **London & County** won considerable critical acclaim as a result of trebling its asset base for an addition of 42% to equity by acquiring industrial/financial conglomerate **Drakes**, built up by Christopher Selmes (27), the financial "whizz kid" reputed to have made a fortune after starting with £200 as a 15-year-old schoolboy. After reporting interim profits in 1972/73 of £1.58 million, up from £412,000, Lex commented that the bulk of this gain had come from growth in the traditional banking business, not from dealing profits, and that the current climate looked favourable for the "high risk/reward make-up" of the group. At 300p the shares were on a prospective P/E of 16 on the likely total for the year of £3.5 million.

BTR and Racal prosper

Meanwhile back on the apparently less glamorous industrial scene, **BTR** managed to make up for the first half slowdown in 1971, beating its forecast of a maintained £2.84 million total for the year by planned cost reduction moves involving a 15% cut in the workforce. The outcome of £3.55 million for 1971 was handsomely beaten at £4.1 million in 1972 with BTR's management skills evident in this 15% increase in pretax profits being achieved on no more than a 1.5% boost in turnover. At 105p, the historic P/E was 14.8. Thanks to the remarkable success of its latest product line, the Clansman VHF manpack radio, **Racal** exceeded its £2.9 million profits forecast for 1971/72 with a total of £3.12 million. The shares were then 216p and by the time of the interim statement for 1972/73 in December they were 224p for a prospective P/E of 22 on a forecast £3.9 million total for the year. Racal, said Lex, is maintaining its "supergrowth" status.

Bids and deals

The biggest bid of the year was that of **Grand Metropolitan Hotels** for **Watney Mann**, following hard on the heels of Watney's own £126 million bid for **International Distillers & Vintners**. The opening price was £353 million, but **Rank Organisation** countered with a £430 million on offer, only to drop out two weeks later just before Grand Metropolitan came back with an ultimately successful final bid of £435 million. Breweries were in the firing line again in August when **Imperial Tobacco** bid £286 million for **Courage**. **United Drapery Stores** failed with a £111 million offer for **Debenham's**, but Rank agreed a £43 million takeover of **Butlins**, and **Amey**, the aggregates group, went to **Consolidated Goldfields** for £58 million.

Mothercare and Comet come to market

The two most popular new issues of the year were **Comet**, the discount electrical goods retailer offering 4.7 million shares or 38% of its equity, at 110p, and the ever popular **Mothercare** raising £13.2 million by an offer for sale of 25% of its capital at 165p. Despite the issues being priced at relatively high P/E multiples of 18.2 and 28.2 respectively, they both scored runaway successes with premiums of 37p and 25p on the first day of dealing.

1973

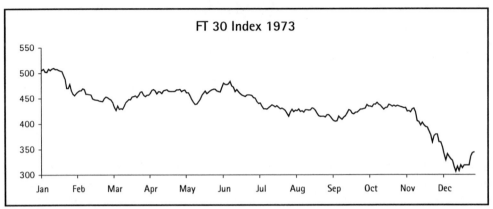

FT 30 Index 1973

Source: Thomson Reuters Datastream

The cracks begin to show

During the first three weeks of the New Year, most commentators were prepared to give the market the benefit of the doubt, arguing that company profits were recovering strongly on the back of productivity gains in the context of a 5% growth rate, money supply growth was slowing and the government had no choice but to bring interest rates down in order to fund its budget deficit. There were also some indications in early January of a slowdown in the consumer boom and a slight pickup in industrial investment. Wall Street was no discouragement either, reaching a new record peak of 1051.7 on 11th January on expectations of an imminent end to the war in Vietnam and the success of President Nixon's wages and prices policy.

The FT 30 managed to hold above the 500 level until 18th January, when Prime Minister Heath unveiled Phase Two of his own anti-inflation policy, described by the *FT* as "the most comprehensive set of economic controls since the War" as the government assumed powers to regulate prices, pay, rents and dividends for the next three years. The next day the FT 30 dropped 10.5 to 495.1 and was not to see the top side of 500 again for another five years. The problem was that although the market had appeared to recognise the need for a tough wages and prices policy in order to break the vicious circle of inflationary expectations, the new measures were so far-reaching that at the same time as casting doubt on the future for company profits, they also called into question the chances of maintaining the target growth rate. Industry was not at all happy, for example, with a Prices Code which permitted companies to pass on in price increases only 50% of allowable wage increases and which also stipulated that any fall in raw material and other allowable costs should be fully reflected in price reductions. The picture was further complicated by the fact that the TUC, as usual, would have no truck with any sort of pay restraint, and by the end of February the index had fallen to below 450 with the government seeming to have got the worst of both worlds, alienating industry while failing to appease the unions.

A new dollar crisis

As if all this was not enough for the market to cope with, a new world currency crisis blew up in the first week of February as billions of dollars flowed into the central banks of Europe, particularly into Germany, and also into Japan. The heart of the problem was that the realignment of December 1971 had failed as yet to produce an appreciable restoration of the balance of payments equilibrium between the major industrial countries. Even accepting the inevitable time lags, it was still disturbing to see the US trade deficit rising so sharply in 1972 with no prospect of a reduction in 1973, and capital flows to those countries with corresponding surpluses were to a large extent inevitable. By the middle of the month, a new currency package had emerged involving another dollar devaluation against gold, this time from $38 to $42.22 with a new joint float by the principal EEC currencies, excluding the pound and the lira, and with the yen floating on its own. The reaction of Wall Street to this new devaluation was to slip below the 1000 mark again, seeming to heed President Nixon's warning that it was "no substitute for discipline in the economy".

Still gambling on growth

To some degree the fact that the pound was already floating had served to absorb the shocks that would otherwise have overwhelmed it had parities remained fixed, but the latest currency upheaval still managed to provide an unsettling background to the Budget of 6th March. Interest rates were rising again, the trade surplus was disappearing rapidly, and clearly it was no longer possible to pursue an abnormally rapid growth path and sustain a large public sector deficit, without fear of the external consequences.

Despite these caveats, the Chancellor still opted for an expansionary budget with the aim of maintaining a high growth rate while keeping up the fight against inflation. There were to be no cutbacks in public spending, which involved an increase in the borrowing requirement from £2.8 billion in 1972/73 to one of £4.4 billion in 1973/74, arising not from this budget but from the spending boosts and tax reductions implemented in 1971/72 when the Chancellor was responding to the sharp rise in unemployment. Despite having implemented his promise to impose VAT on a wide range of goods and services, it was increasingly difficult to see how this greatly enlarged borrowing requirement could possibly be funded without falling inflationary expectations and rising gilt-edged prices. Lex in the *FT* called this an "imperative rather than an objective", seeming to believe in the Chancellor's ability to do what had to be done. Gilts knew better as usual and the Government Securities index fell 1.54 to 69.71, its lowest point in two years.

Riding the tiger

During the second quarter of the year, the magnitude of the task facing Mr Barber became increasingly obvious. The trade balance deteriorated sharply thanks to a soaring import bill in terms of volume and price even before the expected revival in industrial stockbuilding and capital investment had begun to get underway. At the same time the consumer boom showed no signs of abating and in the absence of positive measures of restraint, there was little scope to shift resources into investment and exports at a time when shortages of labour, materials and productive capacity made it vital to do so. A freak April trade surplus, together with a £500 million cut in public spending, indications of a slightly more cooperative attitude by the TUC and a reduction in Minimum Lending Rate back to 7½% sparked a rally in mid-June, but once again gilts were less easily influenced and failed to respond. In retrospect this rally provided the equity investor with the last chance to sell before things began to get really difficult. But at the time it all looked very different. The National Institute for one confessed to being 'remarkably optimistic' and to believing that fears about overheating were exaggerated in the context of a prices and incomes policy coupled with a floating exchange rate.

The US was having not dissimilar problems. Output was surging ahead, but so were prices and President Nixon had no easy task in implementing an effective wages and prices policy against a background of a weak dollar, a soaring gold price, and the Watergate scandal which cast doubt on the standing of his administration and its ability to regulate the economy. Sentiment on Wall Street was further upset by the sudden and unexpected collapse of Equity Funding Corporation, a popular growth stock, following revelations that roughly two thirds of its $3 billion in life policies were fictitious and that $25 million had been obtained by reinsuring them with other insurance companies. As a result the Dow was back to the 900 mark by mid-June, unimpressed by a 60-day price freeze which, with its system of audits and price reporting requirements, looked positively damaging for corporate profits.

Interest rates start to take off

The third quarter of the year was marked by renewed currency turmoil with the trade-weighted depreciation of sterling reaching a level some 20% below the point at which it stood at the time of the Washington agreement in December 1971. The size of this depreciation had tended to be obscured by the fact that the pound was floating and also by the habit of measuring it against the dollar, which was also weak, but it is true to say that the floating pound under Mr Heath had sustained a bigger fall than under

Mr Wilson after three years of desperate rearguard action. It was doubly unfortunate that a depreciation of this magnitude happened to coincide with a worldwide boom in commodity prices, which meant that UK imports of food and raw materials became very expensive. Exports were rising strongly but not enough to compensate for this adverse shift in the terms of trade, and in any case, they were being held back in volume terms by labour and capacity shortages aggravated by the persistence of the consumer boom.

Despite urgings by most economic commentators, including top government adviser, Lord Rothschild, but not of course the National Institute, Messrs Heath and Barber insisted that no curbs on domestic demand were necessary. Their pledge was to "go for growth" and to pay no attention to the "prophets of gloom", but knowing that they could not allow the pound to float down any further without causing an unacceptable deterioration in the terms of trade, they decided to protect the pound by letting interest rates rise. In late July, there was another 1% call on Special Deposits taking £260 million out of the banking system, and simultaneously MLR was hoisted 1½% to 9%. Within days it was up again to 11½%, putting the finishing touches to the FT 30's sixty-point decline from its mid-June level and leaving gilts friendless and struggling to find a floor as the Government Securities index slipped to the lowest level recorded since its compilation in 1924.

Waiting for "something to turn up"

In retrospect it is clear that the Government was putting too much reliance on commodity prices topping out and actually falling, and on some sort of agreement being worked out over wages and prices in Phase Three. Indeed it was as puzzling then as now, why Mr Heath should have expected any cooperation from the unions over pay. They had made no secret of their outright opposition to any sort of freeze and to be fair to their leaders, it would have been practically impossible to carry their members against a background of soaring retail prices, especially food prices. Delegates were being withdrawn from pay talks, strikes were a daily occurrence, and the miners, after raising some hopes earlier in the year by returning a "no strike" ballot, in July announced that their latest pay claim would be pursued by a policy of confrontation, not negotiation. Neither did commodity prices show much sign of turning down to any significant extent, and with oil prices still rising and supplies tight, there was even talk of petrol rationing being introduced in August. Thus with both pay and commodity prices largely outside the government's control, most responsible economic commentators continued to stress the need for direct action by making substantial cuts in public expenditure and by keeping the money supply under much stricter control. Indeed, they argued that such action would actually help business confidence whereas the indiscriminate use of the interest rate weapon posed a threat both to growth and to the Government's electoral chances. In response, the Prime Minister reaffirmed his "go for growth" pledge, insisting there would be "no going back, no loss of nerve".

The oil drama takes centre stage

All the while this debate was going on, another drama was being played out around conference tables in Geneva and Vienna. This was the confrontation between the Western oil companies and the producing states, now organised in OPEC (Organisation of Petroleum-Exporting Countries), over the question of raising the return to the latter to compensate for the recent dollar devaluations. In fact the dispute went much deeper, involving both the matter of economic relationships between the industrial world and the developing world, and that of the former's attitude towards Israel. It was also only too obvious to the producers that while prices of practically every other commodity were soaring, the price of oil was effectively pegged.

There was nothing new about the idea of using the "oil weapon" to put pressure on the West. In August 1967, just after the Six-Day War, Iraq had tried unsuccessfully to get its Arab neighbours to support an oil sales ban and a boycott of Western goods for a period of three months. Then in February 1971, after further talk of an embargo, OPEC members signed a five-year agreement with the oil companies for a considerable increase in revenues to the producing nations. However, in the wake of the subsequent dollar devaluations it was hardly likely to hold. A 6% increase was agreed at Geneva after the first devaluation, but when demands for an 11% rise were rejected by the oil companies following the second devaluation, the "oil weapon" began to be brandished in earnest.

Libya takes the lead

Libya had already nationalised all BP's interests in the country in 1972. In May 1973 pumping operations were halted in Libya, Iraq and Kuwait, then Libya proceeded to expropriate 51% of the assets of all the US oil companies. In September, President Nixon warned that Arab action could lead to a Western boycott of their oil, but in the absence of adequate alternative sources of supply, it must have seemed an empty threat. All eyes were now focused on the OPEC meeting in Vienna in September. There had been speeches by the Arab delegates referring to the "scandalous" profits being made by the Western oil companies at the expense of the producing nations, and unofficial indications were that OPEC would demand a straight oil price rise in the 15-20% range. No one was prepared for what was to follow.

Egypt and Syria attack Israel

The trigger was the so-called Yom Kippur War which broke out in the first week of October when Egyptian and Syrian forces simultaneously attacked Israel on two fronts. Remarkably, markets were undeterred by the event and equities and gilts both extended their recovery from the September lows, more concerned with hopes that interest rates had peaked and news that industrial profits for the first nine months of the year were up 24.3%. Wall Street's reaction was much the same, with the Dow extending its advance to 978 even though Iraq promptly seized US oil interests in the country the day after the war had started. The element of surprise in the initial attack had led to some early Arab successes, and the US began an airlift to Israel to replace the military equipment lost in the first days of the war. By the end of the week Israel had regained the initiative, stabilising the Syrian front and launching a devastating counterattack against the Egyptian forces in the Sinai. Egypt immediately called for the Arab producers to use their oil weapon against the "friends of Israel" by stopping exports at once. The Gulf States were the first to act, breaking off talks on the renegotiation of the five-year agreement and unilaterally raising the price of their crude oil by 66%, taking it from $3 to $5 a barrel.

The FT 30 exhibited some nervousness during the first week of the war, pulling back from 441.6 to 428.2 when commentators pointed out the dramatic implications for industrial costs and for the balance of payments of a rise in the price of oil of this magnitude. However, it rallied to 437.7 on news of a quarter per cent reduction in MLR, seemingly rating the event as more important than Libya adding $4 to the posted price of its oil, double the increase just imposed by the Gulf States, and the start of the embargo with a 5% cut in oil supplies. Wall Street, too, had its head in the sand, actually reaching a new recovery peak of 987 on 27th October, the day Venezuela decided to go along with the Arabs and raised its own oil price by 56%.

The moment of truth

Whatever the efficient market theory may say about all the news being discounted in the market at any given point, there can be no argument about the fact that if in October 1973 all the news was known, its significance was not appreciated for some days. The moment of truth arrived on the last day of the month when the Arab producers announced that oil supplies to the West might be cut not by 5% but by 20%, with nothing at all going to the Netherlands, because of its overtly pro-Israeli stance. Within a week the Dow had lost 67 points to 919, then rallied briefly to 930 on the acceptance by both parties in the conflict of the Kissinger peace plan, before plunging below 900 again after a belated awakening by investors to the serious consequences for the economy of the cutback in oil supplies and the increase in prices. London had even more problems to contend with. The power workers had been taking industrial action throughout October and then in November the miners imposed an overtime ban in pursuit of their pay claim which was well above the Phase Three limits. Nevertheless, the Chancellor insisted that there would be "no slamming on of brakes" and that the use of Special Deposits would be adequate to control the expansion of bank credit to the private sector.

Action at last

It was not until the middle of November that both the government and the market got the message and on the same day the October trade figures came out showing a record £298 million deficit, Mr Heath declared a State of Emergency over the oil and coal crisis. Simultaneously, a major credit squeeze was inaugurated by lifting MLR to a record 13% and by adding another 2% to Special Deposits bringing them up to 6% to take £600 million out of the banking system. The FT 30 plunged 17.4 to 405.5, gilts lost as much as 4.5 points, knocking the Government Securities index back to 62.39, and only golds gained. Rumours that these measures would soon be followed up with a mini-Budget, the threat of industrial action on the railways, and the first manifestations of the secondary banking crisis, all against the background of Wall Street sliding towards the 800 level, took the FT 30 back to 365 by the end of the month.

The first half of December brought no respite. Distribution problems created by the rail dispute deepened the energy crisis, and in a televised address to the nation on 14th December, the Prime Minister announced the immediate introduction of a three-day week to conserve fuel supplies. There were by now real signs of distress selling and with sentiment further disturbed by the collapse of London & County Bank and the November trade gap indicating that the total deficit for the year was going to be close to £2.3 billion even before the oil price rise had taken effect, the index touched a seven-year low point of 305.9 by the middle of the month. Then a few days before Christmas, a new package of measures was unveiled. Public spending was to be cut by £1.2 billion, consumer credit was to be severely restricted by the reimposition of HP controls, and the overheated property sector was singled out for special treatment in the form of a development tax and a clampdown on the granting of office development permits. Most commentators thought the moves were not drastic enough, but the market rallied strongly to end the year at 344 on hopes that they would serve to cool the economy without tipping it into recession. Once again, domestic considerations obviously carried more weight than the news released on Christmas Eve that the Gulf States had increased the price of their crude yet again, this time from $5 to $11.50, or four times the pre-War level in early October.

On the last day of the year the FT 30 was down 32%, gilts had lost 14% with the Government Securities Index at 61.05, and only golds gained with a 117% rise to a new peak of 207.1 in response to a bullion price up 73% to $112.50. Once again it was the shares of the marginal producers which benefited most, and while **Western Holdings** and **East Driefontein** doubled, **Durban Deep** more than trebled to 780p.

Goldsmith goes for cash

The unexpected developments towards the end of the year had a major impact on the fortunes of a great many companies. In some cases it was to be a fatal impact. Jimmy

Goldsmith, however, was to enhance his reputation in 1973 for always staying at least one step ahead of the game by selling two of his City properties for £11.7 million in March, and then by disposing of some 1600 shops, mostly acquired via Allied Suppliers, to Guardian Properties for £17.5 million in May. In the meantime, he had bought another 30% of French food giant, Générale Alimentaire, taking his holding up to 48%. In June, Cavenham announced pretax profits of £22.5 million, comfortably exceeding most forecasts, leaving the shares at 151p on a P/E of 15. Market capitalisation was now £135 million with £50 million represented by cash. Goldsmith, like Hanson, had his eye on the US and in December he made his first successful deal there by making a $62 million cash bid for 51% of Grand Union, an East Coast supermarket group with a billion dollar turnover and a poor earnings record. Half year profits were announced just before Christmas but even a 45% gain at the pre-tax level to £16.2 million was not enough to stop the shares ending the year well down at 147p.

Slater Walker and Hill Samuel plan to merge

Pretax profits of **Slater Walker** in 1972 were up by only 8% at £17.6 million but earnings per share rose by 22% to give a P/E multiple of 16 at 250p. Gross assets in commercial banking and in property had doubled and with a net worth of 160p with probably another 30p surplus on book value of quoted investments, Lex saw the rating as taking into account "precious little goodwill" regardless of the group's one-man image. Then towards the end of April, the City was stunned by the news that Slater Walker was to merge with **Hill Samuel**. The merchant bank had been extensively courted in 1970 when it rejected a £120 million bid from Commercial Union. The result would have created London's biggest merchant bank with a market capitalisation of £260 million and £1.5 billion of gross assets, £1 billion under management, £230 million in insurance funds, and combined net profits of £17.5 million. The initial reaction from the financial establishment was favourable. The Bank of England was ready to give its support and Jim Slater's readiness to defer to Sir Kenneth Keith by acting as his deputy and to agree to the name of the Hill Samuel Group was seen as a welcome move to "depersonalise" the business. The *FT* referred to the move as marking the phasing out of "one of the truly great financial innovators". The government decided that no reference to the Monopolies Commission was called for and joint statements were made professing the international ambitions of the new group, particularly with an eye to Europe, the US and the Far East. Then on 20th June, two days before the closing date of the offer, it was announced that the merger had been called off because of "differences of workstyle and personalities" between the two companies.

It was at this point that the formerly fairly muted criticism of the proposed deal became overtly hostile, largely on the grounds that the incompatibility of the two groups had always been obvious. It was not good news for Sir Kenneth Keith who, under institutional pressure, had been forced to abandon a proposed merger with Metropolitan Estates in 1970, and neither was it for Jim Slater, in that it appeared that his ambitions had been thwarted for the first time in his meteoric career. Supposedly as part of an "image mending" exercise, Slater Walker offered to buy back shares at a premium in the relatively disappointing Dual Trust originally formed to hold stakes in the group's satellite companies and as a result nicknamed "Dustbin Trust". Strategic stakes in companies were also detailed as part of a new disclosure policy, and they were seen to include Spillers (10.8%), J. Bibby (24%) and British Ropes (11%). Despite the Hill Samuel setback, Slater Walker still looked to be ending the year in good shape despite a share price practically halved to 140p in reaction to the secondary banking crisis.

London and County Bank collapses

The other financials began the year in fine form but ended it in very different shape, affected in varying degrees by the credit squeeze and soaring interest rates. Gerald Caplan's **London & County**, for example, proceeded to beat its 1972/73 profits forecast by reporting a total of £3.58 million, indicating a pre-tax figure for the current year of probably £7 million, which would drop the P/E from 16 to 10 with the share price at 250p. The company announced that it planned to set up a chain of regional offices to service industrial and commercial borrowers, and with deposits having trebled in the past year to £76 million, the future was widely judged to be bright. Fears that it was about to darken became very evident in November when the share price fell dramatically from 200p to 58p. The company put out a statement saying that it knew of "no reason for the extreme fluctuations in the share price", but the market paid more attention to the abrupt resignation of the recently appointed head of the banking department reputedly because of a "clash in operating style" with Mr Caplan.

On 1st December the shares were suspended at 40p, valuing the company at £4.67 million, and urgent rescue talks were reported to be underway with London & County's bankers, National Westminster, and large shareholders, Eagle Star, First National Finance and Keyser Ullman. United Drapery Stores was also involved as a result of having granted London & County a licence to operate banking departments within many of its stores. Within days a rescue plan had been devised by a consortium led by Pat Matthews' FNFC which bought 25% of the capital from some of the major shareholders (including Mr Caplan) for a nominal £1, and pledged to make up to £30 million available in order to overcome the liquidity crisis.

Other secondary banks under pressure

The troubles of London & County cast a shadow over the rest of the financial sector, prompting a run on some of the smaller ones which were then caught out as a result of their dangerous mismatching of short-term borrowing with medium and long-term lending. **Cedar Holdings**, a banking and second mortgage specialist, was the next to fall to the great embarrassment of its prominent institutional shareholders.

Save in terms of share price, the more highly regarded **FNFC** and **Keyser Ullman** continued to forge ahead. **First National Finance** turned in almost doubled profits in 1972 of £13.23 million, excluding property dealing gains, mainly stemming from a massive increase in banking profits as lending volume expanded sharply. The first half of 1973 recorded a further substantial gain to £9.02 million indicating a probable total for the year of around £19 million on the back of hugely expanded advances mainly to "non-bank borrowers". In December, the company was applauded for having pulled off something of a coup by striking a deal with British Rail to provide banking services at up to forty mainline stations over the next four years. Significantly, the shares demonstrated relative weakness within the sector, ending the year 60% down at 42p. **Keyser Ullman** also appeared to be well on course, reporting profits of £8.69 million for its first part-year together with Dalton Barton, compared with £4.06 million, and then selling Central & District Properties to Town & City for £97 million, realising a handsome profit on the original acquisition price. At the time of the London & County collapse, Keyser Ullman was widely congratulated on its timely property sales, and as a cash-rich group with a net worth of some £130 million against a market capitalisation of £96 million, it was judged as unlikely to be disturbed either by stock market weakness or the recent softness in property values.

Vavasseur bails out Barclay

Just like the other financial groups, **Vavasseur** had been keen to expand its asset base in 1973, and in January it made a surprise £17 million bid for John Bentley's **Barclay Securities**. John Bentley, one of Jim Slater's early lieutenants, then 28, had taken control of Barclay in mid-1969 when it was refloated with the aim of reorganising and rationalising a chain of wholesale chemists and expanding the business by making further acquisitions. This he managed to do very successfully and then began to branch out into other areas. In November 1971 he bought the Lines toy business from the liquidators for £5.3 million, a deal which made Barclay the biggest toy maker in the UK. It was his rationalisation moves there and again at Shepperton Studios following the takeover of Lion International that began to give the whole Slater-inspired "asset stripping" technique a bad name, not least because at Shepperton John Bentley ran up against the outspoken left- wing union leader, Alan Sapper. In the event, having reputedly exclaimed "Vava ... who?" when told of the bid, John Bentley accepted the offer after getting it upped to £18.5 million, placed his new Vavasseur paper with institutions and neatly avoided the financial holocaust that was soon to follow.

More excitement for Hanson

After a quiet 1972 in the wake of the abortive Costain bid, **Hanson** began 1973 with an agreed £12 million offer for BHD Engineers, simultaneously making a forecast of a 34% rise in pretax profits to at least £6 million. In May a £4.8 million bid was made for unquoted specialist pumps maker, Sykes Lacey-Hulbert. Also in May, Hanson put together a £34 million consortium bid for Rolls Royce Motors, which the government was planning to sell following its rescue of Rolls Royce Group two years before. The Government turned down Hanson's proposal and went ahead with a stock market flotation. In June, a 140% rise in interim profits prompted a full-year forecast of a minimum of £7.5 million. Then in mid-June **Bowater** cum **Ralli** bid £51 million for Hanson, offering fourteen of its shares for fifteen of Hanson's. Hanson shares jumped 20p on the news to 172p, and it was announced that the Hanson interests controlling 13.4% would accept, as would Slater Walker with between 5% and 7.5%. It was vigorously denied by the Slater camp that this was in any way a contrived marriage created by Jim Slater "moving the pieces around the chess board". In any case, the objection became academic when five weeks later the proposed merger was referred to the Monopolies Commission and Bowater bowed out. Then in September, Hanson sold two of BHD's principal divisions for £13.6 million cash, retaining a rump worth £2 million earning £500,000 a year, and the market wondered why Hanson would have wanted to accept a bid from anyone. The shares now stood at 121p, backed by net assets of 100p of which 50p was in cash and were on a 1972/73 P/E of 9. In December it became clear where Hanson's ambitions lay. Two acquisitions were made in the US. The first was a 24% stake in building materials group, Gable Industries, for £4.5 million, and the second was J. Howard Smith, a producer of edible oil and animal foodstuffs, for which £13.7 million was paid. The latter acquisition has a special significance in that it brought into the Hanson fold David Clarke, one of the family owners, later to be nominated in 1992 as Lord White's successor on his planned retirement in 1997. Vice Chairman Gordon White justified this substantial move into America on the grounds that the country was "better equipped to withstand crisis than any other", adding that it would not be long before at least 50% of the group's earnings would be coming from overseas. Full year figures announced at the same time came out at £8.25 million, handsomely beating the £7.5 million forecast, and leaving the shares at 90p on a modest P/E of 6.7.

Sainsbury comes to market

One of the most popular new issues of the year, and the biggest one to date, was **Sainsbury** offer for sale of 27% of its equity at 145p for an overall valuation of £117 million. There was no forecast for the coming year and the P/E on the 1972/73 figures was a lofty 20.6 compared with Tesco's 17, but the offer was 14.5 times oversubscribed, pulling in a record £495 million. The shares opened with a premium of 17p in very active trading. Frozen food group **Bejam** also attracted an enthusiastic response when it offered 25% of its equity or 2.75 million shares at 72p. The P/E was a relatively modest 16.5, and on the first day of trading the shares opened at 118p. 1973 was also the year in which Asil Nadir (29) made his first public appearance in the role of Chairman and Managing Director of **Wearwell**, a "cash and carry" wholesaler of mens' wear from stock. Out of an equity capital of 8 million shares, 3.2 million were offered for sale at 46p on a P/E multiple of 10.9. The issue was well received and after opening at 53p, the shares quickly settled down to around the 50p level. **House of Fraser** agreed to accept a £225 million offer from **Boots** but the Monopolies and Mergers Commission stepped in and the offer lapsed.

1974

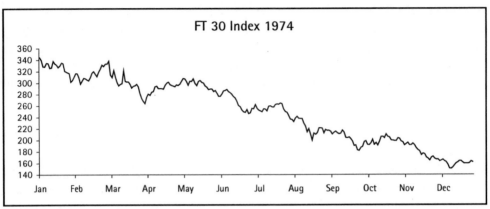

FT 30 Index 1974

Source: Thomson Reuters Datastream

Into the abyss

Wall Street saw a New Year rally which carried the Dow up 37 points to 880, boosted by a flurry of Prime Rate cuts, a reduction in margin requirements and President Nixon's so-called "oil initiative" designed to promote co-operation between the oil-producing and the oil-consuming nations. London, on the other hand, took a gloomier view, influenced by estimates that the oil price rise would add another £1.8 billion to the UK's already soaring import bill. There were also no signs of the miners or the railworkers moderating their demands, lay-offs topped the million mark as energy-starved industries cut production, and there was renewed anxiety over sterling, which by the middle of January had plunged to a new record low against the dollar at $2.18. The decline in industrials was slowed to some degree by a 0.25% reduction in MLR leading to an easing of liquidity fears and by increased oil supplies heightening prospects of a move to a four-day working week before long, but they caught up with a rush in the last days of the month when it became clear that a full-scale miners' strike was inevitable, and the FT 30 crashed to a seven-year low of 301.7. The fall made history in that the level of 305.3, which had marked the end of the 1968/71 bear market, had been breached, the first time that such a reversal had occurred since the introduction of the index in 1935. With a fall of 44.5% from the May 1972 all-time peak of 543.6, the decline had exceeded the extent of all previous post-War bear markets. Simultaneously, gilts achieved a new record low, losing nearly four points in January to 57.45, with yields topping 13%.

Mr Heath seeks a fresh mandate

Pressure now began to intensify for the Conservatives to call a General Election. The dramatic change in external circumstances created by the oil crisis seemed to be largely unappreciated by the miners, and the whole of the TUC, and since it was clear that the government would be forced into taking drastic measures to deal with the new situation, it was clearly vital to seek a stronger mandate. National Union of Mineworkers' Vice President, Mick McGahey, heightened the political tension in the country by calling for the TUC to "mobilise support for the miners, to burst Stage Three, to defeat the Tory government, and to elect a Labour government committed to the progressive policies of the Left". Furthermore, referring to the prospect of troops being brought in to keep coal supplies moving, he called upon them to remember their working class origins and to disobey orders. Both statements proved to be more embarrassing to Labour than to the government, prompting Messrs. Wilson and Callaghan to issue a statement "utterly repudiating" the subversive nature of McGahey's appeal. The index reacted by penetrating the 300 level, thereby wiping out all the gains since late 1959, and then rallied on the announcement that the election date was to be 28th February.

Expectations of a Conservative victory carried the FT 30 up to 337.8 on the eve of the declaration of the poll despite the miners' strike having begun and a TUC statement to the effect that it had reached an "understanding" with the Labour Party. The shock result with Labour five seats ahead of the Conservatives, but with no overall majority, caused the market to achieve yet another record, this time with a 24-point one-day fall (after 32.8) to 313.8. Mr Heath's failure to retain office with support from the minority parties, led to the return of Harold Wilson to Downing Street with Denis Healey as his new Chancellor, asserting that their immediate priorities were to get the miners back to work and the rest of industry back to normal working, the repeal of the Industrial Relations Act, and the introduction of a budget as soon as possible. Henceforth, industrial relations were to be regulated by a strictly voluntary "social contract" whereby both sides of industry would work together in the national interest.

The miners go back to work

After a further dip to 309.6, the market rallied to 321.6 and sterling gained nearly 5 cents to $2.33 on relief that a period of uncertainty had ended and on hopes that the miners' strike would be quickly settled. The miners did indeed return to work, but only after winning a generous pay award that drove a coach and horses through Stage Three, but the uncertainty remained thanks to the inflationary fears rekindled by the settlement terms with its almost immediate impact on coal, steel and electricity prices.

It soon became clear that the "social contract" was destined to be a very one-sided affair when two days after the NUM had accepted the new pay award, the Yorkshire miners demanded another £20 per week, their leader Arthur Scargill adding that the only "social contract" he recognised was the one between him and his members. If Prime Minister Heath had called the election to decide who ran the country – the government or the trade unions – the answer was now clear. It was not the government of the day, whether Conservative or Labour, and with "their" government in office, the unions were determined to have their say. Furthermore, with Michael Foot as Minister of Employment, Anthony Wedgwood Benn as Minister for Industry talking of planning intervention in the country's top one hundred companies, and Denis Healey promising to squeeze the rich until "the pips squeaked", they were not going to be seriously opposed.

No help from Healey's budget

The market was becoming increasingly unsettled by these developments, and the new government's first budget at the end of March confirmed its worst fears. Admittedly, Chancellor Healey's task was not an easy one. He had to curb home demand and turn round the balance of payments without generating massive unemployment, restrain the monetary printing presses without producing a new wave of bankruptcies, placate the IMF and foreign bankers without alienating his own followers, and at the same time reconcile his avowed aim of squeezing the rich without creating a crisis in the capital markets. In the event, he chose to let private industry and higher income groups bear the brunt of his deflationary measures. The basic rate of income tax was increased by 3p while the top rate went up from 75% to 83%, and to 98% for investment incomes. Corporation Tax was raised to 52% with an advance payment element, employers' National Insurance contributions were increased, and sanction was given to a broad range of price increases for the nationalised industries. And of course there was the Green Paper on the Wealth Tax. Coming on top of the price curbs introduced immediately after the election involving a 10% reduction in gross margins for all retailers, the first of the threshold pay awards, and another record trade gap, this was too much for the market to bear. Already bumping along just below 300, equities assessed the impact of these new impositions on company liquidity and promptly nosedived to 267.4 by the end of March, their lowest level since October 1962. Gilts followed suit, falling to a new low of 54.2 with yields at the long-end nudging 15%. Once again, gold shares were the only bright spot, approaching the 400 mark as the bullion price soared.

The calm before the storm

Adding to investor anxiety was a new wave of rumours about many of the secondary banks, and the hammering of stockbrokers Mitton Butler & Priest. The US economy was also becoming a source of worry as Prime Rates began to rise again, threatening the downtrend in UK domestic rates. However, with sterling holding up well at around the $2.40 mark, thanks to a $2.5 billion foreign loan arranged through the clearing banks and a $3 billion swap agreement, the government continued to reduce MLR in quarter point steps and to release Special Deposits in an effort to ease industry's liquidity problems. Encouraged by the prospect of further cuts in interest rates and by the belief that after an unprecedented 50% decline the bear market had to have run its course, the FT 30 quickly regained the 300 level by mid-April and managed to hold it, give or take a few points, until the third week of May. Gilts rallied strongly over the same period, with buyers taking heart from evidence that the money supply was at last being strictly controlled. This phase of relative optimism failed to last out the month.

No way out

By the end of May it was no longer possible to ignore what the CBI referred to as the "horrifying rate" at which industrial costs were rising and the implications for company profits at a time when world trade was declining and the government was dedicated to a policy of strict price controls. Any chance that the Labour government might have had of stabilising the situation was doomed to failure by its inability to impose any degree of wage restraint on the trade unions. As the retail price index rose, the timebomb of threshold pay awards left behind by the Heath administration now began to be triggered, pushing wage inflation up towards an annual rate of 30%. Furthermore, those unions that had not had the foresight to sign threshold pay agreements were threatening strike action in order to obtain them now.

Against such a background, there was no prospect that industry, the powerhouse of the economy, could achieve the shift of resources into exports and capital investment necessary to correct the balance of payments deficit and to maintain it in surplus. Sentiment was further damaged by a renewed wave of collapses in the finance and property sector. **Vavasseur** was suspended "pending reorganisation following a substantial fall in the value of its assets", the £130 million **Lyon Group** was taken over by its creditors, and the £200 million **Stern Holdings**, one of London's biggest residential property groups, announced that it was having "cash difficulties". **Guardian Properties**, the group that had bought the shops from Jimmy Goldsmith, was suspended. **Keyser Ullman**, itself the subject of rumours about property lending problems, was forced to take over management control of **Grendon Securities** to protect the £17 million it had lent to Christopher Selmes to buy it, and **FNFC**, now down to 22p, yielding 12.5% and on a P/E of 3, admitted that its provisions against losses had probably been inadequate. And, after two more hammerings, every member of the Stock Exchange had to chip in with another £200 for the compensation fund in June, followed by £350 in October.

Cash is King

Already back into the 280/290 range by the end of May, the FT 30 paid less heed to further interest rate cuts than to Jim Slater's much publicised speech at Slater Walker's AGM when he announced disposals so far in 1974 totalling some £50 million, adding that "cash is the best investment now". Wall Street was also no help at this stage. Hopes that interest rates had reached a plateau were dashed as the Federal Reserve Board made it clear that the control of inflation would take priority over expansion, and Prime Rates began to rise again. Other countries' problems also made themselves felt with the collapse of Germany's Herstatt Bank, and on the last day of June the FT 30 was close to 250, gilts were challenging their all-time low, and the Dow was barely holding the 800 level in the wake of the collapse of the Franklin National Bank. There were now real fears that the fall in markets could become self-feeding.

The £500 million 'lifeboat' for the secondary banks created by the Bank of England in the wake of the London & County collapse plus another £50 million pledged by the Crown Agents, itself a heavy property lender and a major shareholder in FNFC, was beginning to look woefully inadequate. As for the private industrial sector, there seemed to be no hope of solving its liquidity problems. The fall in share prices and the huge rise in interest rates had effectively killed off the new issue market and the bond market, and banks were in no mood to lend money, especially to those companies which really needed it. The suspicion of the Lex column voiced on 25th May that "something nasty is about to happen" appeared to have been very well founded.

Heading for below 200

A few commentators wondered whether staying on the sidelines after such an unprecedented fall in equities would in due course be seen as a classic case of lost opportunity. However, their views lacked conviction in the context of a corporate sector caught in the trap of excessive taxation, sharply rising production costs, strict price controls, and the almost daily evidence of its results with its devastating impact on confidence soon came to be known widely as the "Doomsday Machine".

There was a modest rally in gilts and equities, ahead of Chancellor Healey's minibudget on 23rd July, but despite his announced intent "to attack inflation at its source", the measures, which included a reduction in VAT from 10% to 8%, a slight easing of dividend controls, doubling of regional employment premiums and more food subsidies, did not impress the market. It was much more concerned with rumours of further trouble in the finance and property sectors, talk that even tighter price curbs were under discussion for inclusion in the Labour manifesto, and a fall in the Dow towards 750 as Dr Burns of the Federal Reserve Board warned of yet higher interest rates to counter inflation, with sentiment further unsettled by the moves to impeach President Nixon. By the end of July the FT 30 was back to a 16-year low of 236.4 and gilts had lost all their pre-budget gains. August was even worse. The month saw the country's premier HP company, **United Dominions Trust**, forced into degearing with a £30 million rescue package; once high-flying **Triumph Investment Trust** reporting a near £20 million loss after provisions against loans and write-offs; and the collapse of **Court Line**, the country's second largest tour operator.

On the political front, Minister for Industry, Anthony Wedgwood Benn, unveiled his plans for intervention in industry, designed to greatly increase the degree of State control. His targets were the 25 companies which in his view constituted the "commanding heights" of the economy. The Prime Minister wanted and obtained a less specific commitment, mocking Benn and his left-wing friends for "planning to raise Marks & Spencer to the efficiency of the Co-Op". With an eye to a likely October election, the president of the powerful engineering workers' union, Hugh Scanlon (later to become Baron Scanlon of Davyhulme), called the Tories and the Liberals "enemies of the working class" and warned of industrial chaos if Labour lost. The July trade gap was a near record £478 million thanks to a fading of the export boom and a growing non-oil deficit, causing concern about sterling and severely restricting the scope for any sort of reflationary budget in November. And in America, the resignation of President Nixon and his succession by Gerald Ford failed to help markets there and the Dow lost another 100 points to 656 by the end of August. This atmosphere of universal gloom pushed the FT 30 to 199.8 on 19th August, wiping out 16 years of gains. With a decline of 63%, the 1972/74 bear market was now the worst on record, beating that of 61% from November 1936 to June 1940, and the 52% drop from 1929 to 1932. The Government Securities index also hit a record low of 53.13 during the month as yields on undated stocks topped 16%, thereby maintaining a very large yield gap with equities returning an average 9.62%.

The Arabs start buying

September opened with the news that wage rates had doubled during the first seven months of the year and were now rising at an annual rate of 19%, and an FT Business Opinion Survey which revealed that fears about the impact of rising costs and controlled prices upon profit margins and earnings on capital employed were now widespread throughout industry. There was also another hammering on the Stock Exchange, this time of brokers Tustain L'Estrange, making the fifth this year; an unconvincing denial from another HP company, **Mercantile Credit**, that it was in financial difficulties; and **Lloyds Bank** reporting a loss of £33 million due to "irregularities" at its Lugano branch. The only bright spot of the month was a Kuwaiti bid of £107 million for **St Martins Property**. Coming so soon after Abu Dhabi's £36 million payment for a 44% stake in Commercial Union's head office building, this raised hopes of further reinvestment of Arab oil money bearing in mind that at their current valuation, all the constituents of the FT 30 could be bought by Saudi Arabia out of six months of oil revenues.

The setting of the election date for 10th October immediately ushered in a new period of uncertainty and there was little comfort for investors at a time of national crisis to read in Labour's manifesto that the Party's main objective was "to bring about a fundamental and irreversible shift in the balance of wealth and power in favour of working people and their families". Meanwhile, Wall Street was fast heading towards the 600 level, destroying the myth of the "glamour stock" and the two-tier market in the process. Thus Avon and Polaroid were now down by 50% on the year, Fairchild and Dr Pepper by 30%, and even such proven growth stocks as Xerox and IBM had lost 25% and 15% respectively. The Dow ended the month at 607 with the FT 30 similarly depressed at 188.4, and markets around the world down by an average of 40%, seeming to heed Dr. Kissinger's warning that the strains on the world economy were threatening "to engulf us all in a general depression".

The "Doomsday Machine" rolls on

In the days ahead of the election, the market steadied in the belief that whichever party won would have no choice but to take urgent action to ease the corporate liquidity situation and to restore profitability as well as keeping wages and personal consumption under strict control. This view gained credibility from the news that corporate profits, which had risen 30% during the first nine months of the year, were now falling sharply, but the more cynical thought that industry was being deliberately weakened to the point where it would fall into the outstretched arms of Mr Benn and his National Enterprise Board. There was also no evidence that if Labour won, as seemed likely, it would use anything stronger than exhortation to get the unions to live up to their side of the social contract and moderate their wage demands.

In the event, Labour retained office with a majority of 3 and the FT 30 rallied to over 200 on Mr Wilson's promise that he would take measures to help industry and stimulate investment. However, the Queen's Speech made no mention of any such priority while nationalisation plans figured largely, and by the end of October the index was below 200 again with gilts hitting new lows in reaction to the inevitable increase in the borrowing requirement and the latest inflationary pay awards. All eyes were now on the budget scheduled for mid-November, but its £1.6 billion of relief to industry failed to offset the huge prospective increase in the PSBR, now quantified at £6.3 billion compared with the March forecast of £2.73 billion. Even the Chancellor admitted that the figure was "disturbingly large", and equities, gilts and sterling all fell sharply on fears that overseas confidence would be upset, making a continuation of high domestic interest rates necessary to attract capital to finance the trade deficit.

National Westminster in the firing line

During the remainder of the month, the decline accelerated. The FT 30 fell into the 160/170 range to a 20-year low, the All Share index went into new low ground, the gilts index came within a whisker of the 50 level and the pound reached a record 20.8% weighted depreciation against its December 1971 benchmark. Adding to the gloom were the triggering of the latest threshold pay increases, this time for another 10 million workers, serving to push the rise in wage rates up to 26.4%, and indications that the miners were preparing another huge pay claim with no regard for the social contract or a productivity deal proposed by the National Coal Board. Confidence was further damaged by the collapse of **Triumph Investment Trust**, the suspension of **Jessel Securities**, and renewed fears over the financial stability of **Slater Walker**, **FNFC** and **Keyser Ullman**, as well as practically every property company, all accompanied by falling share prices. But most damaging of all were the rumours about the clearing banks, and **National Westminster Bank** in particular.

By the end of the month, NatWest and Lloyds were both below their par values and the Bank of England took the unprecedented step of issuing a denial that the former had requested or been offered large-scale support. Apart from talk of foreign exchange dealing losses, the principal source of anxiety was over property lending. It was plain to see what bad debts in this area had done to the secondary banks, and the clearing banks were estimated to have lent some £2.8 billion on property in the context of capital and reserves of the Big Four plus the two Scottish clearers of £2.7 billion in total, all at a time when their normal lending to industry was looking none too secure.

The last lap

No one was looking for a pre-Christmas rally in London or indeed in New York where the Dow had just crashed through the 600 level for the first time in 12 years on growing signs of a deepening recession. The first week of December saw the publication of an FT Business Opinion Survey showing that industry expected the trend of costs and prices to worsen; British Leyland, the country's biggest exporter, going cap in hand to the government for financial assistance; and the National Institute forecasting a 25% inflation rate in 1975 and for once offering no solutions. The Stock Exchange called for monthly returns from its member firms in order to detect any liquidity problems as early as possible.

Almost the last straw was the November trade gap which, at £534 million, was the highest ever, and the FT 30 slumped to 150 while the Government Securities index slipped below 50 for the first time. Above all, there was no sign whatsoever of any action by the government to produce a credible anti-inflation policy which relied upon anything more than pious and obviously misplaced hopes about the value of the social contract. The vanity of these hopes was underlined by the strike record for the first 11 months of 1974 which with 13.9 million lost working days was rather more than twice that for 1973 under a Conservative administration. Not surprisingly, against such a background, 1974 turned out to be the worst performing year ever for the stock market. The FT 30 at 161.4 was down 53% and no less than 70% from the May 1972 high of 543.6, while the Actuaries indices were all down 54%. At 49.8, the Government Securities index had lost 18.4% in 1974 following a 14% drop in 1973. Consols now yielded 17% while equities returned a strictly historic 12.5%. Only gold and gold shares gained, beneficiaries of anxiety over monetary stability, and bullion closed the year up 65% at $186 with the FT Gold Mines index adding 70.6 at 353.5.

What went wrong?

There was no shortage of post mortems on 1974 but at its most fundamental level the problem was simply a massive erosion of real corporate profits at a time of accelerating inflation when rigid price controls coupled with a penal tax system made it impossible to earn a real return on investment. Lex attempted to put some figures on it by calculating that between 1968 and the second quarter of 1973, trading profits of the corporate sector before depreciation and tax expressed as a percentage of Gross National Product net of stock appreciation, fell from 12.7% to 10.1%. By the second quarter of 1974, the figure had fallen to 5.7%. In the space of a year, cash flow of industrial and commercial companies had dropped from an annual rate of £4 billion to £1 billion while capital spending had been slow to respond, still running at an annual rate of £5 billion.

Disappointment with this drop in real profitability led to the collapse of the new issue market and the long-term bond market, and while in 1972 new issues in each category were £300 million, in 1974 redemptions of long-term debt were greater than both of them together. This resulted in a huge increase in the importance of bank finance and in the year to November 1974, advances to manufacturing industry rose by £2.7 billion or 40%. If this unhappy combination of inflation and recession triggered by the massive and unexpected cost in the price of oil was a worldwide phenomenon as evidenced by the collapse of stock markets everywhere, the impact in the UK was much worse thanks to the coincidence of political factors. Thus the monetary free-for-all unleashed by the revolution in credit and competition introduced by the Conservatives, clashed head on with Labour's free-for-all policy on wages coupled with one of strict control on prices. Fortunately, the Conservative party in opposition – or rather one vital section within it – had seen the light and was busy laying the foundations for what was to become known five years later as the "Thatcher Revolution". Minister of Health in the last Conservative administration, Sir Keith Joseph, gave a speech at Preston in September 1974 entitled "Inflation is caused by Governments". It was seen as a challenge to the Heath leadership, reminding the party that it had lost its way and forgotten the case for the free market economy, monetary restraint and strict control of public spending, policies it had advocated in 1966 and 1970.

The "X" factor

Even though the market was just days away from its biggest rise in history, at the turn of the year few authoritative commentators were prepared to venture a forecast. Lex did not feel confident enough of the sort of climate that 1975 would bring to list any New Year selections. It should not be forgotten that at the time there were real fears that Britain was heading for social and political chaos. Official indulgence of the ugliest elements on the left of the Labour Party and the unions was causing great concern in the Establishment, and there was an 'unofficial' resurgence of potential counter-movements by the Right. Harold Wilson publicly denounced "smear" campaigns against him and there was serious speculation about a coup. Retired NATO commander, Sir Walter Walker, urged the setting up of a 'citizen army' to counter anti-social elements in the event of a breakdown in law and order – while Colonel David Stirling, the war hero known as the Phantom Major for his exploits behind enemy lines, formed "Great Britain '75" made up of former professional soldiers who were ready to infiltrate picket lines to keep essential services going in the event of large-scale trade union disruption. Condemned by Labour minister, Reg Prentice, for his "provocative" action, Colonel Stirling assured the country that he would not deploy his team unless requested to do so by the government of the day.

Financials count the cost

In 1974 the chickens came home to roost for the finance and property sector. The year began with **Cornhill Consolidated** admitting to liquidity problems at the same time as it was being sued for $8.5 million by an American insurance company for conspiracy to defraud. Also in January, **P&O** bailed out **Bovis** with a £25 million bid, or one fifth of what it had been prepared to offer two years earlier, all thanks to the problems of finance subsidiary, **Twentieth Century Banking**. In early March, FNFC reported profits up from £13.23 million to £18.42 million despite heavy exposure to property sector lending, but at 37p with estimated net worth of 40p a share, the group was widely considered to be stable, especially bearing in mind its 50/50 share with the Bank of England over the London & County rescue operation. Nevertheless the chairman referred to the group's "uncertain outlook", adding that the emphasis in the coming year would be more on consolidation than expansion, and immediately began disposing of some of its industrial interests for cash. The interim figures were well down at £3.8 million against £9 million, after provisions out of profits, and it was pointed out that a large part of the £5 million contributed to the consortium loan for London & County would be "irrecoverable". The share price was now in single figures as investors worried about the apparent lack of provisions against losses on the group's £400 million loan book.

By contrast **Keyser Ullman** was judged to be a model of conservatism, having made provisions of 12% against total loans in 1973/74 with £17 million, or an effective 30%, against the property element despite having made a profit of some £30 million on the sale of Central & District. A press conference had been called in July to announce the results and at the same time the resignations of the two principal Dalton Barton directors largely responsible for the property book, Jack Dellal and Stanley van Gelder. Nervous ahead of the press conference, the shares rallied to 115p on news that the Prudential had increased its stake in the bank by buying shares from the resigning directors. The shares continued to weaken during the rest of the year in common with those of other secondary banks, and at the end of December were back to 34p on the interim statement that further provisions would have to be made against property lending and that profits in the first half of 1974/75 were substantially lower with the trend not likely to be reversed in the second six months.

Doubts grow about Slater Walker

There is no question that Jim Slater was quicker to sense trouble ahead than were his fellow bankers, primary as well as secondary. In February he sold his remaining 50% stake in Crittall Hope Engineering to Norcros for £6.3 million in loan stock, and it was clear from the 1973 results announced at the end of March that banking and money market profits had taken over from those formerly supplied by dealing. Profits were only marginally higher after adjustments at £23.4 million, but it had been a difficult year and, having reduced much of the group's equity exposure before the worst of the market slide and with a £50 million cash pile, Slater was considered still to be in a position to weigh up his options rather than be forced to concentrate on survival like some. The shares then stood at 140p, selling on a P/E of 8, and were regarded as a bid target for one of the larger banking groups looking for innovative management. In quick succession, the satellite companies in America, Australia and South Africa were all sold off to local interests. The half share in South Pacific Properties, a leisure development venture, was sold to P&O, the other partner, and the German interests comprising an industrial holding company and a small merchant bank were sold to Bowater for £3.5 million. Jim Slater explained the rationale behind his move into cash in very striking terms at his AGM on 30th May, saying: "Many people in recent months have found you cannot always turn property into cash, you cannot always turn large lines of shares into cash, you cannot always turn pictures into cash. Cash you can always turn into other things". Privately he is reputed to have used even more forthright language, recommending investment in gold coins and tins of baked beans, all to be tucked away in a mountain hideout with a machine gun to protect them!

In July he sold his controversial stake in Singapore-based Haw Par for around £10 million, but despite all the disposals to date, the interim figures announced in August showed that even though short-term loans and creditors had been reduced by a third to £205 million, the group was still highly geared with £142 million of unsecured loan stocks and long-term loans. Rumours about the group's liquidity position in the context of a share price that had fallen dramatically to 50p, prompted a statement from the company in October reaffirming its "inherent financial strength" and making reference to "completely uncharged free assets" of £65 million or 86p a share. Lex concluded that there was "no reason to be concerned" about the financial state of the Slater Walker Group but expressed some puzzlement about the decision to inject another £5 million into the insurance side given that it was reported to already have £21 million in cash.

In November, Slater completed the withdrawal from the Far East with the sale of Slater Walker Overseas Investments to Hutchison for £4.4 million. The deal was described as a "further movement in the retrenchment of the group". Later that month the first acquisition in over two years was made with the purchase for £1.58 million cash of Jessel's Unit Trust Management Company, thereby doubling Slater Walker's funds under management to £80 million. Some saw this as Slater going back to what he did best. Then just before Christmas, the 20% stake in Costain was sold to a group of Arab investors for £4.17 million, albeit at a £3.2 million loss on the original purchase price. Still, Slater had never been averse to taking a loss when he thought it necessary, a policy given point a few days later when Bowater announced that it was winding up the German merchant bank bought from Slater in June. Despite these disposals, the share price continued its relentless decline, ending the year at 35p.

Property shares become "penny stocks"

Among the worst performing stocks in 1974 were those of the highly geared property companies. Huge development programmes embarked upon with borrowed money at low rates of interest at the top of the market, had become disaster areas. Rising interest rates coupled with collapsing property values wiped out profits, generated staggering losses and uncovered loans on an almost heroic scale. John Ritblat's **British Land** ended the year at 9.5p, down from a 1974 high of 122p, **English Property Company** fell to 32p from a high of 112p, and even Jeffrey Sterling's **Town & City**, into which he had merged his **Sterling Guarantee** in a £34 million reverse bid in April, dropped from 59p to 11p despite a string of very timely disposals by the new chairman. Even the blue chips in the sector suffered. **Land Securities** fell from 212p to 89p and **Hammerson** from 470p to 175p, but they were in the vanguard of the recovery while the position of some of the most highly geared companies actually continued to deteriorate.

No problems for BTR and Racal

BTR may have suffered in share price terms in 1973 and 1974, but this reflected no disappointment with the group's performance. Despite a difficult year in automotive products because of rising raw material prices and the price freeze, pretax profits for 1973/74 were up 38% at £6 million on sales only 20% higher overall but 46% higher overseas. The first half of 1974 continued this remarkable trend with pretax profits up two thirds at £4 million on sales 42% greater at £50 million. £10 million was considered to be the target for the full year and at 52.5p the shares were yielding 9.1% and selling on a prospective P/E of 3.7. Thanks to its electronics tag, **Racal** always had a more glamorous image than BTR and a higher rating to match. The £3.9 million forecast for 1972/73 had been comfortably exceeded at £4.27 million, and then in 1973/74 the forecast of £5.3 million was beaten handsomely again with a total of £6.25 million. At this point overseas sales and exports represented 50% of the total and, at 137p, the shares were selling on an historic P/E of 11.7. By December, when the interim results were announced, the share price was back to 100p despite a 46% advance in pretax profits and a forecast of "in excess of £8 million" for the full year. Racal's equity market capitalisation was now £24 million, the dividend yield 4% and the historic P/E 9.4.

US acquisitions pay off for Hanson and Goldsmith

Rising overseas sales, especially in the US, served to more than make up for **Hanson's** problem areas in the UK and first half figures for 1973/74 showed profits up 11% to £5.5 million with £10 million in prospect for the full year. J. Howard Smith, now renamed Seacoast, revealed bumper post-acquisition results thanks largely to a dearth of rival Peruvian fishmeal, and its contribution in the second half of the year brought the year's total to £10.4 million. In spite of holding cash balances of £22 million, Hanson's share price was not spared the widespread declines of the second half of the year, and at 55p with an equity market capitalisation of £17 million, the yield was 14%.

    Cavenham suffered much more in share price terms than the other proven growth stocks. To a large extent this was due to the complex nature of the group's controlling companies, and to the close links with Anglo-Continental, Goldsmith's banking arm, itself very much involved with Slater Walker's financial and property interests. After reporting 1973/74 pretax profits of £30 million, the interim figures for 1974/75 showed only a modest increase at £16.4 million after sharply higher interest costs, but sales were swelled to £800 million by the inclusion of Grand Union. The shares ended the year at 40p to yield 13.8% on a P/E of 2.8.

1975

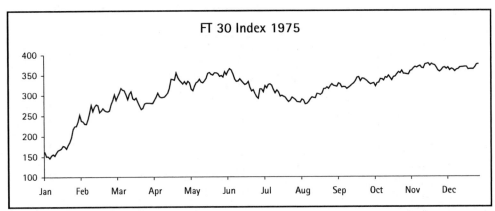

FT 30 Index 1975

Source: Thomson Reuters Datastream

No bell rang

The first trading day of the New Year opened inauspiciously with the suspension of **Burmah Oil** at 100p when the company was forced to call for government assistance to help service its huge US loans. This came as a shock to the market in spite of an 80% decline in the share price during the year, since first half profits in 1974 of £28 million compared with £57 million for the whole of 1973. There had been a warning about a "substantial loss" from the tanker side in the second half but no indication that it would create an overall loss.

In the event, the story of Burmah was of a gamble that failed. The two acquisitions that were intended to catapult Burmah into the major league were the huge tanker operation and Signal Oil and Gas in the US. They were financed by $650 million in loans from American banks but the resulting heavy gearing left Burmah unable to cope with the sharp downturn in trading conditions in 1973 and the gaping hole in its balance sheet created by the fall in the value of its holding in BP from £443 million to £182 million. The Bank of England agreed to guarantee the loan but in return Burmah had to hand over 51% of its North Sea operations, its 21.6% holding in BP together with its 2% in Shell. Nervous speculation about the size of the likely loss for the year meant that the shares were changing hands at around 45p in unofficial dealings. The FT 30 lost 10.8 to 150.6 on the news and by the end of the first week had shed another 4.6 points to 146 on 6th January as **Bowater** crashed 20% to 51p after 44p on rumours of liquidity problems and losses on commodity trading. This was the bottom of the market but true to form, no bell rang. In retrospect it was argued that the market was absurdly cheap and with the FT 30 yielding 13.4% and selling on a P/E of 3.8, there was no doubt that it was discounting almost every conceivable disaster.

Bargain Basement
6th January 1975

Stock	Price (p.)	Div Yld%	P/E	Mkt. Cap (£m)
British Oxygen	17	19.5	3.3	35
BP	196	12.8	2.6	755
Grand Met	23½	20.1	2.4	57
ICI	118	14.0	3.5	575
Lloyds Bank	96	10.1	2.1	125
Nat West	96	12.1	1.9	175
Trusthouse Forte	41½	26.4	2.9	35

The recovery begins

The recovery began slowly and cautiously. Legend has it that the turn was engineered by a buying programme initiated after a lunch given by Prudential at their High Holborn office attended by fund managers from the other leading insurance companies. On 7th January the index rose 7 points to 153 with rises outnumbering gains by only 5 to 4, but significantly markings were the highest for six weeks, and Government Securities added 1.21 to 50.86 encouraged by more Prime Rate cuts in the US and clear signs that the Federal Reserve Board was moving towards a less restrictive monetary policy. The Dow had bottomed at 584 just before Christmas and had added 50 points in heavy trading during the first two weeks of the New Year. London's advance now began to gather momentum, aided by hints from the Chancellor of a tightening of the social contract and two 0.25% cuts in MLR, bringing it down to 11%. Activity also picked up sharply and by the end of the month the FT 30 had topped 250 for a 73% gain on its 6th January low point while the Dow had crossed the 700 level on record volume. The Bank of England now had an £86 million profit on the BP shares taken over from Burmah just three weeks earlier! It was time for a pause, and it came with the publication of the White Paper on Government Expenditure which provided a reminder that its apparently inexorable rise meant that after claims on available resources had been met, there would be very little left over for personal consumption and that tax rises were inevitable.

The setback was short-lived, and encouraged by a much reduced trade deficit in January together with a compromise settlement on the latest miners' pay claim, equities surged ahead again, crossing the 300 level on the last day of February with the Government Securities index reaching 58 in the wake of a further cut in MLR to 10.5% and indications of a continuing worldwide downtrend in interest rates. One political event of great significance during the month was the ousting of Edward Heath from the leadership of the Conservative party, and his replacement by Margaret Thatcher. For the first time in British history, a woman had become the leader of one of the great political parties.

Sterling passes judgement

Companies were not slow to take advantage of this new-found enthusiasm for equities to try to rebuild their balance sheets and in the three weeks to mid-March there were calls for £180 million in rights issues. They were relatively easily absorbed but kept the index below 300 until the budget in mid-April when expectations of action by the Chancellor on wages and public expenditure prompted a renewed advance. In the event a £1.25 billion increase in taxes through 2p on the standard rate and surcharges on drink and tobacco with VAT up from 8% to 25% on luxury items, was taken as evidence that Mr Healey meant what he had said about raising taxes unless the social contract was more strictly observed. There was also a promise of a £1 billion reduction in public expenditure – but given that the PSBR for 1975 had more than tripled to £9 billion since he had become Chancellor, and looked like heading for £12 billion in the current year, this carried little weight. Equities received a further boost in early June from the Referendum resulting in a 2-to-1 vote in favour of the UK staying in the EEC and from further gains in the US, taking the Dow well above 800, but after peaking at 365.3, the index began to slip as investors turned their attention to what sterling was saying about the economic situation.

The momentum of the recovery in equities and gilts to a large extent had masked the deterioration in sterling, where the weighted depreciation had increased from 21.7% in early January to 28.9% by the end of June. But if the domestic market had been impressed for a time by Chancellor Healey's "tough" budget, clearly the international community had not. Thanks to the plight of sterling, the message had got through at last to the domestic market, Mr Healey and the TUC included. To cure inflation by demand reduction alone would cause such severe unemployment that there was seen to be no alternative but to introduce a workable incomes policy combined with a reduction in public expenditure to put government financing back on a sound footing and to leave room for resources to be diverted for the improvement of the trade balance and for productive investment. The demotion of Mr Benn from his post as Minister for Industry to the Department of Energy was another step designed to rebuild business confidence.

Biting the bullet

Even the TUC saw which way the wind was blowing and came up with its own plan to fight inflation which TGWU General Secretary Jack Jones referred to as necessary "to avoid the destruction of the Labour movement". Chancellor Healey seized his opportunity and introduced a voluntary 10% (or £6 per week) pay limit backed up by a veiled threat of statutory action, the latter to the great dismay of Employment Minister Michael Foot. The aim was to reduce inflation from 24% to 10% by the time of the next pay round in September 1976 and to single figures by the end of that year. Many Members of Parliament did not regard the pay limit as applying to themselves but amid scenes of uproar in the Commons, the majority voted to reduce the proposed 78% rise of £3500 to £8000 per annum to one of only £1250, to £5750. This new mood of realism by the Government and its grudging acceptance by the TUC, marked a turning point for the market. The FT 30, which had fallen below 300 in July, stayed there throughout the first half of August, recrossed that level before the end of the month, encouraged by the first signs of a slowdown in the rate of wage rises and a consequent pick-up in business confidence. Even a continuing rise in unemployment and a further decline in sterling failed to dent the market's recovery as investors saw each new shock as likely to push the government further into following the unaccustomed path of financial rectitude. A rise in MLR to 12% in October prompted some nervousness, but taken in the context of hints of a request for an IMF loan, this was seen as further evidence of the government facing up to its responsibilities, and the market surged into the 360/370 range on rising volume.

The IMF takes a hand

In early November, Chancellor Healey made formal application to the IMF for a $2 billion loan and a team from that international body flew into London to "look at the books". Another rise in unemployment had prompted calls from the TUC for the imposition of import controls and rumours of a pre-Christmas reflationary package embodying such controls were seen as a possible threat to the granting of the loan. But with sterling now close to a 30% depreciation level and to a $2 exchange rate, Mr Healey could not take any chances. His package involved only very selective and temporary import restrictions in the textile sector together with an easing of HP curbs on consumer durables, cars excepted, but most important of all, he had won Cabinet agreement to public spending cuts of up to £3 billion. This was widely seen as the most important area of all given that the unplanned and out of control growth in public expenditure since the Government took office, meant that the public sector had become the chief engine of inflation. It was here that the deficit ran riot and where inflation was financed. The bailing out of **Chrysler** with a £180 million package designed to avoid embarrassing job losses indicated that the public purse was still open for really hard luck cases, but the huge operating losses in the coal, rail and steel industries had begun to drive home the lesson that overmanning and inefficient operation in the public sector could not be allowed to continue, whatever the trade unions might say. As Mr Healey had said at the Labour Party conference in October, capital investment in industry, public or private, is simply wasted in situations where there is persistent overmanning and constant strikes, adding that such laws of arithmetic are not changed by elections, an observation prompted by the fact that he had just been voted off the National Executive for these unsocialist views.

The year ended with the equity indices very close to their November highs, the FT 30 at 375.7, up 133%, and the All Share at 158.08, up 154%. Gilts, not surprisingly in the light of the obvious temptations for the government to keep spending, closed below the year's best, but at 59.83 the Government Securities index was still up 20%. Golds had a very see-saw year, with the FT Gold Mines index hitting a new peak of 442.3 in May, then relapsing sharply following the abolition by the IMF of the "official" gold price, to end the year at 243.2. The metal closed at $140, a disappointing level for gold bulls who had thought that the opening of the physical market to US citizens for the first time since 1934 would have created strong demand throughout the year.

Despite the strong rise in the domestic market, the year also saw significant buying of overseas securities as a currency hedge. As a consequence, the dollar premium – the additional cost to UK residents of acquiring the necessary foreign currency from a limited pool of funds – almost doubled in 1975 to just over 120%.

FNFC and Keyser Ullman clear the decks

Welcome though the upturn in the market was, it could do nothing to help the secondary banks and reflex gains in share prices in January were quickly lost as it became clear that their problems persisted. In May, **FNFC** provided some idea of the extent by reporting a loss of £8.3 million for 1974 after provisions of £33 million had wiped out trading profits of £27.3 million, but even after such drastic write-offs, a question mark still hung over the loan book totalling £390 million. The figures for the first half of 1975, released in October, provided a partial answer when the loss rocketed to £73 million after £91 million was provided against the loans. The shares were back to 2p by the end of the year with the Bank of England "lifeboat" continuing to provide support to avoid the further shocks to the banking and property sectors which would come from a forced liquidation. In fact almost half the £1.3 billion of support funds was taken up by FNFC and by leading HP company, **United Dominions Trust**. In the case of **Keyser Ullman**, too, it soon became obvious that there were still problems to solve and that provisions made at the time of the departure of Messrs Dellal and van Gelder had not been adequate. In July, with the share price now down below 50p, directors Ian Stoutzker and Roland Franklin announced their resignations, and two weeks later the company reported a loss of £61 million after provisions of no less than £82.5 million. This was very much a deck-clearing operation and in December the bank announced operating profits for the first half of 1975/76 of £2.4 million, which translated into a £1 million loss after provisions. The share price ended the year at 45p after touching a low point of 32p.

Slater Walker begins to fade

Slater Walker staged a remarkable recovery on the back of the turnround in the market that began on 7th January, and from 27p on that day the shares rocketed to 79p five weeks later. Disposals totalling £5.75 million were made in March alone and after the 1974 results released later that month showed a £9 million drop in pretax profits to £14.5 million, the group was widely judged to have weathered the storm remarkably well. Net worth, which had fallen from 81p to 60.8p in the course of 1974, was now up to 83.6p, a performance that practically no other financial group could even approach. Disposals over a 15-month period now totalled £140 million and despite book losses of £40 million, bank balances still comprised a third of current assets, but a warning was given at the AGM in June that profits in the current year would be 'very low indeed'. The big question was in what direction Jim Slater would now go, and there was some speculation about the identity of the "new and attractive" investment areas he had recently mentioned.

Unfortunately, it was at this point that the Haw Par issue, first raised in Singapore in 1971, came live again. Investigations by the Singapore authorities had led to allegations that there might have been "misappropriation of company funds" and illegal share dealing for the personal benefit of the Slater Walker directors, including Jim Slater and Dick Tarling, through the medium of a company allegedly specially formed for the purpose, namely Spydar Securities (Hong Kong). If this hint of a scandal muddied the waters more than a little, the interim results released in August did nothing to help matters. Profits were down from £10.1 million to just £2.2 million thanks to the absence of dealing profits and to losses in the property portfolio. Sentiment was further unsettled by news that Jim Slater was selling some of his other shareholdings and his agricultural land investments in order "to reduce personal borrowings". Farmland had been a great favourite of Slater and there is a story that his agent, after querying just how much land he was expected to buy, received the answer, "Stop when you reach the sea"!

Jim Slater resigns

By October the share price was back to around the 50p mark, and then on 24th October Jim Slater stunned the City by announcing his resignation, not just from the company he had created but from City life, in order to devote more time to his "family and other interests". The share price lost 11p to 35p and the market fell 10 points on the news but recovered for a loss on the day of 2.7 at 354. Slater's friend and business associate, Jimmy Goldsmith, took control of the group and Lord Rothschild and Charles Hambro joined the board. Goldsmith announced that a "close scrutiny" of Slater Walker would be undertaken over the next three to four months, and the share price fell back to 20p on fears of what might be revealed. In December, the new board decided to cancel the interim dividend declared in October, and the shares fell back to a new low of 17p.

Just to complete the picture of an end of an era, a month earlier Malcolm Horsman had relinquished his executive appointment at Bowater which he had taken up when it had merged with Ralli International in 1972. Ralli's diverse interests had failed to fulfil their early promise and the combined group had put in a creditable performance only by virtue of Bowater's traditional activities.

Hanson and Goldsmith consolidate in the US

1975 was the year **Hanson** made his major move into the US. Former Vice Chairman, Gordon White, had already set up office in New York with the purpose of looking for suitable acquisitions. Those he had found so far proved their worth at the time of the interim results for 1974/75 when their contribution more than offset the downturn in property and building materials in the UK. As a result pretax profits were up from £5.5 million to £5.7 million and a total of at least £11 million looked attainable for the full year. Then in July, an £8.6 million rights issue was announced with the aim of facilitating further expansion in the US. On the back of a forecast doubled dividend, the shares jumped 22p to 162p, although one leading commentator described the move into the US as a "high risk strategy". Before the end of that month a $35 million deal had been agreed to purchase the textile interests of Indian Head. This was a cyclical business being bought very advantageously at the trough of a recession — 1974 profits had just halved to $6 million — at a 40% discount on net assets. Then in November, $7.5 million was paid for a 27% interest in Hygrade Foods, the well-known meat-packers, and when the 1974/75 results were announced in December, two thirds of the £12.1 million profits were seen to have been made in the US. With the shares at 122p, the market capitalisation was now £82 million and the group still had £21 million in cash.

 Cavenham had not scored quite such an immediate success with its US acquisitions as Hanson, and Grand Union, the East Coast supermarket chain, needed a $9 million write-off which resulted in a drop in 1974/75 profits from £29.5 million to £25 million. A significant improvement was forecast for 1975/76 and interim profits duly came in 18% up at £19.9 million, indicating a total for the year of £33 million for a prospective P/E of 8 with the shares at 130p.

BTR and Racal ignore the recession

BTR's overseas sales rose 74% in 1974/75 to represent 60% of total sales producing a pretax profit of £9.9 million. A further improvement was forecast for the current year, and the interim results in September showed that it was well on target with profits up 60% at £6.3 million on sales 50% higher. There had been a rights issue in July to raise £5.7 million but the object of the company's ambitions did not become clear until 1976. **Racal's** profit forecast of "in excess of £8 million" turned out to be £9.5 million, a gain of 56% on sales up by 45%. There was also a one-for-one scrip issue. In December, first half profits weighed in at £6.24 million as against £2.8 million for the previous period, and a full year forecast of £15 million was made. Like BTR and Hanson, one of the secrets of Racal's success was the large overseas sales content which was now roughly 70%. The other was the absence of borrowings of any kind. BTR ended the year at 153p and Racal at 235p.

Saatchi & Saatchi step out

September saw the entry of Maurice and Charles Saatchi into the public arena with a reverse takeover of quoted advertising agency, Compton Partners, leaving them with 35% of the new holding company to be called Saatchi & Saatchi Compton. The Saatchis were already the wunderkinder of the advertising world having built up billings from zero to £11 million since 1970, and profits to £300,000. The merger with Compton Partners would give them total billings of £30 million and make them the third largest agency in the UK after J. Walter Thompson and Ogilvy, Benson & Mather.

1976

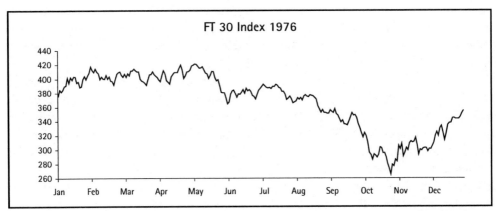

FT 30 Index 1976

Source: Thomson Reuters Datastream

A flying start

The year opened on a high note. The FT 30 crossed the 400 level and reached 417.4 at the end of January, joining in the worldwide rally led by Wall Street on expectations of a continuing decline in interest rates. There was a lot for the London market to be hopeful about. Industry was more confident than at any time since November 1973. Inflation was under some degree of control, thanks to the pay and prices policy and the recession, and there were real signs of an export-led boom developing. This latter point seemed to be fully confirmed by the December trade deficit, which at £79 million was less than half that of November, bringing the 1975 total to £1.7 billion, or half that of the previous year. The coming oil bonanza was another major bull point. Only eleven years had passed since drilling in the North Sea began and despite much earlier scepticism, the area had proved to be one of the most productive oil and gas basins in the world. By the end of 1974 oil was flowing at the rate of a million barrels a day, just when it was most needed, and oil shares were booming.

Company profits had risen just 4.3% in 1975, but for 1976 expectations were of a rise of around 20-25%. Unemployment was rising fast but while the TUC's response was to call for a £2 billion reflationary package, the Prime Minister avowed that the Government's anti-inflation drive would not slacken, hinting at a tough Phase Two. The aim, he said, was to reverse the UK economy's 30-year decline in order to enter the coming economic upturn with inflation under control and domestic resources not overstretched by excessive public spending. Any major reflationary moves were out of the question. To underline this tough message, the Chancellor's White Paper referred to his planned £2.4 billion cuts by 1978/79, as a "long, harrowing, but necessary process". Jack Jones pressed for a continuation of the £6-a-week limit against strong opposition from TUC colleagues. Equities had also been boosted by a rapid succession of cuts in MLR which by the end of January had fallen to 10%. Significantly, while the Government Securities index responded positively to this last reduction, rising 0.82 to 65.21, it took no notice of subsequent cuts and was back to 62.47 when MLR reached 9% on 5th March.

The problem was sterling, which had just fallen below $2. By the end of the month it was down to $1.93, with the authorities making no attempt to stem the decline in line with the then policy of accepting depreciation as long as the rate of inflation in the UK remained substantially higher than in other industrial countries. France blamed its withdrawal from an already very shaky "snake" that month on the UK's "uncontrolled devaluation" of the pound and also on Germany's adamant refusal to revalue the DMark. The aim of the policy was to stimulate export-led growth and keep interest rates down to encourage investment, thus buying time for an excessive rate of monetary expansion to be adjusted gradually to inflation goals.

Confidence begins to wane

Overseas holders of sterling seemed to be taking the view that whatever a Labour Government might say about cutting public expenditure, it was neither willing nor indeed able to do so. Furthermore, plans for funding the public sector deficit looked certain to run into problems as the economic recovery picked up and industry began to compete for funds. In any case, the much-vaunted "cuts" announced so far were not immediate but only reductions in future planned expenditure, which was already more than the economy could bear. Overseas opinion was also influenced by the chaotic state of the UK motor industry, especially British Leyland, which had become a symbol of the country's industrial weakness and of the Government's inability to cure it. In receipt of Government funds and run by Government appointees, the company was still a hotbed of industrial unrest, crippling the country's principal export earner. Two factors now added to the uncertainty. One was the surprise resignation of Harold Wilson and doubts about the succession. The other was the April budget where tax cuts were rumoured to be linked to acceptance by the trade unions of a 3% pay norm. The election of James Callaghan two days before the budget removed one uncertainty and provided some relief even though the enhanced position of Michael Foot in the new cabinet continued to cause anxiety. The budget, however, did not help in that the trade-off between tax cuts and pay restraint was seen to accord to the trade unions a pivotal role in the formation of economic policy.

Sterling continues to slide

A flood of rights issues, including one for £200 million from ICI, helped to subdue the market in April and May, but also keeping it in check were real doubts that the Chancellor could persuade the TUC and its members to agree to a Stage Two incomes policy. After all, incomes restraint at a time of recession when the connection between the wage explosion of 1974 and the sharp rise in unemployment in 1975 had become obvious to all, was one thing. Quite another would be to gain acceptance for such a policy when an upturn was underway. There were also doubts that the Government's newfound enthusiasm for the role of the private sector could be maintained in such circumstances. The budget had provided some useful concessions in the form of tax relief on stock appreciation and promised revisions of the Price Code, but the idea that industrial investment was a precondition for the eventual ability to indulge in social expenditure was totally lost on the left of the Labour Party. Relief that the TUC had agreed to compromise on a 5% pay norm helped to keep the FT 30 above 400 until the end of May, but the sight of sterling continuing to fall despite a 2.5 point rise in MLR, now began to erode investor confidence.

The problem was now seen to be a lack of monetary or fiscal support for the pay policy, hampering its present effectiveness and in due course ensuring its demise as well as that of the inflation reduction targets. There had been further talks with the IMF about a loan but the inevitable and predictable conditions attached to the granting of one were bound to cause such political problems for the Government that it was reluctant to endanger the delicate rapport that it had achieved with the TUC. Instead, in June, it opted for a $5.3 billion stand-by credit from the central banks for six months, effectively buying time to put its house in order and thereby avoiding the necessity of going to the IMF. Sterling rebounded 5.5 cents to $1.77 on the news but gilts and equities remained largely unmoved, staying in the 62/63 and 370/390 range respectively until late August.

Public spending cuts become a priority

The central bankers might have expected the implementation of a tighter fiscal policy in return for their loan, and coincidentally the BIS in a European report added that Britain should set money supply targets and cut back on its PSBR. Unfortunately, however good the Chancellor's intentions may have been, his resolve was soon to be severely tested. Jack Jones responded to hints of a Stage Three wages and prices policy by asserting that he would not support it and wanted an "ordered return to free collective bargaining". Then the monthly trade figures began to deteriorate alarmingly in May and June, forcing Mr Healey to look again at the idea of public spending cuts. Unfortunately just when he and the Prime Minister had steeled themselves to pushing them through, the unemployment figures soared to a new post-War record at 1.46

million. Their conviction that priority must be given to the strengthening of the country's industrial base and that the Party's supporters must "accept the cuts or see Labour driven from office", appeared to have moderated somewhat by the end of July when the first definitive cuts were announced. A planned £1 billion cut in the PSBR from the expenditure proposed in 1977/78 was to be offset by raising the employers' National Insurance contributions by £910 million.

The reaction of the markets was to believe that the Government once again was looking to the corporate sector's developing surplus to fund its public spending ambitions, and a month later the index was down to 350 with the pound coming under pressure again. The picture was complicated further both by a drought so severe that a three-day week was on the cards, and a challenge to the pay policy by the National Union of Seamen which served to undermine the whole accord between the Government and the TUC. Activity in the equity market was abysmally low at this point and of three new issues in July, **Hambro Life, Molins** and **Borthwick**, all were trading at a substantial discount to their offer price. Oils were a firm exception on North Sea exploration hopes.

Trying to square the circle

The problem for the Government was that it had a huge public spending programme to fund and that to do so, it needed to sell an equally huge amount of gilts. Its relative lack of success in doing so had led to a succession of interest rate rises, but as MLR rose another 1.5 points to 13% in mid-September, the question began to be asked whether the reliance on high interest rates alone to fund the Government deficit did not serve to perpetuate the recession which the burgeoning deficit was intended to offset. In fact, by this time it seemed clear that what lay behind the Government's difficulty in funding the PSBR had less to do with the level of interest rates, than with simply a lack of confidence in the stability of the pound and the Government's whole economic strategy. Thus a high rate was not going to prove attractive to investors if it sparked fears of a still rising trend. The policy of pushing up rates to a level from which it was hoped they would be expected to fall, known as the "Grand Old Duke of York" strategy, did not work for Mr Barber in 1972, and there was much less reason to think that it would work for Mr Healey in 1976. After all, everyone now knew what heights inflation could achieve under a lax monetary and fiscal regime, and there were no guarantees that the recent decline from those heights was going to persist. Indeed, the present policy actually threatened to reverse that decline.

In early September it was announced that the Government would apply to extend the $5.3 billion credit facility for a further three months but markets were not impressed at this further attempt to buy time and by the middle of the month the FT 30 was back to 335, Government Securities to 60.03 and sterling to $1.7350. The feeling was that the Government was simply waiting and hoping for "something to turn up".

"Crisis? What crisis?"

With yields at the long end of the gilts market now topping 15%, the Government launched a new tap stock with a 14.5% coupon, the highest ever. It was comfortably oversubscribed at an issue price of £96.50 and there were hopes that this modest success in funding a rapidly accumulating deficit would continue.

A week later, the Government's funding programme lay in tatters. A wave of selling from across the world had driven sterling below $1.70 and the new tap stock was now at a one-point discount as yields neared the 16% level. The spark for this new slide in sterling had been a "special case" treatment of the National Union of Seamen's claim which they had won by the simple expedient of threatening to strike, knowing full well that this was the last thing the Government wanted at such a critical juncture in its fortunes. An inflationary settlement, however, was almost as dangerous and a 4 cent fall in sterling on 28th September prompted Mr Healey to abandon his trip to Hong Kong for the Commonwealth Finance Minsters' Conference, while the Prime Minister countered reporters' questions with "Crisis? What crisis?" as his Chancellor returned to Downing Street to formulate an emergency package preparatory to the now inevitable application for a $3.9 billion loan from the IMF. The timing was particularly unfortunate for the Chancellor from a political point of view in that the Labour Party Conference was in full swing, and while the delegates gave his policy their backing, they insisted that no strings should be attached to the loan, especially those concerning cuts in public spending. On the same day, they also voted overwhelmingly in favour of a resolution to take over the banks and the insurance companies!

Markets now began to take fright and by the end of the first week of October, the FT 30 breached the 300 level as MLR was raised 2 full points to a record 15% and £700 million of Special Deposits were called for. Gilts fell by between 3 and 4 points and the 14.5% tap stock now stood at a 4-point discount to its offer price just three weeks earlier as yields edged over 16%. Home loans soared to their highest ever level of 12.25% and a new tap stock with a 15.5% coupon was launched.

Grasping the nettle

The Government now had no choice but to grasp the nettle of public spending cuts regardless of the threat to Party unity, but it still took one further panic at the end of October to make them decide to do so. The Prime Minister appeared on the Panorama television programme, warning of the grave political consequences if the IMF were to try to force the Government to adopt policies which would be so harmful to the economy that it would go into a downward spiral. The next day there were rumours of an imminent rise in MLR to 18%, a devaluation to $1.50, and a split between the Chancellor and the Prime Minister leading to the resignation of the former. The Treasury took the almost unprecedented step of formally denying the resignation story, but by then sterling had fallen to $1.57, Government Securities to 56, and the FT 30 to 265.3. The Chancellor promised an economic package for late November, and on the bold assumption that it would contain the necessary measures, markets began to recover, seemingly on the idea that the worse the news, the more effective the package was likely to be. By this time Mr Healey was perhaps influenced more by the Conservatives winning two of the three by-elections in November, than by his own National Executive voting 13 to 6 to oppose any cuts in public spending and a motion to the same effect tabled by 100 Labour MPs. Within a week the FT 30 was over 300 again and gilts and sterling had risen sharply as talks with IMF representatives got underway. News that the 15.5% tap stock had been sold out gave a boost to the gilt market, as did a new squeeze on bank lending in an attempt to bring the growth of money supply under stricter control. The first stage of the Government's monetary restabilisation programme had been judged in the market to be a relative success, and before the end of the month, MLR was reduced by a quarter of a point to 14.75%.

Going straight

The gains in sterling, gilts and equities were consolidated and then extended as December progressed, gathering pace after the IMF-tailored package in the middle of the month. There was an initial but short-lived disappointment with its provisions which were thought to be half-hearted and likely to make no more than a marginal contribution towards correcting the fundamental imbalances in the economy. However, second thoughts concentrated on the novel sight of a Labour Government actually agreeing to cut back on its public spending programme by £1 billion in 1977/78 and by £1.5 billion in 1978/79, targeting such sacred cows as food subsidies, roads, new housing and school buildings. This would mean reducing the PSBR by £2 billion in 1977/78 to £8.7 billion, and by another £3 billion in 1978/79 to keep it at that level. Furthermore, the rate of growth of the money supply, which had crept up to an annual rate of 27% in September, was to be firmly controlled within a 9-13% band. And perhaps most important of all was the fact that the Government was now firmly in hock to the IMF and subject to its supervision. It was not enough for Minister for Overseas Development, Reg Prentice, who resigned from the Cabinet on the grounds that the government was too obsessed with appeasing the trade unions, was not firm enough with its public spending cuts and persisted in indulging in irrelevant measures like nationalisation and devolution. Echoing Sir Keith Joseph's September 1974 speech, he went on to blame governments of both parties and both sides of industry for the country's thirty years of economic decline. Another quarter point off MLR just before Christmas gave a further boost to sentiment and the year ended on a high note, encouraged by the Dow breaking through the 1000 level on expectations of the newly-elected President Carter providing a major stimulus to the economy. The FT 30 ended the year at 354.7, down 6% over the period but up 34%

on the October low. The Government Securities index was practically unchanged on the year at 60.27 but this was up 8% on the October figure. Golds were the worst performer of all, with the FT Gold Mines index practically halving to 119.8 on fears about the long-term effect of demonetisation and the new official sales policy for physical gold.

Slater Walker – the final chapter

In January, Slater Walker's new chairman, Jimmy Goldsmith, arranged for the transfer of Jim Slater's personal holding of 2 million shares at 23p to his own stable of interests. This deal effectively ended Jim Slater's relationship with the company he had created. The company, however, continued but despite drastic job cuts the new management was unable to turn the operation around. The share price began to weaken significantly in September and later that month a loss for 1975 of no less than £42 million was announced. Insolvency was only avoided thanks to the cooperation of the Bank of England, which not only made available a £70 million borrowing facility but also guaranteed £40 million of potential bad debts in the loan portfolio. The price dropped 9p to 7p on the news, and little encouragement was provided by the accountant's report. The banking side of the business was described as "inherently weak with too high a proportion of loans to 'in house' companies and their affiliates" and the insurance investment portfolios were criticised for having too high a property content and too many shareholdings of questionable value. There was also criticism of loans to directors, and loans to affiliated companies allegedly for the purpose of share support operations contrary to Section 54 of the Companies Act. Only the investment management and unit trust side, run by Brian Banks as a largely independent operation, received a completely clean bill of health. Slater eventually was charged on six counts, but all were dismissed on the basis that there was "no case to answer", and Singapore's application for extradition was rejected. Dick Tarling was not so fortunate and had to serve some months in Changi jail.

In August 1978 it was announced that the Bank of England was going to buy Slater Walker Limited, the banking operation, together with some properties and "other group assets". All the prior charge holders assented to the terms, and the ordinary shareholders agreed to a change of name to **Britannia Arrow Holdings** for their equity interest. Thus ended, not without some dignity, perhaps the most remarkable financial phenomenon of the post-War years.

Hanson boosts its US interests

Hanson's first move in 1976 was to make a tender offer for the balance of **Hygrade Foods**. Despite some legal obstacles the offer was successful, doubling group sales to £350 million, 80% of which now arose in the US. The acquisition focussed more attention on the group's US activities and in particular on the role of Gordon White whose 10% interest in Hanson Industries, the company controlling US operations, had not been disclosed to shareholders despite the fact that it had come to account for four fifths of total sales. Furthermore, given his obvious importance, the fact that he was not a director of the UK company also caused some concern. Later in the year, it was disclosed that Gordon White had bought his 10% stake for £265,000, or just £265 on the basis of 0.1% paid, and that a formula was being devised to buy him out. The fact that he had been practically solely responsible for the creation of the US side of the business and its remarkable contribution to the success of the parent company, now received less attention than the huge profit he would make on his modest investment. Interim profits were comfortably ahead at £7.8 million and a "substantial increase" was forecast for the full year which resulted in a figure of £19.2 million, establishing the group firmly among the top 300 US companies.

The final act of the year was an £8.5 million bid for the 75% of **Whitecroft Industries**, the Midlands based conglomerate, that it did not already own, the original stake having been purchased from Slater Walker. The bid was rejected by the Whitecroft board and its supporters as inadequate and, unwilling to pay up, Hanson dropped the bid. The shares ended the year at 108p.

Control of Cavenham shifts

1976 saw the first step in Goldsmith's plan to move control of Cavenham into French hands. His master company Générale Occidentale bought out the balance of shares in Générale Alimentaire publicly held, and passed them on to Cavenham in return for Cavenham shares, thus bringing its holding in Cavenham up from 39% to 51%. The 1975/76 results came out in June and showed expectations of £33 million comfortably exceeded at £34.7 million. The interim figures for 1976/77 recorded a 14% improvement at £22.7 million, but by then the share price had slipped back to 93p to yield over 9%. In Goldsmith's eyes this was too modest a rating for a company which had grown in ten years from practically nothing to become an international food giant, and the second stage of his plan began to take shape.

BTR and Racal go from strength to strength

Two weeks after revealing pretax profits for 1975 up by 62% to £16 million, **BTR** took its first step along the path of expansion into the US market with a £15.5 million bid for SW Industries, a leader in elastomeric roll coverings and web control systems. The acquisition came too late to have a great effect on the interim results for 1976, but on sales up just 19% pretax profits showed a 37% gain to £8.6 million. The shares then stood at 138p, yielding 8.1% on a P/E of 6, but by year-end had advanced to 150p. As usual, **Racal** beat its forecast of £15 million for 1975/76 by turning in a figure of £19.65 million, but it was the first half result for 1976/77 that really excited the market. Sharply rising demand for its military communications equipment and a relatively fixed cost base, sent profits soaring 85% to £11.5 million, prompting a forecast for the full year of more than £28 million. At the time of the announcement at the beginning of December, the shares stood at 208p yielding 1.25% on a dividend covered 17.5 times by earnings, but by the end of the month they were up to 240p.

The secondary banks limp on

Continuing provisions still hampered the chances of recovery at **FNFC** and **Keyser Ullman** despite the notable absence of the sort of investigations and allegations that had accompanied the demise of London & County and Slater Walker. Still, the losses were equally staggering, and while history seems to look upon the "secondary banking crisis" as an exceptional episode in the country's financial development, it should not be forgotten that at their peak all these companies possessed the enthusiastic backing of the financial establishment. All had major institutional shareholders, some of which were represented on the board. Eminent Conservative politician, Edward du Cann, was chairman of Keyser Ullman, leader of the Liberal Party, Jeremy Thorpe, was a non-executive director of London and County and Sir Gordon Newton, chairman of the *Financial Times*, was also chairman of Vavasseur. As top City journalist Ivan Fallon wrote in the *Sunday Telegraph* in October 1975, "At one time to be a Slater associate was akin in the City to being a companion to Alexander the Great". Indeed, given the huge provisions that had to be made by the Big Four against the loan portfolios built up in the early 1970s, it was as much a crisis for the primary banks as it was for the secondary, with the former surviving only by virtue of their much larger reserves.

Poseidon sinks beneath the waves

As a sad postscript to the heady days of the Australian nickel boom when Poseidon was known as the "share of the century", in September 1976 its quotation was suspended at 155p on grounds of "liquidity problems". The following month a receiver was appointed and the company was reported to have accumulated losses of A$16 million and debts of A$28 million. Western Mining and Shell subsequently acquired the Windarra prospect as a joint venture, and two years later Poseidon returned to the market as a gold mining company.

1977

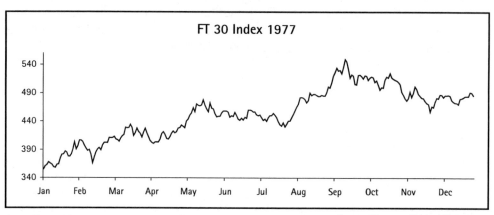

FT 30 Index 1977

Source: Thomson Reuters Datastream

North Sea oil proves its worth

The New Year began with high hopes. On the external front, Saudi Arabia was acting as a moderating voice within OPEC, keeping oil prices down, and expansionary moves in the US boded well for Britain's exports. At home, sterling had recovered to the $1.70 mark after the Chancellor's November package and overseas confidence had been buoyed by the knowledge that the IMF was looking over his shoulder. There was also a growing realisation of what North Sea oil could be worth to the balance of payments given that the country was no more than two years away from self-sufficiency. It was only two years since the economy had emerged from its gravest post-War crisis and it was now clear that the policies of deficit financing intended to avoid recession, had in fact, served to perpetuate it. Even though gilt yields were high, apparently providing little incentive for investment in equities, there were grounds for hoping that the latter would be a longer-term beneficiary from the more realistic appraisal of the economic facts of life forced upon the Government since 1975. Sentiment was given another boost by the BIS agreeing to provide a $3 billion facility as security against a further rundown of foreign official sterling balances, and also by the plan to reduce sterling's reserve role by banning its use as a trading currency for transactions in which the UK was not directly involved.

News of a £21 million trade surplus in December, followed by further cuts in MLR to 12%, prompted a strong advance in equities to over 400 and in the Government Securities index to 65.5 at the beginning of February. But while capital markets responded quickly to Government action, inevitable time lags meant that neither the rate of inflation nor the numbers of unemployed could do so immediately. Thus with price rises comfortably outstripping the rise in earnings, there were going to be difficulties in negotiating a deal with the TUC over a third phase of wage restraint at a time when real incomes were being so severely squeezed. However, further falls in MLR and another trade surplus in February, ensured a rising trend in gilts and equities ahead of the budget at the end of March. Restrained by a still high rate of inflation, by the limitations imposed by the Letter of Intent to the IMF, and by the need to reach agreement over Stage Three, the Chancellor brought in a broadly neutral budget with £2.3 billion of tax cuts, £1 billion of which were conditional on a satisfactory Stage Three, and a rise in personal allowances and thresholds to help the lower paid, balanced by an £800 million boost to indirect taxation, largely on drink, tobacco and petrol duties. Markets were now subject to a two-way pull. The optimists argued that the fact of the Government observing the limitations on its actions imposed by the IMF guidelines at a time when there was so much slack in the economy, was bound to mean a continuing decline in interest rates, while the more cynical suggested that the Chancellor had been happy to introduce such a cautious budget since it left him with the scope to be more reflationary in the event of an election being called.

Time for a pause

Falling interest rates proved the more powerful influence for a time and by mid-May, after MLR had dropped by stages to 8%, the FT 30 reached a new peak for the year of 477.4, its highest point since June 1973. Meanwhile gilts had topped out with the Government Securities index at 71.48 as institutions, heavy buyers of gilts in the final quarter of 1976, had swung back to equities, seeing them as better value when the downtrend in interest rates apparently had run its course and inflationary trends had not.

But now uncertainties began to dominate both markets. The Retail Price Index in April rose by 17.5%, showing that there were still plenty of price increases coming through in the wake of the collapse of sterling in the last quarter of 1976. Short-term rates were rising in the US as the Federal Reserve Board reimposed a tight monetary policy to try to combat the persistence of inflationary pressures, and the Dow slipped below 900 to a new low for the year. And potentially most serious of all, union after union rejected the idea of a third phase of wage restraint, preferring a return to free collective bargaining in an effort to redress a situation where earnings were now rising at just about half the rate that prices were increasing. There was the further anxiety that the Labour Government's hold on office was looking increasingly tenuous. The so-called "Lib/Lab" pact had collapsed, the Conservatives had made gains of landslide proportions in by-elections and local elections, and the Finance Bill had been thrown out, upsetting a not insignificant part of the Chancellor's budget arithmetic. While a change of government no doubt would have been welcome in many quarters, the market's attitude was that with Labour following IMF guidelines and engaged in negotiating Stage Three with the trade unions, maintenance of the status quo at this stage was greatly preferable to the uncertainty of a General Election. By the end of July the FT 30 had lost nearly 50 points to 430 and Government Securities just over 4 points to 67.

Markets get their second wind

Then in August the mood of the markets changed abruptly for the better as fears about the Government's ability to secure a third stage pay deal and control the money supply without a rise in interest rates, suddenly seemed to melt away. The trigger was the decision of the authorities in the last week of July to abandon the policy of linkage with a weak dollar at $1.72, embarked upon at the beginning of the year as a rough and ready way of cushioning export margins. The support peg was now shifted from the dollar to the trade-weighted average providing a general index of sterling's value. The effect on confidence was dramatic and the result was the rapid establishment of a virtuous circle of further currency inflows, falling interest rates and booming gilt sales. £1.5 billion of gilts were sold in August as MLR dropped to 7% but equities were the biggest beneficiary. There was no "tap" to supply whatever the market wanted and a wave of buying sent the FT 30 to 500.9 on the last day of the month. Up to a point, nothing succeeds in the stock market like success and that point was still some way off. Overseas money continued to flow in, and reserves rose to a new record of £14.85 billion, reflecting confidence that the recession in the UK economy had bottomed and that with the benefits of North Sea oil already flowing, the prospects were bright.

In mid-September, the FT 30 hit a new all-time high of 549.2, on the same day a record trade surplus of £316 million was announced, and two days later MLR was reduced to 6%. However, the picture was soon upset by a run of disappointing profits statements from such industrial leaders as **GKN**, **Dunlop** and **Vickers**, and within a matter of days the index was heading back towards 500 again despite further reductions in MLR to 5%, its lowest level for five years, and another trade surplus in September indicating a probable surplus for the year as a whole.

Success brings its problems

Doubts centred on the likely difficulty of keeping the growth of money supply within the target range now that so much overseas money was pouring into the country, and fears that if this problem was countered by letting the exchange rate rise, then industrial competitiveness would suffer. The dilemma was partially resolved on the last day of October, immediately after the Autumn 'package' announcing more tax concessions and reaffirming the lower public spending targets embodied in the Letter of Intent to the IMF. The pound was to be cut loose altogether, clearly indicating that, for the moment at least, observance of monetary guidelines had priority over exchange rate stabilisation and industrial competitiveness. Sterling jumped six cents on the news to $1.8405, gilts remained steady, but equities dropped like a stone, losing 33 points on the week to 476, only to bounce back over 500 again a week later just as gilts began to weaken in anticipation of a reversal in the downtrend of interest rates.

The decision to free the pound worked to a degree. Currency inflows peaked at £20 billion, and the diversion of 'hot money' into the DMark and the yen meant that the UK's competitive position was relatively unaffected, but the market found it difficult to shake off its anxieties over the money supply and about the chances of Mr Healey managing to keep the growth of average earnings within his target limit of 10%. The raising of MLR by two full points to 7% at the end of November seemed to clear the air and at year end the FT 30 was up 36% at 485.4, gilts were up 30% at 78.09, and the FT Gold Mines index, up 11%, enjoyed a modest revival on the back of a strongly recovering bullion price, benefiting from a weak dollar and flying in the face of IMF sales.

Cavenham goes home to France

After asserting a corporate philosophy of concentrating on food companies, Jimmy Goldsmith surprised the market in January by taking a 35% stake in **Beaverbrook**, the Express Newspaper group, at a cost of some £2 million. The size of the deal was insignificant in relation to the whole group, but it still worried some investors who saw it as a perverse reaction to the blocking in the US of his attempted $350 million takeover of Schenley. By now **Cavenham** shares had an abysmal market rating totally out of line with the company's meteoric growth record, and there was little surprise when Goldsmith's master company, Générale Occidentale, made a bid of 120p for the 49% of Cavenham that it did not own. At the time the shares stood at 93p yielding 8.75% and were selling on a P/E of less than 5, and most commentators regarded the bid as woefully inadequate for a company with net assets of 150p earning 20p a share in 1977. It was an attempt, said Lex in the *Financial Times*, by the top of the pyramid to absorb the base. In the face of such adverse comment, Goldsmith dropped the 120p bid, but returned to the fray two months later with a partial bid of 155p cash designed to take his holding up to 75%. Despite further criticism, the bid was successful and then in August he proceeded to mop up the 25% rump with an offer in Cavenham preference stock valued at 127p a share against a suspension price of 81p. The net result was that for a total outlay of £40 million, the cost of the partial bid, Goldsmith had brought Cavenham, one of Europe's leading food groups making annual profits of very close to that figure, under his personal and private control. The top of the pyramid had indeed absorbed the base and it had used the latter's own capital to do so.

Racal looks to the US

In January, **Racal** made its first major bid, which proved to be a double diversification, taking the group into the US and into a new product. The target was Milgo, an American computer peripheral equipment manufacturer, and after a hard fought battle Racal succeeded with a $63 million offer. Simultaneously, a £14.7 million rights issue was announced, accompanied by a full year forecast of £32 million, against an earlier one of "more than £28 million", and the shares rose 22p to 305p on the news. The actual outcome was £32.7 million, up 67% on a sales increase of 53%, there was a 1 for 1 scrip issue, and at 380p, the shares were selling on a P/E of slightly less than nine. Another foray into the US electronics market was made in October with a £3.5 million bid for Dana Laboratories, makers of voltmeters and systems counters. In December the interim figures showed a 68% jump in pretax profits to £19.4 million, and the forecast for the full year was "in excess of" £45 million. The shares ended the year at 208p after the 1 for 1 scrip, recording a 73% gain.

Another £12 million for BTR

BTR reported 1976 profits up by 51% to £24 million and at the same time announced a £12 million rights issue, the second in eighteen months. The terms were 1 for 5 at 140p, against a market price of just under 200p, giving an ex-rights yield of 7½%. The interim results announced in mid-September revealed a useful advance in profits from £10. 1 million to £13.3 million. Then in early December a £9.5 million bid was made for **Allied Polymer**, an industrial rubber products group originally formed by Slater Walker out of Greengate & Irwell, P.B. Cow and Frankenstein Group and floated in 1971. The group had run into problems in 1975/76 and BTR was making an offer at a one third discount to the original flotation price. BTR shares ended the year at 256p yielding 5.4% on a P/E of 9.6.

Hanson increases its US interests

Hanson's interim profits for 1977/78 were up by 43% to £11.23 million and a "substantial improvement" was forecast for the full year with £23 million the consensus target figure. In the intervening period, a number of tactical disposals were made in the US, cutting borrowings by $8 million. In October, an unsuccessful approach was made to **Lindustries**, a UK engineering, rubber and textiles group, and then in November a $29 million bid was launched for Interstate United Corporation, a US specialist foods group. Full year results exceeded most expectations with profits at £24.4 million, but the cyclical nature of the US operations prompted caution from most commentators. At year end the shares stood at 154p, yielding 6.2% with a P/E of 7.6 and equity market capitalisation at this point was £100 million.

The Sir Eric Miller Story

The scandal of the year involved **Peachey Property** and its Chairman, Sir Eric Miller. Sir Eric, a keen supporter of Labour Party fund-raising and social activities, knighted during the Wilson premiership, suddenly resigned from his position as Chairman of Peachey Property, London's largest residential property company and owners of the Park West block in Edgware Road. The resignation had been forced upon him by his three fellow directors following Sir Eric's failure to give what they considered to be a satisfactory answer to questions concerning a missing £282,000. His explanation was that the money had been expended in pursuit of an abortive European acquisition and that £130,000 had been deposited in a bank which then had sent a letter to the board acknowledging receipt. The three directors denied categorically that they had ever seen such a letter and Sir Eric was unable to provide evidence of its existence, as indeed was the bank concerned. As a result of his inability to refute the charges against him, Sir Eric lost a proxy fight to remain on the board, and the Department of Trade and Industry embarked upon an investigation. Just before its findings were published, Sir Eric shot himself in the garden of his Kensington house.

1978

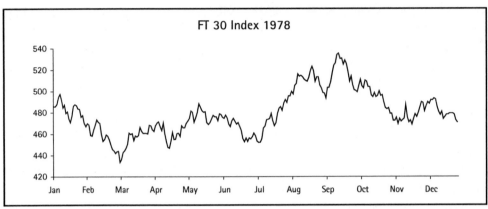

FT 30 Index 1978

Source: Thomson Reuters Datastream

Trying for a pay policy

Given that the rate of inflation was coming down, that the economy was beginning to stir, and that the balance of payments was considered certain to improve thanks to the bonus of North Sea oil, prospects for 1978 were widely regarded as more encouraging than for a very long time. However, Lex in the *FT* pointed out very prophetically that the two principal dangers would turn out to be the excessive weakness of the dollar and growing domestic demand pressures.

It did not take long before the first of these dangers became only too apparent. At the end of the first week of January, it was announced in Washington that the term of office of Dr Arthur Burns at the Federal Reserve Board would not be renewed. The departure of this strict advocate of sound money was taken as a sure sign that the Administration was giving lower priority to the control of inflation and maintenance of the exchange rate, and the dollar fell sharply, taking the Dow Jones with it. A ½% cut in MLR to 6½% failed to help the London market, which was becoming increasingly concerned about export prospects as the pound rose ten cents in a month to $1.95. February brought further shocks with the release of the January trade figures showing a £179 million deficit, and banking figures which indicated that the growth of the money supply had already exceeded its upper limit. The anxiety now was that the bull position in gilts could be rapidly unwound as last year's big overseas buyers rushed to sell while sterling was still strong, thereby making it very difficult for the Government to sell gilts on a falling market. In the event, equities took fright first, following Wall Street down and hitting the year's low point of 433.4 at the beginning of March. The slide in gilts began later in the month after it became clear that the money supply was rising much faster than originally thought and sterling fell sharply. The prime concern was that sterling's fall could turn into a rout just as it had two years previously, but markets recovered and stabilised ahead of the budget in the reasonably confident expectation that the Chancellor would act positively to rebuild foreign confidence.

A confident budget

In a budget designed to "encourage the level of economic activity" and achieve a 3% growth rate, the Chancellor introduced a £2 billion package of tax concessions, raising allowances and widening bands. Simultaneously he announced a new growth target for money supply in the range of 8-12%, adding that the progress of his pay policy would determine whether it could be tightened further in the autumn. He also raised MLR to 7½%.

Markets were not impressed. They were understandably sceptical about his ability to finance an £8½ billion PSBR at the top end of the range, given the strong possibility, on past performance, of exceeding the money supply growth target and of running into difficulty selling enough gilts against a background of rising interest rates. Doubts were increased two days later when the March trade gap was announced to have been £164 million, largely as a result of another increase in the volume of imports. Clearly a great deal depended on the Government managing to continue to convince the trade unions of their mutual interest in maintaining a moderate pay policy, and in a May Day speech, the Prime Minister confidently declared that Labour had found the key to controlling wages without precipitating a trade union revolt. It was a bold claim that was soon to be severely tested. Meanwhile slow gilt sales, despite long yields up to 13%, prompted another hike in MLR, this time to 8¾%, but with money market rates already pointing to a higher figure, there was little conviction in the market that this level was going to prove a peak.

The Opposition rocks the boat

Later in May, the Chancellor's already suspect budget arithmetic was upset further by two Opposition amendments, one to knock a penny off the standard rate of income tax to 33p and the other to raise the starting point for higher tax rates by £1,000 to £8,000. Their effect was to reduce revenue by £500 million in a full year, and speculation began about where the Chancellor would look to make up this deficiency. His first move was to raise MLR to 9%, but again the market judged this level not to be one from which interest rates might be more expected to fall than to rise and selling gilts remained an uphill struggle for the authorities. News of a record trade surplus of £336 million in April and of the Retail Price index rising just 7.9%, its lowest rate for five years, helped to some degree but markets were not prepared to ignore the fact that the money supply was rising at over 16% on an annualised basis, that wholesale prices were up again and that the rise in earnings had now overtaken that of prices. Since these latter factors were capable of reversing the favourable trend of the former, it was clear that some new initiative was necessary to enable the Government to reassert monetary control.

The problem lay in the difficulty of convincing the City that public spending plans could be reconciled with monetary objectives without endangering the natural recovery of the private sector by starving it of credit, but the Chancellor's June package of fiscal and monetary measures, designed to rescue his budget strategy, demonstrated once again that the public sector took absolute priority over the private. MLR was raised to 10%, the "corset" was reimposed on the banks, limiting the expansion of their interest-bearing deposits in order to squeeze bank lending, and employers' National Insurance contributions were raised by 2½% to offset the loss to revenue resulting from the Opposition's tax amendments. It did not work. Gilts enjoyed a short-lived burst of buying enthusiasm which evaporated within days, and equities fell back at the prospect of this new tax on labour and investment driving up prices and slowing down the recovery of the private sector.

The pay policy collapses

In July and August the revival in consumer spending began to pick up sharply with retail sales heading for their peak levels of 1973/74. The buying enthusiasm embraced equities and, encouraged by Wall Street hitting a new high for the year of 888 and a similar revival by most world markets, the FT 30 rose above 500 again. Commentators rationalised the moves by pointing out that equity values were still trailing far behind the rate of inflation, retail prices having risen by 50% since 1973 in the US and by 100% in the UK, and that P/Es were less than half the figures ruling in 1973. The FT 30 peaked at 535.5 in mid-September and the All Share index achieved a new all time high, but significantly gilts, sensing dearer money on the way, failed to participate in the rally. By this time it was clear that a monetary and fiscal policy, however strictly implemented, was not an acceptable alternative to a pay policy and there was now no chance of the Government achieving the latter. Messrs Callaghan and Healey had argued hard for one but in the face of determined opposition both from the TUC and individual unions, for all practical purposes, the policy was a dead letter.

If the decision not to go for an autumn election but to postpone it until the following spring, had been a gamble on winning trade union support for Stage Four, it was one which was seen to have failed by the end of September when the Ford manual workers greeted a 5% pay offer with an immediate all-out strike. A week later the TGWU made the strike "official", and recognising a fait accompli, the Chancellor hinted at easing his 5% earnings increase guideline in an effort to avoid further confrontations. After seven weeks on strike, the Ford workers eventually agreed to accept the employer's "final offer" of a 17% increase. The miners promptly filed a claim for a 40% increase and the engineers one for 33% while the TUC contributed to the debate by proposing a change in the Government's anti-inflation strategy whereby rigorous controls would be put on prices rather than on wages. Public sector workers, who had borne the brunt of the wage restraint policy over the past three years, now looked for the promise of "comparability" to be made good. The stage was set for the "winter of discontent".

The monetary squeeze tightens

The net result of the abandonment of pay policy while monetary policy remained firm was to leave private industry squeezed between soaring credit costs and ever rising wage demands, a development which gilts seemed to suspect immediately after the April budget but equities did not. Rather than relieve the pressure on credit demand by cutting back on public spending, in November the Chancellor renewed his efforts to fund an excessive PSBR by raising MLR to 12½%, tightening the credit squeeze further and maintaining the money supply growth targets. Home loans shot up by 2% to 11¾% and base rates by 1% to 12½%. The Government broker managed to satisfy a large demand for gilts, but equities stagnated at around the 480 level as buyers held off in the face of so many uncertainties, content to collect a return of over 12% in the money market.

Events on the other side of the Atlantic provided no encouragement on the interest rate front. Worldwide concern about the continuing weakness of the dollar in the face of persistent inflationary pressures in the US economy, prompted President Carter in November to introduce an anti-inflationary package which constituted the most sweeping moves to help the dollar since those of President Nixon in 1971. The discount rate was raised from 8½% to 9½%, currency swaps with other central banks were doubled to $15 billion, gold sales were to be increased, and a $3 billion loan was obtained from the IMF. Unfortunately, the impact of the measures was largely negated by the onset of a new oil crisis as the Shah's regime in Iran collapsed. It rapidly became obvious that the event would have a profound effect on the world economy in 1979, and not surprisingly the year ended on a dull note with international investment sentiment upset by OPEC's decision to raise oil prices by 14½%, an act inspired both by a new militancy following the Iranian revolution and by a wish to compensate for the decline in the dollar.

The FT 30 closed the year at 470.9, 3% lower on balance after reaching extremes of 535.5 and 433.4, while the Government Securities index fell by 12% to 68.89. The Dow Jones index stood at 805 against 831 at the start of the year. Gold did best of all, benefiting from a growing distrust of paper currencies – especially the dollar – gaining 37% on the year to $226 but the FT Gold Mines index rose by only 3.7% to 138.

Racal buys more in the US

In April, **Racal** announced another important US purchase, this time of data communications company Vadic, for £5.4 million. Two months later, the South African subsidiary was sold to local interests for £6 million, a move emphasising the new concentration on the US, the world's biggest market for electronic equipment. Later that month, the 1977/78 results showed a 52% gain in pre-tax profits to £50 million as against a forecast of "in excess of £45 million". Sales were reported to be still booming and Lex described the company as the market's "only real remaining growth stock". At 248p, the P/E was 11 and the market capitalisation £282 million.

The interim figures in December saw another strong advance to £24.3 million, up 25% and less dramatic than the market was used to, but very creditable nonetheless for a company still in the process of digesting its recent acquisitions. Milgo was a key contributor this time, increasing its share of profits from 25% to 29%. The whole balance of the group had changed dramatically since 1976 and data communications plus electronic equipment, other than military communications, now accounted for some 45% of profits. By now the shares had risen to 332p where the dividend yield was 2% with a prospective P/E of 12 on the forecast for the full year of £57 million.

...and so does BTR

BTR continued to forge ahead in 1978, demonstrating that it too deserved to remain firmly in the growth stock category. Full year profits were up 20% at £29 million, putting the shares at 213p on a modest P/E of just 6½. Then in June, BTR made its biggest bid yet in the US with a $48 million offer for Worcester Controls, a manufacturer of ball valves, pneumatic and electric activators. Another rights issue was announced in August, the third since 1975, to raise £24 million. It was well received by a market which recognised BTR's ability to combine rapid organic growth with an aggressive acquisition policy, and looked to be well on the way to making £40 million in 1978/79.

Hanson consolidates in the US

1978 was a relatively unexciting year for **Hanson Trust** and first half profits only just managed to keep the rising trend unbroken at £11.4 million against £11.2 million as the US acquisitions began to demonstrate the cyclical nature of their businesses. However, forecasts of £25 million for the full year were well beaten at £26.1 million even though the contribution of the US side had slipped from 65% to 50%.

BCCI comes clean

The *Financial Times* in May carried a special feature on Bank of Credit and Commerce International (BCCI) including an interview with General Manager, Agha Hassan Abedi. Explaining why his fast-growing bank was looked on with suspicion by the financial establishment, he observed with remarkable candour, "Western banks concentrate on the visible, whereas we stress the invisible..."!

1979

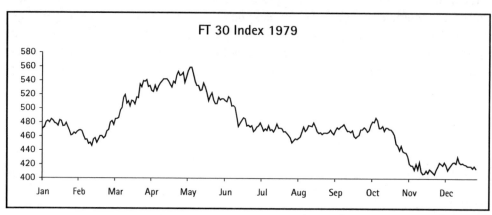

FT 30 Index 1979

Source: Thomson Reuters Datastream

A year to remember

Markets entered 1979 in an uneasy frame of mind. On the domestic front, the breakdown of the Government's pay policy was a major concern giving rise to fears of increasing industrial disruption and the prospect that inflation would soon be back into double figures. Externally, worries centred on the Iranian situation and the further threat that it could pose to the stability of the Middle East as well as on the implications for the industrialised world if it led to oil shortages accompanied by a new wave of price increases. Against such a background, the Government's scope for manoeuvre was seen to be strictly limited. January quickly showed that fears on both counts were well grounded.

The first week of the New Year saw 25,000 lorry drivers on strike, virtually paralysing the nation's distribution services, and leading to speculation that the Government would be forced to declare a State of Emergency and use troops to keep essential services running. This eventuality was narrowly avoided, but the Chancellor's "peace package" promising more cash to the lower paid, reaffirming the pledge of comparability with the private sector for public sector workers, and tougher price controls, was widely judged to undermine his basic policies by granting concessions when he should have been standing firm in the face of importunate trade union demands. Meanwhile, bank lending had risen sharply as companies were forced to borrow to finance the build-up of stocks during the haulage strike, and by mid-February pressure on money market rates, coupled with the Government's need to complete its funding programme, prompted an increase in MLR to 14%.

During all this time, equities proved remarkably resilient as a result of buyers being more impressed by the UK's new oil wealth than depressed by the latest round of industrial disruption. Even the record spot prices being paid for oil and the delivery cuts of up to 45% imposed by BP, Shell and Exxon, harmful though they were, still served to emphasise how much better off the UK was than the rest of the industrialised world. Gilts were dull initially but picked up sharply as the funding operation in the wake of the boost in MLR proved a resounding success. The pound was now around $2 and a petrocurrency carrying one of the highest interest rates in the world was irresistible to overseas buyers.

Pre-election optimism boosts the market

The boom in gilts now began to instil a renewed confidence into the equity market as investors took a view of the longer-term effect of North Sea oil on the economy and on profits and dividend prospects. From 450 in mid-February, the FT 30 had recovered to 500 by the end of the first week in March. Activity was at its highest level for eighteen months, and the All Share index actually broke into new high ground, unhampered by the FT 30's bias towards heavy capital goods constituents.

At this point a new factor emerged to add momentum to the rise. This was the near certainty of a spring election and expectations of a Conservative victory. The open challenge to the Government by the unions and the industrial chaos it had caused, had effectively destroyed Labour's claim to be able to manage the trade unions better than the Conservatives. It had also hardened public opinion against the Labour Party's basic premise that the governance of the country was only possible with the advice and consent of the trade unions. Mountains of rubbish on street corners, pickets preventing the delivery of food to hospital patients and daily disruption of essential services, had made the public much more sympathetic to Mrs Thatcher's determination to place reform of the trade union movement at the top of the Conservatives' list of priorities. The announcement at the end of March that the election was set for 3rd May sparked a further advance in the FT 30 towards 540 and saw the All Share index at another new peak. Two reductions of 1% in MLR, bringing it down to 12%, helped but so did a comparison of the manifestos of the two parties. Labour's renewed pledges to seek further control over industry, to impose a wealth tax, to abolish the public schools and to extend the powers of the Price Commission, looked doctrinaire and irrelevant. On the other hand, the Conservatives' plans to pursue reform of the trade unions, to cut taxes, to control the money supply and to advocate a return to responsible pay bargaining between employers and workers with no government intervention, appeared to be not only eminently practical, but also long overdue.

Mrs Thatcher takes over

In the days immediately preceding the election, all the main indices moved ahead with both the FT 30 and the All Share reaching new records, and Government Securities topping 75. The actual result, giving the Conservatives a 43-seat majority, exceeded their most optimistic expectations. Nevertheless, it had been well discounted. The FT 30 responded with a 5-point rise to a new all-time peak of 558.6 but the reaction was swift as the magnitude of the task facing the new administration began to be appreciated. Margaret Thatcher, the first woman Prime Minister in British history, was not going to have an easy ride. Clearly it was not going be possible to make significant cuts in public spending "at a stroke" and with money supply still growing too fast, interest rates were likely to continue to rise, putting pressure on both gilts and equities.

Attention now was firmly focused on what the new Chancellor, Sir Geoffrey Howe, would do in his first budget on 12th June, but before then the market had to absorb three items of bad news. The first was the report that earnings were rising at an annual rate of 14.2%. The second was Iran's decision to start a new round of oil price increases, and the third was the announcement that the trade deficit for the first four months of the year was just over £1 billion. Because of a strike by Civil Service statisticians, there had been no trade figures for four months and the cumulative total came as a shock. The FT 30 was down almost to 500 on the day of the budget, and concern over the Chancellor's radical change of direction prompted a decisive penetration of that level.

The keynote of the budget was a major shift from taxes on income to taxes on spending. The basic rate of income tax was cut from 33p to 30p, personal allowances were increased, the threshold for the 40% tax rate was raised from £8,000 to £10,000 and the top rate of tax for those earning over £25,000 was slashed from 83% to 60%. All these reductions added up to £4.5 billion and they were to be offset in part by increasing VAT to a unified rate of 15% and raising the excise duties on beer, wines and spirits and tobacco. Simultaneously, the Chancellor raised MLR by two full points to 14% and announced that money supply growth would be restrained within a 7-11% target range, thereby demonstrating his urgent need to cure the current surge in private sector credit demand and to establish a new level from which funding could resume. Public spending cuts of up to £1.5 billion were promised, as well as the first in a series of asset sales led by BP. Also, the first steps were taken to dismantle the system of exchange controls, a move which initially boosted sterling. The Chancellor described it as an "opportunity" budget, but the market worried about the extent and severity of the impending credit squeeze, the impact of high interest rates and a strong pound on corporate profits, and the chances of further industrial unrest. Accordingly, the FT 30 slipped into a 450-480 trading range to await developments, an attitude that appeared to be fully justified a month later when Sir Geoffrey, in reaffirming his determination to cut public spending down to size, described the immediate outlook as "almost frighteningly bad".

The Federal Reserve Board gets a new Chairman

In July an event occurred on the other side of the Atlantic that was to have a profound effect on the economies of the US and of the world. It was the appointment of Paul Volcker as Chairman of the Federal Reserve Board. Mr Volcker had very determined ideas of how to achieve domestic price stability and restore international confidence in the dollar. It was by the application of "disciplined, persistent and consistent monetary policy" which, in effect, meant tight money accompanied by whatever level of interest rates might result. His predecessor had pursued policies of relative monetary stringency, but the dollar had been undermined by a disastrous over-expansion of dollar credit through domestic and overseas channels for years, and the authorities had been slow to realise just how drastic measures to check it would have to be. Furthermore, the role of the dollar as the international trading currency meant that monetary policies everywhere were at risk unless the dollar was controlled. Hence the importance of Mr Volcker's new approach to the problem. His appointment was greeted with a ten-point rise in the Dow to 839, but one particularly prescient commentator noted that this was "like throwing a party to celebrate the arrival of your executioner".

Recognising that the source of US inflation was domestic and had to be tackled by the effective control of domestic credit growth, Mr Volcker's inaugural package in October involved a 2% hike in the discount rate to 12%, an increase in bank reserve requirements to 8%, acting rather like the UK "corset", and very importantly, a change from managing interest rates on a day-to-day basis by the so-called federal funds rate, and instead using the monetary base as a yardstick. The significance of this last measure was not only that interest rate moves would no longer be predictable but also that they could reach any level. The sky was the limit. The reaction to all this was a sharp rise in the dollar and a sharp fall in bonds and equities as prime rates topped 15%.

The Chancellor tightens the squeeze

Whatever the longer-term benefits of the new US monetary policy might be, the abrupt rise in interest rates over there posed some shorter-term problems for Chancellor Howe by effectively sabotaging his funding operations as bank lending rose and the growth in money supply strayed well above the top of the 7-11% target range. The situation was not helped by the fact that following removal of the remaining exchange controls, sterling had lost all its immediate post-election gains. Erstwhile foreign buyers were paying more attention to the UK's continuing balance of payments difficulties and the prospect of a new wave of exorbitant wage claims accompanied by the threat of industrial action now that retail prices were rising much faster than earnings as the budget increases filtered through. CBI surveys were universally gloomy, showing business confidence at its lowest level for two years and forecasting a sharp drop in corporate profitability in 1980. At least the setback in sterling had brought some relief to hard-pressed exporters, but the question was being asked whether the monetary squeeze would have its impact on inflation before it destroyed the profitability of large parts of UK manufacturing industry. At the same time, industry striving to protect its margins in a high interest rate recession by shedding labour and closing down unprofitable activities, was likely to do less damage to productivity and profits than to output and employment. However, doubts about the answer caused the FT 30 to drop below 450 at the end of October.

Against such a background, gilt-edged prices continued to be eroded until mid-November when the Chancellor acted to regain the initiative in financial markets. MLR was raised by 3% to the unprecedented level of 17% and mortgage rates promptly rose to a record 15% as the price had to be paid for the Chancellor's budget tax cuts. After some initial hesitation the tactic worked and by mid-December, gilts were rising strongly on news of a sharp slowdown in the rate of monetary growth and a run of prime rate reductions by the US banks. Encouragement was drawn also from some signs of moderation on the labour front. British Leyland workers voted not to strike over the dismissal of Communist shop steward, Derek Robinson, known as "Red Robbo", albeit under the threat of plant closure if they did, and the miners, after rejecting an 11-15% pay deal, agreed to accept an offer of 20%. On the other side of the fence, welcome signs of managerial firmness were noted in British Steel refusing to improve on its 2% offer, despite strike threats.

All in the same boat

Equities were less enthusiastic than gilts about these supposedly encouraging developments and by mid-November the FT 30 was getting uncomfortably close to the 400 level. The 20% settlement for the miners was considered by many to establish a "going rate" for future claims, giving rise to the belief that the coming recession would impinge more on profits than on incomes. It was also a reminder that there were those in the Conservative ranks who believed in the omnipotence of the trade unions and who would go to any lengths to appease the miners or indeed any other group of workers with enough muscle to bring down a government. At the same time markets took some comfort from the fact that interest rates were rising in all the industrialised countries as part of a general determination to check the growth of money and credit in an effort to conquer inflation. Furthermore, a recession endured in the cause of fighting inflation was likely not to be so deep or obstinate and once inflation began to respond, the natural forces of recovery would start to make themselves felt.

Such consoling thoughts were much needed in December, a month which had seen a warning from the Bank of England that companies were facing a financial squeeze as severe as that of 1974/75, Libya raising the price of its oil to $34.50 a barrel, Russian tanks rolling over the border into Afghanistan and the train drivers' union, ASLEF, blacking steel imports, not to mention the rate of growth of the Retail Price index practically doubling on the year to 17.4% in November. This was not the sort of background to provide much of a Christmas rally, and the FT 30 ended the year at 414.2, down 12%, while the All Share index actually managed a 4.2% rise to 229.79. Gilts, as measured by the Government Securities index, lost 5.2% to 65.10. Golds were the star of the year. Beneficiary of a growing distrust of all paper currencies, especially the dollar, and of the highly unstable situation in the Middle East, the bullion price rose by $300 to $526 an ounce, while the FT Gold Mines index gained 90% to 268.6. The Dow Jones index managed to add a modest 33 on the year to 838 despite the persistent weakness of the dollar and the political problems posed to President Carter by the Iranian hostage situation.

BTR powers ahead

In 1978/79 **BTR's** "constellation of unglamorous but formidably efficient businesses" turned in profits of £42.5 million, a 43% advance, as contributions began to flow from its fifteen plants in the US. BTR still had acquisitive ambitions in the UK and in June launched a surprise £26 million bid for **Bestobell**, the fluid engineering and insulation group. Bestobell's record had been uninspiring in comparison with that of BTR, but its management convinced enough institutions that it could do better by retaining its independence and the bid failed, although leaving BTR with a 25% stake. Interim figures showed that BTR's growth momentum was undiminished with pre-tax profits up 50% at £27.4 million on sales just 33% higher. The shares ended the year at 287p, well down from the year's high of 347p, yielding 5% and selling on a P/E of 11.3.

Racal slows down

Iran's drastic cut backs in defence spending showed the wisdom of **Racal's** efforts to reduce its dependence on the military communications market, and profits for 1978/79 easily topped the £57 million forecast at £61.6 million. First half figures for 1979/80, however, were much less exciting but they too underlined the management's foresight in diminishing the importance of its UK manufacturing base. Held back by strikes and the strength of the pound, profits were up by only 4% at £25.3 million, indicating a total for the year of perhaps £65 million. The shares fell sharply on the news and closed the year at 183p as against a high of 276p, yielding 2.9% on a P/E of 10.9.

Hanson consolidates

Hanson accompanied its modestly better half year results of £12.4 million, up 10%, with a £17 million rights issue, obviously with an eye to acquisitions. The terms were a deeply discounted 1 for 2 at 50p against a share price of 168p and the issue was not underwritten, thereby saving expenses in a dull market which had just seen 75% of Thomas Tilling's £57 million rights issue left with the underwriters. Then in August a successful £27 million offer was made for **Lindustries** and the following month its biggest bid to date, $163 million, was made for Barber Oil Corporation in the US, although it was subsequently dropped because of legal complications. The year also saw the settling of the terms for Sir Gordon White's 10% stake in Hanson Industries, the group's US operating arm, and he received 4.3 million shares in Hanson Trust, then valued at £5.5 million. Full year profits were £31.2 million, boosted by a cyclical upturn in the US market and a strong recovery in brick demand in the US. The shares ended the year at 123p, yielding 8.5% and with a P/E of 6.8.

1980

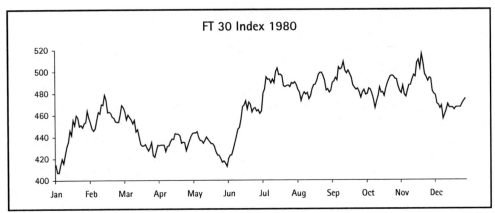

FT 30 Index 1980

Source: Thomson Reuters Datastream

Return to Go

The onset of the steelworkers' strike in the first week of the New Year provided a clear indication that the Government's resolve to make loss-making industries confront the reality of their situation was going to be severely tested in 1980. A gloomy assessment by stockbrokers Phillips & Drew, based on the assumption that the next five years would show average earnings rising at an annual rate of 15%, just as they had in the last ten, did not help sentiment. However after falling to 407, equities suddenly embarked upon a strong rally, adding 50 points in three weeks. With the steel strike spreading, the latest earnings figures recording a rise of 19.2% and the gold price soaring to over $800 in response to international tensions, it was difficult to believe that the market was doing anything other than looking into the distance, accepting that things would have to get worse before they got better. The hope and expectation was that the Government's efforts to contain monetary growth as a first step towards reducing inflation, would establish the preconditions for tackling the real economic challenges, principally the imbalance between the public and private sectors, and the idea that the government of the day could and should use public funds to rescue any and every hugely unprofitable industry, public and private, just because it happened to be a large employer of labour. These were challenges which previous governments had either refused to recognise as such or simply ducked for reasons of political convenience.

"Medium–Term Financial Strategy" unveiled

By mid-March the upward spiral of dollar interest rates had taken some of the heat off sterling as well as breaking the back of the boom in commodity prices, thus relieving some of the cost pressures on UK industry. However, with MLR at 17% and average earnings rising at almost 20%, such pressures remained acute, and hopes of some relief in the budget at the end of the month were soon dashed. The principal feature of the budget was the unveiling of the Chancellor's "medium-term financial strategy" (MTFS) which, in the words of an *FT* editorial marked "an historic break in economic management". The MTFS formally abandoned the illusion that economic growth, price stability and full employment are in the gift of the government, accepting by implication that all a government can do is frame its policies in such a way that business can operate in a climate conducive to the achievement of these desirable objectives. It was the long-awaited embodiment of the ideas put forward by Sir Keith Joseph in his epoch-making address in September 1974. Its keynote was to give total priority to reducing monetary inflation by keeping money supply growth within the 7-11% range, setting a target of 4-8% by 1983/84, and at the same time ensuring that the Government's own demand for credit remained consistent with these aims by planning to reduce the PSBR's share of national income from 5½% in 1978/79 to 1½% by 1983/84.

This ambitious programme would be made possible only by using North Sea oil revenue to reduce the public sector deficit instead of distributing it around the economy. Assuming everything went according to plan, by 1983/84 debt sales would be minimal, and huge savings flows would be released for industrial investment both at home and overseas. The downside was that if it would allow only modest room for growth, industry might have a hard time surviving the transitional period, and the budget provided no comfort beyond minor concessions on stock relief and the long-term prospect of lower interest rates. The remainder of the budget was concerned with taxing welfare benefits, raising excise duties on beer, wine, spirits and tobacco, and while raising personal allowances and thresholds, still letting fiscal drag increase the real burden of income tax.

Signs of success

Disappointed at the absence of a cut in MLR, the market fell immediately after the budget but rallied on the ending of the steel strike in its thirteenth week and on renewed hopes of a cut in late April as world interest rates showed distinct signs of peaking. These hopes were encouraged by the fact that money supply growth, after hovering just above the target range all year, had at last fallen within it.

As a result, the first anniversary of the Conservatives taking office appeared to have witnessed at least a modest success in round one of the battle to contain monetary growth, while the real economy was withstanding the monetary battering it had received rather better than many had forecast. However, by July there were distinct signs that Government borrowing in 1980/81 was going to be well above target, and also that money supply growth was once again creeping above the 11% upper limit in response to the buoyant demand for credit from the private sector. But in the context of falling US interest rates, unemployment topping the 1.5 million mark for the first time, indications that both the rate of growth in earnings and in prices were peaking and two successive months of trade surpluses, the Chancellor felt he had enough leeway to take his first step to ease the credit squeeze and took MLR down one point to 16%. The market responded positively to the cut with the FT 30 crossing the 500 level once again in mid-July while the All Share index achieved a new peak of 286.5. Gilts, too, moved ahead strongly, convinced that inflation and interest rates had topped out even though the Government's funding needs probably ruled out another reduction in MLR in the very near future. This conviction was strengthened later in the month when the rate of growth of the Retail Price index, at 21%, down from 21.9% in May, recorded its first significant fall since 1978 and the growth in average earnings was also checked.

Straying off course

Banking figures released in August showing money supply rising at an annualised rate of 22%, twice the upper limit of the target range, quickly took the steam out of gilts. They were hit again later in the month following further evidence of overshoot in the PSBR, both excesses underlining the tendency of public and private sector borrowing needs to rise with a fall in economic activity with the one undermining the other. The root of the problem was that a year ago it might have been assumed that either the pound would fall or wage increases would be sharply reduced, and that one way or another the competitive position of manufacturing industry would be restored, its financial position improved and its need for new borrowing fall. In the event, margins continued to bear the brunt of the adjustment, leading to dreadful profit figures, wholesale closures and redundancies, and reliance on the banks for day-to-day finance. As if to prove the point, at the end of the month, ICI announced a 52% fall in profits between its first and second quarters, and the unemployment total topped two million as the labour shakeout continued.

The Government was now coming under increasing pressure from both the TUC and the CBI to abandon policies, the harsh effects of which on the real economy now cast serious doubt on the validity of the whole "medium-term financial strategy". The Labour Party was too involved with its own leadership struggle to take much part in the argument, but with the TUC warning of "uncontrollable social unrest" and the CBI chairman threatening the Government with "a bareknuckle fight" unless there were major policy reversals, equities held their ground remarkably well and the FT 30 did not stray far from the 500 mark while the All Share made new highs. Investors seemingly were less influenced by the rhetoric of vested interests than with the straws in the wind of falling pay settlements and falling inflation, albeit both recession-induced, and the dramatic improvement in the balance of payments. Furthermore, with the spot price of oil now below OPEC's "official" levels, even the outbreak of war between Iran and Iraq was not regarded as such a potentially dangerous development as it might have been. The depth of the recession, too, was not necessarily being contemplated with despair. Rather it was being seen as a measure of the scope for recovery available to companies forced to rationalise and reorganise to a point where they were now much more capable of taking advantage of an improving business climate.

Markets contrast with the real economy

Thus in the last week of October, when ICI reported a £10 million loss in its third quarter, the first in its 54-year history, the All Share index moved into new high ground. November saw money supply up sharply again but the measure (M3) was now widely reckoned to be erratic and misleading, and markets paid more attention to a record £534 million October trade surplus, another fall in the retail price index and hopes of a cut in interest rates in the Chancellor's economic package promised for the end of the month. A two-point reduction in MLR to 14% was accompanied by measures designed to put the MTFS back on course and to lighten the burden on the private sector. The savings net was widened to pull in another £3 billion for an attractive National Savings scheme, National Insurance contributions were increased for employees but not for employers, and a supplementary tax on North Sea oil profits was introduced to raise another £1 billion. The need for such fund-raising provisions became obvious when it was announced simultaneously that the PSBR for 1980/81 was likely to be around £11½ billion compared with the £8½ billion aim at the time of the last budget. After holding above 500 for just five trading days, and buoyed also by the Dow Jones crossing the 1000 level in the wake of the Republican victory, the FT 30 suddenly fell away as US interest rates began to rise dramatically after President Reagan gave Paul Volcker free rein to pursue his anti-inflation policies.

Dollar interest rates soar

The first half of December saw the FT 30 back to 460 with the upsurge in dollar interest rates dominating financial markets everywhere and prompting speculation about a new worldwide bear market after the Dow had lost almost 100 points in less than a month. Gilts fell away, too, on fears that the US rate rises - prime rates had reached 21½% – made the latest MLR cut look misjudged in the context of a still rising PSBR and could lead to another funding crisis for the Government.

The last days of December brought slightly better news with the rate of growth in average earnings at 20% slowing appreciably for the first time since 1977, another drop in the retail price index to 15.3% and US prime rates reacting from their peak levels. The FT 30 closed the year at 474.5, up 14.5%, but the All Share index at 292.22 recorded a gain of 28.5% as the stock market took due note of the huge structural changes that had been taking place in the economy over the past couple of years.

While many commentators with a political axe to grind, deplored the decline in Britain's traditional manufacturing industries, the stock market was quietly acknowledging it as a fait accompli, reflecting the shift of resources into service industries and oil extraction while so much of the burden of manufacturing was being assumed by Japan and the fast developing economic powers of South East Asia. This change of roles was both inevitable and inexorable, and as one commentator put it, there was no doubt that "the moving finger was firmly attached to the invisible hand"! Organised labour was not happy with the situation but the first phase of the promised industrial relations legislation, the Employment Act of 1980, was now in place and no one could miss the fact that the number of strike days lost in 1980 was less than half the 29.4 million total of 1979. The Actuaries Oil share index, having crossed the 1000 mark for the first time in October was still up 35% on the year at 933, the Financial Group index was up 28.5%, while the Metals & Metal-forming sector index was down by 4%. Gilts were below their best levels but still cautiously optimistic about the outcome of the Government's policies, and at 68.69 the Government Securities index recorded a gain of 5.5%. The gold price continued to reflect international tensions and currency fears, hovering around the $600 mark, and FT Gold Mines was up by 52% at 407.5, undeterred by the collapse of the silver price following the failure of the Hunt brothers' attempt to corner the market.

Racal buys Decca

Corporate activity in 1980 kicked off with **Racal**, now capitalised at £467 million, making a bid approach to pioneer electronics company **Decca** which recently had slipped into losses. GEC was also interested but Racal still managed to win the day with a £101 million cash offer. Even though there were a few more problems than expected to sort out at Decca, there was no doubt that Racal chairman, Sir Ernest Harrison, was pleased with his prize, and after reporting 1979/80 profits up by just £2 million to £63.6 million, he confidently forecast that with Decca breaking even, the current year would be the "best for years". At the time, the shares stood at 259p yielding 2.3% with a P/E of 19, and despite considerable comment about a slowdown in earnings growth in the wake of the Decca acquisition and a worldwide recession, Racal attracted major institutional support, ending the year at 330p.

BTR also continued a "gravity-defying profits performance" in 1979/80, reporting a 43% advance in pre-tax profits to £57.2 million despite suffering industrial disruption at its UK-based manufacturing operations. As usual it was the overseas side that made the running and at the time of the interim results in September, showing profits of £36.4 million, it was announced that substantial gains had been made in all countries with the exception of the UK. Meanwhile, two acquisitions had been made in the US, carbide cutting tools manufacturer Adamas Carbide for $10 million and disposable clothing manufacturer Huyck for $143 million, but a £60 million rights issue in September was reckoned widely to be the prelude to a renewed offer for Bestobell. Like Racal, BTR had built up a devoted institutional following and the shares closed the year at 364p, yielding 4. 1 % with a P/E of 13.6.

Hanson buys McDonough

An initial contribution from Lindustries, together with a strong performance by the UK industrial services operations, helped to offset a cyclical downturn in the US and **Hanson Group**'s first half profits came in 29% up at £16.1 million. There was still a lot of comment about the dullness and the cyclical nature of most of the group's businesses but in the context of an all-embracing recession, it was difficult to fault the achievement of a total of £39.1 million for the full year. In October a major US acquisition was made in the shape of McDonough Co. for $180 million. Makers of footwear, cement and handtools, the company was bought at the bottom of a cyclical trough after profits had halved, and funded with debt secured on its assets. The shares ended the year at their high point of 208p, although the rating was still modest with a yield of 5.8% and a P/E of 9.2.

Asil Nadir takes control of Polly Peck

In February an obscure paragraph in the *FT* reported that Restro Investments, a private company based in Jersey, was making a cash offer of £470,000, or 9p per share, for troubled ladies' fashion business **Polly Peck (Holdings)**. The directors, including the founding Zelker family, agreed to accept the offer for their 57% shareholding, and Asil Nadir, who was chairman of Restro as well as of clothing concern **Wearwell**, said that he intended to "continue and develop" the business of Polly Peck and maintain the listing. At the time Asil Nadir did not have a reputation as a stock market operator, but the shares moved strongly ahead in thin trading conditions and eventually were suspended at 83p in mid-June "pending an announcement". The following month a 1 for 5 rights issue at 75p was announced. The £1.6 million raised was to pay for the acquisition of Uni-Pac, a company owned by Mr Nadir and engaged in the production of corrugated packaging from plants based in Turkish Cyprus. As the first and only producer of corrugated packaging in the region, the company was expected to be the principal supplier to the local agricultural industry with one third of production being absorbed by Cyprus and the balance going to mainland Turkey. On the basis of Cyprus sales alone, pre-tax profits of £2 million were forecast for 1980/81 and the shares of Polly Peck returned from suspension at 128p. September saw a flurry of activity in **Cornell**, a small loss-making London dress company, on rumours of a bid for a controlling interest from another of Asil Nadir's companies, Jersey based Azania Investments. A bid of 19p was eventually made in December, by which time the shares were already over 50p. Polly Peck ended the year at 145p with the distinction of being the best performing share of the year, recording a gain of 2708%.

The USM is born

The year was notable also for the creation of the Unlisted Securities Market (USM), designed to provide an easier route to fund-raising and public trading for smaller and relatively untried companies. Principally, the advantages for entrants were, firstly, a 3-year instead of a 5-year record and, secondly, a placing of a minimum of 10% of the company's equity instead of 25%, but in every case the services of a sponsoring stockbroker had to be acquired. The first two companies on the market were **Scan Data International** and **John Hadland**.

1981

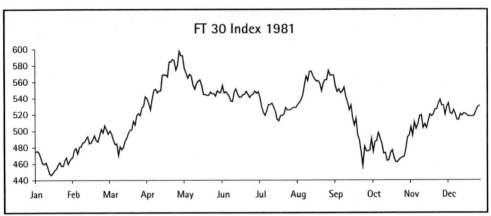

FT 30 Index 1981

Source: Thomson Reuters Datastream

Rationalisation and redundancies rule

Hopes for the New Year were tempered by worries about the impact on the real economy of Government policies should the recession persist, and the test that rising unemployment, together with falling investment and output, would pose for the Government's nerve. Even the most ardent supporters of the MTFS had to admit that it was a failure in the sense that the money supply, public spending and the PSBR were all growing wildly in excess of the original target levels, and that the squeeze on the corporate sector was much worse than intended. On the other hand, the objective of falling inflation was being achieved by the recession anyway with little regard for a policy that seemed to have created every kind of deflation except monetary deflation. The budget, scheduled for 9th March, was confidently expected to remedy at least some of these policy deficiencies and the FT 30 managed to struggle over 500 again just before the event despite further evidence from industry of falling profits, shrinking dividends and redundancies as ICI reported a 54% fall in profits for 1980, cut its dividend, and rationalised many of its operations with huge job losses.

At the same time, a measure of the difficulties that the Government was going to have to tackle during the rest of the year and beyond was provided by the sight of still rising US interest rates, and of striking South Wales miners forcing the National Coal Board to back down on its cost-saving pit closures programme. The more serious problem, and the more intractable in that it was totally outside the Government's control, was US interest rates with their immediate impact on the level of sterling. President Reagan had much the same free market and deregulation policy as Mrs Thatcher, and his programme of big personal tax cuts to be matched by deep cuts in public spending ran into precisely the same problem that was facing her in the

UK. Taxes can be cut at a stroke but government spending cannot, and Paul Volcker had been given carte blanche to bridge the gap. That meant sharply higher interest rates to reduce domestic inflation and protect the dollar. As a result, from $2.40 in January, the pound fell to below $2.20 just before the budget. Capitulation to the striking miners also did nothing for foreign confidence in sterling and served to detract from an otherwise tough and resolute budget.

The market looks ahead

The aim of the budget was to strengthen and advance the MTFS, and at the same time redress the imbalance between the personal and business sectors, and the private and public sectors. To this end the burden of taxation was shifted to the wage earner and consumer, largely by increasing indirect taxation on petrol, drink and tobacco and also by failing to index allowances. MLR was cut from 14% to 12%; a PSBR inflated by recession, by spending on defence and by aid to state-owned industries was forecast to fall back from £13.5 billion to £10.5 billion in 1981/82; and the money supply growth target was lowered into the 6-10% band.

An early fall to 470 by the FT 30 immediately after the budget was followed by a strong recovery. This was helped by another fall in the rate of earnings growth, a trade surplus in February of £614 million, and signs of a fall in interest rates plus considerable merger activity in the US pushing the Dow over 1000 again. Gilts, too, were firm on the tightening of fiscal policy evident in the budget and the Government Securities index rose to a new high for the year of just over 70. Interestingly, the advance in markets was led by the depressed industrials, most of which were still reporting appalling results. **GKN** had just announced a loss of £1.2 million against the previous year's profit of £125 million after a second half slump, and **Tube Investments**, **Turner & Newall** and **Lucas** shocked the City with their figures and dividend cuts. Clearly, investors were taking the view that rationalisation and reorganisation of industries that for years had been grossly overmanned and hence low in productivity, would benefit from this once and for all shake-out of surplus labour and unprofitable operations. The celebrated letter to *The Times* from 364 university economists showed that not everyone agreed with government policy, but their confident assertion that "There is no basis in economic theory or supporting evidence for the Government's belief that by deflating demand, they will bring inflation permanently under control and thereby induce an automatic recovery in output and employment", coincided very neatly with the announcement that ICI's first quarter profits had risen to £52 million compared with just £7 million in the last quarter of 1980, and with the FT 30 almost breaching the 600 level on the last day of April.

The lady's not for turning

For the past year Mrs Thatcher had been under enormous pressure to change course, just like Macmillan in 1962 and Heath in 1972. Furthermore, the TUC's predictions of uncontrollable social unrest had become a reality with the inner city riots, notably in Toxteth, Moss Side and Brixton. But unlike her predecessors, and despite the electoral risks involved, she did not lose her nerve. If expenditure was to go up then taxes had to go up too, and there was to be no pump priming as a temporary palliative for soaring unemployment. The logic of following such a policy had been lost on previous governments, save when faced with the demands of creditors, but paraphrasing the title of a play by Christopher Fry, Mrs. Thatcher insisted, "the lady's not for turning". Her determination alienated the so-called "wets" in her Cabinet, making necessary the drastic reshuffle in September which brought in Norman Tebbit to replace Jim Prior at the Department of Employment. The days of "beer and sandwiches at No. 10" for union leaders were over. Conviction politics had replaced consensus politics and more industrial legislation was on the way, this time tackling trade union immunities.

Fortunately for the Conservatives, the Labour party was not in much of a position to make political capital out of the widespread criticism of Mrs Thatcher. Michael Foot had defeated Denis Healey in the leadership election of October 1980, and the consequent swing towards the left alienated leading moderates within the party, prompting the "Gang of Four" – Roy Jenkins, Shirley Williams, William Rodgers and David Owen – to launch the Social Democratic Party (SDP) in January 1981.

The Chancellor's Stock Exchange Carol
Christmas 1981

Chancellor Geoffrey Howe looked out
On the Feast of Stephen,
When the snow lay round about
Deep and crisp and even.
Cannon Street shut down at noon
Worse, Fleet Street stayed open,
Westminster was full of gloom,
All the wets were fro-o-zen.

***

In your realm of stocks and shares
Confidence yet aileth:
Too few bulls, too many bears –
Doom and gloom prevaileth.
"Slump" you say "will never end,
Maggie isn't learning:
Poor old Geoffrey's round the bend,
His corner's not for turning."

But the indicators show
Policies are working,
Output's up and it's all go
For all those exporting.
Maggie's target is in sight
Don't despair or scorn her,
In the tunnel I see light
We have turned the corner!

***

Come, my friends, and stand by me:
My words are not hollow.
Though the winter bitter be
Gentle spring will follow.
Christmas is the time for hope
Hope is what I'm stressing
Brokers, jobbers, one and all,
I wish you God's blessing.

Sung by Sir Geoffrey Howe at the Stock Exchange Christmas lunch, 1981, accompanied by Sir Nicholas Goodison's son, Adam, on the guitar.

US interest rates call the tune

From this point on it was developments on the other side of the Atlantic that dominated the course of markets in the UK and in the rest of the industrialised world. The rise in the dollar on the back of soaring US domestic interest rates was seen as equivalent to a "third oil shock", threatening to bring both lower growth and higher inflation. On its own, this was bad news for the pound but the effect was greatly aggravated by a sharp fall in the oil price as the worldwide recession slashed consumption. The first week of June saw the pound hit by a wave of selling as foreign holders re-evaluated its role as a petrocurrency. The exchange rate fell below $2 and gilts slipped in sympathy to a 13-month low. Equities, however, remained firm on the prospect of an upturn in profits as a consequence of a sharply reduced cost base and a de facto devaluation. Even the largest rights issue ever, a £624 million call from BP towards the end of June, failed to put buyers off but by late September an almost daily catalogue of rights issues together with a sharp increase in interest rates in response to US prime rates topping 20%, proved too much to bear. In two weeks the FT 30 lost a hundred points and the fall was mirrored in stock exchanges across the world, giving point to BIS calls for the US to stop relying on a monetary policy which caused such high interest rates with their attendant damage to other economies around the world and instead do something about cutting its own huge budget deficit.

Sterling in the front line

It was now widely perceived that with sterling back to around $1.80, interest rates were likely to be at higher levels for much longer than anyone had thought likely earlier in the year. By October UK base rates were up to 16% again (MLR had been abandoned in favour of the Bank of England signalling its wishes via a less obtrusive money market intervention point), but a month later they were down to 14.5% as US short term rates eased significantly, and the FT 30 managed to climb back over 500 again. Gilts were less easily persuaded that lower interest rates were here to stay but after touching a 5-year low of 60.44, they staged a modest recovery only to relapse again as disappointing money supply figures, and the retail price index reversing its downtrend, seemed to put paid to hopes of further rate cuts. The feeling was that the authorities had given up on keeping the money supply within bounds and were now operating an exchange rate targeting policy. Despite official denials that this was the case, sterling strengthened in December, helping markets to end the year on a note of cautious optimism. This mood was encouraged further by indications that the PSBR target was being achieved, a rising trade surplus, and the first significant indications of a pick-up in industrial output.

Anxieties remained over the prospect of serious industrial disruption in the New Year by the miners and the railway workers, but the year which had seen the worst recession in half a century still managed to end with the FT 30 up 11.8% at 530.4 and the All Share up 6.8% at 313.2. This disparity in performance was accounted for by the strong recovery in the industrial stocks which dominated the FT 30 contrasting with only minor advances by the Financials and a 25% fall in Oils. High interest rates took their toll of gilts, and the Government Securities index closed the year down 10% at 62.37. Sky-high dollar interest rates plus signs that the Volcker medicine was going to work were no help to Golds either and with the bullion price down from $600 to $400, FT Gold Mines slipped 40% to 307.5. During the year Wall Street had to cope with far higher interest rates than London and the Dow Jones index ended 1981 with the loss of 100 points at 873.

Racal sorts out Decca

Problems sorting out Decca continued to hold back **Racal's** performance in the first half of 1980/81 and profits were up by only 5% at £26.5 million. The shares fell on the news and at 310p, yielding just 2%, Lex concluded that there was "no margin for disappointment". In the event there was no disappointment with full year profits of £73.2 million accompanied by the announcement that losses at Decca were now under control and that the group was heading for "substantial profits" over the next two years. The shares rose 12p to 384p to yield 1.7%, but by the end of the year they had advanced to 435p on strong institutional support.

BTR acquires a "growth stock" rating

BTR's full year figures came in at £70.3 million, up 23%, with strong growth in the US and Australia more than offsetting a downturn in the UK. Vigorous rationalisation measures involving a 25% cut in employment in the UK factories helped the interim figures to a 20% gain at £41.6 million and a £90 million total was assumed to be within reach for the full year. Then in September, BTR showed that its acquisitive ambitions remained unsatisfied with a £25.5 million bid for Serck Radiators. By now the shares were seen no longer as a dull industrial conglomerate but had been accorded a rating in line with that of Racal, ending the year at 344p selling on a P/E of over 20.

Hanson goes for Berec

Hanson's half year profits gain of 13% to £18.2 million was suitably impressive against a background of recession both in the US and the UK, but what really pushed the group into the headlines in 1981 was its bid for the well-known battery company,

Berec, formerly called by its much better known name of EverReady. With an asset value of more than twice the share price, a strong brand name, a costly investment programme nearing completion, and recession-hit profits, Berec looked a classic target for Hanson, and in July a dawn raid at 90p took the latter's holding to 15%. Reinforced by a £44 million rights issue later in the month, Hanson eventually launched a full bid with a £73 million offer in September. Following intervention by Thomas Tilling, Hanson had to raise its bid to £95 million, a figure which managed to secure the prize. Meanwhile, Hanson's full year figures of £49.7 million, showing a strong second half acceleration, raised hopes of what 1982 could bring once rationalisation of Berec was underway. The shares ended the year at 287p yielding 5.2% ahead of a one for one scrip issue.

Nadir beats his forecast

Polly Peck's forecast of profits of £2 million for its first year of operation in the packaging business was treated with some caution, but the shares had doubled to 325p by the time the actual figure of £2.11 million was announced. This was accompanied by an even more apparently fantastic forecast of £10 million for 1981/82. One analyst computed that there was not enough citrus fruit production in the whole world to utilise the numbers of boxes required to justify that forecast, but the shares of Polly Peck ended the year at 355p, up another 145%, on a prospective P/E of less than 2.

Maxwell takes control of British Printing

Following a dawn raid in July 1980, Robert Maxwell's Pergamon Press had picked up a 29.4% stake in the country's largest printing concern, **British Printing Corporation**. Then, in April 1981, he paid £10 million to take Pergamon's stake up to 77%. It was an audacious move in that Pergamon, with net worth of some £9 million and pre-tax profits of £3½ million a year, was taking on a lossmaking, debt-ridden colossus. BPC had just reported a loss of £11.3 million for 1980 and its debt load had risen to £40 million. What attracted Maxwell was BPC's £200 million turnover and the scope for reorganisation and rationalisation in an industry grossly overmanned and hog-tied by trade union restrictive practices. It was now operating under a Government committed to changing the rules of the game, and Maxwell was ready to make the most of the opportunity. He reduced the loss to £1.2 million by the end of 1981, and the following year reported a pre-tax profit of £12.4 million.

The transformation of W. Williams & Sons begins

In January, Caerphilly-based engineering and foundry company, **W. Williams & Sons**, hard hit by the downturn in the industry, reported a sharp swing from profit to loss in the first half of 1980. There was no improvement in the second half, but rescue for the company and its shareholders appeared in November with a 25p a share offer for 51% of the 3.4 million shares in issue by C. Price, a private building company operating in the East Midlands. The move attracted little attention at the time but within ten years, the company, under its new management of ex-London & Northern executives Nigel Rudd and Brian McGowan, was to rival the achievements of Hanson and BTR.

British Aerospace takes off

Nationalised by the Labour Government in 1976, British Aerospace (BAe), representing some 80% of the UK's aircraft industry, was chosen as the first candidate for privatisation. Half the company was sold to the public for £150 million with an offer for sale of 100 million shares at 150p on a fully-taxed P/E of 9.6 and a prospective dividend yield of 7.4%. Despite Labour's pledge to renationalise the company, the offer was well oversubscribed and attracted a 21p premium when dealings began.

1982

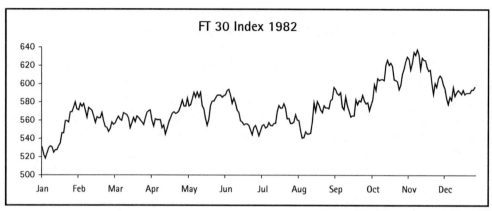

FT 30 Index 1982

Source: Thomson Reuters Datastream

The revival begins

The resilience of equities, especially industrials, during a recession-hit year, pointed to a more encouraging outlook for the New Year than had been the case at the beginning of 1981. At the same time, no one had any illusions about the potential pitfalls that lay ahead, especially those related to the US economy which left that of the UK hostage to another's fortune. Industrial disruption too could prove to be a major stumbling block. Admittedly high unemployment had weakened the trade unions in 1981, but as it continued to rise some thought it could spark a "do or die" degree of militancy, signs of which were already appearing among the miners, now led by the redoubtable Arthur Scargill, and among the railway unions. There was also no widespread evidence of industrial recovery – both Laker and deLorean collapsed in February – despite the pick-up in share prices, and the upturn in industrial production figures reported in December had gone into reverse in the first quarter of 1982. Nevertheless, equities had risen to 564 on the eve of the budget in mid-March, taking heart from a £2.5 billion package, including another cut in base rates to 13%, designed to cut industry's costs, create jobs and promote new investment, to be paid for in part by increased excise duties and balanced by reductions in public spending and additional asset sales. A fall in the rate of growth of average earnings and of retail prices both to 11%, reported later in the month, was accorded more weight than the appointment of a receiver for **Stone Platt** and the near-collapse of **Turner & Newall**, but a strong advance in equities and gilts was stopped dead in its tracks by the outbreak of the Falklands War.

Who dares wins

There is no question but that the decision to order the naval taskforce to set sail was a huge political gamble. There is also little doubt that no other political leader would have had the courage and determination to take that decision. Failure then to achieve an Argentinian withdrawal, either voluntarily or forcibly, almost certainly would have meant the end of three years of Conservative rule and an abrupt reversal of policies. As it turned out, a 20-point fall in the FT 30 and one of nearly three points in gilts was regained within days as US support seemed to guarantee a successful outcome to the conflict. After reaching a new all-time peak of 590.6 in mid-May, 35 points were lost over the next few days as a run of Argentinian successes prompted further consideration of the degree of military and political risk involved.

A rally to 592.6 on the eve of the Argentinian surrender was followed by a near 50-point reaction by the end of June as investors returned to contemplation of the familiar peacetime problems of excessively high US interest rates, still rising public spending, stagnant output and the ever-present threat of industrial disruption. To these worries were now added fears about the impact on the international banking system of the developing countries' debt crises, led by Mexico, and of a spate of bankruptcies among major multinational corporations. All were weighed down by heavy debts accumulated when interest rates were negative and were now cruelly exposed to real rates as recession and disinflation set in. However, there was a silver lining in that these signs that his disinflationary policies were working to the extent that they now threatened a disastrous financial collapse, seemed to persuade Paul Volcker that enough was enough. Accordingly, in late July he announced that the Federal Reserve Board would adopt a more flexible monetary approach by tolerating money supply growth at the upper end of the permitted range, while still maintaining his anti-inflationary goal. The Dow did not respond immediately and after dipping below 800 on a short-lived upturn in interest rates, it rallied strongly, topping 900 on the last day of August in very active trading. At the same time the danger was perceived that a policy of maintaining brutally high interest rates as disinflation takes hold, would create a demand for money in distress borrowing which the banks could not satisfy without putting their own liquidity at risk. On the other hand, not to satisfy it would lead to the collapse of many over-stretched companies and the non-repayment of the bank's existing loans. This was a 'no win' situation as evidenced by the troubles of Continental Illinois and of International Harvester, but to quote former Federal Reserve chairman Dr Arthur Burns, "The banks have been foolish. Let us hope they continue to be so." The popular view was that the shock to confidence of the recent debt crises had gone a very long way towards killing inflationary habits and expectations, and that borrowing and monetary growth would begin to recede naturally. Activity would remain depressed but as debt service costs became bearable for sound borrowers, reconstruction would gradually get underway with any defaults absorbed in banking profits.

In early October, Volcker suspended the money supply growth target while restating his commitment to restraining the growth of money and credit to "appropriate levels" to keep inflation under control, and the next day the Dow broke through the 1000 level on the second highest volume in its history.

Two record breakthroughs

Meanwhile, back in the UK base rates were down to 9% and gilts were seemingly in accord with the US view that the inflationary momentum of the 'sixties and the 'seventies had been broken. Thus on the same day that the Dow topped 1000, the Government Securities index added nearly two points to 82.83, its highest level since 1964. Equities, too, confirmed this measure of world economic interdependence and broke through 600, closing above it for the first time at 606.1. But if the rise in equities was justified by the prospect of falling debt service costs coming straight through to profits, with any rise in sales as icing on the cake, and the rise in gilts by the reduction in inflation, the longer-term future of both depended to a large extent on the Government controlling the growth of the public sector and thereby its tendency to pre-empt available resources. That task still lay ahead, and given that the public sector had been insulated for so long from competitive pressures, it was not going to be accomplished without a struggle.

Earlier governments of both persuasions had tended to avoid confrontation but Mrs Thatcher was determined to get across to public service workers the message that there is a link between pay, productivity and jobs. In any case, the hard-pressed private sector was making heavy calls on available funds, and there seemed to be no good reason for the overmanned, inefficient and often loss-making elements of the public sector to continue to be protected from the pains of disinflation.

By the time of the Chancellor's autumn statement, the FT 30 was up to 630, but despite its cautious tone, the belief by overseas holders of sterling that with the oil price depressed, he might be tempted to allow the currency to depreciate further, forced the rate below $1.60 at the end of November. Equities followed it down to reach 588, but rallied as the pound revived in response to the Chancellor's denial that this was what he had in mind, reinforced by a 1% rise in Base Rate to 10%. With the rise in retail prices and average earnings both below 7% in November and no growth in corporate profits over the year, there was some evidence that the Government's disinflationary goals were being achieved. Accordingly it was thought unlikely to continue to pursue policies which could risk prolonging and deepening the recession. Thus despite the most severe industrial recession since the War, the FT 30 managed to gain 12.5% on the year to 596.7 while the All Share did even better, up 22.5% at 382.2. Gilts, although below the best, plussed a remarkable 30% to 81.19, while FT Gold Mines gained 85% to 556.6 as the bullion price recovered, strongly boosted by the Falklands conflict and a run of sovereign debt defaults seen as threatening to the stability of the international banking system.

Racal pulls Decca around

Racal entered 1982 in fine style with a 45% advance in first half profits to £38.4 million, largely thanks to a £10.5 million turnround by Decca. The momentum carried on into the second half and pre-tax profits for the full year came out at £102.6 million, up 39% on sales up by just 20%. On the announcement in June, the shares added 22p to 450p where the yield was 1.6%, but at year end they had risen to 595p boosted by news that Racal had obtained the cellular radio contract, which before the end of the decade was to add another important division to the group.

BTR consolidates

1982 was a year of consolidation for **BTR** with continuing rationalisation measures in the UK operations serving to prevent profit figures from achieving the most optimistic predictions. As a consequence, the £90.1 million total for 1981, up 28% on sales up 25%, included a £4 million drop in UK profits to £26 million, and first half profits for 1982 showed only a 13% gain to £48.7 million despite a small contribution from Serck. The UK workforce had been reduced from 18,500 to 10,500, and although earlier forecasts of a £110 million total for the year were beginning to look unlikely to be met, the prospect of rationalisation benefits coming through in due course helped the shares to end the year at 378p.

Berec pays off for Hanson

Hanson's first half profits were up by no less than 21% to £22 million and after this demonstration of how good management can weather the worst recession in fifty years, due note was taken of the Chairman's pronouncement that there was evidence of the recession bottoming and signs of recovery. In July a successful £15 million bid was made for **United Gas Industries**, and the following month a move to increase the group's borrowing powers from twice capital and reserves to three times was assumed to be the prelude to further acquisitions. Full year figures also recorded a 21% advance bringing the total to £60.4 million with Berec making a nine-month contribution of £14.2 million. The shares closed the year at 271p, effectively doubling over the period.

Polly Peck expands

The placing of 1.3 million shares in **Polly Peck** out of the Restro holding brought in £4.5 million from a consortium of Middle East investors in January. The placing price was around 350p but at the time of the release of the interim 1981/82 figures in June showing a profit of over £3 million, the shares were still only 342p and selling on a P/E of under 5, a rating considered by the *FT* to be "overdoing the caution" for a company which had proved the sceptics wrong by turning a moribund East End rag trade outfit into a major force in international packaging. At the same time expansion plans were announced for the packaging plant in Northern Cyprus and in mainland Turkey, and the £10 million forecast began to look no longer unrealistic. Sister company **Cornell** had been suspended in August at 165p and came back in September with a £2.76 million rights issue designed to fund its investment in a 64% stake in a mineral water bottling plant at Niksar in Turkey with the aim of tackling the huge market in the Middle East.

This rapid expansion of the Polly Peck empire now began to attract a great deal of speculative as well as investment interest, and the share price rose in a straight line, topping £16 by the end of November when the full year profits were revealed to be £9.04 million. The accompanying statement referred to expanding packaging production and also to plans to exploit the substantial market believed to exist in Turkey and the Middle East for locally manufactured products, particularly in the field of television and video and in pharmaceuticals. A merger of the three companies, i.e. Polly Peck, Cornell and Wearwell, was said also to be under discussion. The degree of official backing from the Turkish government was emphasised in the form of an 8-year tax holiday in acknowledgement of Polly Peck's key role in the economic development of the region. The prospect of profits of around £20 million for 1982/83 was now being aired and the shares advanced further in the final quarter to end the year at £23.

Williams goes to first base

The new managers of **W. Williams** wasted no time in rationalising the business and at the interim stage they had cut the deficit from £599,000 to £199,000 on turnover practically halved to £1.55 million. By this time the share price had risen to 40p as a number of institutions gave their backing to Rudd and McGowan. Then in November, they made their first big move with a £3.1 million agreed cash bid for loss-making **Leys Foundry**, a Derby-based foundry and engineering company best known for its Ewart chains and Beeston boilers.

Bio-Isolates makes its debut

Bio-Isolates was a start-up flotation on the USM by Chandra Singh's London Venture Capital group. Operating from rented space in a Swansea dairy, the company had devised and patented a process for extracting protein from whey, and although the value of the product was questioned by local food producers the concept managed to catch the imagination of the public. Floated at 33p in an offer for sale of 41% of the company's equity, the shares established a 16p premium on the first day of dealing, and ended the year at 270p with a market capitalisation of just over £20 million. Interestingly, shortly after the flotation, one of the family of the founders disposed of a large holding in contravention of the undertaking given in the prospectus.

Among the year's new issues, the most notable were **Amersham** and **International Signal & Control**. The former was unique in that it was the first flotation of a "high-tech" company involved in radioactive materials used for medical and industrial research purposes. At the offer for sale price of 142p the P/E was a relatively demanding 19 and the yield a modest 3.5%, but the issue was well oversubscribed and the 40p premium established on the first day of dealing prompted a political row about the shares being sold too cheaply. Neither was there anything on the London market quite like International Signal & Control. Founded by US entrepreneur Jim Guerin in 1971, the company specialised in defence electronics and had a glittering record. Since 1978 pre-tax profits had risen five-fold to £5.3 million on sales trebled to £75.8 million and the P/E of 18 at the offer price of 155p was not considered overdemanding for a company in its line of business. Guerin had brought ISC to London because the SEC in the US insisted on fuller details of his principal customers, which he was not prepared to supply for security reasons. Investors thus had to take the company on trust. They were happy to do so, bidding the shares up to 226p when dealings started.

Index-linked Gilts

Introduced for the first time in 1982, index-linked gilts are designed to protect capital from erosion by inflation, by increasing both capital and income in line with the Retail Price Index (RPI).Thus, while all conventional gilts are redeemed at their nominal value of £100 on maturity, an index-linked gilt will have its par value adjusted over its life to take account of the rise in the RPI. Similarly, the coupon will be adjusted in line with the RPI increase on each pay-out date.

1983

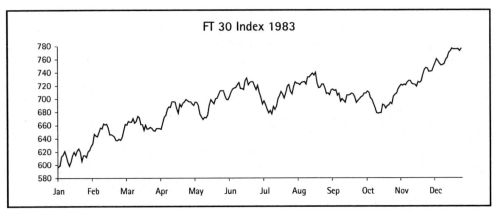

FT 30 Index 1983

Source: Thomson Reuters Datastream

New peaks for the indices

With markets having made modest progress in the last three recession-hit years, hopes were high that a more significant advance would be recorded in a year which looked likely to see the end of recession. Even the Chancellor's uncompromising New Year message, promising no relaxation in the fight against inflation and designed to discourage speculation in the City that the March budget would be expansionary, failed to deter buyers and the end of the first week in January saw both the FT 30 and the All Share at new record levels of 621 and 396. The pound and gilts, however, both fell sharply on oil price weakness and on Labour's pledge to devalue, but steadied after a 1% hike in Base Rates to 11%. As a measure of the change in sentiment, whereas not so long ago weak sterling and a weak oil price might have been interpreted bearishly, the first was now seen as boosting corporate profits and the second as aiding world recovery as well as having a negligible impact on national revenue. Thus ahead of the budget on 15th March, on OPEC's agreement to a $5 cut in the oil price to $29 a barrel, the FT 30 actually rose 2.5 points to 665.8 in recognition of the fact that the fall in the pound, since the autumn, had more than offset the decline of the dollar-denominated oil price.

A Conservative landslide

The budget made some useful personal concessions in terms of raising tax allowances and child benefits as well as increasing duties on petrol, drink and tobacco again, and although it was well received by markets, all eyes were now on the impending election called for 9th June. With Mrs Thatcher's standing boosted by the Falklands victory and CBI surveys reporting a "substantial recovery in business confidence", the Conservatives were odds-on favourites but if there were any doubts, they were dispelled by Labour's election pledges. They included withdrawal from the EEC, renationalisation, reimposition of exchange controls, repeal of industrial legislation and closure of all nuclear bases in the UK, as well as an immediate increase in public expenditure by £7.5 billion and an increase in the PSBR from £8 billion to £14 billion. Labour veteran, Peter Shore, called the manifesto "the longest suicide note in history". A more Macchiavellian view was that this was not a serious attempt to unseat Mrs Thatcher but another move in the Labour party's internal struggle. The policies of the left were being put forward so that they could be seen to be rejected by the electorate. Those policies would then be dumped and Labour's leaders could prepare to fight another day on a new platform. The FT 30 crossed the 700 mark for the first time in the fortnight ahead of the poll, but reacted sharply after topping 730 following the Conservatives' re-election with a 144-seat majority. Profit-taking was only to be expected after such a well discounted outcome, but the new Chancellor, Nigel Lawson, managed to create some anxiety, not least among his Cabinet colleagues, by demands for massive public spending cuts out of expenditure planned for 1984/85 in the wake of reports that 1983/84 borrowing was already well above target. Another unsettling factor at this time was the miners' call for a "substantial pay rise" and the threat of a strike if it was not met.

By the end of July, the FT 30 had moved above 700 again, encouraged both by a parallel revival in the US economy to which the Dow had responded by successfully challenging the 1200 level and by President Reagan's continuing commitment to sound money evidenced by Paul Volcker staying on for a second term of office at the Federal Reserve Board.

If markets remained hesitant throughout the summer, there had been a record number of rights issues to absorb as well as the £525 million BP tender offer scheduled for late September. It sold effortlessly, and then towards the end of October the market suddenly sprang to life in response to **ICI's** third quarter profits which were up over 150% at £147 million, showing an acceleration of the trend evident in the first two quarters. Investor enthusiasm was helped by another flurry of takeover activity with **BAT** vying with Allianz for control of **Eagle Star** and on 28th November the FT 30 reached a new peak of 743.9 on growing confidence that a spontaneous economic recovery promoted by market forces with the minimum of government assistance, was now underway. In the run-up to Christmas, the jobless figures fell again, as did the Retail Price index. The November trade figures pointed to a surplus for the year of over £1.5 billion, and further good company results confirmed expectations that corporate profits would show a gain of around 25% on the year with dividend growth restored in real terms.

After several years of disappointed hopes, it appeared that the UK industrial recovery had arrived, and with the OECD confirming that prospects for world recovery were showing "a big improvement", the FT 30 closed the year at 775.7, up 29.5%, with the All Share trailing at 470.5 for a gain of 22.5%. The superior performance of the FT 30 was due to the fact that the painful rationalisation and reorganisation of 1980 and 1981 had begun to show through in dramatic productivity gains and profit rises, particularly among the capital intensive cyclicals, led by ICI, which dominated the index. This was also the year in which US fund managers had discovered the UK, becoming big buyers of stocks like ICI and Glaxo after the decisive election win by the Conservatives in June. Gilts put up a less impressive performance in 1983, held back by anxieties over the US deficit and by the downtrend in sterling over the year, and recorded a modest gain of just 2% at 83.12.

Racal slows down

Racal's interim figures for 1983/84 showed a very creditable 22% jump in profits to £47 million on an 18% sales gain, but warnings of a second half slowdown due to the recession and growing competition in the field of data communications disappointed the market and the shares fell 62p to 485p on the announcement. Full year forecasts were scaled down from £120 million plus and the eventual total of £112 million was not greeted with any enthusiasm. Orders from OPEC countries were well down and data communications remained a problem area, but also affecting investor sentiment was a patent dispute between Racal-Milgo and Motorola-Codex which looked like being settled in the latter's favour.

Tilling falls to BTR

BTR, by contrast, had an excellent year. Profits for 1982 came out at £106.7 million, up 18%, and taking advantage of the fact that it was now a firm favourite of the investment community, in April BTR launched a dawn raid on industrial conglomerate Thomas Tilling. Having picked up only 6%, a week later BTR made a full bid which valued Tilling at £576 million. The target argued that the offer price was "totally unreflective of its underlying worth and assets", but after raising its bid to £660 million, BTR won control. Interim figures of the combined group recorded a 20% gain to £58.3 million but they included a loss in the period for Tilling which contrasted sharply with a £95 million full year profit forecast in its defence document. BTR also announced a 100% scrip issue, and the shares ended the year at 424p, an effective gain of over 100%.

Hanson expands in the UK

Hanson Group began the year with a £264 million agreed counterbid for **United Drapery Stores**, then the subject of an approach by a consortium led by Heron. In the course of the contest, Hanson made a full year profit forecast of £75 million which was already looking conservative at the time of the interim figures in June, which showed a 53% jump to £34 million. Hanson wasted no time in trying to recoup the major part of the UDS purchase price, and by the end of September had agreed to dispose of the Richard Shops, John Collier, Timpson and Orbit for some £152 million. In December full year figures revealed an overall 51% advance to £91 million, a sparkling result that proved to be the prelude to a £170 million bid for **London Brick**. During the year the market capitalisation of the whole group topped the £1 billion mark for the first time.

Polly Peck grows and grows

The announcement of Asil Nadir's plans to double capacity at Uni-Pac and to acquire two cargo planes and two cargo ships to strengthen its monopoly position in the region, together with his confident statement at the AGM in mid-February that **Polly Peck** was "on the verge of becoming a very large international concern with unlimited trading potential", sent the shares soaring to a peak of £35. Before the end of that month, however, they had collapsed to £17, at which level they were suspended pending a statement to answer charges that the company was exploiting sequestered Greek property in Northern Cyprus, thereby prejudicing a political settlement, and that the claimed tax holiday did not have the official blessing of the Turkish government. A brief statement answering the charges in general terms was made, and the suspension lifted, but the shares plunged afresh to £10 before rallying into the £15-£20 range. Even interim profits rocketing to £8 million did not help matters greatly and the accompanying statement was criticised as being woefully inadequate in the light of the rapid expansion of the group. In September, £13 million was raised by a placing of 6.3% of the group with a consortium of Middle East investors and brokers to the company, L. Messel, then began a series of institutional presentations. By the time of the announcement of the results for the full year in early December, Polly Peck's share price had recovered to £24 where the market capitalisation was £175 million. Profits came in at £24.7 million on turnover of £62 million, and much was made of the expansion of activities serving to make Polly Peck a much more widely based manufacturing and trading group. Legal & General disclosed that it held a 5.1% stake, and just before Christmas Asil Nadir announced a 10 for 1 share split and another placing with Middle East investors to raise £5 million. The shares had recovered their poise and closed the year at £26½, or 265p in their new form.

The Turkish Connection

In 1983 the phenomenal success of Polly Peck prompted investors to look for others that might follow the same path literally, given Polly Peck's origins, from rags to riches. Their first target was **Mellins**, an obscure loss-making manufacturer of lingerie and babywear in which Mr Tukar Suleyman, a gentleman of Turkish descent, acquired a 29% stake. Despite his declared intention to return the company to profitability by remaining in the same area of operations, the shares rose from 6p in November 1982 to a peak of 246p in February 1983 on rumours that Mr Suleyman was related to Mr Nadir and on the confident expectation that new businesses would be injected into the company. A rights issue in April at 100p to raise £660,000 seemed to be nothing other than confirmation of these expectations, but the subsequent purchase of a stake in loss-making store **Bambers** gave rise to doubts when the deal was shelved following revelations of exceptional losses at Bambers. By the end of the year, Mellins' share price was back to 62p as investors changed their allegiance to late runners, **Bellair Cosmetics** and **Harold Ingram**, both of which became subject to bids from Wasskon, a Liechtenstein-based company run by Mr Akcay and Mr Tecimer, both of Turkish origin. Wasskon had paid 8p for a controlling stake in Bellair in April and the shares soared on the news to end the year at £11¾. During the intervening period no announcement was made beyond "the company knows of no reason for the rise in the share price". The case of Harold Ingram followed much the same pattern. Wasskon's controlling stake was acquired at 65p a share in August and the shares promptly rose to 350p by the end of December, again on no news.

A darling of the market

Sinclair Research was riding high in 1983 on founder Sir Clive Sinclair's reputation for imagination, innovation and salesmanship, and in January a £20 million placing of 10% of the company (to exclude the electric car project) was made with institutions. The valuation had been made on the basis of pre-tax profits of £10 million in 1981/82 on turnover of £27 million, and a forecast of practically doubled turnover in 1982/83. Profits for the year rose to £13 million and expectations were boosted by booming home computer sales, news of a new mini-TV to sell for £50, and of course hopes for the revolutionary electric car. A public quotation was said to be scheduled for the following year.

New directions

Many of the new issues during the year were indicative of the new directions the UK economy was taking in the eighties. **Pineapple**, the dance studio company, got off to a fine start, and was soon followed by Eric and Julia Morley's **Miss World.** Placed at 60p, the shares had the rare distinction of opening at more than twice the issue price, touching 132p on the first day of dealing. Then came Michael Green's **Carlton Communications**, which achieved a quotation on the USM via a reverse bid for Nigel Wray's **Fleet Street Letter**. The declared aim was "to expand in TV work." Later in the year, **Tottenham Hotspur** came to market, but while it received an enthusiastic reception from the small investor with its offer for sale at 100p, it failed to gain significant institutional support.

1984

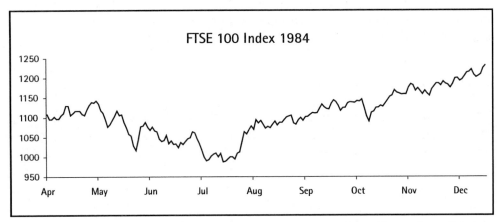

FTSE 100 Index 1984

Source: Thomson Reuters Datastream

The last battle

Expectations that the economic recovery would continue and broaden in 1984 did not go hand in hand with a widespread belief that the stock market would repeat its sparkling performance of 1983. Rights issues were not considered likely to match last year's record of £2 billion but there was no doubt that they would still lay claim to a large slice of available institutional cash, as would the continuing stream of privatisations scheduled to include the record breaking £3.9 billion **British Telecom** offering. However, January soon demonstrated that institutional buyers had more than enough resources to cope with anything the market might throw at them, and equities advanced on a broad front on record volume. Within a matter of days the 800 level was penetrated decisively with US buyers prominent, and by the end of the month the index had topped 840 in company with other markets around the world also hitting new highs.

A sharp setback on Wall Street in response to Paul Volcker's expressions of concern over the inflated US budget deficit led to a reaction in London but it was shortlived and a renewed buying wave carried the FT 30 up to 865 ahead of the budget in mid-March. The market was delighted with the new Chancellor's tax-reforming measures, especially the phased reduction in Corporation Tax to bring it down to 35% by 1986/87, the halving of Stamp Duty to 1%, and the abolition of the investment income surcharge. The phasing out of first-year capital allowances and the removal of artificial incentives in the savings market, including the axing of premium relief on new life insurance contracts, did not pass without criticism but there was no question that industry was the gainer in this budget. The PSBR target for 1984/85 was set at £7.25 billion or 2½% of GDP, the money supply growth range was to be 6-10%, and the Retail Price index was expected to be growing at no more than 4.5% per annum at year end as against 5.1 % in February. A week later the FT 30 had crossed the 900 level for the first time with the new FTSE100 share index, launched in January with a base figure of 1000, touching a peak of 1130.7.

Scargill rocks the boat

The market had risen too far and too fast since the beginning of the year and it was time for a pause. No one needed to look very far for reasons for caution. At home the miners' strike, which had started in the first week of March, was becoming more bitter and protracted, seriously hitting output and the balance of payments and undermining foreign confidence in sterling. Continental Illinois, America's eighth largest bank, had to be rescued by the Federal Reserve Board after sustaining huge losses on South American and energy-related loans, and a soaring dollar and a weakening oil price aggravated the situation by ruling out the chances of any decline in interest rates. The atmosphere was one of all-embracing gloom. A sharp increase in oil imports to combat the shortage of coal pushed the April trade deficit to a record £835 million, unemployment reached a record 3,029,000 and the latest round of pit talks collapsed. But after dipping briefly below 800 at the end of May, the FT 30 recovered in June only to collapse again in July as a run on the pound prompted a sharp rise in Base Rates to 12%. At the same time the dockers decided to throw in their lot with the miners, and in late July and early August, the fortunes of Mrs Thatcher's government were at their lowest ebb. The docks were at a standstill, the miners' strike was in its 23rd week with no sign of a settlement, and sterling was making new lows by the day. It was now her turn to call off a 14-day tour of the Far East to stay in London to deal with the crisis. However, better money supply growth figures led to a rapid reduction in Base Rates to 10½% in mid-August and, interestingly, the cuts continued despite sterling becoming progressively weaker in line with a still falling oil price. Perhaps the market sensed the implications of the defeat of the miners' challenge to the Government, seeing it as a test case the outcome of which would settle the issue of "who governs the country" once and for all.

By this time the public sympathy which the miners could claim at the outset of the dispute had all but disappeared. The scenes of violence witnessed daily on TV together with the reluctance of other unions to become involved in the strike to the detriment of their own members were factors which tended to isolate the miners and to refute their argument that they deserved "special case" treatment. Scargill's fund-raising efforts in Libya and Russia did not endear him to the general public either, evoking memories for some of the Betteshanger colliery strike in 1941 during the darkest days of the war, and of the fact that such industrial action did not diminish until Russia joined the Allies following the breakdown of the Nazi-Soviet Pact and the German invasion in June of that year.

Mrs Thatcher stands firm

By September things were beginning to look a lot better for the Government. The dock strike had crumbled after more and more dockers decided to cross the picket lines, and the miners' strike seemed more likely to end with a whimper than the bang so desired by Scargill as the drift back to work gained momentum. Markets survived the **Johnson Matthey** collapse, taking heart from the speed with which the Bank of England came to the rescue. There was another nasty moment in late October when the pit deputies' union debated whether or not to strike, but the threat was lifted and by November the FT 30 was over 900 again. Sterling was still drifting down towards $1.20 under the influence of a weakening oil price and the fear that the miners might still be bought off on the lines of the 1974 settlement, but sentiment improved by the end of the year on OPEC's agreement to production cuts and Mrs Thatcher's refusal to negotiate over the issue of pit closures or to introduce a new Plan for Coal. The landslide re-election of President Reagan on his "You ain't seen nuthin' yet" platform and the Dow's surge above 1200 again was another plus for the London market, but the overall firmness throughout the year owed more to two other factors.

One was the sheer magnitude of the recovery in corporate affairs under the Conservative administration. Trading profits had doubled since 1980 and were likely to rise another 20% in the current year. Corporate liquidity was at its highest level for six years, while balance sheet gearing at 20% and a strong cashflow meant that capital spending could be financed without recourse to bank borrowing. Admittedly, the recovery was from a low base, but it was nonetheless real, and the extent of the previous state of endemic overmanning was demonstrated by the fact that unemployment was continuing to rise. What had happened was that the burden of supporting it had moved from the private sector to the public sector with all that it implied for the borrowing requirement.

The other factor was sterling seemingly coming to terms with its place in a floating currency world in which the UK economy was fully exposed to world competition in a capital as well as a goods and services market. In such a context capital would go wherever it found the best return and an exchange rate was no longer an instrument of adjustment but simply a market price. Hence the Chancellor's efforts to cut back on public spending overheads and to combat wage inflation to ensure that excessive costs did not squeeze the profits of UK Limited and in turn lead to capital outflows which would rapidly undermine the pound. The fall in the pound since its heyday as a petrocurrency in 1981 was part of the process of finding a new market price, and judging from the strong recovery in exports and orders, it was close to doing so. The fact of an exceptionally strong dollar pushing sterling to too low a level temporarily then became a matter for internal adjustment, and once again the process would become self-correcting as the level of the dollar made US industry uncompetitive and that country ultimately less attractive to foreign capital. At least, that was the idea.

The Chancellor's autumn statement forecasting growth of 3½% and an inflation rate down to 4½% in 1985, and hinting at tax cuts of up to £1½ billion in the coming budget, helped the market to end the year on a very firm note. Investors also took heart from the enthusiastic reception accorded to the huge **British Telecom** offering, when the partly paid shares practically doubled on the first day of dealing, the last in a line of outstandingly successful privatisations in 1984 including **Enterprise Oil** and **Jaguar**.

The FT 30 ended the year at 952.3, up 23%, much in line with the FTSE at 1232.2, while the All Share beat them both by gaining 26% to 592.9. Gilts had a quiet year but, down only 2% at 81.7, had stood up remarkably well in the face of the slide in sterling from $1.40 to nearer $1.15, although a further drop in base rates to 9½% helped at the end of November. The Dow was actually down on the year at 1211, but recovering strongly as the new Republican administration, with the cooperation of the Federal Reserve Board, began to shift the emphasis of its policy from fighting inflation to resuscitating the economy, cutting a point off the discount rate to 8% in December.

Racal buys Chubb

Racal's half year figures for 1984/85 continued to reflect the problems that had caused the slowdown in the second half of the previous year. Up only 2½% to £48.7 million, profits had been hit by a dearth of new tactical radio orders, but reports of a strong recovery at Racal-Milgo and a growing order book for defence and marine radar helped to keep the share price steady at around 210p. Earlier estimates of a total for the year of around £130 million were revised to £120-125 million, but the actual figure of £119 million was accepted with good grace with an eye to the potential of the cellular radio division expected to move into substantial profits in 1988/89. Expectations of additional delayed benefits were aroused in August when Racal bid for **Chubb**. Given the trend towards electronic security systems, the expertise of Racal allied with the customer base and celebrated brand name of Chubb, promised to prove a winning combination.

Tilling pays off for BTR

The second half of 1983 began to demonstrate the benefits of the Tilling acquisition for **BTR** and full year profits came in at £170 million, up 60%, with a contribution of £44 million from Tilling. At the interim stage, profits doubled to £115 million and "marked progress" was forecast for 1984, a phrase which analysts interpreted to mean a total for the year of something like £270 million. Crewe House, the magnificent building in Mayfair that had been Tilling's HQ, was sold during the year for £37 million to Saudi Arabia for use as its embassy. The shares ended the year at 614p, having added 130p since the interim announcement in September.

Hanson wins London Brick

Despite forecasts by **London Brick** of a remarkable recovery in profits for the coming year, **Hanson** managed to win the day but only after boosting its offer to £247 million in cash or convertible stock and by requesting an extension of the period for acceptances. This success was followed in April by a $400 million bid for US Industries, a diversified manufacturing group, typically just completing a major reorganisation and getting back into profits after a major loss in 1981/82. Hanson eventually had to pay $530 million, but then offset part of the increase by selling Seacoast, one of its first US acquisitions, for $30 million. **US Industries** added $1 billion to Hanson's US sales, taking them up to $2.2 billion. In June, interim profits weighed in at £64.4 million, up 90% on a sales gain of 40% at £900 million. Analysts pencilled in a full year figure of £150 million, only to see it handsomely beaten at £169 million. This was Hanson's 21st year of operations. Sales now totalled £1.7 billion, evenly divided between the UK and the US, and at 278p the shares were selling on a prospective P/E of 11 assuming profits of around £220 million in the current year. Hanson rounded off 1984 with an ultimately unsuccessful £150 million bid in the week before Christmas for **Powell Duffryn**, a diversified engineering group with a lacklustre record, further depressed by the miners' strike.

Williams returns to profits

The new management at **Williams** had spent most of 1983 rationalising and integrating Ley's Foundries with the original business. High-volume, low-margin work was dropped in favour of smaller production runs carrying increased prices, and losses gradually fell to £76,000 for 1983, down from £312,000, on turnover up from £5.6 million to £27 million. Then towards the end of 1983, the first profitable business was acquired. This was **Garford-Lilley**, a specialist engineering, plastics and woodworking group operating in a number of relatively underexploited niche areas. The acquisition neatly supplemented the recovery trend in the rest of the group, and the first half of 1984 saw a dramatic return to profits with a total of £753,000. By this time Rudd and McGowan were winning increasing institutional support and the shares had risen to around 165p to give a market capitalisation of some £16 million.

Polly Peck pauses

1984 was a year of consolidation for **Polly Peck**. The long-awaited merger with Wearwell took place in May when the half year figures were announced. They were in line with expectations at £18.6 million, up from £8 million, on sales 150% higher at £45.3 million. Analysts' forecasts for the full year centred around a figure of £50 million, and the actual total of £50.5 million was regarded as disappointing for a company accustomed to exceeding rather than meeting forecasts. At the AGM in December, Asil Nadir said that he planned to spend £40 million in 1985 and that he was in discussions with Daihatsu about manufacturing their cars under licence in Turkey, and with Racal over a defence electronics project. The shares ended the year at 220p where the P/E was still a cautious 4.

The year was not a good one for the Polly Peck look-alikes. **Mellins** was suspended at 30p in February while refinancing negotiations were embarked upon and a month later the receiver was called in. **Bellair** was also suspended, but at its peak of £13¼, on the failure of the directors to provide any explanation or substantiation of the extraordinary rise. At the AGM in August, mention was made of plans to manufacture cosmetics under licence in Turkey and of the purchase of a 5.8 acre factory site to this end, but the developments were judged by the board to be "not sufficiently mature" to justify application for restoration of the listing at this time. **Harold Ingram** made no mention at all about moving away from its rag trade origins and after reaching 450p in January, fell back to close the year at 120p.

Two not of a kind

Among notable new issues of 1984 were **Body Shop** and **Blue Arrow**, both on the USM. Body Shop's novel concept of natural-based beauty products in simple refillable packs caught the public imagination and despite the exceptionally high prospective P/E of 24.4 at the 95p offer price, the shares practically doubled on the first day of dealing, boosting the market capitalisation to almost £10 million. Blue Arrow began public life with a placing of 18.4% of its capital at 75p a share to give a market capitalisation for the collection of 34 staff recruitment agencies of just over £3 million. The shares were bid up to 89p on their first day.

Fatal Distraction

Lonrho's seven-year tussle with **House of Fraser** appeared to have ended in November when Tiny Rowland agreed to sell his 29.9% stake in the stores group to the Al Fayed brothers for £138 million. However, within a matter of weeks Rowland had begun buying again, building up a stake of over 5% to enable him to carry on the battle with House of Fraser's prospective new owners.

Tiny Rowland is the most enduring of the controversial characters of post-War years. Starting in 1961, he transformed the obscure London & Rhodesia Mining and Land Company (Lonrho), then making a profit of £160,000, into a pan-African enterprise embracing many of the mining and agricultural activities of the developing countries in that Continent. Businesses acquired in the UK and in Europe included the exclusive importing concession for Volkswagen and Audi cars, as well as a string of hotels and casinos, and by 1979 Lonrho's annual profits had risen to over £90 million. But while Rowland's buccaneering style had won him the admiration of Lonrho's small shareholders, it had upset a large and influential section of the political and financial establishment. The problems began in 1973 when unilateral actions on his part came to light involving overseas payments to directors designed to avoid tax, and led to accusations that he regarded Lonrho as his own private domain. They even prompted Prime Minister Heath to say that the affair represented "the unpleasant and unacceptable face of capitalism". A DTI enquiry was launched, and although the boardroom battle that followed was won by Rowland, thereafter he remained an outsider as far as the City was concerned. His unorthodox courting of Harrods, which began in 1977 did not help, although paradoxically his aim was to achieve international respectability by owning the world's premier department store.

Rowland's initial acquisition in 1977 of a 24% stake in SUITs, which owned 10% of House of Fraser, and Sir Hugh Fraser's agreement to step down as chairman in favour of Rowland, who also became Deputy Chairman of House of Fraser, caused consternation both in Parliament and in the City. Within months Rowland had boosted his holding in SUITs to 30% and bought the 20% stake in House of Fraser held by US stores group, Carter Hawley Hale. His decision to bid £40 million for the whole of SUITs prompted a reference to the Monopolies Commission. After a year of argument, it was decided that he could go ahead with his bid, now revised to £60 million, but by that time Sir Hugh Fraser had bowed to family and City pressure and turned against Rowland. A new boardroom struggle ensued, but Rowland managed to win Sir Hugh over yet again to his side. Thereafter, Rowland's tactics were based on extending his control over House of Fraser, but he continued to meet fierce opposition from the bulk of the board and from their adviser, Warburgs, who planned to install a new Chairman, Professor Roland Smith, in place of Sir Hugh, now the subject of widespread criticism for his gambling problems. Faced with losing both his reputation and his position, in 1980 Sir Hugh decided to back Rowland's £230 million bid for House of Fraser. Victory seemed at last to be within Rowland's grasp, but the City establishment still had one decisive card to play. The bid was referred to the Monopolies Commission. His bid earlier that year for *The Observer* had succeeded but it still managed to stir up more controversy and helped to lose him a favourable judgement on the House of Fraser bid. The Commission's grounds for rejection were not convincing, and even the popular press now sided with Rowland. The contest between Rowland and the House of Fraser board continued, and then in 1984 yet another Monopolies Commission was set up to investigate a Lonrho bid for House of Fraser.

This time Rowland was hoping for a decision in his favour but once again was disappointed. It was at this point that the Al Fayed family came on the scene and apparently having given up all hope of ever attaining his goal of winning control of House of Fraser and Harrods, Rowland agreed to sell his 29.9% stake to the Al Fayeds for £138 million. Everyone thought that was the end of the matter, but they were wrong...

Sinclair falls from favour

Things began to go wrong too for Sir Clive Sinclair in the second half of 1984. Capacity had been expanded rapidly in 1983/84 and costly marketing strategies put in place to meet booming demand in the home computer market, but there was a flood of new entrants and competition became intense. As sales fell, so did the share prices of the other players, and in February the postponement of the planned flotation was announced on the grounds of "adverse stock market sentiment towards companies in the computer sector".

But there was still the electric car. Barrie Wills, managing director of Sinclair Vehicles, and a former de Lorean executive, said that at under £1000 it would appeal to a wide market, embracing commuters, shoppers and the younger generation, and could be expected to have as big an impact on the vehicle market as the inventor's low-cost products had had on electronics. In the event the C5 Electric Car was not at all what the market had been led to expect and even at the low price of £399, no one except the manufacturers believed that the sales target of 100,000 a year was a realistic one. In June Robert Maxwell decided not to proceed with a £12 million rescue operation for Sinclair Research, and in October a receiver was appointed for Sinclair Vehicles. Only 4500 C5s had been sold, there were another 4500 in stock and the company had debts of £7.75 million. Six months later Amstrad was to buy the computer interests for just £5 million.

Bids Galore

1984 was also a very busy year for bids, with a total value of £5.24 billion, twice the level recorded for 1983. **Woolworths** pushed **Harris Queensway** off the scene to win **Comet** for £177 million. **Dixons** had to raise its cash and shares bid from £178 million to £248 million to get **Currys**, but was helped by a near-doubling of its share price after convincing institutions of the benefits it could wring from this old-style electrical retailer. Less controversial was **Ward White's** purchase of **Halfords** from **Burmah** for £52 million. Like a latter-day Charles Clore, Ward White chief executive Philip Birch had acquired and rationalised a number of footwear manufacturers and retailers since 1972, and his first move in a carefully targeted diversification into motor and cycle accessories was to pick off the top brand name in the industry and triple his high street selling space at a stroke. **Carless Capel** was less fortunate with its hostile £100 million bid for **Premier Oil**, even though it had US arbitrageur Ivan Boesky on its side. Shareholder loyalty to Premier's larger-than-life American chairman Roland Shaw was too strong. He was a great favourite with the company's many small investors who had seen him build it from an unregarded 'penny stock' in the mid-'seventies to become an important player in North Sea and UK onshore exploration. By the bid deadline, Carless Capel had picked up acceptances of just over 30%.

FT Stock Exchange 100 Share Index (FTSE)

To meet the need for a market barometer capable of instant computation in order to support a new futures contract based on the UK equity market, the FTSE was introduced in February 1984 with a base figure of 1000. It is made up of the country's top 100 shares, i.e. those with the largest market capitalisations. Like the Actuaries indices, the FTSE constituents are weighted and subject to change from time to time.

1985

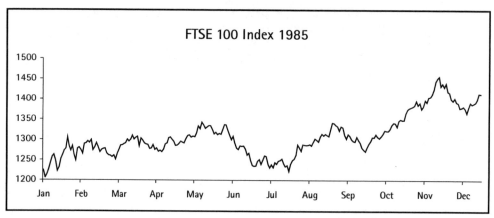

FTSE 100 Index 1985

Source: Thomson Reuters Datastream

FT 30 crosses the 1000 barrier

Hopes were high that the New Year would see a continuation of the favourable trends in growth, inflation and corporate profits established in 1984, but if there were doubts, they centred on the price of oil, sterling, the US economy and the Chancellor's strategy. OPEC was still in some disarray faced with an oil price that looked likely to continue to weaken, sterling showed no sign of arresting its downtrend, the twin deficits appeared to threaten the US recovery, and the record level of unemployment, at over 3 million, meant that the Chancellor would be under intense political pressure to reflate with all the attendant dangers.

In the event, anxiety over a continuing slide in sterling to $1.12 in the first half of January and a 2½% hike in base rates to help stop it, quickly turned into something like euphoria on further consideration of the benefits to UK industry of a lower exchange rate. The FT 30 crossed the 1000 mark for the first time on 18th January, held above it for a week, and then slipped below it again as the pound continued to fall and base rates were raised another 2% to 14%. The index lost over 40 points in the next two days but then steadied in the belief that a brief period of high interest rates was a necessary corrective action and that it would not have much adverse effect on a corporate sector in such a strong financial position. Even a renewed plunge of sterling towards parity with the dollar at the end of February failed to spark any further decline in equities and by mid-March the FT 30 was over 1000 again, helped by some excellent company results, bid activity, strong US buying of the leaders, and the official ending of the miners' year-long strike.

The dollar peaks

Paul Volcker's hints of official intervention at the end of February as the dollar continued to soar and the pound touched $1.0525 (70.9 on the trade-weighted index) marked the end of the dollar's extraordinary rise and simultaneously saw the Dow break into new high ground at 1299. This move heralded the start of the worldwide equity boom fuelled by cheap oil, cheap money and a cheap dollar that culminated in the crash of October 1987. For the moment, however, the event came as a considerable relief, assisting Chancellor Lawson in the task, outlined in his Budget speech in March, of resisting any further fall in the pound by keeping interest rates at whatever level might be necessary to maintain the downward pressure on inflation. In addition he reaffirmed his commitment to the MTFS, tightening the money supply growth targets to 5-9% for M3, the broad measure, and to 3-7% for M0, the narrow measure. Next year's PSBR target was £7 billion now that the figure for the current year had overshot so alarmingly as a result of the miners' strike. In an effort to reassure financial markets only £700 million, less than half what had been expected, was to be given away in tax cuts, leaving room for incentives and job creation measures. Duties were increased on drink and tobacco, but 400,000 people were taken out of the tax net altogether, and National Insurance contributions were restructured to reduce the cost of hiring lower paid workers. Capital gains were to be indexed. The next day base rates were cut by half a point to 13½%, and a week later they came down to 13% as investors switched out of a falling dollar, pushing the rate up to $1.24.

Problems for the Chancellor

A stream of rights issues kept the equity market subdued in April and May but the FT 30 managed to stay close to the 1000 level until June. Then a flurry of heavyweight offerings, totalling almost £2 billion, together with some shockingly bad results from the electronics sector and a pound soaring towards $1.40, started a slide in the index which saw it back almost to 900 in late July. **ICI** blamed a fall in second quarter profits on the strength of the pound and given that some 40% of the profits of the constituents of the Actuaries Industrial Group represented overseas earnings, with another 10% coming from direct exports, the reaction was understandable. At the same time, the market had to bear in mind that the pound's plunge towards $1 had undermined the Government's anti-inflation strategy by sending the rate of growth of the Retail Price index up to 7%, or twice the level achieved in 1983.

This de facto reflationary effect carried all the disadvantages in the form of higher prices with no benefit at all to the unemployment figures, and the Chancellor's room for manoeuvre in this area was limited further by the fact that his £5 billion public spending contingency reserve was already pre-empted thanks to lower oil revenues as the dollar price fell. Furthermore, the degree of overspend was a clear threat to his promised tax cuts, and he needed either more economical methods of funding or to continue disposing of public assets at attractive prices as a substitute for tax revenues. The political dimension of the Chancellor's problems was emphasised in July when the Conservatives lost their seat at the Brecon-Radnor by-election, a result widely taken as a verdict on his economic policies.

New highs all round

In August events began to take a turn for the better. As sterling continued to rise, half a point was taken off base rates in mid-July bringing them back to 12%, and the rate of growth in the Retail Price index slowed and then reversed to 6.8%. There was a further fall to 6.2% in the figure for August and the view was gaining ground that the policy of keeping short-term interest rates relatively high together with a stable exchange rate in order to restrain inflation would enable the Chancellor to relax his fiscal stance in the coming budget. After all, growth was already well established, industry seemed to be able to live with the current level of interest rates, and so did the public, judging from the record rise in retail sales on the back of a record level of consumer debt. And reservations about the fact that the money supply growth targets were being exceeded month by month could be countered by stressing that methods of calculating them were known to be highly unreliable.

Dollar Exchange Rates 1985 Currency Units per $		
1st February		**1st September**
3.17	Germany (DMark)	2.62
9.68	France (Franc)	7.97
2.68	Switzerland (Franc)	2.15
255	Japan (Yen)	211
0.89	UK (£Sterling)	0.69

The dollar, too, was no longer a worry. The Plaza accord of the G5 nations in September had agreed on a policy decision to push it lower and get the locomotive of the US economy rolling again. In fact, the dollar had topped out at the end of February, so although the accord is still hailed as a triumph for US Treasury Secretary James Baker and a shining example of international monetary cooperation, the G5 nations were pushing on an open door. The market had already spoken. But whatever remaining doubts there may have been in investors' minds had disappeared by the end of November as the FT 30 swept through 1100, the FTSE through 1400, while the Dow crossed the 1400 level for the first time.

December was an exciting month, witnessing three of the biggest bids of all time with **Argyll** offering £1.8 billion for **Distillers**, **Elders IXL** £1.8 billion for **Allied Lyons**, and **Hanson** bidding £1.9 billion for **Imperial Group**. **GEC** also made an ultimately abortive £1.2 billion offer for **Plessey.** The economic numbers seemed to set their seal of approval on this enthusiasm as the rate of inflation fell to just over 5%, and the trend in the unemployment figures at last began to turn down.

The FT 30 closed the year at 1131.4, slightly below its November peak of 1146.9, but still up 20% influenced by its preponderance of bid targets, while the FTSE was up 14% at 1412.6. Gilts steadied after dropping below 80 in February during the pound's slide and the raising of base rates to 14%, and recovered to end the year at 82.81, up 2%. The Dow reflected a growing optimism about the outlook for the US economy in the context of the recent G5 accord and a falling oil price, ending the year at its peak level of 1546.7, a gain of 27.6%.

Racal shocks the market

The shares of **Racal** fell 48p to 240p, taking them back to their level in 1982, on the shock announcement in January that profits for the year would be "substantially below expectations" following a £1.55 million fall at the interim stage to £47.2 million. The reason was a "major hiccup" in the US at Racal-Vadic involving a loss of £15 million. Chubb was not pleased with the news and complained to the Takeover Panel about the forecasts made in the offer document, but Racal was cleared on the grounds of genuinely unforeseen circumstances arising. The share price continued to weaken and full year profits eventually came in at a very reasonable £123.6 million, but the announcement was accompanied by yet another warning that interim profits for 1985/86 would be below last year's £47.2 million. The shares did not take kindly to this second disappointment, falling 36p to 156p and taking the whole sector down with them. The reasons given for the expected setback were the increased costs of cellular radio development, higher interest charges, and an exceptionally slow order intake in the US. Further confusion was caused by the prediction of record sales and profits in the year as a whole and the share closed the year at 160p after falling as low as 120p in November on reports of problems at Racal-Milgo.

BTR takes Dunlop

BTR began the year with a £34 million bid for debt-ridden **Dunlop**, quickly opening negotiations with the target's bankers to get them to continue their support if BTR won. Given that Dunlop's debts totalled £500 million, this was no mean achievement, and encouraged BTR to pay up to £101 million in order to secure an agreed deal. Meanwhile BTR's profits for 1984 managed to exceed all expectations at £284 million and the shares plussed 21p to 664p. Interim profits announced in September did not disappoint either, recording a 31% gain to £151 million.

Hanson boosts its war chest

Hanson Group's interim profits for 1984/85 announced in June were a little below best expectations at £106 million, but the market was worried much more by the mammoth £520 million rights issue which came out a week later. It knocked 50p off the share price and depressed the whole market to such a degree that 50% of the issue was left with the underwriters. It was the largest private sector rights issue ever, just topping **Barclays'** £513 million offering earlier in the year. No specific reason was given for this cash-raising exercise but it was widely regarded as designed to boost Hanson's war chest with a view to another major acquisition. In the words of one commentator, now that Hanson can spend £1 billion, "hardly anyone is safe any more". In fact, Hanson's ambitions were soon seen to be even greater when it was revealed subsequently that in May, Lord Hanson had approached the Chancellor with a proposal to buy the government's remaining 31.5% stake in **British Petroleum** for £6 billion.

July saw the sale of **Interstate United**, originally acquired in 1977, for $92.5 million, and then in August Hanson launched its biggest US bid yet with a $745 million offer for **SCM**, the group best known for its Smith Corona typewriters but also with important interests in foods and chemicals. The company tried hard to avoid Hanson's clutches, using complex defence systems and appeals to the US courts, but eventually was forced to capitulate after the offer was raised to $926 million. Hanson's full year figures published in December showed profits up 5% to £253 million. The whole group now had an equity market capitalisation of £3 billion.

Williams expands

In March, Rudd and McGowan were able to report profits over £1 million for the first time at £1.17 million, and later in the month launched their biggest bid yet with a £24 million offer for the forgings and plastics group, **J & HB Jackson**. To secure agreement they had to raise the paper and cash alternative bid to £32.4 million. The acquisition was especially important to **Williams** in two respects. It took the group into the US where Jackson was a major distributor, and it also brought in a lot of cash which served to reduce Williams' gearing from 100% to 33%. Interim profits for 1985 duly rose by a remarkable 88% to £2.7 million, and by this time the shares had risen to 340p where they sold on a prospective P/E of 16 assuming a total for the year of close to £6 million. The last two months of the year saw both a £11.5 million purchase of Rawlplug from **Burmah Oil**, the first big-name acquisition in the important DIY and home care market, and an agreed £7.3 million bid for **Spencer Clark**, manufacturers of structural and special steels. The shares now stood at a little over 400p.

Polly Peck misses a forecast

Polly Peck boosted its cash position in February with a £40 million rights issue, and then in May pleased the market with a 32% increase in interim profits to £28.2 million. The shares were a firm market at 280p following a company visit to Turkey by over fifty London fund managers earlier in the month. Margins continued to hold up at around the 40% level, and it was pointed out that while costs were denominated mainly in Turkish lira, receipts were in harder currencies. The rest of the year did not proceed quite so smoothly. Brokers to the company, L. Messel, reduced their profits forecast for the full year from £85 million to £68 million because of the likely "adverse impact of currency movements". The shares dropped 52p to 173p on the news but managed to maintain that level even though profits eventually turned out to be no more than £61 million.

F.H. Tomkins is transformed

In 1983, Greg Hutchings (35), a former corporate development manager with the Hanson Group, had become a major shareholder and chief executive of **F.H. Tomkins**, an industrial fasteners distribution company. At that time the share price was around the 50p mark. His first purchase was Ferraris, a distributor of motor parts, for £2.2 million, a deal that helped profits in Tomkins' first year under his control to rise by 50% to £2.4 million. His second was Hayters, the well-known private manufacturer of lawnmowers, for £4 million, and in May 1985 an £11.7 million rights issue was made, giving a clear indication that more acquisitions were on the way. The following month Hutchings paid £14 million, half in shares and half in cash, for seven engineering and distribution subsidiaries of GKN. Full year profits for 1984/85 announced in July came to £3.5 million and on the basis of confident predictions of a total of over £7 million in 1985/86, the shares at 200p were selling on a prospective P/E of 18.

What Reebok did for Pentland

In August 1981, Stephen Rubin of tiny Pentland Industries had made what must rank among the most successful investments of all time. He paid $77,500 for a 55% stake in a start-up venture struggling to establish itself as a distributor in the US of athletic and leisure footwear. The name of the company was **Reebok**. After a slow start, Reebok's sales really began to take off in 1983/84 on the back of the fitness boom and its fashion associations. Thanks to Pentland's experience of manufacturing in the Far East, Reebok was able to cope with the meteoric increase in demand for its products, and in that year accounted for 70% of Pentland's turnover and a rise in profits of 65% to £1.65 million. Meanwhile Pentland's shares had risen from 55p at the beginning of 1984, to just over 100p in May. There was talk of a total of £2 million in the current year, but when first half profits came in at no less than £2.5 million, sights were raised to £5 million. The shares were still relatively slow to respond and by the end of August had risen only to 128p even though in March Stephen Rubin had obtained Reebok's world distribution rights. From that point on, however, the share price began to rise almost as fast as Reebok's sales. From £3 at the end of 1984, the share price had reached £10 in mid-June of 1985 when a six-fold increase in Reebok sales, to £57 million, helped Pentland's profits to £12.9 million against earlier estimates of £5 million. The decision was made to let part of its holding go in a US flotation of Reebok to value the company at over $300 million while Pentland still retained over 40% to keep producing profits as an associate.

WPP is born

May 1985 saw Martin Sorrell move into **Wire & Plastic Industries**, a manufacturer of supermarket trolleys and baskets and animal cages, that was soon to become **WPP**, the largest marketing services company in the world. In company with stockbroker Preston Rabl, Sorrell took a 27% stake in Wire & Plastic as a result of issuing themselves with 1.36 million shares at 38p. Martin Sorrell had already made a name for himself as finance director of Saatchi & Saatchi and the idea that he wanted to branch out on his own proved an attractive one to investors. The shares doubled to 75p on the news and moved up throughout the year to reach 290p in December when the first acquisition was made. This was graphics company VAP, for £2 million in shares, and at the same time it was announced that Saatchi & Saatchi had taken a 10% stake in WPP.

New issues in 1985

A record £6 billion was raised in the London securities market in 1985, up 72% on the previous year, and among the more notable new issues was **Coloroll**, the fast-growing home furnishings group run by Business Man of the Year, John Ashcroft. Half the capital was offered for sale at 135p a share giving a market capitalisation of £36.8 million. The issue was ten times oversubscribed but still managed to open at small discount.

Laura Ashley's popularity was less in doubt even though the P/E, at the 135p offer price, was a heady 23. Queues up to a hundred yards long formed the day the prospectus was issued and the issue was forty times oversubscribed. The shares touched 200p on the first day of dealing, closing with a premium of 59p.

JS Pathology also received a warm reception. Founded by Dr Jean Shanks in 1958, the company provided a comprehensive range of pathology services to the private sector and had a remarkable growth record. At the placing price of 160p the shares were on a prospective P/E of 16.7 and the issue was substantially oversubscribed.

1986

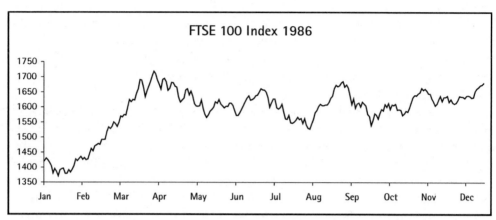

FTSE 100 Index 1986

Source: Thomson Reuters Datastream

Stoking the furnace

With an election looming in just over a year's time, few doubted that the Chancellor would manage to keep the economy on a growth track until then, and at the same time spread his largesse a little more widely wherever it might be needed. A further decline in the price of oil could pose a problem but it was a development where the benefits to the non-oil sector and to the world at large were still seen as outweighing the disadvantages on the revenue front. Asset sales could always fill the gap. Anxiety over sterling also seemed to be unnecessary. The pound had weathered the storm that the fall in the oil price had created in 1985, and there was little reason to doubt that the Chancellor would be able to maintain a stable exchange rate in order to achieve his inflation target of under 4% by year-end. As for the equity market, the prospect of low inflation and a reasonable rate of growth looked certain to provide the rise in earnings and dividends required to validate a prospective yield of around 5% and a P/E of 11.

Not surprisingly the markets opened the New Year with a broad advance, but after hesitating on the political upset created by the Westland affair, which led to the resignation of two Cabinet ministers, Michael Heseltine and Leon Brittan, and a 1% increase in base rates to steady the pound after a sharp drop in the oil price, they recovered to close the month at record levels. There was no doubt that sentiment was aided by the sight of predators being willing to compete with each other and pay ever higher prices for what had once been thought of as rather dull companies. Thus **Imperial Group** and **Distillers** went for £2.5 billion each, some 25% above the opening bids, in hard-fought and no holds barred contests between determined bidders.

The oil price continues to fall

Despite an oil price now below $20 and still falling, an event that might have been expected to prompt another rise in interest rates, markets continued to surge ahead in February in company with the Dow which crossed the 1700 level on the last day of the month. The fact that buying of gilt-edged was pushing yields below 10% seemed to point to lower, not higher interest rates on the way, a view given substance in early March when the Federal Discount Rate was reduced to 7%.

The budget in mid-March provided markets with yet another boost. A penny was taken off the basic rate of tax bringing it down to 29p, the 25p target was reaffirmed, and thresholds and allowances were raised by just over 5% to provide a £1 billion fiscal boost where it was most likely to be spent. Significantly, the M3 target growth range was raised to 11-15%, Personal Equity Plans (PEPS) were introduced, and base rates were lowered to 11½%, moves which prompted Lex in the *FT* to call it a "budget for equities". Within days the FT 30 was over 1400, the Government Securities index over 90 and the Dow into 1800 plus territory.

Meanwhile, the price of oil had collapsed to below $10, a level not seen since 1974. However, worries had not disappeared completely. The rapidity and extent of the fall in the price of oil was certain to cause problems in the US banking system given the huge amount of energy-related loans, and while the Chancellor had said that he could live with halved oil revenues on the basis of $15 a barrel, $10 might prove to be quite another matter regardless of what the OECD might say about benefits to the world. At that price revenues from the North Sea would be no more than £3 billion in 1986/87 compared with £11.5 billion in 1985/86.

Red lights on the M3

April was a significant month in that it witnessed a further cut in base rates to 11% on the day that the money supply figures were released, showing it rising at an annual rate approaching 20%. The clear implication was that monetary targeting was a thing of the past, and when in May the rate of growth in M3 rose even more sharply, only to be met with a 1% reduction in base rates to 10%, there was no doubt. The fact that the same month had seen no improvement in the unemployment figures and also an unexpected drop in manufacturing output, suggested the reason for this policy change. The industrial world was still in recession. To the surprise of politicians and investors, it had not responded to lower oil prices as quickly as they had expected. Inflation had been conquered – RPI growth was down to 2.8% in May – but the problem facing the politicians in particular, with electoral timetables to keep, was how to combine low inflation with full employment. They had fallen victim to the Butler Miller Paradox (so-called after the two economists who had detected it) which states that since people want to hold more money when inflation is falling because it then represents a better store of value, a greater supply of money is going to be needed to finance activity during this period. The politician is thus faced with two more problems. One is that the store of liquidity built up as inflation was falling is not necessarily going to be held on a lasting basis but is likely to be spent, thereby adding to the excess liquidity already being pumped into the system. The other is that it will then add to the difficulty of imposing an effective monetary squeeze to reduce the ensuing inflation.

Preparing for the election

These warning signs did not go unremarked but since a bull market needs nothing more than its own existence to justify it, the investor in mid-1986 was not overly concerned about the fragility of its foundations. After all, the time for them to be tested was still some way off, and meanwhile there was money to be made in a brave new world of low inflation, low interest rates and rapid growth to be built on the ruins of OPEC.

April and May saw a 100-point fall in the FT 30 after the market had to absorb £1.8 billion in rights issues in a month, but after a strong rebound in June and July on signs of the private investor taking the place of the institutional investor, whose liquidity had shrunk to practically nil, buying petered out and the index spent the rest of the year mainly in the 1200-1300 range. The price of oil falling below $9 and a sharp deterioration in the balance of payments did not help, and with output still falling and unemployment still rising, for a time markets seemed to be anticipating even laxer financial controls with all their attendant dangers.

Nerves steadied in August after OPEC managed to agree on a plan for production cuts and the oil price rose by almost 40% to $13.95. Then in mid-October, base rates were raised by 1% to 11%, a move which the Chancellor said should be "enough to keep the anti-inflation strategy on track". His autumn statement the following month seemed to confirm the worst fears of those who thought he might be tempted to spark a pre-election mini-boom. By announcing plans to increase public spending by £10 billion over the next two years, and asset sales of £5 billion a year for the next three at the same time leaving the PSBR for 1986/87 unchanged at £7 billion, Nigel Lawson was suspected of following much the same pre-election path as his predecessor who had set tight spending targets and then allowed them to be overrun. To be fair to both Chancellors, however, they had to cope with exceptional events in the form of the Falklands War, the miners' strike and the collapse of the oil price, making overruns inevitable, and at least the money was going to a public sector that had undergone a measure of reform. It was no longer money down the drain in the form of a subsidy from taxpayers to protect nationalised industries and public services from the consequences of the huge losses incurred as a result of grossly inefficient operations. Nevertheless, the low PSBR was largely an illusion created by the Government's asset sales. Public spending had risen steadily in real terms over the past seven years and, as a percentage of Gross Domestic Product, was higher than in the last year of the Labour government.

There was a cynical view current in the closing weeks of the year that the Chancellor had abandoned monetary and fiscal restraints, accepted devaluation and let loose a consumer boom as a gamble to secure an election victory. Once this had been achieved, it was argued, the screws could be put on again in order to repair the damage done in the shape of higher inflation, higher interest rates and the first balance of payments deficit since 1979. If getting unemployment down was more important than adding a point or two to inflation in an election year, it was perhaps a gamble worth taking, especially since figures released in mid-November showed the first real decline in the numbers of jobless as well as a pre-election poll giving the Conservatives a one-point lead over Labour.

School for scandals

Markets were under something of a cloud in November and December as one scandal after another came to light. First of all Geoffrey Collier, a senior executive at Morgan Grenfell, resigned after insider dealing allegations. Then US arbitrageur, Ivan Boesky, who had been an active participant in many of the year's big bids in the UK, was fined $100 million by the SEC. After weeks of rumours, December saw a DTI investigation ordered into the **Guinness** takeover of **Distillers**, closely followed by the revelation that Guinness had "invested" $100 million in Boesky's arbitrage pool of funds. On the last day of the year, Roger Seelig, the Morgan Grenfell executive who had looked after the Guinness bid, resigned from his post at the bank. Although these events were truly exceptional in the light of the high standing of the persons and the companies involved, they did not prevent a good Christmas rally developing in a market which also had to absorb the £5.6 billion offering from **British Gas**. The advent of dual capacity and automated quotations with Big Bang in October seemed to have no particular influence on the course of markets at the time. The FT 30 closed the year at 1313.9, well below its peak, but still a gain of 15.5%, while the broader-based All Share and FTSE were up 20% and 23.5% at 835 and 1679 respectively. Government Securities were up a modest 1.25% at 83.62. The Dow recorded a gain of 22.5% closing at 1896.

Hanson wins Imperial Group

Imperial Group and **United Biscuits** both thought that Lord Hanson was being kept too busy in the US courts over his takeover of SCM, to concern himself with their proposed merger. His £1.9 billion bid therefore came as a surprise, although he had had his eye on Imperial for a long time. It was one of the few remaining asset situations in the UK market and an obvious target for the Hanson treatment. The referral of the Imperial-United merger to the Monopolies Commission, but not **Hanson's** bid, was a major victory for the Hanson camp, but Sir Hector Laing of United Biscuits countered by proposing a reverse £2.5 billion bid for Imperial and getting over the Monopolies hurdle by agreeing to dispose of Imperial's Golden Wonder subsidiary. A rise in the price of Hanson's shares in the ensuing weeks put the value of both bids on a par, and a combination of a balance of institutions favouring the Hanson option and buying in the market, eventually delivered the prize.

Within the next six months, Hanson managed to dispose of enough parts of SCM to recoup the whole $926 million outlay and still retain half the original group. Boise Cascade bought the paper interests for $160 million, ICI the titanium dioxide division for $580 million and Reckitt & Colman paid $120 million for Durkee Famous Foods. The Park Avenue head office was sold for $36 million. Meanwhile Hanson Group's interim profits for 1985/86 had come in at £157 million, up 50%. The second half of the year saw the beginning of disposals from Imperial Group. In July, the hotel and restaurant division was sold to Forte for £190 million, and two months later Elders IXL paid £1.4 billion for Courage. Golden Wonder went next for £87 million to Dalgety. There were also some relatively minor disposals in the US but they went a long way towards funding the $200 million purchase price of Kaiser Cement, that country's fifth ranking cement producer. Full year profits totalled £464 million, a gain of 83%, leaving the shares at 190p on an historic P/E of 11.

Racal recuperates

In line with the warning given the previous June, **Racal's** interim profits more than halved to £23.2 million, but to sweeten the pill "very satisfactory" results were forecast for 1986/87. Profits for the full year were £90.2 million, representing the first reduction in profits since 1955, but once again Racal followers demonstrated their loyalty and the shares not only held their ground but edged ahead, reacting to analysts' forecasts that profits for 1986/87 would be back to around the £130 million mark. In December the announcement that Racal was buying out its minority partners in Vodafone for $161 million cash, indicated that Racal was in control, and the shares ended the year on a firm note at 192p.

BTR goes for Pilkington

BTR opened 1986 with the sale of Tilling's insurance subsidiary, Cornhill, for the very good price of £305 million. Rationalisation and integration of recent major acquisitions helped provide a 47% gain in final figures for 1985 to £362 million and then the half year figures saw a further strong advance to £203 million. BTR was very long on cash and in a climate where the megabid had now become almost the order of the day, everyone was waiting for BTR to pounce. The selected target turned out to be **Pilkington**, manufacturers of an everyday product but with an unimpressive record, and an ideal subject for the BTR treatment. The £1.16 billion bid was rejected immediately.

Williams and Tomkins extend their Empires

In January, **Williams Holdings** laid the foundations for its biggest bid yet, by taking a 6% stake in **McKechnie**, an engineering group twice its size, already involved in a bid of its own for **Newman Tonks**. The following month Williams made a £140 million offer for McKechnie conditional on the Tonks bid being dropped. In the event, McKechnie shareholders voted for the bid to go ahead, and Williams' consolation for its first failed bid was a £2 million profit on the sale of its share stake. Its own shares were riding high, adding 26p to 548p on the news in March that 1985 profits had topped best expectations at £6.4 million. Its next move was the purchase of Fairey Engineering from **Pearson** for £22 million and then in April an agreed £79 million bid was made for **Duport**. It was hardly surprising that first half 1986 results were up by almost 200% at £8.5 million, or on recent experience, that the announcement was simultaneous with a £58 million offer for **London & Midland Industries** (LMI). Before the end of the year, 21 of LMI's subsidiaries had been sold for £20 million, a move that effectively reduced Williams' gearing from 20% to zero. The next major bid could not be far away.

 F.H. Tomkins also had a busy year. Profits for the first half of 1985/86 doubled to £2.4 million and the shares at 237p were selling on a prospective P/E of 21. With £12 million in cash another bid was expected before long, but few expected anything quite so ambitious as a £175 million all paper bid for **Pegler-Hattersley**. After upping the price to £200 million, Tomkins managed to secure its prize. Full year figures comfortably exceeded expectations at £7.4 million, and by then the shares had risen to 310p where the prospective P/E was down to 14.

Polly Peck goes shopping

Shares of Polly Peck were a nervous market in 1986. They began the year with an unexplained 20p drop to 138p, but confident statements about trading saw them back to 200p at the end of May in time for the interim report. Profits were slightly below expectations at £31.2 million but an accompanying announcement about expanding produce sales into Western and Eastern Europe and improving currency management, served to reassure the market. Full year profits revealed in December were up by 15% to £70.4 million and were closely followed by news of the purchase of TI's small appliance division comprising Russell Hobbs and Tower Housewares for £12 million cash. The acquisition was welcomed for providing some top brand names to boost Polly Peck's consumer sales in the Near East as well as a UK earnings base. The shares closed the year at 180p, still on a P/E of no more than 3.5.

The Guinness Affair

Ernest Saunders was appointed Chief Executive of Guinness in 1981 with the task of reversing the group's ramshackle and unsuccessful diversification policy which had left it with over 250 operations ranging from film finance to babywear. Within five years more than half of these had been disposed of and Guinness was firmly established in just three key areas – namely brewing, retailing and publishing. In the process, profits recovered dramatically and market capitalisation rose from £90 million to £500 million.

The merger with Distillers in 1986 was to be Saunders' crowning achievement and he was to stop at nothing to push rival bidder, Argyll Foods, off the scene. This he succeeded in doing but the methods he employed soon came under scrutiny, and in January 1987 he was forced to step down along with his Finance Director, Olivier Roux. Apart from upsetting the Scottish lobby by failing to honour an undertaking to appoint Sir Thomas Risk as Chairman, his big mistake was to ensure success for his bid by covert means. There was nothing new about trying to persuade institutions to support the share price of one bidder rather than that of a rival in the case of a paper bid, but it was usually done by a nod and a wink over lunch or at informal meetings. The subsequent court proceedings revealed that Saunders' support had been won not only by using Guinness's own money but also by offering 'no loss' guarantees and performance fees – which were readily accepted – to helpful financiers, including the already discredited Ivan Boesky. It has since been contended that Saunders' means were simply not covert enough, and that, in the past, merchant banks had looked after such routine details, wrapping up 'no loss' guarantees in a general fee package to the successful bidder. Until this point, no authority would have been expected to question seriously the conduct of the City's leading merchant banks, stockbrokers and their clients. What the Guinness/ Morgan Grenfell/ Cazenove case did was shatter the belief that the customary test of legitimacy was who you were, not what you did.

Microsoft goes public

Meanwhile on the other side of the Atlantic, history was being made with the Initial Public Offering (IPO) of Microsoft. The stock was offered at $21 and oversubscription led to a rise to $28 on the first day of dealing. At this price the company had a market value of $520 million, making founder Bill Gates with a 45% stake, a multimillionaire. The rapid achievement of the company's mission statement, 'a computer on every desk in every home running Microsoft software', would soon make him a billionaire.

1987

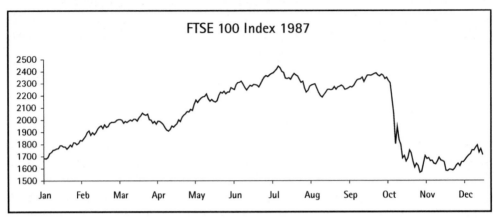

FTSE 100 Index 1987

Source: Thomson Reuters Datastream

Jeux sans frontières

Prospects for the New Year looked promising, not only in the UK but in all the major industrial nations. There were high hopes of what the Plaza Accord might achieve in terms of getting the surplus countries, principally Germany and Japan, to stimulate their economies in order to help reduce the trade imbalance between themselves and the US. Markets were prepared to take a great deal on trust and by the end of January practically all of them were at new peaks. The Dow had cracked the 2000 level for the first time, the Nikkei Dow, 20000, and in London the FT 30 and the FTSE had broken through the 1400 and 1800 levels respectively. Leading UK industrials, like Glaxo and ICI, were becoming firm favourites with international fund managers impressed by the remarkable transformation of the country's economic status. Export-led growth was accelerating, productivity was continuing to improve, government revenues were above estimate, the trade account was in balance and unemployment was falling. In addition, political continuity and stability were virtually assured by the prospect of a renewed term for the Conservatives.

The picture looked almost too good to be true, but for every commentator who thought it was just that, there were two or more ready to justify a continuing rise. Thus the potential problem posed by the high rate of growth in average earnings was explained away on the grounds that it was merited by improved productivity and overtime working in certain industries, while the level of output was said to be understated since the figures gave too much weight to declining industries. As for the renewed decline in the dollar and the possibility that it could force the Federal Reserve Board to impose another squeeze at the risk of causing another world recession, clearly it was the duty of Germany and Japan to take on the locomotive role by stimulating their own economies more. In any case London was cheap by international standards as the wave of foreign buying demonstrated. There was also a distinct air of excitement in markets as the public climbed on the privatisation and new issue bandwagons. Long queues formed outside the issuing houses for prospectuses and multiple applications became the order of the day. Since an allocation invariably resulted in an instant profit, the new private investor soon came to see the stock market as a moneymaking machine. Even the scandals became a bull point by making the whole business of "investment" risqué and alluring.

Betting on a Conservative win

By early March, markets had surged to new record levels ahead of a budget likely to predate the election only by a matter of weeks. Helped by a ½% cut in Base Rates to 10½%, the FTSE crossed the 2000 level for the first time in the week before the budget, then paused and regrouped ready for another run in anticipation of a Conservative victory in June. The budget did nothing to harm this prospect. The basic rate of tax was reduced by 2p to 27p, and thresholds and allowances were raised. Both moves were widely regarded as "fiscally responsible" in that the Chancellor was using half his buoyant revenues for tax cuts and the other half to reduce borrowing. The PSBR target for 1987/88 was now down to £4 billion, 3½% growth was forecast for the non-oil economy, inflation was expected to fall to 4% by year-end, growth in M0 (bank deposits with the Bank of England and notes and coins in circulation) was to be targeted in a 2-6% range, and the current account deficit was considered unlikely to exceed an acceptable £2.5 billion. Gilts liked the package too and the Government Securities index stood at 90.9 on budget day, having risen steadily since the beginning of the year. Within a week of the budget, base rates came down another half point to 10%. Some anxiety was expressed about the rapid growth of private credit and the consumer spending boom, but that too was rationalised by the consideration that, unlike corporate or government borrowing, consumer borrowing is eventually repaid.

New worries about the dollar

It was a sudden fall in the dollar at the end of March that began to spoil this apparently rosy picture. A further meeting of the Group of Five in Paris in February had produced the so-called "Louvre Accord", whereby in return for a US commitment to stabilise the dollar, the Germans and the Japanese had promised once again to undertake their own expansionary measures. However, this renewed fall in the dollar gave rise to the suspicion that the US authorities were reverting to the policy of "benign neglect" of the early years of the Carter administration, in an attempt to force the issue. That suspicion became a certainty when it became known that Paul Volcker was not to be invited to carry on for a third term as head of the

Federal Reserve Board but was to be replaced by a supposedly more pliant Alan Greenspan. The worry now was that the US would overplay its hand in this game of international financial poker, and fail to win an improvement in its trade deficit since a whole series of devaluations meant that the adverse impact of the latest rise in import prices would always serve to mask the benefit of a turnround in exports.

By contrast, the UK had managed a very successful devaluation against the D-Mark over the past two years without courting inflationary dangers because it took place at a time of falling oil and commodity prices and when the labour market was particularly slack. Not surprisingly, the pound now became a firm favourite with overseas investors, giving great importance to the Chancellor's supposed exchange rate targeting policy. It seemed clear that a link with a non-inflationary currency like the D-Mark provided the ultimate backstop against inflation, for as long as the exchange rate target was maintained, a lid would be put on all costs and prices subject to international competition. Furthermore, on the domestic front selective monetary easing could be carried out without too much risk of inflationary side effects.

A landslide victory for Mrs Thatcher

The ramifications of an exchange rate targeting policy took very much second place in the minds of investors, institutional and private, in the weeks ahead of the election on 11th June. Two half-point reductions in base rates had brought them down to 9% by early May, **Sock Shop**, oversubscribed 53 times, opened at more than double the 125p offer price, and **Tie Rack** did even better, attracting subscriptions of over £1 billion for the £12½ million of stock on offer. **Rolls-Royce** was hugely oversubscribed and opened at 147p partly paid against an offer price of 85p, while **Polly Peck** at last moved into new high ground thanks to a wave of buying of its new ADRs by US investors who did not share in London's "residual scepticism". Against the trend and with masterly timing in May, co-founder of **WPP**, Preston Rabl, placed his 5.6% stake in the company with institutions, and two months later Saatchi & Saatchi followed suit.

The Conservative win with a majority of 100 seats was up to the best expectations of the market and the FT 30 added another 27.1 to a record 1767.9, the FTSE 40.2 to 2289.5, and the Dow provided moral support by advancing 17.6 to 2377.7. But with the yield on equities at just over 3%, or one third of that obtainable on long-term government stocks, the ratio was now at a record level. In addition, money supply growth of M3 was rising at well over 20% a year, oil prices were firming, commodity prices had stopped falling, and growth in earnings was edging over 8%. Not surprisingly consumer spending was at record levels and house prices were soaring along with those of other non-financial assets.

Twin peaks

There was still a month to go before London hit its peak for the year, and yet another six weeks before New York did the same, but although the warning signs multiplied there was no broad consensus that markets were riding for a fall. Oddly enough Tokyo had taken a 10% tumble between June and July, and given its status as the most expensive of all markets, its rapid recovery to a new record was seen as a vote of confidence in world share prices. Also the downward drift of the dollar had halted and a degree of stability had returned to currency markets, giving rise to hopes that with its trade imbalance no longer widening, the US would be able to survive the strain of its double deficit pending further progress in the field of international monetary co-operation. Even fears of a Third World debt crisis began to recede as commodity prices firmed, thus relieving the pressure on the hard-pressed debtor countries while the Western banks began to make multi-billion dollar provisions against potential loan losses. But as far as London was concerned, these global factors were less important than a deluge of new issues and rights which the market was simply unwilling and then unable to digest, as well as a run of disappointing, even alarming, economic numbers.

Nearing the summit

The indices peaked on 16th July with the FT 30 at 1926.2 and the FTSE at 2443.4, but significantly with the Government Securities index at just under 91, some 2½ points short of its high. On the same day the Dow reached a new record of 2496.97 but from then on London was more concerned with its own problems.

A week later markets were shocked by a dramatic increase in the trade deficit for May to £1.16 billion after a steep rise in imports. At the end of the month, top stockbrokers Barclays de Zoete Wedd called an end to the long bull market, the Government Securities index had fallen another three points to 87.66, and the yield ratio had risen to a multiple of 3.3, higher than the peak in 1972. There was also an enormous and growing settlement backlog aggravated by the active trading of small investors in penny stocks with an insatiable appetite for rights issues.

Then in the first week of August, just three years after joining the USM with a market capitalisation of £3 million, **Blue Arrow**, still with net assets of only £21 million, announced the biggest rights issue ever of £837 million to finance the takeover of Manpower in the US, the world's leading recruitment agency. The *FT* described the move as one of "stunning audacity" and warned that the surplus liquidity in the system that made such deals possible carried the danger that increased leverage in the securities and property markets would make any setbacks very painful. **WPP's** £177 million rights issue to help finance Martin Sorrell's bid for J. Walter Thompson, of which only 35% was taken up, did not bode well for the Blue Arrow issue, and the uncertainty was compounded two days later when a surprise 1%

rise in base rates to 10% in response to "domestic monetary conditions" knocked the FTSE back to 2261, 56 points down on the day. Along with a rights issue of £700 million from **Midland Bank**, and the **British Airports Authority** (BAA) £500 million issue, underwriters were calculated to be coping with some £3 billion, two thirds of which they now seemed likely to be left holding.

Over the top

Still ready to look on the bright side, investors took the view that with the mammoth sale of £7.2 billion of **BP** stock scheduled for the third week of October, the Chancellor was following the Grand Old Duke of York strategy by knocking markets down in August ready for a run-up ahead of this much-publicised offering. In any case the Dow was still marching onward and upward, reaching a peak of 2722.42 on 25th August.

London began to rally in early September, survived another horrendous set of trade figures both in the US and at home, and entered October approaching the 2400 level with sentiment aided by **TSB's** £777 million bid for **Hill Samuel**, **AB Foods'** £767 million offer for **S & W Berisford**, and **Benlox's** £2 billion break-up bid for **Storehouse**. Meanwhile **Saatchi & Saatchi** had made an abortive approach to **Midland Bank** as well as to **Hill Samuel**, and **Blue Arrow's** rights issue was reported as only 48.9% taken up with the balance placed by Phillips & Drew with "outside investors". In a climate of such frenetic activity, the feeling was that a rising share should not be sold in case there was something about to happen and that a falling share should not be sold either in case it attracted a bid.

With manufacturing output now rising strongly, unemployment still falling and confident CBI surveys, markets were looking forward post-BP to a period of calm and consolidation with no privatisations for at least six months. This reasoned appraisal of the investment situation changed abruptly at the end of the first week in October when a sudden rise in US prime rates from 8¾% to 9¼% coincided with an all-embracing "sell" recommendation by respected Elliott Wave analyst, Robert Prechter. The Dow responded with a record points drop of 91.55 to 2548.63, and a hesitant recovery at the beginning of the second week was snuffed out abruptly by another disappointing set of trade figures followed by a renewed slide in the dollar. On Wednesday 14th October, the Dow lost 95 points, the following day another 57, and no relief was in prospect for Friday after a hike in prime rates to 9¾%.

At one with the elements

The London market had not been upset very much by the news from New York, and the FTSE closed at 2322 on Thursday 15th October. There was a widespread conviction that "they" would ensure a firm market for the BP sale later in the month at 330p but any investor who might have been tempted to cut and run on Friday morning after learning of the prime rate rises would have found it practically impossible to deal. The previous night had witnessed one of the worst storms in living memory with London and the South East especially hard hit. Falling trees had disrupted road and rail services as well as telephone lines, and most stockbrokers and marketmakers were unable either to get to their offices or even to communicate with them. As a result Friday in London was a non-event for all practical purposes and the news next morning that the Dow had fallen a record 108.36 ensured that there would be pent-up panic selling on Monday. Systems failures meant that there were no figures available for Friday, and Monday's record 249.6 drop in the FTSE was measured against Thursday's close.

There was worse to come on Tuesday following Wall Street's Black Monday when the Dow dropped 508.32 points to 1738.42, its worst ever fall, inviting parallels with the Great Crash of October 1929. The FTSE lost another 250.7 bringing it back to 1801.6 and Tokyo fell by a record 3836 to 21910. With BP back to around 280p against almost 350p a week earlier, the outlook for the offer at 330p was not promising, but appeals by the US underwriters to have the issue abandoned were rejected by the Chancellor. Instead a buy-back floor price was conceded which meant that the Government actually benefited from the Crash by buying back at 70p shares it had sold three weeks before at 120p in partly-paid form.

Rescuing the dollar

To the extent that it was the continuing weakness of the dollar as a result of the failure of the US authorities to live up to their part of the Louvre Accord that had set the scene for the October Crash, the event inevitably made the problem more acute and the dollar promptly fell to new record lows against the currencies of its major trading partners. The latter, already fretting that the huge amounts expended on trying to support the dollar earlier in the year had done nothing but boost their own money supply and undermine their own low inflation policies, now had no alternative but to continue to play the game according to the American rules. Accordingly, they embarked upon a round of interest rate cuts on the post-Crash assumption that everything possible had to be done to halt the dollar's slide and restore confidence in the international financial system. The US authorities had won their poker game but the danger remained that it would prove to be a Pyrrhic victory unless a programme of fundamental corrections was embarked upon in the US as a quid pro quo for the supportive actions of its trading partners.

The aftershock of the quake that hit world stock markets on 19th October continued to reverberate for the rest of the year and beyond. However, fears of a rapid initial impact on consumer confidence and on investment as a result of the sharp reduction in financial wealth and the increased difficulty of obtaining equity finance appeared to have been exaggerated when evidence of any adverse effect on real activity proved hard to find. Indeed, the concerted efforts to avoid recession served to prolong artificially a boom that had already outlived its natural life. The day of reckoning had been postponed, not averted, but many took comfort from the thought that the Crash had occurred as a result of the temporary breakdown of a relatively untried, oversophisticated computerised trading system faced with a sudden and dramatic increase in cross-border activity. Also blamed was the huge amount of trading in futures and "derivatives" with their unquantifiable effect on "real" shares in the here and now. It was even suggested – with considerable justification – that the collapse had been a blessing in disguise in that it had pricked the bubble of asset speculation arising from five years of irrational concentration on capital gains rather than income, and heralded a return to more orthodox values.

Chancellor Lawson's contribution to this international rescue operation for the dollar was three ½% reductions in base rates, one at the end of October, one at the beginning of November and one at the beginning of December, bringing them back to 8½%. With the exchange rate at $1.86 at year-end against $1.68 at the time of the Crash, the reductions did not do much to help the dollar, but they may have eased the after-effects of Black Monday by helping to restore a degree of confidence in some investors, private and institutional, burdened by underwriting commitments and nursing massive losses on shares bought only weeks earlier. County Natwest, for example, reported losses of £69 million, £49 million of which was accounted for by Blue Arrow. Certainly an upbeat Autumn statement provided no case for base rate reductions, and the market remained nervous on fears that the Chancellor was following the example of the US and putting other policy objectives above the fight against inflation. Still, such anxieties did not prevent a useful rally developing in December, taking the FTSE out of its 1550-1650 trading range up to nearly 1800 before closing at 1712.7 for a gain of just 2% on the year but down 30% on the mid-July peak of 2443.4. Over the same period the average dividend yield had risen from 3.3% to 4% while the P/E had fallen from 15.1 to 12. **Eurotunnel**, however, was substantially undersubscribed and opened at 100p discount to the 350p offer price. Gilts ended the year at 88.99, well below their peak on inflation fears, but still up 5% overall, demonstrating the appeal of quality bonds for investors who had witnessed the devastating vulnerability of even the most blue chip of equity investments. Wall Street's performance was much in line with that of London, losing practically all the year's gains and ending not much better than at the start of the year, up just 2% at 1938.8.

Hanson buys Kidde

Hanson had another successful year. A run of relatively minor disposals preceded the interim figures which exceeded best expectations with a 97% advance to £312 million, including a six-month contribution from Imperial. Then in August came the biggest US bid yet with an agreed $1.7 billion offer for Kidde, a conglomerate with over a hundred subsidiaries all operating in basic industries and ripe for rationalisation. Hanson's earnings growth in 1988 was now assured. Results for the first nine months of 1986/87 announced in late August saw the shares up to a peak for the year of 195p on a prospective P/E of 14 given a likely full year total of around £725 million. This remarkable performance did not prevent the savaging of the shares in the wake of the October Crash, and even though the annual profits came out at £741 million, they ended the year at 127p, down 35%. Hanson also took two "investment" stakes during the year, one of 3% in **Morgan Grenfell** and one of 5% in **Midland Bank**, typically both "name" companies fallen on hard times.

Vodafone underpins Racal

Racal's 8.4% gain at the interim level to £25.2 million was notable for the first move into the black by the telecommunications division based on Vodafone. The figure was a modest £97,000 against a loss of over £7 million, but forecasts of a £10 million profit were made for 1987 ranging up to £100 million in 1990. Even the failure of group profits to match estimates of £110 million for the full year by 10% failed to dent investor enthusiasm, and the shares surged ahead to a peak of 348p in September on confidence that Vodafone would ensure a total of at least £150 million in 1987/88. The shares suffered more than most leaders in the post-Crash shakeout and ended the year at 222p, down 36%.

Pilkington gets away

BTR's year began with a disappointment for new Chief Executive John Cahill, who had taken over from Sir Owen Green in November, when they were forced to drop the Pilkington bid. The proposed takeover had raised a major political storm as a result of the Government's failure to refer the bid to the Monopolies Commission, even though there were no obvious grounds for doing so. The Pilkington family had a lot of political clout and made good use of it in a climate where sentiment had turned against the megabid in the wake of the Guinness affair. The full year figures for 1986 provided some compensation in that they were considerably above best market expectations at £505 million, a 40% advance marking the company's twentieth successive year of growth. Interim profits for the current year announced in September showed a continuation of this trend with a 38% gain to £280 million and most commentators agreed that at this stage, BTR had the edge over Hanson in the "organic growth" stakes. The shares peaked at 374p in September and managed to lose 100p, or 27%, in the final quarter.

Williams and Tomkins keep buying

Williams achieved the peak of its popularity in 1987, overcoming any disappointment that might have been caused by the narrow failure of its £540 million bid for veteran engineering conglomerate, Norcros. Profits for 1986 more than tripled to £22.9 million on turnover doubled to £206 million, and the shares rose another 10p on the news to 738p where the market capitalisation was £347 million. Then in June the shares were suspended at 835p ahead of the purchase for £250 million, to be funded by a share placing, of Reed International's DIY division, comprising some of the best brand names in the business in the shape of Crown Paints and Polycell as well as the paint interests in North America. This deal was widely regarded as a major coup for Rudd and McGowan and the shares continued to gain ground ahead of the interim results due in September. They did not disappoint either and the figure of £18 million was taken as an indication of full year profits of over £50 million, leaving the shares at 927p on a prospective P/E of 15. After a 2 for 1 scrip, the shares topped out at 347p and ended the year at 219p, down 37% as the high-flying conglomerates tended to fall out of favour with investors.

The year was also a brilliant one for Greg Hutchings and **F.H. Tomkins**. January saw interim profits for 1986/87 practically quadrupled to £9.3 million, and in May he announced the purchase of US gun makers Smith & Wesson for $112 million in cash and shares. This 135-year-old company, with one of the best known brand names in the world, had a 30% share of the US market but had recently run into problems, losing an important US Army contract to Beretta. The deal had been masterminded by Hutchings' alter ego in America, Richard Carr, in a partnership clearly based on the Hanson-White model. Full year profits once again exceeded best expectations at £30 million, also quadrupling, and estimates for the following year were pencilled in at £42 million plus, as rationalisation benefits continued to flow. After peaking at 320p, the shares ended the year at 220p, down 31%.

Polly Peck finds new friends

Continuing with his plans to diversify geographically and to reduce **Polly Peck**'s dependence on the Near East, in March Asil Nadir contrived a £20 million placing of stock at 203p with institutions, the proceeds to be spent on expanding the produce distribution network in Western Europe. The shares moved ahead steadily in the first half of the year, passing the old £36 peak in May thanks to vigorous buying of the new ADRs by US investors whose shareholdings now topped 20%. The interim results, with profits up 18% at £36.9 million, did not disappoint and at 296p the shares were selling on a prospective P/E of around 6 assuming a full year total of £83 million. The shares continued to advance throughout the summer, eventually reaching a high of 422p just before the Crash on the announcement that the electronics business was being expanded four-fold by the acquisition of Capetronic in the US for $35 million. Full year profits revealed in December were above target at £86 million, and the shares, now back to 260p, were on a prospective P/E of 5. They rallied strongly during the rest of the month to close at 288p.

Picking up the pieces

Among the principal casualties of the October Crash were the "shells", tiny quoted companies with a vestigial business, control of which had been bought by one or more entrepreneurs. Suspended pending reorganisation and refinancing, they would then return to the market after tranches of the increased capital had been placed with friends of the new management and favoured institutions. The first day of dealing would see a mad scramble for stock by small private investors, alerted to the situation by the City pages and by the specialist 'penny share' publications, resulting in a meteoric rise in the share price.

There was nothing new about the idea. Slater had done it in 1964 with H. Lotery, and more recently so had Asil Nadir with Polly Peck. But now with a bull market roaring away and mass public participation, everyone was trying to get in on the act. Entrepreneurs of whom no one had ever heard had to do no more than announce that they had gained control, raise some money on the strength of as yet unspecified acquisitions, and the share price would soar away. They were then in a position to use their paper to take over established companies and to come out with rights issues to raise even more cash.

The South Africans, always keen to sense a favourable business climate, were early on the scene following in the footsteps of Michael Meyer who had made such a success in building up **Emess Lighting**. Kenneth Maud took control of tiny **Peek Holdings** in August 1986 with the aim of turning it into a leader in applied electronics and industrial technology, and after a rights issue at 2½p saw the shares soar to 160p at their peak in the summer of 1987. Over this period he managed to make some useful acquisitions, but too late to do so were Daryll Phillips who tried to build a media services empire with **Acsis**, and Bruce McInnes who planned to turn **Charles Baynes** into a specialist engineering group. They did not make their move until late in June 1987 and although the impact on their respective share prices was instantaneous and dramatic, it did not last long enough to enable any really advantageous acquisitions to be made. More successful was Hugo Biermann with **Thomson T-Line** which, thanks to a well-structured acquisition policy taking in bookmakers J. Coral, he managed to sell to Ladbrokes.

Other darlings of the small private investor – and of more than a few large institutions – were **Blacks Leisure**, **Platignum**, **Eagle Trust** and **James Ferguson** of Barlow Clowes fame, along with a number of fast-growing property developers like **Dares Estates**, **Randsworth**, **Speyhawk** and **Marina Developments**. The October Crash was a watershed for these speculative favourites as investors clamoured to sell in an unwilling market where the size had contracted and the spread had widened alarmingly.

A Week to Remember
October 15th-26th, 1987

Stock	Closing Price	Change					Closing price	
	Thur 15th	Mon 19th	Tue 20th	Wed 21st	Thur 22nd	Fri 23rd	Mon 26th	Mon 26th
FTSE	2301.9	-249.6	-250.7	+142.2	-110.6	-38	-111.1	1684.1
Barclays Bank	605	-84	-52	+37	-15	-7	-35	443
Br Telecom	262	-17	-20	+14	-15	+5	-4	223
BP	349	-34	-31	+11	-14½	+4½	-21	266
Glaxo	£143/8	-11/2	+13/8	-17/8	-5/8	-1/4	-1/8	111/8
Hanson	174½	-27½	-28½	+23	-5	-5	-5	124
ICI	£16	-113/16	-19/16	+½	-17/8	-3/8	-3/4	103/4
Land Secs	573	-50	-45	+20	-23	-27	-18	430
Marks & Spencer	251	-20	-18	+7	-13	+5	-9½	202

1988

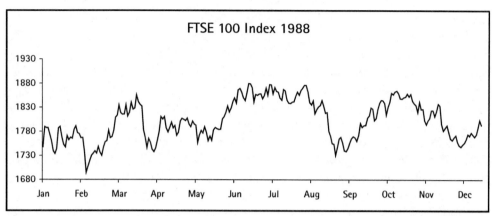

FTSE 100 Index 1988

Source: Thomson Reuters Datastream

Fuelling the spending boom

As far as the real economy was concerned, Black Monday witnessed the "crash that never was". The vision of world recession and financial collapse that had seemed so frightening then had quickly faded as consumers continued to spend and profits kept on growing. The rate of growth in 1987 looked like exceeding the estimate in the budget, actually accelerating in the second half, but for many commentators this remarkable performance evoked memories of the last days of earlier "dashes for growth" in 1964 and 1974 and their aftermath. The key question was over the nature of the motive power behind the boom, and in particular whether it owed more to rapid money growth and credit expansion than to increased productivity and competitiveness. The consensus seemed to be that it was a mixture of both, in which case the Chancellor would have to be ready to apply a touch of the brakes by raising interest rates and at the same time going easy on his promised tax cuts.

The situation was made even more delicate by the fact that the dollar was continuing to fall, still with no visible effect on the trade imbalances and thus the background remained as unstable now as it had been in the run-up to the October Crash. The consolation for investors, however, was the thought that a dollar that had halved against the yen and the D-Mark since 1985 was bound to have a dramatic effect on the competitive position of US exports before long, and that with stock markets in London and New York both down by some 30% from their 1987 peaks, the downward adjustment was in line with the post-War bear market average and the scope for a further decline had to be limited.

The Chancellor's dilemma

A sharp rise in the dollar in mid-January after a 25% fall in the US trade deficit was taken as some indication that policies were beginning to work and both markets rose, but London quickly relapsed when the Chancellor reacted to record bank lending figures and a higher than expected trade deficit in December, by raising base rates by half a point to 9%. Thereafter the London market became increasingly dominated by concern over the deteriorating trade deficit, the excessive growth in money supply, and the unrelenting pressure for higher pay in key public and private sectors. The Bank of England was already issuing warnings that interest rates might have to go up again in order to bear down on inflation but during the second quarter of the year the Chancellor chose to let an appreciating exchange rate do the job, at the same time giving himself room to compensate industry by cutting interest rates.

This phase began with the "radical, reforming" budget in mid-March which took 2p off the basic rate of tax bringing it down to the promised 25p, and slashed the top rate to 40%, as well as indexing allowances at twice the rate of inflation, all adding up to a £4 billion giveaway package. The equity market responded to the reduction in interest rates to 7½% by mid-May, rising above the 1800 level on the FTSE, but was unable to maintain it for long after the Chancellor abruptly changed tack. The problem facing him was two-fold. One aspect was that lower interest rates were much less important to low-geared UK industry than a high exchange rate, and the balance of payments deficit continued to rise alarmingly. The other was that lower interest rates helped to inflate domestic demand by fuelling a private sector borrowing binge, thus adding to inflationary pressures. The situation was aggravated further by the absence of a PSBR which had the reverse effect of "crowding out", leaving the field clear for the private sector, and by the fact that foreign investors saw sterling as a one-way bet.

Double jeopardy

Thus faced with the choice between letting the pound appreciate and further hurt the competitive position of industry, or cutting interest rates and abandoning his anti-inflation policy, the Chancellor decided to hang on to the anti-inflation policy at all costs and opt for a high exchange rate and high interest rates. Base rates rose in four half-point steps in June from 7½% to 9½%, and were increased progressively to reach 13% by the end of November, their upward march accompanied by an ever-widening trade deficit and rising inflation figures, as August's "temporary blip" at 5.7% began to take on a permanent air. The risk was that in due course an unsustainable "go" phase in the economy would be brought to an all too sustainable "stop" as a rising exchange rate reversed much of industry's competitive gains since 1986, and rising interest rates hit a personal sector that was historically grossly overextended, particularly in an obviously vulnerable property market.

The Autumn Statement, however, was looking for a controlled slowdown with a "soft landing" for the economy in 1989 as GDP growth slowed to 3% from 4½% in 1988, and the inflation rate topped out at 7% the following summer, falling back to 6¼% in the fourth quarter before returning to 5% in 1990. The dramatic expansion of the trade deficit was not explained away altogether satisfactorily by the official view that the balance of payments provided a safety valve for excess demand at home, and that the deficit would ultimately be self-correcting as inflationary pressures were tackled at their source. Indeed, a rise from £1 billion in 1986 to £2.7 billion in 1987 rising to a likely £15 billion in 1988, seemed to indicate that the "teenage scribblers" in the stockbrokers' offices had been much more prescient than Mr Lawson in June when they predicted a £10 billion trade deficit and base rates rising to 12%.

The year ended on a relatively cheerful note, helped by a buoyant Wall Street in the wake of the re-election of the Republicans, and by a sharp reduction in the November trade deficit, but there was no runaway enthusiasm. The massive intervention in support of the dollar since the October 1987 Crash had had an expansionary effect on the world economy in 1988, but while US trade performance had improved, the familiar pattern of current account deficits in the US matched by surpluses in Japan and Germany persisted. The problem had been managed, not solved, and it was clear that hopes for future macro-economic coordination rested very much on the working out of the international political process.

All in all, it had been a year of low activity in London with the institutions tending to sit on the fence and top up their holdings by way of rights issues, while the majority of private investors had gone to ground completely, switching their allegiance from shares to property. Even so, the £2½ billion public offering from **British Steel** was more than three times oversubscribed and the shares opened at a small premium in December. The FTSE closed the year at 1782.8, up just 2%, while the FT 30 was barely changed at 1447.8. Gilts continued to reflect inflation fears and Government Securities lost 1.5 points to 86.85. Gold shares remained depressed with FT Gold Mines down from 296 to 161 on the continuing failure of the bullion price to derive any benefit from the Crash. The Dow at 2144 gained over 10% on the year on growing expectations that the dollar was bottoming out and that the US economy was on course for a soft landing. Tokyo managed the best performance of all, crossing the 30000 level on the Nikkei Dow into new high ground by year-end.

Hanson prefers to be a seller

Hanson opened 1988 with an agreed £69 million cash bid for UK brickmaker, George Armitage, but it proved to be the sole purchase in a year which Lord Hanson later referred to as one for selling rather than buying. The following month another part of Kaiser Cement was sold for $195 million, a deal which meant that the whole of the acquisition price had now been recouped leaving Hanson with a rump making $20 million a year. First quarter profits were well up to expectations, recording a 12% gain to £169 million, but conglomerates were still out of favour, and at 137p the shares were selling at a 15% discount to the average market rating. A total of £800 million was pencilled in by analysts at this point, but this estimate was raised to £840 million after first half profits came in at £356 million, up 14%. August saw the sale of Kidde Fire Protection to UK's **Pilgrim House** for $254 million, and a nine-month profits total of £605 million which promptly raised full year hopes into the £845-850 million range. Before the end of the year another division of SCM, Durkee Industrial Foods, was sold to Unilever for $185 million bringing the total proceeds from the $926 million acquisition in 1986 to $1.3 billion, and Kidde Credit brought in another $70 million. A proposal almost to double the group's borrowing powers to £11 billion raised speculation about the next bid target, and the year ended with the encouraging news that profits for 1987/88 had exceeded all estimates at £880 million. The shares were now 157p and the P/E was in single figures.

Racal floats Vodafone

Racal's figures continued to be dominated by the extraordinary growth of its telecom division, and first half profits recorded a gain of 73% to £43.4 million, confirming hopes of a likely total for the year of around £150 million. In April the decision was made to float 20% of **Vodafone**, now to be called **Racal Telecom**, in order to generate cash for the parent company to pursue its ambitions to expand its security and datacom operations in Europe. The shares rose 72p on the news to 319p on the expectations of the effect on Racal of a growth valuation being accorded to its remarkable offshoot. Full year profits of £159 million did not disappoint, but everyone was waiting for the terms of the Racal Telecom flotation in October. At the 170p offer price the new shares were being sold on a prospective P/E of 30.5 on a forecast of profits practically doubling to £71.7 million. This put a valuation of £1.7 billion on the new company, which meant that with Racal still retaining an 80% stake, the whole of the rest of Racal was being valued at no more than £300 million, an anomalously low figure even bearing in mind a static profits performance. Interim profits announced in December were up 44% at £62.4 million, a gain due entirely to a further dramatic advance by Racal Telecom. Given their high rating at the flotation price, Racal Telecom shares received a cautious welcome from investors but quickly attracted buyers and closed the year at 184p.

BTR's results for 1987 proved something of a disappointment when the 17% gain in profits to £590 million fell short of forecasts ranging up to £700 million. The discrepancy was blamed on exchange rate effects, and did not prevent the shares from out-performing the averages later in the year as investors acknowledged the attractions of BTR's diversity of businesses and locations at a time when domestic concerns were dominated by rising interest rates and a consumer squeeze. The last quarter of the year saw two significant overseas purchases in Rockwell's measurement and flow control division for $437 million cash, and New Zealand carpet and soft furnishings company, Feltrax, for $572 million. The shares recorded a modest gain on the year at 294p.

Williams collects more "names"

The year opened for **Williams** with the completion of the purchase for £138 million of Berger Paints from Hoechst, a deal which left them as the country's second largest paint business. By the time the 1987 results were due, the shares had advanced to 274p and profits of £57.2 million did not disappoint. Estimates for the full year fell into the £115-120 million range, and interim profits of £50.5 million in September indicated that they were well on course. Meanwhile, in pursuit of market-leading brand names, Williams had taken a 3.9% stake in **Yale & Valor**, and added upmarket kitchen supplier **Smallbone** to its collection. The final deal of the year was the acquisition of electrical and electronic group **Pilgrim House** for £330 million in cash and convertible stock. The move was seen as providing Williams with a better balance of interests, effectively doubling the size of its industrial and military products divisions and increasing overseas exposure. The shares ended the year practically unchanged at 225p.

Tomkins looks to the US again

First half profits up 81% to £16.8 million pleased followers of Greg Hutchings and prompted forecasts of a total of around £44 million for the full year. This figure was comfortably exceeded at £47 million with the help of a $16 million contribution from Smith & Wesson, and the acquisition of Murray Ohio Manufacturing for $224 million was seen as providing scope for further substantial earnings growth in 1989. However, the shares did not do well over the year while investors chose to stay on the sidelines to see how the newer conglomerates fared in less favourable trading conditions.

Polly Peck expands its network

1988 was the year in which Asil Nadir began to expand his fresh produce distribution network. In February, a Spanish packer was bought to complement recent acquisitions in Marseilles and Rotterdam, in May a base was established in the Far East by buying the Rainbow Orient Company in Hong Kong for £36 million, and in June an American and another Dutch distributor were added.

Interim profits were well up to best expectations with a 30% advance to £48 million and the shares rose 29p to 318p on the announcement. In October, a £133 million rights issue was launched with the declared object of reducing borrowings in preparation for a series of acquisitions designed to increase the company's geographical diversity and to raise the quality of earnings. The move was welcomed both for cutting gearing from 135% to 60% and for reducing the dependence on the Near and Middle East from 36% to 10%. The make-up of the whole group now looked much better balanced with Agriculture falling to 39%, Electronics rising to 48% and Textiles static at 13%, with Leisure and Pharmaceuticals expected to grow to 10%. In addition, next year's profits were forecast to top £142.5 million on over £1 billion of turnover. Profits for 1987/88 were £107.3 million and the shares ended the year not much changed at 268p ex-rights.

1989

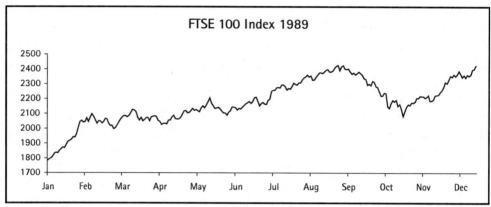

FTSE 100 Index 1989

Source: Thomson Reuters Datastream

You can't buck the market

Equity markets greeted the New Year with considerable enthusiasm, casting aside the caution of the last days of 1988, and the FTSE surged through the 2000 level at the end of January on record volume. The confident expectation seemed to be that high interest rates were working and that growth would slow to a more sustainable level of around 3% while inflation would fall back below 5% again. In any case, an average P/E of a little under 10 and a yield of over 5% was not taking too much on trust. Sentiment was boosted further by takeover fever when **GEC** and **Siemens** launched a £1.7 billion bid for **Plessey** which was promptly followed by a £7 billion consortium bid for GEC as part of Plessey's defensive tactics.

After reaching 2072 at the end of the first week in February, the market began to have second thoughts when inflation registered yet another upward 'blip' as the Retail Price index rose 0.7% to 7.5%. Worse was to come later in the month, when the Richmond by-election saw the Conservatives' majority slashed from nearly 20,000 to just over 2,500. The index dipped below 2000 again and fears were expressed that a credit-based boom as well entrenched as this one would not succumb quickly or easily and that the persistence of inflationary pressures could lead to a new round of rate rises with the attendant risk of overkill. However, the setback proved very short-lived and the FTSE rebounded to 2125 in mid-March in response to a budget designed to be tough on inflation as well as providing help for the lower paid and for savings. There were no changes in the basic rate of tax but thresholds and allowances were raised at a cost of £2 billion. The trade deficit was forecast to remain broadly unchanged at £14½ billion, inflation to fall to 5½% by year end and growth of money supply (M0) was to be held in the 1-5% target range. Growth in GDP over the year was scaled down from 3% to 2½%.

Too much, too late

The budget estimates were viewed with a degree of cynicism by many commentators who suspected that to date the Chancellor had chosen to give short-term growth priority over the longer-term battle against inflation, and that his choice had left the economy of the UK as the odd man out in an industrialised world where policy-makers remained determined to keep up the fight in spite of rising unemployment and painfully high interest rates. The further implication was that he would soon be forced to change tack as the UK fell increasingly out of line with its trading partners and sterling came under pressure. This is precisely what happened towards the end of May when the pound fell sharply against both the dollar and the D-Mark, and base rates were raised to 14%.

The dilemma facing the Chancellor was given even more point the day after when the April trade deficit was seen to have widened dramatically, indicating a total for the year approaching £18 billion against the budget estimate made barely a month earlier. A deficit at this level looked much more than a symptom of excess domestic demand. There was a much publicised clash of opinion between the Chancellor and the Prime Minister backed by her personal adviser, Sir Alan Walters, over the management of the exchange rate, with the former wishing to peg the pound at close to DM3 while the latter wanted to let it find its own level, and if this had a lot to do with the deterioration of the trade deficit as Mrs Thatcher prevailed and the pound soared to over DM3.20, Mr Lawson also came in for criticism for underestimating the strength of demand in the wake of the abolition of credit controls and his failure to reduce wage inflation. Now he found himself unable to bring down interest rates without precipitating another sterling crisis, and if he kept them where they were or even raised them again, then he would run the risk of tipping the economy into recession.

Weight of money rules

Throughout the summer months the problems facing the Chancellor and the economy made no impact at all on the equity market. By the end of July the FTSE had crossed the 2300 mark to record a new high for the year, totally ignoring gloomy surveys from the CBI, falling retail sales figures, and a further deterioration in the trade deficit. A much greater influence was the strength of institutional cash flow, relatively few rights issues and a number of major bids including the £13.5 billion consortium bid for **BAT**, **Boots** paying £900 million for **Ward White**, **Bass** buying **Holiday Inns** for £2.6 billion, and the sight of the Dow actually surpassing its August 1987 high point.

On 1st September the FTSE moved above the 2400 mark, but a month later worse than expected August trade figures, followed by a 1% rise in German interest rates, prompted an increase in base rates to 15%. The index lost over 100 points in three days as the pound failed to benefit but instead fell sharply to below the DM3 level. Simultaneously, Wall Street took its worst knock since Black Monday with a 190-point fall on news of the collapse of the United Airlines buy-out following the failure to syndicate the required $7.2 billion financing. The Bank of England added to the general air of despondency with a warning that base rates at 15% "challenged the assumption" upon which much of the record £30 billion of bank lending for property development had been based. Then Nigel Lawson rocked the market at the end of October by announcing his resignation as Chancellor. The news sparked an 80-point fall in the FTSE to 2082, not least because it served to emphasise the deep divisions within the Cabinet, but within three days the index had made up all the ground lost as the new Chancellor, John Major, declared his commitment to the defeat of inflation and the maintenance of a "firm exchange rate".

John Major becomes Chancellor

The ex-Chancellor made no secret of the reason for his resignation, which essentially was over exchange rate policy and the Chancellor's "right to manage", although less generous commentators thought that, knowing his policies had initiated and continued to fuel an unsustainable private sector credit-based boom, he was simply getting out from under before it all came tumbling down. All eyes were now on John Major to see how he would manage both the economy and Mrs Thatcher. The autumn statement in mid-November made it clear that it was not going to be a simple task. A sharp slowdown was forecast for 1990 with domestic demand stagnant and inflation rising to over 7%. The balance of payments deficit, now likely to total £20 billion in the current year, was expected to fall to £15 billion in 1990 while growth, which had already been downgraded to 2% in 1989, was predicted to fall further to 1¼% in 1990 or ¾% ex-oil.

This depressing picture was given substance a week later when **Coloroll** reported halved interim profits, **Tarmac** issued a profits warning, and a whole string of companies announced lower earnings or losses and dividend cuts. Equity buyers, however, looked at Ford's £1.6 billion bid for loss-making **Jaguar**, sterling being allowed to slip below DM2.80, questioned the strength of Mr Major's dedication to a firm exchange rate, and pushed the FTSE to over 2400 again by year end, oversubscribing £5.24 billion of water privatisation issues in the process. The Christmas rally was given further impetus by the failure of a Thatcher leadership challenge in the first week of December and by the Dow moving back into new high ground to 2753.2 on the back of prime rate reductions and the lowest trade deficit in five years. Given that the forecasts at the beginning of the year for inflation and the trade gap had both turned out to be gross underestimates and that the growth prediction also had to be scaled down drastically, equities did well to record a gain of about a third in 1989, taking the FTSE to 2422.7. Expectations still favoured a slowdown in growth rather than outright recession, and gilts similarly looked upon inflation as a greater threat than deflation, their index losing 3% over the year to

84.29. Tokyo rounded off an exciting year by hitting a new all-time high point in December of 38915.

Measure for Measure

One of the problems arising from the pursuit of monetarist policies was the difficulty of establishing a yardstick upon which to base those policies. A growing realisation of this fact led the Bank of England to conclude that "any choice of dividing line between those financial assets included in, and those excluded from, broad money is to a large degree arbitrary, and is likely to be invalidated by developments in the financial system." By the end of the decade, M3, M4 and M5 had come to be regarded simply as a useful source of information, not as indicators whose behaviour should prompt an automatic policy response. M0, the narrow measure comprising mostly notes and coins in circulation and bank deposits at the Bank of England, was now the only monetary aggregate targeted by the Government to judge if high interest rates were working.

Hanson buys Goldfields

The year began quietly enough for **Hanson** with a string of US disposals from Kidde, SCM and Kaiser totalling some $33 million, and then Hygrade Foods was sold for $140 million. First quarter profits were well up at £195 million, a rise of 15%, and net cash holdings of over £1 billion were reported. The next few weeks saw this figure augmented by £224 million from an MBO of Allder's plus £25 million from Elizabeth Shaw Chocolates, with another £26 million coming from the sale of Barbour Campbell in Northern Ireland. Before the end of June $400 million came in from the sale of Smith Corona and the stake in Midland Bank was disposed of for a "substantial premium". Then came the biggest bid ever with a £3.1 billion offer for **Consolidated Goldfields**, already strenuously resisting a £3.2 billion offer from rival South African mining house, Minorco. That bid had been deadlocked first by a reference to the Monopolies Commission and then by complex challenges in the courts, and typically Hanson timed its intervention to maximum advantage. Goldfields finally agreed to accept an offer of £3.5 billion and Hanson walked away with a considerable prize. Disposals were not long in coming and simultaneous with the release of the nine-month figures showing a 23% advance to £742 million, the sale of the South African Goldfields assets for £368 million was announced. By November the London head office had been closed down and all the staff dismissed, and four of the US subsidiaries went for $650 million. Hanson rounded off a bumper year with profits topping £1 billion for the first time against £880 million. The shares were now 228p, well up on the year but still selling on a modest enough P/E of 11.

Racal Telecom takes over

Despite some relatively minor acquisitions in the US and an ADR listing for **Racal**, 1989 was still very much **Racal Telecom's** year. Thus the latter's profits surge from £37 million to £85 million helped the parent to a 29% advance for 1988/89 to £178 million. Accelerating demand resulting in a 72% rise in RT's turnover to £194 million had much the same effect in the first half of 1989/90, when its profits rose 146% to £75 million and Racal's, 32% to £82.5 million. During the year RT's share price reached a high of 557p, more than three times the original issue price, while Racal's also benefited from its popularity, topping 575p.

BTR back in the fast lane

If **BTR's** 1987 results had caused some disappointment, the company redeemed itself with those for 1988. A 39% advance to £819 million on turnover up by 32% was in the best BTR tradition, fully justifying the 75p rise in the share price during the first three months of the year to 370p. Organic and acquisition growth figured roughly equally in this result and with £1.5 billion to spend in the current year, there was no hint of a slowdown. Two European acquisitions were announced in March, one for $28 million in Italy and one for $10 million in France, both makers of roll covers for paper-making machinery. August saw a sharp rise in the share price to over 450p on a statement from US financiers and deal-makers, Kohlberg Kravis & Roberts, that they intended to buy 15% of BTR with the aim of creating a partnership of their financial clout with BTR's industrial management skills. Given BTR's superb track record it was difficult to see what KKR could do for the company, and some commentators saw it as an attempt by a speculative and opportunistic operator in a nearly played out market to hitch its wagon to a more solid and reliable star. BTR's interim figures were well up to the mark at £513 million, a gain of 40%, and the shares closed the year at 465p.

Williams takes it easy

Williams' profits for 1988 announced in March fell neatly into the target range at £116 million to record a 101% advance on turnover up by 78%. It was announced that no major acquisitions were planned for 1989, and the emphasis in the following months was much more on disposals. In April, four engineering businesses were sold to B. Elliott for £22.5 million, and in May, American Electrical Components went in an MBO for $40 million. Then at the time of the interim figures in September, up almost 50% to £75 million, it was announced that the motor distribution business, **Pendragon**, would be given to shareholders. The shares did not live up to best expectations, and after a brief flurry in November on a false takeover rumour which sent them up to over 300p, they closed the year at 267p with a P/E of under 10 on fears that the DIY slump would affect profits in the current year and beyond.

Tomkins consolidates

Interim profits of £19.1 million, up from £16.8 million, were not as spectacular as followers of Greg Hutchings had come to expect but nonetheless they demonstrated solid growth. This low profile but creditable performance continued in the second half and full year figures came out at £65 million for a gain of 38%. The shares rose 11p to 266p on the announcement with buyers reassured by the fact that the group had done well over a difficult period, was ungeared and had £300 million to spend.

Polly Peck buys Del Monte

Asil Nadir continued his buying spree aimed at expanding Polly Peck's geographical network. In January, a West German fruit importer was bought for £15 million, 90% in shares, together with one on the West Coast of the US, and March saw the acquisition of a 21% stake in a Hong Kong supplier of household appliances. Results for a 16-month period to end December 1988 announced in April saw the forecast total of £142.5 million comfortably exceeded at £144 million, and Lex commented that as Polly Peck "continued to raise the quality of its earnings and reduce its geographical dependency on the Near East, it was shifting from an erratic and opportunistic trading group into a truly international electronics and agricultural business". The writer added prophetically that the group had "not entirely put its reputation for nasty surprises behind it", and expressed concern that borrowings continued to rise to pay for capital expenditure yet to be reflected in earnings. He added that the group had generated less cash in the last 16 months than in the previous 12, partly because of inexplicably large cash adjustments of £99 million to compensate for the weakness of the Turkish lira, but that a P/E of 7 with the shares at 320p took "that sort of thing" into account. June saw a listing obtained on the Swiss exchanges, and also the unexplained resignation of managing director, Tony Reading. Then in September a £283 million rights issue was announced to help fund the purchase for $875 million from Nabisco of Del Monte fruits. The shares surged to 369p on the news given the obvious strategic logic of buying on 12 times earnings probably the world's leading fruit brand name which could be used to cover all Polly Peck's produce. Since Del Monte was No. 1 in pineapples and No.3 in bananas, the deal made Polly Peck into the world's third largest fruit company. There was an added bonus in that Polly Peck would continue to benefit from the huge advertising budget of Del Monte's canned fruit operations retained by Nabisco. At the same time interim profits of £64.4 million were announced, representing a gain of 34% on turnover up 65% to just over £500 million.

Nadir reaches his zenith

Asil Nadir was now achieving for his company the aura of respectability that had eluded it for so long, and during the remainder of the year he continued to make all the right moves. A 30% stake was taken in Sansui, the troubled Japanese electronics company, rescuing it and at the same time providing Polly Peck with tied manufacturing capacity to feed into its distribution network. Then the textile division was sold for £38 million and a sale and leaseback of Del Monte's cargo ships was planned to bring in another $200 million plus, all with the aim of reducing gearing, which had crept up again thanks to recent purchases, to 105% this year and to below 75% by the end of 1990. The shares closed the year at around 400p, near to their best ever level. Polly Peck now had an equity market capitalisation of some £1.5 billion and had joined the FTSE100 index of the country's leading companies.

Ferranti bites the bullet

In September 1987, defence electronics and missile manufacturer **International Signal & Control** (ISC) had merged with **Ferranti**, a move widely acclaimed as one of mutual benefit with the marketing abilities of James Guerin and his team being enhanced by Ferranti's technical skills. All seemed to be going well until May 1989 when Mr. Guerin and associate Claude Ivy announced that they were quitting the group to "pursue their private interests in the preferred environment of a small, privately owned company". The shares fell 3½p to 104½p on the news and on County Natwest's modest downgrading of their profits estimate, but Ferranti was still regarded as a "good two-way bet" on a bid and on its order prospects. A month later the shares fell 15p to 82p on a statement from the company that profits could fall by as much as 20%, and in mid-September they were suspended at 73½p given the likelihood of "a substantial loss on overseas contracts managed by ISC subsidiaries", unofficially estimated to be around £150 million. Later in the month Ferranti quantified the figure by writing off £185 million, and legal proceedings were launched against Mr Guerin who, it now transpired, had sold all his 31.8 million shares in July and August.

The giant killers

1989 was the year the fee-driven superbids came to Britain. Devised by merchant bankers, they targeted well-known conservative companies with the avowed aim of "maximising shareholder value", and the necessary cash was provided by a consortium of banks, institutions and companies specially created for the purpose. The first bid was unveiled in January as a tactic in Lazard's defence against **GEC's** unwelcome approach to **Plessey**, but the £7 billion counterbid failed to get off the ground. The plan to break up a cash-rich and admittedly rather staid GEC with a view to giving the company "a new strategy and direction and maximise shareholder value" was not convincing in the light of Lord Weinstock's obvious achievements, and one by one the consortium's prospective members dropped out or joined the GEC camp. Within ten days it was all over, to the considerable embarrassment of Lazards and of Barclays which was to lead the consortium.

Then in July came a £13.5 billion bid for **British American Tobacco**, making it the biggest ever launched in the UK. It had been thought up by Jimmy Goldsmith, Jacob Rothschild and Kerry Packer, who planned to unbundle what they saw as an untidy mix of Third World tobacco interests and First World financial services, once again with the ostensible aim of benefiting shareholders. BATs put up a vigorous defence and shareholder loyalty won the day for Sir Patrick Sheehy and his board. Shareholders of both companies clearly viewed their conservative managements as to be supported rather than prodded into more adventurous paths. Before long, the banks and institutions that had created **Isosceles** to pay over £2 billion for supermarket chain **Gateway**, with only a 10% equity base, must have wished that their bid too had failed.

The collapse of the $7.2 billion financing plan for the buy-out of United Airlines marked the end of these attempts to channel all the loose money in the system into frankly speculative deals, but did not prevent the BIS from commenting ruefully on the "apparent propensity of the banking system to make repeated mistakes on a rather grand scale".

1990

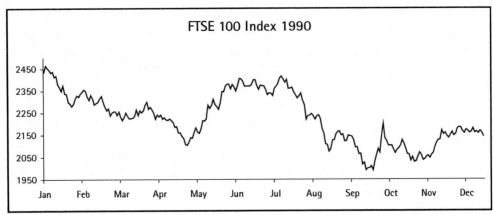

FTSE 100 Index 1990

Source: Thomson Reuters Datastream

'If it isn't hurting, it isn't working'

An *FT* survey of analysts' forecasts at the beginning of January revealed that most believed the UK economy would still manage to avoid a recession in 1990 and return to steady growth in 1991. Base rates were predicted to fall to 13% by the end of the year and to 11% in 1991, while inflation was expected to fall from the present rate of 7.7% to 5.5% in 1990 and to 4.8% in 1991. A similar downward path was forecast for the trade deficit from £20 billion to £15 billion to £12.5 billion. However, little change was looked for in the number of unemployed at 1.7 million. Chancellor Major's New Year message included the celebrated phrase "if it isn't hurting, it isn't working" but the clear implication that the earlier excesses which had resulted in a huge balance of payments deficit and an inflation rate well above the OECD average would have to be paid for by a corresponding period of below average growth, failed to upset the market, at least initially.

The first week of the New Year saw the FTSE at last breaking through its July 1987 peak to reach 2463.7 accompanied by the Dow moving above 2800 for the first time. Frankfurt, too, was hitting new highs as investors took the view that a united Germany would create a new powerhouse in the European bloc. This burst of enthusiasm proved to be short-lived as bond markets worldwide suddenly weakened dramatically on fears that inflation was more likely than recession as governments found it difficult to maintain their resolve in the face of an economic downturn. By the end of the month the Dow had lost some 250 points and Tokyo over 2000, while London's FTSE was back to 2322 on growing signs of corporate distress in the retail sector as a result of the virtual collapse of consumer demand. **Lowndes Queensway** and **Magnet** were finding out all too soon the double disadvantage for leveraged buyouts in industries where demand is also interest rate-sensitive.

Given a continuing run of adverse company news and economic numbers pointing to a far more serious slowdown than had been expected, the London market held up surprisingly well throughout the spring. Institutional investors still seemed to be taking the view that the means of achieving lower inflation had to be painful and thus apparently bad news was regarded as indicative of good news further down the line. This resilience was tested just as severely by the Government's political problems as the storm over the poll tax raged and Labour opened up a nineteen-point lead ahead of the Mid-Staffordshire by-election and then won it, overturning a 14,654-seat Conservative majority in the process. Leading "wet", Peter Walker, quit the Cabinet at the beginning of March.

The budget was seen as neutral with a touch of laxity, evidencing John Major's preference for gradualism in contrast to overkill, but anxiety began to grow in mid-April when both the earnings and inflation figures rose sharply to 9.5% and 8.1% respectively, putting paid to hopes of an early cut in interest rates. Another big rise in the trade gap for March plus news that a receiver had been appointed to major construction company **Rush & Tomkins**, knocked the FTSE back almost to 2100 at the end of April. It then staged a rapid recovery into the 2300-2400 band on growing speculation about the benefits to the economy that would flow from joining the European Exchange Rate Mechanism (ERM). This was what Nigel Lawson had wanted to do in 1989, but now that Mrs Thatcher had dropped her opposition to the idea, the way was clear for John Major to do so.

To join or not to join...

The pros and cons of joining the ERM were debated vigorously throughout the summer months. Those in favour saw it as the surest way to introduce a degree of monetary discipline into an inflation-prone economy with a long tradition of "muddling through". They had no illusions that it would be an easy process since industry would have to learn to take decisions on no-devaluation assumptions instead of looking for a lower exchange rate to validate their failure to control costs. In fact, they saw ERM membership as presenting the only possible remedy for the long-standing defects of the UK economy in that a combination of rising costs with a fixed exchange rate would soon solve the problem of excessive wage rises, and do so the hard way. After all, Chancellor Lawson had done his bit by sharply reducing direct taxation and it was now up to the private sector to fulfil its part of the bargain by accepting the discipline of a firm exchange rate in the absence of any credible policy based upon voluntary restraint.

Those who opposed entry did so largely on the grounds that the country's financial and industrial systems were incapable of producing sustainable non-inflationary growth and that the greatest economic successes had taken place during periods of devaluation. Furthermore, they argued, giving up the freedom to juggle with the exchange rate would be the last in a long line of abdications ranging from import controls, exchange controls, incomes policies, low-cost food imports and credit controls, leaving the UK economy rudderless.

Iraq invades Kuwait

Given that informed opinion believed ERM entry would take place some time in the autumn and that the equity indices remained close to the tops of their trading ranges, it was clear that markets saw membership as a bull point. Certainly it was enough to offset a run of corporate disasters as **Coloroll** and **Lowndes Queensway** went to the wall and rumours swirled around **Parkfield**, but the Iraqi invasion of Kuwait at the beginning of August added a quite different dimension of uncertainty and markets fell sharply. A rocketing oil price seemed to assure both higher inflation and a global economic slowdown and the consequences if a shooting war developed were almost too awful to contemplate.

By the end of August, the FTSE had dropped to 2100 while the oil price had risen to over $30 a barrel, reviving sterling's petrocurrency status and evoking memories of what high interest rates, together with an overvalued currency, had done to UK industry in the early 'eighties. The Dow was a little more resilient on ultimate safe haven considerations outweighing normal economic calculations, but Tokyo, which had been falling throughout the year, crashed through the 25000 level. Worries about the course of the oil price were relieved to some degree by OPEC's agreement to raise production to counter the shortfall from Iraq and Kuwait, but fears remained about what would happen to oil production if a full-scale war broke out in the Gulf.

Meanwhile in the UK, evidence of acute corporate distress was mounting almost daily. **Parkfield**, once the best performing share in the All Share index, collapsed under the weight of its bank debt, **Polly Peck** was obviously in serious trouble, and the share price of prominent property development companies nose-dived as asset values sank and debt servicing costs rose. The FTSE responded by dipping below 2000 at the end of September. Interestingly, this gloomy background failed to deter **Ratners** from continuing to demonstrate its "insatiable appetite for deals" and paying $400 million for Kay, the loss-making US jewellery store chain.

The good news on the anti-inflation front, if it could be called good in such a context, was that money supply growth in terms of M0, the narrow measure, was back into the 1-5% target range. It was now clear that the monetary squeeze, begun in mid-1988, was working by curbing output and demand with distressing consequences for companies and individuals but as yet with no discernible effect on prices and wages, both now rising at rates in excess of 10% per annum. This left the Chancellor with the unenviable problem of how to head off a wage/price spiral developing later in the year without precipitating a recession, which could prove disastrous for the Conservatives' electoral prospects, all at a time when a degree of relaxation looked essential after base rates had stayed for a whole twelve months at 15%.

Sterling joins the ERM

John Major chose to try to solve the problem on 8th October by joining the ERM, and at the same time lowering base rates to 14%. The joining rate was DM2.95 in the wider band with a permitted 6% fluctuation either side. Despite the immediate obviously adverse impact on the open market sectors of the UK economy, markets welcomed the move and the FTSE recorded a gain of 130 points over the next two days to 2200. All of this and more was lost by the end of the month, partly on fears of full-scale war breaking out in the Gulf but also on John Major's admission that the slowdown had turned into recession after a fall in output for two consecutive quarters. ICI's 48% profits fall in the third quarter plus the announcement that it planned to cut capital spending by 10% in the coming year, did not help and neither did the loss of a Conservative safe seat to the Liberal Democrats at the Eastbourne by-election.

Discontent in the Conservative party was growing by the day and with the public opinion polls showing Mrs Thatcher to be the most unpopular Prime Minister in history, she became the obvious scapegoat. Her vigorous and uncompromising approach which had produced both victory in the Falklands and the defeat of the miners also served to alienate many of her Cabinet colleagues who did not appreciate themselves becoming the regular targets of the "smack of firm government". The pro-Europeans were particularly upset by her hardline stance against closer European union and her ringing denunciation of Jacques Delors' vision, "No! No! No!" in the Commons on 30th October. That speech, together with Sir Geoffrey Howe's smouldering resentment at his demotion from his post of Foreign Secretary the year before, provoked his resignation, accompanied by a personal statement to the House which launched a devastating attack on the Prime Minister's style of government. The event precipitated a full-scale leadership crisis. It was the last straw for the market and the FTSE reacted almost to the 2000 level.

John Major becomes PM

The rapid resolution of the leadership issue by the election of John Major in place of Margaret Thatcher was greeted with great relief by the markets and the FTSE rebounded to around the 2150 mark. The recovery was maintained until the end of the year, buoyed by UN backing for the use of force to expel the Iraqis from Kuwait and by the first decline of the year in the rate of inflation as the Retail Price Index fell from 10.9% to 9.7%. Nevertheless, the background was not encouraging enough to spark the sort of Christmas rally needed to prevent 1990 from becoming the first year out of the previous twelve in which the equity indices had not recorded an advance.

Hopes that interest rates had peaked were being balanced against a CBI survey revealing that industrial confidence was at its lowest level for ten years and that the recession was spreading with retailers reporting their biggest sales slump since 1980. It could still be argued that the recession was in the price, but the argument lacked conviction given the uncertainty surrounding the probable length and depth of the downturn together with the huge question mark that hung over the situation in the Gulf. This last factor threatened to dash all the hopes of the "peace dividends" that had been expected to flow from the break-up of the Communist bloc and the reunification of Germany. In the event the FTSE closed the year down 11.5% at 2143.5. Gilts, by contrast, although still down 2.5% on the year, had staged a significant recovery from their low point in the summer as bonds worldwide strengthened on "safety first" attractions and UK gilts specifically attracted buyers on post-ERM considerations that they now represented a clearly definable and lower currency risk.

Wall Street fared much better than other world markets, declining only 4.3% to 2633.6, buoyed by its growing "safe haven" characteristics, patriotic fervour and lower interest rates. Tokyo, on the other hand, went from bad to worse on fears over the stability of its banking system and the impact on the Japanese economy of the sharp increase in the price of oil. The Nikkei Dow closed at 23848, down 39% on the year.

Hanson proposes and disposes

For **Hanson**, 1990 was a year for sorting out some of the more complex aspects of its recent acquisitions, especially those arising from the takeover of Consolidated Goldfields. The release of first quarter results, up 15% to £225 million, was accompanied by the news that $504 million was to be paid for a large stake in Peabody Coal, the company which held the balance of the shares in Newmont Gold acquired by Hanson via Consgold. Later the rest of Peabody was bought for $715 million, giving Hanson full control of Newmont, the biggest gold producer in the US. A plan to make a public offering of Newmont failed to get off the ground, and then in a surprise move in October, a swap was arranged with Jimmy Goldsmith for his US timber and oil interests. Further disposals were made during the course of the year, notably of the housewares group Tucker (ex-Kidde) for $185 million. Serious discussions also were entered into with the Government over the possibility of Hanson buying **Powergen** ahead of the planned public offering.

Full year figures recorded a useful 21% advance to £1.29 billion and with cash balances of almost £7 billion plus an enlarged borrowing capacity, it was clear that nothing was out of Hanson's range. Nevertheless, the shares ended well down on the year at 185p, overshadowed in the final weeks by talk of vastly enlarged provisions at Peabody Coal to cover possible health claims.

Racal talks of demerger

Racal Telecom's full year profits for 1989/90 recorded a 95% gain to £165 million, while those of **Racal** were up only 13% at £201 million. It was clear that the offshoot would soon overtake its parent, and demerger talk became rife when interim profits for 1990/91 showed those of Racal Telecom at £122 million surpassing Racal's figure of £97.5 million and also making it clear that but for its share of the former's profits, Racal would have made a loss. In a dull market, the shares of both companies closed the year well down from their highs at 172p and 257p respectively.

BTR gets a new Chief

BTR's 1989 results, showing a 22% advance to £1.06 billion, were accompanied by the launch of its biggest bid since the abortive one for Pilkington. The target was **Norton Inc.**, a US abrasives, plastics and ceramics business with 113 plants in 26 countries and operating on margins of less than half those of BTR. The $1.6 billion offer was rejected but while acceptances continued to mount, the French glass giant St. Gobain entered the contest and managed to get Norton's agreement to a much higher offer. This was another major setback for BTR's ambitions and a $10 million profit on the sale of its stake in Norton was no consolation. BTR's urgent need to get its teeth into an important new acquisition was demonstrated by the half-time figures in September showing only a 6% gain to £530 million with earnings growth down to just 4%. The shares fell 40p to 318p on the news, which also led to a downgrading of full year forecasts and was taken as having adverse implications for the whole market.

In December, John Cahill stepped down from the post of Chief Executive in favour of Alan Jackson (54), who came in from BTR Nylex, the Australian associate which he had built from almost nothing in 1984 into Australia's largest industrial manufacturer providing 40% of BTR's overall pre-tax earnings. The appointment was widely welcomed but the shares still ended the year well down from their high point at 320p.

A testing time for Williams

Williams' profits advance to £153.5 million in 1989 was viewed as strictly historic for a group with a 40% exposure to the UK consumer market, and in order to justify its reputation as another Hanson or BTR it would have to do more than simply consolidate in a recession. Some fast footwork by Messrs Rudd and McGowan in May saw the sale of the UK and Irish paint interests for £240 million cash, a deal which at a stroke cut their dependence on the UK consumer to 25% and also reduced gearing from 60% to zero. The move, however, did nothing for Williams' popularity and when the interim profits in September showed an £11 million fall to £61 million, the shares dropped 13p to 217p for a prospective P/E of 9 on a downgraded total for the year of £120 million.

Tomkins survives a difficult year

With 35% of operating profits arising in the UK, **Tomkins** was reckoned to have done well to record a 22% gain to £23.3 million for the first half of 1989/90. The US side was also doing well with Smith & Wesson winning an important FBI order which served to compensate for its earlier pre-Tomkins loss of a US Army contract to Beretta. Then in June a major US acquisition was made in the form of Philips Industries, a diversified Ohio-based industrial company, for $550 million. At the same time a full year forecast was made of "not less than" £76 million, a figure that turned out in due course to be £77.1 million. The shares held up well for the first part of the year but suffered along with the other conglomerates, large and small, to end the year at 225p.

The bid that never was

Polly Peck began the year promisingly enough with the purchase of a Dallas-based fruit distributor, and the establishment of a joint venture with a French company to manufacture colour TVs in Turkey. The results for 1989 announced at the end of March showed profits well ahead at £161 million and Lex commented that this was a "familiar picture of startling but slightly impenetrable success with as usual no detail to speak of on the group's operations".

The shares were now 393p for a P/E of 7.6 and reservations about the still 100% plus gearing began to fade as, first, the sale and leaseback of the Del Monte ships brought in £142 million, and then the flotation of Vestel on the Istanbul market, together with the injection of all the electronic interests into Sansui, raised another £100 million. The shares reached a peak of 462p shortly afterwards but were back to just below 400p on Gulf influences in mid-August when Asil Nadir made an unscheduled announcement about his plan to stage a buy-out for the balance of the group he did not own. His declared reason was that Polly Peck was undervalued by the market, and the shares duly responded by rising 24p to 417p. Less than a week later he said he had dropped the idea after approaches from "significant institutional and private shareholders". The shares reacted instantly, losing 78p on the day to 324p.

An inspector calls

Things now began to go badly wrong for Asil Nadir. For one thing, the Stock Exchange was concerned that he did not appear to have discussed his buy-out plan with Polly Peck's board or its advisers and for another, the fact that funding for the buy-out was not in place, meant his announcement on 13th August could constitute an offence under Section 47 of the Financial Services Act by giving a false impression of the value of the shares. The company's fall from grace had been so rapid that considerable confusion and uncertainty existed. Even Polly Peck's Head of Public Relations, Dominick Henry, was quoted as saying "None of us here has any idea why the hell this is happening", as the share price fell another 15p to 265p at the end of August. All eyes were now on the half-time results due on 3rd September. They were better than expected with a 72% gain to £110.5 million after a £29 million first contribution from Del Monte, but the fact that net borrowings were still high at £864 million pointed out the problems of financing a buy-out. The following week saw exceptionally heavy trading in the shares on reports that Asil Nadir was buying at around the 285p level, and 21 million shares changed hands on a single day.

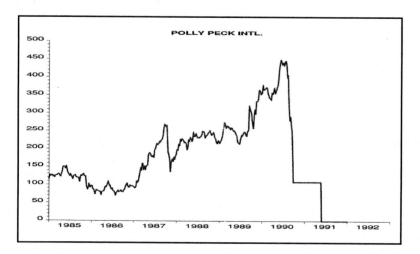

Then towards the end of the third week the shares began to slip and after falling 135p to 108p on 20th September, they were suspended on the Polly Peck board's request for a DTI investigation into recent events. Simultaneously, Asil Nadir was interviewed at the Serious Fraud Office. There was a statement from the board in early October that a liquidity problem existed but hopes of a bail-out by the Turkish government were soon dashed and loan payments were halted. The shares were still being traded on the Zurich exchange but they had collapsed to 1 cent by 24th October when administrators were appointed, offering little hope for UK investors. Subsequently Asil Nadir was arrested to face a number of charges relating to theft and false accounting, although he claimed that the downfall of his empire was the result of a Greek-inspired political conspiracy.

The rise and fall of Polly Peck ranks as the most spectacular of all booms and busts in stock exchange history, going from practically zero to £1.5 billion in nine years and then back to zero in five weeks. The full story has yet to unfold, but large and constant capital spending funded by debt seems to have stayed persistently ahead of returns from normal trading operations, with the true picture concealed in a fog of figures involving exchange rate juggling which regularly understated the former and overstated the latter. Once again quite where the auditors fitted into the picture is uncertain.

Parkfield overwhelmed by debt

The other principal corporate disaster of the year was as much a shock to the company's devoted fans as the downfall of Polly Peck was to its followers. It involved **Parkfield**, transformed by the American, Roger Felber, since 1983 from a loss-making foundry company by a series of acquisitions into a specialist engineering and distribution group making profits of £23 million in 1989. In the process it had become the best performing share in the All Share index, turning a stake of £1000 into one worth £120,000 by early 1990. The group's most recent move was into video distribution where it had become the market leader with a third share of the 60 million videos sold or rented in the UK. 1990 began encouragingly enough with the report of interim profits up 79% to £13.9 million, but the *FT* commented on the company's "irritating habit of taking profits from asset sales above the line", and then added that the prospective P/E of 12½ reflected a balance between growth prospects and the "long overdue corporate mistake". A few days later the shares touched their all-time high of 518p at which level the equity market capitalisation was just over £260 million. In fact it was not such a fair balance in that the "corporate mistake" when it came was of such magnitude that it destroyed the company.

By mid-February the shares had lost nearly 60p to 465p, but the first hint of real trouble came – as it so often does – with the sudden and unexplained resignation of a director. The shares fell another 30p on the news to 430p, but nothing more was heard from the company until late June, by which time the shares had slipped back to around 360p on persistent rumours of problems in the entertainment and video division, originally headed by the resigned director. This first official statement warned that following a sharp fall in second half profits for 1989/90, profits for the current year were unlikely to exceed last year's total of £23 million against widespread expectations of around £35 million. Attributing the prospective shortfall to management problems in the entertainment and video subsidiaries, Roger Felber added, "we are not talking about a disaster". The shares responded to the news by plunging to around 150p but persistent selling on what the company called "unfounded rumours" eventually led to their suspension at 48p in mid-July "pending clarification of the company's financial position". A few days later administrators were appointed, to discover that liabilities, mainly in the form of bank borrowings and leasing commitments, were far higher than expected at over £300 million. They certainly were talking about a disaster, and over the ensuing months the company was sold off division by division while Mr Felber departed for South America.

Sunk without trace

After making his name as boss of highly successful moneybroker, **Exco**, in the early 'eighties, John Gunn was invited to join the board of the long-established and conservatively run **British & Commonwealth** shipping and insurance empire founded by the Cayzer family. Before long he was appointed Chief Executive and the share price rose dramatically in anticipation of what new blood could do for this asset-rich but relatively undynamic group. Unfortunately a string of diverse acquisitions included **Atlantic Computer**, a leasing company, for the hefty sum of £417 million. Questionable accounting practices at Atlantic subsequently suggested that it was probably worthless at the time of purchase and its collapse in April 1990 brought a critical spotlight to bear on all the businesses bought by John Gunn. A vigorous disposal programme was already underway but it was too late to save the group and a year later administrators had to be appointed.

Savings & Loans looted

Wall Street fared surprisingly well during the year considering it had to deal with two of the biggest scandals in US history. The one that made the most headlines internationally was the collapse of **Drexel Burnham Lambert**, the country's fifth largest investment bank, following charges of stock manipulation, insider dealing and illegal trading in 'junk bonds', the creation of the company's highest profile employee, **Michael Milken,** and much used in hostile takeovers fuelled by debt . Far more serious was the scandal that engulfed the whole Savings & Loans industry , the US equivalent of UK building societies ,designed in the 1930s to promote home ownership. With assets in the form of long term, fixed low interest mortgages, they soon found themselves unable to compete with money market funds for deposits when interest rates began to rise in the 1970s, and inevitably a gap opened up between their funding costs and the income from their assets, threatening insolvency. The owners of S & Ls saw deregulation as the answer to their problems and in 1980 lobbied for a looser solvency and risk capital regime to enable them to pay market rates to depositors and lend into more potentially lucrative (if more risky) areas. This was a green light for practically every real estate developer in the country and over the next ten years some $150 billion was looted from the S & Ls in schemes involving fraud and corruption at the highest level, resulting ultimately in the collapse of over one thousand institutions. The affair came to an end with the formation of the Resolution Trust Corporation in 1989 to acquire the bad loans of the insolvent S & Ls at a cost to the US taxpayer of $124 billion.

1991

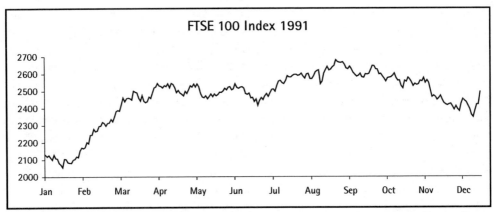

FTSE 100 Index 1991

Source: Thomson Reuters

The shooting war begins

The New Year opened on a cautious note with investors apprehensive ahead of the 15th January deadline for Iraq to begin withdrawing from Kuwait. The feeling was growing that force would have to be used and the first air strikes came as a positive relief to markets with the FTSE adding fifty points to 2105 and the Dow 115 to 2623 while Tokyo plussed over 1000 to 23450. After an immediate upsurge in the oil price to $35, within a couple of days it settled at around $20 after the US announced that it would release its reserve stocks. Gold, too, after a quick flurry to $411, fell back into the $360-370 range, which was below the level at the time of the original invasion last August.

The start of the land war two weeks later saw another sharp rise in London and New York which was extended as the war rapidly progressed to a satisfactory conclusion. In fact the war had gone better than anyone had dared to hope, and with oil price worries out of the way the prospect was for a further reduction in inflation which in turn would permit an easing of monetary policy worldwide and the removal of some of the pressures on the banking system. Thus the first week in March saw the FTSE into new high ground at over 2450, the Dow flirting with the 3000 level and Tokyo topping 26500.

Back to the economy

Unfortunately the victory celebrations could not sweep away entirely the idea that the recession in the UK was unique in the sense that the traditional means of stimulating a recovery, namely devaluation and cutting interest rates, were strictly limited by reason of having joined the ERM. This was all the more worrying given that the recession was showing signs of being more widespread and more severe than earlier predictions had suggested. The last six months had not helped, with UK exporters squeezed between a weak dollar and a strong D-Mark while facing slumping demand and high interest rates at home, and the reversal of the dollar's decline at the end of the Gulf War together with the first of a series of base rate cuts seemed to have little ameliorating effect. The budget with its 2-year phased reduction in Corporation Tax to 33% was welcomed but the forecast recovery in GDP growth to 2% from mid-1991 to mid-1992 was viewed with considerable scepticism as the numbers out of work rose to over 2 million in March and bank lending collapsed to its lowest level in fifteen years. In this context, the extra 2½% on VAT was not regarded as helpful either.

But perhaps the most worrying point of all was that the supposed constraints on stimulative action since joining the ERM had not prevented a cut in base rates from 15% to 11½% and an 8% depreciation against the dollar by the end of June, quite apart from the stimulus implied by the return to substantial deficit financing announced in the budget. A surplus of £800 million was to turn into a deficit of £7.9 billion in 1991/92, rising to £12 billion the following year before falling back to zero again in 1994/95. Taken in conjunction with CBI surveys revealing that the recession was bad and getting worse, that retail sales figures were casting doubt on the prospect of any consumer-led recovery and that money supply (M0) growth had practically stopped, this meant that the FTSE at close to 2500 on a prospective P/E of 17.5 looked as out of line with the real economy on the upside as it had been for months after the 1987 October Crash on the downside. Further substance to this view was given by ICI's 52% drop in first quarter profits and the fact that half of the £3 billion contingency reserve had gone in the first three weeks of 1991/92 to help fund rising unemployment and public sector pay deals. The implications of this second point for the budget's PSBR forecast were clear.

Wall Street shows the way

The obvious conclusion was that the London equity market was taking a lot on trust, following Wall Street's lead as the Dow moved above 3000 on indications that the recent cuts in the Federal Discount rate to 5½% were beginning to stimulate the flagging US economy. It may also have been giving some credence to Chancellor Lamont's predictions of an early recovery on the assumption that he still retained some power to assist it, all in the context of an election likely to be postponed until the late autumn or even the spring of 1992 as a result of Labour's recently established lead in the opinion polls.

Time was now on the Chancellor's side and it seemed a reasonable bet that some degree of recovery would manifest itself by then. The corporate sector had been quick to take advantage of the strength of the equity market – as indeed had the

Government with its hugely successful power company privatisation – and rights issues of over £5 billion in the first six months of the year had already exceeded the annual totals for 1990 and 1989. But July still saw new peaks for the FTSE and the All Share index with confidence boosted by another half-point cut in base rates to 11%, a surprise swing from deficit to surplus in the June trade figures, a 1.3% pick-up in retail sales in June, and the Chancellor's forecast of inflation down to 4% by the end of the year. The headline-making collapse of BCCI seemed to have little effect on the broad market despite its devastating impact on the Asian business community.

August and September saw the FTSE staying comfortably above the 2600 level – apart from a one-day rout on the Russian coup – assisted by another half-point reduction in base rates to 10½% and the Federal Discount Rate coming down to 5%. There were also numerous pronouncements from the Chancellor and the Prime Minister to the effect that the economy was "on course", that inflation was "licked", and that the "clouds of recession" were beginning to lift, views with which the Bank of England, the CBI and the *FT* poll of 23 economists all now concurred. Even the IMF predicted that the UK economy would grow by 2.3% in 1992.

Recovery? What recovery?

It was in the final quarter of the year, coincidentally around the anniversary of the UK joining the ERM, that faith in an economic recovery began to wane. Inevitably the level of the market then came into question since it had risen in anticipation of a recovery and of the increased chances of a third term for the Conservative administration that such a recovery implied. By mid-November the FTSE was bumping along the bottom of the 2550-2650 range and then a shock 120-point fall in the Dow on recession fears there, pushed it straight through the 2500 level. Three by-election defeats earlier in the month, a further fall in manufacturing output in the third quarter and a drop in October's retail sales did not help sentiment, and with deflationary worries now coming to the fore, neither did the October Retail Price Index showing the rate of price inflation slowing to 3.7%.

Those who had opposed ERM membership tended to blame the lack of recovery on the Chancellor's inability to apply the traditional stimuli of devaluation and interest rate cuts, contrasting his position with that of his US counterparts who were able to use both measures. The supporters of ERM membership continued to maintain that there should never have been any illusions about it being an easy option or one likely to show quick results. On the contrary, it involved a long and difficult process of adjustment, but it was already showing signs of working as UK interest rates and inflation levels converged towards the German levels. As for the US model, there was just as much anxiety there over a "no show" recovery, despite a weak dollar and the lowest interest rates for 25 years. This last point raised a question that was to concern markets well into 1992. What if the recovery was not just delayed but postponed indefinitely while consumers took the "cold turkey" treatment for structural inflation, giving debt reduction and the rebuilding of savings priority over present consumption? If this was indeed the case then the sharp increase in public spending announced in the budget and again in the Autumn statement – the PSBR was heading for £10.5 billion in the current year with double that in prospect for 1992/93 – did not threaten to "crowd out" private and corporate claims on funds, but rather filled what would otherwise have been a void.

Weighed down by evidence of a general industrial malaise aggravated by incidents like the death of Robert Maxwell, the failure of the **British Aerospace** rights issue and the problems of **Brent Walker**, the FTSE fell below 2400 at the beginning of December and against such a depressing background there was little expectation of a pre-Christmas rally developing. The signing of the Maastricht Treaty, with its initial favourable impact on the standing of the Prime Minister, sparked a 2-day advance to over 2450, but fears of a German interest rate rise which were soon fulfilled prompted a reaction of 100 points in the week leading up to Christmas.

What eventually turned the tide in the closing days of the year was a surprise cut in the US Federal Discount Rate of one whole point to 3½%. The effect was to send the Dow soaring back up through the 3000 level to end the year at 3168 for an overall gain of 20%. Fired by this example and inspired by the idea that Wall Street was signalling a recovery in the US economy that would give a jump start to the rest of the world, the FTSE recovered to 2493 by year end to record an advance of 16.3%. Gilts seemed to have put inflationary fears behind them and after peaking at 87.94 in September, closed the year at 86.26 for a gain of 5%, reflecting a growing interest in bonds on the view that a prospective permanent low inflation environment would mean a fundamental change in the relationship between bonds and equities to the advantage of the former. Golds once again disappointed with the FT Gold Mines index down 6% at 140 after bullion had lost nearly $40 over the year to $353. Tokyo continued to reflect anxieties about the health of the Japanese banking system in the wake of the further asset deflation that had taken place during the year, particularly in property and stocks. The Nikkei Dow at the end of December stood at 22,437, practically unchanged on the year, and unlike New York and London, demonstrating no signs of recovery.

Now Hanson slows down

Confirmation of the severity of the recession for those who still needed it, came with the release of **Hanson's** first quarter profits for 1990/91. At £241 million, they were up by only 7%, and by the end of the first half the figure of £586 million showed that the rate of advance had slowed to 3%. Estimates for the full year suggested that the group would be doing well to exceed last year's £1.29 billion by even the narrowest of margins. Still, Lords Hanson and White, who earlier in the year had announced their intention to stay in control for another five years, retained their capacity for surprise by taking a 2½% stake in ICI at a cost of £240 million, ostensibly "for investment purposes only". Despite this statement, a bid was widely expected and ICI immediately went on the defensive. Already partially reorganised and rationalised under John Harvey-Jones's chairmanship, ICI was undergoing a second wave transformation under his successor, Sir Denys Henderson, who was determined not to succumb to a bid from Hanson. Also helping ICI's defence was the fact that the political climate had changed and a megabid for a company that was practically a national institution could have proved a serious embarrassment to the government with an election looming. An undeclared battle was fought by the companies' respective PR agencies, generally considered to have ended in a victory on points for ICI. The tussle did not prevent Hanson from carrying on business as usual and in September a £350 million bid was agreed for **Beazer**, the UK's fourth largest housebuilder, now struggling with debt incurred in its recent takeover of Koppers, the second largest aggregate producer in the US. The deal was financed by part of a $4 billion loan from a consortium of banks over a 7-year period clearly raised with a further US acquisition in mind. Hanson's full year profits managed to maintain its 28-year growth record intact with a 3% gain to £1.31 billion but the shares ended the year only marginally ahead at 200p, with their standing not helped by the criticism levelled at the company by ICI.

The crack-up

The mysterious death of Robert Maxwell served to dispel a great deal of the mystery surrounding his media empire and simultaneously destroyed his reputation. Although never a popular figure, Maxwell was still admired for the ability and energy that had brought him fame and fortune. His early success in building up scientific publisher Pergamon Press was not without controversy when he clashed with would-be bidder Saul Steinberg of Leasco, but he went on to rescue British Printing Corporation and to defeat the powerful print unions in the process. In 1984 he won control of the ailing *Daily Mirror* and restored its circulation and its profitability. America was his next target and in rapid succession he bought the official Airlines Guide for $750 million and Macmillan's US publishing operations for $2.6 billion, both on borrowed money. As the recession took hold, debt servicing costs soon overtook cashflow and the share price of his flagship company, Maxwell Communication Corporation, began to fall. When a string of strategic disposals failed to stem the slide in the share price, Maxwell, it was subsequently revealed, resorted to a share support operation using money looted from the *Daily Mirror*'s own pension fund.

Racal fights off a bid

Racal, with its shares already well down on the threat to its markets posed by the Gulf War, took another tumble in January on its withdrawal from a potentially very profitable contract to install an internal telephone network linking government departments. However, by the time full year profits for 1990/91 were due in June, the share price had recovered to 230p thanks entirely to a much greater pick-up in the shares of Racal Telecom to 390p. The disparity in performance was explained by RT's 48% profits advance to £245 million beating Racal's £223 million total and confirming indications at half time that the rest of the latter's businesses were making losses approaching £25 million. The demerger terms announced in July were 57 shares in RT, now to be called **Vodafone**, for every 100 Racal. Almost immediately the Racal rump attracted bid speculation on the grounds that it represented an interesting mix of defence and marine electronics, the original core strategic radio business, data communications and security, all with great recovery potential and all undervalued as a result of being overshadowed for so long by Vodafone.

Then in September **Williams Holdings** made a surprise £703 million all-paper bid. Racal's chairman, Sir Ernest Harrison, immediately rejected the bid as "inadequate and opportunistic" and refused to meet or to provide Williams with any additional information. In early December he backed up his case by revealing first half profits recovering to £11.6 million and forecasting a total for the year of "not less than" £50 million, adding that ahead of a proposed demerger of Chubb, an offer of £450 million had been received. Williams promptly raised its bid to £739 million and a war of words began. Sir Ernest Harrison criticised the Williams management on the grounds that they were buyers not builders of businesses, and also for their accounting practices. Williams countered by relating the number of forecasts Racal had missed in recent years, but despite Williams' proven ability to extract higher margins from all its acquisitions, institutional loyalty to Sir Ernest was too strong and only 25.8% acceptances were received.

Third time lucky for BTR

In January a run of aggressive downgradings by analysts of earlier estimates of **BTR's** full year figures due in March knocked the share price below 300p, but it recovered rapidly to 375p ahead of the event. While still recording an 8% fall to £966 million, the first drop in full year earnings since 1968, the figure showed that the analysts had been overcautious and the shares rose to 402p on the news. There was some speculation that perhaps BTR, in company with Hanson, had reached a size which placed a limit on its capacity to grow, but new chief executive Alan Jackson's declared policy change towards a more aggressive acquisition and disposal programme seemed to carry more weight with investors. August duly saw both the disposal of Pretty Polly (ex-Tilling) for £117.5 million, and an agreed £197 million offer for **Rockware**, the UK's leading manufacturer of glass containers. BTR's interim profits recorded a 1.2% advance thanks only to the inclusion of a £90 million profit on the Pretty Polly sale being taken above the line, a move widely criticised for "jumping the gun" on a policy change currently under discussion by the Accounting Standards Board, but all was forgotten the following month when the long awaited "big bid" came along with a £1.5 billion cash and share offer for **Hawker Siddeley**.

The Hawker board had got off to a bad start by forecasting a fall in profits just ahead of the bid announcement and rapidly had to try to redeem the position. BTR spoke of Hawker's "decade of disappointment", and Hawker countered with criticism of BTR's record, implying that it owed more to accountants than to managers, and then came up with a vigorous acquisitions and disposals programme of its own together with a forecast of only a modest decline in profits. The outcome seemed to remain in considerable doubt even though it should have been obvious to the objective observer that Hawker had an uphill struggle on its hands, and a marginally increased bid won the day for BTR with 70% acceptances. BTR now had its major acquisition for the new chief executive to cut his teeth on.

Williams goes for Yale and Valor

Messrs Rudd and McGowan confirmed their reputation for rapidly changing the size and shape of **Williams** to fit in with new business conditions, by opening the year with an agreed all paper £330 million bid for **Yale & Valor** on a modest exit P/E of 12. This gave Williams market leadership in two more established products and boosted group turnover to £1.2 billion divided 44/44 between the UK and the US with 12% in Europe. Net assets of £450 million could be set against borrowings of £50 million, and profits for 1990 came out at £125 million, comfortably ahead of analysts' downgraded forecasts of £120 million. Interim profits announced at the end of August showed that Williams' management was back in form with a 26% advance to £76.5 million despite static sales. The failed bid for Racal had left them with a £77 million stake and a loss of £14 million on cost price, but in the context of Williams' size and Racal's recovery potential, it seemed fair to regard it as a valuable strategic interest not only in Racal but also in the soon to be demerged Chubb.

Tomkins pulls ahead

First half profits for **Tomkins** exceeded best expectations in a difficult market with a 34% advance to £31.2 million, showing that it did not deserve to lag behind its fellow conglomerates at 220p on a prospective P/E of 7½ given likely full year profits of around £108 million. In the event, the total came out at £112 million thanks to a strong performance from the US interests, especially from the recently rationalised Philips Industries. Greg Hutchings began to attract more fans for his quietly effective acquisition and management style which had not seen one false move since he began the expansion of Tomkins in 1983. The shares ended the year at 414p to record the biggest gain of any of the conglomerates and also the highest rating.

1992

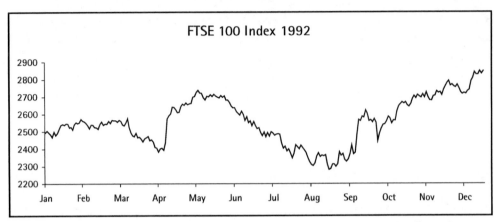

FTSE 100 Index 1992

Source: Thomson Reuters Datastream

Dragons' teeth

The New Year opened with the Prime Minister admitting that the recession was proving to be "deeper and longer" than expected but adding that a "jagged and irregular" recovery was underway. Given the uncertainty surrounding the election outcome, with both parties running neck and neck in the opinion polls, there appeared to be little upside in equities on a P/E of 17.25 and yielding just 4.5% at a time when dividend cuts were beginning to be presented as prudent policy in line with earnings trends. Thus the push through the 2550 level by the FTSE in the second half of January perhaps owed more to the extraordinary strength of Wall Street, where the Dow was consolidating its move above 3000 and reaching new highs by the day.

By the end of January the FTSE had picked up by 10%, recovering all the ground lost since early December when hopes of an imminent recovery had all but disappeared. Expectations of investors now seemed to be pinned on an election-winning budget, albeit one in which any vote-winning concessions could not be represented by the Opposition as political bribes. The weeks leading up to the budget, now set for 10th March, did nothing to ease the problems facing the Chancellor. The unemployment figures announced in mid-February saw a rise to a new peak of 2.6 million, indicating that employers were finding it easier to fit into the straitjacket imposed by the ERM by cutting jobs than by reducing pay awards, which were still running at over 7%. Then towards the end of the month the trade figures showed a practically doubled deficit in January thanks to a sharp fall in exports. Against such a background there was probably nothing the Chancellor could have done to keep everyone happy, but his reduction of tax to 20p in the pound on the first £2000 of taxable income was a benefit bestowed on the lower paid without tampering with the 25p basic tax rate. Of greater significance was the announcement of an increase in the PSBR for 1992/93 of £4 billion to £28 billion, or 4.5% of GDP as corporate tax receipts halved and unemployment continued to rise, an increase which Labour, while saying that it was a figure they would accept, still represented as a bribe to the electorate.

The election looms

The election date was now set for 9th April and the campaign began to heat up. The market did not see the budget as an election-winning one and after losing over 50 points to 2522 on the day, the FTSE quickly slipped below 2500 as Labour pulled ahead in the polls. But if Norman Lamont's budget did not win the election, there is a case for believing that John Smith's "shadow budget" lost it. Although Neil Kinnock had pledged to repeal any cut in the basic rate of tax that the Conservatives might have introduced in the pre-election budget, and the Labour Party's plans for increasing the higher rate to 50% had been well aired, the publication of the budget Labour would introduce if elected was a "first", leaving no one in any doubt at all about their intentions. It was a move of extraordinary naivety and a gift to the Conservatives who, without fear of contradiction, could portray Labour as the party of high taxation. The idea that the electorate would be prepared to pay higher taxes in return for improved public services might have carried some conviction if people had believed that Labour's plan to "invest" more money in public services would produce any improvement. Rather they suspected that it would result in nothing other than fatter pay packets for public service workers in line with Labour's parallel promise of comparability in pay with the private sector.

Given the depth of the recession, the Conservatives were simply not able to present a very convincing case for re-election. However marginally better news on the recovery front in the form of rising business confidence, suggestions from the CBI of an improvement in manufacturing order books, retail sales up for the second month running and a slightly smaller February trade deficit, helped to narrow Labour's lead during the final countdown.

A fourth term for the Conservatives

The Conservative victory, with a 21-seat overall majority, still came as a complete surprise to markets, and shares, gilts and sterling all soared. The consensus view was that the decisive removal of a serious degree of political uncertainty had created a much more favourable climate for an economic recovery. The FTSE rose 136 points to 2572, gilts were up to four points better as overseas investors snapped up the latest offering, and the pound pushed up towards the DM 2.90 level again. New York and

Tokyo also seemed to be celebrating the event as the Dow added 30 points to 3255 helped by another cut in the Federal Funds rate, and the Nikkei plussed 1252 to 17850, shaking off concern about the banks' exposure to the property and share collapse.

This post-election honeymoon continued well into May with the FTSE peaking at 2737.8 around the middle of the month just after another half a point off Base Rates had been greeted as an indication that everything was going according to plan. CBI reports that home and export order books were at their best levels since August 1990 and that the economy was "on the turn", helped to keep the index above 2700 for most of the rest of the month, but by mid-June it had lost nearly 150 points on growing fears about the timing and strength of the recovery. The sight of the Dow crossing the 3400 level for the first time was not enough to offset an unrelenting flow of unsettling economic news, which included the Danish rejection of Maastricht and the collapse of Canary Wharf developer Olympia & York, and was even counterproductive to a degree in that the rise looked out of touch with reality in the US economy where huge cuts in interest rates and a rapidly depreciating dollar had still failed to produce a recovery.

Disinflation or deflation?

Despite the American example, critics of ERM membership were calling for precisely these "remedies" to bring the UK out of recession, reluctant to recognise that the situation could be one in which such traditional measures simply would not work here any more than they appeared to in America. The ERM continued to take much of the blame but by July there were signs that the real problem was coming to be seen as far more intractable and one less likely to be responsive to any short-term stimulative actions. Quite simply the UK consumer had stopped consuming. Overloaded with personal debt, afraid for his job, and seeing the value of his principal asset, his house, continuing to fall, spending was strictly confined to the essentials of life.

With inflation down to 3.9% in June and base rates still at 10%, real interest rates were actually rising, widening the gap between income and debt-servicing costs and causing asset values to shrink further. With much the same process going on at the corporate level, manifesting itself in disappointing results and dividend reductions, it was not surprising that investors should shy away from new issues like the consumer oriented **MFI** and **Anglian** as well as causing the withdrawal of the once eagerly-awaited **GPA** offer, and that by the end of July the FTSE should be below 2400 albeit still on a P/E of 17 and a yield of 5%. Gilts showed the other side of the coin by hitting a new peak for the year of 89.75 in early July, and although the yield ratio, at 1.73, was now at its lowest level since the depths of the bear market in 1974, few commentators were prepared to regard it as a buy signal. At last the realisation was dawning that the name of the game had changed for the first time in sixty years from "disinflation" to "deflation", and any doubts that this was the case should have been expunged by the sight of the Dow falling on 3rd July when the Federal Discount Rate was cut to 3% in a near-panic response to the worst June unemployment figures in eight years.

Something's gotta give!

Given that the problems of the individual and the corporation in the shape of rising costs and falling income were mirrored at a national level, the divergence of performance between the stock markets of Tokyo, New York and London presented an obvious puzzle, sharing, as they did, the same problems of slow growth, trade disputes and political disillusionment, all within the confines of the Global Village. Indeed, Tokyo, down 60% from its late 1989 peak, was considered by some observers to have come to terms with the new situation rather better than either London or New York, especially a New York which had acquired P/Es more reminiscent of Tokyo in its heyday than of a grid-locked US economy. While the P/E on the Standard & Poor 500 was a forward-looking 29, that on the Dow Jones Industrial index (supposedly more representative of America's industrial heartland) was an incredible 61, assuming a potential for recovery that looked increasingly far-fetched as the likes of General Motors and IBM caused analysts to downgrade already cautious forecasts.

By contrast London looked reasonable value but with a history of downward revisions of growth estimates over the past year with their implications for unemployment and the PSBR, together with the reporting of "financial accidents" by such blue-chip companies as BP and Barclays Bank, few were prepared to take the plunge. To the extent that the case for the bulls rested upon the chances of an enforced policy change, they could point to the fact that the Government Securities index had come back almost two full points from its July peak while sterling at DM2.82 was over eleven pfennigs below its immediate post-election figure, but by now the US example looked much less convincing as dreadful corporate news began to undermine the Dow and the dollar continued to slide.

Into the unknown

Thus the London market entered August with the feeling that the course through uncharted waters had been set back in October 1990 when the UK had joined the ERM, but increasingly voices were heard suggesting that the dangers of holding to that course now far outweighed those of abandoning it. The chief argument of the dissidents was that the background had changed dramatically since October 1990. Germany now had to keep its interest rates high in order to counter reunification-induced inflationary pressures while the US administration in the run-up to an election felt compelled to reduce rates in an attempt to end a recession which was proving much more persistent than originally expected. The pound was caught in the middle, pegged at a hopelessly uncompetitive exchange rate while the Government was forced to maintain interest rates at a level which threatened to turn recession into slump. The result was a ballooning balance of payments deficit, a PSBR out of control, and unemployment heading towards 3 million, all serving to create a situation which was economically and politically unsustainable.

The storm clouds gather

The last week in August saw an intensification of world currency turmoil with the dollar plunging another 7 pfennigs to a record low of DM1.40, while the pound rose to almost $2.00, simultaneously dropping through DM2.80 towards its ERM floor. Speculation grew about the prospects of a UK interest rate rise and the FTSE responded by falling almost to the 2300 level, seemingly convinced by unequivocal statements from the Prime Minister and the Chancellor alike that ERM membership was sacrosanct and that leaving it was unthinkable, as indeed was even the prospect of realignment within the system. However, though the market was considered to have discounted at least a one-point hike in base rates, no rise came and the pound kept on falling. This anomalous situation was seen as casting doubt on the strength of the Government's commitment to the ERM and speculative pressure continued unabated.

In the first week of September, news that the Government was borrowing £7.3 billion in D-Marks to be used in support of the pound, sparked a rally back to DM2.80 (and a low-volume reflex 68.9 point rise to 2381.9 in the FTSE) but it was shortlived. The foreign exchange market was simply too big for any sort of intervention to have any lasting effect, save for an adverse one on the credibility of the authorities. The situation remained fragile throughout the second week of September although the 7% devaluation of the Italian lira, followed by its departure from the ERM, together with a quarter point reduction in Germany's key Lombard rate to 9.5%, prompted some hopes of lower interest rates all round and further realignments serving to let sterling off the hook. But despite further heavy intervention, the pound continued to fall to within a fraction of its ERM floor of DM2.778, pulling equities and gilts down with it on renewed fears of a rise in interest rates. Sterling had now become a one-way bet on devaluation and the speculators moved in for the kill, convinced that no interest rate rise could avoid it. The 2% hike on the morning of 16th September proved their point, and when the announcement of a further rise to 15% later in the day failed to lift sterling off the floor, the Government bowed to the inevitable, cancelled the second rate rise and dropped out of the ERM. The pound fell immediately to DM 2.64.

Dancing amid the ruins

The confusion surrounding events leading up to sterling's departure from the ERM had left investors uncertain which way to jump but the return of base rates to 10% the following day cleared the air and the FTSE leapt 105 points to 2483.9 while gilts added nearly a point to 89.22. It might have been a 'Black Wednesday' for the reputations of the Prime Minister and his Chancellor and for the credibility of the Government's whole economic policy, but there was little doubt that the markets saw the move as opening the way to the adoption of policies more in tune with the state of the economy of the UK rather than that of Germany.

Over the next few days talk of an early return to the ERM faded and when the Chancellor reduced base rates to 9%, declaring that "operating a floating regime is not an easy and not a soft option", or in much the same terms as he had spoken previously about ERM membership, it became clear that he was intent on making a virtue of necessity. The U-turn was complete. However, the political fallout augmented by the storm over the pit closures, restrained investor enthusiasm throughout the first half of October, but then another one-point cut in base rates to 8% and hints of more to come, prompted a wave of buying taking the FTSE almost to 2700 and the Government Securities index to over 94. All eyes were now on the Autumn Statement scheduled for 12th November, in which Chancellor Lamont was confidently expected to re-establish a framework for the Government's economic policy and fill the 'policy vacuum'.

Plotting a new course

This he broadly succeeded in doing by setting forth measures seemingly consistent with going for growth at the same time as keeping up the pressure on inflation. A political as much as an economic package, the mix of monetary and fiscal policies was welcomed by Conservative backbenchers and industry alike, who saw it as restoring the Government's credibility as well as paving the way for recovery. The 1% reduction in base rates to 7% was seen as easing the burden of the debt overhang, while the specific measures targeted at the motor industry, industry generally and housing were regarded as bringing relief to where it was most needed. The 1.5% ceiling in public sector pay settlements also won broad approval.

The one aspect of the statement that caused most anxiety and criticism concerned public sector finances, given no change in the level of public spending for this year and next with the PSBR forecast to rise to £37 billion and then to £44 billion, and in the absence of new revenue-raising measures, everything appeared to depend upon the early development of a strong and lasting economic recovery. In this context, the revised Treasury forecast of 1% growth in GDP in 1993 was not particularly encouraging and less so, given the implications for export-led growth at a time when the current account deficit was already expected to rise from £12 billion in 1992 to £15.5 billion in 1993. Still the market was prepared to give the Chancellor the benefit of the doubt and the FTSE moved up 29.6 points to 2726.4, its highest level since the record of 2737.8 achieved in May.

The next few days witnessed some hesitancy, but later in the month optimism was rekindled by more encouraging economic data on retail sales and wage settlements and by speculation on the prospects for corporate earnings growth in a recovery phase as inflation continued to fall. Some satisfaction was also derived from the sight of sterling apparently enjoying life outside the ERM, while inside chaos still reigned with one currency after another coming under pressure.

On to new high ground

On 25th November the FTSE surged to a new peak of 2741.8 on high volume, and encouraged by good news from the US in the form of a revision of third quarter growth from 2.7% to 3.9%, it kept going to reach 2792 on 1st December. The pattern beginning to emerge was one of accelerating recovery in the US and the first signs of an upturn in the UK, while Germany and the rest of Continental Europe remained mired in recession. Against such a background, the UK equity market was regarded as having it both ways in that any signs of hesitancy in that upturn would almost certainly prompt a further reduction in interest rates by a Government now firmly committed to a growth strategy.

In the third week of December the FTSE crossed the 2800 level for the first time boosted by yet another fall in headline inflation in November to 3%, its lowest level in six years. There was a new surge of buying in the final week of the year, sparked by reports of a dramatic 30% increase in new car sales in December and of a hectic start to the post-Christmas sales, and the FTSE closed 1992 at 2846.5, up 14.2% on the year and just 1.3 points short of its all-time high reached two days before. Gilts too ended on a firm note with the Government Securities index at 94.34, although below its high point of 95.54. Sterling ended the year at DM2.44, 17.2% down on its ERM joining rate, while against the dollar it was practically unchanged at $1.51. With the gold price down $20 on the year to $333, gold shares remained out of favour and FT Gold Mines closed 54% off at 63.9. Wall Street provided some background encouragement, ending the year at just over 3300, still below its June peak but on a rising trend on expectations of continuing recovery and a favourable start for the Clinton administration.

When the going gets tough...

There are some recessions that even the best-managed conglomerates cannot withstand, and **Hanson's** first quarter fall of 6% in pre-tax profits to £226 million came as no surprise. Neither did the decision not to launch a bid for **ICI** and to sell its stake in the company. The disposal proceeds of some £280 million, making a profit of £40 million in the process, helped to reduce net debt which had risen to £1.5 billion as a result of the acquisition of Beazer, and the move fitted in well with the new declared policy of disposing of peripheral interests in order to concentrate on building core businesses, including natural resources, through organic growth and acquisition. Thus Jacuzzi (ex-Kidde) was to be floated off and Beazer's US housebuilding side sold to bring in almost $1 billion, and the temptation to bail out Canary Wharf was resisted. By the third quarter the decline in profits had accelerated to 21.2%, aggravated by the sharp fall in the dollar, a performance which appeared to give point to the new strategy. However, the surprise £780 million cash bid for **RHM** in October prompted many commentators to wonder whether Hanson had broken away completely from its predatory past despite the much-publicised change in policy and the appointment of Derek Bonham and David Clarke as heirs-apparent to Lords Hanson and White. The counter offer by Tomkins and Hanson's subsequent withdrawal came as something of a relief to Hanson fans, offsetting any disappointment with the small drop in full year profits to £1.29 billion, the first year-on-year decline in the company's history. The shares ended 1993 at 234p selling on a P/E of 11.9 and with a dividend yield of 6.3%.

BTR, with a rather greater concentration of similar core businesses under its belt and a recent major acquisition to work on, proved more recession-resistant than Hanson in 1992. Pre-tax profits for 1991 had come in 3% down at £917 million, but following vigorous rationalisation measures worldwide, interim profits for 1992 announced in September were up 7% to £548 million on sales 33% ahead at £4.3 billion as benefits from the shakedown of Hawker Siddeley began to flow. The company reported little sign of recovery in the UK, but the downward revision in November by one leading stockbroker of 1992 estimates from £1.03 billion to £984 million carried little weight with BTR followers, and after dipping briefly to below 500p on the news, the shares ended the year at 550p where the P/E was a forward-looking 19.3 and the yield a modest 4%. Estimates now began to be revised upwards again, and buyers were attracted further by speculation that BTR was limbering up for another important acquisition, with Lucas the most likely target.

Despite rumours to the contrary, in June **Racal** made good its bid-inspired profits forecast of "not less than" £50 million for 1991/92 with a total of £55.6 million, and then kept the excitement going with plans for the imminent demerger of Chubb. The scheme involved consolidating five old Racal shares into one new Racal share plus one Chubb, leaving original Racal shareholders with one share of each company. Debt was to be divided equally between the two companies, a fair split given that Racal had nurtured Chubb with its cashflow since the acquisition in 1984. Both shares advanced strongly following the demerger in early October, and then the first interim results in December seemed to prove the point that the sum of the parts was greater than the whole. Racal turned in pre-tax profits of £23.1 million against a loss of £2.4 million while Chubb's figure almost doubled to £26.9 million, and both declared the same dividend. Meanwhile, in the earlier part of the year Vodafone had come in for some brokers' downgradings as the recession took the shine off the more optimistic estimates of cellular phone demand, but in the event first half profits were well up to best expectations at £160 million, a gain of 23%, and the shares ended the year at a new high of 427p.

Williams Holdings had a relatively quiet year as the management busied itself consolidating recent acquisitions, many of which were to a greater or lesser degree affected by recession. Profits for 1991 were up 42% at £168 million, but first half figures for 1992 announced in September showed a 6% fall to £72 million despite a further improvement in margins. At the same time a policy change was indicated as a result of the diminishing chances of success of future paper bids given the then-modest rating of the company's shares at 247p with a P/E of just 12.3. Accordingly, long-term borrowing facilities were put in place with the aim of helping to fund future acquisitions, but the rapid recovery of the share price in the final quarter of the year to 335p to provide a P/E of 17 suggested that both options remained open for Williams.

Tomkins opened 1992 in fine style, reporting a 40% advance in pre-tax profits for the first half of 1991/92 to £43.7 million on sales up 52% thanks to a continuing strong performance from the US interests. Full year figures announced in July confirmed Tomkins' position as the most recession-resistant of all the conglomerates with an 18% rise to £132 million. Analysts were now estimating a total of £144 million for 1992/93 and the shares rose towards 500p ahead of a 100% scrip issue. Given net cash of £112 million another acquisition was thought to be on the cards before long, but the £935 million agreed counter offer for RHM dismayed many of Greg Hutchings' most devoted followers. The cash and share offer involved a 1 for 2 rights at 200p to raise £653 million net, and Tomkins' shares lost 50p to 212p on the announcement. Despite the fact that he had not put a foot wrong since taking control of Tomkins in 1983, many observers were convinced that with RHM, Greg Hutchings had gone one bid too far. On the contrary, he argued that basic products are basic products and that the same principles of efficient production and distribution apply as much to bread and cakes as they do to nuts and bolts. As the acceptances rolled in with the pattern indicating that Tomkins would end up with little or no net debt, this latter view began to gain ground and the share price had recovered to 256p by year end.

Per Astra ad Ardua

Apart from a few political careers, the biggest casualty of the 'arms for Iraq' affair was **Astra Holdings**. This long-established fireworks manufacturer had gained a stock market listing by reversing into Francis Sumner early in 1986. Then under chairman Geoffrey James, it began to expand into military pyrotechnics with groundburst simulators, smoke pots, thunderflashes and practice bombs. Sales grew rapidly, particularly in the US, and the share price soared. All might have been well had the company stuck to simulated weaponry, but it was the move into munitions proper that brought it down. A £22 million rights issue in 1990 to fund the purchase of loss-making Belgian arms group PRB was quickly swallowed up, and in 1992 Astra went into receivership with debts of £54 million. PRB had been engaged in making parts for the Iraqi supergun, and the subsequent DTI investigation uncovered many more skeletons in Astra's cupboard.

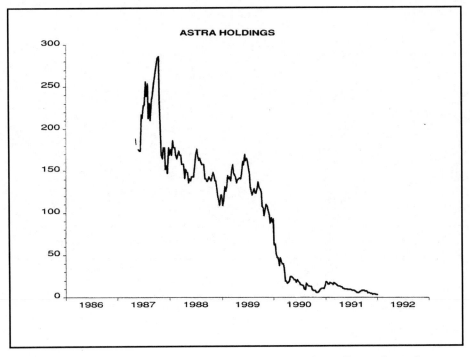

Source: Thomson Reuters Datastream

1993

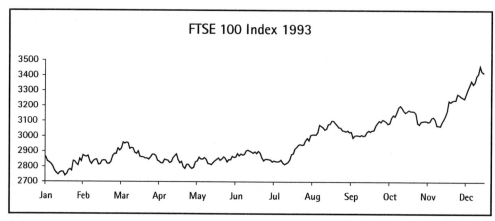

FTSE 100 Index 1993

Source: Thomson Reuters Datastream

The recovery begins

The Prime Minister's New Year message spoke of clear signs of recovery that could mark the start of a "virtuous cycle" of sustainable growth and prosperity thanks to the success in reducing inflation and to the opportunities created by the coming into being of the Single European Market. But while the equity market seemed to agree with him by reaching new highs in the first days of 1993, there were plenty of sceptics who believed that given the existence of the country's huge trade and budget deficits, even a modest recovery would quickly run into serious problems. Their argument was that given the sharp diminution in the UK's manufacturing base in recent years, rising consumer demand would feed straight through to imports instead of benefiting domestic industry. For the same reason, any post-devaluation surge in export demand would run into supply constraints. The net result would therefore be very little if any expansion in activity to the continuing detriment of both deficits, a situation likely to be aggravated and perpetuated by the urgent need to fund a still growing PSBR at the risk of starving the private sector of funds for expansion. Companies would also be keen to rebuild their balance sheets and any advance in the equity market was likely to be subdued by a flood of rights issues.

Those of a more optimistic frame of mind countered the apparent inevitability of this doom-laden scenario by saying that consumer confidence was likely to remain at a low level thanks to a combination of a still-high debt burden, a depressed housing market and fear of unemployment, and that the real beneficiary of lower interest rates and low inflation would be a corporate sector already leaner and fitter from the economy measures undertaken during the recession. Thus they argued that perhaps for the first time, a UK Government was in a position to take the action necessary, if devaluation is going to work, of curbing domestic demand and public spending in order to shift resources into productive investment and exports. Indeed the Government no longer had any choice in the matter and to pursue this course was a simple policy imperative.

Fortunately, the Government had a lot going for it. For one thing it was still in the first year of the electoral cycle and growing signs of industrial recovery were already benefiting sterling which, now that it had "escaped" from the ERM, was being spoken of as a "safe haven" currency. Furthermore, the two budgets in 1993 gave the Chancellor the opportunity to use the first one to boost recovery and the second to start to repair public sector finances. Also there was little prospect of widespread industrial unrest forcing the Government to alter its plans as it had in previous devaluations. Add in the prospects of a continuing decline in inflation and there was a real chance that overseas capital could flow in and tide the country over until real growth led to a significant reduction in both deficits.

At first the bulls seemed to have the better of the argument and on 4th January the FTSE reached a new high of 2861.5. But their triumph was shortlived. Two weeks later the index had shed almost 100 points as investors worried about the prospect of "paper heading towards the market from all directions". The Retail Price Index for December also caused some consternation. The 2.6% rise was the lowest in 6½ years but the underlying rate (excluding mortgage payments) had risen 3.7% over the year as a whole. This figure was uncomfortably close to the top end of the Chancellor's target range of 1-4%, largely thanks to the effect of devaluation on prices of raw materials and fuels as well as seasonal food price increases.

A new Governor for the Bank of England

But after falling below 2750 on fading recovery hopes sparked by disappointing December retail sales figures and a shock rise in unemployment to just short of 3 million, equities rebounded sharply at the end of January in response to a surprise 1% cut in Bank Rate to 6%. Despite its welcome by the market, the cut drew some criticism for being a panic reaction to the jobless figure, and Governor-elect of the Bank of England, Eddie George, was quick to caution against expectations of further rate cuts. This view appeared to be well-supported by the news that the Retail Price Index rose only 1.7% in January, the lowest figure in 25 years, that private sector pay was rising at a rate of only 3.6%, and that the public sector pay limit of 1.5% looked like being accepted, albeit reluctantly. Chancellor Lamont expressed his agreement with the Governor, but it was a falling pound that effectively ruled out the prospect of further rate cuts at this stage. Clearly, the foreign exchange markets were not convinced that the UK was entering a new era of non-inflationary growth and in mid-

February the pound fell to $1.42 and to DM2.35, establishing a new trade-weighted low of 75.7 against the basket of currencies. The Chancellor's priority in the forthcoming budget was to present a convincing enough fiscal package that would serve to put a floor under the pound by attracting global capital flows, thus leaving scope for more rate cuts in due course. This still left him with the problem of how to strike a balance between measures that would help to establish the Government's anti-inflation credentials and those that might hinder the fragile recovery process. A steady rise in the Government Securities Index from 93 at the beginning to around 98 ten weeks later, suggested that inflation was the lesser fear, but the debate continued.

Six out of the "seven wise men" – economists appointed as special advisers to the Chancellor in the interests of open government – were not in favour of tax rises on the grounds that they would inhibit recovery but all thought that interest rate reductions were needed. Mr. Lamont's dilemma was partially solved by a German rate cut, an unexpected fall in unemployment, and a rise in January's figure for manufacturing output, and by the end of the first week of March optimism was back in fashion. The FTSE surged to 2922 and buyers clamoured to buy gilts yielding 8.5%. Additional data showing increased consumer lending, growing business confidence and subdued wage pressures, prompted a further rise to 2957.3 and to 98.04 with sterling recovering too in the week leading up to Budget Day.

A courageous Budget

The Government's defeat in the Maastricht debate put an extra political onus on the Chancellor, and he rose to the occasion by staking all on the recovery taking hold before the financial situation could get any worse. His 'wedge' of rising tax revenues, led by the extension of VAT in two stages to domestic fuel and power, to raise £6.5 billion in 1994/95 and £10.5 billion the following year, clearly relied upon the adventurous assumption that gradually improving labour and housing markets would enable the population to take these deferred tax increases in their stride. The rise in employees' National Insurance contributions from 9% to 10% was the measure proposed in John Smith's "shadow budget" a year earlier, and the fact that Mr. Lamont had adopted it, as well as provoking the wrath of his own backbenchers by extending VAT to domestic fuel, did him credit by demonstrating that he saw the nation's finances as a problem to be solved rather than just as a political balancing act.

The budget was broadly welcomed by the markets but over the ensuing weeks both gilts and equities retreated under the influence of conflicting economic numbers. An FT editorial made the point that unfamiliarity with the sight of a recovery led by manufacturing output and exports instead of being consumer-driven, had served to confuse forecasters. Nevertheless, investors still paid more attention to the third successive monthly rise in retail sales figures and to the inflation fears it aroused, than to still rising industrial output. At the end of April the FTSE fell below 2800 again and Government Securities slipped below 95.

Going for gold

However, the early summer was not lacking in excitement. In mid-March, the gold price had fallen to a 7-year low point of $325, prompting many analysts to predict another drop to $300 and even lower. Thanks to the explosive growth of the derivatives market, gold was no longer regarded as the hedge it had once been. Furthermore, the supply/demand fundamentals appeared to leave no scope for upside potential, and in the words of one dealer quoted by Reuters, "gold is awful, whichever way you look at it". As is so often the case in the markets, such a damning indictment marked the precise bottom of the downswing. Six weeks later, the price was nudging $360 thanks to the buying impetus provided by the well-publicised action of fund manager George Soros in paying $400 million to Sir James Goldsmith for a sizeable stake in Newmont Mines, the largest gold producer in the US. Sir James then added fuel to the flames of speculation by revealing that he had used $300 million of that sum to purchase bullion options. Despite what Lex called "these somewhat dubious origins" behind the rise and analysts reiterating that the physical supply/demand situation did not justify any upward movement, the gold price continued to advance as fund managers climbed aboard the Soros/Goldsmith bandwagon. The peak of $405 was reached on the last day of July, and then reports that China's central bank was selling gave the signal for a general sell-off. By any standards, this engineered rise in the gold price was a textbook example of how a speculative operation should be carried out. A neglected commodity, but one with latent appeal, was selected, the price target was modest, and the timescale was brief enough to leave minimum scope for upsets to occur. If the Hunt brothers had employed the same tactics with silver in 1980, they would have made money instead of losing the lot. It should also be noted that money was made out of gold shares. The FT Gold Mines index had already risen 50% to 97.6 by the time bullion hit its low point, a move indicative of accumulation, and touched 250 as the price topped $400.

Nightmare on Elm Street

The other principal diversion for investors in May and June was the news that former Polly Peck chief, Asil Nadir, had skipped bail and flown to his base in Northern Cyprus. Mr. Nadir's avowed reason for putting himself outside the reach of British justice was that he could not be sure of getting a fair trial. Remarkably, despite evidence of extensive insider dealing in Polly Peck shares through the medium of a Swiss company, and of illegal transfers of many millions of pounds from company funds in the UK to Turkey and Cyprus, Mr. Nadir and friends still contrived to portray the Serious Fraud Office (SFO) as the villain of the piece.

A new Chancellor takes over

Meanwhile back in the real economy, in May the FTSE had managed to re-establish itself above 2800 again despite the prospect of more and more rights issues to add to the total of £7 billion so far in 1993. Mr. Lamont greeted the announcement of a 1.3% rise in the Retail Price Index for April as "an outstanding achievement", and it was somewhat ironic that when Kenneth Clarke replaced him as Chancellor a few days later, the event should have been followed by a flow of economic data, including a surprise narrowing of the trade gap, confirming the prospect of modest growth without a revival of inflation. These reports saw the FTSE respond by advancing towards 2900 as gilt yields shrank to 8%. In fact, a half-year round-up showed gilts outperforming equities, rising 10% against the latter's 7%, as the forces of disinflation were seen to have developed more strongly than originally expected against a background of relatively disappointing economic growth.

Up, up and away

July was the month investors decided to put aside their worries and embrace the belief that the industrial recovery was now well established and was going to continue without a resurgence of inflation. That belief was not confined to the UK. In the US investors had experienced the same doubts and fears about recovery and inflation, with the Dow Jones index ebbing and flowing in response to every new set of economic numbers. Now the thirst for yield that had driven both bond and equity markets to their present levels, intensified as the conviction grew that low inflation and low interest rates were here to stay and that corporate earnings were set to rise. Two more factors added impetus to the rise. One was the Group of Seven breakthrough during the Uruguay round of the GATT talks, widely expected to usher in a new era of world prosperity on the back of trade liberalisation. The other was the near collapse of the ERM, untying Europe's depressed economies from the restrictions of German domestic monetary policy, and opening the way for interest rate cuts just like those embarked upon by the UK in September 1992. A forty-vote victory for the Conservatives in a confidence motion called over the Maastricht ratification may also have helped to resolve many of the political doubts raised by earlier disastrous losses in by-elections and at local council elections.

New highs across the board

The advances by gilts and equities were swift and dramatic. Both the Dow and the FTSE consolidated their moves into new high ground and by the last day of July they stood at 3537 and 2926 respectively. The Government Securities Index also touched a new high of 99.17 on that day. Two weeks later, despite a sharp fall in manufacturing output in June and a rise in unemployment, the FTSE crossed the 3000 mark, buoyed by the belief that such news made an interest rate cut more likely. Gilts powered ahead to 102 and by then the Bank of England had sold enough stock in the first 4½ months of the financial year 1993/94 to cover 60% of its £50 billion requirement. Also there was no problem for the market in digesting the £5.3 billion total of the third British Telecom offering. Much of it, like gilts, went to overseas buyers.

Money talks

The liquidity-driven nature of the boom prompted some commentators to warn that liquidity flows have a habit of reversing themselves rather abruptly. Thus any sign of an upturn in US rates could cause the managers of mutual and pension funds to take their profits and repatriate their funds. The argument, sound though it was, did not find much support from investors at this time. Apart from a sharp but brief setback at the end of October, markets here continued to move ahead on hopes of further rate cuts if the economic data was disappointing, and of a strengthening economic recovery if it was not. A half point cut to 5½% duly arrived in the last week of November, and against this background the new Chancellor's budget, scheduled for the last day of the month, held no terrors. On the contrary, it caused the year to end in fine style with both gilts and equities embarking upon an almost unbroken run. The keynote was big spending cuts, allied with more slow-burn tax rises designed to take effect as the recovery gained pace. Mr. Clarke's avowed intent to tackle the PSBR "once and for all" caused some surprise but markets were not displeased with the prospect of borrowing being cut by £5.5 billion in 1994/95, £7 billion in 1995/96 and by £10.5 billion the following year, and aiming at zero by the end of the decade. These targets were well below those of his predecessor, just as the tax rises were a significant addition. Gilts added 1½ points on the day taking the index to 104.18, and the FTSE plussed 31.1 to 3166.9. Sterling firmed to $1.485 and to DM 2.5475.

At the end of December, the FTSE stood at 3418.4, down from the high point of 3462.6 touched two days earlier, but still up 20% on the year. Much better performances were recorded by individual interest rate-sensitive sectors, and Building Materials and Contracting and Construction rose by 59% and 65% respectively. Financials also showed exceptional strength and while the Financial Group as a whole was up 56%, Properties plussed 85% (aided by the revelation that George Soros regarded commercial property as a good bet), and Merchant Banks gained 80%. There was a great deal of speculative activity among the smaller companies which included many of the year's new issues, and the Smaller Companies index added 32%. The Government Securities index achieved a high of 107.6, up 14%, and the yield fell from 8.42% to 6.37%. With equities yielding around 3.4%, the yield ratio was comfortably under 2, a figure which helped to relieve any anxieties that might have been aroused by a P/E of 24. The Dow Jones index appeared equally cheerful, achieving a new high of 3794.33 in December before shading to show a gain of 14.7% on the year. Gold managed to hold on to much of its advance since mid-March, and at $390.75 was up 17.5% over the year as a whole. Gold shares fared even better and the FT Gold Mines index quadrupled to 257.7.

Constructive divorce in action

There was relatively little excitement among the select band of top growth stocks, the fortunes of which we have followed from the day they embarked upon the acquisition trail. With the megabid no longer practical nor fashionable thanks to a dearth of suitable targets and a degree of political unacceptability, minor bolt-on acquisitions accompanied by selective disposals became much more the order of the day. **Racal** had set the pattern back in 1988 with the flotation of **Vodafone,** followed by that of **Chubb** in 1992. Since then the value of **Vodafone** has trebled and that of Chubb more than doubled, demonstrating what Lex termed "constructive divorce in action". **ICI,** in the wake of the Hanson approach, was prompted to follow a similar course of action, hiving off **Zeneca,** its pharmaceutical arm. The move was popular with ICI shareholders, and deservedly so. Within two years, a re-rating of the pharmaceutical sector had put a £10 billion price tag on Zeneca, more than that of the old ICI before the split.

Hanson changes down

Still, **Hanson** managed to have an active year. The planned disposal of Beazer Homes USA was carried out (following the purchase and inclusion of Watt Housing for $116 million in April), and a parallel flotation was scheduled for the UK in early 1994, to bring in around $600 million in total. Beazer's aggregate businesses were retained and consolidated with others already owned by Hanson. Both moves followed the new policy of establishing Hanson as a focused industrial group, as distinct from an opportunistic wheeler -dealer; and served to reduce gearing substantially. The coal interests were added to significantly as a result of purchasing Costain's Australian holdings for $300 million, and then by swapping Consolidated Goldfields' remaining US gold operations for Santa Fe's mining and quarrying intersts. In the process, Hanson had become the largest private sector coal company in the world.

Then in September came an agreed $3.7 billion bid for loss-making, debt-ridden Quantum Chemical. It was the biggest bid to date in the US and very much in the Hanson tradition in that it was an ideal subject for remedial treatment. Quantum's debt load was immediately refinanced with the benefit of Hanson's superior credit standing and borrowing powers, and a drastic cost reduction programme was embarked upon with the aim of restoring the company to profitability as soon as possible. Profits for the full year to end-September were down for the second year running at fractionally over £1 billion pre-tax thanks to the continuing recession, and in spite of the failure to raise the dividend for the first time in the company's history, the shares performed well over the year, closing at 268p, just below the year's high of 288p and well above the low point of 222p. The feeling was that, with so much of the profits decline recession-related, there was considerable scope for a cyclical upturn enhanced by Hanson's famed ability to cut costs – and furthermore, Quantum would come into play the following year. Forecasts for 1993/94 settled in the £1.1 - £1.15 million range for a prospective P/E of around 16 and a dividend yield approaching 6%.

BTR had a quiet year but it was a notable one in that the full year profits for 1992 revealed in March confounded the downward revisions of some stockbrokers to less than £1 billion, by weighing in 18% up at £1.078 billion pre-tax. Despite tough conditions worldwide, the group's ability to achieve production and efficiency savings served to maintain margins and to actually improve them at Hawker Siddeley. Continuing progress was evident in the interim figures announced in September. Pre-tax profits were up 9% at £598 million on sales 13% ahead at £4.87 billion. In December an agreed $820 million bid was announced for Rexnord, a US manufacturer of material conveying systems, power transmission equipment and industrial and aerospace seals. This was BTR's biggest bid since Hawker Siddeley, and was expected to be earnings-enhancing from the outset, as Rexnord's marketplace was widened to take in Europe and Asia. Adjusted for a 2 for 3 scrip issue, the shares ended 1993 at 373p, down from a high of 410p, but well off the low of 318p. Forecasts for 1994 centred around £1.25 million for a prospective P/E of 16.

In its first full year post-Chubb, **Racal** demonstrated that it remained a leader in the electronics industry in its own right, with pre-tax profits of £51.5 million on sales up only marginally at £950 million, 70% arising overseas. Higher operating profits, lower exceptional costs and a £6.9 million currency gain more than offset £3.8 million demerger costs and a cut in investment income. Chairman, Sir Ernest Harrison, stated that the results had been affected by the recession and aggravated by the worldwide constraints on defence expenditure, but still looked forward to a further improvement in operating profit based on the "ongoing cost reduction and profit improvement programme". Most observers took this to mean a total of around £58 million in 1993/94, but not for the first time Racal wrong-footed the analysts by announcing a small loss at the interim stage in December against estimates of a profit in the £16-£22 million range Despite the fact that the adoption of the new accounting standards obscured the underlying trading picture, and there were closure and dispersal costs of £20.2 million incurred at Racal-Redac, the market took the news badly and the shares lost 29p on the day of the announcement to hit a new low for the year of 160p on 20 million volume. Encouraged by the chairman's forecast of operating profits similar to the previous year's, and by the prospective benefits of the company's participation in the Army's Bowman communications project and the Camelot lottery bid, analysts pencilled-in £45 million for the full year and the shares rallied by end-December to 185p for a hugely discounted P/E of 11.

Tomkins' interim figures for 1992/93 were less dramatic than the market was becoming accustomed to, but creditable for all that. Sales were down 3% but with a firm US performance outweighing tough times in the UK, pre-tax profits still managed to increase by 8% to £47.1 million. Most observers continued to express reservations about the previous year's RHM acquisition, worried that it would serve to undermine the quality of earnings of the rest of the group. They remained unconvinced by full-year figures showing pre-tax profits up 30% at £171 million on sales up 62% (or 10% ex-21 weeks of RHM) and the announcement that the rationalisation of RHM was running ahead of schedule with the workforce already cut by 10%. Profits were a little below earlier estimates of £174 million and the shares continued to languish close to the low for the year at 220p despite brokers' forecasts of £250 million in 1993/94. Sentiment improved towards the end of the year, however, thanks to press comment that any credibility gap was more than adequately accounted for by the fact of the shares trading at a 15% discount to the market and a 15% premium on yield.

Williams Holdings' full-year profits for 1992, announced in March, came out at £161 million, a figure flattered to some degree by accounting changes, but still demonstrating management's skills at bearing down on costs, keeping up capital outlays and gaining market share. Weaker aerospace markets took the shine off the fire and safety divisions, but strong consumer specialist product sales in both Europe and North America boosted profits. The group was reckoned to be well-positioned for a broad recovery led by the US (44% of sales) and closely followed by the UK, which had shown an improvement in the last quarter of 1992. Forecasts of a gradual improvement throughout the year with an emphasis on the second half were reinforced by a string of small acquisitions designed to strengthen Williams' position in its core businesses of building, security and fire protection products.

In August, founder director Brian McGowan left the company to head up the relaunched House of Fraser. He was succeeded as Chief Executive by Roger Carr, who also had been with the group from the start and had set up the celebrated 'hit squad' that reviewed new acquisitions. Interim figures revealed in September were a little below best expectations at £76.1 million but the comparable period in 1992 had been augmented by a £6.1 million gain on the sale of the Racal stake, and £2 million had already been spent on reorganisation at Hammerite and Thorn Fire Protection, acquired earlier in the year. Full-year forecasts were scaled down from around £174 million to £168 million, which would provide a prospective P/E of 17 at 326p. The share price advanced strongly, however, in the final quarter to end the year at 374p.

1994

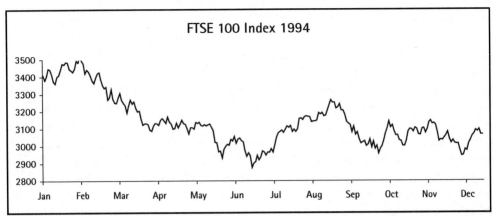

FTSE 100 Index 1994

Source: Thomson Reuters Datastream

Inflation fears rule

End-year enthusiasm was rife, and forecasts by the usual panel of experts of where the FTSE might stand at the end of 1994 ranged up to 4000 with an average of 3700. Even those who looked for a rise in both inflation and interest rates still expected the market to go higher on the grounds that such developments would arise as a consequence of faster economic growth. Doubts, such as they were, centred upon the fragility of consumer confidence given the insecurity induced by the high level of unemployment and the impact of the deferred tax burden imposed by the last two budgets. A few of the more cautious commentators foresaw a fall in the market later in the year, as the cycle of low interest rates turned in response to pre-emptive counter-inflationary action by the Federal Reserve Board. These cautious commentators were right and anxieties on this score were to dominate markets for the rest of the year. However, the bulls managed to have it all their own way for the whole of January and the first two days of February, but for no longer. The FTSE hit a new record high of 3520.3 on 2nd February, apparently buoyed by Governor of the Bank of England, Eddie George's statement that: "prospects for sustained growth in output and gradually falling unemployment are better than at any time in my professional career." Also on 2nd February, the Dow reached a new peak of 3978.36 coinciding with news that in the fourth quarter of 1993, US GDP had grown at the rate of 5.9%, its best level since 1987.

All change at the Fed

Everything changed the next day when the Federal Reserve Board tightened monetary policy for the first time in five years by raising the Federal Funds rate (the interest rate banks charge each other on overnight loan money) from 3% to 3.25%. The move, said chairman Alan Greenspan, signalled "a less accommodative stance in monetary policy in order to sustain and advance the economic expansion". To the extent that the direct cause of the global bull market in 1993 had been the flow of capital out of low-yielding deposits in the US, first into domestic securities and then into overseas stocks and bonds, it also signalled the top for capital markets worldwide. Henceforth, every apparently bullish US economic number carried with it fears of another interest rate hike. The FTSE lost 28.8 on 3rd February and by the end of the month that loss had risen to over 300 points, unchecked by a controversial cut in UK base rates to 5.25% on 8th February. Given that the US had initiated the change in trend for world interest rates a week earlier, the Chancellor's quarter per cent reduction was criticised for making little sense, since it simply increased the likelihood that the next move in UK rates would be upward. Gilts certainly took this view and by the end of February, the Government Securities index had lost nearly five points to 101, while the yield had risen to 7.3%.

Reversing the flow

The declines in both gilts and equities continued as the Federal Reserve edged interest rates up to 3.75% at the end of April, and then up half a point to 4.25% a month later. Alan Greenspan's accompanying statement that this latest increase served to "substantially remove the degree of monetary accommodation which prevailed throughout 1993" was greeted initially with cautious enthusiasm. After a prolonged period during which the US monetary authorities had held short-term interest rates at an artificially low level in an effort to restore a badly battered banking system to good health, it seemed reasonable to hope that they were ready to adopt a neutral stance now that their object had been largely achieved. Of course, if this was not going to be the case, then it was bad news for countries lagging the US recovery if they had to continue to cope with rising interest rates.

After a brief rally, UK equities resumed their decline, losing 160 points in the last week of May and taking the FTSE below 3000. Gilts suffered too, with the index slipping to 91.04 causing the yield to rise to 8.4%. The realisation was dawning fast that the tidal outflow of dollars created by the Federal Reserve's extended regime of low interest rates was certain to continue to reverse in the wake of the change in monetary policy inaugurated on 2nd February. After all, the Bank of England had sold £14 billion of gilts in 1993 to overseas buyers as yields tumbled from 9% to 6.5%. What were its chances of repeating the performance this year and next on rising yields? The question appeared to be answered by news that overseas holders of gilts were net sellers in April to the tune of £1.3 billion as compared with December 1993 when they had been net buyers of £2.7 billion. Furthermore, against this sort of background, equities yielding no more than 3.7% still looked vulnerable.

Sentiment was not helped by the domestic political scene, where the Conservatives had just suffered the worst local elections defeat in fifty years, lost five parliamentary by-elections in a row, and then had to face the prospect of the charismatic Tony Blair taking over the leadership of the Labour Party following the death of John Smith. The market was totally unaffected by the 12-week long railway signalmen's strike. Given that the number of working days lost in strikes was the lowest since records began over a century ago, this series of one-day strikes masterminded by trade union diehard, Jimmy Knapp, was an irrelevancy. As usual, the strikes seriously inconvenienced the travelling public but if they were designed to embarrass the government, they signally failed to do so. Indeed, they had precisely the opposite effect, proving far more embarrassing to the Labour Party under a new leader keen to distance itself from the sort of irresponsible trade union action that had contributed to the defeat of the last Labour government in 1979.

The dollar starts to slide

The dollar now began to cast a shadow over world markets. It had been weak in the first half of the year, but in the first week of July it slipped below the key DM160 and Yen100 levels despite intervention and an encouraging (if ambiguous) statement from Alan Greenspan that the economic outlook was "as bright as it has been for decades". Nevertheless, a weak dollar fuelled rate rise fears and markets continued to fall, with the FTSE dropping below 2900 and the Dow approaching 3600. However, these levels then became floors as observers began to pay more attention to the brighter aspects of the economic picture. In the US, recovery was well under way with steady growth of output and employment in prospect for 1995. Inflationary pressures were subdued, demand did not need to be restrained, and the nascent recovery in Europe and Japan made the current account deficit less of a problem. As for the dollar, the G7 countries had decided that a support programme was not necessary. In any case, the US currency was down sharply against only the D-Mark and the yen whereas it was up against both the Canadian dollar and the Mexican Peso, their countries ranking No. 1 and No. 3 in the list of US trading partners. Thus, talk of imported inflation was just that, and 'benign neglect' was the best policy for the US to pursue, if indeed (as always) they had any choice in the matter.

In the case of the UK, recovery had gained momentum in the second quarter, seemingly unaffected by the April tax rises, and underlying inflation was holding steady at 2.4%. This sort of background meant ever-improving prospects for earnings and dividends and should have been more than enough to counterbalance the adverse influence on equities of a further modest increase in interest rates designed to inhibit inflationary pressures. After all, inflation can be beaten only in advance, not in arrears.

Rates still rising

This more balanced and sensible approach to markets survived another half-point increase in the Federal Funds rate to 4.75% in August, and by the end of the following week both the FTSE and the Dow had posted their highest levels since their declines began at 3265.1 and 3891.41 respectively. The optimism engendered by the fact that in both countries real growth was exceeding predictions and inflation undershooting them was severely tested in September in the UK when the Chancellor raised base rates to 5.75% in a pre-emptive strike designed to "take no risks with inflation at a time of strong growth". The FTSE dipped fractionally below 3000 again and the Government Securities index slipped to 89.99, but both quickly recovered. More evidence of strong growth in the US economy sparked expectations of a further rate rise in November, but the three quarter point hike to 5.5% caught markets off balance and equities took another nosedive with both the FTSE and the Dow losing over 100 points each by the end of the month. The severity of the falls in equities while bonds firmed invited yield ratio comparisons with October 1987 when it last exceeded its normal 2.2 to 2.6 range on the upside just before the Crash. In the views of more than a few market observers, Wall Street was "an accident waiting to happen". The big worry was that money had poured into equities on the strength of the economic recovery continuing to push up corporate earnings, but that the cycle was about to turn down. Only a few days earlier disappointing figures from General Motors had seen $2 billion wiped off its capitalisation in seven times normal volume.

Steady as she goes

The UK budget at the end of November was designed, said Chancellor Clarke, "to keep the economy on track to achieve the great prize of sustainable growth...that does not pass through illusory boom to painful bust". He forecast sharp cuts in future government spending and borrowing aimed at creating a public sector surplus by 1998/99, but the fact that the current PSBR was £34.5 billion against expectations of no more than £30 billion raised some eyebrows. The antics of the small band of Tory rebels who forced him to drop stage two of the fuel tax rise during the passage of the Finance Bill a week later, served to heighten the now ever-present political worries and the first week of December saw the FTSE below 3000 again. Another half-point on base rates, bringing them up to 6.25% on 7th December, and then the 29% swing against the Government revealed by the Dudley West by-election result, completed the shakeout. A vigorous end-year rally now began, encouraged by a number of high-profile bids including that by **Trafalgar House** for **Northern Electric**, the first of the many to come in the regional utility sector.

At the end of December, the FTSE stood at 3065.5, down 10.37% on the year, while the less internationally-oriented Mid-250 and Small Cap were down by only 7.6% and 6.5%. Not surprisingly, the big losers were the interest rate-sensitive sectors that had topped the bill in 1993, and Building and Construction lost 24.8% while Properties fell by 21.5%. The other notably dull sector was Insurance, down 23.2% on regulatory fears and worries about the effect of increased competition from low-cost, direct selling newcomers. Sector winners were Minerals Extraction and Oils, up 5.5% and 6.6% respectively on the back of the overall rise in commodity prices over the year.

Gilts as reflected in the Government Securities index ended the year at 90.87, down 16.5%, almost precisely reversing the gain of 1993 as the yield rose to 8.5%. With Equities yielding 4.2%, a yield ratio of no more than 2 did not look uncomfortable in the context of an historic P/E of 16.3. The Dow demonstrated considerable resilience, confounding many forecasters swayed by a weak dollar, and ended the year up 2% at 3834, unaffected by the devaluation of the Mexican peso on 20th December. The gold price took a back seat as interest rates rose, closing at $382.75, off just 2% in dollar terms but considerably more in that of most other currencies.

Playing by new rules

An easing of the recession, coupled with the effects of the reorganisation and rationalisation that the principal conglomerates had imposed upon their own sprawling empires, began to bring benefits in 1994 but investors remained sceptical.

BTR's 1993 results, announced in March, with pre-tax profits up 17% at £1.28 billion just topped most analysts' forecasts, and they were encouraged by reference to a general improvement in all areas during the second half. Interim figures revealed six months later recorded a worthy 16% gain at the pre-tax level to £694 million on sales, down 4%, but the picture was spoilt by mention of pressure on margins resulting from difficulties encountered in passing on rising raw material prices to customers who were themselves struggling to sell to reluctant consumers. The *FT* referred to the results as a 'debacle', and the share price fell 54p to 329p, cutting the group's market capitalisation by £1.6 billion and accounting for 10 points of a 40 point drop in the FTSE. Brokers' estimates for 1994 were trimmed from £1.4 billion to £1.3 billion and the shares remained under a cloud for the rest of the year. The gloom lifted a little in early December when a more upbeat trading statement was made but the end of the year left the shares close to their low at 293p with a middle-of-the-road P/E of 15.5 and a yield of 5.3%.

Hanson's interim figures in May pleased its followers with a 35% advance at the pre-tax level to £683 million thanks to a maiden contribution from Quantum and an upturn in the considerable building-related businesses in the US. With the costly Peabody Coal strike now history, things were looking good for the second half and a pre-tax total for 1993/94 of £1.35 billion was well up to best expectations. Quantum continued to show its worth with volume and prices both up strongly, and gearing was down to 58% after a string of disposals totalling £945 million. Nevertheless, the share price continued to decline, ending the year at 230p for an undemanding prospective P/E of around 12 and an above-average yield of 6.7%. Most commentators believed that the company had lost its edge and become a collection of solid but rather unexciting businesses.

In 1994, **Williams** made further progress with its planned transition from acquisitive conglomerate to focused industrial manufacturing group. However, the process involved considerable exceptional charges which served to obscure creditable gains in operating profits. At the pre-tax level full-year profits for 1993 announced in March registered a modest fall at £153 million, reflecting a slow pick-up in its major market areas and resulting pressure on prices which left growth prospects still dependent on higher volumes coupled with tighter cost controls. During the year, the engineering businesses were sold for £40.3 million and bolt-on acquisitions were made in the shape of **Corbin** and **Russwin** for £80 million and **Solvay** for £64 million, both funded by a £267 million rights issue of 1 for 7 at 330p. The former boosted Williams' share of the US commercial lock market from 9% to 20% and was expected to be earnings positive from Day One. Solvay fitted in neatly with Cuprinol in the European building products division. Interim figures showed a 13% lift in pre-tax profits to £86.2 million, calming City worries about Williams' ability to pass on higher raw material prices in difficult market conditions. Taking into account integration costs, most observers were looking for profits to top £200 million in the full year, regarding the shares as 'good value' at 314p on an historic P/E of 19.4 and a yield of 5.2%.

Tomkins' half-year figures to end-October 1993 slightly exceeded market estimates at £94 million and, excluding RHM's contribution, sales were up 28% and operating profits 22% ahead at £47.4 million, thanks to good progress in the US offsetting dull markets in the UK and even duller ones in Continental Europe. RHM chipped in £38.5 million, pointing to around £100 million in the first full year as rationalisation and integration proceeded. Again, most observers remained sceptical about the ability to make RHM live up to the sort of returns they had come to expect from Tomkins' non-food side. They were also concerned that the low share rating would make impossible the acquisitions for paper that would be necessary to power future growth. However, one useful acquisition was made in March of Noma Industries for $115 million cash. Noma was a Canadian company making lawnmowers and snowblowers and as such was an ideal bolt-on to Murray Ohio which was suffering from capacity shortages. Then, in May, £14 million cash was used to boost a 37.6% stake in Cobra to 62.4% making it a subsidiary and significantly increasing Tomkins' interests in South Africa. Full year profits announced in July were better than expected, up 50% at £257 million, with all divisions ahead but the major push still coming from the US. The share price barely budged from 218p, prompting chairman Greg Hutchings to comment, "we win every match but we are still bottom of the league". Critics continued to focus on RHM, saying that its integration looked like taking four years rather than the originally planned three, and that the price war in the volume bread market would continue to be a drag on the group. Forecasts of £300 million for 1994/95 failed to encourage the market and the shares ended the year at 220p on an historic P/E of 14.1 and a yield of 4.2%.

Racal's 1993/94 pre-tax total of £26.4 million after £19.6 million of disposal and closure costs as well as acquisition goodwill written off, although well below original expectations, was well received by the market and the shares rose 10p to 248p. Although some commentators noted that 'jam tomorrow' had become a habit with Racal, this time there was a lot to look forward to now that revitalisation of the core datacom businesses was under way and the networks side was set to benefit from the 22½% stake in Camelot. £70 million pre-tax was reckoned by some analysts to be the measure of the 'very substantial improvement' in 1994/95 forecast by chairman Sir Ernest Harrison. A useful acquisition announced also in June was an 80% stake in Techno Transfer Industries of Singapore for £9.7 million cash. The company built and operated remote control submarines used in the offshore oil industry and already accounted for more than half of the drilling rig support market in East Asia. Unfortunately for the high hopes engendered by the chairman's statement six months earlier, the interim figures in December revealed that the problems of the datacom division were proving more intractable than expected and that it would fall "substantially short" of its stated targets for margins of "well over 5%" on turnover of around £400 million. The shares fell 13p to 203p on the news as analysts scaled down forecasts for the full year to £60 million, but given the group's tendency towards over-optimistic forecasts the below-average prospective P/E of 16 on the end-December price of 223p was considered about right.

1995

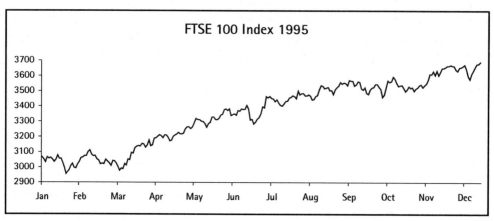

FTSE 100 Index 1995

Source: Thomson Reuters Datastream

Climbing a wall of worry

The fact that their bullish predictions for 1994 had been so soon confounded made for a more restrained assessment by analysts of the prospects for 1995. However, caution rather than pessimism was still the keynote, with most observers acknowledging that the UK economy was being 'rebalanced' away from consumer-led growth towards a more healthy and sustainable export and industry-driven recovery. The doubters concentrated on the political tensions that would arise inevitably from this apparently desirable economic scenario and on their belief that more rate rises were going to be necessary to subdue inflationary pressures. The turbulence in world markets throughout January soon appeared to justify this more cautious approach.

Congress's opposition to the $40 billion Mexico aid package emphasised the dangers of investing in vulnerable countries and suspect currencies, and Latin American and Asian-stock markets plunged, victims of a continuing 'flight to quality' as the high-risk/high-reward view of emerging markets was reassessed, now putting the emphasis on the former. Stronger-than-expected economic numbers fuelling rate rise fears unsettled both the Dow and the FTSE, with the latter dipping briefly below 3000 in late January. However, when the fears became a reality as the Fed Funds rate was raised half a point to 6% and London immediately followed suit by putting base rates up to 6.75%, both markets rallied strongly on hopes that perhaps rates had peaked at last. Currency markets were less hopeful on this score and the D-Mark became the one and only 'safe haven' now that the Kobe earthquake disaster had taken the shine off the yen. Nevertheless, the Dow continued its advance, topping

4000 by the end of February as Federal Reserve Board chairman Alan Greenspan opined that the US economy "may be slowing to a sustainable growth rate".

Barings goes belly-up

London was faced with new trials and tribulations when Barings, arguably the UK's most prestigious merchant bank, announced that it was ceasing trading after the whole of its capital and reserves had been lost as a result of open-ended trading losses in the Singapore-based derivatives market. The difficulty of capping the losses and thus crystallizing the trading deficit militated against a bail-out operation and Barings was allowed to go to the wall. Anxieties about a systemic problem in the banking world were well-aired, but predictions of up to a 100 point fall in the FTSE were shrugged off and a fall of 16 to 3009.3 was more than recovered the next day when the index closed at 3041.2.

Dow v. Dollar

Still influenced by the Fed chairman's statement, which indicated that perhaps there were no more rate rises in the pipeline, US bonds and equities continued to rise, totally ignoring warnings from observers who saw the advance as anomalous and perverse, given that the dollar appeared to be in free fall against the D-Mark and the Yen. There was a hiccup towards the end of March when the Dow lost 60 points and bonds a full point on reports of an imminent emergency Federal Reserve Board meeting to raise interest rates to defend the dollar. But instead, a batch of weak economic data emerged and markets recovered. Many commentators now began to try to rationalise the Dow's strength against a background of a still-sliding dollar, down 10% already in 1995 against the D-Mark and the Yen. The problem, they decided, had to be seen not just as one for the US but one for Germany and Japan as well. After all, a weak dollar feeds only very slowly into higher US inflation, given that imports make up no more than 14% of US GDP and much of these are priced in weaker currencies. A strong D-Mark is not a worry. On the other hand, if the Japanese were upset at having to bear the brunt of the dollar's decline,they should set their own house in order by liberalising imports and loosening their own monetary policy. If they were reluctant to do so, then the strength of the yen would force them to do so ultimately. Given that the restructuring of the US industrial economy since the 'eighties had made it much more competitive and productive capacity had probably grown much more than traditional measurements suggested, then a weak dollar had become a powerful weapon for redressing the trade imbalance with Japan. Thus there was no point in looking to central bank intervention and a new Plaza Accord to stem the dollar's decline. The economic fundamentals would simply have to correct themselves through the operation of the market. But for the moment, the Dow was simply enjoying a devaluation bull market whereas the Nikkei Dow was suffering a revaluation bear market.

Taking chances

Wall Street's rise and rise to over 4400 was a factor in the FTSE's continuing advance in company with gilts and by the end of May the former had topped 3300 and the latter, 95. The progress was marked with a high degree of volatility as conflicting economic data emerged week by week and the Government's political fortunes waxed and waned, with the emphasis on waned. Headline inflation perking up to a 2½-year high at 3.5% in March prompted expectations of a base rate rise when the Chancellor and the Governor next met in the first week of May, and the fact that rates were left unchanged at the insistence of the Chancellor was widely criticised at the time by practically every commentator. His 'no change' decision was seen as a politically-influenced one, coming in the wake of disastrous local election results, and sterling slipped to DM2.19, leaving it down 4% against the basket of currencies since the last base rate rise.

But as usual the market knew better, and later economic data soon appeared to validate the Chancellor's judgement. Of course indications of restrained domestic consumption and the likelihood that, thanks to rising exports, the UK was on-track to record in 1995 its first annual trade surplus for a decade, did nothing for the 'feel good factor'. The Government's political problems grew worse throughout the month of June, with John Major's leadership abilities coming into serious question. His bold decision to stand down as leader and put himself up for re-election against all comers threw the market into a state of confusion as the political and economic credentials of possible challengers were examined by the media. Equities, gilts and sterling all lost ground on fears that any outcome short of an overwhelming endorsement for John Major would lead to a weakening of the Government's anti-inflation resolve as electoral priorities took over. Former Welsh Secretary John Redwood's intervention was seen as a serious threat to the Prime Minister and by the last week of June, the FTSE had lost 120 points from its high achieved two weeks before.

Clearing the air

The outcome of the leadership election saw a considerable, if not overwhelming, endorsement of John Major, but it was enough to calm the market's political anxieties. The Conservatives were doubly fortunate in that, in the same week, the Fed Funds rate was trimmed by a quarter point to 5.75%, and Chancellor Clarke became the hero of the hour for holding out against a base rate rise in May. The FTSE surged

34.6 to a new peak for the year of 3463.9 on 7th July, and on the same day the Dow plussed 38.73 to reach a new all-time high of 4702.73. The big question was that after only eighteen months since the rate rise from 3% on 2nd February 1994, had the impetus of the recovery been tamed enough to eliminate inflationary pressures? 6% was not much of a peak by the inflationary standards we had become accustomed to (it was last seen in 1966) but the US economy had slowed in first half 1995, inflation clearly was subdued, and return to a 'safe' 2.5% growth trend should not be seen as overoptimistic. A cheap dollar was still boosting US exports and Japan had started to come to heel. The threat of trade sanctions (which would have virtually doubled the price of a Lexus in the US) seemed to have worked, and alarmed by the fall of the Nikkei Dow below 15000 to a 3-year low, the Japanese Finance Ministry continued with its rate cuts. The feeling was one of relief all round, for if the country with the world's weakest currency can cut rates at the same time as the one with the world's strongest, the clear indication is that rates are on the way down worldwide. The dollar then began to rally in earnest, particularly against the yen, and gained a new impetus in the first week of August when restrictions on Japanese institutions investing overseas were lifted.

Bids boost the FTSE

With sterling down 5% on a trade-weighted basis so far in 1995 and down 16% since leaving the ERM in 1992, the boost to UK industry's competitiveness and output given by this degree of devaluation was clear. But the other side of the coin was that the slide must in time be reflected in domestic prices, especially if the hoped for 2.5% to 3% growth rate was to be sustained.

It was worries on this score that kept the base rate debate going throughout the summer, with the Bank of England warning that the 2.5% inflation target was likely to be exceeded in the absence of a rate rise, and the Chancellor arguing that there was more than enough evidence of a slowdown to justify resisting calls for any rise. If equities would have been hit by an increase in base rates, or their attractions dulled by the impact on corporate earnings of a slowing economy, the fact that they continued to advance was interpreted by more optimistic observers as evidence that perhaps the economy was capable of achieving the elusive goal of non-inflationary sustainable growth. At the same time, it had to be admitted that the market owed a part of its strength to a very high level of bid activity, principally involving the big capitalisation regional utility companies, which not only resulted in the reinvestment of proceeds but also pushed up the prices of other likely bid targets. The FTSE swept through its previous all-time high of 3520.3 recorded on 2nd February 1994 to close at 3535.7 on 21st August, reacted almost immediately to below 3500 following a series of cautious trading statements from high-profile companies about the effect of rising raw material prices and unit labour costs on margins, and then surged to a new all-time high of 3570.8 on 13th September. Gilts continued their recovery too, the Government Securities index reaching 94.81 on the same day, albeit below its high for the year of

95.51, seemingly not too worried by further reports that the 1995/96 PSBR overshoot from the original £21.5 billion forecast made in November 1994 was likely to exceed the Treasury's revised figure of £23.5 billion by another £5 billion at least.

Another attack of nerves

This renewed bout of enthusiasm suffered a setback in the second half of September, when gilts fell back to below 93 and the FTSE shed almost 100 points to 3479 on nervousness inspired by further currency turmoil as the European Union Majorca summit underlined the difficulty that many countries would have in meeting the strict Maastricht convergency criteria for a single currency. This sparked yet another 'flight to safety', targeting the D-Mark and the Swiss franc, a move leading to a new setback for the dollar which slipped back to DM1.42 and below the psychologically important Y100 mark. The pound suffered too, falling sharply against both the dollar and the D-Mark and thus dimming the prospect of base rate reductions. Observers who had called the dollar's turn back in April, 'a major trend reversal', began to get cold feet, expressing fears that the rally could completely unwind thanks to a combination of unchanged fundamentals: namely a record US trade gap, a disappointing Japanese fiscal package and the problems of achieving European Monetary Union so well-aired in Majorca. However, following the pattern that had become established at the beginning of the year, setbacks provide buying opportunities and by the middle of November the foreign exchange markets had stabilised, the FTSE had topped 3600 for the first time, the gilts index was up to 95 again and the Dow was within a whisker of the 5000 mark. Buyers were further encouraged by a sharp fall in the headline inflation figure for October to 3.2% against 3.9% in September, a development which suggested that the Chancellor now had greater scope for generosity in the budget due at the end of the month.

Free as a bird

The budget provided a little something for everyone, although most commentators professed to be disappointed at the absence of more vigorous stimuli to an economy they saw as becoming increasingly sluggish, lamenting that it bore the hallmark of all post-Lawson budgets, namely a greater concern with inflation than recession. The Chancellor's forecast of 3% growth in 1996 was greeted with considerable scepticism especially since he had done little in his budget to pave the way for growth of this magnitude, and if it were to be achieved then his projection for underlying inflation at 2.5% looked overoptimistic. The dilemma posed was that if 3% growth demanded interest rate cuts, 2.5% inflation required subdued growth and the restraining hand of the Governor of the Bank of England. However, these initial doubts were quickly swept away as the market responded to a renewed advance on Wall Street and a flurry of major bids at home, pushing the FTSE to a record closing high of 3680.4 on 1st December. With the building societies having trimmed their mortgage rates by 0.25% on budget day, the market now had good reason to look for a base rate reduction before the end of the year. On 13th December it duly arrived with a quarter point cut to 6.5%, apparently agreed amicably this time between the Chancellor and the Governor, the latter clearly influenced by yet another fall in the rate of inflation to 3.1% in November. Two days later, sentiment gained a further boost as the Bundesbank cut its rates to their lowest for seven years, and then to create a perfect end to a year, on 19th December the Fed Funds rate was cut by a quarter point to 5.5%. Shares had plunged the day before on fears that there would be no rate cut without an agreement between President Clinton and Congress over the plan to balance the Federal budget by 2002, but rebounded sharply on the announcement that an agreement had been reached.

The FTSE100 closed the year at a record high of 3683.3 for a gain of 20.3%, outpacing both the FTSE Actuaries All Share, up 18.5%, and the FTSE Mid-250, up just 14.8%, thereby demonstrating the popularity of the leaders over second line stocks and in part the effects of an unprecedented takeover boom. Gilts as measured by the Government Securities Index were up 5.6% at 95.94 with the long gilt yield falling from 8.7% to 7.7% to provide a gilt/equity yield ratio of slightly under 2, a figure putting equities in the 'good value' category. Wall Street outperformed all other markets with a 33% advance to 5117.12 although this figure was 100 points below the peak of 5216.47 reached on 13th December. There too, the long bond yield had fallen over the year from 8% to below 6%. The NASDAQ Composite index was up 42% thanks to an outstanding performance by technology stocks. Even Japan joined in the fun with the Nikkei 225 closing 37% up at 19868 on its low point of 14485 posted on 3rd July. However, this performance confounded most forecasters who had looked for a rising index on the back of a strong yen, whereas the rise did not take place until the yen began to fall. Sterling ended the year at $1.55 practically unchanged, but against the D-Mark it fell from DM2.43 to DM2.23. Gold managed no more than a $2.75 rise over the year to $387.05 despite being strongly tipped on the back of increasing demand pushing spot prices above forward ones depressed by heavy producer sales.

A record year for takeovers

Merger mania gripped the City in 1995, with deals totalling some £66 billion, more than double the figure for 1994 and comfortably ahead of the previous record total of £45 billion achieved in 1989. By far the biggest bid was **Glaxo**'s agreed £9.1 billion offer for pharmaceutical rival **Wellcome**, and **Lloyds Bank** managed to spend almost as much by buying **Cheltenham & Gloucester Building Society** and **TSB**. The merchant banking sector also received more than its fair share of bids. Stricken

Barings went to Dutch bank **ING** for £1, **Warburgs** sold out to Swiss Bank Corporation for £800 million, **Kleinwort Benson** accepted £1 billion offer from Germany's Dresdner Bank, and **Smith New Court** went along with top US stockbroker Merrill Lynch for £526 million. Many of the relatively newly-privatised regional electricity companies decided to join forces in £1 billion-plus deals, with the water companies soon becoming involved.

AIM

June 1995 saw the introduction of AIM (Alternative Investment Market), designed as a replacement for the USM (Unlisted Securities Market) but with even cheaper and less demanding entry qualifications. One essential qualification, however, was that every would-be entrant had to find a sponsor, usually a stockbroker, who would also be responsible for the company's behaviour following admission. AIM was to prove a popular junior market, especially for start-up companies in the high technology and biotechnology fields.

The long-expected bid for **Fisons** eventually came in August with a £1.7 billion price tag from Rhone-Poulenc, but the most exciting and acrimonious bid of the year promised to be **Granada's** hostile £3.3 bllion offer in December for **Forte**.

If technology stocks provided much of the excitement on Wall Street, they did much the same in London, with biotech and computer-related companies heading the Best Performing tables in 1995. However, their relatively small market capitalisations prevented them from influencing the indices to the extent they did in the US. Their volatility also proved unsettling to many investors. Some who remembered the boom-and-bust associated with the personal computer market in 1984 when astronomical profit forecasts two and three years ahead were to prove unattainable for one-product companies in highly competitive markets, especially when burdened with huge current losses and development costs. Murphy's Law – what can go wrong, will go wrong – operates with great reliability in the field of high technology.

All change at Hanson

1995 was a year of significant change for **Hanson**. In February, the demerger of its non-core US businesses was announced. This involved the creation of US Industries, shares in which were allotted to Hanson shareholders on a 1 for 100 basis and David Clarke, Lord White's nominated successor, was to leave the Hanson orbit to run the new group. However, the principal interest in the deal from the point of view of the London market was the fact that the demerger removed £855 million of debts from the parent company's balance sheet, thus reducing gearing to some 38%. Coupled with the passing on of £587 million of goodwill, this meant that Hanson was now in a position to make a substantial acquisition of up to £3 billion without overstretching itself. United Biscuits (its old adversary in the battle for Imperial Tobacco) was a popular prospective target, but most observers thought a contracyclical like one of the big regional electricity companies was most logical. The shares rose strongly ahead of interim figures in May, which were well up to best expectations. Operating profits surged from £353 million to £662 million thanks to rising demand and price rises for its basic products in both the UK and the US, and to the continued benefit to margins of cost-reduction programmes. Quantum Chemical's profits at £213 million were actually up sevenfold, but the momentum was expected to slacken in the second half with most observers looking for a full-year total of around £1.3 billion for a prospective P/E of below 13 at 250p. The well above-average yield of 6% was widely regarded as a further prop for the share price.

Then at the beginning of August came the long-awaited 'big bid', with a £2.5 billion agreed offer for **Eastern Group**, one of the major regional electricity distributors, and incidentally one of three to attract a bid that month. The deal was regarded by some commentators as a typically cautious and unimaginative one devised by Lord Hanson's chosen successor, Derek Bonham. But others saw it as a classic cash generating and earnings enhancing acquisition needed by a group with strong cyclical characteristics. The fact that it was not in the freebooting tradition of earlier Hanson deals was simply a sign of the times. The death of Lord White, "the principal architect of the company's success", in the words of Lord Hanson, seemed to underline the impression that this was indeed the end of an era. Since by this time the share price had declined steadily to below 200p, it was clear that the market had difficulty in coming to terms with Hanson's status change, and the full-year results announced in the first week of December, creditable though they were, did little to bolster the group's image. Broadly unchanged at £1.275 billion pre-tax, the results continued to benefit from rising profits at Quantum Chemical, but an unchanged dividend and consideration of gearing post-Eastern soaring to 130% seemed to carry more weight with investors. Derek Bonham's revelation of plans to raise £2 billion by disposals over the next twelve months made little difference initially, but sentiment quickly improved when within days he announced the sale of Cavenham Forest Industries and a majority stake in Suburban Propane. Proceeds of around £1.5 billion would reduce gearing "considerably" and, despite a minor earnings dilution, the shares responded to close the year at 192p, comfortably above the low point of 180p, and seemingly on an improving trend although still down 16.5% in 1995. With a below-average P/E of 10.5 and an above-average yield of 7.8%, more than one commentator tipped the shares for recovery in 1996 on the grounds that the out-of-fashion phase had been overdone and Derek Bonham's management skills underrated.

Back to basics for BTR

BTR opened 1995 by announcing the planned retirement of Chief Executive Alan Jackson at the end of the year and the appointment of Ian Strachan, former Deputy Chief Executive of RTZ, in his place. Full-year figures for 1994 revealed in mid-March pleased the market as pre-tax profits rose 11% to £1.41 billion, confounding earlier pessimism about margins which in fact improved from 15.2% to 17.2% between the first and second halves as volume gains accrued. With gearing down from 64% to 35% over the past two years, thanks to a string of disposals designed to focus the group more towards industrial manufacturing, BTR was widely seen as standing high in the organic growth stakes and under no pressure to seek out a new acquisition to exploit. Cash flow was rising rapidly and exercise of the remaining warrants would bring in another £1.3 billion before 1999. The share price responded to this broadly favourable view to reach a high for the year of 348p in May. Then in July, it was revealed that BTR was to buy out the 37% of Australian-based BTR Nylex that it did not own for £2 billion.

The deal was seen in part as demonstrating the scarcity of suitable bid targets, but met broad approval as facilitating BTR's planned expansion in the Far East. The fact that gearing would rise to 100% again as a result of the cash and shares offer appeared to cause little anxiety given that more disposals were assumed to be in the pipeline. Interim profits in September were in line with most forecasts, up 5% to £729 million after a £21 million provision relating to recent acquisitions, and the group was reckoned to be on target for a full-year total of around £1.5 billion. There was more action on the acquisition front later that month, with £56 million being paid for the industrial battery side of Varta, loss-making but still Europe's biggest manufacturer, and £60 million for leading Brazilian automotive component manufacturer, OSA, doubling BTR's sales in that country. Unfortunately, a reasonable share price performance over the year was wrecked by a statement in the first week of December that profits in the current year would "not meet expectations". Vulnerable areas were said to be the automotive and construction industry in Continental Europe, the housing sector in Australia, and chemicals in Taiwan and mainland China, but more worrying was an expression of concern about the global economic background where early signs of recovery had faded. The shares fell 14p to 320p on the statement as analysts trimmed their full-year forecasts from £1.5 billion to nearer £1.4 billion. However, the shares ended the year on an upbeat note on news of the disposal for £330 million of **Tilcon**, its UK aggregates business, and then of **Slazenger** (ex-Dunlop) for £300 million. The resulting sharp reduction in gearing encouraged analysts and the shares rallied to reach 329p at year end, where the yield was a useful 5.3% and the P/E a modest 14.3. Alan Jackson's five years at the top had resulted in BTR becoming refocused on industrial manufacturing following a programme of strategic disposals and acquisitions.

Williams puts down roots

Williams Holdings' pre-tax profits rise in 1994 to £200.3 million was in line with most forecasts, and Lex complimented the group on achieving the desired transformation from "sprawling takeover vehicle to focused global industrial group". At the same time, the concentration on three core businesses was considered to take away some of the excitement, given that suitable acquisitions would be hard to find and the fact that gearing heading for zero by end-1995 made them both practicable and desirable. Despite "very challenging conditions" in building products, interim profits announced in September recorded a useful 20% gain to £103.1 million, a performance prompting most analysts to pencil in a total for the year of around £220 million for a prospective P/E of 15 and a yield of 5.5% at 323p. Expectations of continuing recovery in most areas of operation caused the share price to firm over the next few weeks as forecasts were revised upwards to £230 million, but in early December a third quarter trading statement to the effect that profits in the current year would be "at the lower end of market expectations", knocked the share price back to 315p as analysts quickly trimmed their forecasts to £228 million. However, the shares recovered on the back of a firm market background to close the year at 329p, still modestly rated on a P/E of 15.3 and yield of 5.3%.

Tomkins pulls it off

Tomkins made a good start to the year by revealing surprisingly good interim profits for the six months to end-October 1994, up 22% to £114.5 million pre-tax with the dividend raised from 2.08p to 2.43p. The share price edged ahead from end-year levels but picked up strongly in July when full-year profits exceeded forecasts at £303 million. The figures were helped by a £16 million gain at RHM plus improved margins. Commentators were impressed by an overall 50% increase in capital expenditure to just over £120 million, but still hankered after a deal putting the group's £289 million cash pile to good use by helping to fund an acquisition of around twice that sum. The logic was that such a deal was necessary to offset below-average earnings growth as the US recreational vehicle and housing markets went into cyclical slowdown. However, news in August that the company was seeking permission to buy back up to 10% of its own shares won broad approval from the market even if it meant that Tomkins could find no better use for its money, and the share price advanced again. Then, in mid-December, Tomkins fans got what they wanted with a $1 billion agreed bid for Gates Rubber, a US manufacturer of rubber automotive components, mainly hoses, transmission belts and seals. With sales per employee some 20% below Tomkins' average, the deal provided ample room to boost margins and with two thirds of Gates' sales in the replacement market there was little concern about the cyclical nature of the car market. Funding the purchase by a convertible preference issue instead of equity meant that the deal would be earnings enhancing from the outset in the 5-10% range, providing Tomkins with the opportunity to reverse three years of underperformance. The share price responded instantly and closed the year at 282p, up 28% with all the appearance of being destined for higher levels in 1996. At this point the P/E was 15.7 and yield 3.8%.

Racal back in favour

Racal redeemed itself in the eyes of many of its followers in 1995. Last December's warning statement served to take the sting out of the apparently disappointing profits total of £58.3 million reported in early June, though it was below even the revised estimate, and the shares slipped only 8p to 250p. As expected, problem areas continued to be data products but the division was rescued to some extent by Racal's 22.5% stake in Camelot's first year profit of £10.8 million and the capitalisation of its £6.4 million investment. in the National Lottery operator. Radio communications managed a 15% rise in profits to £20.5 million but warned of "reduced profitability in the current year". On the defence side, the acquisition of Thorn Sensors in March for £18.9 million involved a £22 million provision for reorganisation costs and contract liabilities and was considered unlikely to contribute to that division's forecast profit of £10 million on £170 million turnover in 1995/96.

Most commentators took the view that with tough trading conditions likely to persist in its two core businesses of data products and radio communications, the shares might have problems sustaining their premium rating of a prospective P/E of 15.5 at 250p on estimated pre-tax profits of around £70 million. In the event the share price drifted back to below 220p in late summer but picked up strongly ahead of the interim figures in early December. Profits were a little above most estimates, up 28% at £30.1 million thanks to an £8.2 million contribution from Camelot, but the 23p rise in the share price to 276p owed much more to the announcement that Racal was to buy **British Rail Telecommunication** (BRT) from British Rail for £132.8 million. The deal was seen as the means to achieve the rebalancing of the group towards communications network services, thus diminishing the importance of the dull and difficult data products division. BRT operates BR's internal telecom system which is one of the largest and most comprehensive in the country. Already returning profits of £17.6 million on turnover of £174 million, the network was substantially underutilised and, while retaining BR's custom, Racal would be able to compete aggressively for new contracts. Earnings enhancing from Day One, the rise in gearing from around 17% to almost 100% resulting from the deal caused no worries among commentators and the shares remained in favour, ending the year at 285p, up 31% from their low point. With a P/E of 21.8 and a yield of 2.8%, the shares were highly rated, but bulls pinned their hopes on the shift away from manufacturing evidenced by the runaway success of the Camelot participation and then the BRT deal. One analyst was looking for profits of £72 million in the current year, rising to £92 million in 1996/97 with £130 million in prospect for the year after that.

1996

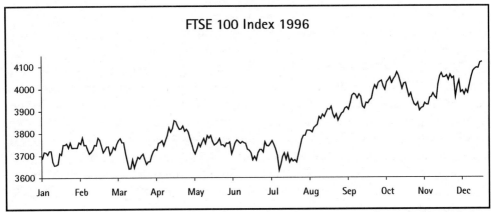

FTSE 100 Index 1996

Source: Thomson Reuters Datastream

Exceeding expectations

Nothing succeeds in the stock market like success and few commentators were prepared to call the FTSE lower twelve months hence. Having been over-optimistic about the way things would go in 1994 and pessimistic about 1995, most of them decided to follow the middle path for 1996. The consensus was for a first-half advance under the influence of continuing, albeit sluggish, non-inflationary growth massaged by further small interest rate cuts, while the second half was considered likely to see these positive trends overshadowed by political anxieties as the election loomed ever-nearer. These political fears looked like surfacing much earlier than expected when a second high profile defection reduced the government's majority to crisis level and John Major's leadership abilities once again were called into question. The unveiling of Tony Blair's 'stakeholder' concept also worried many who feared the impact on industry's competitiveness of a future policy likely to be biased against profits and dividends and to be in favour of a minimum wage. The fact that it was welcomed by the trade unions set alarm bells ringing for those who remembered Harold Wilson's one-sided 'social contract' of 1974. However the market had become accustomed to the Tories' troubles as well as to Labour's 'policy initiatives', and took them in its stride, surging through the 3700 level in the first week of the year. A brief setback prompted by a sharp fall on Wall Street was quickly reversed by the Chancellor's decision to trim base rates by another quarter point to 6.25% and on 31st January the FTSE recorded a new closing high of 3759.3, with more bids and rumours of bids playing their part in the advance. The Dow continued to set the pace for world markets, closing at an all-time high of 5394.94 on the last day of the month following a cut in the Fed Funds rate from 5.5% to 5.25%.

Second thoughts

A note of caution now began to infuse commentaries on the London market. The second rate cut in five weeks was widely believed to have been made against the better judgement of the Governor of the Bank of England, who, earlier in the month and probably with an eye to the high wage settlements just announced at Ford and Vauxhall, had warned of the dangers of stoking up inflationary pressures. The Chancellor on the other hand had perhaps been tempted to cut rates sooner rather than later in the hope of seeing his party's fortunes rise in line with the growth of real personal disposable incomes and increased consumer spending in the second half of the year. After all, suggested Lex in the *FT*, if the deteriorating performance of UK exports was due to the slowdown in European growth rates, the situation would not be improved by rate cuts here. Another commentator, pointing out that broad money growth in the year to November 1995 had risen above the Chancellor's 3-9% target range, hinted at a parallel with early 1986 when, at a time of weak growth and low inflation, the government had sought to regain its electoral appeal by boosting the elusive 'feel good factor' and abandoned monetary targeting. It was further suggested that if the Chancellor was right to look for an above-trend 3% annual growth rate in the second half of 1996 and yet had no intention of raising interest rates ahead of the election, then the prospect of the economy bumping up against its capacity ceiling loomed large, with all its implications for inflation and the balance of payments.

Another brick in the wall

Of course, such fears could have proved to be simply an extension of 1995's 'wall of worry' that a continuing bull market was destined to climb. But if they turned out to have real substance, then there could be serious trouble ahead for the economy, just as in 1986. Such developments would not necessarily be bad news for the equity market, or at least 'not yet' seemed to be the view the market was happy to take. But the next base rate cut to 6% in the second week of March was greeted with even less enthusiasm. The Chancellor's rationale was that with inflationary pressures continuing to ease and the economy growing at below what he considered to be its sustainable long term rate, then he was still on course to meet his 2.5% inflation target by the end of his government's term. Unfortunately, in the same week, the closely-watched US employment figures came in as the strongest in thirteen years, triggering a dramatic share and bond sell off on Wall Street. The Dow lost 171.24 to 5470.45 and bonds fell as much as three points. Inevitably, there was a knock-on effect in London and over the next few days the FTSE slipped through the bottom of its 3650-3750 range with sentiment further depressed by the political and financial fall-out from the beef crisis. Gilts suffered too, with the Government Securities index losing two full points since February to 92, pushing the yield up to 8.3%.

Dead man walking

Gold provided a little, but only a little, excitement in January as a $10 advance in the first week of the New Year, with the spot price ahead of the forward ones, brought the usual small band of gold and chartist fanatics out of the closet. However, a flurry of speculative activity failed to spark any substantial physical demand – and, unlike the Goldsmith/Soros foray in 1993, there was not the muscle in financial or publicity terms to sustain the advance. This time, top South African producer **Western Areas** blew the whistle by announcing that it had sold forward its entire production for the next 8½ years, i.e. 7.3 million ounces, equivalent to Australia's entire annual output. This constituted the industry's largest-ever forward sale and effectively overwhelmed any idea that the price backwardation owed its existence to anything more than short-term technical factors. After peaking at $417.75 at the beginning of February, within a matter of days the price had dropped back to below $400 again.

Unwilling suspension of disbelief

Most commentators had difficulty in reconciling their experience of UK economic history with the idea that a recovering economy was consistent with the persistence of low inflation and assumed that a reversal of the downtrend in interest rates would stop the bull market dead in its tracks. It was not a matter of 'if' such a reversal would begin, but 'when'. Thus a general feeling of unease was engendered by the obvious conclusion that markets, led by Wall Street, were living on borrowed time. This less-than-optimistic view was encouraged by consideration of the government's all-too evident difficulty in bringing down the PSBR to fit in with the Treasury's earlier forecasts, and of the problem common to all the governments of the industrialised world, ie. that of fiscal consolidation as they try to reduce the ratio of gross public debt to GDP to a more manageable level. The Chancellor's budget forecast of a PSBR for 1995/96 of £29 billion (already revised from November 1994's figure of £21.5 billion and the Treasury's midsummer forecast of £23.5 billion) was now looking more like £32 billion as the cut-off date approached, a disparity the magnitude of which cast doubt on his forecasts for 1996/97 and 1997/98 and the chances of meeting the Maastricht convergence criteria by the mooted target date, however academic the latter problem might appear to be at this stage.

The final cut

But if contemplation of such serious matters was enough to keep the FTSE locked in the 3650-3850 range during the first half of the year, at the beginning of the second half they had begun to look positively esoteric. Contrary to popular expectations, US interest rates were not raised, Fed chairman Alan Greenspan preferring to employ exhortation to achieve his anti-inflationary ends; and criticism of Chancellor Clarke's quarter point cut in base rates to 5.75% on 6th June as unnecessary in the context of strengthening consumer demand was to a great extent defused by appreciating sterling and the belief that a rate cut now was preferable to politically-inspired tax cuts in the forthcoming budget. There was more agonising to come throughout July and early August, but by the middle of the month investors had decided that the pluses in the economy outweighed the minuses and the bull market was back, albeit with the aid of a number of high-profile bids and rumours of many more. The FTSE broke out of its trading range to reach a new closing high of 3872.9 on 16th August and by the end of the month had crossed the 3900 level. Another batch of strong US data in September, coupled with the story that eight out of twelve US Federal banks were demanding a rate rise, kept the Dow subdued for a time and pushed the yield on the 30-year Treasury bond over 7% again, but when rates were left unchanged, the Dow pressed on towards 6000 and bonds recovered strongly. A rate rise was now considered highly unlikely so close to the November election.

Views from the mountain top

In the first week of October, the FTSE breached the 4000 level for the first time, unaffected by any pronouncements made at the Labour Party conference, but the advance sparked a renewed debate about whether markets were too high. A 0.1% rise to 2.9% in the underlying rate of inflation in September was seen as evidence that the recovery in consumer spending was putting pressure on prices, the continuing rise in sterling was bound to adversely affect the competitive position of UK exports, and the growth of broad money supply at over 10% was not compatible with continuing low inflation in an economy growing at its current rate. Political fears reasserted themselves, too, on the grounds that while Tony Blair sought to reassure industry about New Labour's policies on public spending and taxation, an actual election victory would soon see him in conflict with Old Labour's only too well-known views on those same subjects. As for Wall Street, a spate of articles sought to drive home the message that the market was too high and riding for a fall. The so-called 'Q ratio', for example, which compares stock market valuations with the replacement cost of corporate assets, now stood at 1.5, its highest level since 1915. The Standard & Poor dividend yield was 2.13%, the lowest figure recorded this century and well below the 2.6% ruling in October 1987, just before the Crash. Such figures, the argument went, left equities expensive relative to bonds which were themselves expensive as a result of failing to factor-in the interest rate rises likely in 1997. The over-enthusiastic reception given to new issues like **Planet Hollywood** and **Yahoo!** were seen as evidence of speculative excess, and the unprecedented inflow of money into mutual funds that had fuelled the stock market rise in the first half of the year had now diminished significantly.

Action v Exhortation

But, as usual, while the critics propose, the markets dispose, and the Chancellor's quarter point increase in base rate to 6% at the end of October served both to reinforce his anti-inflation credentials and reassure investors that a cautious and responsible budget was in prospect four weeks hence. The increase was seen as going some way to allaying the frequently expressed anti-inflationary concerns of the Bank of England, while the boost it had given to sterling was certain to lessen pressure for further increases. A sharp rise in the underlying rate of inflation to 3.3% in October provided a sobering prelude to the budget and the FTSE achieved an intraday high of 4094.4 just before the Chancellor rose to speak. His budget package involved £1.7 billion in cuts from 1996/97's spending total, a reduction in the basic rate of income tax from 24% to 23%, a widening of the 20% reduced rate band and increased duties on petrol and tobacco. Given that consumer spending was estimated to rise by 4.25% in the coming year, many commentators thought tax cuts of any sort were uncalled for; but overall, the budget was welcomed as well-judged given the political context in which the Chancellor found himself. The FTSE continued to hover just above the 4000 level until the first week in December when, along with practically every market in the world, it was knocked for six by Fed chairman Alan Greenspan's comment that asset markets were in a state of "irrational exuberance".

Given his position, the remark was widely taken to imply that the day was not far distant when he would raise interest rates to curb that exuberance and head off inflationary pressures. Nevertheless, a turbulent week in the wake of this pronouncement was soon forgotten as markets embarked upon a traditional end-year rally which took both the FTSE and the Dow to new highs. On the last day of 1996, the FTSE reached a record high of 4118.5, up 11.6% on the year and almost exactly in line with the performance of the All-Share index and the FTSE 250. The best performing sector was Oil Exploration & Production, up 55% thanks to an unexpectedly firm oil price and a spate of bids among the smaller exploration stocks with a final burst of strength provided by the cold snap. Financials, led by banks and composite insurers, were the other star performers as consolidation continued to dominate the sector. Gilts as measured by the Government Securities Index were down 1.45% at 94.54 and the 10-year yield of 7.55% provided a modest gilt/equity yield ratio of 2.02. The Dow closed at 6448.27, up 26% on the year, after a last-minute bout of nerves induced by stronger home sales and consumer confidence data triggered another triple-digit loss of 101.4 on 31st January, leaving the year's high at 6560.9 recorded on 27th December. Bonds were hit by the news too, and the yield on the 30-year Treasury bond edged over 6.6%.

Japan, a popular choice for recovery at the beginning of the year, remained the

Cinderella of world stock markets and after touching 22666 in June, ended 1996 at 19361.35 for a loss of 2.5%. Clearly the Japanese economy was still suffering from the bursting of the bubble of 'irrational exuberance' that had infected its own share and property markets in the late 'eighties and now called into question the stability of its whole financial system. In currencies, sterling stood out, reaching $1.69 and DM2.61, up from $1.55 and DM2.23 twelve months earlier, reflecting both a re-rating of the UK economy and the expectations of interest rate rises for a currency already yielding in excess of most others. The dollar weakness in the first half of 1995 was now almost totally forgotten as it forged ahead against the D-Mark and the Yen, closing the year at DM1.54 (DM1.43) and Y116 (Y103), reflecting the strength of the US economy. After its abortive burst of strength back in January, gold continued to drift throughout the year, losing $20 to $369.50 with sentiment further dampened by the prospect of European central bank sales to help their countries meet the single currency criteria.

Mixing and matching

1996 was a significant year for bids and mergers, opening with **Granada** winning its hostile £3.6 billion bid for **Forte** and **Rentokil** taking out **BET** for £2.6 billion. On a more amicable note, **United News & Media** agreed a £3 billion merger with **MAI** (formerly known as Mills & Allen International) and in May, **Sun Alliance** and **Royal Insurance** got together to form a £6 billion grouping. The biggest merger that did not go all the way was between **BT** and **Cable & Wireless**, but BT still managed to acquire the global muscle it needed by linking with America's **MCI** to create one of the top three telecommunications companies in the world. The utilities were in the forefront of bid action, and by the end of the year only two of the twelve regional electricity companies floated six years before remained independent. There is no doubt there would have been even more activity in the sector but for the DTI blocking bids for **National Power** and **PowerGen** in May, and then calling a halt to any more water company bids in October.

Notable new issues in 1996 were led by mobile telephone company **Orange** in March. The company floated 26.5% of its capital at an issue price of 205p to provide an equity market capitalisation of £2.5 billion. The issue was ten times oversubscribed and the shares opened at 244p on the first day of dealing with the popularity of the offer totally unaffected by the fact that Orange's huge development costs meant that its £140 million loss on sales of £229 million in 1995 had brought its cumulative loss over the past three years to £500 million. By contrast, Racal's flotation in 1988 of 20% of Vodafone had seen only a modest 14p premium on an offer price of 170p for a valuation of £1.75 billion. At the time, this high rating of a prospective P/E of 30 was seen as daring for a company forecasting no more than a doubling of profits to £71.7 million in 1989. **Railtrack**, owner of former British Rail's land and track, got off to a slow start in May thanks to a barrage of criticism from Labour's Shadow Minister of Transport, Clare Short, but investors ignored renationalisation and regulatory fears and oversubscribed the issue three times. The shares established a 20p premium on the first day and went on to double by the end of the year. Less popular on launch day in July was nuclear power group **British Energy**. Offered at 100p, the shares opened at a 6p discount before moving up substantially on yield considerations to end the year at 147p. In September, a much lower-key issue was **AEA Technology**, the research arm of the Atomic Energy Authority and the last privatisation ahead of the General Election. Institutional demand leading to a seven-times oversubscription ensured that the placing price was set above the projected target range of 240p-270p at 280p, and after opening at 310p, the shares forged ahead to close the year at 400p.

Fantasy Football

1996 showed that football had come a long way since the lacklustre launch of **Tottenham Hotspur**, the first club to come to the market, back in 1983. It was soon followed by **Manchester United**, which received a more enthusiastic reception but more than ten years were to pass before football became accepted as an investment-grade subdivision of the leisure sector. That transformation was directly attributable to the impact of BSkyB's satellite broadcasting and the subsequent deification, globalisation and total commercialisation of the game. Tottenham Hotspur rose from 222p to 630p and Manchester United from 188p to 667p during the course of the year, performances triggering a flurry of activity in the junior markets as other clubs rushed to cash in on the game's new-found popularity with investors as well as with fans

The sum of the parts...?

Lord Hanson marked the closing chapters of his and his company's remarkable career by announcing the demerger of its principal components ahead of his planned retirement in the autumn of 1997. The slogan attached to the policy was 'divide equals multiply', but the market's reaction failed to justify the equation as the combined value of the demerged companies slumped after they went their separate ways in October. **Millenium Chemicals** traded up to £16 3/4 before closing the year only a shade above its low point of £10 3/4. **Imperial Tobacco** fared little better with the prospect of a high yield and assured dividend growth overshadowed by BAT's class action lawsuits, and the share price ended 1996 at 377p, well off its high of 429p. Most disappointing of all was the performance of the **Hanson** rump, containing the energy division (Eastern Electricity and Peabody Coal) and building materials, where the share price fell from 134p to 80p ahead of their demerger early in 1997. All the components were now considered to look vulnerable themselves to bids.

   BTR was another notably poor performer over the year as doubts persisted about the likely success and the timescale of its proclaimed strategy of disposing of non-core businesses to concentrate on industrial manufacturing and expansion in emerging markets. A 5% boost in 1995's pre-tax profits to £1.5 billion was welcomed by the market, but the fall from favour gathered pace after a profit warning in May, analysts' predictions of a dividend cut, and rumours of discontent in the boardroom. Despite the company's denial of the dividend cut story, in September the interim dividend was slashed by 35%. The fact of the company biting the bullet appeared to encourage the idea that new chief executive Ian Strachan was in control and determined to see his strategy through, and in the final weeks of the year the share price continued its recovery from a low point of 229p to close at 284p, albeit down from 329p twelve months earlier.

Williams Holdings pursued a similar course to BTR, disposing of what it saw as non-core businesses to concentrate on its three chosen activities, fire protection, security, and home improvement products. Since the disposals made considerably greater impact on Williams' debts than in the case of BTR, the market treated the company much more generously and the shares rose 4% over the year to 343p. This was hardly an impressive performance relative to the market as a whole but better than that of any of its fellow 'diversified industrials', the histories of which we have recorded. However, real enthusiasm for the prospects of 'new look' Williams was muted by the fact that the disposals included businesses like Rawlplug, Valor and Swish, which to many investors were 'core' to their image of the company if not to that perceived by the management.

Tomkins remained the only example of the traditional unreconstructed conglomerate among those whose fortunes we have followed since they first embarked upon the acquisition trail. This had not made it more or less popular with critics who saw all conglomerates as tarred with the same brush, but Chief Executive Greg Hutchings could still point to fifteen years of steady profits growth and was justifiably unrepentant about a strategy that continued to work. The acquisition of US rubber group Gates in July has proceeded smoothly and its contribution to the half-year ending November pushed pre-tax profits up 34% to £168.8 million. While ready to dispose of a handful of small operations as always, Tomkins still had a £350 million cashpile available for suitable bolt-on acquisitions, rather than return it to shareholders in a buy-back as critics regularly urged.

Racal embarked upon the demerger route long before it became fashionable or even obligatory. **Vodafone** went first in 1988 and 1991, followed by **Chubb** in 1992, leaving the original communications and network services business amplified by marine radar (Decca), avionics and a 22½% stake in National Lottery operator Camelot. Nevertheless, concentration on a narrower range of activities failed to diminish Racal's well-practised ability to upset the market and wrongfoot the analysts with shock profits warnings. The announcement in December that pre-tax profits for 1996/97 would come out at around £50 million instead of the £70-75 million widely expected, knocked 50p off the share price to 225p, and prompted critics to speculate that it was high time outside interests looked at Racal with a view to break-up. Traditionally, Racal has always bounced back from such setbacks and the shares recovered strongly to close the month and the year at 257p.

1997

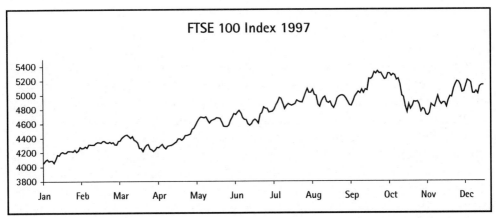

FTSE 100 Index 1997

Source: Thomson Reuters Datastream

Brave new world?

With many stock market forecasts having got the two halves of 1996 back-to-front by looking for a strong first half followed by at best a pause in the second half as political doubts and fears grew during the run-up to the election, most now favoured the idea of a modest rise in the FTSE of around 5% over the course of 1997. Those of a more bearish persuasion stressed that Alan Greenspan's cautionary words in early December had gone unheeded, and that when he did signal a turn in the interest rate cycle, Wall Street would nosedive, taking world markets with it. On the domestic front, their fears centred on the prospect of a 'double whammy' from Labour if it won the election in May. Base rates would be raised immediately to establish the new government's anti-inflation credentials in the wake of what would be portrayed as Tory complacency, the windfall tax on utilities would prove to be the thin end of the wedge for a new regime of corporate taxation, and in due course the party's trade union backers would demand their reward and minimum wage and other 'social' measures would be introduced to the detriment of industry's competitiveness. On the other hand, many of the most enthusiastic bulls took a global perspective, seeing world stock markets rising thanks to the enhanced profitability of the corporate sector in the wake of new technology and more flexible labour markets, all in the context of low inflation and low interest rates. The UK stock market, they argued, could prove a magnet for international investors in 1997 after Wall Street's exceptional run, continuing disillusionment with Japan (down another 1500 points in January) and the attractions of a strong pound. Furthermore, the building society and insurance company flotations were bringing in a new army of small investors, thus giving a renewed impetus to the cult of the equity.

Goldilocks v. The Bears

The opening days of the New Year saw the bulls firmly in the ascendant. By the end of January the FTSE had plussed 100 points and the Dow had surged through 6900 intraday before being hit by computer selling programmes. The continuing strength of sterling, while recognised as causing problems for exporters, was also seen as lessening the chances of any more rate rises ahead of the election. Sentiment was further improved when the three main monetary meetings in the US, Germany and the UK in the first week of February all passed without interest rate increases, and on 7th February the FTSE crossed the 4300 level for the first time to close at a record 4307.8, well-supported by strong gains in gilts. Markets continued their advance during the rest of the month with the Dow moving above 7000 and the FTSE adding another fifty points, taking in their stride another Delphic utterance from the Chairman of the Fed. Initial sharp falls were quickly regained on consideration of the fact that the US economy was in excellent shape and Alan Greenspan was simply hinting at pre-emptive, not remedial, action. There would be no replay of February 1994. This was still a 'Goldilocks economy' with growth not too fast to cause inflation nor too slow not to create jobs and lift corporate profits. London actually reached a new peak of 4444.3 on 11th March but then lost 170 points during the week in which the election date was announced. This reaction prompted some commentators to suggest that a Labour victory, despite the party's huge lead in the opinion polls being apparently confirmed by a 17% swing in The Wirral by-election, had not been fully discounted in the market. With unemployment and inflation still falling, and output rising along with house and other asset prices and real personal disposable incomes, perhaps a change of government was much more of a leap in the dark than it had seemed a few months ago.

The Turn of the Screw

Although widely regarded as inevitable sooner rather than later, the first hike in the Fed Funds rate for two years came as a shock to Wall Street. A quarter point rise to 5.5% on 25th March saw the Dow down over 200 points on the week as observers began to look for the next increase against a background of increasing economic activity, and the yield on the 30-year Treasury bill topped 7% again. Clear evidence that the UK economy was hotting up in the shape of rises in average earnings and retail sales against a background of sharply falling unemployment also stoked interest rate rise fears in London. A rise ahead of the election was considered highly unlikely but an increase of at least a quarter of a point was seen as certain immediately after, whichever party won. Both markets remained nervous until the last week in April when they began to recover towards their mid-March peak levels. Wall Street was encouraged by bi-partisan progress on methods of achieving a balanced budget by 2002 combined with further evidence of strong growth with little sign of inflationary pressures and the Dow moved above 7000 again. London shrugged off initial worries about the sheer scale of Labour's victory on 1st May, greeting the result by hitting a new high the following day of 4455.6, well supported by gilts, seemingly convinced that Prime Minister Blair and Chancellor Brown would honour their electoral campaign pledges.

The running man

Gordon Brown's first days as Chancellor of the Exchequer did nothing to jeopardise New Labour's instant honeymoon with the City. He had promised to 'hit the ground running' and did precisely that with a quarter point increase in base rates to 6.25% a day ahead of schedule followed by an announcement that from now on power to set interest rates will be transferred from the Treasury to the Bank of England. The base rate increase had been well discounted but the move to pass operational control over interest rates to the Bank of England surprised and pleased both domestic and international investors. Gilts, sterling and the equity market all surged on the expectation that the change would reduce long-term inflationary pressure on the economy. Medium to long gilts rose between two and five points, the pound moved sharply higher, and the FTSE plussed 63.7 to close at a new high of 4519.3. Second thoughts focusing on the enhanced prospects under a Labour government of joining European economic and monetary union (EMU) quickly took the shine off sterling, but gilts and equities continued to advance. Equities were led higher by heavy institutional buying of bank and insurance shares ahead of the forthcoming building society flotations led by **Halifax** and **Norwich Union**. Given the importance of these impending additions to the indices, institutions had to increase their sector weightings now before also becoming buyers of the newcomers on launch day. **Alliance & Leicester** had already gained 20% since dealings began just a month earlier. Thus in the week following the election, the FTSE had plussed 175 points to a record 4630.9, prompting a number of stockbrokers to revise their end-year target forecasts up to the 5000 mark. The mammoth **Grand Metropolitan/Guinness** merger looked like keeping the pot boiling for a time but nervous speculation about the contents of Chancellor Brown's first budget a month hence seemed likely to introduce an unaccustomed element of caution into the proceedings. But while commentators urged caution, investors continued to push the market to new highs, and the not infrequent sharp setbacks were followed by even sharper recoveries. The Halifax and Norwich Union flotations were hugely successful, serving to boost investor confidence further. Similarly, the quarter point hike in base rates to 6.5% in the first week of June was no deterrent, rather being regarded as enhancing the Chancellor's credibility in the context of his new arm's-length relationship with the Bank of England.

They think it's all over

The week leading up to the budget now scheduled for July 2nd produced some extraordinarily bearish predictions given that the most feared measures were widely regarded as odds-on bets for inclusion in the Chancellor's speech and thus largely discounted in the market place. 'Market poised for Budget slump' was the headline in the Business section of one Sunday newspaper on June 29th above a report that a fall of up to 400 points was in prospect if Gordon Brown cut or abolished the tax credit on dividends. The next day, on the eve of the budget, the FTSE gained a remarkable 123.7 points and its response on July 2nd when the Chancellor did his worst and abolished the tax credit altogether was to add another 23.1. The budget was subjected to a good deal of criticism in the press the following day. The promised windfall tax on the utilities at £4.8 billion was at the lower end of market expectations, but the counter to the fact that the amount was at least tolerable for the companies involved was that it was inadequate to fund the government's spending plans. The abolition of the tax credit on dividends was seen as an undeserved slap in the face for the pension funds, more than outweighing the unexpected and welcome cut in corporation tax from 33% to 31%. The fiscal measures taken to tackle buoyant consumer spending were regarded as wholly inadequate in the context of demutualisation bonuses totalling some £35 billion in the course of the year, and even the lowered PSBR targets were seen as simply an overoptimistic extension of the previous Chancellor's planned reductions.

The popular conclusion was that Gordon Brown had abdicated responsibility for the control of inflation to the Bank of England and its new Monetary Policy Committee. Higher interest rates were now considered to be inevitable with their concomitant effect on sterling, already at a level seriously damaging the prospects of our exporters. This general thumbs-down from the City experts accompanied by an overnight 6 pfennig rise in the pound to DM2.95 and a 4 cent boost to $1.69 prompted a heavy mark-down in shares at the opening of July 3rd, pushing the FTSE down 62.6 points. However, buyers failed to share the pessimism of the market makers, and as they piled in the index soared 112.2 at one stage before closing up 80.3 at a new record of 4831.7. Wall Street added to the fun by gaining 100 points in the first hour of trading to achieve a new high of 7984 in response to benign US jobs data regarded as lessening the chances of a rate rise next month.

Liquidity rules

With the FTSE already well above the best that end-year forecasts made just six months earlier and with the Dow similarly confounding market commentators who had been predicting a crash since July 1996, the bulls had had things all their own way in 1997 and they were to continue to do so. When the next base rate rise came in the second week of July with a quarter point hike to 6.75%, sterling strengthened again and, despite the CBI reporting that export orders were falling at their fastest rate since 1991 and that exporters judged their prospects to be the worst since 1980, by the end of the month the FTSE was clearly heading for the 5000 level. Even a further rate rise to 7% on 7th August was defused by an accompanying statement that 'upward pressure on the exchange rate should be reduced by the perception that interest rates have reached a level consistent with the inflation target'. This clear hint that there were no more rate rises in the pipeline was greeted with a sharp setback in the pound from $1.66 to $1.59, a 13 pfennig drop to DM2.92, and a surge in the FTSE to a new peak of 5086.8 on the day after the Dow had reached a record high of 8259.31.

With the FTSE now up 32% since the start of the year, hitherto cautious commentators tried hard to rationalise this continuing strength in equities, citing the plethora of megamergers, share buybacks, and the high level of institutional liquidity, but they persisted in voicing their reservations. The abolition of the tax credit on dividends was seen as potentially reducing the attractions of equities for tax exempt investors like pension funds since net yields now stacked up very differently from gross yields, stretching the gilt/equity yield ratio from 2.15 to 2.7 as the dividend yield on the All Share fell from 3.31% to 2.65%. Given that the Dow had risen by 50% in the last twelve months, the Continental European markets were at new peaks and Russian, Asian and Latin American markets were all soaring, it was clear that the liquidity phenomenon was being played out at a global level as money sought new opportunities for investment in the wake of the death of communism and the opening up of markets worldwide. But while globalisation and the opportunities it presents are here to stay, liquidity is not a permanent state of affairs, and by mid-August markets were beginning to have second thoughts, paying more attention to the growing problems of the Asian so-called 'Tiger economies'.

The Tigers stumble

In July, Thailand had devalued the baht, and within days the Philippines had followed suit and devalued the peso, a sequence strongly suggesting that problems were not going to be confined to these two countries. Apparent confirmation of these fears came as the Hong Kong market, after peaking post-handover at 16673 on 7th August, promptly lost 2500 points by the end of the month. On the home front, the Bank of

England did nothing to help by warning that base rates might not yet have peaked since inflation risks still 'appeared to be more on the upside' as unemployment fell. A similar statement from the Bundesbank warning about 'inflationary trends' coupled with anxiety about impending US economic data sparked rate rise fears on both sides of the Atlantic and stock markets worldwide went sharply into reverse. On 15th August the FTSE lost 125.5 to 4865.8, the Dow shed 247.37 to 7694.66 and City editors speculated that perhaps this was the start of the long feared 'Crash'. Lex concluded that Asia's problems represented 'a further unwelcome strain on nerves already frayed by inflated valuations and rising volatility', and much attention began to be focused on the precarious position of Japan with some 40% of its exports going to the region. The Nikkei-Dow, after a shaky start to the year, had topped 20000 in May and managed to hold on to that level until the end of July when the Thai crisis broke. One of the principal worries was that, with Japan trying to export its way out of recession, any marked slowdown in the region could force the country to repatriate its huge dollar assets, mainly in Treasury Bonds, in order to shore up domestic balance sheets, thereby threatening a collapse of the dollar and, as T-bond yields rose, hitting US equity valuations. However, a more reasoned view saw US bonds as the ultimate safe haven, especially for the Japanese with their abysmally low domestic returns.

EMU hopes dashed

Markets remained nervous and volatile throughout the rest of August and September but the Dow was soon edging back towards 8000 and the FTSE towards 5000 as the belief grew that the Asian crisis could be beneficial by helping to reduce inflationary pressures, thus postponing the turning point for short term interest rates. Falling gilt and US bond yields seemed to confirm this view as did a run of benign US economic data supporting the 'goldilocks' scenario. Then, in the last week of September, an apparently authoritative press report that Chancellor Brown favoured joining the Euro soon after the scheduled launch date saw the FTSE rise over 300 points to 5367.3 and gilts rise strongly in anticipation of a 'convergence play' with interest rates moving to lower Continental levels and sterling falling on expectations of a lower joining rate. The euphoria and the uncertainty lasted until the third week in October when the Chancellor insisted that the government's 'wait and see' Europolicy remained unchanged, whereupon the FTSE promptly lost all its gain and dipped below the 5000 level again. No support was forthcoming from Wall Street after Alan Greenspan made another of his now familiar studied pronouncements. He said that the US economy was on an 'unsustainable track' and added that 'it was clearly unrealistic to expect the continuation of recent stock market gains'. The Dow reacted by slipping well below the 8000 mark again, and then, as if all this was not enough for the markets to bear, Hong Kong went sharply into reverse losing practically a third of its value in the second half of October on fears of a deepening crisis in Asia leading to the collapse of Hong Kong's dollar peg and a devaluation of the Chinese currency. On 28th October, the Dow crashed a near record 554.26 to 7161.15. The following morning, the FTSE lost a staggering 457.9 points before both staging a partial recovery. Things looked even worse the next day when Hong Kong fell another 1438 points to 9059 but after opening 200 down, the Dow rallied to end up 337 at 7498 on a record billion shares traded as the 'buy on dips' policy was implemented by the institutions.

Japan on the rack

Nerves may have been steadied by this performance but they remained badly frayed for the rest of the year as investors tried to balance the counter inflationary impact of the Asian slowdown against the possibility, even probability, many thought, that it could get much worse and spread well beyond the region. 'Contagion' became the new watchword as investors contemplated the fact that globalisation inevitably means more exposure through links with other countries, making one market subject to another's problems. After all, since 1990, investments by the developed world in the emerging economies had risen sixfold to $336 billion in 1996 which meant that we were all riding tigers. As if to emphasise this point, South Korea went into freefall as one after another of its leading companies revealed that they were hopelessly over indebted and technically bankrupt. A bailout package from the IMF was quickly negotiated and some encouragement was taken from the fact that it was tied to the implementation of economic and structural reforms. However, the principal effect of this latest crisis was to put the spotlight back on Japan, the key country in the region where a further deterioration could jeopardise the recovery of the whole of Asia. The Nikkei Dow slipped below what was widely regarded as the danger level of 16000 as the country continued to endure a situation of wilting domestic consumer demand coupled with a slowdown in its leading export markets, all exacerbated by erosion of collateral resulting from depressed asset prices. A series of financial packages unveiled by the government were widely considered to be inadequate given that the most essential requirement was for a root and branch restructuring of the whole corporate and financial system, but in late November following a brief dip below 15000, the Japanese market rallied to over 16000 again as overseas investors interpreted the authorities' decision to allow Hokkaido Takushoku Bank to go under as an indication of a willingness to accept the inevitable. The collapse of brokers Sanyo and Yamaichi had been well flagged and caused no great stir in the market but at the same time no great confidence was created by the Finance Minister's statement that there would be no more collapses following the Bank of Japan's injection of liquidity to avert rate rises and its setting up of secret bilateral loans to companies in trouble.

Hanging together

In this context of global stress and strain, the MPC's decision in the first week of November to raise base rates to 7.25% came in for a great deal of criticism for tightening in the face of the twin deflationary influences of falling share prices and the Asian economic collapse. Fortunately for markets worldwide, there was little indication that the Federal Reserve was contemplating a rate rise. Alan Greenspan calmed contagion fears by describing the impact of the Asian crisis on the US economy as 'modest' although still stressing 'interdependence in today's world economy and financial system' and the consensus appeared to be that with 3% growth, stable prices and jobs for all, the US would continue to grow, more slowly perhaps but with inflation less of a threat. At the same time, many believed that the impact of the Asian crisis had the potential to be very much more than 'modest'. Major international companies like **Nike**, **Oracle**, **BTR** and **3M** had already warned of lower profits as a result of lower shipments to the region and, with apparently little or no prospect of a quick recovery in Asian economies, such warnings looked likely to proliferate, making nonsense of present optimistic corporate earnings forecasts. Furthermore, given that one effect of the crisis had been to scare investment away from the emerging markets just at the time they most needed to raise capital, weak growth would depress imports and further devaluations would make them more competitive in world markets. This would be the sort of situation where contagion became a reality as other emerging markets came under pressure, and when that happened, the West could not remain unaffected as 'interdependence' came into play. Such considerations kept the London market subdued but in the first week of December, the FTSE crossed into 5000-plus territory once more, holding comfortably above that level until the end of the year.

The rationale for this excellent performance rested in part on the UK's 'safe haven' status (shared with the US) in a global context, in the eyes of the managers of huge funds of mobile capital, on the high level of institutional liquidity and also on the country's relatively benign economic climate. To quote a circular from Morgan Stanley Dean Witter raising its end-1998 forecast for the FTSE to 6000, 'UK profitability and creditworthiness are on a secular uptrend and as the convergence play holds down gilt yields into the longer term, equity investors are getting the best of both worlds'. Indeed, the UK was seen as offering better value than the US with average dividend yields of roughly twice and P/Es half those ruling on Wall Street, although it was widely acknowledged that in both countries equity valuations were at unprecedentedly high levels. The fact that long bond yields in the US and in Europe had fallen to their lowest levels for thirty years while over the past three years earnings in the US had risen by 13% p.a., provided all the evidence investors needed that the 'new paradigm' of high growth accompanied by low inflation now ruled and fully justified equities achieving this 'new and permanently high plateau'. More sceptical commentators pointed out that the strength of the bond market was due in part to lower growth expectations and that the spectacular growth in earnings seen in recent years was simply not sustainable, especially now in the wake of the Asian slowdown. Chase Manhattan actually issued a 'Goodbye Goldilocks' circular forecasting that US growth post the Asian crisis would fall to barely 1% in 1998.

At end year, the FTSE stood at 5135.5 to record a gain of 24.7%, well in excess of all the experts' forecasts made twelve months earlier and just ahead of the Dow which was up 22.6%. The FTSE also outperformed the 250 and Small Cap indices as investors concentrated their firepower on the big battalions of the banks, insurances, pharmaceuticals, international oils and utilities. The Government Securities index gained 7.47% to 101.53 as the 10 year gilt yield fell over the year from 7.5% to 6.28%. Both Tokyo and Hong Kong demonstrated the damage from the Asian upset by falling 26.2% and 35.6% from their mid-year highs. Gold once again failed to fulfil its traditional role as a safe haven in times of crisis and lost $80 to $289 as country after country announced plans to dispose of large parts of their gold stocks. Gold shares fared badly too but not simply as a result of a falling gold price. The collapse of Canadian developer **Bre-X** adversely affected confidence in gold shares generally after its initial in-house resource estimate of 30 million ounces at the 'gold discovery of the century' at Busang in Indonesia was downgraded to 'insignificant amounts' after independent tests. The involvement in the project of members of the ruling Suharto family and the death of the company's chief geologist following a fall from a helicopter prompted the Canadian authorities to launch a full investigation.

There was plenty of corporate activity in 1997, all of which helped to keep the equity pot on the boil. Among the erstwhile conglomerates, **Williams** paid £1.26 billion for **Chubb** and disposed of its substantial DIY interests in order to concentrate on security and fire protection, thereby divesting itself of its unfashionable conglomerate tag and at the same time eliminating debt. **BTR** confirmed its intention to sell its non-core activities for around £2.5 billion and to restrict itself to control systems, power drives and autocomponents. For BTR's shareholders, this was a step in the right direction but the company still had a long way to go to restore its once glorious image. **Tomkins** remained the unreconstructed conglomerate, resisting pressure to return part of its £350 million cash pile, and then buying US autocomponents manufacturer Stant Corporation for $600 million. On what one might call the financial supply side, Morgan Stanley got together with Dean Witter in a $24 billion merger to create the biggest US securities and investment business, and **Merrill Lynch** bought **Mercury Asset Management** for £3.1 billion to form one of the largest fund management groups in the world.

1998

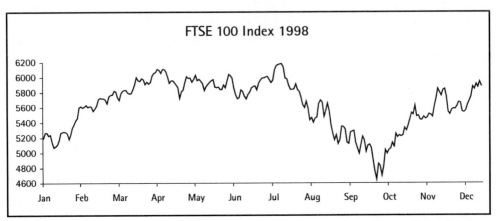

FTSE 100 Index 1998

Source: Thomson Reuters Datastream

A question of balance

The New Year opened on a hesitant note, on fears that Indonesia's and Malaysia's economic and political problems would greatly exacerbate the Asian crisis, and after the Dow fell 400 points in the second week of January, there was real concern that the 'bear market' was actually under way. Falling bond yields helped the case for the bulls as the return on 30 year Treasuries fell to 5.7%, the lowest level since its inception in 1977, and that on long gilts went below 6% for the first time since 1964. The bears remained confident that the full extent of Asia's problems had not been taken into account by Western markets, a belief reinforced by the fact that practically every day brought further bad news from the region. Hong Kong continued to slide with the latest fall sparked by the collapse of Hong Kong based financial conglomerate Peregrine which revealed that a quarter of its net assets had been wiped out by the default of a single Indonesian borrower. The bears argued that a collapsing currency, as in the case of Indonesia where the dollar rate had gone from 4000 rupiah to 9000, would do considerable harm in such an open emerging economy, squeezing already precarious living standards for the masses to a degree that would inevitably create serious political problems for the country's rulers. Thus IMF prescriptions might not prove acceptable in this case or indeed in many others yet to arise, a view that foreshadowed the subsequent accusations of Prime Minister Mahatir of Malaysia that they were an unwarrantable restraint on national policies and a form of neo-colonialism imposed after the machinations of Western speculators had created the problems in the first place. And as if all this was not enough for the markets to deal with, the Lewinsky scandal and its threat to the US presidency began to dominate headlines across the world.

Bulls on top

Nevertheless, despite this apparently threatening international backdrop, by the middle of February both the FTSE and the Dow, in company with the Continental European markets, had achieved new record highs and all the Asian markets were rallying strongly. By now even the most enthusiastic bulls were looking on incredulously as the FTSE headed for 6000 and the Dow for 9000, taking heart from a pronouncement by Warren Buffett, the sage of Omaha, that 'there is no reason to think of stocks as generally overvalued as long as interest rates stay this low and returns on equity this high'. The problem for the objective investor was that neither of these preconditions looked like remaining in place for very much longer and the real reason that equities were continuing to rise was that cash was continuing to pour into the markets. The institutions had gone into 1998 with high cash levels and since then a run of big ticket mergers and share buybacks had boosted their liquidity further creating a situation where weight of money was simply overruling traditional concepts of value.

On the home front the March budget was well received by markets despite the absence of help for exporters struggling with sterling at a 9 year high ($1.66 and DM3.05) and the biggest trade deficit in goods since 1990, the lowest confidence among exporters since 1980 and pleas from the CBI for the Bank of England to say that interest rates have peaked. Unfortunately, April figures showing average earnings rising by 4.9% and underlying inflation at 3.0% in the context of the Bank's warning in January that anything over 4.5% was not compatible with its inflation target of 2.5% did not paint a picture of a slowing economy and put a rate rise firmly back on the cards. It duly came in the first week of June with a quarter point hike to 7.5%, a move apparently justified by May's numbers revealing a further rise in average earnings to 5.2% and underlying inflation to 3.2%, prompting Governor George to say that he 'may have made a mistake' in delaying his support for a rate rise. The London market remained subdued in the face of these uncertainties but topped 6000 again in mid-July as the June inflation figures fell back to 2.8%.

Similar potentially inflationary data in the US with average earnings up 4.4% in April, the highest rate of increase since 1983 and unemployment falling from 4.7% to 4.37%, raised the probability of a rate rise but some commentators speculated that the Federal Reserve would be reluctant to act because it would serve to strengthen the dollar against the yen thus worsening Japan's delicate position. Furthermore, it could even trigger a stock market slump if a collapsing yen led to a Chinese devaluation and a further deterioration in the whole region that would make contagion inevitable. The Nikkei Dow was already having great difficulty in holding above the 15000 level and the yen had topped Y140 to the dollar as successive reform packages were judged inadequate to deal with Japan's deep seated problems. And with company after company in the US coming up with profit warnings, Alan Greenspan's cautionary words in the third week of July that Wall Street 'needs to adjust to a less optimistic view of earnings prospects' seemed to suggest that the broad economic numbers giving rise to inflationary concerns were perhaps largely historic. Certainly the new record highs for the Dow at 9337.97 and the FTSE at 6174 on 17th July were very soon to become historic.

Midnight in Moscow

Given that the Asian crisis had been around for a full twelve months, that high profile profit warnings had been a regular feature of the corporate scene since last November, and that the overvaluation of Western markets was a matter of record, the slide that began in the last week of July came as a surprise only by virtue of the fact that investors had become accustomed to seeing bad news ignored. The straw that broke the camel's back was the latest twist to the Russian crisis that had begun in March when President Yeltsin fired Prime Minster Chernomyrdin and his whole administration. The event had raised fears that the country could descend into political and economic chaos leading to the return of power of the Communists and an abrupt end to the reform process. In the ensuing months short term interest rates rocketed in an effort to support the rouble while at the same time negotiations were entered into with the IMF over a rescue package. Russia had attracted a huge amount of foreign money since 1994 on the principle that it was the last great emerging market and that with a total equity capitalisation slightly less than Glaxo's, it presented an outstanding opportunity for the bold investor. As a result, it became the best performing market of 1997 and with Western banks accounting for over a third of the country's $60 billion of short term finance, a rouble devaluation would create a lot of casualties. In mid-August financier George Soros warned that a 15-25% devaluation was inevitable and within days the Russian authorities did indeed devalue and for good measure declared a 90-day moratorium on foreign debt repayments while carrying out a restructuring that meant creditors had to write off 80-95% of the principal. The moves cost George Soros's interests an estimated $2 billion, and American, German and British banks all incurred significant losses.

Follow me down

The most serious effect of the Russian debacle was that it now acted as an accelerator for the incipient crises in other emerging markets. And next in line was Latin America, a region of much greater importance to the US economy, taking over 14% of its exports and with its banks ten times more exposed than was the case in Russia.

If a serious collapse occurred in, say Brazil, the contagion would inevitably spread to the US,tipping the whole world into recession. Such fears dominated the markets throughout August and September and three figure falls in the Dow and the FTSE became common events, attracting TV and newspaper comment which served to spread a sense of unease and uncertainty from the investment community to the wider public. By mid-September bank shares both in London and New York were down by around 40% on average and similar falls were recorded by major international players like **Coca-Cola**, **Gillette** and **Procter & Gamble**. **Shell** closed down its London headquarters warning of spreading Asian woes, and **Whitbread** announced that it was halting the pub and restaurant expansion programme embarked upon in May, citing recessionary fears. By this time the FTSE was down to just over 5000, the Dow to around 7700, while in Tokyo the Nikkei Dow had dipped below 14000 after Okura, one of Japan's oldest trading houses had gone bust for $1.8 billion. There were calls from financial commentators for interest rate cuts but the best Alan Greenspan could manage at this stage was to confirm that the Fed was 'no longer biased towards tightening', and similarly London's MPC left base rates unchanged at 7.5% while hinting of easing.

The 'hedge' fund that didn't hedge

The event that turned September's unease and uncertainty into outright alarm and despondency in October was the collapse of **Long-Term Capital Management**, a US so-called 'hedge fund' that had built up a $200 billion exposure on a $5 billion equity base. As the flagship of the US hedge funds backed by a large number of the country's blue chip financial institutions, LTCM's failure was widely interpreted as a sign that the problems of Asia, Russia and Latin America had spread to the heart of the US financial establishment, marking a new and even more serious phase in what had now become a world crisis. Excessive leverage coupled with 'irrational exuberance' had proved to be a deadly combination. It was no longer enough to steer clear of high credit risks. Any investment that could prove to be illiquid was now too hot to handle. Hence the 'dash for cash' and the stampede into US Treasury bills which had pushed the long bond yield below 5% despite the sudden depreciation of the dollar against the yen of 20% in a week as 'yen carry trade' positions were unwound under duress. (For months traders had accepted a strong dollar and a weak yen as the norm and in order to profit from this apparently stable relationship, they would sell yen and buy dollars, the whole operation being carried out with bank finance. Once the banks became nervous and demanded repayment, the positions had to be unwound by selling dollars and buying yen). Recognising the seriousness of the situation and its potential for growing worse, the Fed was quick to act. Almost immediately it joined with a 14 bank consortium to inject $6 billion of new capital into LTCM and cut the Fed Funds rate by 0.25% to 5.5%. A jump of 330 points by the Dow on the day the rate cut was announced was followed by heavy selling on rumours about the damage LTCM's failure was likely to uncover and little encouragement was taken from President Clinton's statement that we were facing our worst crisis in fifty years. Within a week, London followed suit with a quarter point cut in base rate to 7.25%. It was accompanied by a communiqué from the MPC referring to the deterioration in the international economic and financial environment and an almost simultaneous pronouncement from Chancellor Brown that he was halving his growth forecast for 1999 from 2% to 1%. Alan Greenspan expressed his own concern by saying, 'I've never seen anything like this...we are clearly facing a set of forces that should be dampening demand going forward to an unknown extent' – and then took another quarter point off interest rates ahead of the Fed's next regular meeting.

Into calmer waters

The FTSE had touched its low point of 4648.7 on 5th October amid a deluge of bearish comment about shares in general and the worldwide economic situation, but recovered almost 800 points by the end of the mouth as investors took heart from the speed with which interest rate cuts had been initiated and rescue packages approved. Also by the last day of October the Dow had gained 1000 points on its end-August low, interestingly not having plumbed new depths in the first week of October like London, Tokyo and practically all the Continental European markets. The extent of the recovery invited speculation that we were seeing the beginning of the end of the global financial crisis. The Thai market was up 50% since late August and South Korea 23%, helped by the fall of the dollar against the yen and the US rate cuts, and generally encouraged by G7's moves to underpin the financial systems of countries prepared to follow IMF 'approved' policies. In fact in less than a month, terror of global financial meltdown had changed to mere apprehension at the prospect of an economic slowdown. Another cut in base rates, this time by an unexpected half a per cent to 6.75%, in the first week of November, was greeted on the day by a 143 point fall in the FTSE but the market quickly recovered ahead of the Fed's next meeting when rates were slashed to 4.75%. This was the third rate cut in seven weeks and it was enough to power the Dow back to its July high despite the wide assumption that the outlook for corporate profits was now very much worse. The beginning of December saw sharp falls on both London and New York as investors took fright at a string of profit warnings from high profile companies but once again recovery was swift as the traditional pre-Christmas rally developed. London received an additional boost from another reduction in base rate, this time by half a per cent to 6.25%, but some commentators took the cut as an indication that the MPC was sensing progressive weakness in the economy rather than a reason to be cheerful. They believed that the rate cuts had come too late to avoid a slide into recession, and that the Chancellor's forecast that the economy would grow between 1% and 1.5% in 1999 was far too optimistic with a contraction of around 1% much more likely given a prolonged period of sterling overvaluation, depressed business and consumer confidence, and a scary global economic backdrop.

At year end the FTSE stood at 5882.6, up 14.5%, dramatically outperforming the FTSE 250 (+1.4%) and the Small Cap (-10.47%), but only just beating the Government Securities index which closed up 14.2% at 115.98. The Dow gained 16% on the year to 9181.43 but was beaten handsomely by the computer and internet stock – dominated NASDAQ, up 85%, and by the S&P 500, up 26%. Japan disappointed yet again with a 9.3% fall to 13842 as did Hong Kong, down 6.3% at 10048. The consensus among commentators reviewing the year was that the return to relative peace and stability after the terrors of the late summer owed practically everything to the enthusiasm of the US consumer and the skills of Federal Reserve Chairman, Alan Greenspan in keeping the US economy up and running and thereby heading off a global recession. The big question was whether or not the US 'locomotive' would run out of steam in 1999. *FT* editorials and the Lex column remained steadfastly sceptical just as they had done for the past two years. They were convinced Wall Street was in 'bubble territory' driven by excessive liquidity and 'irrational exuberance' as investors continued to pour money into mutual funds in the expectation of continuing annual returns in the mid-teens. This was an expectation doomed to disappointment, the writers believed, as deflationary forces spread through the global economy. A rising stock market had underpinned the strength of consumer demand but it could not continue to rise indefinitely given a negative savings ratio, a yawning current account deficit, and a merger boom which was by definition finite. Furthermore, there was considerable irony in the fact that Alan Greenspan fired his warning shot about 'irrational exuberance' almost precisely two years earlier when the Dow stood at around 6400 (the FTSE at 4000) and yet today with the index at over 9000 after three rate cuts since last October, investors could be forgiven for thinking that the aim of the Federal Reserve's monetary policy was to sustain the current level of equity prices. Such thoughts could therefore prompt investors to assume a higher degree of risk and push prices still higher. FTSE100 forecasts for the coming year showed that if the institutions shared the *FT's* scepticism, they did not foresee a bursting of the bubble with its inevitable knock-on effect on the UK market in 1999. The change of sentiment within the space of the past three months was particularly striking when December's forecasts are compared with those of October.

Big is beautiful

The biggest prospective deal in corporate history was the **Smith Kline Beecham/Glaxo** merger plan announced in January to create the world's largest pharmaceutical company. In the event, disagreement among top management, as to who would be running the new group, led to the deal being called off in the following month. There was keen competition from US buyers for **Energy Group**, the former

Hanson constituent made up of Peabody Coal and Eastern Electricity, and it eventually fell to Texas Utilities for £4.5 billion. The automobile industry saw plenty of headline-making activity with Chrysler getting together with Daimler-Benz, and then Volkswagen upsetting BMW's plans to buy Rolls Royce Motors. The latter dispute was settled by Volkswagen buying the company for £430 million, selling the Rolls Royce brand to BMW for £40 million and keeping the Bentley marque. The oil industry's response to an oil price falling below $10 at one point during the year was to table more mergers with a view to rationalisation of operations and drastic cost cutting. Top of the list was BP's £30 billion offer for Amoco, thereby creating the world's biggest industrial merger to date. And **BTR** apparently resolved its problems by completing its disposal programme, then merging with top engineering group, **Siebe** and changing the name of the new group to **Invensys**.

'The deal of the century'

The big news coming out of the world of American banking in 1998 was the merger between Citicorp and Travelers when the former's international consumer and commercial lending operations would link with the insurance, brokerage and securities operations of the latter to create an all-purpose global financial conglomerate. It was described at the time as 'the deal of the century' and the combined group had a market capitalisation of $155 billion.

1999

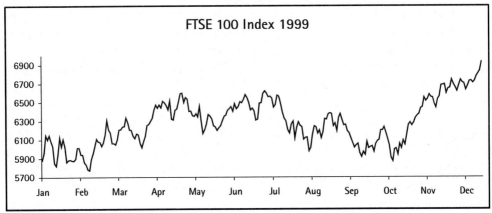

FTSE 100 Index 1999

Source: Thomson Reuters Datastream

More warnings from the Fed

The first week of the New Year seemed to augur well for the experts end-year forecasts with the FTSE and the Dow hitting new highs on 8th January of 6195.6 (intraday) and 9643.3 respectively, the FTSE encouraged by a reduction in base rates to 6%. However, the second week saw markets in a panic at the prospect of a Brazilian devaluation upsetting its neighbours both north and south of the border. The FTSE shed 287 points at one point on 13th January while the Dow lost 125 on the same day and another 228 the next, before recovering strongly on Brazil's decision to float, only to be hit again a few days later by a warning from Alan Greenspan that the high level of US share prices 'would appear to envision substantially greater growth of profits than has been experienced of late'. Then on 4th February, the MPC made its fifth reduction in interest rates since October 1998, with a half per cent cut to 5.5%. The motive for this larger than expected cut was widely attributed to the MPC's wish to give the economy every chance of avoiding slipping into recession, a fate many commentators still regarded as inevitable. The market appeared to think that a soft landing was on the cards and the FTSE rallied back into 6000 plus territory, reaching a new record high of 6207.6 on the 24th February. At this point London was outperforming New York where higher bond yields had acted as a depressant on US equities – the yield on the Long Bond had risen by half a per cent to 5.5% within a month – and given that the bond/equity yield ratio was 4.3 in the US compared with just 2 in London, there was no doubt which was the most attractive market to a degree prompting Lex to conclude that it could take the Dow which had flirted with its all-time high earlier in the week, 'a little while before it saw such rarefied levels again'. Such statements are guaranteed to tempt fate and the Dow plussed over 600 points the following week bringing it to the brink of the 10000 mark despite a profit warning from **Caterpillar** and poor results from **Oracle**. Once again analysts had difficulty in evaluating a market which long ago had left behind all traditional concepts of fair valuation and contented themselves with saying that all the good news was already priced in and that the continued strength of the economy – it had grown at 6.1% in the final quarter of 1998 – would force the Fed to tighten monetary policy sooner or later.

The Dow moves above 10000

Meanwhile, London had a budget to contend with and although a reduction in the basic rate of personal income tax from 23% to 22% and the introduction of a 10p starting rate provided headline appeal, the energy levy and road fuel duty increases looked to many observers to be positively anti-business. However, the market was in no mood to be critical and accepting the Chancellor's forecast of growth of 1-1.5% for 1999 rising to 2.25-2.5% in 2000 all in the context of a 2.5% inflation rate, the FTSE followed the Dow into new high ground. The beginning of the air strikes on Yugoslavia caused some initial nervousness but markets quickly recovered their poise and by the end of the first quarter, the FTSE was showing a gain of some 7% which was extended to a new peak on the first day of the new financial year as investors looked to the MPC to take note of the struggling engineering industry and the strength of the pound against the Euro, and cut rates again at its meeting on 8th April. The cut duly arrived, this time one of a quarter per cent to 5.25%, powering the FTSE through the 6500 level just as the Dow crossed into the even more 'rarefied levels' above 10000. These exuberant performances invited speculation in the US that the booming economy was perhaps more in need of rate rises than rate cuts, and that the autumn 1998 reductions would make the Fed's task much more difficult in the months ahead. After all, the economy was eight years into its current expansion, still accelerating, broadly based on consumer spending, housing, business investment, and although as yet there was little evidence of a revival of inflation, it was a leap in the dark to assume that the link between growth and inflation had been broken. However, it was also argued that anxiety about the Fed's next move had already pushed the yield on the Long Bond up to 5.8%. Thus the market was already doing the Fed's work for it since the yield is used as a bench mark for pricing credit card debt and mortgages, and it also ought to act as a brake on rising equity prices. Benchmark it may have been but brake it was not, and less than a month after crossing the 10000 level, the Dow had moved into 11,000 plus territory.

Will the bubble burst?

This new high sparked a flood of articles with titles on the lines of 'When will the bubble burst?', given that the fate of Wall Street was of critical importance to stock markets around the world. In practically every case the writers' conclusion was that while there were sound economic reasons for higher share ratings, Wall Street was not a perpetual motion machine with stock market gains fuelling consumption and investment which in due course drive share prices higher. Shocks and interruptions are part and parcel of the economic scene and the more other countries rely upon the strength of the US economy and its rising stock market, the more vulnerable they become. In the words of David Smith, Economics Editor of the Sunday Times, 'US investors have become complacent and convinced that their country has entered a period of untroubled, inflation-free growth with the Fed standing ready to supply any interest rate cuts needed to keep the rally going. It looks too good to be true. And it is.' In the same week, Alan Greenspan apparently concurred with this opinion when, referring to the record $300 billion US trade deficit, he announced, 'There are imbalances in our expansion that, unless redressed, will bring this long run of strong growth and low inflation to a close'. Then a few days later towards the end of May he signalled his anxiety over inflationary pressures in the economy by changing his neutral position on interest rates to a bias towards raising them, a move which caused the Dow to lose 300 points in two days and bond yields to push up towards 6%. So many well-aired expressions of concern about the state of the economy meant of course that a rate rise had already been priced in. When it came in the first week of July with a quarter point hike to 5% the Dow soared to a new record to close above 11200 and bond yields eased, encouraged by the Fed's accompanying statement that it was reverting to a neutral bias.

With the threat of recession fading fast as business and consumer confidence rose against a backdrop of consistently low inflation and unemployment, much the same interest rate concerns beset the UK market in June and July. However, with the example of Wall Street to follow, equities were capable of coping with such uncertainties, managing to reach a record closing high of 6620.6 on 6th July. This more ebullient form was assisted by strong recoveries in the emerging markets and signs of a pick-up in France and Germany, just as US growth showed signs of slowing. But if these relative performances could be indicating that world growth was becoming more balanced, the downside of such a development in the view of many commentators was that the US would suffer disproportionately as the hot money for which it had proved such a magnet flowed out again as more attractive investment areas appeared. Their views gained substance from the fact that in the last three weeks of July, the dollar had lost 6% against the yen and 5% against the Euro. Alan Greenspan now weighed in with a statement to the effect that the June interest rate rise did not mean that the danger of inflation had been eliminated, and that the current wave of euphoria in equity markets ran the risk of driving prices to levels that would be unsupportable once the inevitable adjustment occurred. Even though he partially softened the severity of his warnings by adding that in the event of a serious correction it would be the Fed's job 'to mitigate the fallout and hopefully ease the transition to the next expansion', markets were due for a summer break and by the end of July the Dow had lost nearly 600 points from its peak and the FTSE nearly 400. And as a result of the Tory gains in the Euro-elections in June, the London market had also lost, temporarily at least, the convergence prop as the prospects of EMU entry receded into the 2003-05 range. Within a matter of weeks, however, growing signs of recovery in Europe suggested that the Euro debate was going to re-opened sooner rather than later. The official Conservative hardline anti-Euro policy was now beginning to look positively reactionary in the context of the corporate restructuring going on in Europe together with a new wave of cross border mergers and acquisitions, many involving UK companies. It was clearly no longer a case of the Europhiles pushing the UK into the embrace of a clutch of ex-growth, sclerotic economies plagued by inflexible labour markets and state-dominated industries After all the French stock market had risen 18% so far in 1999, while the German market was up 8%, much the same as the FTSE100.

More rate rises on the way

By the end of August the Dow had achieved a new high at 11326.04 despite a further quarter point hike in the Fed funds rate to 5.25% with the markets apparently accepting that Alan Greenspan knew best and was on their side. Once again he managed to balance cautionary words about the dangers of asset price inflation and their relevance to monetary policy, with the observation that US corporate profits were widely understated as a result of the accounting treatment of software investment. London recovered into the 6200/6400 range, after one unsettling dip below 6000 in the middle of the month, on further evidence of recovery in output against a background of subdued inflation pointing to growth of 2.5% in 2000. But while these latest forecasts thoroughly wrongfooted the pessimists of autumn 1998, the dramatic nature of the turnaround clearly rang alarm bells for a majority of the MPC who sprang a surprise quarter point rate rise on 8th September. The accompanying statement referred to the Committee's concern about the rapid rise in house prices along with the strength of domestic consumption and tight labour markets, but few commentators applauded the rise. Most saw it as likely to exacerbate the economy's two-tier problem of strong services and weak manufacturing and as a defeat for the 'give growth a chance' element in the MPC. Within a matter of days interest rate worries came to dominate stock markets worldwide and by the end of the month the FTSE was below 6000 again and the Dow was getting uncomfortably close to the psychologically important 10000 level.

Anniversary blues

Worse was to come in the first few days of October as fears grow that rates could rise simultaneously in the US, the UK and in Europe. A strong rally developed when the week passed without a single rate rise but the relief was shortlived as investors anxieties began to focus on the impending anniversary of Black Monday in October 1987 and also, of course, of the Great Crash of October 1929. Alan Greenspan did nothing to allay this nervousness by advising banks to set aside funds as insurance against a market sell-off and as the long bond yield rose to 6.3%, the Dow lost 200 points intraday on 15th October, and the FTSE shed a similar amount before both markets recovered smartly to end above the day's worst at 10135.91 and 5907.1 respectively. The latter's recovery was encouraged by yet another megabid, this time one of £18.5 billion for mobile phone operator **Orange** from German conglomerate **Mannesman**, following hard on the heels of **Bank of Scotland's** £22 billion hostile bid for **Natwest Bank**. By now sentiment tended to have a bearish bias given that both the Dow and the FTSE seemed unable to stage any lasting recovery from a 10% discount on their mid-summer peaks, and predictions of 12000 and 7000 by Christmas were no longer heard. Furthermore, activity was also considered likely to be depressed by the approach of the Millennium (Y2K) over fears that the 'bug' could create financial chaos, although the other side of the coin was that if the fears turned out to be groundless then the New Year could be greeted with a surge of buying.

At the end of October no one seemed willing to place any bets. However, the fact that in the first week of November the market took a quarter point hike in base rates in its stride together with the flying start given to the new 'techMARK' index of high tech stocks, strongly suggested that it was too early to give up hopes of a traditional pre-Christmas rally. At the same time few commentators would have predicted the extent and volume of the end-year advance dominated by IT, internet and telecom stocks. It seemed that the sharp setbacks in the FTSE and the Dow culminating in the lows of mid-October had anticipated and discounted the rate rises which were widely acknowledged to be inevitable before the end of the year. After one step backward the scene was now set for two steps forward. Thus in the second week of November the FTSE topped 6500 for the first time and when a week later the Fed raised interest rates by a quarter point to 5.5% completing the takeback from the October '98 cuts, the Dow had already climbed above 11000 again and was clearly heading higher encouraged by Alan Greenspan's statement that the US was 'experiencing a virtuous circle of new investment, rising productivity and rising profits'. He also pointed out that the rising rate of return on US assets was attracting private capital flows, thus defusing at least part of the perceived problem of the huge current account deficit.

Making a case

Indeed since a bull market requires no more than its own existence to justify itself and the bears had been so consistently wrong-footed since well before the Fed chairman's cautionary words about 'irrational exuberance' back in December 1996, the phrase 'rational exuberance' now began to make its appearance. The argument was that the consistency of the superior return of equities over bonds in recent years meant that the decline in the 'equity risk premium' – the extra return of stocks over bonds required to compensate for the supposed additional risk posed by holding stocks – was more than justified and that there was no reason why it should not fall to zero. After all, the bulls pointed out, monetary and fiscal policies are now dictated by global capital flows in the context of a benign disinflationary process in which revolutionary technology plays a new and vital part. One or two lone voices observed that this argument is comparable to saying that because a householder has not suffered any fires or burglaries in the past there is no need to keep paying insurance in the future.

Bids galore

The momentum of the advance in November and December was greatly boosted by a renewed wave of high profile mergers and hostile bids, many across borders and designed either to achieve global scale in growth industries or to produce economies by reducing overcapacity in cyclical industries. The Natwest Bank situation rumbled on with The Royal Bank of Scotland entering the contest amid speculation as to the identity of other interested parties. **Carlton TV** and **United News & Media** announced an agreed merger and everyone waited to see what **Granada** would do about it. **United Biscuits** put itself up for sale and immediately attracted a flurry of interest. And then **Vodafone Airtouch** entered the record books with an £85 billion hostile bid for Germany's **Mannesman**, planning to create a European telecommunications giant. As a result of all this activity in the last two months of the year, a stock market that had appeared to be going nowhere in mid-October managed to post some very respectable percentage gains by the last day of the year. The FTSE closed up 17.8% to a new record high of 6930.2 with both the FTSE 250 and Small Cap also at new highs. With an historic P/E on the All Share of 27 and a dividend yield of 2.2%, valuations were firmly at the top and bottom of their respective ranges, but the consensus among the analysts was that such ratings were now justified by low inflation and low bond yields (the Government Stock index was down 10% on the year), and the prospect of sustained earnings growth in the 8-14% range in 2000 after a patchy 1998 and 1999. Some reservations were expressed about pressure on margins from higher energy costs, wages and internet-related competition, and of course interest rates which were expected to peak at 6% at best and at 7% at worst. And with output per head in UK manufacturing rising against all expectations at over 5% in 1999 little concern was registered about the high level of sterling at DM3.14 and FF10.5, figures which would have been considered very worrying at the start of the year. High profile takeover activity was also thought likely to spill over into the New Year and to be a supportive factor for the market. End-2000 forecasts for the FTSE ranged from 6300 up to 7800 with the great majority nearer the upper end of the scale.

The Dow managed a 25.2% gain on the year to a record 11497.12, aided by the inclusion of **Microsoft** and **Intel** which replaced old timers **Chevron**, **Goodyear**, **Sears Roebuck** and **Union Carbide** in order for the index to be more representative of 'the evolving US economy'. The fact that IT stocks (ex-telecoms) now represented some 25% of the US stock market by valuation, also helped to push both the S&P500 and the NASDAQ indices to new highs. With a P/E of around 40 and a dividend yield of slightly less than 1%, S&P valuations were at historic highs and lows just like those in the UK but even more extreme, and much the same factors were cited to justify them.

Of the other major world markets, Japan outdid most with a 37% rise to 18934, a figure still slightly less than half that reached ten years earlier. Hong Kong bettered even this performance gaining 69% to 16962 to finally retrieve all the ground lost since the handover and move into new high ground.

Ancestral voices . . .

By any historic standard, the frenzied buying of internet stocks and of 'shell' situations in the closing weeks of the year must set alarm bells ringing. In many cases the sums involved are so vast that it has to be doubted that many investors look beyond the share price to the actual market capitalisations of the companies into which they are buying. A billion pounds, i.e. a thousand million pounds, is by definition a high value to place on a company that is losing many millions of pounds, irrespective of the brilliant prospects that are assumed to lie ahead. They may be in the vanguard of the 'new economy' but since the 'old economy' is not going to disappear and should be the principal beneficiary of business to business e-commerce applications, then it is irrational to value new and largely untried companies so much more highly than those that satisfy all the traditional investment criteria. Indeed values of the newcomers have reached a level which means that they are likely to qualify for the FTSE 100, replacing a number of household name stocks in the process. If this is soon to be the case, at least these new 'blue chips' will have greater claim to an appellation that derives from that of the highest value chip on the gaming table.

Apart from the inherent challenges posed to these new companies as a result of operating in highly competitive fields where technological changes occur almost at the speed of light, there is the ever present scope for problems to arise in the realms of management and accounting – problems to which fast growing companies are particularly prone.

As for the 'shell' situations, buyers who push valuations up from almost nothing to hundreds of millions of pounds are acting in precisely the same way as did those who subscribed to the unspecified project launched in 1720 at the time of the South Sea Bubble 'to carry on a design of more general advantage...and of more certain profit.... than any undertaking yet set on foot'.

Of course it may be that anyone over twenty five is a step behind events and simply incapable of understanding that the internet changes everything. However, remembering the blind panic that overcame investors across the world in the autumn of 1998, it has to be doubted that it will change human nature...

2000

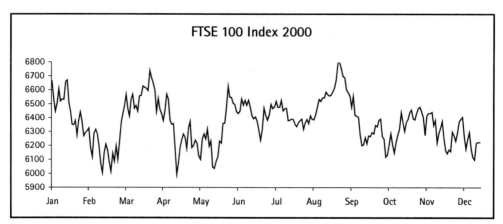

FTSE 100 Index 2000

6800
6700
6600
6500
6400
6300
6200
6100
6000
5900

Jan Feb Mar Apr May Jun Jul Aug Sep Oct Nov Dec

Source: Thomson Reuters Datastream

Heaven's Gate

It was the best of times – for the first three months of the year. It was the worst of times – for the remaining nine. The mood was cautious after the pre-Christmas euphoria. Relief that the Y2K bug had failed to bite and create computer and hence financial chaos, was tempered by consideration that excessive pre-Millennium spending on the latest software in anticipation of possible problems would mean a slowdown in such spending in the months ahead. Some commentators expressed dismay about the demise of P/Es and dividend yields as standard evaluation yardsticks for equities, and their fears appeared to be more than justified in the first days of the New Year as sharp falls in the IT and telecoms sectors were accompanied by strong rises in many of the 'old economy' stocks. By the end of the first week in January, the IT hardware sector had lost 15%, software just over 10% with many individual stocks down over 20%, while stock market stalwarts like **Diageo**, **Scottish & Newcastle** and **Imperial Tobacco** rose by between 10% and 15%. Similarly, in the US the technology based NASDAQ Composite shed 10% of its value with leaders like **Amazon** and **Oracle** down around 20%, while the Dow surged ahead to a new high of 11,522 on 7th January.

Unfortunately, this apparent return to investment sanity failed to last out the month and after reaching a new record of 11722.98 on 14th January, a week later the Dow lost 500 points in response to a quarter point hike in the Federal Funds rate to 5.75%, and the NASDAQ took up the running again to achieve a new record. London followed much the same pattern. The FTSE slipped back towards 6000 in anticipation of interest rate rises, which duly arrived by mid-February in the shape of two quarter point hikes in MLR, raising it to 6%. But the techMARK 100 index then got its second wind and surged ahead to new highs as buyers, both private and institutional, returned in force for the TMT stocks. Lex was a voice in the wilderness observing 'this is just the beginning…rates will keep rising until the stock market bubble bursts…it is a miserable prospect for stocks'.

However, those investors who were happy to make hay while the sun shines were convinced it would keep shining. There was no sign of the US economy slowing down, they argued, and in the new economy of huge equity returns and free venture capital funding, interest rate rises were largely irrelevant. In the UK, many successful old economy stocks were already down over 40% in the past year, yielding more than gilts and with single figure P/Es. History of success counted for little when compared with the prospect of spectacular success in the future, seemingly regardless of the high risks involved. New valuation methods were devised for high tech stocks involving generous allowances for forecast rates of earnings growth, and calculations were made to prove that the more a company invests and spends to gain market share, the bigger it will become.

However, these were too sophisticated for most investors to understand and for them the name of the game was 'momentum', i.e. if it starts to go up, climb aboard. And until the end of the first quarter of 2000 it worked, with many stocks, principally in the software and computer services sector and telecoms, rising tenfold. Such stocks came to be known as 'ten baggers'. Voice technology company **Vocalis** having spent most of 1999 around 100p with a market capitalization of some £30 million, suddenly took off in the last quarter of the year and actually topped £10.50 in March 2000. Even more striking was the performance of **Recognition Systems**, a designer of discriminating software. Down from over 60p to under 10p in 1998/99, when it looked like running out of money, the advent of substantial new financing sent the shares soaring to 660p at their peak in March. New issues which had anything to do with the internet were guaranteed a huge following on launch day. **Interactive Investor International** was issued at 150p, touched 600p, and then pulled back to 338p, at which price it had a market capitalisation of £555 million despite making a loss of £6.3 million on net revenues of just £2.6 million in 1999. Its principal business was running a website disseminating financial news. But the most high-profile new issue was travel company **Lastminute.com**, the launch of which, at the upgraded price of 380p, has been widely credited as marking the peak of the dot.com boom. The shares touched 562p on the first day of trading before closing at 487p. At this price, a company not expected to turn a profit until 2004, was capitalized at some £730 million, or rather more than **Unigate** which had just reported profits of £155 million for 1999.

Out with the old, in with the new

Ironically, it was perhaps the realization of the event foreshadowed towards the end of 1999, namely the inclusion of the heavyweight stocks (in market capitalization terms) of the new economy into the FTSE100, that signalled the beginning of the end of the high tech boom. Thought by many that the event would bestow the stamp of respectability on these relative newcomers, to many more it seemed to demonstrate the absurdity of replacing nine household name stocks with combined profits totalling £3.73 billion, with nine relative unknowns, four of which were still making heavy losses, but overall making profits of just £500 million. Internet security specialist **Baltimore Technology**, for example, now capitalized at over £4 billion and whilst losing £31.4 million on £23.3 million of sales went into the FTSE, while brewing and leisure giant **Whitbread**, making profits of £360 million, went out.

For many investors, however, high tech shares still remained the only game in town. As the FTSE briefly dipped below 6000 on 15th February, the techMARK index powered ahead to top 5700. Similarly, in the US the Dow dipped below 10,000 towards the end of the month after Alan Greenspan warned of higher interest rates to combat overheating, but the NASDAQ Composite continued to gain ground, eventually peaking at 5048.62 on 10th March as SEC Chairman Arthur Levitt castigated the market's 'casino mentality', and interest rates were upped another quarter point to 6%. Old and new economy stocks then reversed their roles once more, and by the end of the month the Dow had topped 11,000 again as the NASDAQ lost 10%. In London over the same period the FTSE recovered to 6738, while the techMARK shed over 500 points with many of the high tech sector's favourite counters taking serious hits. **Baltimore** dropped from £140 to £108, Misys from £13 to £8.50 and local telecoms provider **Kingston Communications** from £16 to £11. Stockbroker and internet company issuing house **Durlacher**, which seemed to have it every which way during the high tech boom, fell from £40 to £26.50.

Falls of such a degree were beginning to sow seeds of doubt in the minds of even the most confirmed believer on the new economy and the momentum theory of investing. Their share prices were not supposed to act this way. But by definition momentum, once lost, can never be regained, and of course with no conventional valuation basis to fall back on, a share price that has lost momentum has no obvious support levels on the way down. Rather, analysts began to look more closely at the numbers that didn't seem to matter as long as stock was going up. Now the 'spend, spend, spend' policy designed to grab market share and establish a company as a leader in its field came to be called 'cash burn', and calculations were made as to how long it would be before that cash ran out. Such companies were seen to be locked in a race against time. There was not enough cash left to expand sales, still not enough sales to generate profits, and with that problem out in the open and share prices crumbling, no venture capitalist or shareholder was willing to put in more money. The warning signs had been evident in the US for some time: E-retailer **Peapod** found itself in exactly that situation and the shares had already crashed from $16 to $3 in the first quarter of 2000; internet toy retailer **e-Toys** had reported sales up 360% to $107 million for 1999 but losses were up 700% to $70 million; and a company with a $200 stock price in mid 1999, making it bigger than **Toys-R-Us**, was now trading at $16.

Keeping the faith

But if investors were worried, they were not prepared to give up hope that the TMT sector was still the place to be. In the words of a note from Warburg Dillon Read, 'the no boom/no bust approach keeps us focused on growth which, like it or not, remains concentrated in the TMT area of the market'. The first half of April provided little substance for such a view, for by 14th April the techMARK index at 3528 was down 38.7% from its March peak, while the NASDAQ Composite was down 34.2%. The FTSE and the Dow, after holding firm at the beginning of the month, also went into reverse in that second week, with the former losing 391 points to 6178 and the latter 806 to 10,305, influenced by fears that a jump in US headline inflation to 3.7% and a 5% year on year growth rate in the first quarter could lead to more aggressive rate rises. However, the meltdown predicted by some commentators failed to occur, and by the end of April a partial calm had returned to markets largely inspired by confidence in Alan Greenspan's ability to engineer a soft landing for the US economy. Investor confidence, at least in the US, was also evident in the fact that with an inflow of $115 billion in the first quarter, mutual funds had already taken more than their total for the whole of 1999. Initially, too, a degree of euphoria was induced by the large sums paid by Europe's leading telecom companies for the Third Generation mobile telephone licences. However, the total of £22 billion was too far ahead of expectations and it was not long before analysts began to work out that with another £4 billion to be spent on infrastructure, the companies would be so cash strapped that this spending would have to be scaled down to meet debt repayments and that profit generation would be put back by years.

The stage was set for another sharp fall in high tech stocks. In March the sell-off had been led by the software and internet-related companies, but this time it was the telecoms sector that led the field on the downside. **Vodafone**, which following its takeover of **Mannesmann** in February was now the country's biggest company representing some 14% of the FTSE100, lost 8.6% and with sentiment further damaged by the collapse of leading internet retailer **Boo.com**, the techMARK index fell to 3052, a fall of 47% from its March peak, and the FTSE slipped back to close to the bottom of its 6000/6600 trading range. But continuing in its now well-established roller coaster fashion, 22nd May marked a temporary low point for markets and the next ten days saw the FTSE shoot up 9.8% to the top of its trading range, with **Vodafone** up 30% and accounting for a substantial part of the points rally. The justification for this sharp recovery was cited as recent evidence that the US economy was slowing and the belief that interest rates had peaked after a half point hike in Fed Funds to 6.5% in mid-May, and also that 6% was going to mark the top in the UK. The Dow and NASDAQ recorded similarly dramatic rises, but more sceptical commentators saw the US economy in a Catch 22 situation with signs of a slowdown boosting stocks and causing consumer confidence to rise, thus threatening to revive the spending boom and increase the chances of the Fed tightening again. From the corporate point of view, while the near term outlook for earnings appeared favourable, the valuations were already stretched and if longer term prospects had deteriorated with successive rate rises, then a slowing of the growth rate would inevitably produce a further negative impact on earnings. It was not long before this cautious view appeared to be borne out by profit warnings from Goodyear, expressions of anxiety from two of the big banks about the impact on the sector of higher interest rates leading to rising loan losses, and earnings shortfalls from Unisys and EDS showing that high tech stocks were not going to be immune in the slowdown. King of the e-retailers, Amazon, actually fell 20% on 23rd June after an analyst's warning that it could run out of money by the first quarter of 2001, given the massive spending required for advertising and marketing ahead of the all-important Christmas season.

Swan song

Such influences made for quiet markets on both sides of the Atlantic throughout July and the first half of August, but more bullish pressures were building up. The conviction was growing that following a growth rate of 8.3% in the final quarter of 1999, reduced to 4.8% in the first quarter of 2000, the 5.2% in the second quarter was a blip and the forecast of 3.5% in the third quarter told the true story about a slowing US economy in the wake of interest rate hikes. There was also much talk about Europe taking up the running as the US economy slowed, with a 3.7% growth rate predicted for 2000, against a background of subdued inflation. The UK was calculated to be in the vanguard of this advance thanks to its success in achieving the ideal combination of steady growth, low inflation, low unemployment, and rising productivity as a result of embracing the technological revolution. It was also felt that the fall in TMT stocks had been overdone. After the excesses of 1999 and the first quarter of the year, a correction was certainly in order but falls of 50% on average, and up to 80% in some cases, were perhaps in themselves excessive. But probably the most significant factors were the continuing massive mutual fund inflows of $231 billion in the first half of the year, against just $103 billion for the whole of 1999, allied with the residual bullishness of self-interested market operators.

The scene was set for a major rally, and in the second week in August the Dow led the way, adding 260 points to top 11,000 for the first time since April. Over the next few weeks the mood of optimism spread and on 4th September, the FTSE actually hit a new high of 6798.1 on volume of 2.4 billion shares, the heaviest since the mid-March peak. Both the techMARK 100 and the NASDAQ Composite crossed the 4000 mark again, and the Dow at 11,310 came to within 3.5% of its January all-time high. That was the end of the rally. Two weeks later the FTSE was back in the 6000/6600 box at 6400, the Dow below 11,000 again, and the techMARK and NASDAQ indices had both pulled back to around the 3800 mark. The setback was blamed on the oil price soaring to a 10 year high of $35 a barrel and consideration of its effect on margins and hence corporate profits, already under pressure to judge from a string of high-profile profit warnings. But some were not downhearted. Alfred

Goldman, Chief Market Strategist of A.G. Edwards proclaimed, 'if there's one thing we should have learned about this bull market over the last 20 years is that when they knock 'em down…you buy 'em'. The oil price rise had a particularly adverse effect in the UK, as a combination of farmers and lorry drivers organized protests against fuel tax increases and blockaded key distribution depots. Their action prompted panic buying of petrol by the public and demonstrated the vulnerability of a fine-tuned economy, and indeed of the government itself when New Labour saw its first decline in popularity in the opinion polls since taking office in 1997. Critics also saw the pound as a major problem. It was strong against the euro to the detriment of the UK's principal export market, and at a 7-year low against the dollar, in which imported raw materials including oil are priced. As a result, the manufacturing industry was getting the worst of both worlds. And there was no indication that the situation was going to change. Concerted intervention earlier in September by the central banks had failed to boost the euro, which was now worth $0.87 against $1.18 at its debut in January 1999, and the renewed round of Middle East trouble looked like keeping the oil price high and even threatening a repeat of the crisis of 1973.

One darned thing after another

A flood of profit warnings and earnings downgrades during the rest of the month appeared to confirm all these fears. Chemical giant **Dupont's** warning about the impact on industry of the high oil prices knocked **ICI** for six. Once regarded as the bellwether of UK industry, **ICI** was on the ropes and its share price was now at a 15-year low, giving a market capitalisation of just £2.6 billion in contrast with one of £60 billion for **Zeneca**, its former pharmaceutical division spun off in 1993. **Invensys (BTR cum Siebe)** also rocked the boat with a profits warning that saw the shares down 7% on the day to 156p, a far cry from last year's peak of 356p. By the last day of the month, the FTSE at 6294, along with the All Share, had recorded a loss for a third consecutive quarter of the year, an event that had not occurred since 1974. In the US, too, the profits warnings came thick and fast led by **Intel**, the world's leading chip producer. Its announcement that revenue growth would be in the region of 3-5% against analysts' expectations of 9-10% upset the whole technology sector, and **Intel** fell 22% on the day to $48. On 1st October, **Dell** warned of reduced sales but said it was still on course for in-house estimates of profits for the year. The market took the news badly and the shares fell 15% to a level now 60% below their April high. Then **Xerox** forecast a third quarter loss in the place of an expected profit, and the shares dropped 29% to a point where they were now 80% down on the year. **Lucent**, the world's largest telecom equipment maker, caused an even bigger stir, warning that fourth quarter earnings were likely to be 30% below earlier forecasts. The shares dropped 26% and were now down 73% from their high. **Motorola's** warning that sales of its mobile phones were likely to be 6% below forecast added to the stream of bad news and the FTSE just avoided breaching the 6000 level, while the Dow on 18th October actually lost 435 points before closing down 114 points at 9975.

It looked as if the penny had dropped at last. The downgrading of sales and earnings forecasts from key players in the high tech sector meant that there was no justification for their earlier stratospheric valuations, and even more importantly today, no basis for their current levels given that things could only get worse thanks to declining investment spending, the high oil price and a strong dollar. The UK high tech sector was in much the same bind. Now that the background situation had changed so dramatically for the worse, the 'buy on dips' policy that had worked so well in the past could only mean chucking good money after bad when historic earnings multiples (where there were earnings to multiply) were already at daunting levels and prospective P/Es were pie in the sky. Nevertheless, after plumbing the depths on 18th October, markets rebounded and by the end of the month the Dow had climbed back over 1000 points to 10,971, and the FTSE was up to 6400 again. This recovery occurred despite leading network equipment maker **Nortel Networks** reporting third quarter sales below analysts' expectations. The news wiped 30% off the value of the shares, but investors were heartened by good results from optical equipment manufacturers **JDS Uniphase**. Furthermore, lower than expected US gross domestic product figures fuelled hopes that the slowdown was underway and interest rates had reached the top of their cycle. The mood was summed up by the equity market strategists of Deutsche Bank, who in a paper assessing the chances of a full-scale bear market developing, observed, 'As long as core inflation remains subdued and the global economy is set for a soft landing – which we firmly believe will be the case – then equity markets are unlikely to fall much further'.

The bears continued to focus on what they saw as growing signs that the US was heading for a hard landing, which would inevitably have a knock-on effect on the rest of the world. They argued that the welfare of the stock market and the economy was more closely linked than ever before, and this time the decline of the former could be the cause of recession rather than its consequence for as stock prices crumbled, a negative wealth effect would kick in and consumer spending would dive. In addition, falling sales and earnings in the high technology sector, and in old economy manufacturing like automobiles, would mean cutting output and thus investment and the lay-offs involved would in turn hit employment and consumer spending. Almost every week earnings forecasts were being subjected to downward revision. In mid-November, the S&P fourth quarter figure of +11.2% compared with one of +15.6% made just a month ago, and forecasts for 2001 were now logged at +12.6% against an earlier figure of +19.1%. Goldman Sachs also cut its GDP growth forecast for the US economy in 2001 from 4% to 3.3%, making the generous assumption that it was on a glidepath for a soft landing in time to avoid overheating and another round of interest rate rises. Little credence was given to the view that this deceleration of growth and earnings would prompt overseas investors to divert capital flows to other trading blocks, no longer offsetting the country's huge trade deficit and sustaining the dollar. After all, given the relative weakness of Japan and Euroland, if the US slowed, they would slow even more.

The miracle worker

Hopes were beginning to fade that December would bring the traditional Christmas rally, but Alan Greenspan's pronouncement that he was 'alert to the possibility that greater caution and weakening asset value...could signal or precipitate an excessive softening in household and business spending', inspired confidence in many quarters that he would save America and the world as he had done so many times before by lowering interest rates. Another run of disappointing earnings from what were once the darlings of the high technology sector actually bolstered this confidence and provided investors once more with something to look forward to. Less attention was paid to the Fed chairman's description of the stock market increases in recent years as 'extraordinary gains' or his pointed observation that 'our current circumstances are in no way comparable to those of 1998', when a rapid series of rate cuts by the Fed accompanied by rescue packages for countries in trouble served to avert a global financial crisis. At that time, the US economy was still growing strongly and could play the locomotive to pull along the rest of the world's economies. However, from this point on the market seemed to display a touching faith in the ability of Alan Greenspan to control the situation, and although there was not the hoped for reduction in interest rates, just before Christmas a proclaimed shift to an 'easing bias' was enough to keep hopes alive and the Dow managed to end the year at 10,876, down only 5.4%, but still recording its first annual loss in ten years. The NASDAQ Composite was down 40% on the year and 50% from the March peak, with many of its high-profile constituents joining 'The Ten Percenters', i.e. recording losses of 90% plus from their 1999/2000 highs. London fared a little worse with the FTSE losing 10.2% to 6222.5, while the techMARK 100 at 2564 shed 55.3% from its March spike of 5743.3. Telecoms and IT companies were by far the worst performers in the FTSE, led by Anglo-French IT services company **SEMA**, down 75%, closely followed by cable operator **Telewest**, down 68%, and third in line was **British Telecom**, which lost 62% to 570p on concerns over its huge debt burden. Signs of a return to normality in markets was the expulsion of **SEMA**, **Bookham** and **Baltimore** from the FTSE100, and the return of **Rolls-Royce**, **Smith Industries**, **AB Foods** and **Safeway**.

Against such a background it was not surprising that the Long Bond yield stood at 5.4% compared with 6.5% at the beginning of the year, and the 10-year gilt yield at 4.9% (5.5%). Bonds might not beat equities in the long run, but in a low inflation climate they were seen to provide a safe heaven from profit warnings in so-called 'growth' sectors that could halve an investor's money in the blink of an eye.

European markets were also well down on the year, with the Paris CAC 40 off around 15%, and German's DAX down 20% with the high technology Neuer Markt crashing over 60%. In Asia, where technology and electronics companies dominate the stock markets, Japan's Nikkei 225 fell 27% to 13,785, South Korea more than halved to 500, while Hong Kong's broader based index managed to hold above the 15,000 level, down 11% at 15,095, buoyed by the hopes of rate cuts and the benefits of structural reforms in mainland China.

Among the commodities, oil closed the year at $23 a barrel, the $35 spike in late summer having proved to be a short-lived aberration. Gold remained in the doldrums at around $272, as its classic hedge role continued to be eroded by financial instruments unheard of in its heyday.

Looking ahead

Despite having been spectacularly wrong in their forecasts for the FTSE100 level at the end of 2000 – they had ranged from 6900 up to 8800 – the leading brokers continued to project much the same degree of optimism into 2001, with a range from 6600 all the way up to 8125. Governor of the Bank of England, Sir Edward George's pronouncement that the US slowdown 'may be sharper than we needed and sharper than is desirable for the world economy', apparently cut little ice with market professionals only too eager to pin their hopes on the Federal Reserve Chairman's prospective interest rate cuts, and the new administration's tax rebates to keep the ball rolling. Interestingly, in another poll of experts conducted by the *FT*, the most downbeat forecast for the coming year (at 5900) was made by stock market historian David Schwartz, the sole member of the panel without an axe to grind. At the same time, despite putting so much faith in the power of rate cuts, not one of the FT's panel of experts was looking for a Fed Funds rate below 5% by year end, or an MLR rate below 5.5%.

2001

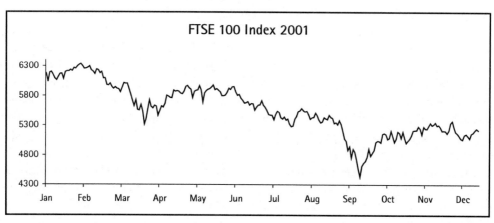

Source: Thomson Reuters Datastream

'Somebody stole the economy'

Despite the hopes that had rested on a rate cut by the Federal Reserve, when it came on 3rd January with a larger than expected half point reduction to 6%, the stock market's reaction was decidedly mixed. After an initial surge of 300 points on the announcement, the Dow lost 250 points and the NASDAQ 159 the following day on widely expressed concerns that the cut, far from being designed to head off a recession, was in response to a recession that had already arrived. Support for such a view came that same week with earnings downgrades from top US brokers on **Hewlett-Packard**, **Intel** and **Applied Micro Circuits**, casting a shadow over the whole tech sector. Consensus forecasts for earnings growth in the fourth quarter of 2000 were now down to 4.3% from 15.3%, neatly illustrating that even without an actual recession, slower growth means lower earnings, and lower earnings and lower dividends in turn leading to lower share prices. To cap a bad week, trading in the shares of **Bank of America** was temporarily halted as rumours of trading or loan losses knocked the share price. The Bank denied having experienced 'any significant losses in derivatives or other trading activities'. In short, the rate cut did nothing to restore confidence but rather the opposite, as markets interpreted Alan Greenspan's comment about 'tight conditions in some segments of financial markets' as evidence that the banks had been lending too freely and were now seriously exposed to credit risk.

Follow my leader

As for the London market, its reaction to the Fed's rate cut was muted, but at least the event helped to avoid a 'difference of opinion' between the MPC and the Chancellor over the advisability of a reduction in MLR ahead of the spring election. It was the Fed's second rate cut at the end of January by another half a percentage point to 5.5% that prompted UK investors to look for parallel action here. When it came on 10th February with a quarter point cut to 5.75%, the FTSE100 was sufficiently underwhelmed to close below the 6200 floor at 6104.3, down 1.5% on the week. The reason for the absence of an enthusiastic response to once eagerly awaited rate cuts was a continuing stream of worrying economic and corporate news on both sides of the Atlantic. Indeed, on the day the Fed's second cut was announced it was revealed that US GDP had grown at just 1.4% in the final quarter of 2000, much slower than expected. And the day before, **DaimlerChrysler** topped the latest run of job losses by announcing 26,000 lay-offs over a 3-year period, compounding a severe profit warning from **Nortel Networks** and more caution from **Dell** and **Hewlett-Packard**. In the words of one US analyst, 'Betting on a rosy scenario tilts the market towards risk', and in those of another contemplating the huge size and importance of the "new economy" companies, 'the negative microeconomics of the tech sector might be stronger than the positive macroeconomics of the Fed'.

By mid-February, the FTSE had slipped below 6100 and was lower than it had been in February 1999, a situation that owed a great deal to the slump in telecom shares which now had such a significant weighting in the indices. Unfortunately for anyone thinking the market had to be worth buying at this level, **Vodafone**, once the biggest company in the UK with a market capitalization of £240 billion, was still selling on a P/E of 50 after halving in price over the past year. The software sector's historic P/E remained over 80, and leading constituent **Logica's** P/E was 120 with a prospective figure on analysts' current projections of 73, even though the share price had halved from its peak. Given the climate of an increasing number of profits warnings and the example of what was happening in the US, there was little evidence for calling a market bottom. All eyes were now on the psychologically important 6000 level, and its breach on 24th February sparked a number of articles in the financial press postulating a new investment era. Their line was that returns from shares were no longer going to beat returns from bonds and cash as they had since 1980. The collapse of important household name stocks in the last twelve months had demonstrated to institutional and private investors alike that there was no such thing as a stock for 'widows and orphans', and both would want to adopt a much more conservative approach in their investment strategy for the future. Furthermore, it could take years to rebuild confidence in a market system that provided full listings, and even entry to the FTSE100 index, to shares of companies that would have been shown the door ten years ago – and for very good reason as had now been so painfully demonstrated.

March was not a good month for stock markets anywhere. The anniversary of the peaking of the TMT boom seemed to concentrate the minds of investors and financial journalists on the frightening extent of the disaster that had overtaken technology stocks and the dot.coms. The techMARK 100 and the NASDAQ Composite were both down 60% from their 2000 peaks, while many of the high tech leaders in both indices had sustained even larger percentage falls. **Freeserve**, the UK's first quoted internet service provider, after touching 930p last year to enter the FTSE100 with a market capitalization of £6.1 billion, was now valued at less than £1 billion, while America's **Yahoo!**, which at its peak was bigger than **General Motors**, **Boeing** and **Heinz** put together with a market capitalization in excess of $100 billion, was now down to under $10 billion. Many of the smaller companies had fared much worse. Internet auctioneer **QXL**, once set to rival America's **eBay**, had fallen from a peak of 778p to 8p, and optical chip designer **Bookham**, floated at £10 in April 2000, soared to £42 before making a secondary placing in August at £30, then touching £54, was now down to £4. And things showed no sign of getting better with the second week of March seeing warnings from leading US chipmakers **Intel** and **National Semiconductors**, and the announcement of a substantial cost-cutting programme from **Cisco**. The weakness now appeared to be generalised and was neatly summed up by CEO of **Sun Microsystems**, Scott McNealy's cri de coeur, 'Somebody stole the economy!'

All the king's horses...

The big worry was that if the US tipped into recession, then with Japan still in the doldrums, something like two thirds of G7 economic activity would be hit simultaneously, with inevitable adverse effect on the rest of the global village. These anxieties now became increasingly reflected in stock markets everywhere, and even before a further half point cut in Fed Funds to 5% on 20th March, the FTSE had lost over 500 points to just below 5400, and the Dow had slipped under 10,000 again. The fact that this third rate cut failed to boost markets, but rather the reverse as the Dow and NASDAQ fell again, prompted speculation that the setback had gone well beyond a simple correction of high tech "over exuberance" and was now creating negative feedback in the real economy. The ability of the central banks, primarily the US Federal Reserve, to steer the world's economies away from recession was now being called into question. Their success in the battle against inflation in the early eighties had invested the central banks in the US and Europe with a degree of 'almost mystical authority', and generated a widespread confidence in their powers to avert trouble. This time, however, things could be very different and simple monetary easing might not be enough to stop recession developing from the current downturn, which was the result of a classic credit cycle squeeze caused by the end of "over exuberant" spending and investment. This time around too, the stock market casualties were much bigger fish compared with those hurt in the crash of 1987. When many of the biggest companies in the world are losing billions of dollars and laying off thousands of workers, and their share prices are down around 70% or even more, the economy is obviously going to suffer rather more collateral damage than when just a handful of over-ambitious mini-conglomerates bite the dust.

...and all the king's men

The CBI added its voice to the calls for further interest rate cuts. Worried that the American slowdown would have a serious impact on the UK, already reeling from the foot and mouth outbreak, the director general expressed the hope that the MPC would continue to reduce rates to 5% by mid-summer, following the quarter point cut to 5.5% on 5th April. The European Central Bank was also urged to cut from 4.75% to 4.25%, and most observers were looking for a further reduction by the Federal Reserve ahead of its next scheduled meeting on 16th May, after a sharp fall in US employment figures for March. **Dell** had cheered markets in the first week of April by announcing that it was on course to meet its first quarter sales and profits forecast, but the rally was quickly snuffed out by disappointing employment data and by a new round of profit warnings from high tech heavyweights. The gloom was compounded in Europe where software group **Autonomy** lost 245p to 345p after warning of a sharp drop in first quarter sales, news which also provided the first real indication that the slowdown in technology spending had spread across the Atlantic. The statement upset the rest of the software sector and the techMARK 100 lost 56 points to 1780.

Nevertheless, the second half of April saw a renewed advance in London and New York on hopes that perhaps the worst was over for the high tech sector following better than expected results from **Intel, IBM** and **Apple**, and on expectations of more help from the Federal Reserve. A surprise half-point rate cut to 4.5% on 18th April boosted markets further, with the Dow rising 400 points to 10,615 and the NASDAQ 156 points to 2079 on record volumes. While in London the FTSE plussed 129 to 5890 and the techMARK soared 147 or 8% to 1984. The news from Intel that business was beginning to improve was especially welcome to the embattled high tech sectors everywhere, and in Japan the Nikkei Dow shot up 574 to 13,641 and Hong Kong's Hang Seng gained 366 to 12,972.

However, a number of commentators interpreted the Fed's action as an indication that Alan Greenspan and his colleagues were more concerned about the economic outlook than they were prepared to admit. They also considered that **Intel's** optimism was more than cancelled out by job cuts and quarterly earnings downgrades from **Cisco** and **Hewlett-Packard**, and also from "old economy" companies like **General Motors** and **Gillette**. It was also suggested that the Fed's move ahead of the next scheduled meeting had caught the bears on the hop and the sharp rise in the US indices was simply the result of a classic bear squeeze. There also seemed little doubt that despite the massive percentage declines in many of the high tech leaders, their valuations remained too high given the earnings outlook for the rest of the year and probably well into 2002. A V-shaped recovery was no longer a scenario to bet on.

'A curiously bullish bear market'

Markets received a further boost at the end of April when US first quarter growth was revealed to have bounced back to 2% from a low of 1% in the final quarter of 2000. Treasury Secretary Paul O'Neill hailed the figure as 'nothing but good news' and testimony to his belief that the US economy was 'wonderfully resilient', and remained a 'strong engine for growth for the world economy'. More objective commentators thought it was a mistake to place too much reliance on the continuing strength of consumer spending against a background of falling business investment, rising unemployment and the ultimately inevitable negative wealth effect of a weakening stock market. They also believed that such circumstances meant that the already fairly sharp downward revisions of earnings forecasts for 2001 were still too optimistic. In the words of a note from Credit Suisse First Boston, 'This was a curiously bullish bear market'.

The corporate news round of continuing job losses and the publicity given to analysts' fears about the viability of the big telecom companies clearly supported the more bearish view, but markets appeared to have regained their faith in Alan Greenspan's ability to work miracles and forged ahead in May in anticipation of more rate cuts. These duly arrived in the middle of the month with a UK base rate reduction of a quarter point to 5.25%, and a surprise cut of the same degree to 4.5% by the ECB, followed a few days later by a half point cut to 4% by the Federal Reserve. The markets responded enthusiastically with the Dow topping 11,000 again and achieving a new high for the year of 11,337 on 21st May, 20% up from the March low and only 4% off its all-time high of the previous year. The NASDAQ Composite also took heart, rising to almost 2300 at the end of May despite profit warnings from **Dell**, **Palm** and **Agilent**. The dollar reflected this reaffirmed faith in the US economy by rising strongly. In London, the FTSE pushed close to 6000 and the techMARK 100 managed to get up to 2100 again, but overall the advances failed to match the enthusiasm shown in the US, muted perhaps by the month's huge cash calls in the shape of a £5.9 billion rights issue from **BT** and a £3.5 billion placing by **Vodafone**. The election scheduled for the 7th June did not appear to introduce any element of uncertainty into the proceedings, given that another Labour landslide was widely taken for granted.

Second thoughts

By the middle of June, optimism about a rapid recovery from the global downturn was fading fast. Earlier indications that the high tech slowdown in the US was bottoming out were seemingly thoroughly disproved by another bout of disastrous news from the sector. **Nortel Networks**, one of the leading makers of telecommunications equipment in North America, entered the corporate record books, warning of a second quarter loss of $19.2 billion on revenues, down 27% on this first quarter, and of another 10,000 job losses on top of the 20,000 already announced. **Nortel's** problems were now seen as typical of those plaguing the whole telecoms sector, i.e. a collapse in the level of demand required to justify the massive debt-funded capital spending of the past couple of years. **JDS Uniphase**, the top maker of components for optical communications networks, found itself in the same boat, revealing that sales in the third quarter would be less than half those of the year before. **Philips**, the Dutch electronics group, reflected European difficulties by announcing a dramatic slide in its semiconductor sales, and **Nokia** slashed sales forecasts for its mobile phones. The need for retrenchment in the sector had prompted the leading US and European manufacturers, **Lucent** and **Alcatel**, to explore the possibility of a merger but talks broke down and shares of both companies fell sharply. Fears that the UK's largest telecommunications equipment maker, **Marconi**, would not be immune from the malaise apparently affecting the whole industry, caused its shares to lose 15% on the week to 290p. Alan Greenspan clearly took note of these developments and, concluding that the US economy was 'unacceptably weak', on 27th June cut the Fed Funds rate by a quarter of a point to 3.75%. The move failed to cheer markets and at the end of June, the Dow was back to around 10,500 and the FTSE100 was bumping along the bottom of its 5600/6000 trading range. The break through the 5600 level came a few days into July when **Marconi's** shares were suspended ahead of an announcement that the current year's operating profits would halve and another 4,000 jobs would go. The FTSE100 constituent's shares dropped 53% the next day when dealings were resumed, and ended the week at 104p, over 90% down from the previous year's peak of £12.50. Given the lack of visibility in the industry, many commentators thought that there was certain to be bad news on the way. There was. Clearly the strategy devised by Lord Weinstock's successors, Lord Simpson and John Mayo, to transform GEC from a leader in electronics and defence into a global player in the telecoms industry had been a costly failure. The chairman and financial director were now widely criticised for making confident statements as late as mid-June, when it was already obvious that all its US rivals and BT were in serious trouble.

Outside the high tech field, **Invensys** showed that nuts and bolts businesses were not doing very well either by issuing its third profits warning in ten months and announcing the resignation of its CEO. The shares promptly fell 23% to 79p. In the US, **JDS Uniphase** justified its warnings earlier in the year by posting full year losses of $50 billion and laying off another 7,000 workers, while **Lucent** and **Hewlett-Packard** added 20,000 and 6,000 dismissals respectively to their totals to date. These results were well in tune with the latest economic data, which showed sharp slowdowns in both the US and UK economies with the downturn spreading from high technology to general manufacturing and to service industries.

Against this background, markets still managed to hold their ground in anticipation of yet another round of interest rate reductions. They did not have to wait for long. On 2nd August, the Bank of England trimmed rates by a quarter point to 5%, explaining this surprise move by reference to the deteriorating international economy. The surprise element arose from the fact that house prices were still rising strongly and that therefore the MPC would not want to boost consumer demand, and thus the cut invited speculation that 'they knew something the rest of us didn't'. With high tech flagship **Cisco** reporting a 13 cents a share loss for the year end to July against a profit of 39 cents in 1999/2000, and "old economy" stock **Procter & Gamble** logging its first quarterly loss in eight years, it was less of a surprise when the Federal Reserve cut rates by another quarter point to 3.5% on 21st August. This was the seventh cut in eight months, and since the previous six appeared to have done nothing for the economy or the stock market, stocks sold off on the announcement and by the end of the month, the Dow was below 10,000 again. Concern was also expressed in some quarters about the problems the slowdown in the US, Japan and Europe must generate for the emerging economies. Argentina, Brazil and Turkey were seeing the steepest falls in their currencies since late summer of 1998, and most of Asia was already firmly in recession. With a weakening dollar and the leaders of the industrialised world in no mood to boost their imports, this was global contagion in reverse as the downturn threatened the economic and political stability of the developing world.

Black September

By the end of the first week in September, markets across the world were clearly in trouble. On 7th September, the US Labour Department revealed that the unemployment rate for August had risen to 4.9%, up sharply from July's 4.5%, and the biggest monthly rise in six years. The news was immediately taken as a sign that consumer confidence and spending would now begin to crumble and take away the last bastion between the US and recession. The Dow lost 235 points to 9605 and the FTSE100 tumbled 134 to 5070 on high volume, with practically every sector affected. Particularly hard hit was the debt-laden telecommunications sector, with analysts expressing concern about the viability of **Marconi** and the impact on its lead banks if it went under in the light of debt totalling £4.4 billion. The techMARK 100 recorded a new low point of 1366, down 5.7% on the week, and all the European markets slipped to 30-month lows. In Asia, Japan's Nikkei Dow and Hong Kong's Hang Seng indices both headed towards the 10,000 mark, with the decline of the former influenced by a 0.8% contraction in GDP between April and June.

Further interest rate cuts were clearly on the cards but few commentators were prepared to call a market turn in the face of a continuing stream of adverse corporate and economic news. On Monday 10th September, the FTSE plunged below 5000 for the first time since 1998, hitting an intraday low of 4895.9 as Wall Street opened 100 points down, but ended just 36.6 lower at 5033.7 as the Dow recovered to close practically unchanged at 9605. Airlines were a particularly weak sector. **British Airways** was down 11% on the week to 270p against a high of 463p in January, after a flurry of sell recommendations from analysts forecasting a substantial loss for the current year, and a likely dividend cut as increasing competition from the budget airlines sabotaged BA's efforts to cut capacity to match falling traffic volumes. In the US, **AMR**, the parent company of American Airlines and TWA, warned that its third quarter loss would top that of the second quarter, when it lost $105 million. In Europe, **KLM** and **Swissair** both met heavy selling on anxieties over their debt levels. Further afield, Air New Zealand was looking for buyers for troubled subsidiary **Ansett Australia**, and the Indian government was having difficulty in finding buyers for its loss-making national carrier, **Air India**.

Bolt from the blue

The terrorist suicide mission which destroyed the Twin Towers in the heart of New York's financial district and the attack on the Pentagon, sent a shockwave through stock markets around the world. London, up 95 before the news of the attack, plunged 287.7 to 4746 on high turnover, its largest points fall since October 1987. Sectors hardest hit were airlines, leisure, hotels, banking and insurance. **British Airways** dived to just above the 200p mark, and airports operator **BAA** lost over 100p to 515p. The French and German main indices both declined by over 5%, and in Asia, Japan's Nikkei Dow plunged 682 points to 9610. Hong Kong's Hang Seng dipped 923 to 9493. Gold surged $15 to $290, and the oil price climbed to $31 on fears of what effect US retaliatory action in the Middle East could have on oil supplies. The grey market was looking for falls of 500 in the Dow and 350 in the NASDAQ Composite when Wall Street eventually opened for business on Monday 17th September. The next two days saw a near 200 point recovery in the FTSE, but this was all but wiped out on Friday by nervous selling in anticipation of Wall Street's reaction after four days of enforced suspension of trading. Over the weekend there was some talk of a patriotic rally on Monday morning, but the broad consensus was for a heavy fall. Economically, things had looked bad enough a week earlier and the outlook had to be a lot worse now, quite apart from the further uncertainty introduced by the prospect of an imminent US military response. The consensus was right. The Dow lost a record 685 points on Monday and ended the week down 14.3% at 8235, its biggest loss since 1933. The NASDAQ at 1423 was down 16% on the week. Another half point cut in Fed Funds to 3% and the announcement of an emergency spending package of $40 billion counted for little in a market dominated by risk aversion, pessimism about earnings prospects and fears of recession. No one was in the mood to question Alan Greenspan's judgement that 'for the foreseeable future, the risks are weighted mainly towards conditions that may generate economic weakness'.

Visibility zero

Not surprisingly, the week saw another downward lurch for London and the other European markets. A quarter point off UK base rates to 4.75% and a half point reduction by the European Central Bank to 3.75% did nothing to halt the slide. Once again, airlines, insurance and leisure stocks were in the firing line with **British Airways** falling below its 1987 flotation price of 125p at one point, before recovering to 152p after a deal with insurers and the government headed off the insurance crisis that had threatened to ground its fleet. **TBI**, operator of Luton and Belfast International airports, crashed 20p to 59p as investors took the view that the 90p cash bid from French group **Vinci**, which had been vigorously resisted, would no longer be on the table. Also hard hit were shares in companies where high levels of indebtedness and already collapsing share prices were considered to call into question their financial viability. Prominent in this group were **Invensys**, down 45% over the week to 35p, **Marconi**, down 38% to 20p, and **Cookson**, off a massive 52% to 50p. The FTSE100 closed the week at 4433.7 (after touching an intraday low of 4219 on Thursday 20th September), falling123.2 on Friday on exceptionally high volume of 4.2 billion shares, with a record 222,000 individual trades indicating a "sell at any price" approach by many investors. The mood was summed up by a Credit Suisse First Boston investment report entitled 'Market Outlook: Visibility Zero'.

With all the emphasis on building a global coalition against terrorism ahead of embarking upon military action, stock markets used this breathing space to recover their poise in the final week of September. The climactic falls of 21st September marked a turning point of sorts in the opinion of a number of commentators, as the FTSE and the Dow clawed back some 500 points of their losses. Paradoxically, the unremittingly bad corporate news of closures and job losses, which at first sight hardly seemed to support the belief that markets had turned the corner, was interpreted as doing precisely that. The theory was that because companies in trouble were taking such rapid restorative measures and the central banks were playing their part with lavish interest rate cuts, then the bad times would soon pass and recovery was just around the corner. These actions were seen as clearly differentiating the current slowdown from that which began for Japan in 1990, and had persisted to the present day largely as a result of the authorities' reluctance to embrace change at an early stage. More cautious observers noted that the slackening pace of consumer spending was already evident prior to the events of 11th September and was bound to accelerate again, given that the retrenchment measures announced before and after that date involved many of the biggest companies in the world, and as such would inevitably cause huge collateral damage throughout their industries. This made a V-shaped recovery very unlikely and tipped the balance in favour of a much longer convalescent phase for the global economy of the sort that followed 1929/31 and 1973/74. They also contrasted the relatively optimistic forecasts of governments' "official" economists with the appalling news from industry and company spokesmen telling it as it is at the sharp end, given that the former were compelled to put on a brave face for fear of telling the truth and being blamed for causing a recession.

Sand in the wheels

On 7th October, the bombing campaign over Afghanistan began but stock markets remained relatively firm, helped by another half point off Fed Funds to 2.5%, and a quarter point reduction in MLR to 4.5%, and by the end of the week both New York and London had practically recovered to their pre-September 11th levels. This performance appeared to imply that investors saw September 11th as a one-off event, and was all the more remarkable in that it took place against the background of the anthrax outbreaks, more gloomy economic news, the suspension of **Railtrack** and the bankruptcy of **Polaroid**. With the FTSE up 17%, the S&P up 14%, and the Eurotop 300 up 21% from their September 21st lows, there was no denying that the rally in world markets had been impressive. It was also true that shares were reasonable value, even cheap on the earnings yield/bonds yield ratio.

However, as the month wore on it became increasingly difficult for the indices to make further headway, as the now familiar run of profit warnings and losses continued to compete for dominance in the market place, with expectations of another round of interest rate cuts. Two intraday dips to below 5000 at the end of October along with the Dow barely holding above 9000, suggested that the bears were gaining control, but then a strong recovery from these levels seemed to confirm the belief that floors had been established at these levels. Attention now became concentrated on the upside scope. The argument for an advance to test the top of the 5000/5200 box for the FTSE, and the pre-September 11th level of 9605 for the Dow, relied very largely on investors' appreciation of the fact that stock markets traditionally lead economic recoveries by some six months, and their belief that with still more rate cuts in the pipeline, recovery in the second quarter of 2002 was a done deal. By early November, both these upside targets had been achieved despite an avalanche of appalling corporate and economic news which failed to dim the hopes engendered by a concerted round of interest rate cuts on November 8th from the Federal Reserve, the Monetary Policy Committee and the European Central Bank. All these bodies cut rates by half a point against expectations of no more than a quarter in the UK and the Eurozone, moves which suggested to the more cautious commentators that the authorities had previously been underplaying the seriousness of the economic situation. Economist Sushil Wadhwani, one of the so-called 'doves' on the MPC, expressed concern about 'sand in the wheels' of world trade expansion post September 11th, created by the additional costs to industry of extra security and the necessary trimming of "just in time" inventory policies, coupled with the reluctance of executives to travel as extensively as before.

'Déjà vu all over again'

In the writings of the more serious financial commentators concerned with the long view, as distinct from the day-to-day performance of the markets, there was now to be found more than a suggestion that this was no ordinary bear market but one more on the pattern of those of 1929/1933 and 1972/1975, or even more worrying, that of Japan starting in 1989 and still with no end in sight. Their fear was that lower interest rates were not going to stimulate investment spending by a corporate sector already burdened by excess capacity as a result of its last spending spree, nor borrowing and spending by already heavily-indebted consumers facing the uncertainties now so evident in the jobs market. The unfolding of such a situation would mean that a V-shaped economic recovery was not a bankable proposition and that by treating it as such, buyers of equities had got their timescale wrong and were assuming an unacceptably high degree of risk. Rather, they suggested, investors would be better advised to follow the example of **Boots**' pension fund managers, who had switched the whole of the company's £2.3 billion portfolio into bonds over the past one and a half years in order to guarantee that the company would be able to meet its obligations to fund members. The lesson from their action was that equities could no longer be relied upon to provide the sort of double-digit returns that had come to be expected from them. Furthermore, the hiring of "expert" fund managers was not the answer, as **Unilever's** pension fund's negligence case against Mercury Asset Management clearly demonstrated, an action with which many private investors stampeded into share ISAs by their financial advisors in the first quarter of 2000 would greatly sympathise. Those commentators also believed that the great body of investors, institutional as well as private, had become thoroughly alienated from the investment banking/stockbroking community, and from many of their household name corporate clients where disastrous performances seemed to be no bar to seven figure bonuses for the former, and seven figure compensation payments with huge pension top-ups for the latter. Indeed, as one writer suggested, in a world where "investment" had become indistinguishable from "speculation", and over-optimism, misjudgement and incompetence abounded, then security of capital and peace of mind should be the investor's prime objective. Switching from "cyclicals" to "defensives" and back again earns commissions for the stockbroker, but does not guarantee gains for the investor who has no need to hold equities at all in periods of great uncertainty. After all, a low interest rate from a bond, or even a deposit account in a low inflation environment, was not such a bad deal while waiting to see how things turned out.

Back from the brink

However, by mid-November with the war against Afghanistan going far better than anyone could have expected, investors seemed too scared of missing a buying opportunity to wait and see 'how things turned out' and stock markets continued to rise. The Airbus crash over New York on 12th November created a short-lived panic in the markets on fears that it could have been terrorist related, but the accident verdict saw lost ground recovered quickly. The bulls took considerable comfort from the fact that the oil price was below $20 a barrel for the first time in two years, providing a welcome addition to the two principal motors of industrial recovery, namely interest rate cuts and fiscal stimuli. Also, the bulls continued to argue, the historical evidence that since 1945 the average length of US recession was eleven months and interest rate cuts start to take effect within twelve months, led to the conclusion that the trough of the current recession should be reached in the second quarter of 2002. The rise in the stock market was therefore simply fulfilling its historical role by flagging the recovery due in the third quarter. With the Dow knocking on the door of 10,000 again and the FTSE100 comfortably above 5300 towards the end of November, the scene appeared set for a traditional end-year rally, but the prospect was upset by the collapse of **Enron**, America's leading energy company, creating the biggest bankruptcy in history. Once valued at $80 billion, Enron had been advised and audited by top accountancy firm Andersen, and its sudden collapse prompted anxieties about the financial stability of other companies where accounting practises were being called into question by analysts. Some even speculated that the event undermined the whole basis of equity valuation if accountants and auditors could not be relied upon to present a "true and fair" picture of a company's accounts, and perhaps 'unrealistic calculations of past returns' was much more worrying than Alan Greenspan's latest cautionary words to investors about their 'unrealistic expectations of future returns'! Such anxieties, coupled with another round of profit warnings from the TMT sectors and higher than expected November job losses in the US weighed on equity markets, pushing the Dow below 9800 and the FTSE almost back to 5000 by mid-December. The collapse of the Argentinian economy contributed to the gloom, but with its bonds trading at around 25% of face value earlier in the year, the consensus was that the crisis had been well signposted and thus did not provide the sort of sudden shock that sparks contagion. Another cut in the Fed Funds rate, this time by 0.25% to 1.75%, was greeted initially with some scepticism, but a continuing rise in bond yields demonstrated that the market was placing bets on economic recovery, albeit without too much regard for its timing or strength.

At the end of December the FTSE100 stood at 5242, down 15.8% on the year, while the more vulnerable techMARK 100 had lost 42.8% to 1467. In the US, the Dow was down just 6% at 10,136, reflecting its weighting in so-called defensive and cyclical stocks, and contrasting sharply with a 21% slump to 1987 in the technology biased NASDAQ Composite. The Euroblock 300 index had lost 18%, and in Asia, Japan was down 23.5% at 10,542, and Hong Kong, 24.3% at 11,431. However, the fact that all the indices were up substantially from their 21st September low points prompted a number of observers to conclude that the bear market had ended on that day and we were now in the early stages of a new bull market. More cautious commentators noted that these end-year figures marked the second consecutive year of falling equity prices for the first time since 1973/74, but that today's P/Es and dividend yields were historically at the top of the range, as contrasted with single figure P/Es and double figure dividend yields to tempt investors on the last day of December 1974. Thus, current valuations in the context of weak demand and lingering overcapacity in 2002, failed to provide a very bullish prospect for the coming year. This view was reflected in an average of analysts' forecasts for the FTSE100 a year hence of 5850, indicating a more sober assessment of an economic background which to less professionally involved commentators was just as evident a year ago when the forecasts for end-2001 had been a thousand points higher.

The year also demonstrated more clearly than most that investors were dealing not so much with a "stock market" but a "market of stocks". When "old economy"

FTSE100 constituents like **Marks & Spencer** and **Imperial Tobacco** could rise by 95% and 32% respectively while **Marconi** could fall by over 90% and, along with seven more "new economy stocks", be ejected from the index as their market capitalisations nosedived, such a disparity of performance between the biggest companies in the land tended to undermine the long-term argument for equities. A few commentators suggested that if most investors hold a small selection of stocks, not an index, then one Marconi could wreck the long-term prospects of their portfolio. Furthermore, even if they had invested in a tracker fund, that medium's weighting in a recent big time loser like **Vodafone**, would act as a drag on performance. Thus, they concluded, the obviously superior performance of equities over gilt-edged and building society deposits since 1900, while widely used as an endorsement for the investment industry, nevertheless served as a smokescreen for a multitude of individual disasters. An investor who had been persuaded to put £7,000 cash into a technology share ISA in the spring of 2000, and now saw it worth some £1,800, might be forgiven for believing that the industry's emphasis on long-term gains was a cover-up for an inability to forecast short or even medium-term prospects. To quote legendary economist John Maynard Keynes, 'In the long run we're all dead'.

2002

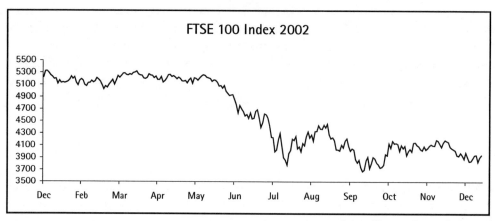

FTSE 100 Index 2002

Source: Thomson Reuters Datastream

As good as it gets

A bout of New Year optimism took the FTSE through 5300 and the techMARK above 1500 on 4th January, but there was no follow through against a background where nothing had changed except the date. Alan Greenspan warned that the US economy faced 'significant' risks in the near-term even if the signals had turned from 'unremittingly negative' to 'far more mixed', but hope that another rate cut was on the cards was counterbalanced by nervousness ahead of an important string of earnings releases and the Dow and the NASDAQ Composite failed to hang on to early gains, peaking at 10,259 and 2059 respectively. The company announcements were even more dire than feared. **DaimlerChrysler** revealed plans to close six plants in the US and cut 26,000 jobs. **Ford** announced five plant closures in the US and 22,000 job losses out of 35,000 worldwide. Then top US retailer **Kmart** came out with disappointing earnings and the shares slid to a 30-year low point amid speculation about imminent bankruptcy. Before the end of January, **IBM, Sun Microsystems, Microsoft** and **Nortel** had all managed to upset the US markets, and in London, profit warnings from **Logica**, **Energis** and **Gateway** added to the gloom. The message of the more responsible financial writers was that while a recovery was inevitable in due course, the time horizon was lengthening. Simple inventory rebuilding did not constitute a true recovery, for which strong final demand was needed. The US consumer had shouldered the burden with private consumption, but could not be relied upon to continue to do so in the context of low personal savings, rising unemployment and a falling stock market. Since the interest rate cycle was at or very near to its low point, the best prospect seemed to be a bottoming out of the inventory and investment cycles followed by a period of anaemic growth. As for the stock market, the reflex bounce from the September lows looked as if it had stalled, an unsurprising development given that equity valuations were something like twice their historic average on trailing P/Es. A further depressant, post-Enron, was provided by doubts about the quality of those earnings that were being accorded such a high rating.

The debate about the long-term merits of equities over bonds was aired again in the *Financial Times* in mid-February following the publication of 'The Triumph of the Optimists', an historical analysis by three London Business School academics showing that over the past century equities had outperformed bonds by an appreciable margin. The fact that this outperformance was more marked in the last fifty years was attributed to the explosion of inflation, which had devastated bond portfolios, and to the birth of the cult of the equity, which had prompted the re-rating of equities both in absolute terms and relative to bonds. Most commentators saw this historical background as not necessarily indicative of the continuing outperformance of shares, noting that the past century had seen bonds outperforming equities over periods as long as 20 years. Another academic, Professor Zvi Bodie of Boston University, contributed to the debate – if not to the advertisements of ISA-selling institutions – by pronouncing, 'Inflation-linked bonds are the only assets that can be relied upon as a hedge against inflation, as they offer a known return at maturity. With stocks there is no certainty of value at any date in the future'.

A further shadow was cast over UK markets by the new accounting rule 'FRS17', stating that pension surpluses and more importantly, deficits, henceforth will have to be reflected in a company's balance sheet. This meant an extreme fall in the value of a company's pension fund could wipe out profits, breach loan agreements and trigger a cash crisis. Hence Boots' switch of its pension fund into gilts with 'a known return at maturity', and the growing number of companies ditching their final salary pension schemes.

Recession? What recession?

Towards the end of February the Dow, which had spent most of the month below 10,000, was beginning to perk up again as the old economy stocks again attracted investors in place of the technology stocks, which continued to sag. Evidence of economic recovery was accumulating in the US, prompting Alan Greenspan to speak of the economy being 'close to a turning point' as fourth quarter GDP growth was revised upwards to 1.4% from 0.2%. This meant that technically there had been no recession according to the usual definition of a downturn over two consecutive quarters, or that thanks to the Fed's aggressive and rapid interest rate cuts and the ongoing productivity revolution, this had been the shortest and shallowest recession on record.

In the UK, the economic news was also more encouraging, especially in manufacturing which was showing signs of expanding for the first time in over a year, thus bringing more balance to an economy seen as overly dependent on consumer spending. After slipping back towards 5000 in February, the FTSE100 was almost up to 5300 again by mid-March, breaking a 2-year downtrend in the process and prompting this headline in one prominent business paper: 'Plunge back into shares, say experts', an exhortation no doubt totally uninfluenced by the fact that the ISA sales season was in full swing. In the US, the Dow topped 10,600, while even the embattled NASDAQ Composite was pushing back towards 2000 again, and some market commentators opined that investor sentiment was turning from 'selling on rallies' in favour of 'buying on dips'. A further revision of US fourth quarter GDP growth from 1.4% to 1.7%, and speculation that first quarter growth could exceed expectations of 2.5%, together with another batch of upbeat production and consumer sentiment data, seemed to bolster this new mood of optimism. However, doubts soon resurfaced as the price of oil surged to $28 a barrel in the first week of April. Iraq had proposed a one month ban on oil exports in reaction to Israeli incursions into Palestinian enclaves, invoking memories of 1973, and lack of Saudi support for the proposal did not totally dispel Western worries given the political turmoil in Venezuela, South America's leading oil producer. The oil price began to ease but remained stubbornly above $25.

Then a new round of corporate bad news dealt another blow to investor confidence. Early in April, **IBM** came out with its first profit warning in a decade and announced that its accounts were the subject of an SEC investigation. The shares fell 5%, but those of **General Electric**, America's biggest and arguably most respected company, slumped 9%, also on rumours of questionable accounting practises. In the UK, huge post-acquisition write-offs at **Vodafone**, contributing to the largest pre-tax loss in the country's corporate history, saw the share price slip towards 100p, at which level it would register a 75% decline from the March 2000 peak. **Nokia** warned of a sales slowdown and the shares fell below €20, more than halving from their January high point. **ITV Digital**, in which Granada and Carlton had invested over £1 billion, was clearly unable to meet its commitments and was effectively bankrupt. In Germany, media giant **Kirch** was in much the same boat, while **Deutsche Telekom**, struggling under a debt load of €67 billion fell below its flotation price of the mid-90s. **France Telecom** was in a similar state and France's highest profile media conglomerate, **Vivendi**, was having difficulty keeping its head above water. By now, investors were becoming accustomed to the fact that many once revered captains of industry had feet of clay, but more disillusionment was in store when in late April it was announced that New York's Attorney General was investigating allegations that Merrill Lynch had urged clients to buy stocks disparaged by their analysts, and that the SEC was looking at conflicts of interest in investment banking operations. In the words of an *FT* editorial, 'the real problem behind the malaise of equity markets was not so much one of economics or geopolitics but one of trust – or rather loss of trust'. The writer went on to point out that, furthermore, in an era of low inflation with companies under severe pricing pressures, the scope to generate rapid profits growth from economic expansion was not great, and that therefore the expected economic recovery could not be relied upon to deliver rising equity prices. Critical comment on the UK budget did not help matters, with observers stressing that Chancellor Brown needed growth and rising tax revenues to fund his ambitious spending plans, and failure to get it would leave a "black hole" in government finances. Giving substance to such fears was the fact that independent forecasts of UK growth for this year and next were well below those made by the Treasury. President Bush faced much the same problem and could take little comfort from Alan Greenspan's observation that the 'strength of the economic expansion remains to be clarified'. There was even speculation that in the current climate interest rates might have lost their effectiveness as an instrument of monetary policy and that maintaining Fed Funds rate at 1.75%, or even cutting it further, would be of little help. Adding to worries was the fact that the dollar was beginning to weaken, perhaps reflecting a loss of confidence in the US economy by overseas investors, and threatening a diminution of the capital inflows required to offset the record, and rising, $400 billion current account deficit.

On 26th April, the Dow fell below 10,000 for the first time since February, supposedly on disappointment that the latest batch of earnings figures and consumer confidence data did not seem to be in tune with the better than expected first quarter GDP growth figure of 5.8%. Similar anxieties might have been expected to upset the London market, but the FTSE managed to cling tenaciously to the 5200 level in spite of first quarter GDP growth coming in at 0.1% after zero in the fourth quarter of 2001, casting further doubt on the Treasury's forecasts of between 2% and 2.5% for the full year. This delicate balance between hopes and fears was broadly maintained throughout May, but by the first week of June the fears had become dominant and the FTSE100 fell decisively through the bottom of its 5000/5350 box. The move invited speculation that the index was heading for the record books by falling three years in a row, an event that none of the market professionals had forecast any more than they had the second year decline in 2001. After a brief attempt by the Dow to re-establish a footing above 10,000 again, as June progressed it was clear that this level was no longer a floor but a ceiling. If the US economic indicators being mixed to positive could inspire some confidence in investors, the unrelenting flow of negative news from the corporate front line had the opposite effect. Such news was very much market specific, and leading chip producer **Intel's** substantial downward revision of second quarter revenues because of weak European demand hit hopes of a second half recovery in the technology and telecoms sectors worldwide. In the same week, the CEO of **Ericsson**, the Swedish mobile phone group, announced that he could see no improvement in market conditions until 2003, and stocks fell across the board as analysts revised their growth forecasts sharply downwards. Then, just to make the point that such downward revision of earnings was not the exclusive preserve of the technology and telecoms sectors, fears about their competitive position, the reliability of patents and even the effectiveness of their drugs, hit a wide range of shares in pharmaceutical and biotechnology companies including industry leaders like **Merck**, **Bristol-Myers Squibb**, **GlaxoSmithKline** and **Biogen**.

With former growth stocks and now classic defensive stocks in full retreat, fears were growing again that stock market woes would feed back into the real economy, hampering recovery by dampening business and consumer confidence and undermining the official line that the fundamentals of the economy were sound despite tumbling markets. By the middle of June, the FTSE100 stood at 4630.8, breaking through the low point of October 1998 plumbed during the Russian crisis and leaving the 9/11 low as the next obvious downside target. Very much in the firing line as markets fell were the life and general insurance companies, many of which were reckoned to be close to breaching their solvency requirements and in danger of becoming forced sellers of their equity holdings. An easing of rules by the Financial Services Authority (FSA), adjusting the level from a straight 25% drop from one point to that from a 90-day moving average, did not do much to reassure investors and insurance stocks continued to slide. The fact that Abbey National had just transferred another £150 million into its life assurance subsidiary, Scottish Mutual, in a repeat of its post-9/11 move, and Credit Suisse had done the same with Winterthur to the tune of SF1.7 billion, showed that the dangers were very real and failed to restore confidence. Questions were raised about **Lloyds TSB** and Scottish Widows, and **HBOS** and Clerical Medical, and it was no surprise that the banking sector was fast losing its "safe haven" status in investors' minds. Days later, **Royal & SunAlliance** switched £224 million from general to life funds to boost its solvency ratio, and **Standard Life** announced it would raise £1.6 billion in the bond market 'to fund growth and help bolster its solvency position'.

A 'perfect storm'

Over on Wall Street, by mid-June the Dow was down to 9407, the NASDAQ Composite had broken through the 1500 support level, and the S&P 500 was below 1000, assailed by what was described as a 'perfect storm' of negative news ranging from disappointing consumer confidence data, more profit warnings, insider dealing allegations at **ImClone** and a considerable hotting up of the ever present geopolitical tensions. Brazil's falling currency, spiralling interest rates and political unrest were also continuing to give cause for concern, much more so than had a similar situation in Argentina a few weeks earlier. In receipt of more foreign direct investment than any other developing country except China, and accounting for a third of US bank exposure in Latin America, a debt crisis in Brazil was considered potentially much more serious than that in Russia, which had convulsed world markets in the autumn of 1998.

But in the last week of June, an event on the home front put even worries about Brazil firmly on the backburner. This was the news that **WorldCom**, America's second largest long distance telecoms carrier, had been guilty of accounting irregularities which involved booking operating costs as capital expenditure, thus inflating profits to the tune of $3.8 billion, and was on the brink of bankruptcy. At its peak two years earlier with the shares standing at $60, **WorldCom** had an equity market capitalisation of $180 billion, making the collapse the biggest in history. The shock waves rocked markets across the world. Telecom shares suffered the most, as France's **Alcatel** simultaneously issued a profit warning in the context of 'continued deterioration in the business environment', thus confirming once again that the slowdown in the US had spread to Europe. **WorldCom** was already known to be in trouble thanks to its $34 billion debt load in an industry plagued by overcapacity and cutthroat competition, but the fraudulent element in such a major company shattered investor confidence in many of the other great names in US industry. It also meant that the existing credit squeeze was going to intensify as banks, many already heavily invested in now practically worthless **WorldCom** bonds, would think twice before providing additional finance for other deeply indebted companies. Even the mighty **GE,** the bellwether of the US economy, fell under suspicion that maybe its 25-year record of profits growth had not been achieved without bending a few accounting rules. In the event, GE reported a 14% rise in second quarter earnings and said it was on target to meet analysts' expectations for the third quarter, but doubts persisted about the outlook for its financial arm, GE Capital, which accounted for some 40% of profits for the whole group.

Markets remained nervous but stable ahead of US Independence Day celebrations on 4th July on fears of a major terrorist incident, and then the Dow went into freefall the following week, losing 700 points to 8684, while the NASDAQ Composite and S&P 500 dived to their lowest levels since 1997. Selling across the board was prompting some commentators to believe they had identified the 'capitulation' phase in the market, when investors simply get fed up and dump all their stocks regardless of merit. Others thought the slide would continue as long as investors still had reason to question the quality of accounting procedures. As if to confirm this view, top drug companies **Merck** and **Bristol-Myers Squibb** both fell under suspicion, the former for inflating revenues and the latter for dubious sales practices, while **Xerox** admitted to overstating revenue by $6.4 billion between 1997 and 2001, as a result of taking immediate credit for income from leased equipment instead of spreading it over the life of the contract.

All for one...

The argument that the UK had much stricter accounting rules and that the corporate sector here was unlikely to produce any of the sort of shocks that were now practically daily events in the US, was used to suggest that the London market might decouple from Wall Street. However, UK investors were clearly in no mood to debate the issue, and the FTSE100 lost 400 points in the same week to 4224, then on 15th July plunged below 4000 to a 5½ year low of 3994.5. A 3-day rally then began which took the FTSE up just over 300 points, but this was brought to an abrupt halt by a 390 point fall in the Dow to 8019 on heavy volume. The triggers for the fall were principally the announcement of a record trade deficit for May, the dollar hitting a new 2½ year low against the euro, negative trading news from **Microsoft** and **Sun Microsystems,** and the onset of a criminal investigation at **Johnson & Johnson,** America's best-known healthcare group. Selling was broad-based, suggesting forced disposals by mutual funds to raise cash to meet redemptions, and withdrawals in June at $14 billion were the third largest monthly figure on record.

Despite encouraging words about the economy from President Bush and musings on 'infectious growth' from Alan Greenspan, US markets continued to fall, with the Dow hitting a new low of 7702 on 23rd July, unsettled by WorldCom's actual bankruptcy filing, earnings warnings from **Bell South**, and a bigger than expected second quarter loss from **Williams**, the energy company. The next day, UK and European stocks also slumped with insurance shares particularly hard hit following a shock profits warning from Dutch insurance company **AEGON**. The impact was two-fold in that it raised doubts about the insurance business generally, as well as solvency concerns in a falling equity market. The FTSE dived 80.9 to close at 3777.1 on record turnover of 3.4 billion shares after being down 232.1 during the day at 3625.9, but then the Dow managed its second largest rise on record, up 489 to 8191. The US rebound was attributed to rumours of a special Federal Reserve meeting which overruled bad news in the form of an SEC investigation into **AOL Time Warner**, the world's largest media group, as well as the arrest of the directors of cable group **Adelphia** on fraud charges. London rallied sharply the following Monday and at the end of the last week in July the FTSE was over 4000 again, while the Dow was apparently comfortably established once again above the 8000 level. It was beginning to look as if markets had discounted the worst. However, few observers were yet prepared to call a bottom, although most were happy to forecast recovery from current levels in the FTSE100 to 5000 at year-end.

Similarly, on Wall Street practically all the market strategists were looking for the S&P 500 to reach 1000 or slightly more by the end of 2002, against its present level of 843. A small band of commentators still thought that both markets were headed lower, principally because the magnitude of falls to date was bound to affect the economy, thus delaying the rises in earnings and dividends required to justify even current levels. One actually predicted a fall in the S&P 500 to 670, if the feared 'double dip' recession occurred, thus paralleling the 55% drop recorded in 1974.

...and one for all

The first week in August saw the biggest 4-day rally in the Dow since 1933, but it faltered on a show of economic numbers pointing to a marked slow-down in the recovery momentum, which cast serious doubt on Alan Greenspan's growth forecast for the year of 3.5%. The FTSE fell in sympathy, briefly dipping below 4000, with sentiment affected adversely by a surprise drop in June's manufacturing output of 5.3% against an expected figure of 0.8%, making it the worst performance since strike-ridden 1979. Thereafter, despite a continuing flow of discouraging economic and corporate news on both sides of the Atlantic and indeed worldwide, progress of the major indices was two steps forward, one step back, as if they were riding the punches thrown at them. All the worries and problems were still there, but while they were not being solved, it looked as if, at least, they were being contained. Thus, in Latin America, Uruguay's banking crisis was apparently speedily resolved by a $1.5

billion IMF loan package, and despite US Treasury Secretary Paul O'Neill's undiplomatically expressed worries about aid to Brazil ending up in Swiss bank accounts, a $30 billion package was provided, coincidentally helping to bail out US banks with massive exposure to the country's debts.

Even going to war with Iraq was being portrayed in some quarters as potentially good for the markets. Credit Suisse First Boston actually described a war as 'a strong positive for investor and business confidence, global growth, the dollar and equity markets', the rationale being that replacing Saddam Hussein's dictatorship with a democratic pro-Western administration would effectively 'liberate' the Iraqi oil fields and place them at the world's disposal. Not surprisingly, this rosy view was not widely endorsed on the grounds that the transitional period before the achievement of this best case scenario could be extremely risky and dangerous, and that Murphy's Law – what can go wrong, will go wrong – has never been repealed.

Markets remained cautious ahead of the 14th August deadline for America's CEOs to certify their companies' accounts, and its passing without incident saw the Dow rise above 9000 again, and the FTSE push above 4400 to complete a chartist's head and shoulders reversal pattern, indicating to some that a shot at 5000 was on the cards. The moves sparked renewed speculation in the popular financial press that markets really had touched bottom and this time the rally 'had legs', even if the economic and geopolitical background had yet to show improvement. More cautious commentators saw a turn for the better in the economic numbers as essential not just for a continuation of the rally from the July lows, but also to justify the recovery in markets to date. After all, they argued, the negative influences were too serious to be ignored and clearly tilted the balance of the equity market firmly towards risk rather than reward. The idea that a market's ability to take bad news in its stride was a sign of strength, was not very convincing when that bad news had the potential to cripple the economy and the stock market.

Three in a row?

In the event, the increasingly hard line being taken by Washington over Iraq, an oil price pushing towards $30 a barrel, a run of high-profile third quarter earnings warnings, at best mixed economic numbers in the US, and continuing stagnation in Japan and the Eurozone economies, played into the hands of the bears. By the end of September it was clear that the rally had failed. The Dow was below 8000 and the FTSE the wrong side of 4000 once more. The London stock market now looked like falling for the third year in succession, an event that last occurred forty years ago in 1960/62. More than one commentator could not resist pointing out that this almost certain outcome called into question the forecasting skills of the City's top equity strategists, who had been unanimous in expecting the FTSE to end the year up around 15% in the 5500/6000 range. An argument now developed between those who thought that enough was enough and this had to be the bottom of the market, and others who feared that an exceptional event reflected exceptional circumstances and that we could be moving into unknown territory. The latter were worried that an ever-rising stock market had become a sine qua non of the whole financial system, and that its unexpected collapse 'beyond the envelope of normalcy' was undermining the foundations of everyday life, i.e. pensions, savings, endowment mortgages, etc. Against such a background, they argued, confidence was certain to fall, businesses would not invest, consumers would not spend, and there was little prospect of a recovery in earnings and dividends to produce a meaningful stock market advance in 2003, or even to sustain current levels.

The bears had it all their own way in the first half of October, and as markets fell insurance shares were hard hit on solvency fears and bank shares nosedived on rumours of large trading losses in derivatives. The FTSE slipped below 3700 in late September, and on 9th October the Dow hit a low for the year of 7286, as did the NASDAQ Composite at 1114 and the S&P500 at 776. Then came a rally out of nowhere, which over the next ten days added 1000 points to the Dow and 500 points to the FTSE. The sudden turnaround was widely attributed to a positive statement from **GE** and a Lehman's upgrade for **IBM**, closely followed by news of a 26% increase in **Microsoft's** third quarter sales, but the balance of good and bad news was much the same as six weeks before and short covering by hedge funds was also believed to have been a major contributor to the speed and extent of the rally. Speculation that a new bull market was underway was tempered by the knowledge that two earlier rallies had failed, by the growing publicity being given to the pension fund deficits of so many major companies (with the inevitable impact on their investment plans, earnings and dividends), by the Bali bombing demonstrating that global terrorism was still alive and kicking, and the prospect of an invasion of Iraq coming ever closer. The broad conclusion of impartial commentators, i.e. those outside the financial services industry, was that this had to be just another bear market rally, but one crumb of comfort for the bulls was that the less than encouraging economic background was likely to convince the authorities on both sides of the Atlantic that further interest rate cuts were required.

By the end of October, a quarter point rate cut by the Federal Reserve was reckoned to be priced in with the Dow looking steady around the 8500 level, but the fact that the half point cut to 1.25% on 6th November was unilateral and not co-ordinated with cuts by the ECB and the Bank of England in a synchronised easing of global monetary policy, was interpreted in some quarters as an indication of the seriousness of the US economic situation. Furthermore, if a rate cut to an historic low of 1.25% failed to get things moving, then the Fed had very little room for manoeuvre remaining. More generous commentators took heart from the global stock market rally and interpreted the fact that this was the Fed's first and only rate cut this year as evidence that monetary policy had done its work and we could all look forward to a "Goldilocks" recovery, i.e. not too hot to stoke inflation and not too cold to boost unemployment. However, with the S&P 500 up 21% from its October low point, European markets up 18%, the UK up 14% and Japan up 10%, investors were clearly taking a great deal on trust. Thus, the big question in the final weeks of the year was: had the economic conditions really changed for the better or were stock markets simply ahead of the game? 'Cash is cash. Everything else is opinion', opined Andy Brough of Schroder Asset Management, neatly expressing the cautious fund manager's view of an equity market that still seemed tilted more towards risk than reward.

Hope springs eternal

With the FTSE100 standing at 4169 and just four weeks to go, a poll of top investment banks and stockbrokers came up with an end-year forecast average of 4380, but before the middle of December, in true contrarian fashion, the index was below 4000 and still falling under the weight of an avalanche of adverse corporate and broader economic news. **BAE** crashed to a 9-year low of 103p as it warned of a £1.6 billion cost overrun and gave its second profit warning in three months. **Cable & Wireless** revealed a previously undisclosed potential tax liability of some £1.5 billion and the share price collapsed to below 50p at one point. Hotel and pubs group **Six Continents** and **JD Wetherspoon** both issued profits warnings, prompting fears of a slowdown in consumer spending. Then **Barclays** and **Lloyds TSB** announced a sharp rise in bad debt provisions, and **Abbey National** warned that it was heading for its first ever pre-tax loss.

The news across the Atlantic was no better, with **McDonalds** saying it was going to make its first quarterly loss since going public in 1965, the imminent bankruptcy of **United Airlines**, profit warnings from **AOL Time Warner**, **Hewlett-Packard** and **Disney**, and unemployment rising to 6%, a 7-year high. Furthermore, the changing of the guard at the US Treasury was widely seen as heralding the abandonment of a strong dollar policy in order to boost the US economy at the expense of exporters in the UK and in Euroland. Even more worrying to the rest of the world was the fact that a weaker dollar would give a further boost to the already daunting competitive muscle of China, where the currency was linked to the dollar. Geopolitical global tensions were also having an adverse impact on markets, as political turmoil in Venezuela and the prospect of war with Iraq combined to send the price of oil above the critical $30 level.

It was now clear that markets were heading for three years down in a row for the first time since 1960-1962 and 1947-1949, and given the depressing background, the superbears were looking for 2003 to make it a fourth year of decline to match 1937-1940. By the last day of the year the FTSE had recorded a fall of 24.5% to 3940.4, making it the worst annual performance since the 55% fall of 1974. The "white heat" of new technology continued to scorch the techMark100 index, which closed the year down 56% at 648. The Dow fared a little better, down 17.7% at 8341, buoyed by its defensive constituents, while the less cushioned NASDAQ Composite fell 33% to 1335, and the S&P 500, 25% to 879. Continental markets were all down about 18-20% on average, as were the Nikkei Dow in Tokyo and the Hang Seng in Hong Kong. The gold price staged a significant advance over the year, but a 26% gain in dollar terms was diluted by that currency's decline against sterling and the euro.

2003

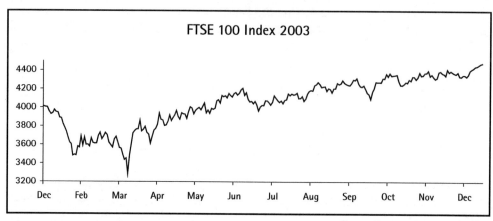

Source: Thomson Reuters Datastream

Deliverance?

None of the leading investment institutions could believe that 2003 would end the year on the downside, and forecasts for the FTSE ranged from 4200 up to 5000. This degree of cautious optimism was inspired by the widespread conviction that a combination of the lowest interest rates in sixty years, low inflation, buoyant government spending on both sides of the Atlantic and a continuing high level of consumer spending, provided a broadly favourable background for equity investment. Accordingly, the New Year opened on a high note with the FTSE moving above 4000 again and the Dow adding almost 500 points in the first two weeks of January, but the rest of the month witnessed a total reversal as indices slumped to below their end 2002 figures. The principal worry now coming to the fore was the realisation that the falls in the stock market to date were having a seriously adverse impact on a financial structure, i.e. pensions, endowment mortgages and savings and investment plans, predicated upon consistent and predictable growth in the stock market.

In short, the FTSE down 48% from its peak of two years ago, the Dow and the NASDAQ Composite down 30% and over 60% respectively, was something simply not planned for. As a result many life assurance companies and the pension funds of even our most respected companies were now unable to fund their liabilities. If such institutions were now forced to follow the pre-emptive action taken by the finance director of Boots in mid-2000, ditch their equity holdings and replace them with bonds, then markets had nowhere to go but down. Overlay these worries with the perils attendant on the now apparently inevitable invasion of Iraq and the declines looked set to become self-feeding.

Straws in the wind

With the FTSE slipping below 3500 and the Dow under 8000, a few brave commentators pointed out that shares were at their cheapest level relative to bonds for 36 years, with the 10-year gilts yield of 4.2% set against 3.8% on the FTSE All Share index. However, for most commentators, "fair value" was not considered to be a buying opportunity given that "overvaluation" three years ago could well be matched by "undervaluation" in today's difficult situation. Then in February, two events occurred to ease this "difficult situation". The FSA decided to change the solvency rules for insurance companies by taking what it called a more realistic view of the problem by adopting a broader definition of liabilities, thereby relieving the pressure on them to dispose of their equities. Lex could not resist pointing out that the last time life assurance companies had turned net sellers was at the bottom of the market in 1974/75. The other welcome event came on 6th February, with a quarter point cut in MLR to 3.75%. It was the first rate move in fifteen months and the least expected. There was speculation that the MPC was taking something of a risk given the ebullient state of the housing market, but on balance most commentators thought it was a good move in the light of weakness in industrial output, exports and investment, not to mention the 10% fall in the FTSE in January.

A string of appalling corporate news over the next few days appeared to confirm the wisdom of a rate cut, but did nothing for investor optimism. **Reuters'** share price crashed to almost 100p, a 12-year low, on news of 1,000 job losses and restructuring costs of £200 million in response to losing out heavily to Bloomberg in its core financial news services division, **Invensys** issued yet another profit warning and the shares halved to 18p as the markets lost faith in the ability of the new management team to rescue what had once been one of the most admired companies in the country. **Corus**, Europe's largest steel producer, recorded a loss of £2 billion and with the share price down to 8p, revealed a restructuring plan involving plant closures, massive job losses, asset sales and a right issue. And **ICI**, once the bellwether company of the UK economy, plunged to below 100p, a 30-year low, after problems with its additives division cast doubts on its new strategy. The world's biggest media group, **AOL Time Warner**, announced a world-class loss for 2002 of $99 billion, but Europe was not to be left out of the record books. France's media giant **Vivendi** reported that country's biggest ever corporate loss, and then **Deutsche Telekom** did the same for Germany. Parallel with all the doom and gloom in the West, the outbreak of Severe Acute Respiratory Syndrome (SARS) was taking its toll on Far Eastern markets as flights and hotel bookings were cancelled.

Turning point

The first week of March saw a small measure of confidence return to world markets, helped by an upward revision of US GDP growth in the fourth quarter of 2002 from 0.7% to 1.4%, and a quarter point cut in interest rates to 2.5% by the European

Central Bank. However, it evaporated in the second week as the final countdown to war began, and markets plunged to new lows on 12th March. When the FTSE100 touched 3287 on that day, the fact that the 10-year gilt yield at 4.00% had fallen below the All Share yield of 4.21% for the first time since 1959, was taken by a few brave souls as a sign that the market had bottomed. The hotly contested bid for **Safeway** together with a growing number of share buybacks gave credence to this view, and the rally from the low point survived the actual outbreak of hostilities a few days later to log a 600 point gain by the end of the month. Half of that advance was surrendered as the drive into Baghdad came to an unexpected halt, but was regained when the city fell in early April. Wall Street performed in much the same manner after the Dow touched a low point of 7286. There was a general feeling of relief that the war had gone better than many had feared. The Iraqi army had employed no 'weapons of mass destruction' against the coalition forces, casualties had been light, the oil fields were intact, and the conflict had not spread into neighbouring Arab states.

The economy was now back on the agenda as the principal concern of investors, and according to the IMF, from a global perspective it was not a pretty sight. The official view was that the impediments to global growth had remained untackled since the bursting of the equity bubble in 2000, specifically global industrial overcapacity, the debt overhang resulting from the excesses of the late nineties and the deflationary impact on the world economy of China. In the case of the US, a sliding dollar, down 17% on a trade weighted basis and down 25% against the euro in the last fifteen months in the wake of a ballooning trade deficit, was reviving fears of a Japan-style deflation taking hold. In fact, deflation became the principal talking point throughout the second quarter of the year, sparking a bond boom which took yields to their lowest levels in over fifty years.

In mid-June, the UK 10-year gilt yield touched 3.88%, while the yields on US 10-year and 30-year bonds slid to 3.1% and 4.17% respectively. More rate cuts were clearly on the cards and the Federal Reserve duly obliged with a quarter point reduction to 1.00% in the last week of June, two weeks after the ECB had responded to a first quarter growth rate of zero for the Eurozone with a half point cut to 2.00%. Then on 10th July, the MPC cut the UK base rate to 3.5%, citing a 'hesitant' global recovery to date as justification for its action. Interestingly, many commentators had been looking for even more substantial interest rate cuts to kick-start economic recovery, but Alan Greenspan's assertion that the Fed was ready to buy bonds to drive yields down in order to head off deflationary pressures was enough to do the trick. This statement, that in effect the Fed was prepared to underwrite the bond market, was a Judas kiss that marked the peak of the bond boom. When a few days later Alan Greenspan forecast growth in 2004 in the range of 3.75-4.75% without triggering inflation and Treasury Secretary John Snow described the US economy as 'coiled like a spring and ready to go', bonds slumped and equities took up the running, consolidating their reflex bounce from the panic lows of March.

'The best recovery money can buy'

With a US-led global economic recovery apparently now taken for granted, equity markets continued to rise and many commentators hailed the dawn of a new bull market as the Dow moved above 9000 again and the FTSE topped 4000. More cynical observers saw the tentative pick-up in the economic numbers as a response to the most stimulative monetary and fiscal policy in a generation, creating in the worlds of Karl Rogoff of the IMF, 'the best recovery money can buy'. As for the signs of a better than expected improvement in second quarter corporate earnings, these were attributed to the effect of vigorous cost-cutting measures rather than to top-line increases in real revenue needed to justify share prices at current levels. And the rally in high tech stocks was regarded as fuelled by panic buying by investors not wanting to miss a turnaround after share prices had crashed to often just a fraction of their 1999/2000 peaks.

However, the bulls were firmly in the ascendant and by mid-August the FTSE100 had topped 4200, while the FTSE 250 was at its highest level since June 2002. Talk about a £10 billion "black hole" opening up in government finances, given the gap between the Chancellor's forecast of his borrowing requirements and the likely outcome, appeared not to worry investors any more than the persistent criticism that the Treasury's growth forecasts were also much too optimistic. In fact, the principal influence on the markets was the growing evidence that a full-blooded US recovery was underway. The blowing up of the United Nations HQ in Baghdad on 8th August was not seen as the start of the full-scale efforts of the Iraqi dissidents to sabotage the reconstruction of the country, moves which were to become a major influence on markets in the second quarter of 2004, and by the end of September all the major world indices were standing at their best levels for eighteen months.

A fourth year down in a row was no longer on the cards. The erratic behaviour of the US non-farm payroll figures prompted some worries about the prospect of a 'jobless recovery', and many commentators believed that markets were getting too far ahead of the economy. After all, interest rates were clearly at the bottom of the cycle and there was now nowhere for them to go but up, with a potentially seriously adverse effect on the over-indebted consumer. Fears of an imminent rise in US interest rates in late October caused the Dow to retreat from an assault on the 10,000 level, and had a knock-on effect in Asia, where Tokyo fell 5% and Hong Kong 4%. However, the setback was short-lived. Markets rallied strongly on the announcement that US third quarter GDP growth came in at 7.2%, the highest quarterly gain in twenty years, closely followed by far better than expected jobs figures, and backed up by a statement from the Federal Reserve that 'in the absence of significant excess capacity and benign inflationary pressures, any policy adjustment need not take place in the near future...the real issue is to allow the economy to grow and use up those unemployed and underemployed resources'. Fed Funds stayed at 1%, but in the first week of November the MPC raised rates by a quarter point to 3.75%, stressing that the July cut had been a 'precautionary' one because of the fears of persistent weakness in the global economy and now that such fears were seen to be groundless, a return to the status quo ante was called for. The move invited speculation about the timing and extent of the next rise, and the consensus seemed to be that there would be a series of quarter point hikes during the course of 2004, peaking at 4.5% or even 5% if the inflation rate showed signs of picking up.

Far away countries...

There were indications that all was not well in some of the more remote outposts of the global village. In the first week of November, the Moscow stock market plunged 15% following the arrest of the boss of oil giant **Yukos** on corruption charges and the seizure of his shares in the company. The action was a clear demonstration of the risks inherent in all emerging markets, an area which had become increasingly popular with the new breed of hedge fund managers. Even Japan, reckoned by many observers to be the best recovery play of the year, saw the Nikkei Dow index slipping below 10,000 again on concerns about the viability of the country's regional banks given their critical role in reviving the depressed provinces. The duration of China's phenomenal boom was also being called into question. Over the past two years, China had to some extent replaced the US as the locomotive for global growth, benefiting not only its South-East Asian neighbours, but commodity producers across the world, as well as sucking in more foreign investment than the US, a flow also led by the US.

A country that was now the second biggest importer of oil and the world's leading importer of copper, tin, zinc and cement, as well as a huge consumer of coal and rubber, cannot slow down without making waves for its worldwide suppliers. With China's currency pegged to the US dollar, its competitive edge had been artificially enhanced to some degree, stoking the boom to an unsustainable level. Some observers compared the enthusiasm for China among fund managers and other big investors with that demonstrated in 1999, as the dot.com boom approached its peak. They also worried about the possible threat to political and financial stability posed by a combination of widespread poverty, authoritarian governance, and a primitive banking system, when subjected to a period of rapid growth. The fate of a more sophisticated and disciplined Japan post-1989 did not, they thought, provide an encouraging example.

Christmas cheer

Such considerations were not enough to derail the traditional pre-Christmas rally and encouraged by the revision of the US third quarter growth figure from 7.2% to 8.2%, the Dow managed to breach the 10,000 barrier for the first time in eighteen months, while the NASDAQ had 2000 firmly in its sights. The FTSE100 broke above 4400 and the techMARK 100 above 1000 in the second week of December, and the year ended on a high note all round. To quote the *FT*'s final editorial of 2003, 'The year ends with the US cruising towards calmer waters, the whirlpools of destructive deflation receding'. And there was more supposedly encouraging news the week before Christmas when the capture of Saddam Hussein was announced.

The year had witnessed a dramatic turnaround from the mood of fear and uncertainty that had dominated the first quarter. The MCI World Index was up 29%, the FTSE100, 13% and the FTSE 250, 33%. The Dow had gained 24%, while the tech-weighted NASDAQ Composite was up an impressive 48%, buoyed by gains in internet leaders like **Yahoo!**, up 172%, and **eBay**, up 88%. Europe had done well, led by Germany's DAX with a gain of 26%, but the emerging markets of South America topped the list with an advance of 62%, followed by Asia with a gain of 34%, with Japan up 21% and Hong Kong up 32%. Of course, given the euro's near 20% appreciation over the US dollar, the Eurozone was the place for global funds to have invested in 2003, but the region's growth performance over the year of +0.5% was hardly a match, and without the global growth recovery led by the US and China, the Eurozone would have stood still. Considering the problems that could stem from France and Germany choosing to ignore the rules of the EU 'growth and stability' pact, the failure to reform the Common Agricultural Policy (CAP), and the slow progress towards the liberalisation of labour and product markets, it was perhaps fair to ask why the euro had risen so much. The answer was that with the ballooning US current account deficit putting downward pressure on the dollar, and Asian resistance to devaluation, the bulk of the currency action had migrated to the dollar/euro rate, a process that would do nothing to help the Eurozone out of its state of near-stagnation.

Once again, gold recorded a useful 19% gain in dollar terms, but as in 2002 it was diluted by the dollar's sharp decline. Oil was a far more serious matter, gaining 7% in December to $30 a barrel and surpassing OPEC's promised $28 cap as a result of the slide in the dollar, continuing demand from China, and a pick-up in US imports as growth returned, not to mention the prospect of disruption of supply from the Middle East if the Iraq situation deteriorated further.

The consensus view for 2004 was that the bear market had ended in March 2003, but after three years of getting it seriously wrong, the pundits' end-year predictions for the FTSE100 were much more muted, although still weighted on the upside in the 4500-5000 range. The rationale was that equities would draw support from robust profits growth on the back of continuing strong recovery in the US economy in the first half of the year, but that things would flatten out as interest rates were raised to more "normal" levels and growth momentum slowed in the second half. Consideration was also widely given to the fact that investors had come to terms with living in a low inflation environment, and that they were going to demand higher nominal yields from equities and resist the appeal of above average ratings. In the context of the NASDAQ selling on a P/E of over 40 on expected earnings for 2004, it was difficult to argue with this cautious appraisal of the year ahead.

2004

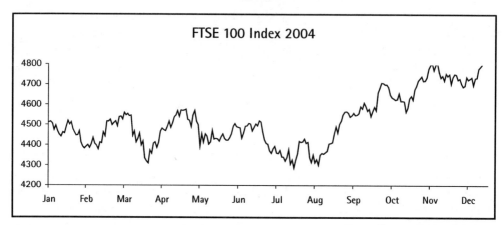

FTSE 100 Index 2004

Source: Thomson Reuters Datastream

Events, events, events...

Encouraged by the resilience shown by the world markets in the past twelve months, the New Year opened on a cautiously optimistic note. However, there were still plenty of sceptics around who thought that the equity gains of 2003 had been 'borrowed' in advance and would have to be paid back now that single digit returns were the best that could be expected from markets. They firmly believed that the productivity-driven momentum in the US was cyclical rather than structural, and that as the government's massive fiscal and monetary stimulus began to lose its effectiveness, the dollar would continue to slide and post the November election, the new administration would have to take some very hard and unwelcome decisions. Such anxieties nevertheless failed to make much impact on the markets, which seemed to approve of a "guns and butter" policy, and in early February, the Dow hit a new recovery high of 10,737, the NASDAQ one of 2153, and the S&P 500 one of 1157. London took a little longer for the FTSE100 to break decisively above 4500, slowed by the Bank of England raising MLR to 4% on 4th February. The reason for getting out of step with other central banks was that the global economic recovery was clearly underway, the UK's 3.5% growth rate in 2003 was above trend, and household spending and borrowing were strong and underpinned by still rising house prices.

The fall in the dollar became an increasingly hot topic in February/March as the euro rose towards the $1.30 mark and sterling touched $1.90, sparking talk of a $2 pound. The latest G7 meeting called for greater exchange rate flexibility, but given the reluctance of China and Japan to let their currencies rise against the dollar to the detriment of their own export-led growth, there appeared to be no way for the dollar to go but down if the problem of America's huge and growing trade deficit was to be tackled. Many of the country's top companies had cleared the decks and repaired

372

their balance sheets, but not America Inc. Typically, it was at precisely this point that the downswing in the dollar reversed, and the move was intensified as its "safe haven" characteristics emerged in the wake of the Madrid train bombings. The atrocity also launched a bout of profit taking and the Dow suffered its biggest 4-day run of losses in eighteen months. Bombings in Bali, Istanbul and Baghdad were one thing, but bombings in the heart of a European capital were quite another, inviting comparison with 9/11 and demonstrating that this new breed of terrorist could strike anywhere, anytime. The Dow reached its low point of 10,048 on 24th March and the FTSE100 hit 4309 on the same day, but both markets then recovered smartly, inspired by March jobs data showing a dramatic 308,000 gain and ending speculation about a "jobless recovery" in the US.

At the same time, a good news/bad news trade-off was created as growing evidence of economic recovery meant that interest rate rises were now firmly in prospect. Rising bond yields in the US were taken as indicating a quarter point rate rise in August, with two more on the cards by December, and in the UK, gilt yields pointed to another quarter point hike in MLR in early May. The MPC duly obliged by raising MLR to 4.25% on 6th May, and there was much talk of a return to 1994, when a series of rate rises on the back of economic recovery depressed stock markets everywhere. The FTSE100 had briefly topped 4600 intraday in late April, but within a couple of weeks it had lost 200 points as the Dow dived to below 10,000 on fears of the fallout from rising interest rates. The broad concern was that rises from abnormally low levels that had persisted for a long time posed considerable risk for financial markets, which had begun to accept them as the norm. Thus with the S&P 500 on a P/E of 30, considerably above the long-run average, the economic recovery had already been factored in and rate rises could pose a major shock to the system. As if all this was not enough to worry markets, the oil price was rising day after day in response to the deteriorating situation in Iraq and the spate of attacks in Saudi Arabia directed at foreign oil workers. Sentiment, too, was depressed by the weakening of the moral case for invading Iraq, which had taken over from the baseless WMD justification, by the prisoner abuse scandal, and the mounting civilian deaths arising from the siege of Falluja. The chickens were now coming home to roost in the White House and in Downing Street, as support for President Bush and Prime Minister Blair plummeted.

Sell in May...?

The rocketing oil price made a great deal of sense of the old market adage about selling in May. British Airways introduced a surcharge on ticket prices, justifying the move by pointing out that its fuel bill had risen from £50 million in 2003, to £150 million in the current year. Many other sectors found themselves in the firing line. Fuel-related costs ranged from 12-14% in transportation, 10-15% in building materials, up to 20% in metals and mining, and 60% in chemicals, plastics, paper and pulp. OPEC's decision in the first week of June to raise output of crude oil to 2 million barrels a day did serve to knock the US price below $40, but serious doubts about the security of oil supplies in both Iraq and Saudi Arabia were considered certain to keep the price uncomfortably high. With higher oil prices fuelling inflation while simultaneously depressing economic growth, the Chancellor was seen to be faced with a serious dilemma in the run-up to next year's election. Threats of disruption by lorry drivers and farmers had already prompted him to promise to reconsider his plan to raise fuel duties in September, but one major decision was already out of his hands and it was left to the Bank of England's Monetary Policy Committee to raise the base rate by another quarter point to 4.5% on 10th June. This was the fourth rise in seven months and all eyes were now on the Federal Reserve, which was widely expected to raise rates by a quarter of a point to 1.25% at its next meeting on 30th June. Alan Greenspan's statement that he was ready to do 'what is required' to curb US inflation had prompted some concern that he might have gone for a half point increase, but most commentators were confident that he would hold to a "softly, softly" approach to rate rises, telegraphing his intentions in advance and then cementing adjustments as necessary. The quarter point hike was the first for four long years and was seen as a major watershed for financial markets everywhere. In the words of a JPMorgan analyst, 'both inflation fears and growth expectations are now bearish for interest rate markets as they require central bank policy normalisation'.

The consensus about the future for world stock markets was that the best of the action had been played out in the first half of the year, based on improving corporate profitability against a background of recovery in the global economy fuelled by a reflationary US fiscal and monetary policy. Prospects for the second half were not going to be so rosy. The fiscal and monetary stimulus was fading fast and the strength and durability of the recovery was under threat from rising interest rates and rising oil prices. The behaviour of Wall Street since the end of June seemed to confirm this view, with the Dow falling decisively out of the 10400/10500 range and the NASDAQ and the S&P 500 relinquishing their hold on 2000+ and 1100+ territory respectively.

As for the FTSE100, the 4500/4600 band was looking like a distant memory by the end of July. The putative bid for **Marks & Spencer** by colourful High Street retailer Philip Green might have been expected to boost market sentiment by demonstrating that key companies could be seen as significantly undervalued, but the controversy surrounding the bid served only to confirm the public's suspicions about the devious way the City works. Bidding for an iconic company always means problems, as Hanson discovered with ICI, BTR with Pilkington and of course Guinness with Distillers, but Marks & Spencer looked to be in a class of its own, with a full-scale investigation by the FSA into possible insider dealing by players on both sides of the fence just days ahead of the takeover proposal. A spokesman for one of the suspected offenders argued that common sense dictated that he would not risk his reputation for the chance of 'making a few quid'. But as one cynic observed, common sense has nothing to do with it. The prospect was simply impossible to resist in the City, where shooting fish in a barrel is a traditional sport! Philip Green's decision not to proceed with his £12.5 billion offer was also believed to have wrong-footed a number of hedge fund operators who had gone long of the stock in the conviction that the aggressive entrepreneur would not walk away. Confidence in the food retailing sector was further undermined by a profits warning by **Sainsbury** and the resignation of its chairman, Sir Peter Davies, who had been appointed two years earlier with the task of turning round the ailing company. **Morrisons**, fresh from its victory in acquiring **Safeway**, also disappointed with a shock profits warning, the first in its 37 year history.

Summer recess

Another sign of a flagging market was a downgraded float price for the once eagerly awaited launch of **M&C Saatchi**, which went to an immediate discount, and the prospect of the same treatment being accorded to **Premier Foods** and **Virgin Mobile**. To what extent the problems of an incumbent government affect the stock market is never clear, but the Governor of the Bank of England's unusually outspoken warning that recent budget deficits were 'higher than is consistent with a sustainable position', no doubt carried more weight with the markets than those of the 'teenage scribblers' who so annoyed Chancellor Lawson, and the mounting evidence that intelligence reports had been 'doctored' to reinforce the case for going to war with Iraq. But perhaps most worrying of all for the future of equity markets was a report by Morgan Stanley that pension funds were continuing to rebalance their holdings away from equities in favour of fixed income instruments simply in order to be sure of funding their long-term liabilities, belatedly following the example of Boots which had made the switch in 2000. The report estimated that the process had resulted in an outflow from equities of some £11 billion between the fourth quarter of 2003 and the first quarter of 2004, and that another £70 billion would have to be divested if the funds' equity weightings were to reach a target figure of 50%, down from the current 67%. Furthermore, a dull or falling market would make the need to switch more necessary and cap any attempt at a rally. Thus, since pension funds tend to hold major FTSE100 stocks, those currently standing at, or close to, their highs are not so much shining examples of relative strength as of anomalies liable to be ironed out when fund managers see them as more easily marketable and disposable holdings.

By the end of July, it was looking as if it was not only parliament going into its summer recess but typically this consensus was wrong-footed by a vigorous, if low volume, rally, which added 100 points to the FTSE and 200 to the Dow by 1st August. A week later, however, both indices were heading down again following a quarter point hike in the UK base rate to 4.75%, July job gains in the US significantly below market expectations, and an oil price pushing towards $50 a barrel, all against the background of a major terror alert in New York. There was even speculation that the Fed might not go ahead with the widely expected rate rise to 1.5% at its 10th August meeting. But when it did, Alan Greenspan's accompanying statement that the economy appeared 'poised to resume a stronger pace of expansion' steadied markets everywhere and provided the basis for a renewed advance. There was still considerable concern among economists and market commentators that the Fed was betting on a rosy scenario and that July's patchy economic numbers and higher than planned for oil price could mean that rising interest rates would be feeding into an already slowing economy. Reports from **Intel** and **Alcoa** that third quarter earnings would fall short of analysts' expectations and a sharp fall in their share prices might have appeared to support this cautious view, but with the Dow back below 10,000 and the NASDAQ at a 10 month low, others argued that such concerns were priced in. In the event, by the end of the month the Dow had plussed almost 400 points to 10,200 and the NASDAQ another 100 to 1860. London followed a similar pattern with the FTSE adding 200 points to top 4500 again, boosted by an €8.5 billion bid for **Abbey National** from Spain's Banco Santander, expectations of a domestic counterbid, bid speculation swirling around Sainsbury, and gains for heavyweight index constituents **BP** and **Shell** on the back of a rising oil price.

In the bag for Bush?

The fact that the Dow was holding its own with the US election just six weeks away created a widespread belief that markets were looking for George Bush to win a second term, if only on the basis that a status quo ante implied stability and that the incumbent was the best bet to keep the show on the road. The size of the US current account deficit continued to cause concern, but the fact that it had been running for the past twenty years amidst frequent warnings of imminent crisis now began to prompt observations that the US had unique advantages that provided it with the ability to weather financial storms capable of overwhelming other countries. Perhaps the US being the world's biggest economy and the dollar the world's principal reserve currency created immunity from the consequences of the Bush administration's financial prodigality, but one sceptical writer could not resist quoting Alan Greenspan back in May 1999, referring to the then record $300 billion deficit, or roughly half this year's likely level, when he had said 'there are imbalances in our expansion that unless redressed will bring this long run of growth and low inflation to a close.' However, the dollar apologists clearly had a point given that the yield on the 10-year Treasury bond had fallen from 4.65%, ahead of the first rise in Fed funds from 1.0% on 1st July this year, to just 4.03% after the latest hike to 1.75%. This sort of behaviour was against the natural order of things, for when official interest rates rise, bond prices are supposed to fall. Some commentators regarded this as evidence that the recovery might not have as much traction as Alan Greenspan believed, and that investors were simply hedging their bets as the Dow retreated towards the 10,000 level under the influence of a renewed rise in crude oil prices, warnings of lower earnings from the three leading consumer goods companies (Colgate-Palmolive, Unilever and Procter & Gamble), and the deteriorating situation in Iraq with its possible implications for the outcome of the US election. On this last point, one trader was ready to call 1250 on the S&P500 for a Bush victory and 950 if Kerry won against 1100 currently.

The London market, still fuelled by bids and rumours of bids, fared relatively better than Wall Street, actually crossing the 4600 barrier to reach an intraday high of 4630 before relapsing, as oil prices resumed their climb and evidence grew of a slowing UK housing market and of a significant fall in High Street spending. Investors chose to interpret this gloomy background as providing a reason for interest rates not needing to be raised much more, if at all, encouraged by the outspoken observations of two members of the Monetary Policy Committee, who had said that this view was implicit in the inflation report. One commentator, David Smith in *The Sunday Times*, wondered if they would have sounded quite so confident were the original RPI inflation indicator, which included mortgage interest payments, still in use and reading 3.2%, instead of the new Consumer Price Index (CPI) coming up with a more reassuring 1.3%, all in the context of average earnings rising at a rate of 3.8%. In the event, the bulls were in the ascendant and on the first day of the final quarter, the FTSE100 recorded its biggest one-day rise of the year, jumping 88.8 points to reach its highest level in 27 months at 4659.6. The Dow also staged a strong performance, rising 112 points to just short of 10,200 again, and all the major European and Asian markets made substantial gains. These moves sparked a debate about whether the FTSE was ready to break out of its trading range on the upside, and the bulls were greatly encouraged when on 5th October it ended the day at 4705.5.

However, investors elsewhere did not share their enthusiasm, being more concerned about the impact of a still rising oil price on world growth prospects, and of a sharp drop in the dollar calling attention once again to the supposed unsustainability of a large and still growing US trade deficit. Thus, towards the end of October, the FTSE was back in its 4400/4600 box and the Dow 200 points below 10,000 again, overwhelmed by uncertainty about how the slowdown in China would play out, the outcome of the US election on 2nd November, and rising insurgency in Iraq. The fact that the regulatory probe into insurance practises ordered by New York's crusading attorney general Eliot Spitzer, could wipe 40% off the market value of **Marsh & McLennan**, America's biggest insurance broker, in a couple of days, was no help to investor confidence. Similarly, the sharp falls in mining shares sparked by plunging metal prices as speculative holders sold out, disturbed by reports of heavy selling on the Shanghai futures exchange, raised worries about the role of hedge funds in increasing market volatility. And volatility remained the name of the game when on 27th October, Eliot Spitzer announced that he would not pursue criminal charges against the directors of Marsh & McLennan, and a $2 fall in the oil price touched off a rally taking the Dow to over 10,000 and saw the FTSE reach an intraday high of 4663. Markets remained firm on the final day of October, with just one day to go before the US election and the very real chance of a dead heat and a rerun of the dispute that had marked the Bush/Gore contest four years earlier did not have the bearish impact many commentators had forecast. Still, fears of a victory for the Democrats were displayed on the day of the election when apparently pro-Kerry exit polls reversed a 60 point gain in the Dow into a 19 point loss.

Only in America...

A clear-cut win for President Bush had not been priced in by the market and the certainty of four more years of a pro-business administration, instead of the US equivalent of a hung parliament, prompted a stampede into equities. By the end of election week, the Dow had added 350 points to 10,387, the NASDAQ Composite over 60 to 2038, and the S&P 500, 36 to 1166, with the rally boosted by both a sharp fall in the price of oil and a 337,000 monthly jobs increase, which was considerably above forecast. A 20 basis points rise in the yield on the 10-year note favoured the view that the bond rally had peaked and that equities were now the only game in town. The quarter point hike in Fed funds to 2% on 10th November was widely expected and seen as consistent with the Fed's plan to remove policy accommodation at a 'measured pace'. The enthusiasm was contagious and markets boomed across the world. In London, the FTSE100 soared through the 4700 level at long last, crossing briefly into 4800 territory intraday in the second week of November, while European markets advanced strongly with the Eurofirst 300 hitting 1034, its highest point since July 2002.

However, while these stock market gains were broadly welcomed, more cautious commentators expressed distrust, seeing them as a reflex response to the removal of US election uncertainties rather than as an unqualified indicator of good times ahead. For one thing, they argued, but for the twin deficits, the US economic picture ought to be reflected in dollar strength. The October job gains pointed to the 'soft patch' being over, the Fed was raising interest rates again, consumer confidence and spending were up, oil prices were down 15% from their October highs, but the dollar was sliding, losing 8% against the euro and 7% against the yen since election day. That was bad news for the Eurozone and for Japan, where growth was stalling as exports were hit, while domestic demand was not picking up the slack. To date, the Asian countries had been buying dollars to keep their own currencies from appreciating and harming their vital export trade, but if they stopped doing so, an uncontrolled fall would force the Fed to take remedial action that would result in a US recession. These same critics admitted that self-interest demanded that the Asian countries simply had no alternative but to carry on supporting the dollar, but at the same time it was clear that the level of depreciation required to make a material reduction in a $600 billion trade deficit was a long way off and would not be reached without creating major problems for America's trading partners. But such considerations were apparently too long term for investors to worry about and markets continued their advance, undeterred by other matters that also might have been regarded as of more immediate concern, like a rebound in oil and metal prices post-speculative liquidations and the spread of insurgency in Iraq, the latter with its implications for the debut election in January and the coalition's exit strategy.

Towards the end of November, the impetus slackened as the dollar continued to slide and Alan Greenspan voiced his concern about an 'increasingly less tenable' current account deficit, prompting speculation about the scale of future interest rate rises.

Eat, drink and be merry...

December opened on a quiet note but hopes of a traditional pre-Christmas rally were boosted as the more bullish market commentators pointed to the prospect of 3% to 3.5% GDP growth in 2005, as predicted by the Chancellor in his pre-budget report, to be backed up by a similar but superior performance by the US economy in George Bush's second term. Once again, the gloomy reports on High Street trading from the retail lobby and the depressed state of the housing market were seen as bull points, and confirming the belief that UK interest rates had peaked at 4.75% and that 2005 would see reductions. Stock markets on both sides of the Atlantic now began to consolidate their gains, helped by the highest level of M&A activity since January 2000, and an upbeat ending to the year looked assured. Fortunately for the pundits who in January had confidently pitched their end-year forecasts for the FTSE100 at the upper end of the 4500-5000 range, a 117 point advance to 4820 in the final two weeks of the year served to match their predictions with unaccustomed accuracy. This represented a 7.7% gain, but it was surpassed by one of 19.3% in the FTSE250, and by one of 19.8% in AIM, the two latter indices benefiting from stock picking taking over from index tracking, and also from having a wider range of constituents and being less burdened by heavyweight casualties among the retailers and pharmaceuticals so prominent in the FTSE100. On Wall Street, the Dow and the NASDAQ Composite were both close to their best levels in 3½ years, but their gains in 2004 were still relatively modest at 3.6% and 8.7% respectively. The S&P500 did better with a rise of 10.7%. European markets held up close to their 2½ year highs, with the Eurofirst 300 at 1041 to record a gain of 8.8%, or one of 17% in dollar terms, reflecting the dramatic rise in the euro.

The devastating tsunami that hit the coastal areas bordering the Indian Ocean on 26th December caused barely a ripple in the financial markets of those countries most affected. Bangkok slipped just 1%, Colombo only 4%, Malaysia was unchanged and Mumbai and Jakarta actually hit new closing highs. Airlines and other travel-related stocks fell slightly on worries about the impact of the disaster on tourism, but the regions' industrial heartland had been untouched, along with the major port facilities. Asian markets thus retained their leadership of the performance tables in 2004 to reach their best levels in seven years, led by Jakarta up 45%, followed by Colombo up 42%, and Pakistan up 35%. India's BSE Sensex was up 18%, Hong Kong's Hang Seng gained 13%, while Sydney rose an impressive 23% thanks to China's insatiable demand for Australia's natural resources. Tokyo continued to disappoint its fans who regularly tip it as the great recovery play, but the Nikkei Dow 225 still registered a respectable 7.6% gain over the year to 11,488, still a long way short of its December 1989 peak of 38,915. Gold at $437 was up 3.5% in dollar terms, but most non-US holders sustained a loss as the dollar declined against all the major currencies. Oil prices, while down some 20% from October's peak level, were still up over 30% since the start of the year and their course in 2005 was unanimously reckoned to be a major influence on world stock markets. Bond yields ended the year lower than they had begun it, despite a succession of interest rate rises and strong GDP growth, an anomalous situation indicating that investors were hedging their bets on the strength of the recovery and adopting a belt and braces approach in constructing their portfolios.

Expecting the unexpected

The prospects for 2005 were keenly debated and the uncertainties, particularly concerning the dollar and the oil price, made for relatively modest end-year predictions for the FTSE100. A panel of 'experts' polled by *The Sunday Times* came up with figures ranging mainly between 5000 and 5400, with the only negative target of 4400 coming from stock market historian David Schwartz, the sole member of the panel without a vested interest in a rising market. Other objective commentators took a similarly cautious view of the year ahead in the belief that geopolitical factors could overshadow simple economic and corporate performance. This belief was strengthened by President Bush's messianic post-election address in which he vowed to use America's power to spread freedom and democracy across the world, raising broader if unquantifiable concerns about possible, even probable fallout from what many considered to be a Mission Impossible. The fact that the President had appointed the same close-knit circle of NeoConservative advisors who had masterminded the invasion of Iraq – with the notable exception of the only multilateralist in the group, Secretary of State Colin Powell – heightened fears that this Team America would favour strongarm tactics over diplomacy in carrying out his mission. Clearly, the use of the term 'crusade' when the attack on Iraq was launched was not just a slip of the tongue, and any further intervention in the region involving Iran or Syria was reckoned to have the potential to cause chaos in the Middle East. Even the possibility, they believed, made a strong case for investors to adopt a 'risk averse' policy for the coming year.

2005

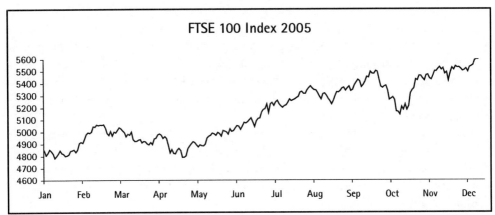

FTSE 100 Index 2005

Source: Thomson Reuters Datastream

Life goes on

Just as share price gains in the opening days of the New Year appeared to favour the bulls, who were quick to cite the old market adage, 'As goes January, so goes the year', perverse as ever the climate changed abruptly in the last week of the month. The trigger was a decidedly gloomy set of fourth quarter results from companies in the US technology sector led by **Motorola** and **Qualcomm**, leaving Wall Street broadly lower with the Dow under 10,500 again and the NASDAQ at 2045, 133 points down from its end-2004 peak. The bad news was not confined to the US. **Sony**, the Japanese consumer electronics giant, shocked markets with a warning that profits in 2005 were likely to be some 30% lower than forecast as a result of an inability to cut costs in line with an unexpected fall in selling prices. European markets were also in the doldrums following a profits warning from **Perlos**, the Finnish maker of handset casings for **Nokia**. The news prompted a near 20% fall in Perlos's share price and a general retreat across the whole of Europe's IT grouping. London fared relatively better, with the FTSE100 remaining within the 4800-4850 range buoyed by a flurry of merger activity, and then in February, markets picked up across the board – an advance attributed by some commentators to the higher than expected turnout for the Iraqi election, creating another 'Baghdad Bounce'.

In the first week of February, another quarter per cent of 'undisruptive tightening' took Fed Funds up to 2.5%, while Alan Greenspan, at a meeting of the G7, opined that the US trade deficit should respond to a 'combination of market forces' along with 'greater budgetary discipline' domestically. Some observers thought that since this latter action would involve drastically cutting spending on education, housing, transport and urban development, President Bush would not have an easy ride through Congress, but the stock market appeared to be unworried and the Dow oscillated around the 10,750 mark, readying itself for a shot at 11,000.

Similarly, in early February the FTSE100 regained the 5000 level, while the FTSE250 actually hit new all-time highs as equities rallied from the 2003 trough and stockpicking took over from index-tracking. However, the FTSE100 failed to hold on to its 5060.8 peak reached on 21st February, and after touching 10,940 on 4th March the Dow backed off from 11,000. The reasons given for this lack of follow through in both markets was principally the recognition that oil prices in the $40-$50 range were a threat to world growth, and that a falling dollar would have a negative impact on the fragile economies of the Eurozone, while at the same time creating inflationary pressure in the US.

On this last point, so called 'expert opinion' was practically unanimous in believing that the dollar had further to fall, despite Treasury Secretary John Snow's assertion that he planned to tackle the spiralling fiscal deficit and that a strong dollar was in the national interest. Forecasts polled from leading international banks predicted a dollar/euro exchange rate in the €140-150 range, and a dollar/yen rate in the Y90-102 range, with a $2-2.05 pound by the end of 2005. Another quarter per cent rise in Fed Funds to 2.75% in the last week of March in response to data with potentially inflationary implications sparked a dollar rally, which simply confirmed the issue by apparently reflecting a conviction that interest rates were heading higher while doing nothing to help reduce the trade deficit, the existence of which was assumed to condemn the dollar to a renewed decline as the year progressed.

A cynical but practical view of the situation by distinguished US economist Catherine L. Mann at the Institute for International Economics, was that since the world's trade deficits and surpluses must all add up to zero, if the US reduces its trade gap, other countries must suffer a shrinkage in their trade surpluses or a rise in their deficits. Thus, foreign countries depend on US imports both directly and indirectly for economic growth, and there is a global co-dependency of the US trade deficit to the extent that they have a vested interest in a large and growing deficit. Their dependency on US demand as a source of growth matches the US dependency on foreign savings to finance domestic investment.

Dollar strength persists

By the end of March this 'realpolitik' view of the supposed dollar crisis had begun to catch on, as 10-year bond yields rose sharply to 4.69%, apparently solving Alan Greenspan's 'conundrum' of rising interest rates going hand in hand with falling yields. Other factors to be accorded some credit for the dollar's recovery was the boost given to its 'safe haven' characteristics by rising geopolitical tensions in the shape of China's threat to use military force if Taiwan declared independence; North Korea's confirmation that it possessed nuclear weapons, coupled with its withdrawal from disarmament talks; and the suspicion of Syrian involvement in the assassination of ex-president Hariri in Lebanon.

Bond yields continued to rise, and by the end of the first quarter 10-year Treasuries had plussed 50 basis points since 1st January, a progress which caused many analysts to warn of the danger of big price falls in corporate bonds where the yield spread, i.e. the margin over the return on government bonds, had narrowed to its tightest in fifteen years. The reasons commonly cited for too many investors chasing too few bonds were firstly that US Treasury bonds were the natural home for the surplus dollars in the hands of Asian central banks, and secondly that insurance institutions were necessarily big buyers, simply to make sure of matching their liabilities in the wake of the disappointing performance of equities over the past five years. The risks inherent in corporate bonds were then highlighted by a profit warning from General Motors, which led to a sharp fall in the prices of its bonds in line with their downgrading to the lowest investment grade with a 'negative outlook'. A week later, **Ford** announced that severe competition, escalating costs and high fuel prices meant that earnings for 2005 would fall well short of earlier expectations, and its shares and bonds suffered a similar fate to those of **General Motors**.

Oils on top

Oil prices soaring to a new record with Goldman Sachs talking up the possibility of reaching in excess of $100 a barrel, did not make for a good start for equities at the opening of the second quarter. The FTSE100 had retreated to just below 4900 on 1st April, and the Dow to around 10400, and even oil and commodity shares were under a cloud despite the booming prices of their products, as many commentators adopted a contrary opinion approach. The speculative oil plays on AIM were very much in the firing line, many of them having achieved apparently absurdly high valuations based on nothing but a handful of exploration licences in the new 'hot' areas of West and Central Africa. The case of **White Nile**, the creation of serial company promoter Phil Edmonds, did no favours for the sector. The shares had been placed at 10p on 10th February and within days had rocketed to 138p on the announcement of the acquisition of a licence to explore vast tracts of desert in Southern Sudan. The shares were promptly suspended by the Stock Exchange on the grounds that details of such an important deal should have been incorporated in the offer prospectus. However, the fact that White Nile had achieved a market capitalisation of over £200 million on the basis of questionable exploration rights (French oil giant Total claimed them too) in disputed rebel-controlled areas, gave strong support to the view that speculative oils were well into bubble territory.

At the same time, while accepting the strictures on White Nile and its fellows, many analysts believed that a strong case could still be made for oil and for established producers and explorers in the context of ever-rising demand from China and India, the practically daily attacks on oil installations in Iraq, the potential for massive disruption of supplies as a result of the implementation of US policy in the Middle East, and of course the unreliability of climatic predictions. This truth of this last point had been demonstrated dramatically in the last week of January as the Eastern seaboard of the US was engulfed in snow and Continental Europe shivered in sub-zero temperatures.

No springtime for shares

Historical data showing that since 1945, UK shares had 'sprung to life' in April no less than 85% of the time, encouraged some bullish predictions as the month began, but hopes faded rapidly. Actual bids like those for **Allied Domecq** and **Somerfield** and even more rumours of bids continued to give a degree of support for the bull case, but bad news soon began to dominate the headlines. Given the healthy state of the rest of the UK motor industry (albeit foreign-owned), the economic consequences of the collapse of Rover were not considered to be too serious, save for the effect on local component suppliers and dedicated dealers. However, it was a political embarrassment for the government with an election date set for 5th May, an event which had to be taken into account in any assessment of the likely course of the stock market. While history traditionally favours Conservative victories, the much trumpeted economic record of New Labour strongly suggested that this time history would be no guide, and that markets were more likely to follow the Bush/Kerry example and be content with the status quo ante on the 'better the devil you know...' principle.

A continuing stream of bad news from prominent High Street retailers like **Boots**, **Dixons** and **GUS** (Argos and Homebase), and then the abandonment by private equity group Apax of its £837 million offer for **Woolworths**, all seemed to confirm that the feared slowdown in consumer spending was now well established. Nevertheless, the FTSE100 managed to hold on to the level at which it had started the year, if not to its mid-February peak, but everything changed on 15th April when a 'tipping point' was reached. This came courtesy of Wall Street, when a swathe of bad news from Corporate America triggered a near 200 point fall in the Dow, effectively wiping out all the post-election gains since November 2004, taking that index down to 10,087, the NASDAQ to 1908 and the S&P500 to 1142. The FTSE100 lost over 50 points and was now back below 4900 again.

US retail sales seemed to be going much the same way as those in the UK, with the March figure up just 0.3% against the 0.7% expected, and the important Michigan consumer sentiment index reported its lowest reading since September 2003. The sales pitches of **Ford** and **General Motors** involving interest free loans and generous cashback were clearly not working, and shares of both companies fell to multi-year lows. GM's pinpointing of sharply higher healthcare costs as one of its major problems had a resonance in a wider context, in that if they were hurting the nation's biggest consumer of healthcare services for its employees and retirees, then they were also hurting the average American. The situation tempted an *FT* columnist to invert the old saying and come up with: 'What's bad for General Motors is bad for America.' This was precisely the most worrying point of all, since if the US consumer was staying away from the malls, it was because the new negatives of rising interest rates, higher prices for gasoline and heating oil, higher healthcare costs and restricted scope for remortgaging as the houseprice boom faded, had at last superseded the old positives of unprecedentedly low interest, tax cuts and rebates, and refinancing on the back of rising house prices. And since in the US, the consumer is king, providing two of the three legs on which the economy stands, then if those two legs begin to buckle, the economy is going to be in trouble.

Big Blue blues

It was doubly unfortunate when on the same day that saw so much bad news emerging about the consumer side of the economy, **Big Blue** (Wall Street's pet name for computer giant IBM) should disappoint markets by announcing first quarter earnings well below expectations, and attribute the short fall principally to a lack of take-up of its core IT products by corporate spenders, thereby casting doubt on the strength of the economy's third leg. **Sun Microsystems** also disappointed, and then when **Samsung** the world's second biggest chipmaker and the No.3 producer of mobile phones, posted a 52% fall in first quarter profits, alarm bells began ringing across the IT industry worldwide, and stock markets took another hit.

As the NASDAQ plunged below 1900, the Dow sank to almost 10,000, and the FTSE100 came uncomfortably close to 4800 again. Far Eastern markets were particularly affected, and as the Nikkei Dow slipped below the 11,000 mark, the Hang Seng barely managed to hang on to the 13,000 level. Japan also had the additional worry that the deterioration in its relations with China over wartime memories and the disputed ownership of potentially oil-rich sea areas might lead to a Chinese boycott of Japanese goods. The only bright spot appearing on the horizon for the global economy was the oil price falling below $50 a barrel in response to OPEC assurances that it would increase investment in production in order to maintain an essential margin of spare capacity to counter unexpected demand or supply disruptions. As a result, oil shares suffered along with those in every other sector, recording falls in the 5-10% range across the board. Leader of the pack, **BP**, had yet another problem to deal with as the Russian tax authorities issued a Yukos-type $1 billion demand dating back to 2001 on TNK-BP, the 50/50 joint venture in which BP had invested $7.5 billion just two years ago. But the dip in oil prices proved to be of the briefest duration and as they moved above $50 again, oil shares quickly recovered lost ground.

Merrill Lynch also did nothing to help market sentiment by scaling back its forecast for first quarter GDP growth from 4.3% to 3.5%, and for the second quarter from 3.5% to 3.2%. The bond market seemed to be in tune with these adjustments, as 10-year Treasury bond yields declined to 4.26% compared with their pre-Easter peak of 4.69%, at the same time re-establishing the 'conundrum' (falling bond yields accompanying rising interest rates) that Alan Greenspan had highlighted at the end of February; although this time around it was becoming increasingly obvious that slowing growth was the answer to the puzzle. By now, most commentators were acknowledging the return of the 'soft patch' in the US economy and technical analysts in the London market were busy adjusting their end-year forecasts for the FTSE100 to around the 4500 mark in response to the likely emergence of a similar 'soft patch' in the UK economy later in the year. Indeed, with the Office for National Statistics reporting growth in the first quarter of just 0.6%, it seemed clear that the Chancellor was no longer on course to achieve his forecast of 3-3.5% growth for 2005. Much independent criticism (including that from the IMF) was directed at the government's expansion of the public sector to the detriment of the private sector, which is the engine of real long-term growth, leading to the inevitable assumption that taxes were set to rise after the election, whoever won.

However, despite a headline in one of the most influential City columns of, 'Chartists forecast stock market slump', the FTSE clung to the 4850-4900 range for a few days, buoyed by bids and rumours of bids, including the prospect of a new contender for drinks giant **Allied Domecq**, but perhaps it was talk of another bid, one from **Provident Financial** for **Cattles**, that held the clue to what was really worrying the markets. The former is the biggest sub-prime lender to what the Americans call a 'trailer park' clientele and Cattles is No.2 in the field. Putting the two together would mean that at a time when private sector debt was at record levels, one of the top 100 companies in the country would be a lender to a section of the public which cannot obtain credit through the normal channels.

In the last week of April, more evidence of a slowdown in consumer spending across the board came with a clutch of first quarter profit warnings from **Kingfisher** (B&Q), **Whitbread** and **Punch Taverns**, and **Carpetright**, leading to falling share prices throughout the retail sector and knocking the FTSE below 4800 again for the first time since its low point for the year on 12th January. The reluctance of the consumer to keep spending was widely attributed to the fading of the houseprice boom and to the prospect of higher interest rates and mortgage costs in the months ahead. More than one commentator was tempted to see this as a major turning point for the economy, following a decade in which the growth in consumer spending had consistently exceeded the growth in GDP. The fact that much the same situation obtained in the US made for a broadly bearish consensus on both sides of the Atlantic, and the FTSE ended the month, after a small uptick, at 4801.7, or at much the same level at which it had started the year. The Dow, on the other hand, at 10,192, was down by 5.6% over the past four months, and the NASDAQ Composite at 1921, a much more substantial 11.8%. If Wall Street sets the pattern for world markets to follow, this was perhaps not a very encouraging sign, one observer dared to suggest, a view supported by yet another fall in bond yields.

Staying on

Markets were steady in the run-up to election day, helped by strong gains on Wall Street which two days earlier had taken the expected hike in Fed Funds to 3% in its stride. Also as expected was Labour's victory, and although the reduction in its majority from 166 seats to 67 was larger than most estimates, investors appeared content with the ending of at least a degree of uncertainty, and the FTSE greeted the news with a gain of 16.6 points, taking the index to 4918.9. However, there was practically universal agreement that Labour's historic third term would meet with far more formidable problems than had the first two, and that the economic virtues of 'stable growth, rising employment, low inflation and sound public finances' that had secured re-election were soon to be history.

As if to confirm this opinion, the next few days brought news of substantial job losses at **Marconi**, **IBM** and **Waterford Wedgewood**, to add to the 6,500 total at **MG Rover**, manufacturing output recording its biggest drop since 1995, and another dramatic fall in High Street sales for April. No one was surprised that the MPC left the base rate unchanged at 4.75% at its first post-election meeting, but few found comfort in a decision they thought had been taken because the economy was already teetering on the edge of a downturn. The implications for government policy were clear: If its ambitions for higher public spending in what it regarded as priority areas were to be met, and the golden rule of borrowing only to invest remain unbroken, then taxes would have to rise sooner rather than later. The prospect extinguished any hope of follow through for the initial post-election gain and the FTSE quickly retreated to below the 4900 level, ignoring an upsurge in the Dow in response to an unexpectedly big increase in the April job creation numbers and strong retail sales figures, prompting speculation that the 'soft patch' was firming up. In the event, the Dow also failed to hold on to its gain, supposedly rattled by rumours of large losses by hedge funds, many of them wrong-footed by the downgrading of the bonds of **Ford** and **General Motors** to junk status, and the simultaneous price-boosting tender offer for GM stock by maverick billionaire investor Kirk Kerkorian.

One commentator could not resist saying 'I told you so', pointing out that today's hedge fund managers are the same ones who failed to make the right calls five years ago, realised that shares could indeed go down as well as up, and decided to go for "positive" returns by going short as well as long, playing both ends against the middle, and making speculative forays into volatile currencies, commodities and derivatives – and all on borrowed money. Their motivation was clear: A 5% front-end load and 1.5% a year from managing a conventional long fund is small beer compared with the 20% to be skimmed off the profits made by a hedge fund. Unfortunately, as the writer points out, this degree of incentivisation can tempt hedge fund managers into going for the big speculative coup instead of taking the more balanced positions that the name implies. To 'hedge' is to 'secure a bet or wager on one side by taking the odds on the other' (OED), a practise employed by conventional bookmakers who thereby ensure a reasonable profit while missing out on spectacular gains, and more importantly, spectacular losses. To depart from this method of operation means that the hedge fund managers are simply gambling with their clients' money.

The month's rumoured disasters were all too believable and unlooked-for redemptions can play havoc with a manager's exit strategy. But perhaps anyone thinking of "investing" in a hedge fund would be wise to consider the implications of a comment made by Christopher Fawcett, chairman of the Alternative Investment Association, which represents over 800 funds. When questioned by a *Times* reporter about the poor performance of hedge funds over the past year, he admitted that 'they tend to find things difficult when there's a change in direction'!

Bouncing back

Such concerns faded into the background in the third week of May, when the FTSE recovered to within a whisker of the 5000 level despite there having been no let-up in the flow of depressing news from the High Street, and both **Barclays** and **HSBC** warning of a 'significant' and 'marked' rise in bad debts on their consumer loans. It looked, therefore, as if the recovery was very much a case of riding on the coat-tails of Wall Street, where the Dow had risen 300 points in five trading days, taking it above 10,500 again in response to further retail sales figures and jobs data, encouraging the belief that the 'soft patch' in the US economy was indeed history. This bullish sentiment was bolstered by a continuing rise in the dollar, taking it to a six-month high against the euro and sterling in anticipation of ongoing interest rate rises in recognition of strength and vigour returning to the economy. The move was, of course, in sharp contrast to the forecasts of the dollar bears made so confidently in January, and there was some speculation that it would further disrupt the "carry trade", i.e. borrowing cheap currencies short in order to buy higher yielding "investments" long, thus potentially creating more problems for the hedge funds.

The decisive 'Non' by the French public in the referendum on the new European Union Constitution provided yet another boost for the dollar. The vote was widely seen as holding back necessary economic and structural reforms and condemning Europe to a further period of stagnation with an inevitable adverse effect on the standing and even perhaps the survival of the euro. Holland's rejection of the constitution two days later served to increase doubts about where the European Union was heading, and simultaneously highlighted the attractions of the UK economy and its stock market, which plussed 47 points on the news, taking the FTSE above 5000 for the first time since February. However, the initial enthusiasm for this event was quickly dampened by a sharp fall on Wall Street, when May's job creation numbers came in well below expectations, raising doubts yet again about the strength of the US recovery and the yield on the 10-year note was pushed below 4.0%. Furthermore, to the extent that the 'No' vote represented a rising mood of national defensiveness in two core EU member states which was certain to spread to others, in the view of an *FT* editorial, to reject the Constitution was to reject a 'better framework within which to conduct the vital political debates on economic reform, social protection and international competitiveness that will determine Europe's future global role'.

The pause in the stock market's advance seemed to reflect a growing conviction that political and economic turmoil in the Eurozone, the UK's principal export market, was not in anyone's interests and a 'wait and see' policy was the only one to adopt at this stage. The oil price was also riding high again, supposedly influenced by reports of lower than expected gasoline stocks in the US at the start of the motoring season, but perhaps more importantly by the illness of Saudi Arabia's 85 year-old King Fahd and the unsettling prospects of a power struggle for the succession in the world's largest oil exporting country, should he die.

Flight of the phoenix

But despite this background of uncertainty, the FTSE was reluctant to relinquish its hold on its 5000 plus territory, and it was given a helping hand in mid-June when Federal Reserve chairman Alan Greenspan, in a testimony to a US Congressional committee, stated that he believed the economy to be on a 'reasonably firm footing' with underlying inflation contained and that he would continue to raise interest rates at a 'measured pace'. The dollar was now firmly back in favour as US fears that the Asian central banks would switch part of their dollar reserve holdings into euros receded, given the uncertainty that now clouded the outlook for the European currency. Indeed, JPMorgan, one of the prominent dollar bears in January, was now forecasting a $ per € rate of 1.20 by December, and of 1.12 by the end of the first quarter of 2006. Interestingly, Continental European stock markets reacted to the political upsets and a weaker euro by surging to new 3-year peaks, with investors motivated by the contrary belief that the 'No' vote had been a wake-up call which would lead to a more rapid implementation of necessary restructuring and reform. Another view put forward to explain the superior performance of European stocks was that, again contrary to popular opinion, their economies were in much better shape to meet the new global challenges than those of the so-called Anglo-Saxon countries. The latter respond to every downturn by cutting interest rates and using fiscal stimuli to increase demand, and thus their impressive growth rates were a snare and a delusion based largely on domestic and public consumption. Europe, by contrast, had not taken this route, and while its resistance to running up consumer debt and running down savings rates had taken its toll in high unemployment across the region, when it did get its house in order it would outperform its Western rivals in the global market place.

By mid-June, the FTSE managed to exceed its February peak of 5060, hitting 5077.6 on 17th June, boosted ironically enough by strong gains in oil shares, which carry a heavy weighting in the index, as they responded to the oil price surging to a new record, a development normally categorised as a bear point for markets. The performance of the oil majors was in sharp contrast to that of many of the smaller oil explorers listed on AIM whose credibility suffered yet again, this time as a result of a 'you couldn't make it up' debacle at **Regal Petroleum** where chairman, Romanian émigré Frank Timmis, resigned after his much-hyped multi-billion barrel oil 'find' in Greece turned out to be a dry hole. The fact that the company had raised £44 million of funding in April at 390p a share, largely on the strength of exploration prospects there and in the Ukraine, left subscribing institutions angry and disillusioned as Regal's share price plunged to below 100p.

Another company to raise eyebrows in the investment commentating community, though for very different reasons, was Gibraltar-based online poker host, **PartyGaming**. While its remarkable ability to bring in the cash – £204 million in 2004 on sales of £331 million – was not in doubt, almost 90% of those figures originated from punters in America, where the activity is illegal; a situation which was certain to create regulatory problems down the line. Although the leader in the industry today, competition and margin erosion as rivals entered the market was another reason for caution, but the principal objection from most commentators was almost a moral one, on the fact that with a prospective market capitalization of close to £5.6 billion, an offshore gambling company would go straight into the FTSE100. In the event, the institutions-only offer was 2½ times oversubscribed, but just to show that all major investment decisions are not always totally objective, rational and calculated, one fund manager is reputed to have decided to pass on the grounds that he could not bring himself to invest in a company whose co-founder was called 'Mr Dikshit'.

Return of Goldilocks

London managed to retain its upward impetus, topping 5100 on 23rd June, fuelled by rate cut hopes and the usual flurry of bid rumours, but after a brief setback triggered by a shock 2-day fall of 290 points by the Dow, the FTSE continued to rise, reaching 5161 on 1st July, its best level since May 2002. The Dow's reaction was widely attributed to fears that US growth prospects were going to be compromised by a triple whammy of rising interest rates (the Fed had upped rates to 3.25% on 30th June), rising oil prices (crude prices had topped $60 a barrel for the first time), and a near 10% appreciation of the dollar – a combination considered capable of knocking 2% of 2004's 4.5% growth figure.

Some observers, however, considered that just as worrying, even if its effects were not easily quantifiable, was the deteriorating situation in the Middle East. The rise of insurgency in Iraq was taking an ever greater toll of US personnel, a development which suggested the military was losing control and inviting speculation about what that would mean for President Bush's political standing. Furthermore, the victory of the hard-line Islamic candidate in the Iranian elections did not bode well for Washington's hopes for democracy in the region.

Such considerations faded into the background over the next few days as a run of positive data on employment, inflation and consumer confidence, backed up by strong earnings reports from across the sectors, encouraged the belief that 'Goldilocks' had come home and that growth was not too hot, not too cold, but just right, so that the Fed could continue to raise rates at a 'measured pace' without hurting growth. A narrowing of both the trade and budget deficits added to this sense of national well-being and underpinned the revival of the dollar's fortunes.

Terror comes to London

The London bombings on 7th July demonstrated that geopolitical risks had not gone away, but the intraday recovery from the initial 200 point fall in the FTSE100 and the advance to a new high the next day, strongly suggested that terrorist attacks, at least those of a limited nature, were now priced-in by the market. An FT columnist speculated that other exogenous shocks, e.g. those involving Saudi Arabia or Iran, would have a far greater effect in that they would create an oil price spike, but that perhaps the greatest danger lay within the system, i.e. an endogenous shock caused by the bursting of the US house price bubble or one arising from a slump in US consumption occurring at the same time as a sharp slowdown in China, a coincidence capable of creating a global recession.

But once again, markets were in no mood to worry about such things and by mid-July, the FTSE was close to 5250, with the FTSE250 reaching a new record high, naively assuming, in the view of many commentators, that the hoped for cut in interest rates to 4% by year end would reverse the slump in export orders in services and manufacturing, and permit the Chancellor to achieve his economic growth prediction for this year of 3% to 3.5% against the 1.7% to 1.8% now being pencilled in by the majority of independent forecasters.

On Wall Street, the Dow plussed 360 points to 10,640 in the first two weeks of July, while the NASDAQ Composite gained 100 points to 2156, assisted by better than expected earnings reports from tech heavyweights **Apple**, **Advanced Micro Devices**, **Intel** and **Texas Instruments**. Mighty **GE** contributed to the bullish mood by reporting an 8% sales growth and a 24% rise in second quarter earnings, figures which, given the company's diversity, were interpreted as reflecting the health of the global economy. The bears were becoming a voice in the wilderness but could just be heard saying that the inflation data were not so benign as they appeared thanks to substitution, i.e. if the price of one index constituent increases sharply, a lower price equivalent replaces it, and to "hedonics", where the price of another constituent can be varied to take account of its greater capability resulting from technological advance. Their concern was that when inflation came to be seen as a threat, then the Fed would have to adopt far tougher policies than those currently contemplated. This ebullient mood on the far side of the Atlantic spread to Europe, where the major equity indices all achieved fresh 3-year highs on an almost daily basis during the first half of July. Tech stocks were particularly in favour under the influence of strong gains recorded by the NASDAQ.

With a repo rate of 2% and the euro weak, the European Central Bank was not expected to trim that figure further, and the bull case for European stocks appeared to rely heavily on the belief that the US economy was back in business, a view that drew some support from the fact that government bond yields were rising again. The 10-year Treasury yield had risen from a low of 3.89% at the beginning of June to 4.18% on 15th July, and if it continued to rise, then the 'conundrum' of falling bond yields accompanying rising interest rates no longer existed. The bulls were now firmly in the ascendant, relying on the familiar, 'It's the economy, stupid' mantra, while the bears continued to keep a wary eye on the geopolitical scene and the possibility, even probability, they thought, of exogenous shocks throwing the markets into disarray.

China makes a move

The long-awaited revaluation of the Chinese yuan had little impact on US markets. Earlier expectations of a change in the 5% to 10% range had already been judged to barely dent the US trade deficit or diminish Chinese competitive advantage, so one of just 2.1% against an unspecified basket of currencies was widely seen as more of a political gesture than an economic one. However, it was not enough to overcome US opposition to the Chinese National Offshore Oil Company's (CNOOC) $18.5 billion offer for California's **Unocal**, which decided to go with Chevron's lower cash and share offer. Cross-border bids were very much in vogue, but if the issue of the control of vital oil supplies was behind the American decision, it would have been difficult for the French authorities to provide a comparable strategic case for its opposition to Pepsi Cola's bid for **Danone**, Chancellor Schroder to justify his outburst about 'vultures' plundering German industry, or for the Bank Of Italy to shut out ABN AMRO in the contest for control of a small regional Italian bank. Interestingly, the only domestic opposition to Saint-Gobain's surprise £3.4 billion bid for **British Plaster Board (BPB)** was one of price.

A second wave of attempted bus and tube bombings in London on 21st July created some initial nervousness in markets, but they quickly recovered and on the last day of the month the FTSE stood at 5282.3, a new 3-year high after a brief sortie above 5300. The momentum for the rise in this final week was provided by a string of upbeat results from blue chip companies, including **Rolls-Royce**, **AstraZeneca**, **Reckitt Benckiser**, **BP** and **British Gas**, all with significant weightings in the FTSE100. However, this apparently favourable corporate picture was spoiled to a degree by an obviously unfavourable outlook for the UK economy, a dichotomy prompting many financial writers to doubt that the momentum could be maintained.

Chancellor Brown's reputation for 'caution and prudence' was now being called into question, as government borrowing tested the limits of acceptability and his 'golden rule' of borrowing only to invest over the current economic cycle managed to remain unbroken, only to be conveniently backdated to the start of the cycle by two years to 1997. Critics insisted that the device was simply deferring the hard choices on tax and spending necessary to maintain fiscal stability as the economy slowed. The latest batch of economic data appeared to justify this cautious view. Second quarter GDP growth came in at 0.4%, the fourth quarter in a row below the long-term trend rate and the slowest in twelve years. A quarter point cut in MLR to 4.5% at the MPC's next meeting was now widely seen as a done deal, but some more cautious commentators were keen to stress that the committee's specific brief was to target inflation. Thus, with the Consumer Price Index (CPI) already at 2%, the top of its allowable range, rising oil and gas prices, and sterling down 10% against the dollar in the past three months, perhaps the case for a rate cut was not so clear after all. Less contentious was the explanation popularly given for the FTSE100's advance against the background of a slowing UK economy, up 8% since the start of the year contrasting with practically 'no change' in the major US stock indices over the same period. Quite simply, it was that the FTSE100's constituents covered so many global industries like oil, mining, pharmaceuticals, banks and financial services, that with some 50% of earnings coming from overseas, it reflected the world scene rather than the domestic one.

Death of a king

Following the death of King Fahd of Saudi Arabia, the transition of power to the new King Abdullah was as rapid and smooth as markets could have hoped for. However, the fact that the oil price notched up a dollar on the news worried some commentators, who saw practically any event in the desert kingdom as cause for concern in that it could disturb the delicate balance between reformists and fundamentalists that preserved the status quo ante in the world's premier oil producing country. A further rise in the oil price to $63 a barrel in the first days of August, supposedly in response to security threats to the US and UK embassies in Riyadh as well as to US refinery problems and likely production disruption by hurricanes in the Gulf of Mexico, did little to discourage the bulls who chose to see it not as a threat to global growth (the prevailing view six months earlier when the price was in the $40-$50 range), but now as a sign of growing global demand.

This favourable interpretation of events was widely reckoned to have some validity as far as the emerging markets of Asia were concerned, given their reliance on commodities and exports and burgeoning trade links with China, and it was no great surprise that the stock markets of South Korea, Indonesia, India and Australia were achieving new record highs.

The UK also had a case to make as the FTSE100 crossed the 5300 mark, powered by the global players in the index with a little help and encouragement from the first cut in interest rates in two years, down a quarter of a point to 4.5% on 4th August.

The US markets continued to forge ahead under the influence of consistently strong corporate earnings and better than expected employment and manufacturing data, undeterred by a rising oil price and another quarter of a per cent boost to interest rates taking Fed Funds to 3.5%, both events which had been considered bear points just a month earlier. The 10-year bond yield had also managed to continue to rise to a 4-month high of 4.4%.

Eastern promise

While the bears seemed to be very much out of step with the mood of the markets, they were not ready to throw in the towel. Apart from the obvious risks that existed in the geopolitical sphere to justify their 'always expect the unexpected' argument for caution, they insisted that the Federal Reserve could not maintain its accommodative policy stance indefinitely while consumers and governments ran up higher and higher debts. The booming US housing market, they believed, was a particular cause for concern, regarding it as already in 'bubble' territory and thus artificially boosting consumer confidence and spending. They also disagreed with the bulls, who said that equities looked cheap relative to bonds because dividend yields were currently very close to bond yields. On the contrary, the bears maintained, to argue thus was to get uncomfortably close to the case for the equity risk premium to fall to zero, one last promoted enthusiastically in the closing months of 1999! Similarly, another commentator noted, the last time 'Goldilocks' was so in vogue was also five years ago.

The extraordinary debut of **Baidu.com**, the Chinese internet search engine, on the US market rang warning bells for some investors with painful memories of the dot.com mania of 1999/2000. At an offer price of $27, a company with revenues of $13.4 million in 2004 was being accorded a market value of $872 million, a heady price many thought, even for an operator in the potentially vast Chinese internet sector. To then rise 350% on the first day of trading and achieve a valuation of near $2.5 billion demonstrated that the appetite for risk was as strong as it had ever been, a view confirmed a few days later when **Yahoo!** paid $1 billion in cash for a 40% stake in **Alibaba**, China's leading e-commerce website. One writer suggested that when Alibaba's founder and CEO, Jack Ma, likened working in the Chinese internet to 'a blind man riding a blind tiger', he might just as well have been referring to China's overseas investors.

To cut or not to cut...

The Bank of England's report in mid-August expressing concern about the inflationary implications of the dramatic rise in the price of oil dashed the hopes of many investors who had been looking for two more cuts to take interest rates down to 4% by the end of the year. They were also disappointed to learn that the MPC's decision to cut had been finely balanced at 5 to 4, with the governor of the Bank voting against. However, there was another school of thought which saw the current oil price as a speculatively-inspired temporary phenomenon, which as it subsided to around the $40 level, would provide scope for the MPC to resume rate cuts to counter the slowdown in growth that the high price of oil had induced. The actual inflation figure for July of 2.3% released just two days later tended to favour the views of the former, and was also credited for checking the FTSE's advance by raising the spectre of 'stagflation' as a high oil price slowed growth, while at the same time creating inflationary pressure.

Much the same situation obtained in the US, as inflation figures came in much higher than expected at 3.2%. The Dow's once promising looking drive towards 10,700 went abruptly into reverse. In the US, too, there existed a division between those analysts who believed the Federal Reserve was on top of the situation, keeping nominal and real interest rates low to maintain the important domestic housing boom and US and global economic activity, and those who distrusted the apparent resilience of the world's economies (and stock markets) in the face of the oil price run-up. The latter saw today's savings-short, asset-dependent, over-indebted US consumer as much more vulnerable to energy-price shocks than in the past, an opinion reinforced as Federal Reserve Chairman, Alan Greenspan, in a keynote speech drew attention to the rise in stock, bond and house prices, which had resulted in a sharp rise in household wealth relative to income with accompanying inflated debt levels, and implying that his successor might be faced with the task of devising a monetary policy to cope with a sharp fall in asset prices. **Wal-Mart**, the world's biggest retailer, also sounded a note of caution, warning of the adverse effect on shoppers of higher petrol prices and trimming its full year profit forecast.

By the end of August, the Dow had pulled back almost 300 points from its 10,685 high touched earlier in the month, while in London the FTSE100 had shaded 150 points from its August 8th peak of 5378. Also weighing on markets as the historically dull month of September dawned, was both the increasing awareness of the American public to the 'no win' situation developing in Iraq with its likely impact on President Bush's second term, and the growing concern over the possibility – even probability many thought – of a SARS Mark II pandemic of Asian bird flu with the potential to create havoc in the world economy.

Stuff happens

But havoc of a different sort was about to be created on America's Gulf Coast as Hurricane Katrina swept in on the night of 29th August, inundating New Orleans, killing thousands and severely damaging port, transportation and storage facilities and offshore oil rigs. The immediate economic impact was reflected in the oil price surging above $70 a barrel, and petrol prices pushing towards $3.50 a gallon in the US and 100p a litre in the UK. With damage losses estimated to exceed $50 billion in America's worst ever natural disaster, insurance stocks slipped along with those of hoteliers, retailers and casino operators, while energy, construction and oil stocks gained, keeping markets broadly steady.

However, more than one commentator believed that Wall Street had its head in the sand, still looking for a cap on the Fed's earlier planned interest rate rises, low inflation and inflated asset prices, now with the added boost from a massive reconstruction programme, to offset the impact on the economy of a $40 increase in the price of oil since January 2004. They argued that abnormally low interest rates coupled with rising asset prices had mitigated the effect of higher oil prices to date, but thought that the point had been reached when they would feed through into higher inflation and damage consumer confidence. One observer even considered that the situation today was akin to that ruling in October 1973, when OPEC delivered the first oil price shock, an event that triggered the severest stock market falls of the post-war period. Few went along with this extreme view, but there was broad agreement that high oil prices were here to stay given the growing demand from the fast developing economies of China and India (not a factor in the seventies) and the ever present threat to production posed by the inherent instability of the Middle East.

Damn the torpedoes...!

If rocketing oil and petrol prices failed to upset the stock market, then neither did the political damage to the Bush administration arising from the delay of the federal reaction to a well-predicted catastrophe. With President Bush's approval ratings already at a record low before the hurricane in response to the situation in Iraq, his popularity and that of the Republican party as a whole took a new dive as the belief grew that an ineffective and even counterproductive 'war on terror' overseas had diverted resources vital to coping with natural disasters at home. The stock market's performance against such an apparently unfavourable background prompted one observer to conclude that perhaps investors had become imbued with the spirit of Admiral Farragut, one of the heroes of the American Civil War, who at the Battle of Mobile Bay had proclaimed, 'Damn the torpedoes! Full speed ahead!'

Meanwhile, back in the UK, the London market was also taking record oil and petrol prices in its stride, with gains in the FTSE100 boosted as usual by the heavy weightings accorded to oils and mining stocks, and those in the FTSE250 by a flurry of merger and acquisition activity among the Mid-Caps. Independent observers, i.e. those outside the financial services industry without a vested interested in a strong stock market, saw this performance as out of sync with a clearly slowing UK economy, which was being faced by yet another potentially inflationary hike in fuel prices and yet another fall in consumer confidence. The August inflation figure then weighed in with a 0.4% increase over July, taking the annual rate to 2.4%, above the Bank of England's 2.0% target for the second month running, and reducing the probability of another interest rate cut before the end of the year.

However, the market was undaunted and by mid-September, the FTSE100 had topped 5400 to reach a 4-year high, aided once again by natural resource stocks and bids and rumours of bids for a number of its constituents. Gold had advanced to its highest level in 17 years, responding supposedly both to supply/demand imbalance and to inflationary concerns, helping to propel the miners in the index into new high ground, while **Deutsche Post's** agreed £3.6 billion bid for logistics giant **Excel**, along with gains by **O2** and **Friends Provident** on hopes of bids from their continental rivals added to the impetus. Wall Street, too, seemed to recover its confidence post-Katrina, with the Dow once again looking at 10,700, but the mood changed abruptly when on 20th September, the Federal Reserve disappointed those who had hoped for a pause in rate rises by upping interest rates by a quarter point to 3.75%. The Dow lost over 100 points on the news but then managed to hold its ground despite Hurricane Rita heading towards Texas, threatening the same degree of devastation on Houston and Galveston as Katrina had visited on New Orleans, and boosting the oil price towards $70 again. In the event, the hurricane diminished in force as it made its landfall, sparking a relief rally which still left the Dow some 250 points below the peak level reached earlier in the month.

The Chancellor comes clean

In the last week of September, Chancellor Brown chose the annual meeting of the IMF as the forum for his first admission that the Treasury's growth forecast for the UK economy in 2005/06 of 3% to 3.5% would not be met. Rather, he explained, the figure would be 'at or slightly below our cautious view of trend' of 2.5%, still optimistic but much more in line with most independent forecasters' estimates of around 2%. The blame was put squarely (if not entirely fairly) on a 'more considerable' rise in oil prices than he had expected, which was 'obviously having an effect on business costs and consumer costs that will be seen in all the major economies'. The Chancellor was also reckoned to be equally well adrift in his public borrowing calculations. His figures of £32 billion in 2005/06 falling to £29 billion in 2006/07, were at odds with those of the most optimistic of the independent forecasters who were looking for £39 billion this year, shading to £38 billion next year.

As widely expected, the Bank of England held interest rates at 4.5% by a unanimous decision in its last meeting of the month, but reports just days later of retail sales volume falling at its fastest rate since 1983, and second quarter GDP growth coming in at its weakest in twelve years, seemed to confirm the view of many commentators who believed further rate cuts were going to be needed to boost a clearly flagging economy. However, for the London stock market such macroeconomic matters seemed to be, for the moment at least, totally irrelevant and the FTSE100 ended the year's third quarter by topping 5500 for the first time since August 2001, bidding to join the bull market being enjoyed by most of our European and Asian trading partners.

But while a number of the country's leading stockbrokers were busy upping their end-year forecasts for the index by 500 or so points, others remained cautious, with veteran fund manager, Patrick Evershed of New Star, describing the market as 'almost an accident waiting to happen'. For a time he was right. After another short-lived attempt to hold above 5500 courtesy of rises in **Boots** and **Alliance UniChem** on their merger announcement, together with vague bid talk boosting **Barclays**, **Whitbread**, and **Sainsbury**, the FTSE100 went sharply into reverse, following the example of Wall Street where the Dow had lost 250 points in the first three days of

October. The sudden fall was widely attributed to fears about rising interest rates after the Fed had expressed concern about inflation, but since the prospect was already on the cards, it looked as if the setback was due simply to old-fashioned profit-taking after an exceptionally steep run-up in the third quarter. This latter view gained substance from the fact that the miners were heavy fallers despite the copper price still climbing. High-flying oil shares were also among the casualties, the decline attributed to their supposedly fading prospects resulting from a lack of investment in exploration and production facilities when the oil price was a lot lower. But once again, profit-taking after a near 40% rise since the beginning of the year as in the case of **BP**, for example, was perhaps a more than adequate explanation.

Macro bad, micro good

Markets continued to decline as the month progressed, as increasing weight was given to inflation fears and the prospect of interest rates being pushed to higher than expected levels, a development which would call into question the ability of the strong run of corporate earnings on both sides of the Atlantic to hold up in a harsher environment. The bears also worried that the inauspicious start to President Bush's second term was putting in jeopardy the whole pro-growth political majority of recent years. This they thought could threaten the establishment of his tax cuts as a permanent feature, just at the time when the US economy would need all its underlying strength to combat higher energy prices and rising interest rates, as Fed chairman Alan Greenspan's successor was forced to make up for what many considered to be the former's mistake of keeping interest rates too low for too long. Alan Greenspan had already expressed concern over the rise in asset prices, particularly those of houses relative to income contributing to the low savings rate and rise in household debt, hinting that the next chairman might be faced with the problem of dealing with a collapse in asset prices. This suggestion of *apres moi le déluge* meant that considerable importance was attached to the identity of his successor. The nomination of White House economic adviser and former Fed governor Ben Bernanke was greeted enthusiastically by Wall Street, where the Dow jumped 172 points on the news on the assumption that he would follow in the footsteps of his revered predecessor. This was perhaps the only piece of good news in a month which had seen the Dow lose some 350 points, but many observers believed that the celebration was perhaps premature, for given the economic legacy he had inherited, the new governor would have no choice but to adopt a more hawkish approach in future policy decisions.

During the course of the month, the FTSE100 had trimmed over 350 points from its high point of 3rd October, influenced not only by Wall Street's decline but also by a further downgrading of the UK's growth prospects as the third quarter figures came in at an annualised rate of 1.6%, and by retail sales volume falling at the fastest rate since 1983. But on the last day of the month the decline was abruptly reversed with a 103.9 rise, the biggest one-day points gain in 2½ years in response to a flurry of megabids for some of the UK's leading companies. Spanish telephone giant Telefónica's £18 billion bid for mobile operator **O2**, Dubai Ports' £3 billion bid approach to **P&O**, and Nippon Glass's talks with **Pilkington** over a possible £2 billion offer, all provided strong support for the argument that UK blue chip stocks, with roughly 50% of their earnings derived from overseas, were well insulated from a weakening domestic economy and should be regarded as global players. Looked at in this light, it was not so surprising that the FTSE100 was becoming a shopping list for foreign buyers, and even while the market was still falling in mid-October, Swiss investment bank, **UBS**, had been happy to nail its flag to the mast and upgrade its 12 month target for the index from 5600 to 6000.

Up another notch

On 1st November, Wall Street called a brief halt to the 'Bernanke Bounce' after the Fed raised interest rates by a quarter point to 4%. The fact that the board's decision was unanimous served to remind investors that the economic background was still much the same and that the Fed's primary duty was to target inflation.

Neither had the political background improved. Top White House aides (unlike government advisers in the UK) were being indicted on charges relating to misrepresentations of the case for going to war over Iraq, the President's popularity rating had slumped to a new low as US military casualties topped the 2,000 mark, and Iran and Syria both seemed hell-bent on creating more trouble in the Middle East.

However, it was only a pause and markets soon renewed their advance, encouraged by more evidence of rising corporate profitability, an oil price still retreating from its post-Katrina high point, and thus to some degree deflating inflation fears, and in the case of the UK market, the prospect of over £20 billion of the latest takeover windfalls being put back into equities. Furthermore, interest rate differentials and its 'safe haven' characteristics continued to boost the dollar, offsetting both the ballooning budget and trade deficits, and taking it to a two year high against the euro and the yen. With the Dow within a whisker of 10,700 again and the FTSE100 almost back to its October 3rd high of 5501, the bears had little option but to fall back on the "15 fat years, 15 lean years" argument that, historically, a prolonged period of outperformance is succeeded by a similar period of underperformance.

Thus, in the wake of the sensational run-up to 2000, the rally from the low point touched in March 2003 to date was destined to be nothing more than a pick-up within a longer term bear trend. The bears also pointed to the fact that after a prolonged period of abnormally low interest rates, central banks across the world were now raising them, a process which was likely to disrupt the "carry trade", i.e. borrowing cheaply to buy higher yielding assets, by prompting the untimely disposal of those assets. Providing more immediate substance for the bear's case was a gloomy forecast from US house builder **Toll Brothers**, but although this was seen in some quarters as a warning sign for the housing market, the principal driving force behind the US economy over the past couple of years, the fallout was entirely sector specific and failed to halt the advance of the leading market indices. Much the same situation ruled in London, where top flight builders' merchant **Travis Perkins** stated that market conditions had 'worsened significantly since mid-October', but while the company's shares fell 9% and depressed the whole sector, the broader market continued to push ahead buoyed by miners, banks and property stocks.

Pressing on regardless

The FTSE100 took a one-day knock in mid-November when heavyweight constituent **Vodafone** slumped 15% after reporting slowing revenue growth, squeezed margins and tough going in Japan, but soon recovered to top 5500 again, as the NASDAQ hit a 4-year high of 2227, and the Dow and S&P 500 broke through their resistance levels of 10,700 and 1240 respectively. The bulls were now clearly in the driving seat, and while most analysts looked for a storming finish to the year with further progress in 2006, some of the more cautious ones were worried by the fact that the yield curve, i.e. the line plotted from the yields on Treasury borrowings from the shortest term to the longest, was practically flat and close to inversion, a state which normally presages a slowdown in economic growth and a recession.

A great deal of comment also focused on the record low yields registered during the month by the UK's new 50-year gilt, a situation that arose as pension fund managers attempted to balance their portfolios away from shares and into a shrinking stock of bonds in order to make sure of matching their long-term pension liabilities, a result that investment in equities could never guarantee. Stephen Lewis of Monument Securities (popularly known as the 'Fifth Horseman') saw this willingness of the pension funds to accept lower returns than the economic risks of their investment would warrant as a 'serious misallocation of capital throughout the economy', aggravating the problem of underfunding and a clear threat to the value of future pensions.

However, this trend had clearly not diminished the attractions of equities for the fund managers who needed them to spice up their returns, and for investors generally who preferred to take a chance on dividend and capital growth rather than accept the relative security of the paltry returns currently being offered by bonds. Furthermore, the bulls argued that a flat yield curve was an expression of investors' interest rate expectations and their confidence in the ability of the Fed to contain inflation, thus implying continuing low bond yields and a situation favourable for equity valuations. Indeed, one commentator suggested that the answer to Alan Greenspan's 'conundrum' of bond yields trending lower while official interest rose was that low interest rates were now a given. Admittedly, a rate of 1% looked abnormally low but in absolute terms, 4% was still historically low. If we accept this thesis, he argued, then continuing growth of the US economy was assured and the Asian central banks which had been piling into US bonds were not to be left holding a depreciating asset as the dollar strengthened, contrary to the practically unanimous opinion of 'experts' at the beginning of the year. Furthermore, the low cost of the 'universal commodity', i.e. money, also served as a counterbalance to the soaring cost of practically every other commodity. Thus, the 82 point fall in the Dow on the last day of November, supposedly in response to a faster than expected third quarter growth rate reviving fears of more aggressive rate rises, he believed, was an aberration, while the 106 point rise the following day was much more of a true reflection of the state of the market and a validation of the case of the bulls.

Christmas cheer

As December dawned, both London and New York marked time around their high points for the year, while most of the markets of Continental Europe continued to forge ahead, albeit in the face of cautionary words from central bankers and a quarter point hike in interest rates to 2.25% by the European Central Bank, the first change in 2½ years. The FTSE100 managed to reach a new peak of 5574 on 7th December, but promptly relapsed to end the day 10 points down at 5528, as heavyweight constituents **British Gas** and **BP** fell back following the Chancellor's move to increase the tax on North Sea oil profits from 40% to 50%. The abrupt reversal was widely attributed to profit-taking, as fund managers elected to lock in gains to establish a creditable end-year performance after a 15% rise in the FTSE100 since January, rather than to Gordon Brown's admission in his pre-budget report that growth this year would be of the order of 1.75%, or well below his forecast in March 2004 of between 3.0% and 3.5%.

As usual, the domestic agenda had little relevance for the global market place that is the London stock market, and in the second half of December the rally got its second wind, managing to reach 5618.8 by year-end for a 16% gain, setting the seal on the third successive year of growth for the FTSE100. Bids and rumours of bids provided support for the final stages of the advance, notably Australian investment bank **Macquarie's** £1.5 billion offer for the **London Stock Exchange**, and talk of a bid being lined up for troubled insurance giant **Royal & SunAlliance**. The much more UK-representative FTSE250 easily outstripped the blue chip index, with a 26.8% gain taking it into new high ground largely thanks to a run of merger and acquisition activity, while the All Share index plussed 18%.

Wall Street's rally faded in the second half of December, and after topping 10,900 in the first week, the Dow managed to end the month at 10,717 or 0.6% down on the year. The NASDAQ Composite fared a little better to close at 2205, up 1.3%, while the S&P 500 plussed just 3% at 1248. The fact that Wall Street had performed relatively poorly compared with the markets of practically every other country, especially those classified as "emerging" was not seen as reflecting a diminution of America's role as the locomotive of the global economy, but simply recognition of the changing face of that economy.

Thus, the apparently insatiable demand for oil, metals and other commodities from China and India, the two most populous countries on earth, destined to be the superpowers of the 21st century, inevitably benefited the countries which supplied these commodities as well as providing a flourishing market for their neighbours' exports. Thus, it was no great surprise to see the Australian market up by 16.7%, with its resource index adding 47%, and Canada following much the same pattern with the main market up 22% and Metals & Minerals up 45%. Similarly, Russia and Brazil, with their vast natural resource base, attracted considerable investor attention, logging gains of 83% and 28% respectively. The *huis clos* stock markets of the Middle East also scored spectacular gains on the back of booming oil revenues, with Saudi Arabia up 100%, Dubai up 220%, and Egypt rising 130%. Everybody's favourite market for 2005, however, had been Japan, where the Nikkei Dow recorded a gain of 40% as confidence grew that the fifteen year long period of deflation was finally ending. The exchanges of Continental Europe also boomed, with Germany's DAX index up 28%, and France's CAC 40 rising 28%, gains not reflecting their largely stagnant economies but investors' hopes that the process of corporate restructuring and cost cutting allied with strengthening domestic consumer demand and exports boosted by a weak euro would soon flow through to earnings.

And in 2006...?

There was a broad consensus among market watchers that 2006 would see the fourth consecutive year of stock market gains, but a regular poll of forecasts by a panel of 'experts' came up with the relatively modest average end-year figure for the FTSE100 of just 5750. The more optimistic members of the panel believed that with global growth certain to be robust, especially in the Asian bloc, and inflation subdued, corporate profits growth would remain strong, and equities would continue to make progress albeit at perhaps a slower pace than in 2005. They saw globalisation and the rise of China and India not as a threat but as a blessing for the economies of the developed world, as their vast cheap labour forces depressed wage costs in the West, serving to keep a lid on inflation and interest rates.

The bears were on the back foot as they had been all year, but unrepentant in their view that rising stock prices, rising commodity prices, especially that of gold, and rising asset prices across the board were being fuelled by the anomalously low cost of money and that this was a situation that could not continue indefinitely. The fact that US consumers had so far managed to keep spending despite terror attacks, hurricanes and soaring energy prices did not mean that they would continue to do so, and the bears were convinced that the longer the reaction was delayed, the sharper it would be. They were concerned that the rising tide of money had floated all the ships, virtually eliminating the prudent margin traditionally required by investors to compensate for risk. And with the interest rate cycle clearly on the turn, a painful restoration of more conventional investment practise was inevitable, they believed, pointing out for example, that the debt multiples on leveraged buy-outs had increased significantly in recent deals, which meant that the new managers were borrowing more against cyclically high profits and repaying on less demanding terms to yield-hungry lenders encouraged by all-time low default rates.

Here be tigers

Geopolitical worries loomed large in the bears' catalogue of "what ifs", and while they acknowledged that the terror attacks of 9/11, the Madrid bombings, and 7/7 had no lasting impact on markets and the risk of more were probably priced in, they still believed that the decision to invade and occupy Iraq had lit a fuse that was still burning and which would before very long create an explosion capable of destabilising the whole of the Middle East. They saw the Bush administration's professed mission to spread democracy throughout the region as bound to be counterproductive, in that it would wreck a structure that had existed for centuries, enabling an autocratic elite to ride the tiger of the tribally-divided and fanatically religious masses of "the street". The advance of the Muslim Brotherhood in Egypt's recent parliamentary elections, of the radical Islamist parties in Iraq in January, and the sweeping victory of Hamas in the Palestinian polls, showed only too clearly that the power and prejudice of religion was not to be underestimated. Iran, too, had now become a major flashpoint, as Western opposition to its nuclear ambitions had enabled the country's hard-line leadership to muster popular support for its defiance. And they were quick to point out that in his latest speech, the omniscient Alan Greenspan had attributed the soaring price of gold not to inflation or supply and demand, but to investors' real fears of a major geopolitical conflict blowing up. Given the huge importance of the region for oil production, any threat to its stability was a threat to the economies – and the stock markets – of the world, and the bears once again cited the precedent of 1973/74, when the quadrupling of the oil price led to the most severe market declines ever recorded in the post-war years. Not everyone agreed that the price of oil was certain to rise. Influential economics commentator Roger Bootle, thought it was more likely to fall in the coming year as production returned to normal after the major disruptions of 2005, as new large-scale production opened up in Russia, Brazil and Canada, and as the expected slowdown in the US economy reduced demand with a knock-on effect on other big users like China and India, all against a background of large speculative positions due to be unwound.

In the final analysis, it would be difficult for a truly objective investor to avoid concluding that if the stock market had managed a significant advance over the past year while being assailed with all of these contradictory opinions, then fortune would continue to favour the bulls in 2006. 'It's the economy, earnings, share buybacks, mergers and acquisitions, stupid!'

2006

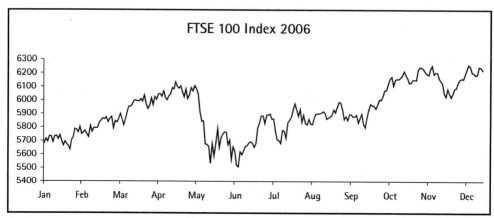

FTSE 100 Index 2006

Source: Thomson Reuters Datastream

A hard act to follow

The New Year opened with a bang. Within the first five trading days the FTSE100 had topped 5700 for the first time in four and a half years and the Dow came within a whisker of 11,000, a level it was to breach in the second week of January. As had been the case throughout 2005, the advance took place against a background of mixed economic and corporate news and rising interest rates, but as far as the UK market was concerned the dominant factor pushing the FTSE100 ever higher continued to be the almost weekly confirmation of the fact that overseas buyers saw it as a shopping list. In mid-January, Singapore's PSA entered the contest for **P&O** only to be foiled two weeks later as Dubai Ports World upped its offer to £3.9 billion; Nippon Sheet Glass closed its deal to buy **Pilkington** for £2.2 billion; early in February, Spain's Ferrovial expressed its intention to bid for **BAA**, the largest airport operator in the UK and the world for a sum approaching £10 billion; and then in March, Germany's industrial gases group **Linde** concluded talks with **BOC** with an agreed £8.2 billion offer. The bulls' argument appeared unassailable. If canny foreign predators were prepared to pay a premium of around 30%-40% to acquire their UK-based counterparts, then the chances were that the whole UK market was seriously undervalued.

The bears' warnings about the eventual adverse impact on markets of rising interest rates across the world went unheeded, as did their concern over an oil price in the $60-$70 range ($40-$50 had been regarded as a threat to world growth a year earlier), simply proving the point that a rising market is its own justification. Indeed, rising interest rates were explained away by a number of commentators as representing nothing more than a return to normality. Thus another quarter point on Fed Funds taking the rate up to 4.5% at the end of January went largely unremarked, as did the ECB's well-flagged increase to 2.5% in the first week of March. The UK's

Monetary Policy Committee was content by an 8 to 1 majority to leave base rates unchanged at 4.5%, despite calls for a cut by representatives of the embattled retail sector. As for the high oil price, its potentially disruptive effect on Western economies was gauged to have been substantially muted by the fact that today it was the result of strong rising demand from fast-growing economies capable of taking it in their stride, as distinct from a reaction to the supply shocks of earlier years, and also by the rising proportion of economic output now accounted for by service industries. Similarly, other potentially problem-creating events that had loomed large in 2005, like the spread of Asian bird flu and the deteriorating situation in Iraq, were also being ignored and by mid-February the FTSE100 was apparently comfortably established above 5800 and the Dow above 11,000.

However, as the index soared through 5900 at the beginning of the second week of March bidding to achieve most end-year target levels in the first quarter, even the most diehard bulls began to think that perhaps enough was enough, for the moment at least. For one thing, the narrowly foiled suicide car bombers' attack on the Abqaiq oil processing plant in Saudi Arabia, in the words of one analyst, would have 'engulfed the world' had it succeeded, forcing governments everywhere to curtail consumption. It was a reminder that 'supply shocks' were still a real threat to the economic order, and one reinforced a few days later by Iran's avowal to inflict 'pain and harm' on the US if its nuclear ambitions were thwarted, something which as one of the world's leading oil producers it was all too capable of doing. For another, the trend towards rising interest rates now began to receive much more attention, largely thanks to the Bank of Japan's announcement that it was going to end its ultra-loose zero per cent monetary policy. A number of commentators interpreted this as marking the end of the 'carry trade', i.e. borrowing cheaply in one currency to chase higher yielding and riskier investments in other currencies and in emerging market assets, a development which could lead to sharp price falls as such speculative positions were unwound. As for the fact that bond yields were rising significantly with the US 10-year Treasury-Bond (T-bond) yield touching 4.80%, its highest level since May 2004, there was potential for an adverse impact on equity prices generally, since the higher yield now available on the Treasury bond was a figure commonly used as the risk-free benchmark for the pricing of other assets.

Size doesn't matter

These concerns had been voiced many times in recent months and the fact that they had been pushed into the background by a rising market did not necessarily mean that they were no longer of importance. At the same time, it was difficult for the investor to take them seriously as company after company, many of them household names and major players in world markets, fell victim to the predators. Nothing seemed too big to be a target anymore, and if not from an overseas company in the same line of business, then from a consortium of private equity funds. Ferrovial's prospective bid for **BAA** was now rumoured to have brought it to the attention of private equity buyers. **Vodafone's** boardroom troubles gave rise to speculation that not only were private equity funds looking to counterbid for its Japanese mobile phone unit but even put together a giant £100 billion plus bid for the whole company, while **BT** shares rose strongly on talk of a £30 billion private equity buy-out. Even mighty **Unilever** was reported to be a target.

Numbers of this magnitude dwarfed those of recent UK deals, like the £4.8 billion buy-out of **Canary Wharf**, the £2.7 billion paid for **Allied Domecq's** pub operations, and the £1.8 billion of the **Debenham's** purchase, and comfortably exceeded the previous world record of $30 billion paid by Kohlberg Kravis Roberts & Co. for food and tobacco giant **RJR Nabisco** in 1989. Indeed, investors with longer memories recalled that 1989 had been the year the fee-driven superbids first came to the UK, when banks and institutions put together a consortium to bid £7.6 billon for **GEC**, and six months later, £13.5 billion for **British American Tobacco**. Both bids failed and were widely regarded as attempts to channel all the loose money in the system into what were seen at the time as opportunistic and speculative deals. The following year, against expectations, interest rates rose instead of falling, and a number of buy-outs ran into trouble on finding that highly leveraged financing and consumer demand were both interest rate-sensitive.

Faraway places...

On March 17th, the FTSE100 drove decisively through the 6000 level to reach an intraday high of 6044 before relapsing to close the day at 5999.4, and this failure of the index to hold on to its initial gain sparked a renewed debate over where the market was going for the rest of the year. Those commentators of a more cautious frame of mind who saw the beginning of the end of cheap credit worldwide as a threat to bull markets everywhere pointed to the sharp shakeouts suffered earlier in the month by many of the more esoteric of emerging markets, particularly in the Middle East and Latin America. Venezuela, they thought, was a good example of hot money flows. Neglected in 2005, and down some 30% by the end of the year despite a booming oil price, it was one of the best performing markets in the first quarter of 2006, rising an astounding 45% before reacting on belated recognition that the policies of the ultra-leftwing, anti-American President Chavez were not foreign investor friendly.

Iceland's double digit interest rates had also attracted a great deal of hot money in recent months, but the emergence of a large and growing current account deficit and a downgrading of the country's sovereign debt by a credit rating agency sparked a dramatic fall in the currency and the stock market in March as overseas investors headed for the exits. Many analysts were worried that despite having diversified their revenue sources by expanding abroad, Iceland's banks remained heavily exposed to the domestic lending market, taking shares as collateral for leveraged purchases of even more shares. Such a situation, they thought, was a recipe for disaster unless the stock market made a dramatic and sustained recovery, since it would lead to forced liquidation of holdings with a knock-on effect on the UK given the extensive holdings there of Iceland's banks and financial institutions. Fears of such a development were already hitting the shares of **easyJet**, **Woolworths** and **French Connection**, where substantial Icelandic stakes had been built up. Other high yielding currencies to suffer as nervous investors withdrew their cash were those of Hungary, Turkey, South Africa, Brazil and New Zealand.

On the last Tuesday of March, the US Federal Reserve reinforced the upward trend in interest rates with a further increase to 4.75%, hinting that there were more rate rises in the pipeline given the positive economic outlook. However, there was little sign of nervousness in London or New York, where markets continued to be dominated by merger and acquisition activity. Cosmetics giant **L'Oreal** made an agreed £650 million bid for **Body Shop**, former BBC Director General Greg Dyke led a consortium of private equity firms in a £5 billion approach to **ITV**, **Aviva** proposed a £17 billion merger with **Prudential**, while **BAE Systems** and **VT Group** got together to make a £750 million bid for defence-related support services group **Babcock International**. On a wider stage, France's **Alcatel** and America's **Lucent** reopened negotiations on a proposed $36 billion merger.

The 6000 level was quickly regained before the end of the month, but despite the market's obvious strength, a poll of pundits at a selection of banks and stockbrokers came up with surprisingly modest revised end-year forecasts ranging from 5000 to 6200. Even the most bullish were ready to concede that the current M&A frenzy could not go on forever, suspecting that the recent breakdown of a number of bids was likely to usher in a period of consolidation, if not an actual setback. The doubters were keener to stress the negatives, believing that they had been pushed into the background by investors' obsession with takeover activity. Thus, soaring commodity prices, while good for the share prices of the producers and for the FTSE100 given their near 25% weighting in the index, were certainly a negative for import prices of practically any manufacturer in the UK, or anywhere else for that matter, and ultimately for profit margins. And in the long run they were not going to do any good for Asia's, and particularly China's, low-cost manufacturing base, which was currently keeping inflation at bay in the West. Furthermore, the price of oil, the commodity with the widest impact of all, was pushing up towards $70 a barrel again and showing no sign of slipping back to what was considered to be a tolerable $50 level in the light of the near civil war in Iraq, the belligerence of the hard-line government in Iran and rebel activity in Nigeria, all of which were providing the potential for continuing major supply disruption.

Raising the bar

After managing to stay comfortably above 6000 for the whole of the first half of April, the FTSE100 continued to confound the bears, many of whom had regarded the passing of the 5% yield barrier by the US 10-year T-bond as a signal that the 3 year upswing for equities from the low point of March 2003 was coming to an end.

However, they still believed that 'sell in May' would be sound advice, given that much of the buying was coming from private investors, who traditionally arrive too late on the scene, and that an index driven higher by the likes of **BP**, **Royal Dutch Shell** and mining stocks including **Kazakhmys**, **Antofagasta** and **Rio Tinto** was not a harbinger of good news for the domestic economy. The bears applied much the same reasoning to the US economy and to Wall Street. While the Dow might look comfortably ensconced in the 11,200-11,400 range, apparently readying itself for an earnings-driven assault on its March 2000 peak, they were convinced that markets were once again in a state of 'irrational exuberance' engendered by easy money and speculative fervour. Markets, they argued, almost by definition are a matter of swings and roundabouts, and it simply made no sense for every asset class to be rocketing in price. It might be difficult to challenge the broad assumption that the supply/demand imbalance meant that the commodity boom was here to stay, but that assumption was in itself dangerous by inducing complacency in investors, similar to that ruling in 1999/2000 when technology stocks were seen as the only game in town.

The last few days of April were marked by a short-lived pause in the advance of equity markets in London and New York, influenced perhaps by oil reaching $75 a barrel, gold topping $600 an ounce, base metals moving to new highs and the IMF warning that the risks for the health of the world economy were 'tilted to the downside'. Nevertheless, investor sentiment remained firmly tilted to the upside, and the IMF's revised forecast of global growth in 2006 from 4.3% to 4.9% prompted Jim O'Neill, Chief Economist of Goldman Sachs, to exclaim that 'in 25 years of looking at the world, I've never seen anything like it'.

With the so-called 'BRICs' (Brazil, Russia, India and China) all booming, Japan growing again after fifteen years in the doldrums, and Germany picking up, the view that the US economy could afford to take a rest from playing the role of the engine of global growth was gaining ground. Thus, in this context, the large and ever increasing US trade deficit was nothing to worry about, in fact, rather the reverse: even the G7's call for a greater measure of exchange rate flexibility in emerging economies to help iron out world trade imbalances could turn out to be a major plus, if growing demand among the BRICs replaced too much emphasis on export-led growth strategies. In short, the exuberance being exhibited in stock markets around the world was seen as entirely rational.

The dollar starts to slide

At the same time, this apparently rational view of how the world scene was likely to develop looked as if it could be severely tested in the closing days of the month, as the slight easing of the dollar against the major currencies evident in recent weeks suddenly turned into a dramatic slide. The trigger was, supposedly, the decision of Sweden's Riksbank to switch a significant percentage of its dollar reserves into euros, a move interpreted as the shape of things to come as Asian central banks followed suit. With the Fed indicating that its rate rise cycle was nearing its peak, and China raising rates by 27 basis points to 5.85%, the dollar was clearly losing interest rate support, and from now on was going to be weighed down by consideration of a growing trade deficit approaching $800 billion, a level widely believed to be unsustainable. To what extent this sudden drop in what had always been regarded as the reserve currency of choice would be a destabilising factor around the world was uncertain. Admittedly, the event had been long predicted but its suddenness still came as a shock to markets, casting doubt on the ability of other trends to persist.

One writer was tempted to extend this doubt to the London stock market, where he considered warning signs to be very much in evidence, particularly in the resources sector where new AIM entrants were being greeted with the same sort of enthusiasm that had been accorded to their dot.com predecessors in 1999/2000. Oil explorer **White Nile**, suspended a year earlier following a meteoric rise on the strength of nebulous claims to exploration rights in disputed territory in the south of Sudan, was a speculative favourite once again to achieve a market capitalisation of some £450 million. Out of the same stable came **Central African Mining and Exploration Company (CAMEC)**, rising eightfold since the start of the year to 90p, producing a market capitalisation of close to £900 million on the back of its first revenues from copper and cobalt interests in the so-called Democratic Republic of the Congo and hopes for its coal and fluorspar projects in Mozambique and South Africa. It was also considered surprising that after allegations of fraud over misrepresentation to investors of the value of its exploration project in Greece, doubts over the ownership of its assets in the Ukraine and the resignation of its stockbroker and auditors, that **Regal Petroleum** should still be in the game with a market capitalisation of £120 million. Even a resemblance to the situation leading up to the great crash of October 1987 was detected. Then, as now, the dollar was falling, interest rates were rising along with trade deficits, there was frenetic trading activity in bids and deals, a rising share could not be sold in case something was about to happen, and poor results were greeted as a buying opportunity since they were regarded as making a company vulnerable to a bid approach. Furthermore, there was also a flood of new issues in the pipeline with BP's £7.2 billion offering of 1987 being matched by **Debenhams'** forthcoming £1.7 billion float, **Standard Life's** demutualisation offer at around £5 billion, and a little further down the line, Russian oil and gas giant **Rosneft** planning to unload a 20% stake onto the public for some £5.5 billion.

As yet there was little sign of indigestion in the market, anymore than there had been in the run-up to the 1987 crash, but sentiment can turn on a sixpence, the writer insisted, especially at a time when so many potentially explosive geopolitical situations existed.

Turn of the screw

And turn on a sixpence was exactly what markets did. The precipitous falls which began in the second week of May occurred across the board, embracing commodity as well as stock markets everywhere with emerging markets particularly hard hit. The trigger for the collapse was ascribed to the news that US core inflation had risen from 2.1% to 2.3% in April, prompting fears that the Fed would continue to raise interest rates and that the '5% solution' designed to keep inflation under control without inhibiting growth was no longer in prospect.

Suddenly the well-documented factors that had been present since at least the start of 2006 came into sharp focus. Until that point, a mergers and acquisitions boom and rising corporate earnings had dominated investors' thinking, keeping them risk tolerant and firmly in a buying mood as a rising market became self-justifying, determining that greater weight should be allotted to the bullish input factors than to the bearish ones. It was the old story that when a rising market becomes accepted as a simple fact of life and share price gains come to be regarded as the norm, then the lure of easy money attracts speculative investors, large as well as small and often leveraged, looking for short-term rewards. Initial success breeds a dangerous complacency, tempting the players to make ever larger bets, a process that always ends in tears.

The stock markets of Iceland, Saudi Arabia and the Gulf States had already taken a severe hit earlier in the year and now it seemed, it was the turn of stock markets everywhere as exuberance, rational as well as irrational, received its comeuppance. By the end of the third week of May, the FTSE100 was down 7.5%, the S&P500, 4.6%, the Eurotop300, 7% and Japan's Nikkei Dow down 8% from their peaks touched earlier in the month. Emerging markets saw far bigger falls with India losing 11%, Indonesia, 8.7%, and Russia, 14%. Volatility, which had been historically low for a prolonged period, suddenly increased dramatically, but while high volatility is supposed to create the ideal environment for hedge funds to operate in, this time the shock reversal of direction was believed to have caught many of them on the wrong foot. In the words of one unnamed manager, 'Everyone is long. There is a lot of illiquidity out there. Stocks have been falling 5% and you can't sell them'. Reports of falls in stock markets became headline news in the last week of May and into June, and the growing conviction that rising interest rates would dash hopes of continuing global economic growth seemed to be confirmed as the ECB hiked rates to 2.75% on 8th June, and countries as diverse as Denmark, India, South Africa, South Korea, Thailand and Turkey all followed suit.

Don't panic!

However, a week is a long time in the history of stock markets and by mid-June, hopes were being expressed that the panic was over. The FTSE100 had found support at the 5500 level, the Dow managed to struggle back into 11,000 plus territory, the Nikkei Dow was holding in the 14,500/15,000 range, and India, among the most important of emerging markets after losing 3500 points from its 12,612 high touched on 10th May, looked like stabilising in the 10,000/11,000 range.

Many commentators, while admitting that Goldilock's recipe of an economy not too hot to stoke inflation and not too cold to inhibit growth might no longer be the only dish on the menu, still maintained that there had been no dramatic change in the global economic background to account for such a severe shakeout in world markets. Some even went so far as to suggest that it might have been a blessing in disguise, purging the speculative excesses that had built up in markets, and thereby perhaps diminishing the extent of further rate rises by central bankers. After all, the outlook for corporate profits still appeared to be favourable and M&A activity, certainly as far as the UK was concerned, was still high, with bids for **AB Ports** and for food machinery group **Enodis** both hotly contested, as well as offers for computer services company **Misys** and brewer, **Hardys & Hanson**.

Furthermore, bond markets were not exactly confirming the fears that inflation was on the way up. The US 10-year T-bond yield had risen barely 50 basis points from its low at the start of the year, and had even slipped below 5% again in the second week of June when the equity scare was at its worst. The 'safe haven' advantage of dollar bonds was not seen as the total explanation for this resilience. Similarly, the rise of the gold price to a 25-year high (discounting the latest dip as the result of the unwinding of speculative positions) was as much a response to geopolitical risks as to fears of inflation.

Further evidence that the May/June falls had been 'just a blip' was provided by an unexpected rise in the latest Michigan Consumer Confidence survey, accompanied by encouraging data on new orders in manufacturing and another boost in job creation figures, all against the background of a narrowing of the US current account deficit in the first quarter. And noting that the oil price had remained relatively stable in the $68-$70 range while other commodities had experienced wild price swings over the past month, it was suggested that there was not a significant speculative premium in the price, and that markets had no choice but to learn to live with this sort of level.

Swimming with sharks

A quarter point hike in US rates to 5.25% in the last week of June accompanied by what were interpreted as dovish comments by the Fed chairman, helped markets everywhere to end the first half of the year in a brighter mood, prompting one analyst to say, 'It's over. We can now get on with our lives'. This more confident mood was bolstered in early July as some of the IPOs in the pipeline made their debut, albeit at the lower end of their projected issue price range. **Standard Life's** price range of 240p-290p back in April was revised to 210p-270p, and then after being offered at 230p, the shares rose to 249p on the first day of dealing. Similarly, healthcare group **Southern Cross** floated at 225p, at the bottom of its indicated 225p-280p range, and gained 18p when dealings began.

With the FTSE100 edging towards 5900, the Dow close to 11,200, and the NASDAQ pushing up to nearly 2200 again, markets appeared to have adjusted to the delicate trade-off between inflation and growth, but just when it looked safe to go back into the water, geopolitical risks suddenly escalated dramatically. Despite warnings from the international community including one from China, its supposedly influential neighbour, North Korea launched a series of long-range missile tests, provocatively starting on 4th July, America's Independence Day. This event upset Asian markets and Wall Street but had little impact on European markets. Their turn was to come just days later when a state of virtual war was declared between Israel and Hezbollah-run South Lebanon, an entity supported by both Syria and Iran.

The very real prospect of the conflict spreading outside the region sent the oil price soaring to $78 a barrel, reigniting fears about rising energy prices combining with rising interest rates to sabotage the hopes for continuing global growth. Markets nosedived and by mid-July, the FTSE100 was back to 5707, the Dow to 10,739, and the NASDAQ to 2037, with oil-importing Japan's Nikkei Dow falling below the 15,000 mark again, practically wiping out the year's gains for all these markets. Then, just to add to the gloom, the earnings prop for the market showed distinct signs of weakening as **Alcoa's** and **Lucent's** second quarter disappointed in the US, while in Germany, software group **SAP** failed to meet expectations. The Mumbai multiple train bombing which killed over 200 people was perversely greeted with a 315 rise in the BSE Sensex to 10930, but did nothing for global sentiment on the terrorist threat.

In fact, the prime beneficiary of an oil price continuing to rise on the prospect of a major disruption of supply occurring in the Middle East was Russia, with its imminent flotation of a stake in its biggest oil company, **Rosneft**. In such a situation as this, the legal challenges to the flotation were swept aside, and the huge demand from the Western institutions effectively made them as shareholders complicit in the dismemberment of Yukos and the creation of a new company under the control of the Kremlin. Most commentators were highly critical of the situation but felt they had no choice but to regard the Rosneft flotation as a commercial/political act in accordance with the 'real politik' of the new global order. The legality of what you did was determined by who you were rather than by the act itself (rather like the City pre-Guinness), and Russia was big enough and powerful enough to get away with practically anything.

A shot in the arm

The Fed gave markets a shot in the arm on 18th July, when chairman Ben Bernanke told Congress that 'our baseline forecast is for moderating inflation' and that a slowdown already underway 'should help limit inflationary pressures over time'. This statement was contrary to the more hawkish one expected and gave Wall Street, and markets across the world, a dramatic boost. The Dow plussed 212 points to take it above 11,000 again, while the FTSE100 rose 96.3 points to 5778, and Asian markets made useful gains. Sentiment was helped by strong earnings reports from **IBM**, **Bank of America** and **JPMorgan Chase**, and by a sharp reaction in the oil price from its recent peak on reports of an unexpected rise in US gasoline and crude stocks. Mining stocks, however, fell back on the news that China was raising bank reserve requirements in an effort to cool its economy.

By the end of the month the FTSE100 was within a whisker of 6000 again, but in the first week of August inflation fears returned to the top of the agenda when the Bank of England surprised practically all the forecasters by raising the base rate by a quarter of a percentage point to 4.75%. In the same week the European Central Bank hiked rates to 3%, and robust US July retail sales figures served to offset slowdown expectations, raising fears that perhaps Fed Funds were not going to peak at 5.25% after all.

Inflation continued to dominate investor thinking throughout the rest of the month, and stock markets ebbed and flowed in reaction to the interpretations placed on incoming economic data. With the Dow hovering around the 11400 level, US markets were widely seen as pricing in a soft economic landing and shrugging off the fears that the long-awaited bursting of the house price bubble would cause a drastic cutback in consumer spending, aggravating a nascent corporate slowdown. In the view of many commentators this was too optimistic a reading of the situation, where a cocktail of higher energy costs, tighter monetary policy, fading benefits from tax cuts and a serious fall in house prices, clearly ratcheted up the risk of recession. UK markets appeared more hesitant, perhaps still rattled by the shock base rate rise a month earlier and fearful of another hike in November if the inflation numbers failed to appease the hawks among the MPC members. David Smith in *The Sunday Times* pointed out, and not for the first time, that the consumer prices index (CPI) measure adopted in 2003 by the Bank of England for targeting inflation flattered the figure by excluding many housing costs, which were included and accorded a higher weighting in the original measure, the Retail Prices Index (RPIX). Thus, while the CPI figure for August rose to 2.5%, that for RPIX climbed to 3.3%, a nine-year high. One writer compared what he called a 'necessities index' covering the costs of housing, domestic fuel, motoring, fares and food, which represented 60% of all spending, producing an inflation rate of 4.8%.

September shocks

September was not a good month for emerging markets, as a string of upsets ranging from a military coup in Thailand to the worst riots in Hungary since the 1956 uprising and the assassination of a top Russian banker, reminded investors that political risk goes with the territory. Stocks, bonds and currencies seen as vulnerable all fell, with anxieties compounded by recognition of the threat to their exports posed by a slowing US economy. To a degree, the fall-out in emerging markets benefited US stocks and bonds by virtue of their 'safe haven' characteristics, and the Dow edged closer to its all-time high while the yield on 10-year T-bonds fell to 4.61%. Markets also took heart from a sharp fall in the oil price towards $60 a barrel and a continuing decline in most commodity prices, although as a result of the heavy weighting of the sectors in the FTSE100, the London index, while still firm, failed to match the performance of the Dow.

More cautious commentators saw this resilience in New York and London as remarkable in the face of a shock $6 billion hit taken by hedge fund **Amaranth Advisors** as a result of making massive leveraged bets that natural gas prices would rise instead of fall, as they did. The scale of the loss was greater than that incurred by pioneer hedge fund Long-Term Capital Management back in 1998, when it was wrong-footed by the Asian crisis, an event that shook markets across the world. They believed that the apparent ease with which the fund was unwinding positions and disposing of half of a €2 billion European leveraged portfolio whilst continuing to obtain credit from lenders, provided a false sense of security for investors in other hedge funds given their long involvement in an energy futures market that had grown dramatically in the past couple of years. They pointed out that **MotherRock**, a $400 million fund, had collapsed in August, again after betting that gas prices would rise instead of fall, and that the two funds were not going to be the only ones to have made the wrong calls in a $60 billion market where speculation now had more influence than the fundamentals of supply and demand.

And then there was the larger issue of how the Amaranth disaster would affect the whole world of hedge funds. After all, until it lost 50% of its assets, Amaranth was among the top fifty funds, regularly recommended as a moderate risk holding by the leading funds-of-hedge fund managers, and yet its risk controls were such that a single maverick trader could operate a strategy no more sophisticated than 'betting billions of investors' funds on red'. Critics also repeated criticisms of the 'two and twenty' fee structure, i.e. a 2% annual management fee coupled with a 20% rake-off from profits made with no penalty for losses. Such a structure, they argued, encouraged managers to go for the biggest and riskiest bets and compared it to a 'Rio trade' without the plane ticket. (This was a practice reputedly used by rogue traders around the time of the Barings collapse. The trader would set up a multi-million dollar 'make or break' transaction, simultaneously booking a one-way flight to Rio de Janeiro. If the deal paid off, then the ticket would be torn up. If it went the wrong way, the trader's institution would take the hit and he (or she) would be safe in Brazil, a country which had no extradition treaty with the United Kingdom).

Carry on regardless

In the event, the Amaranth debacle appeared to worry no one apart from financial columnists, and by the end of September the FTSE100 had topped 6000, the FTSE250 had broken through 10,000, and the Dow at 11,701 was within 50 points of its all-time high touched in March 2000. Within a week that high of 11,750 had been breached, and the move seemed to set the seal of approval on the advances recorded during the year by stock markets across the world. Expectations of global growth slowing to a more moderate pace with inflation tempered by the recent fall in oil and commodity prices were now standard, and seen as providing a favourable background for world stock markets in the final quarter.

With apparently no end in sight for the M&A boom, and practically a deal a day at premium prices confirming the view that equities remained remarkably good value, well-known US market commentator Jim Kramer was tempted into employing the description, 'one of the best markets I've ever seen'. The fact that the market had derated since 2000, as share valuations had failed to keep pace with earnings growth, thus holding out the probability of a re-rating in 2007, appeared to give support to the bull case. The successes of the Democrats in the US mid-term elections, apart from prompting short-lived falls in drug companies on the prospect of regulatory changes and in defence stocks on likely spending cuts, did nothing to disturb the benign market background, and a number of commentators stressed the benefits of 'gridlock government', along with the prospect of regime change in the White House two years hence.

The bears had to resort to the law of diminishing returns to justify their mistrust of current market levels, i.e. with margins and corporate earnings at record levels and bond spreads and property yields so low, the scope for further gains was clearly limited, especially given the excessive use of borrowed money to enhance returns. Add in the ongoing presence of geopolitical risk, the bears maintained, and markets were clearly vulnerable, at the very least, to a setback of the sort of magnitude that had occurred in May/June last.

Rising interest rates in Europe

In the UK, growth of 0.7% in the third quarter marking the fourth successive quarter of above trend growth, accompanied by inflation above target with M4 money rising at 14.5%, its highest rate since 1990, meant that the quarter point hike in base rate to 5% in the second week in November came as no surprise to markets. A month later, the European Central Bank, faced with a Eurozone inflation rate of 1.9% in November, up from 1.6% in October, raised rates to 3.5%, a move that also surprised no one. In fact, central bankers continued to be seen as successfully managing the growth v. inflation balance, gradually returning interest rates from the exceptionally accommodative levels adopted immediately post-2000 to ones that could be described as 'neutral'. Such a policy was not regarded as marking a turning point in the credit cycle and thus threatening the continuation of the bull market.

Another flurry of major bids in the final quarter seemed to confirm this view. Anglo-Dutch steel giant **Corus** received a £5.1 billion bid from India's **Tata**, an offer soon topped by Brazil's **CSN. ScottishPower** fell to Spain's premier energy company **Iberdrola** for £11 billion, **Gallaher** agreed a £7.5 billion offer from **Japan Tobacco, EMI** received a £2.3 billion bid from private equity interests, while the **London Stock Exchange** continued to fend off approaches from rival exchanges. Almost the only shareholders to lose out in this period were those invested in offshore gaming stocks dependent on US punters when Congress more than justified the multiple risk warnings contained in their offer documents by passing a bill making it illegal for banks and credit card companies to process on-line gambling payments. **PartyGaming's** and **Sportingbet's** share prices both more than halved on the announcement.

The bear case received a short-lived boost in the second half of November when the dollar suddenly took a tumble, falling from $1.89 to $1.98 against the pound, and from $1.29 to $1.33 against the euro, moves widely attributed to rate cut expectations encouraged by more evidence of a sharp slowdown in the housing market. The event inevitably focused attention on America's huge current account deficit, reviving fears that Asian central banks would take fright and begin to shy away from the dollar, diversifying their foreign currency reserves. The effect on equity markets was short and sharp, with the Dow losing 100 points and the FTSE100 falling back to just above 6000, but both quickly recovered in the first half of December, when unexpectedly strong job creation figures and upbeat retail sales in the US were interpreted as eliminating the prospect of a rate cut before Christmas and sharply reducing the chances of a cut in the first half of 2007. And such was the mood of the market that a falling dollar – as long as it did not happen too abruptly – was widely seen as beneficial in that is was needed in order to help rebalance the global economy.

A strong finish

Analysts at the leading financial institutions were practically unanimous in forecasting a good year ahead for the global economy, with the FTSE100 ending 2007 in the 6500/7000 range, and December did not disappoint investors looking for the time-honoured Christmas rally. On the last trading day of the year the FTSE100 stood at 6220.8, up 10.7% over the year, while the FTSE250 at 11,177.8 had gained a much more impressive 27%. The Dow at 12463, slightly below a record 12510 touched three days earlier, closed 2006 up 16.6% while the S&P500 rose 14%, and the NASDAQ Composite 9.9%. Given that the Euro had plussed 11.3% against the dollar, it was no surprise that the Eurozone markets topped those of the US with a 23% return, but the star turns were the emerging markets, showing that for 2006 at least, risk taking did bring its own reward. While the broad MSCI Emerging Markets index recorded a rise of 29%, the BRIC Index (composed of Brazil, Russia, India and China) produced the four best performances among all the major stock markets with a combined gain of 53%. China's Shanghai Composite led the field with a catch-up rise of 130% following years of underperformance, setting an example for Hong Kong's Hang Seng which jumped by 34%. Once again, Japan's Nikkei Dow 225 disappointed its many fans who regularly predict every year to be the Year of Japan, with a modest gain of 6.9% at 17,225.

Looking at the year ahead

Lex pronounced that 'overall, equity investors should be positioned for a fairly buoyant macro-economy but a year of reckoning in credit markets', adding that they should be sceptical of banks' claims to have 'bundled credit risk on to third parties through derivatives and securitisation'.

2007

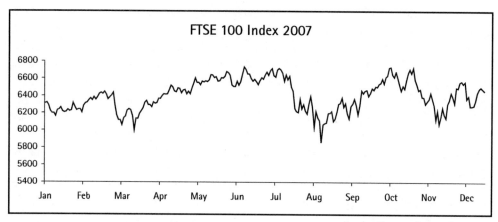

FTSE 100 Index 2007

Source: Thomson Reuters Datastream

A walk in the park?

After touching a new recovery high of 6319 on 3rd January, hopes of the FTSE100 staging a rerun of its storming performance at the start of the 2006, were dashed by a surprise quarter point hike in base rate to 5.25%, as the MPC reacted to evidence that rising energy and food prices were pushing the CPI inflation rate to 3% with the old RPI rate likely to top 4%. An *FT* editorial opined that this was 'a nasty but not fatal bout of inflation', and the FTSE quickly recovered in line with Wall Street and the European markets, which were achieving new records by the day inspired by the prospect of a soft landing for the US economy and the maintenance of a growth v. inflation balance on a global scale.

Emerging markets had a bumpier ride in January after Venezuela's maverick president announced an aggressive nationalisation programme for the country's oil, gas and telecom industries, in most of which the US held important investment stakes, and Thailand's finance minister imposed tighter restrictions on foreign ownership of local companies. The Venezuelan IBC index lost 25% over the next three weeks but the Thai SET index, after an initial plunge, quickly recovered when the government, upset by the market's reaction, cancelled the new restrictions.

London continued to benefit from takeovers, actual and rumoured, as **Countrywide**, the UK's biggest estate agency chain, received a £950 million bid from a US private equity group. **Tata** won **Corus** after upping its bid to £6.2 billion, and rumours swirled around **Cadbury**, **Centrica** and fund manager **Amvescap**. Then, in the first week of February, markets were stunned by the news that a private equity consortium led by CVC had made a bid approach to supermarket giant, **Sainsbury**. The move was to have political and social repercussions, sparking a debate about the new and dominant role that private equity was assuming in the national economy as it acquired more and more major assets. But as far as investors were concerned, the bid was a plus for the stock market, emphasising, yet again, the attractions of UK equities to predators who saw them as stores of unexploited value. At the same time, the controversy surrounding the bid prompted many critics to express their concern that a private equity buying spree fuelled largely by cheap debt and generous tax breaks compounded by excessive leverage and the ability of the managers to offload any risk through the medium of high yield 'no covenant' debt, was a recipe for disaster further down the line. The fact that many of these warnings came from prominent executives within the financial services industry gave them added weight, but there was still no sign of the private equity juggernaut slowing down.

In mid-February, **Blackstone** recorded the world's biggest buy-out winning **Equity Office Properties** for $39 billion, and simultaneously investors demonstrated their enthusiasm for private equity houses and hedge funds, oversubscribing by 27 times the IPO for US hedge fund **Fortress**, which promptly doubled in price on the first day of dealing. This event led to talk of a 'bubble' developing in financial markets comparable to the one that had driven up tech stocks in 1999/2000, and signs that it was ready to burst were seen by many commentators to be evident in the results of **HSBC**, where defaults in the US subprime mortgage market had led to a $1.75 billion increase in the bank's bad debt provisions. The parlous state of the US housing market now became the topic of the month, and given the boost to consumer spending that had been provided by equity withdrawal on the back of ever rising house prices, many commentators saw the slump in prices as the Achilles heel of the US economy.

A short, sharp shock

This view gained credibility on 27th February, when a move by the Chinese authorities to clamp down on stock market speculation triggered a 9% fall in the Shanghai Composite index, an event which was blamed in turn for sparking a worldwide shakeout. The Dow lost over 500 points at one stage before closing down 415 at 12,217, while the FTSE100 shed nearly 150 points. Emerging markets were hit particularly hard, with India's BSE Sensex losing almost 10% and Brazil's BOVESPA nearly 7%. The turmoil continued throughout the first half of March, effectively wiping out all the gains recorded since the beginning of the year, taking the Dow back to almost 12,000 again and the FTSE100 to 6000. The setback prompted commentators to focus on all the negative points that investors had chosen to ignore while markets were rising, and many expressed the belief that China was just a diversion and the real worry was that problems among US subprime borrowers would spill over into the general mortgage market, damaging domestic consumption as a whole with a knock-on effect worldwide in a US-centric global economy. Credit derivatives came in for considerable critical attention given that mortgage loans were regularly pooled, repackaged and sliced into tranches of tradeable obligations carrying varying degrees of risk to be sold into the credit market to yield hungry and risk tolerant investors. The supposed advantage to the financial system of dispersal of risk might get the original imprudent lender off the hook if the loans went bad, but did nothing for the standing of the credit market, something credit agency Moody's clearly had in mind when it opined that the subprime mortgage problems in the US could herald the beginning of the end for the liquidity glut fuelling world markets. Worries about a disorderly unwinding of the 'carry trade' also surfaced again as the yen rose over 3% against the dollar in three days, reviving painful memories of the turmoil created in October 1998, when it had risen 12% leading to heavy losses which then had to be offset by forced sales of equities.

However, the second half of March witnessed a strong rebound in sentiment and stock prices as the M&A bandwagon rolled on and US rate cut expectations revived on 'policy adjustments' talk, replacing earlier reference to 'additional firming'. Fed chairman, Ben Bernanke, was soon to diminish rate cut hopes by restating his concern over the US economy's 'inflation bias', but M&A activity continued to provide a more than adequate counterweight to any uncertainty over inflation and growth, and also to rising oil prices as Middle East tensions rose in response to Iran's capture of fifteen British marines. **Alliance Boots** became the first FTSE100 company to fall to private equity when the board accepted KKR's improved £10 billion offer (albeit laden with £9 billion of debt), **Barclays** announced that it was preparing a bid for the Dutch bank, **ABN AMRO**, and mega companies, **Pearson**, **Whitbread** and **Scottish & Newcastle** were all rumoured to be bid targets. Global deals had reached a total of £1,000 billion in the first quarter of 2007, a 14% increase on the same period in 2006, and nothing seemed to be out of reach for the private equity houses.

Markets were back to business as usual. Shanghai had rapidly recovered its 9% loss to actually post a record high before the end of March, an achievement matched by Russia and Brazil along with most of the emerging markets. The FTSE100 was back above 6400 again and in the final week of April the Dow topped 13,000 for the first time. Even the sharp fall in the dollar, with sterling rising to $2 and the euro to a record €1.36, was now no longer regarded as bad news but again as a 'rebalancing act' for the US trade deficit in relation to the surpluses of China, Japan and the Gulf States. At the same time, the bulls still had to admit that despite US first quarter GDP growth coming in at just 1.3%, its lowest in four years, and with inflation at 2.2%, up from 1.8% in the fourth quarter of 2006, driving the dollar to fresh lows against the euro, the Fed's scope for cutting interest rates was now severely constrained.

Sell in May...?

Such was the mood of the markets as May dawned, that more than one commentator was prepared to counsel investors to ignore the traditional warning about the month presaging a summer lull, arguing that the short-lived February/March sell-off had purged the speculative froth to a high degree and that there was no sign of the M&A frenzy abating. This view quickly appeared fully justified, at least in part, when in the first week of May, **News Corporation** launched a $5 billion bid for **Dow Jones**, **Reuters** announced that it had received an approach, and mining giant **Rio Tinto** soared by 20% on no more than rumours of a bid, an event that suggested that perhaps the speculative froth was still there in abundance.

In such a context, a quarter point hike in base rate to 5.5% on 10th May failed to have any dampening effect on market sentiment, and by the end of the month the FTSE100 had reached a new post-2000 high, with the All Share and the FTSE250 at new peaks. On Wall Street, the Dow touched a new all-time high of 13624 in the last week of May, while the S&P topped its March 2000 record high of 1527. At the same time, a growing number of well-respected market professionals were warning that the good times could not keep rolling in an environment where monetary conditions were tightening by the day and signalling the end, or at least the beginning of the end, of the era of cheap credit that had fuelled the buy-out boom and gains across asset classes. Pronouncements from the International Monetary Fund (IMF) and the Bank of International Settlements (BIS) showed that these august financial institutions had come to much the same conclusion, and the European Central Bank went on to warn of the 'increasing vulnerability' of a system accustomed to a 'very favourable economic environment', if faced with an 'abrupt' loss of liquidity.

This cautious view gained credibility in the first week of June when a dramatic sell-off in the bond market sparked a sharp drop in share prices across the world, but once again the bulls were able to rationalise the situation by interpreting the rise in bond yields as a return to normality, with an upward sloping yield curve reflecting the strong growth outlook for the US economy and the resultant demand for investment capital. They also argued that the rise in bond yields was not large enough to dent the attractions of debt-financed acquisitions, and with the yen at record lows, the 'carry trade' had every incentive to continue. Within days, global equities were climbing again, with the FTSE100 topping 6700, the Dow regaining all the 400 points lost in the first week to cross the 13,600 mark once more, and many Asian markets were hitting new highs.

Brave new world

This stellar performance by markets across the world in the face of such well-publicised reservations expressed by the leading financial institutions invited explanation – and the bulls were ready to provide one. The rise in global liquidity, they argued, was not a temporary phenomenon, but a new and permanent state of affairs arising from a financial revolution bringing liquidity to asset classes, principally real estate, once considered illiquid. Thus in the US and the UK, mortgage loans represent 69% and 74% of GDP respectively, but the figure for France is only 26% and that for Italy, just 14%, providing huge scope for development in Europe before touching the emerging world, where the trend had barely begun. Now consider the 'sovereign wealth funds' of China and the oil-producing states, which were beginning to look beyond gold and dollar bonds to diversifying their holdings or to replace their shrinking natural resources and instead acquire substantial assets in the economies of the developed world.

There was no precedent for such fortunes finding their way into global financial markets, and their presence helped to explain the waterfall of liquidity driving up the price of assets of all descriptions around the world. China's decision to invest $3 billion in top hedge fund **Blackstone**, was typical of this new trend. Furthermore, the argument went, inflation had been tamed by this abundance of capital, and interest rates could safely return to and remain at current 'normal' but historically low levels without taking risks with inflation. All this, the bulls maintained, had created a one-off secular shift benefiting economies and stock markets everywhere.

However, while acknowledging that the bulls had a point and that this apparently benign environment could persist for some time, more cautious observers believed that the tendency of financial institutions to overreach themselves was being seriously underestimated, echoing the comment made by the BIS in not dissimilar circumstances back in 1989, when it lamented the 'apparent propensity of the banking system to make repeated mistakes on a rather grand scale'.

Bear Stearns stumbles

Cue, **Bear Stearns**, one of America's leading investment banks and a specialist in the high yield bond market, and as such an unlikely victim of the fall-out in the subprime mortgage market. Yet in mid-June, two of its managed hedge funds were close to collapse, with the problems of one of them grandly, if unfortunately named, the 'High-Grade Structured Credit Strategies Enhanced Leverage Fund', compounded by borrowings ten times greater than its $600 million capital. The parent company was forced to offload $4 billion of securities to free up capital, while creditor Merrill Lynch went further, seizing collateral and attempting to sell it off to cover its losses. The event appeared to confirm the fears of those who saw the subprime mortgage crisis as a precursor of an even more serious crisis soon to develop in the corporate lending market, where the high loan-to-value ratios in subprime were mirrored in the 'covenant-lite' and 'payment-in-kind' deals in the latter. The effect of Bear Stearns' problems was soon seen in the credit markets, when three 'borrower friendly' bond issues by buy-out groups had to be shelved as investor interest evaporated, **Blackstone's** initial $5 premium on the $31 offer price quickly disappeared, and rating agencies embarked upon a review of subprime related bonds, expected to produce a wave of downgrades.

Interest rates might not be historically high but they had certainly been historically low for a long time, and the return to 'normal' levels clearly had caught many borrowers and lenders on the wrong foot. Even **Northern Rock**, arguably the UK's most innovative building society, and one which might confidently have been expected to know everything about interest rates, warned of a £180-200 million shortfall in the current year's profits as a result of being 'caught out' by failing to anticipate rising rates. The quarter point hike in base rate to 5.75% on 5th July would not have pleased **Northern Rock**, but it failed to deter investors, who after a brief initial hesitation on the Bank's announcement took heart from a new round of M&A activity internationally, and the release of stronger than expected economic numbers from the US economy. At the same time, Blackstone paying $26 billion for **Hilton Hotels**, a private equity consortium setting a new buy-out record with a $48.5 billion offer for Canadian telecoms group, **BCE**, and another bid being lined up for **Sainsbury**, might have set investors' pulses racing, but of more importance for their financial prospects was the fact that interest rates were edging up across the world and the oil price was back towards its highest ever level.

Thus, the 54.9 points gain which led to the FTSE100 ending the first week of July at just a whisker under its high for the year, was fuelled largely by advances in the heavily weighted oil and mining sectors in response to soaring oil and commodity prices, a fact which had to be bad news further down the line for corporate costs and inflation generally. Still, the market is king and investors everywhere seemed content to go along with the view of one leading equity strategist that 'equities should focus on the revenue-making opportunities coming from economic growth in the US and overseas and stop fretting about rates'.

It's tough at the top

The market has a habit of confounding such hubristic pronouncements, and initially appeared to do so when the Dow plunged 148 points and the FTSE100 lost 80 points on news of the first reported downgrades by the rating agencies of a swathe of bonds backed by subprime mortgages. Concerns were also growing over the likely impact of the US housing slowdown on consumer spending, as retail sales for June fell by 0.9% against expectations of a 0.1% rise, DIY retailer **Home Depot** cut its profit forecast, and leading house builder **D.R. Horton** reported a 40% drop in third quarter sales orders. The dollar also slumped, taking the euro to a record high of $1.38, and the pound to its highest level since 1981 at $2.03. Even the yen rallied as the dollar lurched lower, a move that prompted some unwinding of carry trade positions.

However, this mood of despondency endured for less than 48 hours, and investor euphoria returned as **Rio Tinto** launched a $38 billion cash bid for **Alcan**, the Canadian aluminium producer, a move which sent other mines higher on expectations of further consolidation within the industry. Blue-chips led the advance in the Dow as second quarter earnings came in on target for **Alcoa** and **General Electric**, while **Exxon Mobil** was boosted by higher oil prices and all three stocks registered 52-week highs. On the NASDAQ, **Google** and **Apple** both reached new all-time highs, while the Dow was now above 13,900, looking set for an onslaught on the 14000 level. On the home front, after topping 6700 again, the FTSE100 went into retreat as investors began 'fretting about rates' when the fall in the inflation figure for June was much less than expected, and Ernst & Young blamed higher interest rates for the highest level of profit warnings in UK companies since 2001.

The Dow duly topped 14000 intraday on 17th July but ended the day only 20 points up at 13,971, with buyers influenced by disappointing earnings from **Yahoo** and **Intel** and also by **Bear Stearns'** admission that its two troubled hedge funds were now of 'little value'. The FTSE100 continued to find life above 6700 difficult to maintain despite the arrival of the long-awaited offer for Sainsbury with a £12 billion price tag from Qatar's Delta Two, the sight of **Barclays** and **The Royal Bank of Scotland**-led consortium battling for control of ABN Amro, and private equity group, Terra Firma, vying with Warner Music to buy **EMI**.

Downfall

It was not until the last week of July that the now familiar problems in the credit markets moved to centre stage, as high profile deal after deal was reported to be in trouble. Equity investors now realised that if the banks funding KKR's buy-out of **Alliance Boots** could be left with £5 billion of the loan still on their books, then they would not be keen to look at any more leveraged buy-outs (LBOs) for a very long time. The same situation had arisen in the US, where the banks behind Cerberus' $20 billion financing for the purchase of **Chrysler** were forced to postpone the sale of $12 billion of debt after it failed to attract buyers. **Cadbury Schweppes** also had to shelve its plan to sell its American soft drinks business as once eager prospective buyers now struggled to raise the £7 billion purchase price.

The implications for the stock market were clear: If the LBO boom was over, then one of the equity market's principal props that had boosted stock values in the belief that every company was a potential bid target, had been removed. Stocks that had been the subject of recent takeover speculation were hit hard and led the markets down. Brewing and leisure group, **Whitbread** lost 20%, and brewer, **Mitchells & Butlers**, 10%. By the end of the month, the FTSE100 at 6215.2 had lost 500 points from its mid-July peak, and the Dow stood at 13211, compared with its record high of 14017 touched two weeks earlier. Over the same period, Japan's Nikkei Dow lost 1000 points, and emerging markets, many of which had reached record highs only days before, fell sharply.

Just to emphasise investors' reawakened desire to find a safe haven, a weak dollar provided no disincentive for buying US 10-year T-bonds, where the yield dropped from 5.18% to 4.77%. US Treasury Secretary Hank Paulson was quoted as saying that 'we are seeing a reassessment of risk…leading to a market adjustment'. He went on to add that the re-pricing of risk was 'healthy' but that the process would take a little while to make its way through the economy; a judgement no doubt influenced by the existence of a backlog of bond and loan deals agreed by the US banks estimated to amount to some $300 billion on top of around $40 billion already sitting on their books.

Countdown

The bulls took heart from the apparent fact that global growth remained strong and that corporate balance sheets and earnings prospects were healthy, but the July sell-off alarmed a number of fund managers, tempting them to revise their May forecasts of a new peak for the FTSE100 by the end of the year and instead look for a fall of between 10% and 14% from current levels. The prevailing view was that tighter lending standards and the widening of capital spreads resulting from the credit crisis could pose a significant risk to the growth outlook, thus endangering another of the stock market's props. But the real fear was that the abrupt loss of the liquidity on which the private equity groups and the hedge funds had thrived through the creation of a huge derivative credit market, estimated by the BIS to total some $400 trillion, meant that the whole financial system could now be at risk. Following the Bear Stearns debacle, investors were not only wary of taking on new commitments but also looking with deep suspicion at the paper they already had on their books. The rating agencies were now very much in the firing line for bestowing the coveted and confidence inspiring triple-A ratings on structured products created out of subprime loans. The downgrading procedure upon which they had embarked could force the sale of these collateralised debt obligations (CDOs) by banks which had held such AAA-rated paper as a substitute for capital required under the new international banking regulations. And if a top Wall Street investment bank, and one known to be a specialist in high yield bonds could run into trouble, then on the "there's never only one cockroach" principle, there could be a lot of bad news still to come. Given the effect that the initial bad news had already had on markets, a continuing run of failures was considered by some analysts to have the potential to inflict further damage to investor confidence, leading to even steeper stock market falls. Moreover, they thought that the Federal Reserve which had stepped in and restored confidence with the rescue of pioneer hedge fund Long-Term Capital Management back in the autumn of 1998, would find it difficult to stage a repeat performance now that there was such a proliferation of hedge funds, all deeply enmeshed in the financial and corporate systems. In the words of one analyst, 'This time around, there's no one minding the store'.

Further bad news was not long in coming. A brief rally in London and Wall Street in the opening days of August was quickly snuffed out by the news that **American Home Mortgage** could no longer offer home loans after lenders cut its credit lines. Then another mortgage provider, **Accredited Home Lenders**, expressed doubt that it could continue to operate as a result of adverse conditions in the subprime market; Australia's top investment bank **Macquarie** reported that two of its hedge funds were likely to post subprime-induced losses; and private German bank **IKB** had to be bailed out by a group of banks after incurring heavy losses from investing in the subprime market. One writer suggested that this contagion was akin to the environmental damage to host countries caused by the introduction of alien species like American bullfrogs and Japanese knotweed! Reassuring statements from the

Federal Reserve chairman, Ben Bernanke, to the effect that subprime mortgage woes were contained and that the housing slowdown would not prove to be a drag on the rest of the US economy, were treated with a 'they would say that, wouldn't they?' cynicism, and after another rally, the second week of August saw the slide continuing as news from European banks showed that US problems were anything but 'contained'. France's biggest bank, **BNP Paribas**, announced that it was suspending withdrawals from three of its funds invested in subprime-related bonds, saying 'the complete evaporation of liquidity in certain segments of the US securitisation market has made it impossible to value certain assets fairly, regardless of their quality or credit rating'. All eyes were now on the central banks to see what action they would take to calm markets. The Federal Reserve duly obliged by injecting $38 billion into the system to 'provide liquidity to facilitate the orderly functioning of financial markets'. The ECB followed suit with an emergency injection of €95 billion and then another €61 billion two days later. The object of the intervention was to bring overnight interest rates back down to the levels the central banks had set as conducive to growth and low inflation, i.e. 5.25% in the US and 4.00% in Europe. By contrast the Bank of England considered intervention unnecessary and took no action. Most commentators were in agreement that while there was an apparent contradiction between providing whatever liquidity was needed to avert a credit crunch and longer-term counter-inflationary monetary policies, the present action was an imperative and not an option, given that risk aversion had created a blockage in the free flow of money between financial institutions in the US and Europe.

As August progressed the news became steadily worse. **Countrywide**, America's biggest mortgage provider, revealed that it had been forced to call on an $11.5 billion credit line from a 40 bank consortium to stay in business. Goldman Sachs injected $3 billion ($2 billion of its own money plus $1 billion from friendly investors) to shore up its flagship quant hedge fund, **Global Equity Opportunities**, following a loss of $1.5 billion, thus reducing the fund's gearing from six times to three and a half times. And US money management group, **Sentinel**, suspended withdrawals from its $1.5 billion fund. Equity markets now responded to the growing sense of crisis by staging their biggest drop since March 2003. On 16th August, the FTSE100 fell 250 points to close at 5858.9, while the Dow plunged over 300 points at one stage during the day before rallying on rumours of an imminent interest rate cut by the Federal Reserve to close at 12845, down just 15 points. European markets also had a bad day, with the Eurofirst 300 index recording a one-session loss of 51 points, its largest since March 2003, taking it down to 1440. But it was the emerging markets that suffered most, with many Asian exchanges taking their biggest hit since September 2001, simultaneously killing off the idea that the sound economic fundamentals of the region would protect it from troubles in the West. As one *FT* writer pointed out, the world still waits on Wall Street, and as well as being the epicentre of global growth, the US is also the epicentre of global risk. Currencies of emerging economies also tumbled to the benefit of the Japanese yen, thus creating more potential losses for speculators as carry trades were unwound, and debt spreads over US T-bonds widened to their highest since December 2005.

As equity markets tumbled, investors fled to the safety of government bonds and the yield on US 10-year Treasuries fell to 4.60%. With the falls in global stock markets now the lead item on TV news bulletins and headlines in national newspapers, action by the authorities was clearly required, and the Federal Reserve duly obliged on the next trading day, offering a degree of relief by cutting its discount rate to banks from 6.25% to 5.75%, adding that it 'was prepared to act as needed to mitigate the adverse effects on the economy arising from the disruption of financial markets'. This statement was widely interpreted as signalling that the Federal Reserve was ready to cut its key Fed Funds rate. **Bank of America** boosted confidence further by taking a $2 billion stake in **Countrywide**. Global markets soared. The FTSE100 now demonstrated the unprecedented level of volatility in stock market trading by following its biggest one-day fall in four years with its biggest one-day rise over the same period, plussing 205.3 to 6064.2. The Dow climbed an impressive 234 points to 13079, while the S&P500 added 34 to 1445. Asian markets had closed before news of the discount rate cut and continued their decline, with Tokyo recording its biggest daily loss of 875 points since 9/11, taking the Nikkei Dow 225 down to 15273.

The final week of August saw calm of a sort return to markets, but a number of commentators thought this was just the calm before the return of the storm. The rescue of a second German bank, **Sachsen LB**, with an injection of €17.3 billion, after its off-balance sheet 'conduit', **Ormond Quay**, had found itself unable to continue to fund its higher yielding investments by finding buyers for its asset-backed commercial paper (ABCP), sent tremors through the whole banking system. Use of such vehicles had grown dramatically over the past decade and with an estimated global ABCP market totalling $1.2 trillion, the exposure of their sponsoring banks pledged to support them with credit lines, was clearly a matter of concern not just for the banking industry but for the world economy. More worrying still, was that the early success of the operations carried out by these 'conduits' during the good times had spawned the creation of other 'structured investment vehicles' (SIVs), more highly geared and investing in riskier assets, mainly high-yielding US mortgage-related securities. Such SIVs commonly employed leverage of twelve to fifteen times, but always ready to try to make a good thing better (or 'go for broke' in this case), the banks had then devised SIV-lites, with fewer diversification restrictions and the ability to boost leverage to forty to seventy times collateral. Rumours that Merrill Lynch's attempts at selling mortgage-backed bonds from Bear Stearns' stricken funds back in June had realised no more than 11 cents in the dollar, did not bode well for future liquidations. A report in the *Financial Times* that Barclays Capital's involvement in the sponsoring of SIVs meant that it could be exposed to losses of 'hundreds of millions of dollars' if the vehicles were unable to obtain short-term financing by issuing commercial paper, were vigorously denied by the bank which said it was 'flush with liquidity'. But the denial failed to stem concerns about the state of its finances when it was revealed that it had extended a

$1.4 billion credit facility to one of its SIV-lite creations for Cairn Capital, a London-based hedge fund, and had taken out an emergency £1.6 billion overnight loan from the Bank of England, a week after borrowing £314 million from the discount window. One veteran financial writer was tempted to recall the Bank of England's statement in November 1974, that National Westminster had never requested or been offered large scale support as its share price fell below par in the wake of the secondary banking crisis.

Waiting on Wall Street

All eyes were now on September, post the Labour Day holiday in the US, by which time the senior operatives of the investment banks and brokerage houses were expected to be back in the driving seat. Trading volumes had been low in August and almost at Christmas Eve levels, a situation which had led to sharp and perhaps unrepresentative movements in stock prices. At least, that was the view of the more optimistic of market observers like Morgan Stanley's strategists who rated UK equities a 'buy', and those from Cazenove who regarded their outlook as 'weighted heavily to the upside' over the next twelve months. Other observers looked at the central banks' attempts to control the situation and avoid financial panic by flooding the markets with short-term liquidity and lowering the cost for banks borrowing from the discount window, and found them wanting. Money markets had been stabilised only temporarily, and the real test would come with the $370 billion of ABCP requiring funding in September, along with a similar amount of LBO paper. If all this paper had to stay on the banks' balance sheets, then their lending policies would be greatly restricted, as normal lending to customers, both corporate and consumer, was 'crowded out'. Many debt products remained frozen, interbank borrowing rates were still high and buying of US Treasury bonds in pursuit of a 'safety first' policy continued to depress yields. The first test of the money markets in September was reckoned to be the financing of the $22 billion leveraged loan required for the buy-out of credit card processing company, **First Data**.

However, many commentators saw the recovery in world stock markets since their mid-August plunge as a sign that the worst of the credit crisis was over, believing that the actions taken by the central banks led by the US Federal Reserve would quickly restore order to the markets. After all, the governor of the Bank of England had seen no need to intervene, simply pointing out that its standing facilities were always available for banks to borrow however much they wanted, albeit at penalty rates. And the Fed had not been panicked into a rate cut in August at the height of the credit crisis but was content to monitor the situation and take what action it deemed to be necessary at its next scheduled meeting.

This relatively comfortable view of the markets received a rude shock at the end of the first week of October, when the US non-farm payroll data revealed 4,000 job losses for August against an expected gain of 110,000 together with downward revisions for June and July. While notoriously volatile and open to a wide margin of error, the figures are hugely influential on markets and the Dow dived 250 points with the FTSE100 falling 122 in sympathy. The job loss figure was the first negative one in four years and since it covered a period pre-dating most of the credit crisis, it was taken to suggest an economic downturn and thus the certainty of a rate cut by the Fed on 18th September. Stock markets recovered on the prospect but now it was the turn of London to be in for a shock, when the Bank of England revealed that it was to provide emergency funding to mortgage lender **Northern Rock** to enable it to carry on operating.

Northern Rock shares reacted by losing 33p to 639p, to record a decline of 50% from their February peak. Worse was to come as the bank's customers responded to the news of the bailout by queuing at its 76 branches to withdraw their savings; a crisis of confidence which dragged down shares in other banks on fears that the liquidity crunch might not be confined to Northern Rock. Since all mortgage lenders no longer rely on investors' deposits to fund their business but also tap the wholesale money market, in effect borrowing short to lend long, they are pursuing a strategy that relies on guaranteed access to short-term funding. Far more reliant on wholesale funding than any other mortgage lender, the business plan had driven Northern Rock's rapid expansion but also put it at far greater risk than its rivals.

The company's chief executive had issued a profits warning in June after admitting that it had been 'caught out' by rising short-term rates, but in September he was forced to further admit that 'every single market froze' when access to both the 3-month and overnight markets was denied, leaving the Bank of England to fulfil its role as 'lender of last resort'. The situation now proved to be an embarrassment for the Bank of England, which earlier had taken a principled stand against bailing out banks that had got into trouble as a result of pursuing high-risk strategies, therefore creating so-called "moral hazard" by encouraging the belief that such practises could be safely continued given the implied assurance that the central bank would mount a rescue. The Bank was also criticised for not having acted earlier, on the grounds that covert assistance to Northern Rock at the beginning of the month could have avoided the high-profile rescue and the first run on a bank in the country since 1866. The next day saw further turmoil in the markets as **Alliance & Leicester**, the other mortgage lender reckoned to be most reliant on the wholesale market, fell a precipitous 30% in the final hour of trading.

Fortunately, help was at hand and a dangerously volatile situation was calmed by the intervention of the new Chancellor of the Exchequer, Alistair Darling, who in a national television broadcast made a verbal guarantee that not only Northern Rock's but all UK bank deposits were 100% safe. Bank shares rallied sharply, with **Alliance & Leicester** recovering the whole of the previous day's loss, and the FTSE100 extended its rally, adding 100 points to 6283.3. This move was aided by a dramatic 336 point gain in the Dow in response to a half percentage point cut in the key Fed Funds interest rate to 4.75%, designed 'to help forestall some of the adverse effects on the broader economy that might otherwise result from the disruption in financial markets'. The discount rate at which the US central bank lends directly to banks was also cut by 50 basis points.

Federal Reserve chairman Ben Bernanke now received all the plaudits denied to Bank of England chairman, Mervyn King. That the Fed had opted for a half point cut in both the Fed funds and the discount rate instead of the expected quarter was widely welcomed as having a positive psychological impact on markets by demonstrating its determination to 'act as needed' to head off the risk of a slowdown in the US economy. Inevitably, comparisons were made with the actions of the previous Federal Reserve chairman, Alan Greenspan, on the occasion of the collapse of the hedge fund Long-Term Capital Management, in the autumn of 1998, but for every commentator who was prepared to criticise the Fed for riding in to rescue the markets, there were many more who saw it as the Fed's duty to do exactly that. Inaction was simply not an option in such an unprecedented situation and with no commitment made for the run of further rate cuts instituted by his predecessor post-1998, Ben Bernanke still had all his options open. It was at this point that the Bank of England also felt compelled to act and injected £10 billion into the banking system.

By the end of September, stock markets in New York and London were close to matching their mid-July peaks, while those in Asia were setting new records. Investors apparently regarded equities as a one-way bet and were happy to buy on bad news as well as good. The jury was still out over the question of whether or not a slowdown in the US economy was underway and the bulls were greatly encouraged by the September jobs data, which not only showed a 110,000 gain but also revised the August 4,000 job losses figure, which had so upset the markets, to an 89,000 gain. And in any case, they insisted, if the economy does start to slow, then the rest of the world – led by China – can make up for it as a falling dollar boosted the earning of US exporters and multinationals. Admittedly, the big global investment banks were taking severe hits, with losses and writedowns totalling some $18 billion in the wake of the credit crunch, but seemingly 'a billion ain't what it used to be' (to quote Nelson Bunker Hunt on the losses resulting from his failed attempt to corner the silver market), and their shares rose on the assumption that the worst was over.

Of course, the US housing slump was still a worry but the September retail sales figures showed that consumer spending remained buoyant. Even the M&A market was showing signs of revival, with deals being done again, sparking share price rises on rumours of yet more deals. As for the leveraged loans from deals past and pending supposedly clogging up the balance sheets of the big banks, they were beginning to be placed, albeit with new covenants as the balance of power shifted back from borrowers to lenders. Indeed, everything pointed to a return to business as usual, until mid-October when the impending anniversary of the Crash of 1987 reawakened fears of a repeat performance given the similarity of the background. Equity markets then had been at record levels after a seven-year bull market, banks were stuffed with massive underwriting commitments in the wake of a run of high-profile takeover deals, computerised trading was making its debut, the US current account deficit was a big concern and the dollar was in freefall. Veteran financial journalists were keen to draw parallels and to stress that in October 2007, investors also had to worry about a runaway oil price (the trigger for the 1972/1975 bear market), a practically permanent crisis in Iraq, and a potentially explosive situation in Iran. Their fears appeared to have been given substance on 19th October, when US construction industry bellwether **Caterpillar** made a downward revision of its 2007 earnings estimates and warned that a number of industries it served were already in recession.

Wall Street's financials added to the gloom, with **Bank of America** revealing a 32% fall in third quarter earnings and a $2 billion provision for credit losses, while **Citigroup** reported a 57% drop as losses and writedowns topped $3 billion. The Dow slumped 366 points to 13,522, tipping the FTSE100 into an 81.5 point slide to 6527, leaving it down 200 on the week. An 8.5% slide in India's BSE Sensex to 17,559 on the introduction of restrictions on Foreign Investment Institutions (FIIs) using offshore derivatives to buy Indian stocks, was seen by some commentators as evidence that this star of the emerging markets was not necessarily a one-way bet, any more than was China.

Back to reality

However, once again investors seemed determined to place their faith in the ability of the Federal Reserve to cure all economic ills, and shares rallied strongly on confident expectations of another rate cut at the next meeting of its members on the last day of the month. The fact that markets were rising in the face of ever-worsening news on the US housing front, fears of further credit losses on Wall Street following Merrill Lynch's increase in its writedown on mortgage-related securities from $4.5 billion to $8 billion, and a warning from the Bank of England about the 'vulnerability' of the UK financial sector to new shocks from the global credit squeeze, strongly suggested that this was a 'suckers' rally'.

Nevertheless, the announcement of a quarter point cut to 4.5% still saw the Dow rise 137 points to 13,930 and the FTSE100, 62.6 to 6721.6, just 10 points shy of June's seven-year peak. Then reality set in as investors took the view that 'the upside risks to inflation roughly balance the downside risks to growth', which meant that there might be no more rate cuts in prospect. Rumours that more financial institutions were soon to reveal big losses sent bank shares tumbling, along with those of bond insurers, prompting the Fed to inject $41 billion into the banking system, the largest single infusion since 9/11, in a bid to calm markets. **Citigroup**, the world's biggest bank, led the sector down, losing around 7% of its value as analysts calculated that as a result of heavy writedowns, it would have to find another $30 billion to shore up its capital position. Chief executive Chuck Prince resigned, joining Merrill Lynch's Stan O'Neal on the retirement list. This meant that the bosses of two of the world's leading financial companies based in the world's biggest economy and operating on a global scale had been forced to resign after presiding over trading losses and writedowns described by rating agency Standard & Poor's as 'staggering'.

The falling man

With the dollar plunging to record lows against the euro and the pound as oil and gold soared to new heights, the picture the US economy presented to the world was not one to inspire confidence, appearing to justify the observation of one analyst who saw the rise of emerging markets as evidence of 'a permanent shift in global economic leadership'. And just to underline the point, India's BSE Sensex was on the move again, crossing the 20,000 mark for the first time, while Hong Kong's Hang Seng surged decisively above the 30,000 level to a new record at 31,492.

If any thought that the effects of the credit squeeze might be limited to the financial sector had not been totally dismissed as a result of **Caterpillar's** statement, it certainly had to be a few days later when Cisco reported a 'dramatic decrease' in orders for its specialist equipment from US banks. Clearly, banks had quite enough problems of their own to deal with as a result of being over-accommodating in the past to over-ambitious entrepreneurs, as well as to their in-house, bonus-fixated hyperactive traders, and had no desire or now perhaps even the ability to become further involved; witness the ditching of Delta Two's planned acquisition of **Sainsbury** following its last minute inability to raise another £500 million to complete the £10.6 billion offer. It appeared obvious to many observers that a new ultra-conservative, risk-averse approach by banks to the lending of money would extend to the corporate and household sectors, inhibiting both business investment and consumer spending.

If the problems created by mortgage-backed securities had originated in the US, **BNP Paribas** and two German regional banks had demonstrated back in August that they were not going to be confined to that country. Since then, most of the bad news on writedowns and trading losses had featured the big American banks, and analysts were now eagerly awaiting reports from the principal UK banks due in late November and December. In the UK, **Northern Rock** had been the prime casualty to date, and given that its emergency funding from the Bank of England had already topped £20 billion, a figure greater than that reported by any US bank so far, this suggested that the fallout from the credit crunch was going to be much bigger than originally thought.

Then, in the first week of November, Swiss bank **UBS** recorded writedowns of $4.6 billion on leveraged loans and fixed income securities, with another $8 billion still to come according to one researcher, while **Credit Suisse** weighed in with a more modest loss of $1.9 billion, thanks to having heeded warning signs a year ago and reduced its exposure to subprime. Three days later, **Morgan Stanley** put the spotlight back on the US banking sector by announcing it would writedown assets linked to subprime by $3.7 billion, and warned that fourth quarter earnings would take a $2.5 billion hit. Stock markets reacted to the uncertainty over credit losses past and potential by falling sharply, and by the end of the first week in November, the FTSE100 was down to 6304 and the Dow almost to 13,000, with bank shares spearheading the falls accompanied by the formerly highly resilient technology stocks, spooked by fears of a slowdown in capital spending evidenced by the report from Cisco, widely regarded as the bellwether for this sector.

In London, rumours of large losses of up to £10 billion by **Barclays**, an emergency rights issue and the imminent departure of its chief executive, sent the bank's shares plunging by 10% at one point before recovering on the assurance that it was 'awash with liquidity'. Both **Barclays** and **RBS** had now lost 30% of their market value since early August. The only bright spot on the London market was produced by **BHP Billiton's** £70 billion bid for **RTZ**, a move which sparked a sympathetic rise in all the mining giants, temporarily boosting the FTSE100 given their heavy weighting in the index and their role as emerging market proxies.

One world

The extent of the falls in London and New York prompted some top slicing action by investors in Hong Kong and Mumbai, and tempted one observer to draw potential parallels for China and India with what had been happening in London and New York. The argument went that if the current frenetic pace of trading in complex financial instruments as well as ordinary stocks and shares had created a crisis in the two most sophisticated financial centres in the world, the trouble was bound to spread to the BRICs, where trading had been even more frenzied.

When the shares of **Alibaba**, China's biggest e-commerce company, could triple on their Hong Kong debut, and those of **PetroChina** could soar by 160% on the first day of dealing in Shanghai on just a 2% float, making it the world's biggest company by market value at $1,000 billion, equal to Exxon Mobil, Shell and BP combined, then something's gotta give! This sort of share price action spelled trouble wherever it took place, and in the context of a stock market that had risen sixfold in two years, history says instability goes with the territory. The writer recalled that in the second half of the 1980s, Japan was regarded as China is today, and the Nikkei Dow 225 rose fourfold to peak at just under 39,000 in December 1989. Eighteen years later the index stood at 15,583. The conclusion was that today's emerging markets were not guaranteed to provide the perfect hedge for troubled markets in the West.

Against such a background it was difficult to talk markets up, and while most commentators were ready to accept that a slowdown was underway in the US and in Europe, they also knew that governments were inhibited from providing a stimulus by cutting interest rates by signs of a build-up in inflationary pressures in the wake of an oil price approaching $100 a barrel and rising commodity prices, especially foodstuffs. There was also much debate over whether the counter-inflationary pressures arising from cheap goods imported from China were soon to ease, as China itself fell prey to inflation. Food prices there were already up 15% year on year, and producer prices for manufactured goods were up by more than 10% in response to rising metal prices and a 10% hike in the state-controlled price of diesel fuel. With consumer price inflation now topping 6%, much in line with benchmark lending rates which were also well below nominal GDP growth rates, would-be savers had every incentive to try their luck in their local equity markets, further inflating a bubble, the eventual and inevitable bursting of which was widely reckoned to have dire consequences for stock markets everywhere. The feeling was that in the global village decoupling was just a theory and that in practice it applied neither to economies nor to stock markets, and that the present apparent divergence was a strictly temporary phenomenon.

Here we go again

As November progressed, more evidence emerged of the damage caused to UK-based banks as a result of their involvement with subprime-mortgage-related structured credit products. **Barclays** revealed a £1.3 billion writedown, and **HSBC** reported that it had set aside $3.4 billion to cover bad debts in its US consumer finance arm, adding that its emerging market operations would not remain unaffected by the credit squeeze. The Bank of England's quarterly inflation report brought little comfort to the bulls by predicting that growth would 'slow sharply' next year as tighter credit conditions and a US slowdown hit UK consumer spending and business investment, and then warning that stock markets did not appear 'to have priced in the risks ahead'.

Fears of a house price crash in the UK following the pattern in the US were widely considered to be exaggerated, but there was no doubt that the housing market was in trouble judging from sharply lower mortgage applications and the fact that the country's biggest chain of estate agents, **Countrywide**, was closing down branches after being hit by a run of cancelled sales. Hopes of any relief for the US consumer were also fast disappearing. The October payroll data had given some encouragement but it was soon overshadowed by even more depressing news from the housing sector and disappointing reports from mainstream retailers, **J.C. Penney** and **Kohl's**, and a second profits warning from **FedEx**.

It was no surprise that stock markets in London and New York continued to slide, making November their worst month for years. The final week had seen a strong rally based on interest rate cut hopes, but at 6432, the FTSE100 had lost 4.37%, dragged down by falling share prices of **Northern Rock**, the big banks, housebuilders, pubs and retailers, while the Dow and the S&P500 were down 4.4% to log their worst monthly performance in five years. As far as the US was concerned, the two measures instituted for ameliorating the credit crunch and the housing crisis, namely the Treasury-sponsored $100 billion bail-out fund set up by US banks to acquire the most credit worthy assets of orphan SIVs and the 'Hope Now Alliance' scheme to rescue embattled homeowners by delaying mortgage rate rises, had done nothing to allay investors' fears. Interbank lending rates had been rising again since mid-November, topping the crisis levels of August, undiminished by the Fed's two rate cuts and injections of liquidity into the money markets by the Bank of England and the European Central Bank, and fears were growing that the monetary crisis would have an increasingly adverse effect on the real economy.

What lies beneath

Almost daily reports were surfacing of the damage being caused to holders of mortgage-related securities across the world. Ireland's **International Securities Trading Corporation (ISTC)**, a lender to financial institutions, was forced to seek interim protection after a downgrading of its SIV assets resulted in a €70 million writedown and a liquidity crisis which made it unable to write a cheque to repay a €176,000 loan. In Norway, the investment arm of **Terra-Gruppen**, a collection of 80 regional savings banks, declared bankruptcy after its licence was revoked by regulators for failing to inform four small townships of the high risks attached to $84 million of their investments in structured products devised by **Citigroup**. And in Florida, school and municipal officials found themselves short of money to pay staff and utility bills after access to their investment pool was denied following a run of withdrawals from investors alerted to the fact that it had invested several billion dollars in subprime products. Clearly, 'something must be done', and only another rate cut by the Fed would do the trick.

Much the same touching faith in the power of central bankers appeared to apply in the UK, where the clamour was growing for the Bank of England to act in the face of ever more evidence of distress in the domestic economy. And if the task of keeping inflation under control was high on central bankers' list of priorities – and one made more difficult by a falling dollar and record oil, food and other commodity prices – it now had to take second place to that of avoiding the risk of a collapse of the monetary system, with all that that would entail for economies everywhere. In such circumstances, inflation risk seemed to be very much the lesser of two evils, and in any case if a slowdown was already underway, even outright recession, then inflationary pressures would slacken without the need for policy decisions. In confident expectation that the Bank of England would lower base rates for the first time in two years at the next meeting of its Monetary Policy Committee, the FTSE100 quickly made up much of the ground lost in November.

On December 8th, the Bank duly obliged with a quarter point cut to 5.5%, accompanied by the injection of another £10 billion of funds into the money market. The decision was justified by reference to 'slowing growth and the tightening of credit to households and business', and most commentators were confident that this was the first of a series of easings to be continued in quarter point steps in February and May 2008 and beyond. Two days earlier the Bank of Canada had surprised markets with a quarter point cut to 4.25%, but it was no surprise that the European Central Bank held firm at 4%, citing strong upside inflationary pressures for its decision. The Fed was confidently expected to cut rates again at its 11th December meeting, but following their strong run in the first week of December, equity markets paused, suggesting that a move was already well discounted.

Also contributing to the pause was Swiss investment bank **UBS's** announcement that it had written down its subprime-related investments by another $10 billion, a figure greatly in excess of that indicated a month earlier, and clearly a warning of further shocks to come from the banking sector. The **Royal Bank of Scotland's** £1.2 billion writedown was greeted with relief by markets and the shares actually rose – a strange reaction in the opinion of those commentators who tended to agree with Mervyn King that the stock market had not yet woken up to the seriousness of the credit crisis. However, it was already clear that the resilience of the FTSE100 at 6500 plus was more apparent than real, bolstered as it was by heavyweight miners in the middle of a wave of consolidation and classic defensive large cap stocks, and a truer picture of market sentiment was presented by the more domestically oriented MidCaps in the FTSE250, down 14.2% from its May record high and down 4.8% since the beginning of the year.

The quarter point cut in Fed Funds was greeted on the floor of the New York Stock Exchange by boos from traders who had hoped for a half point reduction. The stock market's reaction saw the Dow lose just short of 300 points to 13,432, recover almost all of that at the opening next day, reverse into a 111 point loss and end the day up 41. Clearly, markets did not know whether they were coming or going, a state of affairs which persisted when 24 hours later a consortium of central banks led by the Fed mounted a joint assault on liquidity problems by injecting another $60 billion into the money markets in a bid to unfreeze the credit logjam; something that simple interest rate cuts had not been able to do.

Sovereign wealth funds, which had no liquidity problems, now began to play their part in the drama. Abu Dhabi contributed $7.5 billion for a stake in **Citigroup**, the Singapore government bought a 9% stake in UBS for $11.5 billion, and an anonymous Middle Eastern investor chipped in another $7.5 billion, moves which attracted xenophobic comment in some quarters. On the self-help front, Citigroup took back on to its own books $49 billion of SIVs, following the example of **HSBC**, which two weeks before had reclaimed responsibility for $45 billion of its structured debt instruments. Meanwhile, the **Northern Rock** affair dragged on, but the queue of potential bidders began to thin as the task of raising the many billions of pounds required for the rescue became more difficult. Nationalisation now seemed the most likely option.

Money makes the world go round

Expectations of the traditional Christmas rally were fading fast and as markets sank, more attention began to be paid to the origins of the credit crisis. It was difficult to avoid the conclusion that the real problem was rooted in an over dependence on borrowed money, a facility that had now become severely restricted. As one writer observed, if money makes the world go round, then lack of it is going to slow things down and a knock-on effect for the economy was inevitable. He went on to point out that if the 'securitisation' or the bundling of mortgages, credit card balances and car loans, i.e. any product with a supposedly predictable cashflow, into tradeable packages, had brought the benefits of credit to many more businesses and individuals, essentially it was simply 'monetisation of debt', a process of financial alchemy which transmuted one man's debit into another man's credit. The result had been the creation of an alternative or shadow banking system, largely undisciplined and unregulated, and as such beyond the control of the central banks. Hence, the inability of central bank-inspired interest rate moves and liquidity injections to bring general rates into line with their policy objectives. The clear and present danger now was the threat to the stability of the traditional banking system posed, Frankenstein-like, by its own creation. The asset-backed commercial paper market was virtually paralysed, a state of affairs capable of spelling disaster for those parts of the corporate sector which relied upon it for their short-term financing needs and at the same time burdening the banks with unlooked for financial commitments if they were forced to step into the breach. Even more serious was the potential nightmare scenario arising from the problems of the bond insurers in the shape of counterparty risk. If corporate defaults start to rise as the recession kicks in, what is going to happen if the cash-strapped insurers are unable to keep their end of the bargain?

More massive injections of liquidity into the money markets by the world's central banks coupled with further contributions by sovereign wealth funds to the coffers of America's biggest banks, heartened investors in the three days leading up to Christmas and a rally of sorts was staged. However, the sheer size of the European Central Bank's intervention at $500 billion, or twice the amount originally estimated to be required, served to underline the seriousness of the credit crisis and to diminish the hope that banks would cease to hoard liquidity and capital. Similarly, the news that the China Investment Corporation had pumped $5 billion into **Morgan Stanley** following the bank's increase in its previously estimated writedowns to $9.4 billion, and that **Merrill Lynch** was looking to the Singapore government for a $5 billion boost to its capital reserves, rang alarm bells for one commentator who saw the rescue of the biggest financial institutions of the Western democracies by the sovereign wealth funds of authoritarian, even despotic, regimes as a more extreme example of 'moral hazard', and as far as China was concerned, a huge 'loss of face' for the West.

No Christmas cheer

The pre-Christmas rally proved unable to progress beyond the festival, as markets were forced to digest more bad news on the US housing front along with scaled-up estimates of the losses likely to be incurred by US banks as the subprime crisis continued to unfold. And then on 27th December, they had to face the sharp escalation in geopolitical risks arising from the assassination of Benazir Bhutto on the eve of the Pakistani election, an event that raised serious concerns about the future leadership of the world's second largest Muslim nation, moreover one possessing a nuclear arsenal. As such, Pakistan now took precedence over Iraq and Iran as the top potential flashpoint in the Middle East. The prospect of heightened instability in the region prompted an immediate flight to the perceived 'safe haven' instruments of gold, up $7 to $827 an ounce, and to US Treasury bonds, where the yield on the 10-year issue fell to 4.10%, while the price of oil reversed its recent short-term down trend and mounted a renewed assault on the $100 mark. Equities in New York and London recorded only modest falls, but this time around, the performance was shared by former high-flying emerging markets, which on so many previous occasions in 2007 had soared to new peaks as Western markets fell.

Nevertheless, emerging markets were still the outstanding winners over the year, led by Brazil, Russia and India, all up over 70%, closely followed by Turkey and China, up 66% and 63% respectively, but perhaps it should be noted that China's Shanghai Composite, arguably the most important market index, was 11.7% down from its early November peak along with Hong Kong's Hang Seng index, which was 13% down over the same period. As usual, Japan disappointed its many fans and with a loss of 10.5% became the worst performer among the Asian markets, a state of affairs widely blamed on the political and economic mismanagement of the post-Koizumi administration. By contrast the yen rose dramatically against the dollar in the last six months of the year, a move which did no favours for Japan's exporters. However, a rising yen was also regarded as bearish in a wider context in that by sharply diminishing the attractions of the 'carry trade', it had the effect of reducing the flow of investment funds into world markets.

While not performing as poorly as Japan, US and European markets were still very much at the bottom of the league tables. The Dow at 13,365 was up 7% over the course of the year but still well off its peak of over 14,000, touched on 9th October, a performance matched by the S&P500, up 5% on the year at 1478 but still well short of the October peak. Boosted by the strong recovery in technology stocks, the NASDAQ Composite did better than both by recording a gain of 10.7%. London's showing with the FTSE100 up 4.1% at 6476.9 was widely recognised as a façade, obscuring sharply disparate performances between sectors and owing the fact that it was up at all entirely to gains in the heavily weighted Mining, Oil and Gas and Utility sectors compensating for significant losses among Banks, Retailers and Properties. The Eurofirst 300 index plussed just 1.5% to 1506, but Germany's DAX stood out from the pack with a 22% rise as investors bought into the restructuring story.

Whither 2008?

There was little doubt that the assassination of Benazir Bhutto added an extra element of uncertainty to any calculation of the course of the markets in 2008, a task already difficult enough in the context of the ongoing credit crisis that had been largely unforeseen and yet had betrayed the best hopes for 2007. The Lex column had been remarkably prescient at the start of the year, warning of 'a year of reckoning in credit markets', a pronouncement adding credibility to its view of how 2008 would turn out. The column's opinion was that given the swift action by the banks in writing down the book value of their questionable credit exposure, the timely interest rate cuts by central bankers in the US and the UK, the strong state of profits and balance sheets in the corporate sector coupled with substantial capital injections into Western banks from Asian and Middle Eastern investors, then the banking system should survive and recession be avoided.

However, the caveat was added that if US house prices continued to slide and the downtrend in corporate profits steepened, then banks and the real economy would be 'in a whole lot of trouble'. The opinions of the panels of investment professionals aired in the financial press were broadly split between the bears who saw Lex's caveat as a done deal, and the perennial bulls with a vested interest in a rising market, although in the latter case none was looking for a gain of more than 10% in the FTSE100 to 7200 with most forecasts clustered in the 6500 to 6800 range.

As for the UK economy, a belated appreciation by commentators of the rapid fading of the last decade's so-called 'economic miracle' as current account and budget deficits rose alarmingly tended to cause many of them to back the bears' arguments. One of them was even tempted to say that given the economy's over reliance on the financial services as the main driver of growth, its decline in the wake of the credit crunch as evidenced by a 21% fall in the Bank index should be mirrored in the FTSE100. Add in oil over $100 a barrel, headline inflation boosted by soaring food and energy prices, a falling dollar, the pound at a record low against the euro, and fortune would seem to favour the bears in 2008. And only the most ardent of contrarians would have been heartened by the *Financial Times'* headline in its first issue of the New Year: 'Outlook worst since dotcom bust.'

"If I mistake not, the distress of the year 1857 was produced by an enemy more formidable than hostile armies; by a pestilence more deadly than fever or plague; by a visitation more destructive than the frosts of Spring or the blights of Summer. I believe it was caused by a mountain load of Debt. The whole country, individuals and communities, trading houses, corporations, towns, cities, States, were labouring under a weight of debt beneath which the ordinary business relations of the country were, at length, arrested, and the great instrument usually employed for carrying them on, Credit, broken down."

Edward Everett on the Crisis of 1857

2008

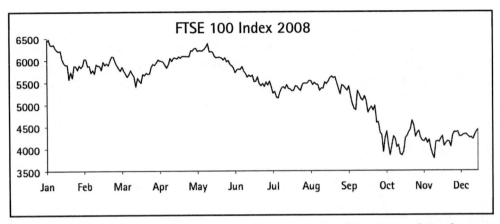

FTSE 100 Index 2008

Source: Thomson Reuters Datastream

There will be blood!

"As goes January, so goes the year", is an old market adage which despite its doubtful provenance provided no "quantum of solace" for the bulls after the FTSE100 lost 130 points (or 2%) to 6348.5 in the first four trading days of the new year. The MidCaps fared even worse, losing 3.7%. The supposed trigger for the falls was further evidence that the US was on the edge of recession, in the form of a record low for home sales for November 2007, payroll data showing a gain of just 18,000 jobs against expectations of one of over 70,000 and the unemployment rate rising to 5% from 4.7%. The news saw the Dow lose 565 points to 12800, the S&P500, 67 points to 1411, and only the price of gold and oil recorded gains. Another rate cut by the Fed before the end of the month was widely considered to be a certainty, an expectation contributing to a further weakening of the dollar.

Worse was soon to come and in particular disappointing reports from the UK retail sector led to extraordinarily high percentage falls in individual stocks. Thus **Marks & Spencer's** announcement that year on year sales had fallen 2.2% in the fourth quarter saw the shares slip below 400p compared with 560p at the beginning of the month and a high of 759p in June 2007. **DSG** (Dixons and Currys) issued a profits warning and the shares slumped 25% to 75p, while **Land of Leather's** share price halved on a warning that profits would fall 'significantly below' expectations. In fact, any company with a "consumer" tag represented the kiss of death for its share price.

As the month wore on, equity markets continued to slide under the influence of a never-ending flow of bad news, unbuoyed by further massive sovereign wealth fund cash injections to shore up the finances of America's big banks, home-grown rescue operations like **Bank of America's** buyout of the rest of **Countrywide**, and hopes of

439

interest rate cuts by the central banks. On this last point, both the Bank of England and the European Central Bank disappointed markets by holding rates steady at 5.5% and 4.0% respectively, failing to react to criticism that they were both 'behind the curve' in not recognising that recession was now a bigger threat than inflation. The Federal Reserve was regarded as a more politicised institution and no one doubted that a rate cut was a certainty at its next meeting at the end of January, especially since Ben Bernanke had already pledged 'substantive additional action as needed to support growth'.

Another Black Monday

However, no one was expecting the worldwide plunge in equity markets that supposedly triggered a 0.75% cut to 3.5%, ten days ahead of schedule. Markets had been falling in the weeks preceding Monday 21st January taking the FTSE100 to below 6000 and the Dow almost back to 12000, but a copycat rout in Asia led to unprecedented falls across Europe and the rest of the world as soon as markets opened on that day. The FTSE100 lost 323.5 points or 5.5% to 5578.2, recording its biggest one-day points fall since the index began in 1983, the Eurofirst 300 slumped 5.8%, Hong Kong's Hang Seng shed 5%, and falls of similar magnitude were seen on stock markets everywhere. India's BSE Sensex, which had soared to a new high of over 21000 against the trend earlier in the month, lost over 2000 points during the day, triggering circuit breakers and demonstrations outside the Exchange calling for the resignation of the Minister of Finance! Wall Street had been closed for a public holiday, and forecasts of a 500 point fall when it reopened on Tuesday were widely believed to have prompted the Fed's action, especially since the announcement was made before the opening bell. Any thought that the Fed had saved the day quickly evaporated as the Dow plunged an initial 465 points to 11634 before rallying to end the day down 128 at 11971. The FTSE100 had more ground to make up and replaced a 240 point loss with a 161.9 gain by the end of the day to close at 5740.1.

The Fed Chairman's accompanying statement that 'broader financial conditions have continued to deteriorate and credit has tightened' and that 'appreciable downside risks remain', was taken as an indication that more rate cuts were on the way, even as soon as the end of January meeting. Most commentators saw the events of the past few days as evidence that equity markets had at last woken up to the severity of the credit crisis and to the fact that it would inevitably affect every aspect of economic life. They also saw them as debunking any idea of 'decoupling' after the falls had left Shanghai's main index 26% off its October high, and Hong Kong's Hang Seng down 32% over the same period.

The Fed's move had taken many observers by surprise but most were ready to accept that given the dangers facing the world economy, the Fed had to risk being accused of overreacting rather than of not reacting at all. The fact that Ben Bernanke had endorsed the President's call for a $140 billion stimulus package of tax breaks revived hopes in some quarters that recession might be avoided, but most saw it as a palliative and not a cure in the context of a credit crisis which had still to run its course.

Société Générale surprises

There were still some surprises to come before the end of "The Week that Shook the World", principally the revelation by Société Générale that a rogue trader had run up losses of €5 billion. The fact that the bank had failed to notify the Federal Reserve of the situation and that its dealers had spent Black Monday unravelling positions to crystallise losses, was eagerly seized upon by investors as being the reason for the dramatic falls that day. Further encouragement was provided by plans to recapitalise the bond insurers to the tune of $15 billion and avoid a de-rating which would force the banks to make further writedowns or set aside their scarce capital against securities insured by the guarantors. Markets promptly rallied, but remained nervous and volatile ahead of the Fed's meeting on 30th January. The half point cut in interest rates to 3% was greeted initially with a 180 point rise in the Dow but it still managed to end the day 38 points lower at 12442, a sequence strongly suggesting that rate cuts were not seen as wholly the answer to the economy's problems. Still, few were prepared to criticise the Fed's moves in the context of the weakest growth figures for five years, slowing consumer spending, inventory reductions by businesses, and a desperately depressed housing market, all against the background of a continuing credit squeeze.

January had proved to be one of the worst months on record for equity markets, but the bulls' hopes were raised in the opening days of February by a flurry of M&A activity. The star turn was **Microsoft's** $45 billion bid for **Yahoo**, designed to challenge Google's dominance in the internet search market. At a 62% premium to Yahoo's closing price, the bid was taken by some commentators as an indication that falling markets were throwing up attractive opportunities for bidders with the resources to take them on. Recent events had already shown that availability of resources was going to be the *sine qua non* of future bids. With default rates rising on many of the leveraged loans issued in buy-outs in 2006/7 and much of it still awaiting syndication, banks were understandably in a parsimonious mood.

Vales' $90 billion bid for **Xstrata** was rumoured to be running into difficulties over funding, given that many of the big banks were already committed to **BHP Billiton's** offer for **Rio Tinto** and had no wish to stretch their finances further. Funding was no problem for China's state-owned mining company, **Chinalco**, which teamed up with Canada's **Alcoa** to pay $14 billion for a 9% stake in **Rio Tinto** in an attempt to derail **BHP Billiton's** offer. The move galvanised the mining sector and helped the FTSE100 to gain 149.4 points, taking it north of the 6000 mark for the first time in two weeks, while the Dow rose to 12743, up almost 800 points from its low recorded on 22nd January.

Property companies suffer

The rally failed to make it into the second week of February as investors were forced to digest yet more evidence of economic slowdown on both sides of the Atlantic. Wall Street was stunned by the news that the index of service sector activity had contracted sharply to register its lowest reading since October 2001. The Dow reacted by shedding 370 points to 12265 and the S&P500 closed down 44 points at 1336, bringing its loss for 2008 to 9%; its worst start to a year ever. Bonds rose as equities fell with the yield on the 10-year US Treasury declining to 3.56%, and credit spreads continued to widen. Confident expectations of a cut in base rates at the next meeting of the Bank of England's Monetary Policy Committee on 7th February provided no support for the London market, and the FTSE100 dived 158 points to 5868 following Wall Street's lead. It was also influenced by reports of a growing risk of defaults on commercial property loans, which would inevitably lead to losses down the line for investors holding commercial mortgage-backed securities.

Australia's **Centro Properties** was already known to be in trouble over the refinancing of $3.8 billion of short-term loans used to buy a chain of shopping malls in the US, and it was now joined by a New York developer who had failed to refinance $5.8 billion of short-term loans taken out to buy seven Manhattan office blocks from Equity Office Properties at the peak of the commercial property boom in early 2007. There were fears that a number of US regional banks could soon be in trouble as a result of being big providers of construction loans to developers. **British Land's** £1.39 billion writedown of its commercial property valuations was seen as further indication that the problem was not going to be confined to the US.

The Bank of England's quarter-point cut in base rates to 5.25% failed to cheer markets which had been hoping for a half-point move, and an early rise in the FTSE100 was transformed into a 150-point fall by the end of the day. The Governor, Mervyn King, once again became the target of criticism for acting as if inflation was a bigger danger to the economy than a slowdown with a high risk of turning into a recession. His counterpart at the European Central Bank was also under pressure to change his priorities following indications of a sharp slowdown in Eurozone service sector activity and a 3.1% fall in the Eurofirst 300 to 1314. Recession fears were heightened by **Ryanair's** gloomy predictions for the airline industry in 2008 and the warning that its own profits could halve, an unusually downbeat assessment by its normally ebullient chairman, Michael O'Leary.

During the past three troubled days in Western markets, most of the Asian markets had been closed for the lunar New Year holiday and on re-opening all of them played catch-up, falling between 2% and 5%. India's BSE led the rout with a 4.5% drop to 16179, in a move that scuppered the once eagerly awaited $3 billion stock market debut of **Reliance Power**, India's largest ever IPO. Australian markets were also faced with a central bank rate rise along with further evidence that the **Macquarie Group** was losing its star status when a subsidiary began ditching securities in order to meet debt covenants, an action sparking falls across the financial sector.

This time, however, there was to be no knock-on effect on Western markets, which were enjoying a strong rally in reaction to Warren Buffett's offer to solve the monoline crisis by taking over the guarantors' $800 billion municipal bond portfolio. The insurance regulator welcomed the offer since it would rescue US towns and states from the threat to their funding of schools and hospitals posed by a credit rating downgrade. However, the monolines themselves saw no merit in a plan that would leave them still holding all the complex structured bonds that had caused the trouble in the first place, virtually guaranteeing a ratings downgrade unless another rescue operation could be mounted by their client banks.

Banks in more trouble

The persistence of such uncertainty ensured that the rally would not get very far and markets relapsed ahead of a clutch of results due from the banking sector towards the end of February. London did not take kindly to **Bradford & Bingley's** revelation that pre-tax profits had halved to £126 million following writedowns of double what the market had expected at £226 million, and the shares dived 56p to 187p, 23% below the flotation price of 245p back in December 2000 and 60% below the 2007 highpoint of 483p. **Alliance & Leicester** shed 42p to 559p – a seven year low – in sympathy and ahead of its results due the following week. Mervyn King had clearly caught the mood of the moment when he said in the Bank of England's quarterly Inflation Report that the pain in the banking system was likely to be 'deeper and more persistent' than he originally thought and that the ability of interest rate cuts to help would be limited.

A similar state of affairs obtained in the Eurozone where the German government intervened to rescue **IKB** in order to prevent it becoming the first Euro bank to be rendered insolvent by the subprime crisis and thus 'create difficulties for confidence and economic growth' for Germany. In the same week France's fourth largest bank, **Natixis**, fell 10% after announcing a €1.2 billion writedown on subprime related holdings, and **UBS** in company with **Commerzbank** also revealed damaging exposure to subprime "assets".

Meanwhile, back in the US, **AIG**, the world's biggest insurance company, admitted that it had been forced to write down its holdings of mortgage-related securities by $4.9 billion, or five times the figure confidently named in December. The reason offered for the discrepancy was a 'material weakness' in its valuation methods, an excuse mirrored a week later by **Credit Suisse** when blaming a $2.8 billion shock loss in its structured credit positions on 'pricing errors' by some of its traders.

Banking news continued to dominate the headlines in February but it was very much a case of swings and roundabouts. The decision to nationalise **Northern Rock** was the lead story and it was greeted with relief by many commentators who thought that the government had done the right thing, if a little late, instead of leaving opportunistic venture capitalists and hedge funds to sort out the mess. They also saw the move as further evidence of a trend already manifesting itself in the US and in the Eurozone of governments stepping in to fill the yawning gap in credibility now existing in vast swathes of the private financial sector, since only the state could bestow a triple-A rating which really meant what it was supposed to mean.

Barclays cheered markets and boosted share prices by reporting profits in line with expectations, a raised dividend payment, and writedowns on credit securities of just £1.6 billion, a figure not much inflated from the £1.3 billion estimated three months earlier. CEO John Varley rated this 'a resilient performance in testing market conditions', adding that 'we feel right on top of risk'. The news helped the FTSE100 to reach another intraday high of over 6000, but a reaction set in ahead of **Alliance & Leicester's** results due the following day. In the event, the building society's fall in profits resulting from a threefold increase in previously indicated writedowns to £185 million sent bank shares reeling again, while **Credit Suisse**'s revelation of further unlooked-for losses simply added to investors' fears that there was still more bad news in the pipeline.

One leading commentator looked at **Barclays'** £36.4 billion total of credit exposure on its balance sheet and suggested that a provision of no more than £1.6 billion was anomalously low compared with those already revealed by its competitors and that he hoped 'the numbers would continue to add up' for Mr Varley. Then **Lloyds TSB** provided a further measure of support for the UK banking sector with results much as forecast, writedowns only modestly up on those indicated in December, and a 5% boost in the dividend, leaving the shares at 452p, down just 27% from their mid-2007 peak to record the best performance among the domestic banks.

Whistling in the dark

Hopes that this marginally more confident mood in the banking sector would lead to the FTSE100 re-establishing a foothold above 6000 received a setback when another run of seriously bearish data on the US economy sent the Dow plunging. However, the downward trend abruptly reversed on news of a $3.6 billion bailout for the monolines which would enable the biggest names in the business to avoid ratings downgrades resulting in another round of writedowns for the banks. The response of stock markets to the rescue of the monolines demonstrated the importance of the issue for investor confidence, but one writer insisted that the very fact of the undercapitalised monolines acting as guarantors of financial asset structures measured in trillions of dollars gave a spurious validity to an essentially insubstantial financial system. Still, in the final week of February, the Dow managed to progress well beyond the 12500 level and the FTSE100 made a decisive move above 6000 on its third attempt, performances mirrored in stock markets across the world.

Nevertheless, more cautious commentators were keen to point out that none of the basic problems facing investors had gone away. The credit crunch was still there and manifesting itself in widening credit spreads which served to offset the beneficial effects of the rate cuts programme initiated by the Federal Reserve and the Bank of

England. Furthermore, oil was over $100 again and the prices of other commodities were soaring, but if the spectre of inflation presented the central banks with a serious policy dilemma, few doubted that they would be deterred from embarking on another round of rate cuts. The prospect of the Fed leading the way caused the dollar to sink to a new record low against the euro, breaching the psychologically important €1.50 level and taking the steam out of the equities rally as investors paused to see what the next batch of economic data would bring.

Sentiment on Wall Street was boosted by **IBM's** announcement of a $15 billion share buy-back, but subsequently depressed by **Google**'s figures for the fourth quarter of 2007, which were widely seen as indicating that its remarkable run of growth was stalling. Competition in the internet advertising business was hotting up and likely to become even more intense if the **Microsoft/Yahoo** proposed merger went ahead, and worries on this score sent **Google's** share price under the $500 mark to $464, 20% down on the month and almost 40% down on its high point of November 2007. It was no surprise that the Dow was soon slipping back towards the 12500 level preparatory to breaching it on the first day of March.

The bigger they come...

Another relatively recent development considered likely to restrain an advance in equity markets was the fact that redemptions from mutual funds in the UK were running at record levels in the final quarter of 2007, and continuing into the current year. Given the unprecedented volatility of the markets over the past year and the exceptionally high percentage falls suffered by household name domestic stocks, it was perhaps not surprising that investors should become risk averse and tempted to cash in their fund holdings rather than risk a further fall in their value.

It was doubtful if anyone seeing **Marks & Spencer** going from strength to strength under the direction of Stuart Rose in mid-2007 would have believed that less than nine months later its share price would have halved to fall below Philip Green's 400p offer made in 2005. Similarly, who would have guessed that with bidders ready to pay 600p or more for **Sainsbury's** in October 2007, six months later the share price would be below 350p? **New Star** was the first fund manager to report hefty redemptions in the wake of poor performances by a number of its popular retail funds, and with markets continuing to fall it was not going to be alone.

Furthermore, such a situation posed an ongoing bear point, since in the absence of large cash reserves, in order to fund redemptions existing stockholdings would have to be liquidated, putting additional downside pressure on market levels. Fortunately for **New Star** and its fellows, conventional unit trusts/mutual funds have assets that are 'marked to market' on a daily basis and thus can be disposed of with relative ease, an advantage denied to hedge funds and other institutions investing in more exotic instruments.

The latter also suffered from the huge disadvantage of being over-reliant on borrowed money, which meant that they were subject to margin calls if the value of their holdings fell, forcing them to sell into a reluctant market. That two funds, founded by the original "Masters of the Universe", **Carlyle Group** and **Kohlberg Kravis & Roberts**, should have found themselves in such a situation and facing possible bankruptcy was seen as evidence of just how serious things had become.

Add in more bad news on the US economy as private sector job losses topped 100,000 in February, the biggest monthly drop since March 2001, and one of a magnitude widely assumed to "scream recession", and no one was surprised to see the Dow drop below 12000. A relentless flow of appalling news from the financials as the cost of default insurance soared to record levels kept up the pressure, pushing the Dow down to 11740 and the S&P500 to 1273, breaching their late January low points. World markets plunged in sympathy with the FTSE100 falling into the 5600/5700 range.

Saving Bear Stearns

But after three consecutive days of declines, markets were looking for an excuse for a rebound and the Fed duly provided one with a $200 billion lending operation in 28-day funds to banks against relatively illiquid mortgage-backed securities as collateral; in effect swapping them for Treasuries and thereby absorbing a great deal of the liquidity risk clogging up the markets. The scale of the emergency funding was described by one observer as 'without precedent in modern times' and another saw it as just another step along an unfamiliar road when 'policy may now have to move beyond liquidity provision and rate cuts to minimise the risk of market failure'. The Dow's reaction was to stage the biggest one-day points rise in five years with a 416 point surge to 12183, but it was not to last.

Too many commentators were ready to point out that the real problem was not one of liquidity but of solvency, a view soon confirmed by the latest round of losses reported by the highly-geared US government-sponsored mortgage agencies, **Freddie Mac** and **Fannie Mae**, encouraging the belief that they would have to be the subject of a government bail-out. Rumours swirled around **Bear Stearns** and many believed that the Fed's support operation had been mounted specifically to avoid the collapse of one of Wall Street's top investment banks with all the damage that such an event would do to market confidence. They were right but the belief served only to highlight the bank's funding problems and as its liquidity position continued to deteriorate, the Fed got together with **JPMorgan Chase** to execute Plan B. This was the provision of emergency funding to **Bear Stearns** through the discount window in a back-to-back arrangement with JPMorgan which resulted in the Fed assuming the credit risk involved in the loans.

However, the Fed's move did nothing to calm the markets but rather the reverse, heightening speculation over which of the big banks was going to be the next to run into trouble, and bank shares tumbled not only on Wall Street but across the world. Even the arranged takeover of Bear Stearns by JPMorgan two days later failed to restore confidence, since to avert a collapse by offering $2 a share in a shotgun wedding with a $30 billion dowry provided by the Fed for a bank priced at $80 a share at the beginning of the month, was still a collapse by any other name. **Lehman Brothers** was popularly believed to be next in line and its shares slumped, but the swift action of the Federal Reserve to date in dealing with the crisis inspired a degree of confidence in its ability to continue to do so and markets paused ahead of the next meeting scheduled for 18th March.

A rate cut was a certainty and the only question was whether it would be one of three quarters of a point or a full one per cent. In the event it was the former, bringing the rate down to 2.25%, and it was accompanied by a cut in the discount rate at which it provides emergency finance to banks to 3.25%, and the extension of the facility to investment banks for the first time in over seventy years. Despite expressions of disappointment that the Fed had not gone for a larger cut, shares soared with the S&P500 recording its biggest one-day gain in five years, adding 54 points to 1330, and the Dow plussed 420 to 12392. This lighter mood was helped by smaller than expected profit declines reported on the same day by **Lehman Brothers** and **Goldman Sachs** along with earnest protestations about the strength of their respective liquidity positions.

However, there was no follow-through in the markets as investors saw the Fed's statement that 'uncertainty about the inflation outlook has increased' as not only severely curtailing the scope for further aggressive rate cuts but also as acknowledging that it faced a major policy dilemma at a time when the dollar was plunging to record lows. As usual, world markets followed Wall Street's lead, rallying and then pausing to see what shocks the next day would bring. London was under particular pressure both as a result of sterling's precipitous decline against the euro and practically every other currency except the dollar, and the all too evident problems experienced by the UK financial sector in recent months; a situation seen as limiting the potential of the Bank of England to deliver the rate cuts seen as necessary to ameliorate the effects of the credit crisis.

Liquidity provision, however, became a matter of urgency in the closing days of March, as rumours (supposedly false) that **HBOS** was in difficulty and seeking urgent talks with the Bank of England sparked a near 20% fall in its share price and sharp falls in the shares of other banks too. A strong unequivocal denial from the Bank of England that neither HBOS nor any other high street bank was in difficulty calmed markets, but there was an element of truth in the rumour to the extent that a meeting between the big banks and the Bank of England had indeed been scheduled to discuss the provision of more generous funding to deal with the credit crunch and also the feasibility of using public funds to purchase mortgage-backed securities. The Fed and the European Central Bank were both involved in discussions over the second option, which would involve an extension of the moves already made by the Bank of England in relation to Northern Rock and by the Fed in lowering capital surplus requirements for Freddie Mac and Fannie Mae from 30% to 20%, thus giving them the scope to add another $200 billion to their mortgage book. One commentator saw the prospect of central banks becoming a 'buyer of last resort' as putting their balance sheets 'in harm's way', but Lex considered that if the bulk of mortgage securities were substantially undervalued, then that prospect could galvanise the market into action and 'encourage the vultures to swoop in'.

'Always look on the bright side'

The Easter break provided a pause for investors to ponder the significance of the week's momentous events and for JPMorgan to rethink its $2 a share offer for Bear Stearns and raise it fivefold to $10. The decision not only lessened the chances of legal challenges to the takeover but also helped to stabilise markets to some degree on consideration of the lengths to which the banking industry and the Fed were prepared to go to look after their own. Some commentators were further tempted to see the Bear Stearns bail-out as a 'cathartic moment' for markets, signalling the point at which confidence was restored to the financial sector, thereby creating the best buying opportunity since March 2003.

The panel of 'experts' polled by the *Sunday Times* at the beginning of the year left their predictions broadly unchanged when asked to review them at the end of the first quarter, looking for a rise in the FTSE100 of some 15% to around 6500 by the end of 2008. Their confidence was contagious and after firming in the last week of March, markets surged on the first day of April. The fact that the trigger for the advance had been the announcement by **UBS** that it was writing down another $19 billion of impaired securities bringing the year's total to $40 billion and had managed to arrange a $15 billion right issue was seen by other commentators as hardly a cause for celebration.

However, the 'turning point' story for the financial sector was catching on, and shares in UBS soared 12% while those of banks in the UK, Europe and the US gained between 5% and 15%, with **Lehman Brothers** adding 17.8% after solving its rumoured capital shortage by raising $4 billion from a sale of new shares. By the end of the first week in April, the Dow was over 12600 again with the S&P500 at 1370, both up over 3%, and the FTSE had managed to top 6000 intraday.

Nonetheless, practically every serious financial writer was prepared to go on record as labelling the recent advance as a counter-trend rally given what they saw as the inevitability of the credit crunch continuing to spread into the 'real economy'. They considered that the bulls' contention that the economy was in good shape, that corporate earnings were rising and the consumer still spending demonstrated a naïve reliance on yesterday's story and ignored the fact that they were all lagging indicators. Far more relevant as a pointer to the future were falling house prices, a mortgage scarcity, retailers warning of the 'really, really terrible' state of current trading, slashed dividends by household-name companies and a string of abandoned deals as banks withdrew from funding commitments, and all stemming from the abrupt transformation of the credit environment from one of plenty to one of famine. And with inter-bank lending rates remaining well above official rates and credit spreads as wide as ever, this was not a crisis likely to respond to the ministrations of conventional monetary and fiscal policies.

A process of credit contraction was always going to be painful but this one was going to be exceptionally so given the degree of illiquidity deriving from high quality assets becoming tarred with the subprime brush and the extent of de-leveraging required before financial equilibrium could be restored. The banks were just the first victims of a mess largely of their own creation, the bears maintained. Now came the turn of the rest of the economy. In the days ahead of the MPC meeting scheduled for 9th April, the FTSE100 managed three more intraday excursions into the 6000 plus territory on rate cut expectations, but the quarter point cut to 5% failed to boost markets, and the accompanying statement that credit conditions had tightened and the availability of credit appeared to be worsening did not help. The rate reduction was widely reckoned to have no effect on mortgage rates with lenders now targeting LIBOR which remained obstinately close to the 6% level, and concern over the prospects for the housing market grew as Halifax reported a 2.5% drop in prices in March, the biggest monthly drop since September 1992. And with credit card charges for purchases and cash withdrawals firmly in the 15% to 30% range, a quarter point rate cut, even in the unlikely event of it being passed on, was going to be of no help to the over-indebted consumer.

The European Central Bank added to the air of despondency by maintaining its key rate at 4%, pushing sterling to a record low against the euro, and warning that the current financial turmoil could last longer and have a bigger effect than anyone now expected. In the same week, top retailer Sir Philip Green described conditions on the High Street being 'as difficult as he had seen' and forecast another fall in profits at his **BHS** chain, while **DSG** (Dixons and Currys) downgraded estimates of the year's profits from £240 million to £200/210 million. Bids and deals provided a small measure of relief to markets, with **RWE**, the German utility company, making an £11 billion cash offer for the UK's nuclear power company **British Energy**, and **Manitowoc** coming back with a bid for Enodis. This demonstrated that FTSE250 companies that had fallen on hard times still had their attractions, boosting the prices of a number of mid-sized engineering stocks that had recently been the subject of bid rumours.

On a wider canvas, the IMF's sharp downgrading of its estimates for global growth made for a more depressing outlook than that engendered by the more hopeful predictions of Treasury officials and central bankers tasked with maintaining public confidence as part of their brief. Most commentators regarded the IMF's view that the US was already in recession, that the slowdown there would endure well into 2009 and that Europe and the rest of the world would follow a similar path, as the more realistic of the two. This opinion was apparently confirmed when **General Electric** reported its worst quarter since 2003 and halved its profits forecast of a rise of 10% in 2008, made just a month earlier, to one of 'no more than 5%'. The results were described by GE's chief financial officer as 'shocking' and the US markets agreed as the Dow dived 256 points to 12395 while the S&P500 lost 37 to 1332. The problem was that as a thoroughly diversified industrial conglomerate with a global spread deriving over 50% of its revenues from outside the US, GE was regarded as the bellwether of the global economy, and thus its 'shocking' results could be seen as the shape of things to come. Some of the blame was laid at the door of Bear Stearns for wrecking the real estate market and scuppering GE's planned property disposals that would have boosted profits, but a credibility problem remained. Stock markets around the world took the hint and followed Wall Street down, with the FTSE100 falling back into the 5800/5900 range.

However, by mid-April investors had shrugged off worries about slowing growth; with the oil price at a record high and other energy and food prices still rising to stoke inflationary pressures, they decided to regard another round of appalling losses and writedowns by the world's biggest banks as a further sign that the worst was over. They were encouraged by US Treasury Secretary Hank Paulson musing that 'in terms of the capital markets, I believe we are closer to the end than the beginning,' and to the relative ease with which the big banks were managing to attract vast amounts of new capital. **Royal Bank of Scotland's** £12 billion rights issue surprised because of its larger than expected size but take-up was widely recommended by City columnists. **HBOS's** appeal to shareholders to contribute another £4 billion was also well received, but a number of writers warned that further offerings from banks would strain shareholders' generosity and that **Barclays**, rumoured to be looking for £3 billion, would be well advised to tap sovereign wealth funds instead.

In the US, **Citigroup's** latest round of losses and writedowns was greeted with a sharp rally in its share price, encouraged by news of the sale of $12 billion of leveraged loans to a private equity group and the plans of the new CEO, Vikram Pandit, to restructure the bank and dispose of up to $500 billion of 'legacy' assets over the next three years. The central banks continued to play their part with a new push to ease strains in the financial markets. The Fed reduced its key interest rate to 2% on 30th April and simultaneously boosted its $100 billion offer of one-month loans by 50% and widened eligibility criteria for T-bond 'swaps', while the Bank of England injected another £50 billion into the markets.

Sentiment was helped by another flurry of bid activity in the mining sector as Kazakh miner **ENRC** tabled a £7 billion offer for rival **Kazakhmys**, which was instantly rejected as 'derisory' by the target. **BHP Billiton** expressed its determination to proceed with its £67 billion offer for a reluctant **Rio Tinto**, and **Xstrata** was rumoured to be planning a $38 billion bid for **Alcoa**. The US tech sector also saw renewed interest in the wake of **Google's** first quarter results coming in above estimates thanks to overseas growth, and **Hewlett-Packard's** offer for **EDS** (Electronic Data Systems) offset any concern over **Microsoft's** withdrawal of its bid for **Yahoo**, a target still widely believed to remain "in play". By the first week of May, the Dow had managed to top 13000 again and the S&P500 had crossed the 1400 mark, while the FTSE100 was looking well-established above 6000 and at 6215 on 2nd May was up 15% on its mid-March low point.

Running on empty

That all this should be going on against the background of soaring prices for oil, metals and agricultural commodities was hardly a bull point and yet it served as one to the extent that it benefited the natural resources producers amongst the index constituents and thus propped up the FTSE100. This rather begged the question of what would happen to the shares of producers and to the index if what many observers believed was a commodity bubble, actually burst. The problem as they saw it was twofold in that commodity prices were being driven not simply by rising demand from the major emerging economies of India and China, but also by speculative demand from Western investors looking for alternative homes for their money following the disappointing performance of equities and real estate and of course much of the bond element in their portfolios.

As a result commodity investors as distinct from commodity users were at risk on two counts. Firstly, with global growth set to slow (if one believed the IMF rather than the perennial optimists), and with the demand for commodities linked to the global consumption cycle, the resulting inevitable reduction in that demand would lead to a falling off in prices. Secondly, that falling off in prices would trigger the liquidation of speculative positions (almost certainly leveraged) and with non-commercial trades reckoned to account for more than 50% of current trading, price falls could be severe. And to the extent that speculative trading was at least in part responsible for the massive price increases recorded by basic foodstuffs like rice and grain, a moral dimension became involved given the devastating impact rising prices were having on the welfare of the billion-plus world population trying to exist on less than a dollar a day when most of that dollar had to be spent on food. To quote billionaire investor and philanthropist, George Soros, commodities are not 'a legitimate asset class for institutional investors'.

As May progressed, stock markets in New York and London and around the world appeared determined to ignore the unrelenting flow of bad news and ever more indications of the knock-on effects that the credit crisis was having on the "real economy". By the middle of the month the FTSE100 had advanced 12.4% to top 6300 for the first time since January and similar rises were recorded by the Eurofirst 300, up 12%, Germany's DAX, up 13%, and by the S&P500, up 9.2%. In the case of the FTSE100, many commentators saw the rise as justified by rising earnings providing a P/E of around 12, well below the long-term average P/E of 15 and thus pricing in a fall in earnings under more adverse conditions.

However, more sceptical observers were eager to point out that sector weightings provided the same level of distortion in FTSE100 earnings as they did in the index itself. Thus, a forecast 30% rise in earnings in the resources sector boosted the average while at the same time masking significantly lower figures in the other sectors. One writer looked at the FTSE100 at 6200, down just 8% from its peak, and detected what he called a 'hidden bear market' in which the big global players with practically no stake in the domestic economy obscured the fate of those which had.

The most convinced of the bears saw the collapse of the financials as the surest pointer to the future for the economy and the markets. Their argument was simply that we live in a credit-driven economy where the banks and the finance houses provide the motive power in their role as the principal purveyors of credit to the corporate sector and to the consumer. The process had driven economies along at a cracking pace for the past twenty or so years and in overdrive for the past ten thanks to the booster effect provided by securitisation and leverage. Now that the engine, i.e. the banks and finance houses, had broken down, the economy would lose its motive power and after allowing for a degree of residual impetus, a sharp slowdown, even a stop, was unavoidable.

The dire effects of the credit crisis were already headline-making news in property-related sectors and those reliant upon discretionary consumer spending, and with no "quick fix" in prospect given a dangerously inflationary background, things looked certain to get worse before they got better.

Flaming June

The strong performance in May recorded by equity markets and the fact that bond yields were rising again as the "flight to safety" urge abated, encouraged the bulls in their belief that the Bear Stearns rescue had marked the nadir of the credit crisis and the only way was up. Within days this belief was undermined by a record quarterly loss and $15 billion of writedowns, or three times the figure estimated in February, from **AIG** the world's biggest insurance company, which planned to raise $12.5 billion while giving no 'assurance' about the scale of future losses. **Bradford & Bingley** launched a £300 million rights issue as its shares sank to an eight-year low, and **HSBC** announced that it was setting aside another $5.8 billion to cover possible bad debts. The governor of the Bank of England, Mervyn King, then weighed in with a pronouncement that 'the NICE decade' was behind us (NICE being an acronym for non-inflationary continuous expansion), and figures were released showing that industry's raw material and fuel costs were up 24.7% year on year, and factory gate prices up 7.5% over the same period.

By the end of the month, many commentators were ready to agree that "Sell in May" would not have been such a bad idea after all and that to do so in June could be an even better idea. Stock markets were already well off the high points of early May, but what was now to send them into significant reverse was a sudden and largely unexpected surge in the oil price to almost $140 a barrel, accompanied by a growing body of evidence of the damage that soaring energy costs were doing to economies everywhere. The airlines had already made it clear that their business models were no longer viable with oil at over $120, and now it seemed that the caveat applied to every other industry too, especially in the light of forecasts of significantly higher prices issuing from apparently authoritative sources like Goldman Sachs and Russia's Gazprom. The fact that the record oil price was achieved on the same day that the US unemployment rate was revealed to have jumped from 5% in April to 5.5% in May, its highest level in twenty-two years, appeared to link cause with effect, and at the same time highlighted the growth versus inflation policy dilemma facing governments everywhere. The European Central Bank made it clear once again that with Eurozone inflation running at 3.6%, fighting inflation was its principal concern and rate rises were more than likely in the months ahead. The Bank of England held rates at 5% on 5th June and in the US, the Fed Chairman Ben Bernanke said that a weak dollar would cause import prices and thus inflation to rise, a statement interpreted as a clear signal that rate cuts were no longer in prospect and even that rises were possible before the end of the year. Such pronouncements from on high strongly suggested that the monetary authorities were more worried about a recurrence of seventies-style inflation than a thirties-style slump, but with the US in an election year and the UK government's need to counter a dramatic fall in the popularity stakes, politicians faced with a "damned if you do, damned if you don't" policy option could not be guaranteed to make the right choice. Rather, they seemed more likely to follow the line reputedly proposed by President Reagan when faced with an impossible situation; 'Don't do something, just stand there.'

If anyone still had any doubts about the devastating impact the credit crunch was having on the real economy, they should have been dispelled by the second week of June when belated warnings from stockbrokers about the prospects for banks, retailers and housebuilders sent share prices tumbling. As a result of being first in the queue, **Royal Bank of Scotland** had managed to complete its £12 billion rights issue just in time, simultaneously spoiling the chances of raising money for any other bank or indeed for any other company. **Bradford & Bingley** had been forced to renegotiate the pricing of its £300 million rights issue and tap private equity as the share price slumped after a profits warning, but this was small beer compared with **HBOS's** £4 billion offering which looked like being left with the underwriters after a one-day 12% fall left the shares 20p below the 275p rights price. Given the high investment standing of HBOS, its predicament held out little hope of raising money for the debt-laden housebuilders, stuck with huge inventories of unsold and currently unsellable houses and flats, and large landbanks subject to massive writedowns. Share prices in the sector were now registering falls of between 80% and 90% from their peak prices of a year ago. As for the retailers, a "sell" note from Citigroup embracing many of the top names in the sector said it all:

> 'With a declining housing market, high levels of debt, low levels of private savings and rising fixed costs, we argue there will be no recovery in consumption patterns until 2010 at the earliest.'

The FTSE100 had slipped below 6000 in the first week of June and the 5800 level was now looking vulnerable.

Parallel falls were registered on Wall Street as the same sectors came under pressure for much the same reasons. Financials headed the declines, with **Lehman Brothers** in the lead, down 13%, closely followed by **Merrill Lynch**, down 7%, both to new lows. One factor raising renewed fears about financials was the much-feared downgrading of bond insurers **Ambac** and **MBIA**, an event which would have created havoc in the markets had it taken place in March. Apparently, price and position adjustments since then had softened the blow but with $1000 billion of bonds reckoned to be affected, more writedowns were in prospect for the insurers' clients. Homebuilders declined 8% to a new 7-year low, and the technology sector lost its recent strength on industry reports of slowing sales growth and increasing competition driving down prices of key products. **General Motors** and **Ford** were also on the slide as consumers rethought their principal discretionary purchase with gasoline topping $4 a gallon. High volatility with many "big name" stocks moving 10% to 20% in a day made for sizeable dips and rallies but the prevailing bias appeared to be to the downside as the Dow fell below 12500 and the S&P500 to below 1350. And the idea that the emerging markets, in particular the BRICs (Brazil, Russia, India and China), would continue to make the running and act as a sort of insurance policy against a slowdown in the economies and stock markets of the developed world, now began to lose its appeal. Signs of overheating in China and India had already prompted central banks in both countries to tighten monetary policy to counter high and rising inflation, a situation shared with most of the emerging economies as oil and food prices raced ahead. Given the much larger share of consumer price indices accounted for by food in the emerging world, inflation expectations were also on the rise, increasing the risk of a wage/price spiral developing and then presenting governments with political and social problems as they tried to maintain control. Stock market performances reflected these difficulties with the main Chinese indices down around 40% in 2008 and India's BSE Sensex off by 25%, both significantly underperforming the S&P500 and the FTSE100.

Meanwhile, back in the UK inflation was also a hot topic, although not in the context of an economy overheating but in one entering a 'very prolonged period of sluggish growth' in the words of the CBI, as it revised its growth forecast for 2009 yet again, this time from 1.7% to 1.3%. The fact that the forecast was contemporaneous with the announcement that the inflation figure for May had hit 3.3%, its highest for fifteen years, raised the spectre of "stagflation", the name coined to describe the low growth, high-inflation situation that had characterised the second half of the seventies. Adding to worries and evoking more disturbing memories of the period was the inflation-busting 14% pay award over two years for tanker drivers extracted after a four-day strike that had brought petrol shortages to many parts of the country, and evidence that other groups of workers were preparing to resort to strike action.

Calls for pay restraint by the Chancellor and by the Governor of the Bank of England did not appear to have much chance of being heeded given the sharp rises that had already been recorded in the prices of food and energy and the prospect of further rises in the case of the latter. Food might not account for as high a proportion of the household budget in the developed world as it does in emerging markets, but add in the need for heat, light and fuel (utilities with little relevance to the lives of the huddled masses in developing economies) and inflationary expectations were going to be much the same.

Faced with such a raft of uncertainties, stock markets continued to drift and one step forward was succeeded by two steps back. The bulls argued that shares were cheap but since that argument had been deployed months ago when prices were a lot higher, it was no longer going to convince anyone. The bears maintained that the world was facing an unprecedented challenge arising out of financial breakdown coinciding with soaring energy and food prices, and that against such a background conventional valuation methods were of little relevance. This was new territory, they insisted, where buyers held the whip hand and the price of an asset was governed by what a buyer was willing to pay.

'Another fine mess'

By the final week of June, practically everything was going the way of the bears. Oil had crossed the $140 level and moved into new high ground, more influenced by fears of supply disruption than by Saudi Arabia's pledge to increase production. The prospect of an Israeli air strike against Iran's nuclear facilities was seen as more than likely in many quarters and **Shell's** Nigerian production was under constant threat.

On the home front, there was growing evidence of the adverse effect that the credit crunch coupled with the sky-high oil price was having on corporate profits and consumer confidence, and the hopes of a second-half recovery that had sparked the March to May rally were fading fast. Banks were looking at a new round of writedowns and **Barclays'** £4.5 billion share issue to a clutch of foreign banks, initially hailed as a coup, was now widely reckoned to prove inadequate to restore its capital base given what was seen as an anomalously generous valuation of its leveraged loan book.

Profit warnings and gloomy forecasts from a number of leading companies in major industrial sectors were seen as clear indication that earnings forecasts that had provided a prop to markets were far too optimistic. If industrial giants like **Rockwell**, **Oshkosh**, **UPS**, and **Oracle** could disappoint along with their counterparts in the UK and the Eurozone, then the second quarter earnings season had to be awaited with some trepidation.

Bearish predictions were now widespread, ranging from just another 10% to go on the downside in the majority, to a few warning of a 1929-style collapse into a depression to rival that of the thirties. Regardless of the questionable value to be placed on predictions made by any of the "investment professionals", there was no doubt that the first half scorecard for stock markets in 2008 was one for the record books. At 5529.9 the FTSE100 was down 14.4% since the start of the year, and the more domestically oriented FTSE250 fared a little worse, losing 14.5%. On Wall Street, the Dow at 11453 had trimmed almost 20% from its October 2007 high of just over 14000 and was down 13.6% in the first half of 2008, while the S&P500 and NASDAQ were both down 12.5%. These performances were much in line with those of markets in the rest of the world and the MSCI World Index recorded a loss of 11.7%, its worst showing since 1982, suggesting that with oil over $140 and other commodity prices soaring, we were all in the same boat and the word "decoupling" would never be heard again.

On currency markets, the US dollar had fallen from 1.46 against the euro to 1.57 and the pound from 0.73 to 0.79, reflecting both traders' perceptions that the European Central Bank's determination to pursue a counter-inflationary policy was greater than that of the Federal Reserve or the Bank of England, and their belief that buying oil and gold was hedging against the prospect of a weaker dollar. And regardless of inflation concerns, government bonds were once again demonstrating their safe haven credentials as the 10-year US T-bond's yield dipped below 4.00%.

Bears on top

The first week of the second half of the year brought no relief for markets but rather the reverse as key indices in London and New York fell to within a whisker of the minus 20% figure, traditionally taken as the signal that a bear market is underway. The Chancellor's proposal to raise the deposit guarantee level from £35,000 to £50,000 appeared timely given that bank shares were on the slide again, unnerved by private equity group **Texas Pacific's** withdrawal from its part in the refinancing of **Bradford & Bingley** following a downgrading of the bank's debt, and by the belated realisation that the problems now being experienced by companies in the heavily indebted consumer-reliant sectors would end up on the doorsteps of the banks.

But what really spooked the markets was a dramatic 5.3% drop in first quarter sales and a profits warning from **Marks & Spencer**, news that sparked a 25% fall in the share price to 240p. Within hours, the normally ever-resilient John Lewis reported an 8.3% slump in sales in the last week of June, confirming, if ever confirmation was needed, that the effect of the credit crunch was spreading into all areas of consumer spending. Share prices of homebuilders, already well down over the year, took another hit when it was revealed that **Taylor Wimpey** had failed to raise the £500 million it needed to shore up its capital position, a failure not altogether surprising given the 64% collapse in mortgage approvals to a record low of 42,000 in May. Purveyors of the second-largest big-ticket item for consumers, the car, were also clearly in trouble, with June sales down 6.1% on a year earlier as higher petrol prices and increased road tax proposals further depressed consumer confidence. Media companies were also suffering as the decline in advertising revenue, already evident in the first quarter, accelerated at an alarming rate, leading to a 30% dive in **Trinity Mirror's** share price on the announcement that profit expectations would be missed by 10%.

It was now obvious to all that problems spread across so many sectors would lead to a growing number of job losses, an outcome that ensured that bad news was no longer confined to the business pages of the national press, further damaging public morale. Calls for the Bank of England to embark on a new round of interest rate cuts continued but without much hope of a response given that the European Central Bank had just hiked rates from 4% to 4.25%, and the best that was looked for was for rates to be left on hold. Despite anti-inflation rhetoric, neither the Federal Reserve nor the Bank of England was expected to follow the example of the ECB and raise rates, both appearing to rely on the sharper than expected slowdown leading to a falling oil price to do the job for them.

Conditions on the other side of the Atlantic provided no help for sentiment here. The giants of the automobile industry, **Ford, General Motors** and **Chrysler**, were all closing plants and laying off workers by the thousands as sales slumped to a 10-year low and all three were rumoured to be running into liquidity crises. And on Main Street, **Starbucks** announced the closure of 600 of its coffee shops with the loss of up to 12,000 staff as it put its urban expansion programme into reverse. Financials seemed unable to pick themselves up from the floor, unsettled by the prospect of further massive losses from **Freddie Mac** and **Fannie Mae** resulting from the continuing deterioration of the housing market and speculation resurfaced that these two government-sponsored mortgage agencies would soon need a $75 billion capital boost to enable them to continue in business. Given their pole position in the US mortgage market, in the event of a liquidity crisis the government would be obliged to step into the breach in order to avoid a credit meltdown, involving the $5 trillion in mortgages backed by the two agencies, that would make the subprime disaster look like 'a modest hiccup'.

The Fed's announcement that it would continue to provide emergency cash as required by the investment banks into 2009, and a sharp fall in the oil price from $145 to $137, helped the Dow to rally from 11200 and the S&P500 from 1250, but having turned a blind eye to recession for so long, buyers seemed to have little conviction now that it was upon them. That conviction waned a little more as the oil price surged ahead in response to Iran's testing of a new batch of long-range missiles and a disappointing start to the second quarter earnings season.

Renewed worries about **Freddie Mac** and **Fannie Mae** and news that the Fed was riding to the rescue to stabilise the current situation by giving both groups access to emergency cash on the same terms as the banks, as well as by seeking authority from Congress to increase its credit lines to them and to invest in their equity, sparked an initial rally of over 100 points in the Dow but it soon went into reverse. There had never been any doubt that the two mortgage agencies were too big to be allowed to fail and that the government would stand behind them. But investors now became concerned about smaller financial institutions "not too big to fail" and shares in the investment banking sector and among the regional banks plunged, the latter panicked by the collapse of California's **Indy Mac Bancorp** after a run on the bank by depositors who withdrew $1.3 billion in a matter of days.

Spain to the rescue

London's FTSE100 saw a similar short-lived advance of just over 100 points to 5350 under the influence not so much of the Fed's rescue plan but of **Santander's** £1.26 billion offer for **Alliance & Leicester**. The fact that the offer price of 299p (plus an

18p dividend) was less than half the price ruling when a possible offer was discussed in December 2007, weighted less with the bulls of the market than the idea that there was enough value around at current levels to attract predators again. The shares moved up to 335p but the premium was reckoned to owe more to short covering than to hopes of a counter bid given that few banks in the current climate had such deep pockets as **Santander**.

Shares of other banks rose for much the same reason, helping the index to a modest gain on the day; but Wall Street's woes, compounded by the dollar falling to a record low against the euro and oil topping $147, now began to take their toll, not just on London, but on markets everywhere. The stage was set for perhaps the most dramatic five days ever seen in financial markets as the popular "buy oils, sell financials" trading strategy went into sharp reverse. The week had opened with an unprecedented collapse in bank shares in the US as traders looked for more second-line banks to follow **Indy Mac** into administration, and in the UK prices plunged and the rights and offer prices of **HBOS, Bradford & Bingley** and **Barclays** were all underwater.

The trigger for a sudden turnaround was the coincidence of a run of better, i.e. not as bad as expected, second quarter results from **JPMorgan, Wells Fargo** and **Citibank**, with the introduction by the SEC of emergency rules limiting short sales of financial stocks and a dramatic slide in the price of oil. The result was what was described as 'the biggest short squeeze ever', and given that other items of news on the housing and inflation fronts were not at all encouraging, the rally clearly owed more to the bear squeeze than to any real evidence that the credit crisis was near its end or that the oil price was on the way down. This view gained ground in the final week of July and markets resumed their downward path.

A false dawn

The real problem seemed to be a lack of investor confidence in the markets, running parallel with the lack of consumer confidence in other areas of the economy. This was very much a traders' stock market, and no place for investors with serious investment planning in mind when the very institutions at the heart of such planning were seen to be in such disarray and so clearly lacking in skill and judgement, a deficiency demonstrated daily as reports rolled in from the banks and other financial institutions.

Slightly better-than-feared results from one would prompt a rally, to be snuffed out a day later by worse-than-expected results from another; but the previous unimaginable extent of their losses and the decline in their share prices tempted a number of commentators to believe that it really was darkest before the dawn and that the capitulation phase had been reached. After all, if **Merrill Lynch** was prepared to sell a portfolio of mortgage-backed securities at 22 cents on the dollar, that had to be a serious deck-clearing operation and capitulation by any other name. Add in the oil price falling below $120 a barrel and the likelihood of it continuing to fall as world economies slowed, and there was certainly a case to be made that a bottom of sorts had been reached.

The bears, however, while acknowledging that such factors could provide scope for a significant rally from a low level, believed that the impact of the credit crunch was only just beginning to be felt in the real economy. The damage had already been done to once well-established levels of economic activity and the banks, the fountainheads of credit, were no longer in any shape to provide the support that was going to be necessary to deal with the fallout. Indeed, as things got tough on "Main Street", they would be hit by a second wave of financial losses as their loan books deteriorated. The problems of the retailers, the housebuilders and the car makers were already well known, but with consumer confidence continuing to fall in step with falling house prices, and rising unemployment, the pain was not going to be confined to those sectors.

Growth forecasts for the US and the UK were in a process of rapid downward revision and with Germany's GDP set to go negative in the second quarter, Eurozone growth was clearly heading in the same direction. And with inflation labelled 'of significant concern' as the Fed held rates at 2%, along with comparable pronouncements from the Bank of England and the European Central Bank as they both stood pat on their respective rates of 5% and 4.25%, no relief was to be looked for on the interest rate front. At the same time, no rate rises were on the cards either, a realisation that served to boost the dollar to its highest level against the euro for five months, a development which, allied with the oil price and that of other commodities continuing to weaken, contrived to power the Dow to over 11700 again and the S&P500 to touch 1300. The FTSE100's gain to just over 5500 was more modest, held back by now out of favour natural resource stocks offsetting gains among the banks where substantial half-year losses had been well signalled and already largely discounted. The pre-rights, pre-offer prices of a month earlier had been left far behind and buyers were comforted by their belief that, by hook or by crook, the banks had managed to pull in the funds needed to rebuild their capital bases.

Black swan rising?

The fact that the markets' advance was not derailed by the sight of Russian tanks rolling over the border into Georgia surprised some commentators, who saw the invasion as creating the most serious East/West confrontation since the end of the Cold War. However, the bulls among them were encouraged by the absence of a major surge in the oil price in response to trouble in the region, given that Georgia was home to two major pipelines feeding into Western Europe, and the reason attributed to this "dog that didn't bark" was that weakening demand for oil was now seen as more important than risks to its supply. One writer was tempted to attribute this stoical performance of Western stock markets in the face of a potentially explosive situation to a growing perception by investors that in uncertain times they were a better bet than emerging markets located in 'far away countries of which we know nothing', where the attendant political risks were perhaps no longer worth running.

After all, rising commodity prices had been feeding inflationary pressures and slowing growth in China, India and other Asian markets, causing their stock markets to underperform those in London and New York, and their recent fall was now taking the steam out of the once more resilient markets of resource-rich Russia and Brazil. Far better to undertake a reappraisal of risk and stick to the stable countries of the developed world where regime change was determined by the ballot box and not by the bullet.

Such an investment strategy appeared to be justified by Russia's rampage through Georgia and the de facto annexation of the breakaway provinces of South Ossetia and Abkhazia in clear defiance of international law. It seemed that the attitudes of the old Soviet Union lived on in the Kremlin, strengthening doubts that Russia was a country we could do business with, something BP knew in relation to its oil interests.

China, too, was fast losing its former fans. Far from attracting an "Olympic bounce", the Shanghai Composite had fallen 10% since the start of the Games, taking the loss from its October 2007 peak to a massive 60%; and the huge security presence coupled with the heavy-handed treatment of foreign journalists and political protesters alike strongly suggested that China in company with Russia had not progressed very far from its repressive, totalitarian past. Clearly for free market capitalism to really work for the common good in a global context, economic reform had to go hand in hand with political reform.

The dollar starts to rise

Within days this perceived relative safe haven advantage for the stock markets of the developed world seemed to be the only argument in their favour as report after report flowed in of the deteriorating prospects for global growth. Second quarter GDP figures for the US and the UK had already been subjected to sharp downward revision and now the Eurozone and Japan weighed in with negative readings, all of which served to confirm fears that the second round effects of the credit contraction were well underway.

The result was to turn attention away from inflation as the global economy's principal concern and focus it firmly back on growth. After all, the argument went, with oil and most other key commodity prices falling and an economic downturn already in train, the recent high inflation figures looked likely to prove a temporary spike and central bankers' top priority had to be preventing the downturn morphing into a global economic crisis. The dramatic resurgence of the dollar since mid-July was seen as the manifestation of a profound shift in investor strategy involving a flight to the relative safety of US assets now that all the other major economies were so obviously in trouble.

Forex dealing up to that point had been based on interest rate differentials, largely ignoring the state of underlying economies, but the latter had now become the decisive factor – witnessed by the fall in sterling from \$2.00 to \$1.85 and in the euro from \$1.60 to \$1.47, albeit still recognising that their rates were likely to fall while US rates were more likely to rise. No one was denying that the ongoing credit contraction would hurt the US economy. It was simply that other countries would suffer more and the US was just the best of a bad lot.

As far as the UK was concerned, the currency moves provided a de facto devaluation of sterling which was precisely what was needed in the wake of the Bank of England's downbeat assessment of the economy's prospects, serving to counter inflationary fears and clear the way for interest rate cuts sooner rather than later. Such hopes might have been expected to buoy the London market but the FTSE100 proved unable to hold above 5500, settling in a 200 point range below that figure with day-to-day movements dominated largely by 5% to 10% fluctuations in banks, miners and oils.

In the US, the main stock indices followed much the same pattern, marking time in a narrow band well below the recent rally peaks of 11700 in the Dow and just over 1300 in the S&P500. Persistent talk of rising prime loan defaults leading to more writedowns for the banks and more problems for **Fanny Mae** and **Freddie Mac** coupled with worries about third quarter earnings, looked like limiting the scope for a further rally. Arguably, as a big user of oil with a consumer population obsessed by the price of gasoline, the US economy would be set to gain if the oil price continued to fall and given its failure to respond positively to recent geopolitical scares most commentators believed the trend would persist.

The old adage "nothing cures high prices like high prices" seemed very appropriate in a context of weakening demand. It was also very applicable to gold, where the price had fallen over 20% from its March peak to almost \$800 an ounce in response to a 19% drop in second quarter demand according to the World Gold Council. However, on 21st August the market suddenly decided that since Russia was second only to Saudi Arabia as the world's biggest oil exporter, the East/West confrontation over Georgia could have serious implications for the supply side and the oil price shot up over \$5 to top \$120 a barrel. The trigger for this delayed boost to the price was the announcement that the US was going ahead with its deal with Poland to site a missile defence shield in the former Warsaw Pact country and prospective NATO member, a move guaranteed to act like a red rag to a bull for a notoriously paranoid Kremlin.

Suddenly, analysts began to take another look at **Goldman Sachs'** forecast of the oil price reaching \$150 by the end of the year and **Gazprom's** estimate of \$200 over the same timescale, with the latter's figure carrying more weight, since as Russia's top producer, it had a degree of influence over the price. Speculation now arose about the prospects for the "buy oils, sell financials" strategy staging a comeback, a possibility that looked more like a probability as **Fannie Mae** and **Freddie Mac** nosed-dived 37% and 51% over the week to new lows on sharply heightened prospects of the need for a government-sponsored bail-out.

However, an abrupt reversal of the rise in the oil price, coupled with Ben Bernanke's use of the word 'encouraging' in the context of the drop in commodity prices and a stabilisation of the dollar, sparked a significant rally in New York and London, taking the indices almost back to their recent peaks.

Talking straight

Dispassionate market commentators saw the rallies as anomalous and making little sense against the background of headlines in the *Financial Times* the next morning, 'British economy shudders to a halt', and American business pages devoted to the multi-billion dollar losses that would hit US regional banks and insurance companies as well as Asian central banks if **Fannie** and **Freddie** went under. The fact that the share price of **HBOS**, the UK's largest provider of mortgages, was alone among the banks in dipping below the figure set for the pricing of its rights offer back in July, also suggested an uncomfortable parallel with the predicament of the US mortgage giants.

It was also apparent from a speech by Christopher Bean, deputy governor of the Bank of England, that unlike the Federal Reserve chairman he did not view the economic situation as at all 'encouraging', demonstrating once again his institution's unusual apolitical approach to problems for which politics had no answer. Rather, he believed the world economy had a 'long way to go' before it recovered from the worst crisis since the 1970s, an opinion Chancellor Darling subsequently endorsed, adding another thirty years to the timescale for good measure and breaking political ranks in the process. The markets seemed to agree and the Dow fell 240 points to 11381, setting the pattern for London and European exchanges to follow as well as for those in Asia.

Sentiment was not helped by **Lehman's** failure to secure a deal with the Korean Development Bank to purchase a stake in the business after the Korean regulatory authorities decided that such an acquisition was too risky for a government agency to undertake. With sovereign wealth funds practically the only buyers in town, **Lehman's** options were now seen to be severely limited and its obvious predicament had a depressing effect on the other big Wall Street investment banks already faced with the damaging implications of credit spreads widening again to top those ruling at the height of the **Bear Stearns** crisis. In any case, the purchase prices attached to the stakes in the banking houses of London and New York acquired earlier in the year no longer looked such a bargain and were likely to discourage further stake building as evidenced by the Bank of China's decision to reduce its holdings of securities issued by the two government-sponsored agencies.

Bids back in fashion

Fortunately for the bulls help was at hand in the shape of a dramatic upward revision of second quarter US GDP growth to 3.3%, coupled with an unexpected gain in durable goods orders, largely as a result of a strong export performance on the back of a weak dollar. Critics were quick to point out that with the dollar no longer weak and domestic consumption likely to tail off as the impact of the tax rebates faded, third quarter figures were not going to be of the same order, and a 200 point rally in the Dow was quickly followed by a 172 point fall to 11543 on the last trading day of August. London fared better, with the FTSE100 holding on to its gains in the 5600/5700 range, thanks to a renewed flurry of largely cash-financed M&A activity.

In the main the predators were cash-rich large-cap companies tempted by the depressed share prices of their targets and by the fall in sterling to launch opportunistic bids for their smaller rivals; witness **Santander's** swoop on **Alliance & Leicester** and **Adecco's** £1.25 billion bid for **Michael Page**. The major companies among the BRICs also were quick to spot an opportunity to extend their global reach, the latest example being India's **Infosys** buying UK software consultant **Axon**, and **Oil & Natural Gas Company of India** making a £1.4 billion cash offer for UK-listed **Imperial Energy**.

Most commentators saw this activity as providing some degree of support to current market levels but were not prepared to see it as a turning point given that the target companies in most cases were possessed of qualities that made them of special attraction to bidders. This was particularly true for the miners, where acquisition was a cheaper and a quicker alternative to setting up a project from ground zero. However, one commentator noted that one huge empire-building deal often marked the top in its sector and wondered if **BHP Billiton's** bid for **Rio Tinto** would have the same effect on Mines in 2008 as **Vodafone's** bid for **Mannesman** had on Telecoms in 2000.

The UK government's housing package was widely seen as more of a public relations exercise designed to lift Labour and Prime Minister Brown's flagging fortunes than as one capable of doing the same for a slumping house market, and as such had little effect on the stock market apart from providing a short-lived boost to the share prices of housebuilders and mortgage banks. Potentially of much more importance for stocks was the sharp fall in the oil price when it became clear that fears of damage to US production in the Gulf of Mexico were unfounded as Hurricane Gustav bypassed the area. With the price of a barrel of oil down from $147 in mid-July to currently below $110, the downtrend was beginning to look well-established and the hope was that it would take the sting out of inflation as well as soften the impact of recession and thus be broadly bullish for stock markets.

But if that was the hope, the realisation turned out very differently as UK investors saw falling sales and profits at **DSG** (**Currys and PC World**) and **Signet**, the world's largest jeweller, compounded with **Punch Tavern's** gloomy forecast and passed dividend, and decided that recession in any degree was not for them and ran for cover. Simultaneously, US markets demonstrated that falling oil and commodity prices carried a sting in their tail given the huge speculative positions held by many of the great and good of Wall Street, and Park Avenue in the case of **Ospraie Management** which closed its flagship fund after losing over $1 billion in the last six weeks as a result of losses incurred on its portfolio of energy, mining and resource stocks. Following just two days after the announcement from fellow New York hedge fund **Atticus** that it had lost $5 billion in the year to end-August, it was clear that the forced unwinding of large leveraged bets concentrated on fashionable market sectors was capable of creating havoc on the exchanges.

The losses were just the latest in a long run of hedge fund disasters which had multiplied ominously since the onslaught of the credit crunch, and raised questions about the validity of funds offering absolute returns and then failing to deliver. As previously noted, the heart of the problem seemed to be the fact that hedge funds simply did not 'hedge' in the precise meaning of the term, i.e. 'secure a bet or wager on one side by taking the odds on the other' (OED), a method employed by humble bookmakers to make a consistent and comfortable return while missing out on the chances of making a huge profit or more importantly, a huge loss. Instead, they were making huge leveraged unhedged bets which, while capable of generating bumper profits in a favourable environment, were certain to end in tears when the gambler's lucky streak ran out.

Interestingly, the **Ospraie** Fund's manager blamed the disaster on 'some of the sharpest declines in a six week period seen in the past ten to twenty years', an event which demonstrated that for whatever reason the lucky streak always runs out in the end due to the appearance of a black swan with a very fat tail. As the chairman of the Alternative Investment Association observed when asked to explain why hedge fund losses had risen back in 2005, 'They tend to find things difficult when there's a change in direction'. On this showing, perhaps the only difference between the abilities of the small investor and those of the mega fund manager lies in the greater claims made for them by the latter and of course the greater losses when he (or she) makes the wrong call. **Ospraie's** problems were doubly unfortunate for **Lehman Brothers**, which had taken a 20% stake in the firm three years previously, in that they cast doubt on the value of its other holdings just at the time it was trying to sell a 50% stake in itself at the best possible price.

Reality breaks in

By the end of the first week in September, the rally was looking to be well and truly over. In the face of an ever-increasing body of evidence that a global economic slowdown was not only inevitable but was also actually underway, investors at last abandoned their willing suspension of disbelief and stock markets plunged led by the Dow, down 3% on the week at 11220 and the S&P500, down 3.2% at 1236, while the FTSE100 lost 396 or 7% to 5240, not surprised but still disappointed by the "no change" bank rate decision. High hopes of an imminent bail-out for **Freddie Mac** and **Fannie Mae** late in the day offset to some extent the shock announcement that US unemployment had risen to a five-year high of 6.1% and a rally in Financials turned a 100 points plus loss in the Dow into a 32 point gain by the close.

In London the FTSE100 was weighed down by heavy losses in its oil, gas and mining company constituents comprising around 30% of the index as the global slowdown story took hold, while the banking sector remained under pressure on fears that a continuing fall in house prices would trigger further losses for banks and building societies as defaults grew. The OECD's report citing the UK as the EU country most likely to slip into recession was no help to sentiment but other European markets also fell sharply in the response to the ECB's introduction of restrictions on the class of collateral it was willing to accept in return for its liquidity provision, and a gloomy statement from Nokia, the world's largest maker of mobile phones, taken as an indicator of a broadening slowdown in consumer technology spending.

Japan also suffered, with the Nikkei225 falling 6.8% to 12212, its lowest level for five months. In Hong Kong, the drop below the psychologically important 20000 level on the Hang Seng index was a cause of more widespread concern, since it was seen as reflecting adverse macroeconomic conditions in mainland China. In India the BSE Sensex fared better, holding in the 14000/15000 band, and the Foreign Investment Institutions (FIIs) continued to be blamed in the local financial pages for repatriating their funds whenever the market dipped. Russia remained in the spotlight post-Georgia, with the RTS index losing 11% on the week, making a total of minus 35% from its high point earlier in the year; and here too there was evidence of a serious withdrawal of outside funding, the most important investment source in all emerging markets. Falling commodity prices hobbled the BOVESPA of resource-rich Brazil, leading to a drop of 6.7% over the week.

Too big to fail

Then came the announcement over the weekend that the US government was going to bail-out **Freddie Mac** and **Fannie Mae**. The action had been widely expected but clearly not fully discounted and it sparked the mother of all rallies with the Dow surging 350 points before ending the day with a gain of 290 points at 11510 with banking stocks the big winners, relieved that the bond holders of the two GSEs were now seen to be protected. In London an initial 200-point surge was maintained for the rest of the day after a connectivity problem put the electronic trading system out of operation for the next seven hours. There, too, banking stocks advanced strongly.

However, it was not good news for all the Financials since under the terms of the bail-out the value of **Fannie's** and **Freddie's** preferred stock was essentially wiped out and the many regional banks in the US which held that stock as part of their capital were going to be forced to raise new capital – not an easy task in the current climate. Another potential problem was the impact of the government takeover on the credit default swap market. Wall Street banks and insurance companies had written derivative contracts on billions of dollars in the two GSEs debt, in effect insuring against default, and since the takeover constituted a credit event equivalent to a bankruptcy, they were now faced with the prospect of payouts estimated to total around £25 billion.

And of course the bail-out did no favours for **Lehman Brothers**, whose ongoing predicament was widely blamed for stopping the rally in its tracks for two reasons.

One was that given the state of public finances, the US Treasury and the Fed would be reluctant to stage another costly rescue operation along the lines of the one for Bear Stearns. Another was that since both the **Bear Stearns** rescue and the **Fannie Mae** and **Freddie Mac** bail-out had protected debt holders but had left shareholders out in the cold, private investors would be wary of putting up money for a bank that could fail, and it would not have escaped their notice that following **Lehman's** capital raising in April, its shares had lost over 90% of their value in 2009.

The lost weekend

At the same time it had to be acknowledged that the fourth largest investment bank on Wall Street, **Lehman**, outranked **Bear Stearns**, which had been number five until absorbed by **JPMorgan**, and it was an even bigger player in the mortgage-backed securities market. As such, its demise would be a major blow to confidence in the already badly shaken global credit markets and clearly this was another case where "something must be done". Action was all the more necessary when the shares of **Merrill Lynch**, the third largest of the investment banks, had fallen to a 10-year low and **Washington Mutual**, the country's top savings and loans institution, was under severe pressure after it was reported that regulators had put the bank under special supervision. And for good measure, mighty **AIG**, once the biggest insurance company in the world, was clearly in trouble as it put $20 billion of non-core assets up for sale and requested access to the Fed's liquidity facility.

Another weekend meeting was called by Treasury Secretary Hank Paulson and Wall Street's top brass dutifully attended at the headquarters of the New York Federal Reserve; but with none of the banks prepared to rescue **Lehman** in the absence of the sort of government support provided in the case of **Bear Stearns**, the decision was taken to let **Lehman** go. Simultaneously, **Merrill Lynch** neatly avoided becoming the next target for short sellers, a group fast coming to be seen as the villains of the piece, by agreeing to be bought by **Bank of America** in a $50 billion all-share deal, and the Fed, along with ten of the biggest banks, announced the creation of a $70 billion pool of emergency funding.

While a surprise to many, the Treasury's abandonment of **Lehman** was broadly welcomed as a courageous move to deal with moral hazard, but taking a moral stand always has a downside and markets took fright the morning after at the prospect of the collapse of **Lehman's** bonds and equity which, just like Fannie's and Freddie's stock, were core holdings of banks and financial institutions from coast to coast. As stocks tumbled and the cost of buying credit insurance soared, **AIG** and its problems now became the centre of attention on fears that its now inevitable collapse would prove to be a far more serious blow to the financial system than anything the markets had seen since the crisis began. By the close the Dow was down a near record 505 points at 10917, a loss of 4.4%, and the S&P500 had dived 4.7% to 1192. London did not escape the fall-out, losing 212 to 5204, led by the banks and insurers where losses were widespread in the 10% to 20% range.

The next day's trading was nervous but not frenetic, with the Fed's decision to hold its key interest rate at 2.00% having a calming effect on Wall Street where the Dow ended the day with a gain of 141 points, though the FTSE100 lost 178 points to 5025 largely as a result of sharp falls among the banks and miners. But it was the calm before the storm. Far from being greeted with relief, the bail-out of 'too big and too interconnected to fail' **AIG** with the US government taking an 80% stake against an $85 billion 2-year loan, was rather seen as evidence of how bad things had become and how wide the financial malaise was spreading. 'Who's next?' was now the big question and the answer came back; **Morgan Stanley** and **Goldman Sachs** as their shares dived 24% and 14% respectively.

The panic was duplicated in London with **HBOS** very much in the firing line as the mortgage bank most reliant on the wholesale funding market. The shares actually halved to 88p at the opening before rallying to over 200p on rumours of a staged merger with supposedly ultra-conservative **Lloyds TSB**. Safety first was the day's dominant theme with government bond yields falling to record lows, and gold and oil reversing their recent downtrends with near-record one day gains in response to a weakening dollar. Overseas markets also suffered, with emerging ones falling the most since they were perceived as the most risky, and the Russian market was forced to close for two days in an attempt to stem the wave of selling.

In London by the close of business the FTSE100 had recovered much of the ground lost during the day to end at 4880, down just 32 points, but the whole scene was to change dramatically after-hours on news of the US Treasury's three-point plan to defuse the crisis. It was to create a government-sponsored agency along the lines of the Resolution Trust Corporation of 1989 to take over the estimated $700 billion of toxic mortgage-related assets on the banks' books that were poisoning the financial system; a move supported by a central bank consortium's injection of $180 billion into the money markets to boost liquidity, and by the banning of short-selling of financial stocks. A further $50 billion was also to be made available to insure money market mutual funds against the danger of breaking the buck, i.e. investors getting back less than the amount they had paid in, something that had just happened to the $62 billion Reserve Primary Fund after writing off $785 million of Lehman debt.

Wall Street instantly reversed the previous day's substantial losses that had taken the Dow back to 10609, soaring 410 points to 11019, and setting the stage for massive advances in stock markets across the world. Next day, London surged 431 points to 5311, an 8.8% gain that set a one-day record for the FTSE100, and comparable advances were seen throughout Europe. Elsewhere, Russia's dollar-dominated stock index topped the bill with a gain of over 22%, and Hong Kong's Hang Seng plussed almost 10% to 19327. The euphoric mood was maintained in New York and the Dow ended the week at 11388, up another 369 points.

The yield gap reappears

Optimism in London was reinforced by the emergence of a popular technical buy signal, as the dividend yield on the FTSE All-Share exceeded the yield on the 10-year gilt for the first time since March 2003, when it had marked the bottom of the last bear market. However, more critical observers were eager to point out that given a deteriorating economic background, dividend cuts were in prospect and that in any case, the origin of the yield gap pre-1959 was that equities ought to yield more than gilts to compensate for the greater risks involved in holding them, a state of affairs which most investors would find acceptable in the light of the dizzying falls in many household name stocks from their 2007 peaks.

Perhaps of greater significance was the boost to confidence provided by the arranged marriage between **HBOS** and **Lloyds TSB**, in that it appeared to avoid the very real possibility of another Northern Rock situation developing.

Warren Buffett shows his hand

A number of commentators were ready to say that two days of record stock market gains should not be seen as an acknowledgement that the credit crisis was going to be resolved by the US Treasury's bail-out proposals. In any case, the plan had to be approved by Congress and quickly, and the idea of taxpayers picking up the tab for the losses incurred by Wall Street bankers was not going to be popular with delegates, who baulked at accepting the principle of 'privatisation of gains and socialisation of losses'.

Markets dived again and were further unsettled by the dollar falling sharply at the prospect of an already bloated Federal budget deficit being additionally inflated by the cost of another rescue operation. A sudden spike in the oil price taking it to $130 at one point before reacting to just above $100 again was no help, but the move was confidently attributed to short covering ahead of a contract expiry date and caused little concern. More worrying was the news from the real economy where August job loss benefit applications rose to a 7 year high, big ticket manufactured goods orders fell 4.5% and new home sales continued to drop, while **GE** cut its profit forecast yet again and fears were expressed about the performance of its financial services division **GE Capital**.

On the plus side, there were events taking place on Wall Street, where the crisis had originated, that were being seen as perhaps pointing the way out of the dark valley and towards the sunlit hills beyond. Most important of all was the decision of **Goldman Sachs** and **Morgan Stanley** to change their status from investment banks to regular commercial banks, a transition that would bring them under the regulatory eye of the Federal Reserve and at the same time provide them with permanent access to Federal funds, thereby validating their business models. Within hours, legendary investor Warren Buffett bestowed his seal of approval by boosting **Goldman Sachs'** capital with a $5 billion purchase of preferred stock, with warrants to invest another $5 billion.

Given Mr Buffett's reputation as the world's most successful investor, his purchase was seen as a massive vote of confidence in Wall Street's top player and thus in Wall Street itself, although one cynical observer wondered if he could detect an echo of John D. Rockerfeller's reassuring statement in October 1929, 'My son and I are buying sound common stocks'. A further boost to the embattled banking sector was provided by **Mitsubishi Financial**, Japan's largest bank, agreeing to buy a 20% stake in **Morgan Stanley**, although its shares still fell on fears that the deal might not go through.

Despite the impassioned urgings of the Treasury Secretary, supported by the Fed chairman and then by President Bush, it soon became clear that Congress was not going to be steamrollered into accepting the rescue plan. Meanwhile, the news was getting steadily worse, topped by the collapse of **Washington Mutual**, the country's biggest savings and loans institution, and the sale of its deposits and mortgage portfolio to **JPMorgan** for $1.9 billion, a deal leaving both equity and bond holders out in the cold just as they had been in the case of **AIG** and **Lehman Brothers**.

The virtual wipeout for both classes of investors did not augur well for the chances of finding new sources of finance for the many other financial institutions looking for capital, a need intensified by the failures of the biggest names on Wall Street and the collapse in value of their stocks and bonds which were in the portfolios of practically every institution in the country. Such negative fallout was blamed on the law of unintended consequences, but given the rapid succession of disaster after disaster, it now looked as if the financial authorities were simply being overwhelmed by events over which they had no control. Hence the air of desperation evident in the presentation of the bail-out plan and one fully justified by the paralysis in the money markets and the almost daily parade of the problems it was creating throughout the business world. After **Washington Mutual**, **Wachovia**, the fourth largest bank in America, was clearly next in line for rescue, with the cost of insuring its debt rising sharply and its share price plunging.

In Europe, shares in the Belgo-Dutch banking and insurance group, **Fortis**, slumped to a 14-year low despite assurances from the Belgian government that depositors' savings were safe. And in the UK, **Bradford & Bingley** was in the headlines again on reports that it was going to follow **Northern Rock** down the nationalisation path unless a buyer could be found. The Bank of England tried to help matters by expanding its liquidity support operations with another $40 billion of loans to banks against a less restrictive range of collateral, but more than one observer pointed out that this was just the latest in a long line of liquidity injections and there was little reason to expect it to do any more than its predecessors. Clearly the real problem lay beyond liquidity and centred more on solvency and hence the reluctance of banks to lend to each other.

The party's over

The actual agreement over the shape of the US bail-out package took place over the weekend of 27/28 September and the all-important announcement was scheduled only hours ahead of the opening of the Asian markets on 28/29 September and just before Wall Street's opening bell. In the event, the news did not receive the rapturous welcome so widely predicted, since Asian markets were preoccupied with growing evidence of problems within their own banking sector, and London and European markets had to face up to the contemporaneous announcements that **Bradford & Bingley** had been nationalised, that **Fortis** had been rescued by the three Benelux governments taking a 49% stake in the group in return for a €11.2 billion cash injection, and that German property giant **Hypo Real Estate** had been bailed out with a €35 billion guarantee by a consortium put together by its bankers after it had run out of funds. The three biggest banks in Iceland also fell under suspicion and their share prices plummeted after the government declared it had taken a 75% stake in **Glitnir Bank** in return for a €600 million infusion of cash. All three had consistently punched above their weight in international markets as a result of supplementing their small domestic deposit base by tapping the wholesale money markets, a strategy now seen as seriously compromising their stability.

Against such a depressing background, stock markets everywhere lost ground but were buoyed to some degree by the confident expectation that the US troubled asset relief programme (TARP) would be approved by Congress as a matter of necessity. The announcement that it had not, albeit by only a narrow margin, took the markets totally by surprise. The Dow recorded its largest ever points fall with a 777 point plunge to 10365 while the S&P500 lost 106 points to 1106, an 8.8% drop, and the NASDAQ dipped below 2000 for the first time since 2003, losing 199 points. London and the European exchanges plunged with the FTSE100 shedding 269 points to 4818 and the Eurofirst 300, 57 to 1047. Dublin fared worst of all with a 12.7% dive spearheaded by the banks with losses ranging from 15% to as much as 45%. Asian markets saw falls in the 4% to 5% range although Hong Kong actually reversed early losses. Trading was halted on the Russian markets for the second time in a week and in Brazil the BOVESPA tumbled by 10%. Bonds gained in the flight to safety with the yield on the US 2-year T. Bill falling to 1.64%, and the gold price topped $900 again while the oil price fell to $96 on expectations that a global slowdown was now inevitable in the wake of the credit crisis.

The world's financial problems were now lead stories in the media and with a two day gap before Congress could be recalled, doubts and fears reigned supreme in the face of yet more evidence of the damage being incurred by financial institutions across the world as a result of the credit meltdown. The Irish government stepped in to guarantee for two years the deposits and debts of its six national banks to ensure the stability of the Irish financial system and on the same day the governments of France, Belgium and Luxembourg got together to provide €6.4 billion of emergency funding for Dexia, the Belgo-French bank specialising in local authority funding, after its shares had fallen 30% in a single trading session. 'There is no need to panic', said the governor of France's central bank.

In the UK, the **Royal Bank of Scotland** continued to underperform the banking sector on concerns that it would suffer from the problems of Fortis, its partner in the takeover of **ABN Amro** in 2007, while **HBOS** fell significantly below the indicated merger price with **Lloyds TSB** on talk of renegotiation or even abandonment of the merger. Further afield in Hong Kong queues formed to withdraw savings from the **Bank of East Asia** on rumours of losses resulting from exposure to the collapse of **Lehman Brothers** and **AIG**, prompting the central bank to issue strong denials and also to inject $500 million into the markets to aid liquidity. In India, the Reserve Bank was obliged to provide additional liquidity to **ICICI**, the country's second largest lender, to stop a run on the bank inspired by Lehman Brothers-related losses.

The day the music died

News that the revised rescue bill had been approved second time around met with a surprisingly negative response by stock markets, given the 78 to 25 majority in favour, but doubts persisted over how the measure would fare in the House of Representatives. Markets were also becoming increasingly concerned about the state of the US economy, with jobs lost in September topping economists' forecasts at 159,000 as employment contracted for nine months in a row and new orders at American factories tumbled.

But most worrying of all, in the view of many commentators, was the paralysis gripping the money markets, as banks continued to hoard cash, unwilling to lend to each other or to anyone else. Much of the blame for this state of affairs continued to be attributed to the decision not to rescue **Lehman Brothers**, thereby effectively wiping out the value of £160 billion in unsecured bonds held around the world. With six household name banks requiring rescue in the US and in Europe in the space of just one week, such caution among their fellow banks was hardly surprising but in the context of the hopes pinned on the passing of the US bail-out bill, the fact that credit was tighter than it had ever been did not suggest that the crisis was anywhere near resolution.

As one writer declared, credit markets overrule stock markets and investors should take their lead from the former when making their investment decisions, something companies were already doing, as evidenced by **Xstrata** dropping its bid for **Lonmin** 'in the light of the current unprecedented uncertainty in the financial markets', **Adecca** deciding not to go ahead with its bid for **Michael Page**, and a private equity consortium walking away from a £1.9 billion bid for **Informa** after struggling to come up with the money.

But perhaps the most depressing of all for the bulls was the reaction of the markets to the approval of the bail-out bill by a convincing majority of 263 votes for and 171 against after the original $700 billion package had been boosted by another $149 billion of politically inspired "extras". For the Dow to have been up 314 points before the vote and down 157 points after suggested to one commentator that Friday 3rd October was fated to become a key date in the economic calendar, namely 'The day the music died', when the full horror of the financial crisis finally got through to the public.

The central banks were no longer the lenders of last resort but had become the lenders of only resort as a result of the money market funds which supply the bulk of the liquidity to the commercial paper markets avoiding lending to any financial institution whose stability was remotely questionable. Thus when credit ceases to circulate, businesses cannot continue to function normally and elect to move into survival mode, hanging on to what cash they have or using it to do no more than pay down debt, cancelling acquisitions, investments, and cutting costs and jobs.

Combined operations

The big question now was would the 'troubled asset relief programme' and the liquidity boosts get credit flowing freely again in the US and would the similar measures instituted by the Bank of England and the ECB do the same in the UK? The announcement over the weekend that the **Hypo Real Estate** rescue had broken down after the consortium had failed to come up with the money did not augur well for a credit revival in Europe, and neither did the uncoordinated and potentially divisive response of national banks to the crisis as one after another pledged to guarantee bank deposits. The IMF now weighed in with a statement to the effect that since 'piecemeal interventions to address liquidity strains have not succeeded in restoring market confidence, a systemic problem requires a systemic solution'.

Plunging stock markets across the world emphasised the urgent need for such a 'systemic solution' as the Dow fell below the 10000 level for the first time since 2003 and the FTSE100 recorded its biggest ever points fall at 491 taking it down to 4589, with bank shares in both countries recording unprecedented percentage falls. In an attempt to provide that solution, the Federal Reserve, the European Central Bank and the Bank of England together with the central banks of Canada, Sweden and Switzerland surprised markets with a co-ordinated emergency action to cut interest rates by half a percentage point. Central banks in Australia, China, Hong Kong, South Korea and Taiwan followed their lead. The Fed also announced that it would intervene in the commercial paper market to assist companies' day-to-day financing, the first time such action had been taken since the Depression. The European Union demonstrated that it too could be co-ordinated with an agreement on bank rescue principles leaving all 27 member states free to adopt measures ranging from recapitalisations to asset purchases to state-backed guarantees.

Still, in a week that was to see the collapse of Iceland's entire banking system as **Landsbank** and **Kaupthing** went to the wall, all these unprecedented co-ordinated measures failed to dispel investors' fears and restore their confidence as stock markets across the world continued to slide. The UK's three-point £500 billion bail-out plan for the banking sector received a good press and became the model for similar action to be taken by the US and the European governments in respect of the provision of public funding to recapitalise the banks and in effect to partly nationalise them. The other measures relating to guaranteeing interbank lending and the provision of yet more emergency liquidity were also widely adopted, but the UK plan was to have a more beneficial effect on the standing of its embattled Prime Minister than on markets, which were to suffer their worst week on record.

By the close of business on Friday, the Dow was down 22.9% to 8451 after slipping below 8000 intraday at one point, the FTSE100 had lost 21% to 3932 and the the Eurozone markets' losses were all above 20%. Tokyo suffered the biggest loss in Asian markets at 24.3% to 8276. As for the BRICs, Brazil was down 22.5%, Russia 21%, both reacting in part to falling commodity prices, while India had lost 19% and China 12.8%.

'Things fall apart'

The sheer extent of the falls resulting from 'the worst financial crisis the world had ever seen' prompted more than one equity market strategist to suggest that it would produce a once in a generation long-term buying opportunity, a view backed by Warren Buffett who had said much the same thing earlier in the month when supplementing his investment in **Goldman Sachs** with a $3.6 billion purchase of **GE** stock. However, it has to be noted that the Sage of Omaha was taking very much a belt and braces approach to his investments in America's leading financial and industrial enterprises by making them in preference stock with a 10% coupon. One writer was also tempted to point out that if 10 years is considered to be a reasonable long-term period, then a hopeful investor towards the end of 1998 (when both the Dow and the FTSE100 stood considerably higher than today's levels) who after ten years of "non-inflationary continuous expansion' might justifiably wonder if the next ten would be any better.

Certainly, the next ten days brought no reassurance as 'the worst week in history' for stock markets was succeeded by huge and illogical swings in individual stock prices and whole indices taking volatility to record highs as funds tried to reconcile their positions. Overshadowing everything were increasing signs that the financial crisis was morphing into an economic crisis of global proportions. Emerging markets' downside performance now began to accelerate at the prospect of disappearing export markets in the developed world, evidenced by the biggest drop in US retail sales in September since 1989 and the belated admission by the authorities in the UK and in the Eurozone that their economies were in recession. Particularly hard hit were the stock markets of resource-rich Brazil and Russia, now plunging in response to the collapse in commodity prices as a result of a dramatic falling off in demand from their principal customers, India and China, now strikingly evidenced by a collapse in dry cargo shipping rates.

Adding to the woes of emerging markets was the flight of capital as Western investors looked at the mounting losses on their investments and the soaring credit spreads of sovereign debt as their currencies slumped and decided that risk aversion was the name of the game. Unfortunately and inevitably, the process served to make matters worse, raising the spectre of debt default and causing the queue of countries lining up for loans from the International Monetary Fund to lengthen. And, of course, one of the results of repatriating funds to what were perceived as safer shores was a sharp rise in the US dollar and the Japanese yen, the currencies of the world's two largest economies.

Meanwhile, governments in the developed world continued to dole out money and provide guarantees for their own embattled financial sectors but all with apparently little effect. Interbank lending rates were easing but still remained tight and with further writedowns in prospect for the second half of the year, there was no doubt that without the pledge of government support, bank shares would have continued to fall. Some encouragement for the banking sector in the US, however, was provided by the sight of **Wells Fargo** stealing **Wachovia** from under **Citibank's** nose, and not being put off by the target's subsequent reporting of a $24.7 billion quarterly loss, the biggest in banking history, and by **Mitsubishi Financial** going ahead with its deal to buy a 20% stake in **Morgan Stanley**.

In the UK, share price movements following the announcement of the terms of the £37 billion share issue for **Royal Bank of Scotland**, **HBOS** and **Lloyds TSB** to be underwritten by the government, suggested that the bulk of the issue would be left with the underwriter. Then in the final week of October, the two banks that had remained largely unscathed by the subprime scandal and supposedly cushioned by their extensive Asian interests suddenly nosedived, with **HSBC** dropping from 840p to under 700p and **Standard Chartered** from 1130p to 658p. Insurance shares took a beating on growing concerns about their capital positions given that all three of their principal asset classes, namely equities, corporate bonds and commercial property, were all in serious decline.

Looking for a rally

No one could now claim that stock markets had not caught up with events in the real economy. Indeed, with the share prices of many of the world's biggest and most revered banking houses collapsing like the busted flushes of the dotcom era, and those of household name companies capable of losing half their valuation in a single trading week, it could be argued that stock markets were overreacting. And if much of the selling was coming from funds forced to raise cash to meet redemptions and from others desperate to deleverage, then any concept of "value" had gone out of the window, making the judgement over whether or not a once in a generation buying opportunity was presenting itself a subjective one on the part of the private investor.

Nevertheless, even though the economic news continued to be as bad or even worse than expected, the sheer extent of the falls in share prices in October argued that a significant rally was imminent. After all, nothing goes down in a straight line, and the only surprise about the blistering rally that occurred on 28th October, taking the Dow up 890 points (10.9%) to 9065, was that it was attributed to expectations that the Fed would cut interest rates the next day, a move that had been widely predicted and regarded as a certainty.

Another reason given for the rally was speculation that the Japanese authorities would intervene to curb the recent dramatic rise in the yen by cutting interest rates from 0.5% to 0.25%, thereby reducing pressure on its hard-pressed exporters as well as on investors who had borrowed in yen to fund investments in higher-yielding currencies and assets. A sudden unwinding of this carry trade was reckoned to be bad news in that it created losses that would then have to be made up by forced sales, further destabilising markets.

Fed cuts to 1%

The Fed's rate cut duly came the next day, with one half of one percentage point to 1%, its lowest level since June 2004. The sharp rise in US markets was contagious, helping Japan's Nikkei Dow rally 6.4% from its lowest level in 26 years as well as boosting all the other Asian markets. Russia's RTS index gained 4.8% while Brazil's BOVESPA rose by 13.4%. London's reaction was more modest initially but the FTSE100 managed to add some 400 points in the next two days to end the month at 4377. Japan now followed the Fed, with a 0.2% cut bringing its key rate down to 0.3%; a move that increased expectations that the Bank of England and the European Central Bank would make further cuts at their meetings scheduled for the following week.

A run of depressing news on the US economy failed to dent this new-found investor enthusiasm and stock markets continued to advance, further buoyed by the prospect of an end to the uncertainty over the outcome of the US presidential election. However, the election day surge that took the Dow up over 300 points, causing the S&P500 to top 1000 again, was not to last. The Obama victory had been well discounted and attention now reverted to the economic crisis gripping America and indeed the whole world, a situation that allowed for no honeymoon period. And just to prove the point, stock markets everywhere went into sharp reverse, with the Dow shedding 486 points to 9139, the S&P500 re-entering three figure territory at 952 and the FTSE100 losing over 100 points to 4532.

Only in America...

While acknowledging the gravity of the problems facing America and the world, commentators were unanimous in believing that the chances for a successful outcome had risen dramatically as a result of the election of Barack Obama to the presidency. The event had demonstrated the ability of America to reinvent itself by elevating to the White House a "man for all seasons", with evidently transnational appeal at a time when the country was still seen as the ideological and economic leader of the free world. The US Federal Reserve was already re-establishing itself as the central bankers' central bank (a position it had never really lost despite the intermittent scares about a collapse of the dollar) with its latest move setting up dollar swap lines with Brazil, South Korea, Singapore and Mexico.

Within days, the European Central Bank, the Bank of England and the Swiss National Bank followed America's lead and launched a co-ordinated series of interest rate cuts amid signs of worsening economic conditions across Europe. The Bank of England's totally unexpected cut of one and a half percentage points to 3%, the largest in that institution's history, taking the rate to its lowest level since 1954, was seen, however, as more of an indication of just how serious the crisis had become rather than as a rescue operation, and the FTSE100 promptly lost almost 6% to 4272. Such fears seemed to be confirmed as the US markets continued to fall, with the Dow losing another 443 points to 8695 and the S&P500 slipping back to the 900 level. The extraordinary rally that had taken both London and New York up just on 20% from their October 27th low points to record a mini bull market appeared to have shot its bolt.

The release of data showing that 240,000 jobs had been lost in October and that the unemployment rate had jumped from 6.1% to 6.5%, a 14-year high, might have been expected to confirm the worst fears about the US economy and hit the Dow for six but instead it managed to add 248 points to 8943. Other markets followed Wall Street's lead, with London plussing 93 to 4365 with similar percentage gains being recorded across Europe. More than one commentator was prepared to call a turn in the London market on the basis that at the previous week's low point the P/E on the All-Share Index at 8.3 was on a par with that ruling at the bottom of the market in 1974.

Furthermore, the recovery from that point had taken place against a background of appallingly bad economic and corporate data, suggesting that it was now all in the price, a view substantiated in part by a week-long rally in **Marks & Spencer** following a shock 43% dip in first half profits amid more evidence of a sharp slowdown in consumer spending. **British Airways** shares pursued a similar path, rising 12% after reporting a 92% dive in interim profits and passing the dividend. Sentiment was also boosted by the government's strong-arm tactics with the banks to ensure that the one and a half point interest rate cut was actually passed on to home owners and the sight of LIBOR coming down to a level which, although uncomfortably high, was back to pre-Lehman levels.

All hands to the pump

But if the general consensus among market commentators was that things would continue to get worse before they got better, there was also a feeling that the actions being taken by governments everywhere were beginning to contain the situation. This view was now to gain support from China's introduction of a near $600 billion economic stimulus package designed to boost domestic demand. The reaction was an immediate boost to Asian markets and then to European markets where mining stocks led the advance on hopes of a reprieve from China's slowdown.

But once again such hopes were dashed as the initial worldwide rally faded in the face of a continuing stream of adverse industrial and financial news. As one writer pointed out, the Chinese Premier calling the latest measures 'our biggest contribution to the world' did not make them so, and they would do nothing to boost the ailing fortunes of **Ford, Chrysler** and **General Motors**, America's top automobile makers. All of them for economic and political reasons were "too big to fail" but would certainly do so without the $25 billion handout they were asking the government to provide. Neither would they help **AIG**, having to up its take from the government with a revised $120 billion bail-out package, nor **American Express**, changing into a bank holding company in order to gain access to the financial rescue package and to Federal funding. Fortunately, for American industry and finance, both seemed to have developed much the same relationship with the government for reasons of necessity as their counterparts in China had with theirs for reasons of ideology.

Back to the future

With the advance of stock markets stalling after their sharp recovery from the depths plumbed in the closing days of October, the debate continued over whether a bottom had been formed or we had seen no more than a rally in an ongoing bear market. In the case of the London market, interestingly, there was no more mention of the supposed "buy signal" that had flashed in mid-September when the yield on the FTSE All-Share index had topped that on UK 10-year Gilts for the first time since March 2003, the starting point of the 2003-2007 bull market. In fact, far from closing again, the gap had continued to widen as markets continued to fall and two months later was over a full percentage point. So, for the first time since going into reverse in August 1959, a date widely regarded as marking the dawn of the cult of the equity, markets had gone back to the old values. Government bonds provided a safe investment with a guaranteed return. Equities, on the other hand, had their ups and downs affecting the dividends they paid and a higher return was demanded to compensate for the risks incurred by holding them, an arrangement that their performance in recent months appeared to validate.

It was difficult not to see this largely unremarked development as signalling a sea change in investment perceptions in the wake of the rollercoaster ride that equities had experienced in the twenty-first century. A portfolio loaded with the technology, media and telecom stocks that were so popular in the first quarter of 2000 was devastated in the 2000/2003 bear market and failed to recover much ground in the 2003/2007 bull market led by mines, oils and financials. Now they were being devastated in their turn, resulting in October seeing the biggest monthly loss in stock markets across the world in twenty-one years. Massive co-ordinated interest rate cuts and liquidity injections coupled with unprecedented government-sponsored bank bail-outs appeared to have had no effect on frozen credit markets and the only gainers over the month were the supposed safe havens provided by the dollar and the yen, short-dated government bonds and cash.

November brought no relief to markets but rather the reverse in the face of a relentless flow of grim economic news. US companies reported the biggest round of job cuts for fifteen years, with another 52,000 to go from **Citigroup** on top of the 23,000 already announced, 9500 from carrier **DHL** as it ended its US-based service, and 43,000 from the country's number two electrical goods retailer, **Circuit City**, as it filed for bankruptcy; all of which meant that the unemployment rate, which had jumped from 6.1% in September to 6.5% in October, still had a lot higher to go. In the UK, the number rose by 140,000 in the third quarter to 1.8 million, a figure estimated to rise to 2.9 million in 2010 in the context of GDP expected to fall by 1.3% or more in 2009.

Retail sales on both sides of the Atlantic plunged to new record lows in a now seemingly well-established trend highlighted by profit warnings from companies as diverse as top mobile phone maker **Nokia, BT** and **DSG** (Currys and PC World), department store giants **Macy's** and **JCPenney**, chipmaker **Intel** and **Sun Microsystems**. Even **Apple** and **Google** were to lose their star status, with the shares of the latter dipping below $300 for the first time in three and a half years. And top European software house, **SAP**, reported that it had 'never witnessed such a sharp decline in customer spending in such a short time'.

Banks in trouble again

Banks continued to be under pressure. They were being urged by the governments providing them with bail-out money, to go ahead and do what banks are supposed to do and lend money to cash-strapped companies. The banks argued that in the current climate it would not be good banking practice to do so, thereby finding themselves in a "damned if you do, damned if you don't" situation reflected in their share prices falling to record lows. US Treasury Secretary Paulson's decision not to use TARP to unburden the banks of their toxic assets but instead to provide them with additional capital and let them sort the problem out for themselves was not widely welcomed since not only did it suggest uncertainty and indecision in high places, but it also sent the asset-backed securities indices into freefall, thereby making the banks' problems worse.

Citigroup was seen as a big loser under the new deal and its shares fell to a 15-year low despite the news that Saudi Arabia's Prince Alwaleed Bin Talal was increasing his stake in the bank from 4% to 5% (although it should be noted that the Prince is not renowned for his stock-picking skills). The other banks were also under a cloud with **JPMorgan's** "fortress" balance sheet failing to save it from falling to a five year low at $23, **Bank of America** dropping to its lowest point since 1996 at $11.25, and even a new look **Goldman Sachs** retreating to $52, a figure below the flotation price of its shares in 1999.

Banks in the UK were also hitting new lows, with **Royal Bank of Scotland**, **HBOS** and **Lloyds TSB** continuing to trade well below the terms set for the government-sponsored share issue, while **Barclays'** share price suffered from the market perception that raising capital from investors in the Middle East was going to prove much more costly and much less shareholder-friendly than it would have been by taking the King's shilling.

No great hopes were pinned on the outcome of the G20 summit held in mid-November given the lengthy timescale attached to its agreement on 'fiscal measures to stimulate domestic demand to rapid effect, as appropriate, while maintaining a policy framework conducive to fiscal sustainability'. The fact that some members were pressing for more regulation in the financial system worried Lex in the *Financial Times,* since the heart of the crisis clearly lay less with unregulated hedge funds than with over-leveraged, regulated banks, suggesting that the need was for better supervision rather than more regulation.

Here we go again!

With the FTSE100 hovering a couple of hundred points above the 4000 mark, the Dow holding above 8000 and the S&P500 just north of 800, the fact that these levels were being maintained in the face of a constant flow of deeply depressing news, revived the "it's all in the price" argument for some commentators who believed the lows of the last week in October would not be revisited, However, that idea was to take a sharp knock over the next few days as the indices crashed through these popular round-number support levels, impelled by growing fears about the severity of the global economic slowdown, evidenced in part by the once unimagined sight of the oil price falling below $50 a barrel for the first time in over three years and a Reuters global benchmark commodity index slipping to a five-year low.

A dip below the end-October low points would mean that the bulls would have to restate their case and perhaps conclude that since none of them guessed that the markets would be where they were today, then it was logical to further conclude that they were in unknown territory. This mood of uncertainty was now to be intensified by the failure of Congress to come up with a quick decision on the $25 billion rescue plan for the automobile industry, suggesting further indecision at a point when time was of the essence.

All these worries contributed to a sudden escalation in the lack of confidence in markets, resulting in a buying stampede for government bonds – pushing yields to historic lows, with that on the 10-year T-bond falling to 3% and that on the 2-year to below 1% for the first time ever. US equities as represented by the S&P500 now yielded more than 10-year government bonds for the first time in fifty years. This sudden reversal of roles for equities and bonds had not signalled a buying opportunity in the London market in September and few expected it to do so on Wall Street in November, especially since the event was widely hailed in the financial press as confirmation of fears that the world was heading for a 'true depression that would bear comparison with that of the 1930s'.

A Thanksgiving for Citigroup

However, in the short-term at least, that expectation was wrong and the US government's decision to bail-out **Citigroup** in the week of Thanksgiving was seen by investors as another reason for celebration, sparking a record two-day points gain in the Dow taking it up to 8443 again and recovering all the ground lost in the previous week. The sheer extent of the bail-out with just over $300 billion devoted to guaranteeing the bank's tainted assets plus another $20 billion cash injection on top of the $25 billion already pledged, raised a few eyebrows but the market appeared to take the view that the outgoing administration did not want another Lehman on its conscience and this was no time for half measures. The Fed's further moves to lend up to $800 billion against mortgage-backed securities and to extend the scope to cover consumer and small business loans were also welcomed in the hope that they would bridge the gap until the new administration's $700 billion stimulus package was up and running under the direction of the President's "dream team" of economic advisers.

The London market had its own excitement in the final week of November as Chancellor Darling unveiled his pre-budget collection of measures designed to provide a stimulus to a clearly flagging economy. However, the market's enthusiastic response with a record percentage one-day rise taking the FTSE100 back into the 4000 plus comfort zone at 4152 did not accord with the views of the bulk of the financial press, where the measures were labelled a '£20 billion gamble'. The idea that such a relatively minor stimulus could offset the downside risks of a recession that was almost certainly going to be longer and deeper than the Chancellor predicted was given little credibility, and the broad consensus was that the country would remain yoked to an increasing burden of public debt as the timescale for economic recovery lengthened.

The fact that public borrowing was now expected to total some £78 billion in the current financial year (against the £43 billion forecast by the Treasury as recently as March) and to reach £120 billion in 2009/10 was defended by the government on the grounds that such spending was necessary to manage the recession, but in that it guaranteed higher taxes in the future, the whole policy was widely seen as New Labour reverting to the "tax and spend" habits of Old Labour. And without regard to political bias, concern at this unprecedented level of public debt was evident in a sharp rise in the cost of insuring against the British government defaulting on its gilts over the next five years, even though such an event had never happened since their creation in 1694.

Woolworths goes under

Meanwhile, back at the sharp end of the economy, all was clearly not going well. On the same day as century-old retailer **Woolworths** and top kitchen maker, **MFI** went into administration, **DSG** reported the first half-year loss in two decades and passed the dividend and **Kingfisher**, Europe's leading home improvement store, announced sharply lower third quarter sales and profits and the closure of its Trade Depot branches. The fallout from the collapse of **Woolworths** was considered likely to hurt the whole of the retailing industry, from High Street stores to suppliers, the former as a result of aggressive discounting as stocks were cleared and the latter from the withdrawal of credit insurance cover.

With official data showing a continuing fall in consumer spending, the whole retail sector was being shunned by investors as **Marks & Spencer's** post-results rally was unwound and **Tesco's** share price fell below the 300p level on fears that it was losing market share in the price war with discounters. US retailers were under similar pressure as consumer spending dipped in the third quarter to record its biggest fall since 1995, and there was little expectation that Black Friday – the day after Thanksgiving when pre-Christmas spending was relied upon to turn stores' losses on the year to-date into profits – would live up to its name save in a doom-laden sense.

The impressive advance in global markets led by Wall Street in the final week of November, to the extent that it had been inspired by an unprecedented run of co-ordinated stimulus and rescue operations by governments in all the big power blocs, raised hopes among the bulls that it would continue into December to form the time-honoured end-year rally. The bears countered with their conviction that all we had seen so far was stock markets reacting to the first phase of the most serious economic crisis in almost a century, namely the breakdown of the financial system. Phase Two, the hammer blow to the so-called real economy, was just beginning to take effect, driving output cuts, rising unemployment and corporate failures from pole to pole.

While admitting the potential for a major stock market rally in the wake of falls of over 50% in the indices of the developed world and of even more in emerging markets, the bears believed that such a rally was precisely what had just occurred and there was no reason for expecting it to continue. They also maintained that the reappearance of the yield gap as bond yields fell to levels not seen in fifty years and commodity prices continued to plunge, clearly signalled a weakening economy with falling corporate profits and dividends, a process that made nonsense of the bulls' contention that equities were now substantially undervalued.

Trouble in China ... and India

One commentator saw dangers, if unquantifiable ones, in the fact that the concept of "de-coupling" when the stars of the emerging markets like India and China would continue to boom, and thus compensate for the slowdown in economies of the developed world, had been turned on its head. Belief in the validity of this concept had sent their stock markets to record peaks a year ago as Western markets stumbled but since then they had fallen dramatically, driven down by collapsing oil and commodity prices and by falling export volumes to the developed world.

The mistake, as the writer saw it, was to have seen the countries as simply larger and more populous variants of the Western and the Japanese models instead of countries the size of continents where the First World and the Third World lived side by side. Theirs was a society divided between the "haves" of a rising, largely urban, middle class, that also formed a ruling elite, and the "have-nots" of the multi-ethnic, multi-religious, and largely rural, masses. The fallout from the credit crunch was going to have much the same effect on the former as it had on their Western counterparts but the latter would suffer much more as development projects were shelved through lack of funds and many more cents of the "dollar-a-day" they lived on would be spent on food.

And any idea that expanding domestic consumption would take up the slack from falling exports was always going to be totally unrealistic. Far more likely was the prospect of domestic unrest as the masses blamed their plight on their rulers, threatening their position and creating a counter reaction from an elite who saw "democracy" in a Western sense as an alien concept. This appeared to be at the root of the trouble in Thailand where protesters were trying to overturn a democratically elected government pledged to support the rural poor. In China, the slowdown in growth had thrown millions of migrant workers from the hinterland out of work and the government of the People's Republic was discovering that having quite such a large disaffected population was not conducive to social stability. The biggest interest rate cut since 1997 and a huge public works programme were therefore measures of necessity, even of desperation.

India's problems were even more complex for a country with over 100 million Muslims within its borders and a Hindu nationalist party bitterly resenting the presence of a single one, a situation where political activism could easily upgrade to terrorism as it had just done in Mumbai. Still, a democracy of 1.2 billion people that owed its apparent cohesion more to a nationwide addiction to Bollywood films and cricket than to a government formed out of a coalition of twenty diverse political parties, was always going to have a fight on its hands.

India and China might indeed become the world's superpowers by 2030, the writer agreed, but on their present showing Western investors not willing to wait that long would be better advised to keep their money where they could see it rather than hazard it in faraway countries of which they knew nothing.

All together now

December dawned and there was little sign of a Christmas rally as the flow of adverse economic and corporate news continued unabated. Another round of rate cuts by the Bank of England and the European Central Bank, of 1% to 2% and of 0.75% to 2.5% respectively, coinciding with similar moves by central banks in Sweden, Australia and New Zealand and by "quantitative easing" on the part of the US Federal Reserve, failed to inspire confidence in investors, whose appetite for buying stocks had been dulled by a conviction that the global slump was deepening and that the news could only get worse.

Even the massive percentage fall in the price of oil and other commodities was no longer seen as primarily beneficial on the counter-inflationary front but as disruptive by reason of its unexpectedness and rapidity; witness the collapse of the **Rio Tinto/BHP Billiton** merger, an event that blighted the whole of the mining sector on the prospect of falling demand for its products as global growth slowed. The slowdown was highlighted in the automobile industry, a key sector along with its myriad suppliers and a major employer in most developed economies, where consumer restraint was leading to cutbacks as unsold stock piled up. And inhibiting every aspect of industrial and commercial activity was the fact that credit was still not flowing in spite of all the co-ordinated best efforts of governments and their central bankers everywhere.

LIBOR had become 'the rate at which banks won't lend to each other', all preferring to accept abysmally low rates on government bonds rather than run any sort of risk. This meant that many companies were heading for serious difficulties when the time came to refinance their loans, and competition to do so was set to intensify as they tried to renegotiate funding in 2009 to keep one step ahead of the coming avalanche of government debt issuance.

Certainly there would be no more of the "borrower-friendly covenant-lite" loans so favoured by the private equity "masters of the universe" pursuing their multi-billion dollar takeover targets in 2006/2007, and many of them were going to face major difficulties in securing refinancing in a trading environment much less benign than that ruling at the time they had secured their deals. In this respect, Canadian telecoms giant **BCE**, the target of a record $48.5 billion private equity buy-out in 2007, had a lucky escape after its accountants ruled that the deal could no longer proceed on the grounds that under the debt repayment terms, the company would be technically insolvent.

Rights issues to existing shareholders were still a possibility for some companies but with memories still fresh of the April 2007 subscription prices of **Royal Bank of Scotland** and **HBOS's** issues at multiples of today's share prices, new money was only going to go to those like **Santander** or **Standard Chartered** where cash requirements were less urgent, falling more into the "would be nice" rather than in the "must have" category.

More job losses

But perverse as ever the markets wrong-footed the bears by staging a strong rally in response to the shock news that US job losses had topped the half a million mark in November, with the Dow reversing a 250 point fall to end the day up 259 at 8635. The turnaround sparked big gains across Asia and the Eurozone with the FTSE100 plussing 251 to touch 4300 again, at the same time reigniting the debate about whether or not markets had bottomed out in the last week of November. The bulls argued that a 20% rise in the S&P500 since its low of 752 on 21st November in the face of irredeemably awful news was a convincing first stage recovery move upon which subsequent advances could build, with the background gradually improving as it surely would given the inevitable bail-out of the US automobile industry and the new administration's massive public works spending programme.

The bears' view was that all the unprecedented measures taken since the credit crisis broke had done nothing to head off a recession or to free-up a credit logjam that would continue to inhibit the recovery process. They also saw the current rally as just a phase in the rollercoaster ride that stock markets across the world had experienced over the past eighteen months and no more than a sideshow in an economic drama of epic proportions that was still unfolding. The failure of Congress to approve a $14 billion stop-gap deal to keep the US automobile industry going until the incoming administration could work out a more permanent solution to its problems, halted the rally in its tracks, echoing the upset caused by the rejection of the $700 billion TARP package in the last week of September.

However, markets steadied on the conviction that a deal of some sort would have to be put together despite the misgivings of those who argued that bail-outs were only short-term solutions to long-term problems. Still, the great majority of commentators were prepared to recognise that in any democracy all economic decisions have a political dimension and especially those that would lead to substantial job losses. Trapped in such a dilemma, politicians had no choice but to compromise and at least impose terms and conditions on those industries that were in receipt of public largesse. The issue was particularly relevant in the UK where the government's planned massive increase in public borrowing to combat the recession was attracting criticism not just from the Conservative opposition but from its Eurozone partners who saw it as not in accord with their growth and stability pact.

Furthermore, the resulting precipitous fall in sterling, down 20% against the euro since mid-2007, was also likely to be seen by them as yet another example of the UK trying to devalue its way out of trouble by gaining a competitive advantage. One writer was tempted to recall a statement made by Gordon Brown when he was shadow chancellor in the mid 1990s: 'A weak currency arises from a weak economy which is in turn the result of a weak government', and then added that the position the country found itself in after ten years of his chancellorship had exposed the delusion that its liberal financial capitalism was superior to the social market model favoured by its Eurozone partners.

No more heroes

Seeming to confirm this view of the UK economy, **HBOS** now revealed that trading had deteriorated alarmingly since its interim statement on November 3rd with writedowns of a further £1.6 billion to add to the £1.7 billion total given at the end of September. This sharp increase in the monthly run rate of impairment charges was interpreted by analysts as a clear sign that the recent recapitalisation measures across the whole banking sector were not going to be enough and further rights issues were inevitable. The share prices of **HBOS** and its merger partner **Lloyds TSB** both fell by close to 20%, reflecting the difficulties they would face in a post-crisis banking world even allowing for their government-sponsored dominant and privileged position. With large portfolios of corporate loans and heavy exposure to commercial real estate, **RBS** and **Barclays** were seen as similarly vulnerable and their share prices also fell sharply.

Just to add to the banks' problems, their skill and judgement was now to be called further into question on the news that many of them had placed clients' investments into the funds run by Bernard Madoff, the Wall Street financier, and alleged perpertrator of a $50 billion fraud. Since Mr Madoff was a former chairman of NASDAQ, one of the biggest stock exchanges in the world, the revelations were a major blow to investor confidence, and more so given that the banks and hedge funds that had steered investors towards his funds appeared to have carried out little or no due diligence. The fact that the regulators had also been asleep at the wheel gave rise to worries that the "black box" operations of the many other hedge funds might have more unpleasant surprises in store for investors even when fraud was not an issue.

As **Amaranth Investors** had shown in October 2006, taking huge bets that go wrong can do just as much damage as an outright fraud and an investor in a so-called hedge fund promising absolute returns regardless of market conditions expects the manager's methods to be more sophisticated than betting the farm (your farm, not his) on the black or the red. And after the virtual collapse of the over-indebted high-profile fund manager **New Star**, the staggeringly high percentage losses recorded by FTSE100 stocks that had to be core holdings of so many other funds, guaranteed that there would be very few "star" fund managers left in the City when the time for portfolio valuations next came around.

Countdown to zero

Hopes that 2008 might end on a happier note for the markets were raised by a 359 point rise in the Dow to 8924 on 16th December in response to the Fed's dramatic slashing of its key interest rate from 1% to a record low in the range of 0.25% to zero and its pledge to use 'all available tools to promote the resumption of sustainable growth and to preserve price stability'. However, the bulls' hopes were tempered by the fact that such a move by the Federal Reserve meant that it had exhausted its capacity to stimulate the economy by the traditional means of cutting interest rates, leaving it with no alternative but to deploy 'all available tools' in a continuing fight to 'further support credit markets and economic activity'.

And in order to drive down interest rates facing households and companies, the means at the Fed's disposal would include the purchase of long-term government bonds, securities issued by institutions like **Fannie Mae** and **Freddie Mac**, asset-backed securities and commercial paper. That would ensure that its balance sheet was kept at the desired high level to guarantee a plentiful supply of money to the financial system to combat deflation, fear of which had supplanted inflation as the greatest danger facing the economy in the wake of plunging prices as the recession deepened.

To have come to this pass also meant that the economic situation had deteriorated significantly in the past few weeks, and that therefore the rise in stock markets was perhaps more a reflex reaction to always popular interest rate cuts than to a reasoned appreciation of economic prospects. A more logical response was the precipitous fall in the dollar against the euro and the yen, especially the former to show that interest rate differentials still have a role to play in foreign exchange dealing, even if risk aversion continued to lead a stampede into US Treasuries pushing 10-year yields below 2.5% to yet another historic low.

Second thoughts by investors saw the Dow lose over 300 points in the next two days with sentiment further dampened by disappointing housing data and news of a weakening economy in Japan. However, markets rallied again on the Bush administration's decision to provide **GM** and **Chrysler** with $17.4 billion from TARP to fund a restructuring programme in lieu of a Chapter 11 bankruptcy process, and to permit **GMAC**, the troubled consumer lender owned by **GM** and by private equity giant, **Cerberus**, to become a bank and thus gain access to funds from TARP and debt guarantees from the **Federal Deposit Insurance Company (FDIC)**. The European Union also recognised the plight of its motor industry by allotting €50 billion of its €200 billion stimulus package to its support.

Blood on the high street

In London, the FTSE100 managed to hold in the 4200/4300 range despite another run of grim housing data and a clutch of High Street retailers following **Woolworths** into administration. An insolvencies company spokesman had forecast that between ten and fifteen retailing chains would be in trouble by the middle of January and the collapse of **Whittard**, **The Officers Club**, **Adams** and **Zavvi**, purveyors of tea and coffee, menswear, children's clothing and CDs and DVDs respectively, before the end of January suggested that he was well on course to being proven correct. Practically every retailer introduced heavy discounts in an attempt to boost trading over the vital holiday period but all the indications were that it was going to be one of the worst on record.

Among other consumer-reliant sectors, the housebuilders and car retailers were especially hard hit, many of them having taken on debt to expand in the belief that the good times would never end, thus demonstrating that boom and bust is always with us. **Taylor Wimpey** became the UK's leading housebuilder in 2007 in a £5 billion merger between Taylor Woodrow and George Wimpey at a time when the 'underlying housing market in the UK and the US was stable' and there was a 'steady demand for new homes'. Since then the shares have lost 95% of their value and the whole group has a market capitalisation of £165 million. **Pendragon** was similarly optimistic about demand for its upmarket vehicles, buying rival Reg Vardy for £500 million in 2006. Its shares have also fallen by over 90% and the group is now capitalised at £17 million.

A final flourish

Against such a depressing background a pre-Christmas rally was hardly to be expected but even more unexpected was a post-Christmas boost resulting in the FTSE100 plussing over 200 points to end the year at 4434, influenced in part by a rise in US markets attributed to the auto bail-out and to expectations of rapid action by the incoming administration. The Dow closed the year at 8776, with the S&P500 topping 900 again at 903 and the NASDAQ Composite reaching 1577. European and Asian markets joined in the rally which helped to trim marginally the enormous losses they had sustained over the year. A final tally revealed that the Dow had lost 33.8% in 2008 while the S&P500's loss of 38.5% was the largest annual drop since 1937. The NASDAQ Composite had been hampered over the year by a relatively poor showing by its technology components and at 1577 was down 40.5%. On the London market, the FTSE100's weighting in Banks and Mines had resulted in a highly deceptive performance in 2008 with the latter providing support in the first half of the year and then joining the former in a second half collapse to wipe 2000 points off the index taking it to 4434, an annual loss of 30.9%. The smaller cap indices fared worse as investors saw companies outside industry leaders as more vulnerable in the downturn, especially if capital-raising was going to be an issue, and the FTSE250 lost 40% of its value. For much the same reasons, investors shunned AIM, which recorded its worst annual loss of 65% since its inception in 1995.

Although already beginning to crumble in the final quarter of 2007, emerging markets led by the BRICs were still star performers of that year but it was downhill all the way in 2008 as the shockwaves of the US recession and credit crisis spread across the globe. Brazil's BOVESPA was down 37% and Russia's RTS index dipped just over 70%, the decline accelerating as the prices of oil and metals dived in the second half of the year. India and China also lost ground, down 53% and 65% respectively as the sharp slowdown in their once double-digit growth rates had the same effect as a recession in the developed world.

Hong Kong's HangSeng index dipped 48.2% and Japan's Nikkei Dow 225 disappointed, as ever, to record its biggest annual decline at 42%, as the strong yen damaged the country's vital export industry, industrial production plunged and the recession deepened. The principal markets in the Eurozone also suffered more than London and New York with the Eurofirst 300 losing 45%, and individually Germany's DAX was down 40.4% and France's CAC40, 42%. Banking troubles led to considerably worse performances by Ireland, off 72%, Belgium, 66% and Austria, 68%. Outsiders, the Czech Republic, Hungary and Poland, all dipped over 50% as a falling currency and rising budget deficit alienated foreign investors.

Exchange rates experienced extraordinary volatility during the year with the US dollar seeming to establish its safe haven credentials during the worst period of the financial crisis and appreciate by more than 20% against its main trading partners in a matter of months. Then came an abrupt turnaround as the Fed took its rate-cutting spree to the end of the line and the European Central Bank appeared to be taking a tougher stance on inflation, with the Eurozone providing its own safe haven for weaker member states. Arguably, the PIGS (Portugal, Italy, Greece and Spain) were making the case for hanging together within the Eurozone rather than hanging separately outside it.

Sterling failed to gain from the reversal of the dollar's rise as concerns about the state of the UK economy grew, but many commentators saw the fall in sterling of 27% against the dollar and 23% against the euro as a much needed de facto devaluation to help the country claw its way back to prosperity.

In dollar terms, the gold price ended the year at around the $850 mark, well down from a peak of $1030 touched in March, but gold enthusiasts were still looking for a renewed rise above $1000 as currency turmoil persisted in 2009. As for the oil price at around $40 a barrel, it was not the problem it had been a year earlier at $95 and clearly heading into $100 plus territory, but in that it reflected a reduction in demand, this lower level raised new concerns over the prospect for global growth.

Looking forward to 2009

Given the undeniable tendency of market "experts" to get it wrong, as they did with their forecasts for the FTSE100 to end 2008 in the range of 6500 to 7200, the more modest targets for 2009 from 4300 up to 5800 had to be looked at with some suspicion. However, to be fair, practically no one within the investment industry, or outside it, predicted a collapse in the UK banking sector that would trim the share prices of **RBS** and **HBOS** by 90% and leave these two revered institutions partially owned by the state.

Some commentators warned that the mining sector was too high and riding for a fall in the context of clear indications of a slowdown in China, but bid activity masked these concerns until they became obvious to all and prices plunged by 50%. The downturn in the property market was also no surprise to many commentators, but its severity; and none looked for the share prices of industry giants, **Land Securities**, **British Land** and **Hammerson** (all FTSE100 constituents) to halve over the year.

And with the consumer reining in spending, High Street retailers might have been expected to suffer, but not to the extent that they did, and the precipitous falls in the share prices of household name companies weighed on the index.

Thus its performance in 2009 would depend very much on how these sectors fared and that in turn would depend on how the economy, not just in the UK but in America and everywhere else, responded to monetary and fiscal stimuli on an unprecedented scale to combat what had come to be recognised as the biggest financial upheaval of the time. The broad consensus among commentators was for a flat first half of the New Year to be followed by signs of recovery in the second half as policy measures begin to work through.

However, citing the totally unexpected and cataclysmic nature of the events of 2008, more than one market professional was ready to stand by his forecast only in the absence of a major negative surprise, an occurrence that the bears saw as guaranteed to be in the financial sector.

2009

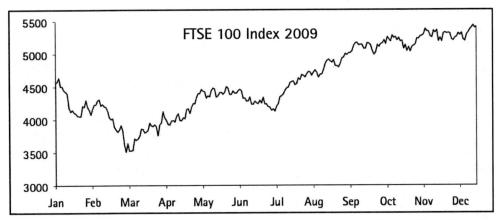

FTSE 100 Index 2009

Source: Thomson Reuters Datastream

On a wing and a prayer

The post-Christmas rally continued into the first week of 2009, raising the hopes of the bulls as the Dow topped 9000 again and the FTSE100 edged over 4600; but all the gains and more were lost in the second week under the assault of a barrage of negative economic and corporate news, shattering investor confidence.

In the US, industrial production fell while unemployment rose to 7.2% – up from a low of 4.1% in 2007 – after the economy lost 2.6 million jobs in 2008, the biggest annual fall since 1945. In the UK and continental Europe the news was just as bleak. The National Institute for Economic and Social Research (NIESR) predicted that UK national income would slump by 1.5% in the fourth quarter of 2008, and Germany, France and Spain all reported sharp falls in industrial output. The first annual loss by **Deutsche Bank** in fifty years, huge job cuts by **Barclays**, and analysts' assessments that **HSBC** would have to raise major capital in 2009, revived worries about the stability of the banking sector, sending share prices into freefall. The performance was mirrored in the US where the KBW Bank index plunged to its lowest level since 1995 after **Citigroup** embarked upon a disposal programme that would radically change its business model, and **Bank of America** was rumoured to be seeking billions of dollars from the Fed in order to complete its purchase of Merrill Lynch as losses at the brokerage business stacked up.

Interest rate reductions by the Bank of England and the European Central Bank, by 0.5% to 1.5% and 2% respectively, had been widely expected and provided no boost to markets. They continued to take their cue from Wall Street, shell-shocked by a 2.7% decline in December's retail sales figures which were much worse than expected. Risk aversion was back in fashion. After rising to 2.5% during the end-December rally, the yield on 10-year Treasuries fell back to 2.2%, as growing signs of economic deterioration countered fears about rising government borrowing leading to oversupply in the bond market.

Don't bank on it!

By mid-January, the Dow had retreated nearly 1000 points to 8000 again and the FTSE100 had lost almost 500 to just above 4000, when a rally of sorts was mounted on the news that the **Bank of America** had got what it wanted in the form of $20 billion to help with recapitalisation, plus a $118 billion backstop for potential losses on tainted assets inherited from Merrill Lynch. These amounts were, of course, in addition to the $25 billion taken from TARP in October and paralleled the $20 billion cash injection and $300 billion loss guarantees provided to **Citigroup** in November. Thus it was difficult to avoid the conclusion that the problems besetting the banks were getting rapidly worse, forcing the Government to ride to their rescue yet again. Given that the bail-out operations of 2008 had not succeeded in stabilising the situation, many commentators believed there was no more reason to think that they would do so in 2009, especially in the context of a global economic slowdown that appeared to be heading for a full stop.

Reports of slumping export volumes from Asia – apparently confirmed by the sight of docksides stockpiled with containers, and harbours full of ships going nowhere – strongly suggested that a lot more trouble was heading the banks' way in the shape of corporate loan defaults, and that the staggering fourth quarter losses just reported would not be the last. The share prices of UK banks also continued to slide on fears that they would have to return cap in hand to a government that was already taking over their job in operational as well as ownership terms by guaranteeing loans of up to £21.5 billion to small and mid-tier businesses. Then just for good measure, within a week of injecting €1.5 billion into **Anglo Irish Bank**, the Irish Government was forced to nationalise it after a run of withdrawals threatened collapse.

Against such a background, it seemed wildly illogical to think that a meaningful rally could have anywhere to go without bank shares joining in, since their failure to do so reflected a lack of confidence in the banks themselves, the fountainheads of credit in all economies based upon the ready availability of that commodity. **Barclays** seemed to prove the point on the last day of the second week of January by plunging 25% to a 16-year low of 98p, with investors spooked by rumours that it had greatly understated writedowns to date and that it would also be excluded from the Government's "bad bank" scheme to house toxic assets, after declining participation in the official recapitalisation plan. **Royal Bank of Scotland** and **Lloyds TSB** also hit new lows, and if the coincidental lifting of the ban on short-selling of financials had to take some of the blame for the sell-off, the fundamentals could have justified it anyway if an RBS analyst was right in claiming that UK domestic banks were 'technically insolvent on a fully marked-to-market basis'.

In a week that concluded in the US with **Bank of America's** share price down 45% after posting its first loss since 1991, and cutting its dividend from 32 cents to 1 cent

– while **Merrill Lynch,** the acquisition it had bought for $50 billion in September, posted a fourth quarter loss of $15 billion – it was clear that Treasury officials and bank bosses on both sides of the Atlantic were going to get together for another "lost weekend" in an attempt to stop the rot.

'Everything that could go wrong, did'

It had been an inauspicious start to the New Year with the disastrous news from the banking world complemented by doom and gloom from industry and commerce. The world's leading chip maker, **Intel**, warned of falling fourth quarter revenue in the wake of a 'dramatic cutback' in technical product spending. Media giant **TimeWarner** slashed its forecast for 2008 after taking a $25 billion writedown on its magazine and internet (AOL) divisions. Charges also related to exposure to recently bankrupted customers including **Lehman Brothers**, a tenant at its landmark Time-Life building. Oil major **Chevron** warned of 'significantly lower' fourth quarter earnings, top aluminium producer **Alcoa** announced it was reducing output by 18% and laying off 13% of its worldwide workforce, and **Boeing** responded to a more than halving of commercial aircraft orders by shedding another 4500 jobs. Once the biggest company on the Toronto stock exchange, telecoms equipment maker, **Nortel**, filed for bankruptcy, laid low by increasing competition and falling demand from its biggest customers and a crippling debt load. **Waterford Wedgwood** falling into administration was no great surprise given that the ailing company had been supported for years by Irish tycoon Sir Tony O'Reilly, who had single-handedly subscribed to a succession of rights issue. But failure after 250 years of history was still a shock. Not a household name but much more important in terms of its economic impact was the filing for bankruptcy protection of the world's third largest petrochemicals group, Lyondell-Bassell, with debts of $26 billion, and more so since the **Royal Bank of Scotland** was said to be a creditor to the tune of £2.5 billion. The group had been created by Russian-born billionaire Len Blavatnik and his comment on the situation, 'Everything that could go wrong, did,' showed every sign of becoming a familiar refrain in the months ahead.

Another shock from RBS

The UK Government's £100 billion loan guarantee and loss insurance package for the banks was not received with any enthusiasm by the stock markets, but rather the reverse. Bank shares plunged again, helped on their way by a staggering £28 billion loss forecast by **Royal Bank of Scotland**, and the Government's decision to boost its stake in the bank to 70% by swapping £5 billion of preference shares for ordinary. Shares in **Barclays** fell 25% to below 100p in a late sell-off sparked by worries that its writedowns to date were disproportionately low given the size of its portfolio of debt securities, and the bank was prompted to issue a reassuring statement on profits and capital position.

However, a brief rally failed to last the day and the share price continued to fall, in company with that of the new **Lloyds Banking Group** following the completion of the merger with **HBOS**. Investors now feared that as losses continued, so would the trend towards full nationalisation, and shareholders would end up with nothing. Sterling plunged too as investors took fright at the apparent open-ended commitment of the government to a succession of bank bail-outs, hitting a 7 1/2 year low against the dollar of $1.37 at one point, and posing the question, "Is this a competitive devaluation or a sterling crisis?"

Royal Bank of Scotland's appalling results – apparently pointing to a dramatic escalation of losses in the final quarter – sent bank shares tumbling across the world. Worst hit were the US banks and financials, where **State Street** appeared to confirm fears about an accelerating downturn by reporting a 71% slump in fourth quarter earnings, and warning that it could face 'billions of dollars' in unrealised credit losses. The news knocked the bank's shares down 59%, spurring a sell-off across the sector that saw **Bank of America** lose another 29% on top of the previous week's 40% dip. **Citigroup** shed another 20% to $2.80, keeping company with **Wells Fargo** down 23.8%, and **JPMorgan Chase** down 20.7%.

Selling pressure was not confined to financials and at the end of the day the Dow was down 4%, penetrating the 8000 level again to 7949 with the S&P 500 just holding above 800 at 805. The fact that the sharp fall had occurred on Inauguration Day for the new President surprised many who had been looking for an "Obama bounce" and it had to be seen as an indication of the seriousness of the economic situation with which the new administration had to deal.

Better than expected fourth quarter earnings and upbeat forecasts from **IBM** and **Apple** sparked a 279 point rally in the Dow the next day but it failed to hold, overwhelmed by disappointing sales and earnings from **Microsoft**, accompanied by the first mass lay-offs in the company's 34 year history; results seen as more representative of the tech market. Jobless claims exceeding forecasts, coupled with housing starts falling to a new low, sapped buyers' enthusiasm and by the end of the week the Dow had breached the 8000 level again, dragging down world stock markets in its wake.

UK in recession – it's official

Official confirmation came that the country was now in recession following a 1.5% drop in national output in the fourth quarter of 2008, after minus 0.6% in the third. This surprised no one, but the speed and severity of the fall and the fact that it was spread across practically every sector exceeded expectations. The news sent sterling tumbling again to below $1.35 at one point, but after dipping briefly below 4000 intraday for the first time since December, the FTSE100 managed to hold above that level; a remarkably resilient performance in the face of a continuing slide in bank shares led by **Barclays**.

Selling pressure on the UK domestic banks had intensified following the Government's decision to up its stake in **RBS** on renewed fears that full nationalisation was on the agenda, a fate that could mean wipe-out US-style for ordinary shareholders, and **Barclays** was seen as unlikely to be able to maintain any "go it alone" capital-raising ambitions. Shares in insurers also slumped since – as some of the principal holders of bank capital debt – they were also in line for substantial losses if nationalisation occurred, a fate already suffered by many US holders of bank bonds.

Biting the bullet

However, what a difference a day makes in the stock market! In the final week of January, London staged a strong rally led by bank shares – inspired by another reassuring statement from **Barclays** affirming its profitability and its capital adequacy. **Barclays'** shares actually doubled from their low point the week before of just under 50p, and those of **RBS** soared 50% to 15p. Wall Street also rallied, taking heart from **Pfizer's** $68 billion takeover of fellow drug manufacturer **Wyeth**, but good news found itself vying for supremacy in an ability to influence the markets with bad news. The latter came in the shape of a string of disappointing fourth quarter results, accompanied by massive job cuts as companies "evaluated their cost structures" to meet the challenges of the year ahead. **GE** revealed a 43% drop in fourth quarter profits and 20,000 job losses in its worldwide workforce – to include 11,000 at GE Capital, its troubled financial arm – while construction giant, **Caterpillar**, logged a 32% fall in profits in the same period, 20,000 job losses and forecast a difficult 2009. Even the **Pfizer/Wyeth** merger had its downside, with 19,500 jobs to go on completion of the deal.

Still, markets were expecting the worst, so it came as no surprise when they got it, a state of affairs that provided a degree of support for the "it's all in the price" argument of the bulls, since how else could they explain a 10% rise in the shares of **AMEX** following its report of a 79% slump in fourth quarter profits? Bear covering was one possible explanation, but markets seemed content to go along with the bulls for the moment, their hopes raised by the prospect of a relatively easy passage for the incoming administration's $825 billion stimulus package through the Democrat-dominated House of Representatives. One analyst was tempted to see soaring job losses as a bull point in that they represented companies' efforts to restructure, a process that would eventually benefit the bottom line, but most saw them as deeply worrying in economies so heavily reliant upon domestic consumption. The latter interpretation appeared to make more sense in that job losses inevitably led to falling consumer spending which in turn resulted in lower industrial confidence and less investment, all leading back to more job losses.

Furthermore, this vicious circle had serious political and social implications and with street protests already seen in January in Athens, Riga and Reykjavik, in Paris and in Russia's provincial cities, clearly it was not only China with ten million unemployed migrant workers that had to worry about maintaining a 'harmonious and stable social climate'. The crisis had begun with the banks, moved on to the 'real economy' and was now entering phase three – when the social consequences would become apparent.

No way out?

The rallies that had taken the Dow up to 8375 and the FTSE100 to 4295 came to a standstill in the final two days of January as investors took heed of a warning from the International Monetary Fund that the world economy was facing its worst year since 1945 with growth coming 'to a virtual halt'. The institution singled out the UK as the country that would suffer most among the economies of the developed world, forecasting that its national income would shrink by 2.8% as a result of heavy exposure to the banking crisis and the housing downturn, compared to an average drop of 2% for the rest. The IMF report was particularly embarrassing for the Prime Minister in that it flatly contradicted his repeated assurances that the country was better placed than others to deal with the crisis, and would start to grow again in the latter half of 2009. Anglo-Dutch steel producer **Corus** added to the Government's discomfort by announcing 2500 lay-offs at its UK plants which were being closed down or mothballed, as did the Society of Motor Manufacturers and Trades (SMMT), stating that it was 'battling for industrial survival' as it pleaded for financial assistance. Job losses now began to dominate the economic picture everywhere.

In the US, **Boeing** reported a fourth quarter loss and let go another 5500 workers. **Starbucks** announced the closure of 300 sites with 6700 job losses and almost every day company after company added to the toll, resulting in US job losses in January of 598,000, bringing the total over the past twelve months to a record high of 3.5 million or 7.6% of the working population.

Another conundrum in the bond market

Policy responses were clearly urgently required and US markets actually rose on the day these record job losses were announced, driven by the confident expectation that the new administration's stimulus package would make it through the Senate without serious opposition. London and the other European markets followed suit with the former buoyed by the Bank of England's move to trim a half percentage point off interest rates taking them to 1%, and the latter by the hope that the European Central Bank would be forced to follow its example at its next meeting in March.

After a couple of short-lived dips below 8000 in the first week of February, the Dow appeared to be re-establishing a position around the middle of the 8000 to 8500 range but then paused on revived concerns that Republican objections could seriously emasculate the package and even if they did not, the situation was deteriorating so rapidly now that it would be ineffective. A number of commentators of the bearish persuasion pointed to the problems posed to the stimulus plans, by the fact that in a month that saw official interest rates managed down to zero, the yield on the 10-year Treasury bond rose from 2% to 3%, despite efforts to talk the rate down by clear hints from the Fed that it was going to buy Treasuries. Since the 10-year T-Bond yield was the benchmark for rate setting across the spectrum of financial instruments, this contradictory move sabotaged the Fed's aim of bringing down the whole structure of interest rates, thus making the stimulus more difficult and more costly to finance. As always, the government proposes and the market disposes.

...without a paddle

News that the Obama stimulus package (now given a more positive spin as the American Recovery and Investment Act) had been agreed by the Senate – albeit in a cut down form and with the minimum support required from the Republicans – coincided with the unveiling of Treasury Secretary Tim Geithner's new $2 trillion plan for a public/private partnership deal to rescue the financial system and supplement the $350 billion he had left to spend out of the original TARP created by his predecessor. Since all the details would have to be thrashed out with Congress before bi-partisan agreement could be reached and the plan implemented, investors took fright at the prospect of delay when the country was in the middle of what President Obama had described as 'a full-blown crisis' and facing 'catastrophe'. The Dow crashed nearly 400 points, taking it to 7888, with the S&P 500 losing 42 points to 827, and markets everywhere following; demonstrating yet again that the world watches and waits on Washington and Wall Street.

A number of commentators expressed disappointment at what they saw as the new president's half-hearted approach to the most serious crisis in eighty years, believing that given the great wave of public goodwill that had taken him to office, he should have been dictating policy solutions and not subjecting them to political horse-trading in Congress. In the light of the comparisons made between the crisis Barack Obama was facing today and that which had confronted FDR on his election in 1932, one writer was tempted to quote from the latter's inaugural address saying what he would do in the event that Congress failed to 'speedily adopt the measures that a stricken nation in the midst of a stricken world may require'; namely that he would request 'broad Executive power to wage a war against the emergency, as great as the power that would be given to me if we were in fact invaded by a foreign foe.'

Exactly what these policy solutions were was still very much a matter of debate, and while governments everywhere were blamed for not identifying and implementing them, it had to be acknowledged that the lack of transparency in the plans already put forward reflected to a considerable extent uncertainty as to the scale of the problem. Most informed critics believed that a worst-case scenario would continue to unfold just as it had over the past eighteen months and that instead of handing out more billions to the banks, there was now no alternative but to subject them to full state ownership and control. Clearly banking was a failed industry, but given the pole-position of the banks in the economy of every country by reason of their function as fountainheads of credit, their survival was essential. And since under private ownership they had failed so disastrously, public ownership remained the only alternative. This view gained ground rapidly as bank after bank in receipt of public funding revealed losses not previously accounted for, while directors insisted on the payment of bonuses to themselves and to senior staff without any relevance to performance targets.

Of pigs in pokes

In the London market, the FTSE100 had managed to struggle back to almost 4300 in the opening days of February, although its strength in the face of Wall Street's decline owed more to random rallies in the banks and miners than to any real enthusiasm among investors. Rights issues totalling £1.3 billion from property giants **Hammerson** and **British Land**, and the prospect of many more to come from the big players in every sector, presented equity investors with the certainty of dilution, as well as the possibility that they might be throwing good money after bad.

Then sentiment took a more decisive knock when the new **Lloyds Banking Group** revealed that it would make a £10 billion loss for 2008, twice the amount expected, as a result of corporate loan losses at **HBOS**, its merger partner. The shares immediately plunged by almost 40%, and sparked declines in the shares of other banks, all of which were exposed to corporate loans. The incident also reopened the question of the competence of **Lloyds'** top management, given that the terms of the merger had been agreed only two months earlier, when **HBOS** had been deemed 'a very good purchase'. Parallels were inevitably made with **Bank of America's** hasty tie-up with **Merrill Lynch** last September, just in time for the latter to reveal far higher than looked-for fourth quarter losses. And in both cases, bonuses remained in line for payment in open defiance of public opinion.

The gathering storm

Investors could find no comfort on the broader economic scene. In continental Europe, the recession appeared to be turning rapidly into the most severe since 1945, with Germany – seen as the powerhouse of the Eurozone – leading the way down, their GDP contracting 2.1% in the final quarter of 2008. This provided some consolation to the UK government, following the IMF prediction in January that Britain would be the worst affected of all developed countries, since it showed that the recession was hurting the strongest economies – and not just those with a bloated financial sector and busted property boom. France recorded a modest 1.2% decline in growth in the fourth quarter, the first of the year, and so remained technically not yet in recession. Italy, however, reported its third consecutive quarterly fall in GDP, with a contraction of 1.8% in the final quarter, and Spain, in spite of its high profile property slump, managed a modest 1% dip.

But it was the countries of Eastern Europe that were seen as posing the greatest danger to the stability of the whole region. With their rapid growth in the boom years of 2005 to 2007, funded almost exclusively by Western European banks, the dramatic reversal of their fortunes left those banks firmly on the hook for losses that matched those suffered by US banks in the subprime debacle. The absence of an EU Federal Reserve, ready to act as a lender of last resort, meant that the situation was bound to deteriorate into one with, 'the capacity to shatter the fragile banking systems of Western Europe' (in the words of one noted market commentator).

No help from Asia

If there remained any thought that Asia might still be in a position to take up the slack, it was dashed by the IMF almost halving its 2009 estimate for GDP growth for the region, from the 4.9% projection made in November to just 2.7% two months later. In Japan, still the world's second largest economy, unemployment soared as the country's (and the world's) leading automobile and electronics companies slashed production in the face of slumping demand. Carlos Ghosn, CEO and President of **Nissan**, Japan's third biggest carmaker, summed up the situation confronting not just **Nissan** but practically every major industrial enterprise everywhere, when he forecast a $2.9 billion loss for the current year, and added: 'In every planning scenario we built, our worst assumptions on the state of the global economy have been met or exceeded.' And just to emphasise the point, **Toyota**, the world's number one carmaker announced that its operating loss for the year to end-March would be three times bigger than previously forecast, largely due to a collapse of more than a third in US demand over the past three months, resulting in the company's first net loss since 1950.

However, China still had its fans despite reports of a 43% slide in imports and a 17.5% dip in exports in January, with their confidence boosted by a dramatic pick-up in dry cargo freight rates (albeit from a very low level), and a positive response by mainland stock markets following the announcement of the big stimulus package in November. By contrast, the Hong Kong market was more inclined to follow Tokyo's lead, and both stock indices dipped towards their October lows, moves suggesting that the advance in the Shanghai markets owed more than a little to government sponsorship.

The stock market's reaction to the President's signing of the American Recovery and Reinvestment Act (ARRA) was far from a vote of confidence in the likely efficacy of the new measures, with the Dow and the S&P 500 diving towards their November lows – something most analysts and commentators had not expected to happen. Worries appeared to centre on the accelerating downturn in the economy, all too evident in the trio of reports on January's housing starts, building permits and industrial production, released a day later and all much worse than forecast. The Fed then added to the gloom by a downward revision of its October growth forecast for 2009, from +1.1% to a range of -0.5% to -1.3%, and at the same time upping its predicted unemployment rate to as high as 8.8% (estimates that profit warnings and job cuts at tyremaker **Goodyear** and farm machinery company **Deere** did nothing to contradict).

On the ropes

Wall Street's slide had its inevitable effect on markets around the world, causing London's FTSE100, for one, to crash through the 4000 level and touch 3938 intraday, before clawing back the loss to trade briefly above 4000 again. Another big rights issue in the shape of a £755 million offering from property giant **Land Securities**, and the certainty of more on the way, weighed on the market – as did fears about the capital position of the big insurers, now taking the place of the banks as the focal point of danger to the country's financial system. Traditionally regarded as successful investment trusts operating a volatile "feast or famine" insurance business on the side, the insurance companies now found themselves trapped in the worst of all worlds as all three of the principal constituents of their investment portfolios, namely equities, commercial property and much of the bond element, plunged in value. And of course an insurance company with not enough capital to fund potential liabilities, is no longer in the insurance business. This dilemma was now being reflected in a dramatic drop in the share prices of the big players in the industry to 10-year lows, and in the case of **Legal & General**, considered to be most at risk, to an all-time low. The slogan used by the industry in the 1970s, 'Get the strength of the insurance companies around you', now had a distinctly hollow ring.

As yet there was no talk of a government-funded AIG-style bail-out. This was just as well – given that the soaring level of public debt was now becoming a matter of national concern, to the extent of making headlines in the tabloids. It was also a huge political liability for incumbent administrations on both sides of the Atlantic, as policies aimed at spending their way out of recession towards economic recovery drew criticism from almost every quarter. Prime Minister Brown's brief recovery in the polls following his "saving the world" plans for recapitalising the banks had gone sharply into reverse, and President Obama's hopes of a bi-partisan approach to national crisis were wilting in the face of Republican intransigence. From a political standpoint, considering the enormity of the problems to be addressed, and the absence of any obvious solution, it was better to be in opposition than in office.

GE in trouble again

In the final week of February an avalanche of disappointing corporate news, and worse-than-forecast economic data, appeared to make sense of falling stock markets.

Mighty **GE** announced that the severity of the financial crisis continued to defy expectations, and slashed its quarterly dividend for the first time since 1938. Its shares fell to $8.80 compared with a price of $38.50 a year ago. **JPMorgan** confirmed that it remained profitable but still made a surprise dividend cut, and top private equity house, **Blackstone**, reported an $827 million fourth quarter loss and no pay-out, after heavy markdowns in its corporate and property investments. The share price at $4.85 contrasted with a launch price of $31 back in 2007, when a Chinese government agency had "invested" $3 billion. Headlining the economic data was a shock 6.2% drop in GDP for the fourth quarter of 2008, well above official forecasts last year of 3.8%, and later revised to 5.4%. The figures cast grave doubts on the new administration's estimates for the economic recovery timetable, judged by one commentator to be 'above the optimistic end of the spectrum'; a cautious view seemingly confirmed by consumer confidence, jobless claims and new home sales continuing to post new lows.

But it was the problems of the banks that weighed most heavily on the market, as nationalisation fears grew with every new bail-out move. The US Government's decision to swap $25 billion of its preferred stock in **Citigroup** for common equity would result in it taking a 36% stake in the bank, and meant a massive dilution for the bank's common shareholders. Shares in the bank slumped 39% to $1.50, and took the rest of the banking sector with them. On the last day of the month the Dow stood at 7062 and the S&P 500 at 735 after crashing through their low points of November 2008 to levels not seen since 1996. The London market with the FTSE100 at 3830 was still holding just above its November low, thanks to earlier anomalous rises in financials, but the Eurofirst 300 lost 2.5% over the week, taking it back to the depths plumbed in March 2003. Japan's Nikkei Dow stood out in Asian markets with a 1.5% rise to 7568 helped by a continuing fall in the yen. But this had to be small consolation for investors in a month which had seen the index flirting with levels not seen since 1983, following reports of a 45% drop in exports over the past year.

More new lows

The travails of the banking industry continued to dominate the UK market just as they did in the US, as governments became increasingly involved. The British Treasury's £500 billion "Asset Protection Scheme" was designed to offer insurance for a bank's riskiest assets. First in the queue was **RBS**, seeking protection for £325 billion of toxic assets on its balance sheet. However, having just reported a £24 billion loss, and with its new chief executive admitting that 'we don't know how deep the economic downturn will go and with each day impairments rise', the bank's ability to pay the likely £10 billion insurance premium without further assistance was in serious doubt. **Lloyds Banking Group** now complicated the picture by revealing a £10.8 billion loss, courtesy of its new HBOS partner, and a request for protection for £250 billion of troubled assets. Reports that negotiations with Treasury officials were not going well, coupled with contemplation of the enormity of the sums involved, did not sit positively with investors; and bank shares fell sharply on the last day of the month.

Another Black Monday

Everything was now pointing to another Black Monday when markets opened on the 2nd of March. Just to make it a certainty, **HSBC** started the day by reporting a 62% fall in profits (after a disastrous performance by its US consumer finance arm), a surprise dividend cut, and a £12.5 billion rights issue (the biggest ever for the UK). Not to be outdone, America's **AIG** revealed a fourth quarter loss of almost $62 billion, to record the biggest quarterly loss in US corporate history. And then they tapped the government for another $30 billion. Since **HSBC** had been regarded as the best capitalised of all the top international banks, with no dividend cut in prospect, and **AIG's** request was its third call on taxpayers' money, investor confidence was badly shaken. The Dow slumped 299 points, taking it below the 7000 mark to 6763 and into territory last visited in 1996. It was accompanied by the S&P 500 dipping below 700, leaving both indices more than 50% down from the highs of sixteen months ago. As usual, this performance set the pattern for markets across the world. The FTSE100 shed 204 points to 3625 and the Eurofirst 300 fell 37 points to 682. Meanwhile, in Asia, Japan's Nikkei Dow crashed to a 26-year low. The Hang Seng at 12033 still managed to hold above the previous October's low point, cushioned by a continuing rally in Shanghai inspired by talks of enhanced domestic spending plans.

These historically low stock market levels inevitably prompted more discussion over the question of whether or not they presented a once in a lifetime buying opportunity. President Obama actually joined in the argument by saying that it was probably the right time to buy stocks if the investor had 'a long-term perspective'. But more than one critic was quick to recall that when Warren Buffett had said precisely that last October, the Dow stood at 8850 and the S&P 500 at 926. Both had lost over 20% of their value since then. Moreover the "Sage of Omaha's" much publicised purchase of preference shares in **Goldman Sachs** and **GE** had boosted the price of their common stock to $135 and $25, respectively, at the time – but five months later they stood at $85 and $6.50. Warren Buffet was ready to admit that he had made a number of wrong calls in 2008. But if the man known as the world's most successful investor could make mistakes, the bears argued, then we were in a very different ball game from the familiar bull market to bear market and back again sequences of the post-War years.

The bigger they come...

Attempts at rallies lacked conviction, and the upswings seemed to represent no more than part of the normal ebb and flow of trading, given that there was nothing in the way of good news to encourage the bulls. Companies everywhere seemed to have moved into survival mode, slashing dividends, launching rights issues, and slimming down operations, all of which made nonsense of the calculations cited by those arguing that equities were cheap. Cheap can always become cheaper, just as had happened since last October. And given the scale of a so-called "long-term perspective" of five to ten years, a 20% plus loss incurred in the first four and a half months gets even the longest-term investment strategy off to a very bad start.

The principal problem overshadowing the markets was the fact that all the measures taken to unfreeze credit flows and kickstart economies appeared to have had little or no effect. Interest rates had been cut to practically zero, billions upon billions had been injected into the money markets to boost liquidity, billions more had been given to banks and financial institutions to save them from collapse, and all apparently in vain. Eighteen months had gone by and many of the biggest banks and financial institutions on the planet were technically insolvent and surviving only thanks to government support. Former giants of the NYSE Big Board, **AIG** and **Citigroup**, had become "penny stocks" that barely qualified them for the Pink Sheets, and national treasures like **Ford** and **General Motors** were in the same boat. Much the same situation ruled in the UK, in Continental Europe and in Japan, where a host of household name companies in banking, insurance, construction, manufacturing and retailing were in desperate straits.

Still not working

Meanwhile, the stimulus packages proposed by governments were criticised on the one hand for being too little, too late and not big or bold enough to tackle the crisis; and on the other hand for burdening countries with a level of debt that would inhibit growth for years to come. In such a context it was hardly surprising that stock markets should lack any sense of direction, and that in consequence the Bank of England's half per cent rate cut to 0.5%, and the introduction of a £75 billion dose of "quantitative easing" for the first time ever, should be greeted with a 116 point fall in the FTSE100 – taking it to 3529, its lowest point since March 2003. News that the Treasury and **Lloyds Banking Group** negotiations had resulted in the taxpayers' stake in the bank being upped to over 70% was no help. But the stock market's lacklustre response to these historic events suggested that investors had little confidence in the ability of authorities to improve the situation. Continental markets reacted similarly to the ECB's move to reduce interest rates by half a per cent to 1.5%, and the Eurofirst 300 index fell to 662, the lowest point since its launch in 1997.

February's US job losses were only a little above expectations, but the rise in the unemployment rate to 8.1% after downward revisions of earlier months still came as a shock. A rate of 11.2% and rising in the state of Michigan, home of the US automobile industry, evoked memories of the old saying, "What's good for General Motors is good for America", resulting in the conclusion that what was bad for the car giant had to be bad for the rest of the country. With so much of American industry geared to the economics of high mass consumption, it was clear that full employment was needed to sustain full employment and without the guarantee of rising consumption, much of industry would grind to a halt, leading to an extension of the recovery time. Such a situation was politically unacceptable in the affluent societies of the developed world where elections were won by governments which gave the people what they wanted. Thus, if the huge industrial complex devoted to the production of automobiles and its myriad related spin-offs is one of the twin engines (the other being the housing and construction industry) of a consumer-reliant economy, then the plight of **General Motors** and automobile manufacturers everywhere was a black mark on any government's record. Both industries were hugely dependent on the banks for credit and, to pursue a mechanical analogy, the engines required the transmission system represented by credit flows to turn the wheels of the economy. With both engines shut down and the transmission system out of order, the economy was going to come to a dead stop. The World Bank now added to the gloom by stating its belief that the global economy was on track to shrink in 2009 for the first time since the end of World War Two, dragged down by a sharp decline in industrial production and trade.

Another false dawn?

Stock markets were by now deeply depressed. The Dow was nudging 6500 and the S&P 500 was well into the 600s. Market strategists were openly discussing the possibility of the Dow going as low as 5000 and the S&P 500 falling into the 400-500 range. And where Wall Street goes, no other market can be far behind. In London, the FTSE100 was down to almost 3500 and a writer in the *Financial Times* actually mooted the possibility of a decline to 2300 to allow for a projected loss in earnings, taking P/Es to a level compatible with other cataclysmic market lows. In Japan, the Nikkei Dow was only just holding above 7000, while in Hong Kong the Hang Seng index at around 11,300 had lost two-thirds of its value since it peaked in 2008 and was a third down from its level at the time of the handover to China in 1997.

Most emerging markets were also suffering and likely to continue to do so, if the World Bank was correct in its assessment that the crisis meant they would have much greater difficulty in accessing financial markets. Even if they could, then they would 'face higher borrowing costs and lower capital flows, leading to weaker investment and slower growth in the future', the Bank said, singling out 'urban-based exporters' as particularly vulnerable, a category covering most of East Asia.

...or perhaps not

But just as the bulls were becoming thoroughly disheartened after twelve days of falls, markets embarked on a dramatic rally, supposedly triggered by news that **Citigroup** was actually operating at a profit, an event that was interpreted as evidence that perhaps the worst was over for the financials. This view was further bolstered by similar statements from **JPMorgan** and **Bank of America** and the rally continued to give markets their best week since the start of the year. The S&P500 and the Dow were both up around 10% at 756 and 7223 while the FTSE100 was 6% to the good at 3753, and the Eurofirst 300 was also up 6% at 702. Asian markets were happy to follow Wall Street's lead, with Japan's Nikkei Dow gaining 5.5% to 7704 after bouncing from the 26-year low touched on the first day of the week, and Hong Kong's Hang Seng plussed just over 14% to 12976.

It was no surprise that the bounce should reopen the debate over whether or not the bear market had at last bottomed out. Everyone had been waiting for a sign that financials were at last back in business as a precursor to a wider economic revival, and a few of the most respected market commentators believed that the US banks' return to profitability was such a sign. **Barclays** strengthened that belief when it too reported that the first quarter had started well. However, it had to be noted that these commentators' views were remarkably well hedged. The UK's own top investment guru, **Fidelity's** Anthony Bolton, welcomed the news from the banks and spoke of the market being 'at or near' its low point, which was perhaps more a statement of the obvious after the dramatic falls of the past eighteen months than an unambiguous "buy, buy, buy" call. He was also reported as saying that quantitative easing was a 'positive' for markets in that it reduced the liquidity premium on credit.

However, both these supposed bull points were not interpreted so generously by more cautious observers. On the matter of the banks making good money in the current quarter, they saw this as inevitable given a near-zero official interest rate policy allied with far higher loan rates, which meant that the standard business of borrowing and lending had to generate good profits. As for quantitative easing increasing access to credit for the general run of businesses, the critics saw that as well intentioned but by no means certain of achieving the desired result. Admittedly, the benchmark 10-year gilt yield had tumbled on the news, but so had that on the US 10-year Treasury Bond when the Fed had proposed a similar policy last December. It was now back to much nearer 3% than 2%. And furthermore, anecdotal evidence from the front line of small business operation indicated that banks were continuing to be impossibly restrictive and uncooperative.

The whirlwind advance stalled as an unaccustomed run of relatively good news managed to achieve a balance with the now familiar clutch of downgrades of national growth forecasts from the IMF and more reports of disappointing earnings, job losses and dividend cuts from the corporate sector. The **Merck/Schering-Plough** merger and reports that **IBM** was in talks with **Sun Microsystems** were a boost to sentiment, and then a surprise jump in February's housing starts reinvigorated the rally on hopes that policy efforts were at last beginning to breath life into the economy. These hopes were now to be enhanced by the Fed's announcement on 18th March that it was going to buy up to $300 billion of Treasury bonds, as well as doubling its intake of mortgage-backed securities with a further $750 billion of purchases. The immediate impact on the Dow was to turn a 100 point loss into a 100 point gain, and much the same effect was seen in stock markets across the world.

However, while the markets clearly welcomed the move as evidence that the Fed was fulfilling its pledge to do whatever it takes to drive down borrowing costs and get credit flowing freely again, many commentators suspected that only a situation much worse than it appeared to be could possibly justify the monetisation of the enormous budget deficit by such means. The fact that the announcement caused the dollar to record its biggest weekly fall in twenty-five years and dollar-dominated oil and other commodities to soar also served to revive inflationary concerns, but since they were less of a worry in the current environment than deflationary ones, the markets were happy to live with them. It was also widely noted that with the Bank of England, the Bank of Japan and the Swiss National Bank pursuing very similar policies – and the European Central Bank likely very soon to join them – the Fed was in good company, and the dollar's fall would be limited and inflationary pressures lessened.

Once bitten, twice shy

Certainly, the effect on the bond market was dramatic and beneficial to the cause of lower interest rates as the yield on the benchmark 10-year Treasury Bond dived almost fifty basis points to 2.54%, its biggest one-day fall in twenty years. At the same time, it had to be recognised that while lower longer-term bond yields were good news for the economy, they had a downside for struggling banks by inhibiting their earning potential from their day-to-day business of borrowing short and lending long. It was also widely noted that at the same time the Fed was buying back $300 billion of Government bonds, it was planning to issue up to $4.2 trillion of debt over the next two years to pay for its costly rescue plans, and lower yields were not going to encourage prospective buyers. However, as one writer insisted, if domestic and overseas investors wanted a secure home for their funds, the safest asset in the financial system was the promise of government to honour its own debt.

Considering the disasters that had overtaken so many other categories of investment over the past two years and longer, currency depreciation risks paled into insignificance relative to the losses piled up by banks accumulating mortgage-backed securities in their reserves and sovereign wealth funds buying into Western banks, hedge funds, mines and supermarkets. Add in the very real prospect of a prolonged period of Japanese-style deflation taking hold, and government bonds were beginning to look like the only game in town. They might be dull and unexciting investments and not provide a topic for dinner party conversation like high-tech and telecom stocks in 1999-2000, and financial and mining stocks in 2007-2008, but they never cut or passed their dividends or halved in value overnight and were as liquid as cash if the need arose to raise money in a hurry.

Kismet or Kaput?

If stock markets were pleased with the introduction of "quantitative easing", they were over the moon about Treasury Secretary Geithner's public-private partnership plan to take up to $1 trillion of toxic assets off the hands of the banks. The idea was that it would leave them with "clean" balance sheets, so freeing them to lend again. The plan was seen as more comprehensive and viable than its predecessors, and stock markets soared. The Dow plussed just short of 500 points to 7775 while the S&P500 put on 54 to 822 and the NASDAQ Composite 98 to 1555. In London the FTSE100 rose 110 points to 3952 and the Eurofirst 300 topped 740. Asian markets also rallied strongly with Japan's Nikkei Dow gaining 272 to 8488 and the Hang Seng 462 to 13,910.

A number of market strategists had been looking for the performance in the final week of the first quarter to provide the answer to the question as to whether we had seen the bottom of the market or just another rally within an ongoing bear trend. 'Kismet or Kaput?' was how one investment letter writer posed the question, suggesting that after so many failed rallies this was going to be a make or break week for investor confidence. Certainly, the week had got off to a good start but given that the main US stock indices had risen by almost 20% since the beginning of the month, a period of consolidation in place of retreat was probably going to be enough to keep the bulls happy. News from the US domestic economy was broadly supportive with a surprise rise in new home sales and the first pick-up of durable goods orders in February for seven months. But mounting job losses continued to act as a brake on any runaway enthusiasm. The Geithner plan also began to attract criticism on the grounds that any price set low enough to attract bids for their as yet unaudited toxic assets could result in further massive writedowns for the banks regardless of whether they were prepared to sell at that price.

This situation revived the question of whether too much of the stimulus enacted so far continued to be misdirected in propping up banks which were technically insolvent and deserved to be treated as such. As a result, they remained deeply flawed institutions incapable of recreating their credit-supplying function without which any stimulus package would be unable to gain traction. This left the state as the lender of last resort, a role it was already fulfilling and it would continue to be lender of first and only resort if the banks fail to gain regain their key position in the financial system. With this in mind, a healthy government bond market was essential, a status that would be jeopardised by further rounds of bond issuance which could have difficulty in attracting buyers. The failure of the Bank of England to see its auction of £1.75 billion of 40-year gilts fully covered for the first time in seven years appeared to be a sign of oversupply that would limit the scope for further financial stimulus and a consequent increase in borrowing requirements. Fortunately for the bond bulls, the auction next day for 13-year indexed-linked gilts was heavily oversubscribed, although its popularity perhaps had more to do with inflation fears following an unexpected, if anomalous, rise in February's CPI figure.

Looking further ahead, those bulls were convinced that the reflationary pressures produced by the politically-inspired stimulus measures would soon be overwhelmed by deflationary pressures resulting from a deterioration in the economic and financial fundamentals.

...and all the King's men

The G20 meeting scheduled for the first week of April would not normally have been expected to have much influence on the markets, but the publicity given to disagreements arising ahead of the event suggested that it might. Prime Minister Brown's whistle-stop world tour to rally support for 'the biggest financial stimulus the world has ever agreed' got off to a bad start when Bank of England governor, Mervyn King, warned that Britain could not afford 'a significant new financial stimulus'. His statement was likened by one political commentator to an 'African coup', an event that often occurs when the leader is away visiting foreign parts. Chancellor Merkel of Germany then added her voice to the debate when she rejected calls to spend more public money as part of a co-ordinated stimulus across the world economy, and suggested that China should do more to help given that it would not even have to raise debt to boost demand. On the fringes, the Chilean leader pointed out to Gordon Brown that by virtue of saving the revenues from its copper exports 'during the good times', it had been enabled to afford its own fiscal stimulus package, while in more colourful terms the Czech president proclaimed that trying to spend the way out of a slump was 'the road to Hell'. President of Brazil Lula da Silva's contribution was to blame the financial crisis on 'white people with blue eyes', an accusation that tempted one commentator to compare the likely consequences of the collapse of the Western financial system to those following the defeat of the Russian Navy by the Japanese in 1905; namely a seismic shift in the balance of power and prestige from the old world to the new.

With only two days to go before the end of the month, stock markets looked as if they were going to hang on to the bulk of the considerable gains recorded since the low points of March 9th, but they were in for a shock. Given all the emphasis in recent days on the need for ever more stimulus, it was the surprise refusal of the US Presidential Auto Task Force to throw more money at **GM** and **Chrysler** and burden the state with yet more debt that set the US markets back on their heels. Government bail-outs of Germany's **Hypo Real Estate** and one of Spain's regional banks added to worries for Continental European markets, while the collapse of Scotland's biggest building society did the same for the London market. The Dow dived 254 to 7522 and the S&P 500 dipped below the supposedly critical 800 level again to 787, while the FTSE100 lost 135 to 3762 and the Eurofirst300 retreated to just above the 700 mark.

However, the next day saw a rally of sorts attributed to a combination of end quarter adjustments to their portfolios by long-only funds and a belated recognition that an end to bail-outs was perhaps the right way to go. London drew strength from **Marks & Spencer's** quarterly report not being quite as bad as expected, and from

Barclays' decision to opt out of the Government insurance scheme along with the disposal of its iShares division, albeit for £3 billion and not the £5 billion initially hoped for.

More controversially, markets could have benefited from hopes for a successful outcome from the G20 meeting in the form of a master plan to restore global growth, but given the pre-meeting grandstanding of many of the leaders and their obligation to protect their own national interests, expectations did not run high.

New quarter, new rally?

Nevertheless, on the first day of the new quarter, the line of least resistance was clearly upwards, with sentiment boosted by manufacturing and housing data suggesting that the US economy might be bottoming out. The UK also witnessed a pick-up in mortgage approvals to the highest level since May 2008 and an increase in house prices of 0.9% in March according to Nationwide (although Halifax reported a fall). These news items were enough to power the Dow above 8000 again and the FTSE above 4000, performances which encouraged those who believed that the depths plumbed by the markets in the first week of March had presented a once in a lifetime buying opportunity.

The result of the G20 was also seen as positive with an aggressive multi-faceted programme to shore up the world's economic system devised in broad agreement between all parties. Bank shares were prominent in the advance, aided by a relaxation by US accounting regulators of the rules over marked to market valuations for financial instruments, giving the banks the latitude to price their "toxic" assets according to in-house calculations – or as one cynical observer commented, 'to price them how they would like them to be, rather than how they are'. The sense of optimism over the prospects for the global economy's recovery spilled over into commodity markets where copper topped $4000 a tonne again on Chinese government purchases to add to strategic stockpiles, and oil extended its gains above the $50 mark.

The rise in equity markets, the $1 trillion boost to IMF funds and the reintroduction of Special Drawing Rights (SDRs) to aid the weaker emerging economies, diminished the demand for so-called safe haven assets and both the dollar and the yen fell back along with the gold price which dipped below $900.

Job losses mount

However, casting a long shadow over recovery hopes was a larger than expected number of US job losses in March, taking the unemployment rate to 8.5%, its highest level since 1983. This figure coupled with the imminence of the first quarter reporting season demanded a necessary reappraisal by investors, the bears argued, of the validity of a rally that clearly had been inspired more by hope than by reality.

There was still a little more positive news to come in the shape of a quarter per cent interest rate cut by the European Central Bank to 1.25% against the half per cent expected. This was taken as evidence that the Eurozone did not see its crisis as quite as serious as that of the US even though emerging industrial data quickly put such a conclusion in doubt. Then **Research In Motion (RIM)**, the Blackberry manufacturer, announced bumper results and **IBM's** merger talks with Sun Microsystems were reported to be going well, events seen as indicating that the hugely important high tech sector was alive and kicking, while news of the successful completion of **HSBC's** £12.5 billion rights issue provided a lift for the banking sector.

But investor confidence proved to be a fragile flower and the rally failed to last out the first week of April and by the second, markets were in retreat again, discouraged by IMF reports that banks were still burdened with some $4 trillion of toxic assets, results from aluminium giant **Alcoa**, pointing to a virtual collapse in global demand, and the now apparently very real prospect of **GM** filing for bankruptcy with all that implied for the state of Michigan – an 'economic Katrina' in the words of one Republican representative – and for the whole US economy. And then just for good measure, **IBM** decided to break off negotiations with **Sun Microsystems**.

The Dow responded by falling back to 7789 and the S&P500 to 815 with the FTSE100 dipping to 3925, but just a day ahead of the Easter break the rally kicked in again. The Dow soared above the 8000 level with a gain of 246 points to 8083, pulling world markets in its wake. The FTSE100 made it back to almost 4000, but the best performing stock markets continued to be those in Asia. Most of them now registered gains in the 20-30% range since the first week of March, taking them to six-month highs, with the Shanghai Composite the leader of the pack and the top performer of 2009. There were rumours of a second Chinese stimulus package and memories of the "decoupling" thesis revived on expectations that China would drive a pick-up in growth across the region. Japan's record $150 billion stimulus package also served to boost investor confidence in Asia.

Mixed messages

Considerably better than expected first quarter results from **Wells Fargo** encouraged the bulls in their belief that the worst of the banking crisis was over and high percentage share price gains were recorded across the sector. **Goldman Sachs** then reinforced the view that the demise of Wall Street had been greatly exaggerated by surprising markets with a profit of $1.8 billion in the first quarter, and the announcement that it would make a public offering of $5 billion of common stock, with a view to getting the government off its back by starting to repay the $10 billion loan from TARP. Outside the banking world, prospects for the US construction industry were regarded as looking brighter on news of the $3 billion merger between **Pulte Homes** and **Centex** to create the nation's biggest house builder, and the granting of access to TARP funding was seen as putting the insurance industry on a surer footing.

However, while every potentially encouraging sign for the economy that appeared delighted the bulls, the bears argued that stock markets were wrongly anticipating a recovery and return to business as usual when all that had been seen so far was, at best, no more than a slowing in the rate of decline. This more cautious view now gained substance, with the release of US retail sales figures for March showing a 1.1% fall embracing a wide range of goods against forecasts of a rise to build on February's 0.3% gain. A profits warning from **Boeing** coupled with plans to cut production of its standard long-haul model 777 by 30% as a result of customers experiencing 'unprecedented declines in global passenger and air cargo volumes', did not suggest even a hint of a slowing in the pace of recession, the bears maintained. In short, they were convinced that at this stage economic data was volatile and unreliable and as the February and March retail sales figures showed, quite capable of stabilising before turning down again.

Furthermore, on a global scale industrial production remained in serious decline, indicating a continuing rise in unemployment that would inevitably depress consumer spending across the board. And as for China taking up the running, the first quarter growth rate of 6.1%, down from 10.1% year on year, was the lowest quarterly reading since records began in 1992, and no cause for celebration.

Calling the bottom

By mid-April the Dow was clearly having difficulty in holding its ground above the 8000 level, as indeed was the FTSE100 in relation to the 4000 mark, but, as one commentator maintained, given the wide range of sectoral variations, these big numbers were largely irrelevant. Thus, the currently popular effort of analysts to call the bottom of the market, he argued, was a meaningless exercise. On the London market, unless the UK was going to become a failed state, with many more household name companies facing total collapse, panic bottoms had already been established in key sectors like banking, house building, retailing and real estate, where many major companies had managed to refinance their once potentially crippling debt loads. The fact that this measure of recovery had been staged from depths plumbed after declines of a once unimaginable extent meant that these sectors still remained deeply depressed and provided no guarantee that the recovery would continue and develop into the next bull market.

Certainly there was money to be made by traders capable of successfully exploiting the high percentage moves experienced on a daily basis by even the biggest stocks, but arguably there was no longer any role for the traditional 'long-term investor' to play in these highly volatile market conditions or at any time in the foreseeable future. Warren Buffett and our home-grown stock market guru, Anthony Bolton, were keen to stress the merits of investing with a long-term perspective, citing a ten year timescale, but unless the next decade was going to be a lot better than the last one, their argument was not very convincing. Ten years ago the FTSE100 was 6500 against just over 4000 today, but even more striking was a comparison of the prices then and now of the darlings of the Technology, Media and Telecoms (TMT) boom, many of them FTSE100 constituents. Computer software and services companies **Logica** and **Misys** had both lost over 80% of their value, media giants **Pearson** and **Daily Mail** were both down by around 75%, while in telecoms, **Vodafone** and **BT** shareholders had seen the value of their shares decline by 70% and 90% respectively. It would take a brave analyst to forecast that any of these shares would recover their 1999/2000 peaks over the next ten years and their performance today, the writer believed, explained and justified the return of the yield gap in September 2008 for the first time since going into reverse in 1959.

Mind the gap

Looking at the precipitous falls in the share prices of companies in almost any sector over the past eighteen months, most investors would agree that equities ought to yield more than gilts to compensate for the greater risks involved in holding them. Certainly for pension fund managers, the appalling performance of equities over this period, with all that it had implied for capital values and income, had presented them with a major problem in guaranteeing that they would be able to meet their obligations to fund members. Do they continue to take a chance with equities, the writer asked, even though, by definition, they can offer no guarantee of any value at all at a defined future date, or do they decide to weight their portfolios towards gilt-edged stocks, confident that the government will honour its promise to pay the bearer? Remembering that the finance director of **Boots** had switched his £2.3 billion pension fund out of equities and into gilts in 2000/2001, and looking at their comparative performances since then, many private investors might wish they had followed his example. And given the need of the government to issue more and more gilts to fund its borrowing requirements designed to battle the recession, the writer argued that the investor could see buying them today as a patriotic duty just as it had been to buy National Savings and War Bonds in the two World Wars.

By the last week of April the jury still seemed to be out on the fate of the six-week long rally that had so raised the hopes of the bulls. In the UK the budget was widely condemned as ineffectual in dealing with a crisis situation and had served principally to raise awareness of the dire state of the public finances. The Chancellor's growth forecasts of a 3.5% contraction in the current year returning to a 1.25% rise in 2010 were considered to be far too optimistic and politically self-serving, and were sharply at odds with the IMF's estimates of minus 4.1% and plus 0.4%. These doubts raised the prospect of a much greater than expected amount of gilt issuance, causing prices of government stocks to fall and the yield on the 10-year gilt to rise by almost 25 basis points to 3.53%, a level that served to counteract the objective of quantitative easing which was to bring down interest rates across the board to get the economy moving again.

Waving, not drowning

Much the same concerns were being aired in US markets where the benchmark 10-year Treasury bond yield had soared to 3.18%, also effectively inhibiting the Federal Reserve's policy aims. Rising bond yields were usually seen as being bad for share prices, as indeed would be a record first quarter fall in GDP of 6.1% against estimates of around 4.7%, Chrysler, the country's number three automobile company, filing for bankruptcy, and the fear at the time of an influenza pandemic stunting global growth.

However, in the closing days of the month, investors appeared to have decided to interpret bad news as good news on the reasoning that now things were so bad they could only get better. Even the most convinced bears were ready to admit that there were some "green shoots" to be seen, even if most of them were in the second derivative class, i.e. represented by a slowing in the rate of deterioration, or in what they considered to be highly subjective and unreliable data like consumer confidence readings. And, as such, the green shoots were still liable to wither in the frost of a continuing credit crunch and rising unemployment. Certainly, for the moment, the bulls held the stage and the remarkable winning streak that had lifted global markets since early March carried into May. The FTSE100 looked to have established a bridgehead over 4000 at 4243 with the FTSE250 at 7571 after a flurry of buying of cyclical Mid-Caps, while the Dow at 8212 and the S&P500 at 877 seemed to have consigned their March lows to the history books after gains of 25% and 30% respectively. The NASDAQ Composite fared even better, up 35% to 1719, thanks to a revival of interest in technology stocks as likely leaders of the anticipated recovery and Oracle taking over from **IBM** as bidder for **Sun Microsystems**. Gains in London and New York were paralleled in financial capitals across the globe, leaving the FTSE All-World index up 31% on its March low.

This groundswell of optimism reflected in rising stock markets appeared to have its roots in a growing belief that concerted government actions had headed off the threat of systemic failure in global banking and that economic recovery was just around the corner. As a result so-called "defensive" stocks, i.e. those whose fortunes were less tied to the business cycle, had taken a back seat, and the "cyclicals" whose fortunes were, had come to the fore in anticipation of a rebounding economy later in the year or early in 2010.

Traders on top

As the advance continued, many analysts were ready to call a new bull market; but, to the extent that their own fortunes, and those of the financial institutions that employed them, were also cyclical, this was perhaps only to be expected. Commentators without a vested interest in a rising market were more cautious. The Lex column in the *Financial Times*, which had been remarkably prescient in forecasting 'a year of reckoning in the credit markets' at the beginning of 2007, was deeply sceptical about the rally and saw it as a trading call based largely on 'cheap credit and government largesse', palliatives that at some point would have to be withdrawn. Like-minded commentators also saw the 'animal spirits' currently being displayed in stock markets as notably lacking in a real economy that continued to suffer the fallout from a badly damaged financial infrastructure where access to credit was severely restricted and subject to penal charges when it was available. At the same time, most agreed that rising markets were in themselves confidence boosting and even if the timing and extent of economic recovery remained in doubt, a degree of stability had been achieved and a counteraction to the panic share price falls of two months ago was more than justified.

However, they still saw the magnitude of the rally as excessive and serving to bestow a favourable interpretation on news that was actually bad or at best ambivalent. Thus, the US jobless figures for April which took the unemployment rate to 8.9%, a 25 year high, were greeted with equanimity by the markets on the grounds that they could have been worse. Similarly, the actual bankruptcy of **Chrysler** was seen as a defining moment, ending months of uncertainty, rather than as a cataclysmic event with a likely post-Lehman-style chain of adverse consequences throughout one of the country's most important industries. The results of the stress tests for America's nineteen biggest banks, too, were broadly welcomed without regard for concerns that they were not stressful enough and had been stage-managed to a degree by the regulators' relaxation of marked to market valuations.

Victor, Uniform of Lima?

In essence, the fate of the nine-week rally and its chances of morphing into a new bull market continued to rely upon economic recovery being just around the corner. Admittedly, the first nine weeks of depression and decline had been wiped out by the rally, leaving markets up on the year and back to square one; but, the bears insisted, the 'promising signs that the pace of decline had moderated' – noted by The Bank of England when it decided to keep interest rates on hold and add another $50 billion to its quantitative easing programme – was not sufficient reason to regard a recovery as a done deal. The monetary and fiscal stimulus, unprecedented in size and scope, enacted across the world was bound to have a booster effect for a time, but as a policy measure it was deeply flawed in that it was trying to resolve a crisis created by excessive liquidity and debt by simply providing more of the same. Flooding the market with cheap credit got us into this mess, the bears argued, and repeating the process could never provide more than a temporary fix, setting the scene for the next crisis, sooner rather than later. Thus, any recovery was likely to be short lived and V-shaped, not U-shaped, before resolving into an all too durable L-shape when the time came round to unwind the stimulus with higher interest rates, higher taxes and public spending cuts in order to head off a return of inflation. Supporting this view was the belief that today's consumers had received a once in a lifetime shock in the Great Financial Crisis of 2007/2009 and were now set on a course of deleveraging to bring down their debts to a more manageable level relative to income and their devalued homes.

Against a background of still rising unemployment, stagnant wages, the threat of higher taxes and the need to boost pension contributions, not to mention tightened credit conditions, spending restraint was no longer a matter of choice but one of necessity, representing a structural change in consumer attitudes. The idea of a wave of asceticism engulfing British consumers, heightened by revulsion at the excesses of greedy bankers and freeloading Members of Parliament, appealed to one writer who saw it as good for the soul and the environment if not for the profitability of purveyors of discretionary purchases. And with consumer spending accounting for two thirds to three quarters of nominal GDP in developed economies and exhortations to "spend, spend, spend" falling on deaf ears, the growth projections over the next five years were going to have to look beyond the consumer for fulfilment. The most stimulative monetary and fiscal policy in a generation had proved the best recovery money could buy, beginning in the first quarter of 2003, but many observers doubted that this even greater stimulus would be able to work the same magic in 2009.

The Governor gets real

By mid-May it was clear that these doubts were shared by the Governor of the Bank of England, who warned that economic output could slump by up to 4.5% in 2009 with recovery to be 'relatively slow and protracted' and even delayed until 2011. The principal reason behind this unexpectedly downbeat forecast was attributed to the fragile state of the banking system, which had led to banks becoming risk averse and more intent on rebuilding their capital ratios than restoring lending to the private sector. The implication was that to get lending going again, the state would have to pump more money into the banks, which would in turn lead to greater state control and possibly full nationalisation.

The FTSE100 lost 94 points to 4331 and the FTSE250, 252 to 7371 in reaction to the Governor's statement, with bank shares leading the decline. On Wall Street, US investors were given reason to think that the stock market had got a little ahead of itself when the April retail sales figures showed an unexpected fall against forecasts of a small rise, while foreclosures continuing to rise gave no hint of relief for the housing market. The Dow pulled back 184 points to 8284 and the S&P500 dipped below 900 again to 883.

Eurozone blues

If hopes of a rapid recovery were beginning to fade in Britain and America, as old problems proved harder to resolve than expected, they were fading faster in continental Europe where such problems, and particularly financial ones, had barely been addressed relative to the actions taken across the waters. The European Central Bank was widely regarded as having been behind the curve in dealing with the financial crisis to date, but appeared to be catching up when, earlier in the month, it had brought interest rates down by another quarter per cent to 1.00% and embarked upon its own version of quantitative easing with a €60 billion covered bond purchase programme. The illusion that the staid and conservative Eurozone could avoid the side effects of what it saw as very much an American problem was never a runner given the global entanglements of its leading banks, but the idea had persisted and, according to IMF calculations, their banks had written down only a fifth of likely losses compared to half by US banks.

Consequently, the Eurozone banks would also have to raise more fresh capital and in increasing amounts if economic recovery was going to be delayed. Germany, supposedly the power house of the Eurozone, now seemed to confirm such fears by reporting a 3.8% fall in GDP in the first quarter, contributing to an overall 2.5% decline for the whole region. Far larger falls were being recorded by member countries in Eastern Europe, serving to aggravate the problems of those in the West given the scale of financing provided by their banks. These concerns were reflected in the performance of the Eurofirst 300 which lost 3% in the second week of May to 839, although this figure still registered a gain of 27.5% on its March low point.

Missing the boat?

However, it soon became clear that the near certainty of a delayed recovery with all that it entailed in continuing job losses which would be bad for consumer spending, corporate earnings and all good things that contribute to a rising stock market, were of concern only to serious financial commentators. Far more important for a great many share buyers was the knowledge that in the stock market it was very often darkest before the dawn and the initial surge in a new bull market was not to be missed. In the space of a couple of days a renewed rise had carried the leading indices in London and New York almost back to their peak levels attained earlier in the month, with sentiment boosted by booming BRICs, headlined by a near 20% rebound in India's BSESensex to top 14000 in response to the Congress Party's election successes.

But as one commentator pointed out, many of the 100%-plus share price moves had taken place at least a couple of months ago and today's buyers were simply letting the early birds cash in. Thus, an investor in mid-May willing to take a bet on the eventual and admittedly inevitable recovery of the bombed out house builders would have been paying prices for shares in **Taylor Wimpey** and **Barratt** that had already risen sevenfold from their November lows. Share prices of British banks had also more than doubled by the end of March from the depths plumbed at the beginning of the month and the same was true of the major US banks. One cynical commentator dubbed the nine week buying spree, 'the dash for trash', an unkind and possibly unfair labelling of many of the leading companies in their fields but one on a par with the public's loss of respect for their elected representatives in the Mother of Parliaments.

Pelion on Ossa

With the end of May approaching, stock markets in London, New York and around the world appeared to be going nowhere, indicating a balance between the arguments of the bulls and the bears. Then for UK investors the issue was resolved in favour of the bears by a downgrading of the country's status from 'stable' to 'negative' by ratings agency Standard & Poor's on the grounds of the deteriorating state of public finances and the uncertainty over how to repair them. The IMF simultaneously pronounced the UK government must be prepared to pump more money into the banking system to enable the banks to 'increase lending sufficiently to underpin a strong recovery', thereby validating precisely what Mervyn King had said only days earlier. The Fund added that banks should do everything possible to preserve their capital by 'restraining dividends and converting preference shares to common shares', a statement that raised the spectre of nationalisation again to haunt bank investors and particularly recent buyers at multiples of the March lows. This double shock sent the FTSE100 into sharp reverse, losing 123 points on the day to 4345 with the decline headed by the banks.

London's dismay was paralleled in New York, following a surprisingly downbeat statement from the Federal Reserve to the effect that rising unemployment and a steeper than expected fall in economic activity would delay recovery. The Fed also revised its earlier forecast that the economy would shrink by 1.3% in 2009 to 2%, an assessment now substantiated by the simultaneous release of housing and employment data significantly undershooting popular expectations, news of the collapse of an important regional bank in Florida, and **GMAC** going cap in hand to the government for another $7.5 billion.

Sentiment was not helped by the downgrading of the UK's economic outlook, since much the same circumstances that had led to the revision applied to all the other countries now burdened with huge deficits as a result of their unprecedented stimulus expenditures. With public debt in the US scheduled to rise from 41% of GDP in 2008 to 75% in 2015, and in the UK to 100% by 2013, and the absence of what the IMF called a 'more ambitious medium-term fiscal adjustment path' to be followed by governments to rebuild national finances, it was not surprising to see the anxiety focus shift from private credits to sovereign credits. In the final week of May, the OECD confirmed the all-embracing nature of the downturn among developed countries by reporting a 2.1% fall in GDP in the first quarter of 2009, the highest figure recorded since 1960, when quarterly readings began.

All together now...

With the IMF, the OECD, the Federal Reserve and the Bank of England all apparently ganging up on the world economy, the bears might have been expected to be in control but, perverse as ever, stock markets everywhere rallied strongly. The trigger for the advance supposedly was a sharp rise in US consumer confidence in

May to an 8-month high, an event which although seemingly contradicted by a record 19.1% fall in house prices in the first quarter, also served to outweigh the imminent collapse of **GM** into bankruptcy. It also outweighed a surge in geopolitical tensions as a result of North Korea's atom bomb test, multiple missile firings and its repudiation of the 1953 Peace Treaty. London was content to follow New York's lead, encouraged by a freakish rise in April's retail sales and undeterred by the sharpest fall in overall household spending since 1980, the biggest drop in wages and compensation since 1955, and capital investment falling for the fifth quarter in a row.

Looking on the bright side, the bulls saw the intensification of the fall in industrial activity as a result of the sharp rundown in inventory, a process that would soon have to be reversed by restarting production to fill shelves again. They also took heart from an apparent easing of credit conditions as interbank lending rates fell back to almost "normal" pre-crisis levels. While acknowledging the benefit the rally bestowed in terms of business confidence, the bears remained convinced that it was simply a reflex response by ever-hopeful investors to unprecedented fiscal and monetary initiatives. As for easing credit conditions, with practically zero interest rates and total state back-up, banks were being given a free ride. They could lend to each other without risk but finding creditworthy borrowers in industry was quite another matter, and, in all too many cases, not worth the risk. And on the question of the effectiveness of the myriad stimulus packages and quantitative easing measures agreed globally at the G20 meeting in March, and earlier at national levels, the sharp reversal of the downturn in 10-year bond yields suggested that not all was going as planned.

Having vilified such a strategy as 'the road to Hell' at the March meeting, the Czech president might at least have agreed that it was paved with good intentions. However, it was an extraordinarily circuitous road in that it started at one window of the Treasury out of which bonds were to be sold in increasing amounts to fund the costly stimulus programmes, providing progressively higher yields in order to attract buyers, while at another window longer-term bonds were being bought back to put money into the system with the object of keeping interest rates down.

Furthermore, while the bond sales were flowing as planned, doubts about the schedule and scale of the buy-back programme were serving to keep rates uncomfortably high and actually reversing the fall in the benchmark US 10-year Treasury bond yield from 2.5%, when the programme was announced in March, to around 3.70% in the last week of May, while in the UK comparable yields had risen from 3.30% to 3.76%. The effect of the move on the US 30-year fixed rate mortgages was to drive the rate up from 5.24% to 5.45% in that week, not a development that would be of help to a still hard-pressed housing market, the recovery of which was seen as the key to revival of the economy.

Road Games

How all this was likely to play out in the markets was a moot point but the bears remained convinced that the road to recovery, if not to hell, was going to be hard and rocky. Most agreed that enough had been done to achieve a degree of stability but insisted that avoiding calamity was not the same as embarking upon the road to recovery. Thus, the entry of **GM** into bankruptcy on the first day of June was certainly a defining moment in the crisis that was gripping the automobile industry worldwide; but, given the collateral damage that would be caused across America and Europe among myriad related industries, it was opening a new phase in an ongoing crisis that would not be resolved until supply fell into line with demand. The German government's subsidy for **Opel** in the GM Europe takeover deal by the Canadians and the Russians (perhaps influenced by a September election) could not be matched by a cash-strapped British government in the case of **Vauxhall**, but regardless of guarantees, job security would remain hostage to market conditions and *force majeure*. Accordingly, a 220 point swing in the Dow and one of 23 points in the S&P500; taking them to 8721 and 942 respectively (and a new high for the year for the latter), hardly seemed appropriate for the occasion, any more than did the FTSE100's rise of 88 to 4506.

Since most serious market commentators were taken by surprise at the magnitude of the rally from the lows of early March, they were tempted to attribute its strength to a combination of late buying by bulls who had missed out on the initial surge and were terrified of being left behind, and by bears who had literally been "caught short" and were closing positions, equally terrified of being squeezed by a further rise. If they were right, then the rally had just about run its course and where it went from here would depend on a more reliable run of economic data than the "up one month, down the next" series that had appeared to date.

Goodbye Armageddon?

The Armageddon crew looking for a retesting of the March and November lows had diminished, with most of them embracing the "flat market" thesis, but a few were still convinced there were time bombs in the financial system with the potential to upset the so-recently-achieved stability. One was the exposure of the banks in America and Britain to commercial property and private equity loans, where refinancing could only take place on terms demanding higher interest rates, tighter covenants and punitive arrangement fees, all of which would make it more difficult for the borrowers to survive. Such a situation meant that the banks had the unenviable choice of taking bad loan provisions and write-offs today or postponing them for another year or so in the hope that a strong recovery would get them off the hook.

Eurozone banks were in a similar position but had the additional burden of loans to Eastern Europe and the Baltic states as well as potential losses arising from not having written down much of the toxic debt on their books. The German regulators had no doubt about the seriousness of the position, reporting potential bad debts of over €200 billion and write-downs of over €800 billion (roughly twice the reserves of their entire banking system) and concluding that things could blow up 'like a grenade'. Sweden's central bank warned of impending loan losses for the country's banks of some €32 billion, much of the sums due to loans to the Baltic states where Latvia was in the most trouble.

Hugely burdened with foreign currency loans and facing the prospect of a 30% devaluation, it was widely feared that Latvia was the template for the rest of the Baltic and the bulk of Eastern Europe where borrowings from Western European banks had totalled some €1.6 trillion during the boom years of 2005/2007. Of course, there was nothing new about this situation; it had just been pushed into the back of investors' minds by a rising market but it had not gone away. Suspicion of capital shortfalls continued to overshadow banks everywhere and the decision by Abu Dhabi investors to dispose of their stake in **Barclays** was taken by some commentators as signalling the top of the sector rally.

Faraway countries...

For those investors doubtful about the merits of investing in the developed markets of the West, the relative outperformance of the BRICs in the recent rally seemed to have revived the "decoupling" story and the belief that they could continue to grow even if the economies of the developed world were in recession. Inevitably, China took centre stage in the thesis that diminished exports could be counterbalanced by expanding domestic consumption, with the same reasoning applied to the rest of the emerging market giants.

However, one writer 'familiar with the situation', strongly disagreed and stressed once again that Brazil, Russia, India and China were not simply scaled-up versions of the developed nations but countries the size of continents where the vast majority of their billion-plus populations dwelt in an impoverished state in an inhospitable hinterland subject all too often to natural disasters of epic proportions. The dirt farmer in Sichuan, China or Orissa, India was not going to be in the market for a car, a refrigerator or a television set, and exports to the developed world would remain the mainstay of their economies for a very long time.

Still, by the end of the first week in June, there seemed to be no reason for the investor with a more modest risk appetite to have sold in May or to look beyond London and New York. In the words of one market commentator, 'the uptrend remained intact, there was a rotation out of bonds, volatility was down and risk taking was back in the market'. The bulls in the UK were heartened by a pick-up in house prices in May and a sharp jump in the service sector's Purchasing Manager's Index (PMI), and apparently undeterred by the virtual collapse of public confidence in the Labour government evidenced by its disastrous showing in the local and European elections. With the next election still probably a year away, business leaders expressed the fear that such a lame duck administration would be unable to tackle the challenges facing the country in the gravest economic crisis since the 1930s. However, the fall in sterling from $1.67 to nearer $1.60 as a reaction to such political uncertainty was not entirely unwelcome to the more export-oriented sectors of industry.

Commodities on a roll

In the US, markets responded positively to a significant drop in job losses in May and to a continuing strong advance in commodity prices led by oil and industrial metals, both being taken as signs that a rebound in the economy was just around the corner. At the same time, enthusiasm was muted by the jump in the unemployment rate to 9.4%, its highest level since a matching rate in 1983, with all that it implied for consumer confidence. As for rising oil and other commodity prices, if they were indicative of recovery they were also an impediment to its progress, especially if the oil price continued to rise to $85 by the end of the year, as forecast by analysts at Goldman Sachs (although it should perhaps be noted that their forecast the previous summer of $150. By the end of 2008 was betrayed by a slide to $40).

Some commentators saw the rise in commodity prices as not so much a sign of global industrial resurgence but more the result of buying by cash-rich China when prices were low, both for simple stockpiling and for investment in massive infrastructure projects in accordance with their stimulus plans to maintain employment while waiting for the eventual upturn in world demand. Given China's continuing dependence on exports to the developed world led by the US consumer, any delay in that upturn would be very damaging for the economy of China and for that of every country in Asia. This mutual dependency between surplus China and deficit America and the maintenance of a supply/demand balance was widely seen as crucial for the future of the global economy and indeed their stock markets.

Render unto Caesar...

Rising bond yields also had a dual aspect. They implied, on the one hand, a growing confidence of investors in risk taking, as they shunned bonds and plumped for equities; but on the other hand they were shooting themselves in the foot by effectively boosting interest rates and making it much more difficult and costly for governments to raise the money needed to create the recovery investors required to justify their risk taking. They also revived fears that rising commodity prices could derail a tentative recovery. One writer saw the situation as another example of the law of unintended consequences, as investors anticipating that recovery would drive demand for so-called hard assets, accumulating them in advance, only to see rising prices actually jeopardising that recovery. He quoted oil industry experts (as distinct from "experts" within financial institutions) as saying that the world was awash with oil and there was no reason for the price to have doubled since the beginning of the year unless it was due to speculative buying by hedge funds and the like. The wild gyrations of the oil price the previous year had made no sense in the context of industrial demand, the writer insisted, and given the destabilising effect of such movements on the economy, perhaps the new breed of regulators should treat oil and industrial metals as vital strategic materials and, just as in wartime, require prospective purchasers to produce end-user certificates. After all, no one needed to buy copper or tin except a metal fabricator, and speculative hoarding inflating prices was contrary to the interests of the manufacturer, the consumer and the whole economy.

Such caveats were not going to be allowed to spoil the party for many investors, who were content to see the rally hanging on close to its peak levels in the major Western markets while new highs were still being made on Asian exchanges. At the same time, it had to be recognised that the advance of the FTSE100 owed a great deal to its weighting in the oil and mining majors, as oil topped $70 a barrel again and copper rose above $5000 a tonne, responding as much to the weak dollar as to recovery hopes. **Rio Tinto's** return to favour with a joint venture over its iron ore resources with **BHP Billiton** and a $15.2 billion rights issue in place of the controversial deal with **Chinalco** sent its shares soaring, simultaneously boosting those of other miners on hopes of more share price enhancing deals within the sector.

Rates on hold

London and the Eurozone markets also derived a degree of support from the "no change" decision on key interest rates by the Bank of England and the European Central Bank, taken as suggesting a return to stability in the financial system. The survival of the Brown government after a threatened leadership challenge failed to materialise also helped sterling to recover, but political uncertainty continued over how to deal with the country's debt mountain in the years ahead. Cutting public spending seemed to be the policy that dared not speak its name, and while everyone knew it had to happen, it was seen by both Labour and Conservatives as politically unacceptable to say so ahead of an election. The also inevitable tax rises were marginally less sensitive, especially for Labour targeting higher earners, but again they were not seen by any party as a vote winner.

However, by mid-June, the inability of the major indices to move out of the trading ranges that had obtained for the past six weeks and their return to the lower end of those ranges, was beginning to worry the bulls. There were still plenty of green shoots among the weeds but the failure of attempts at an upside breakout had sown seeds of suspicion that perhaps markets had got a little ahead of themselves. Taking the ranges as 4300 to 4500 for the FTSE100, 850 to 890 for the Eurofirst 300, and 920 to 950 for the S&P500, by the end of the third week of June all three indices had broken out on the downside. The result of these moves was that just as rising markets had encouraged arguments to be put forward to justify the trend, falling markets now witnessed a concentration on negative influences. Chief among these were the dramatic fall in industrial production in the US, resulting in the lowest level of capacity utilisation since 1967, and the apparently relentless rise in unemployment, both major factors capable of killing the hopes of early recovery engendered by anomalous upticks in monthly data releases and over-optimistic statements by officials, part of whose brief was the maintenance of public confidence.

New game, new rules

The bears were now convinced that they had been right all along. This was no ordinary downturn but one unique in the experience of the politicians and financial administrators tasked with dealing with it. As such a rapid return to business as usual had never been on the cards, a state of affairs regularly evidenced by repeated downward revisions of economic numbers released only weeks earlier. The World Bank's downgrading of its forecast for global growth in 2009, from minus 1.7% made in March to minus 2.9% in June on the back of a 9.7% slump in world trade, coincided with a dramatic reversal of the price rises in oil and industrial metals and upset the markets, prompting a 200 point fall in the Dow to 8339 with the S&P500 losing 28 to 893, and matched by a 111 point loss in the FTSE100 to 4234 and one of 24 in the Eurofirst 300 taking it to 837. Falling metal prices and waning recovery hopes offset benefits to share prices in the mining sector that might have followed from **Xstrata's** £40 billion merger proposal to **AngloAmerican**. Furthermore, the major indices were no longer buoyed by their banking constituents, now overshadowed by the prospect of politically-inspired regulatory reforms dedicated to de-risking the financial system and, in effect, clipping the banks' wings and reducing their profit-making potential in the years ahead. The banks were not alone. The renegotiation of the capitalist tenet of minimum government involvement in industry and commerce radically changed the whole economic landscape for business leaders, who would have to learn to operate more in line with non-commercial factors than they had ever done before. The age-old appeal of industry and commerce to government – asking no more of it than Diogenes did of Alexander, 'Stay out of my sunshine' – no longer had any validity.

To the extent that the stability of the banking system and the ready availability of credit was going to be a key determinant in a sustained recovery, any threat to that stability could not be taken lightly, and since banks and property lending went hand in hand, the staggering falls in commercial property valuations from the 2006/2007 peaks (when much of the lending was undertaken) had to pose a significant threat to all loan-to-value covenants. Worries on this score had been around for a long time but, like so many others, had been sidelined by a rising stock market. They resurfaced dramatically in late June when the problem facing property magnate, Simon Halabi, was revealed by a revaluation of his portfolio of prime City and West End buildings. Valued at £1.8 billion two years ago and providing security for a £1.15 billion loan packaged into bonds, the £929 million revaluation wiped out the equity and triggered a default, requiring a cash injection within 10 days. If a near 50% fall in commercial property valuations was typical, as property insiders believed, then Mr Halabi's default was just the tip of the iceberg and no bank could sit comfortably knowing that around £250 billion of commercial mortgage-backed securities would mature over the next five years and need refinancing or rolling over.

Banks still on trial

The danger that such problems would continue to run and run was reflected in the Bank of England's "Financial Stability Report", which stressed that despite all the hugely costly bailouts, the banking system remained vulnerable and at risk from 'further adverse economic or financial sector developments' capable of inhibiting lending and thus delaying economic recovery. The Bank pointed to rising unemployment, already at 2.2 million, as likely to trigger increasing loan defaults and mortgage arrears serving to deplete banks' capital in the months, even years, ahead. On the same day the report was released, Anglo-Dutch steel giant **Corus** (now owned by **Tata**), illustrated just such 'adverse economic developments', by sacking another 2000 workers in response to a slump in world demand of 50%, while **Jaguar/Landrover** (also owned by **Tata**) announced it was on course for more job cuts as sales plummeted. In the same week **DSG**, the country's number one electrical/electronics goods retailer, reported a £140 million loss and forecast 'no uptick' in business before the end of next year, while making a £310 million cash call to cut its £477 million debt burden.

DSG was just the latest in a lengthening list of household name companies calling on their shareholders for additional capital to tide them over until happy days were here again, but what was going to happen, one cynical commentator asked, if things were still not getting any better by end-2010? The government had no more money to provide, given the still deteriorating state of public finances, and neither the banks nor the shareholders would be eager to contribute to yet another round of financing. And there were worrying signs that politics was being given precedence over economics, as the Brown government decided to postpone its scheduled biennial Comprehensive Spending Review until after next year's election, clearly in the hope that by then a recovery would be well underway, enabling them to go easy on public spending cuts.

In France, Prime Minister Fillon expressed his concern that the country's structural deficit was now 'reaching levels that could jeopardise the very survival of our economic system', a view contrasting sharply with President Sarkozy's rejection of 'austerity' policies and the European Central Bank pumping another €442 billion into the financial system in an attempt to thaw still frozen credit markets.

The OECD seemed to agree with every economist in the UK in urging the Treasury to come up with a 'comprehensive' plan to deal with a public debt load of £775 billion and rising as well as keeping bank nationalisation as 'an arrow in the policy quiver' in case the economy took a turn for the worse. In the same final week of June, the BIS warned that banks' balance sheets were still in urgent need of repair, a process that was 'a precondition of a sustained recovery'.

If politics can triumph over economics only until the situation has become so dire that obfuscation was no longer possible, the markets were poised at a delicate juncture as they entered the second half of the year. Most commentators were happy to sit on the fence and predict markets moving sideways in response to a likely mixed bag of economic data as the year progressed. However, a few looked at the now all too frequent revisions of forecasts made only weeks earlier and the rising total of unemployed, and saw the clear and present danger of a recession within a recession. If they were right, then dashed recovery hopes would send corporate finances reeling along with share prices.

Promises, promises

The run-up to Independence Day on 4th July began well for the markets, but confidence took a knock with the release of the US employment report showing the loss of 467,000 jobs in June, significantly more than the May total of 322,000 and against expectations of no more than a 10% increase. The unemployment rate now stood at 9.5%, a figure that sparked comment about the rationale of a stimulus plan that in February the Obama administration had said was designed to head off unemployment rising to 9% in 2010. The disparity was attributed to the simple fact that 'what they inherited was a lot worse than they thought', according to the Centre for Economic and Policy Research, which added, 'we'll probably be going over 10% in the fall'. With the UK and continental Europe already looking at high and rising unemployment, a situation that could only get worse as the spending squeeze began to bite, more than one commentator was prepared to forecast riots in the streets as the populace lost faith in the ability of elected politicians to deal with the crisis.

The idea that governments everywhere were still trying to come to terms with a situation, the seriousness of which they had so clearly underestimated (or perhaps underplayed for political reasons), was catching on with investors and markets continued to slide in spite of the best efforts of the G8 at L'Aquila.

Exit the dragon?

The fact that the Shanghai Composite index continued to forge ahead as the major indices of markets in the developed world faltered was seen by many commentators as evidence that the Chinese stimulus was working. If this was indeed the case, they said, then China would carry on growing as domestic consumption took up the slack from slowing imports. The economy would act as the locomotive driving the whole Asia Pacific region and de-coupling would become a reality. However, ratings agency Fitch saw things rather differently, expressing concern about the massive lending programme encouraged by the government to ensure that the 8% GDP growth target was achieved. Lending to the corporate sector had doubled in the year to May 2009, and in the context of a 26% fall in exports in that month, instead of being invested in the heavily export-oriented real economy as intended by the central bank, the money appeared to be leaking into the stock market as well as into speculative property and commodity deals. Certainly, the massive oversubscription of new issues following the lifting of IPO suspensions was a clear portent of a market at or near its peak. If the official aim was to keep the factories busy to avoid the social unrest that mass unemployment could bring, then the plan was not working and at the same time it was aggravating the situation by creating a speculative bubble, the inevitable bursting of which would have a devastating impact on global confidence.

Against such a background, the Chinese calls at the G8 for reserve currency diversification away from the US dollar appeared premature on even the most generous interpretation. The US was the world's dominant superpower with a long history of political stability, a precondition for a reserve currency country, and one unrivalled by any other. China was certainly up and coming but it had not arrived in any way to match the US in such a role, and in any case the yuan was not fully convertible whilst it remained subject to capital controls. And as the largest holder of dollar bonds, as another Chinese official had admitted only weeks earlier, China really had no alternative but to keep buying them.

Over there

In other parts of the developing world, markets were underperforming China. Both Russia and India registered falls of around 10% in their markets over the second week of July, the former as its oil export-dependent economy responded to the oil price slipping below the $60 mark, and the latter to investor disappointment at a budget seen as too left-leaning, with loan write-offs for small farmers, rural workfare schemes and costly infrastructure projects in place of the radical reforms needed to sustain rapid growth. Arguably, on a longer-term perspective, the finance minister had got it right, one writer argued, since for political, if not humanitarian reasons, the country's ruling elite would have to adopt some form of welfare system so that a new city centre flyover in Bombay no longer doubled as family accommodation.

As one of the superpowers of the future, India, along with other BRICs, would soon be subject to the same pressures as governments in the developed world, i.e. to provide health and social security benefits for their vast and still growing populations. The process would eventually see the fruits of growth spread more evenly throughout society, although it would mean that their governments would find themselves hobbled with the same ball and chain of social responsibility as those in the West as "two nations" within their borders became one.

Don't worry, be happy!

Meanwhile back in London and New York, markets staged an abrupt turnaround in mid-July, inspired by Intel's bullish forecast about increasing revenue in the second half of the year on the back of rising demand for personal computers. Since other economic data was inconclusive, a great deal of faith appeared to be pinned on the forecast of just one company, albeit a highly important one, but some encouragement was also derived from the US government's rejection of calls for a second stimulus package, and the Bank of England's denial that another dose of quantitative easing was planned. If such measures were no longer considered necessary, perhaps recovery really was underway, and the translation of such hopes into buying orders managed to propel the main stock indices back into the post-spring rally trading bands established in May and June. Within days, markets were bidding to break through the top of these bands as better than expected second quarter profits from **Goldman Sachs** and **JPMorgan** unleashed a 'wave of optimism' to quote from a headline in the *Financial Times*. The prospect of small business lender **CIT** filing for bankruptcy cast a shadow but that was quickly dispelled when the company's bondholders agreed to provide a $3 billion loan to keep the wolf from the door, and then China provided another powerful boost to world markets by announcing that it had achieved 7.9% growth in GDP for the second quarter, up from 6.1% in the first.

While such news items were eagerly seized upon by perennial bulls to justify their belief that a new bull market was in train, more balanced commentators thought they had been cherry-picking the data that suited them and turning a blind eye to that which did not. Thus in the case of the banks, with fewer of them around receiving central bank funds at virtually no cost, it would have been surprising if they had not had a good run in the second quarter. From now on, however, they would start to experience the problems that an ailing economy would foist upon them, in the shape of rising loan defaults, personal and corporate, as the jobless toll mounted. Furthermore, the degree of stability that had been attained in the financial sector meant that regulation and reform were now top of a government's agenda in place of rescue and 'bailout'. Bigger capital cushions, restrictions on the size of trading positions and leverage limits would severely cut back the banks' ability to make money at the same time as trimming the attendant risks. Interestingly, even the upgrade by **Goldman Sachs'** analysts of their forecast for the S&P500 at the end of the year from 940 to 1060 was said to be subject to the state of the 'economic backdrop' and the absence of a 'double dip recession'. Similarly, Fed chairman, Ben Bernanke, in his testimony to Congress, qualified his talk of stabilisation of the economy with forecasts of unemployment staying high until 'at least 2012' and recovery being 'a very long haul'. And a number of analysts thought that rising second quarter earning were not all necessarily a sign of recovery in demand since many were accompanied by a fall in revenue which suggested that the increase was derived from cost-cutting measures involving job losses which would be inimical to demand in the months ahead.

Carry on regardless

Nevertheless, the bulls were not ready to capitulate, and, in the face of mixed messages on the economic and corporate fronts, continued to push markets higher. Wall Street at least had a run of better than expected earnings figures from major Dow components **AT&T**, **3M** and **Ford** on which to base some optimism, but London appeared to have very little going for it beyond the hope that where Wall Street led, it would soon follow. The headline in the *Financial Times* on 25th July, 'Equities surge as economy shrinks', noted the apparent contradiction of the

FTSE100 gaining 10.9% to 4596 in a record breaking 10-day run in spite of the news that the economy had contracted by 5.6% in the year to June, more than twice the amount forecast. Similarly, no regard was being paid to the swine flu pandemic and its possible effect on the economy.

But a market rising as it ignored clearly adverse economic news served to gather more converts to the bull camp, fired by the conviction that it's darkest before the dawn and determined not to be left out of the early stages of a new bull market. Respected analysts now reinstated their end-year targets of 5000 and above for the FTSE100, which had been quietly shelved in the dark days of early March, their confidence boosted by a storming performance by Asian markets. China led the charge, with the Shanghai Composite and Hong Kong's Hang Seng hitting new highs for the year, encouraged by a 7.9% boost to second quarter GDP on the mainland and undeterred by cynical observations that, as a politically-inspired target, it had to be seen to be achieved come what may. Japan joined in the rally and the Nikkei Dow topped 10000 again for the first time since mid-June.

Going with the flow

On Wall Street, **Microsoft** and **Amazon** now clouded the earnings picture, with the former reporting a fall in software sales for the first time ever, and the latter a 10% drop in second quarter earnings. These reports, along with a sharp dip in consumer confidence readings for July, were enough to call a halt to a two-week rally that had seen the Dow and the S&P500 gain 11.5% and the NASDAQ 12%. Nevertheless, there was no marked reaction to a shock 2.5% drop in durable goods orders in June and disappointment at the **Microsoft/Yahoo** tie-up in place of a full takeover. Even a sudden 5% sell-off in the Shanghai Composite on rumours of action by China's central bank to curb the speculative frenzy evidenced by new issues doubling and even tripling on the first day of dealing, failed to trim more than a few points from the US indices and those of other Western markets. Two days later it was all systems go once more and the last week of July saw stock markets everywhere at new highs for the year. The push behind this final flourish to end a momentous month was provided by an unexpected dip in continuing jobless claims in the US from 6.25 million to 6.2 million, a less than forecast 1% fall in second quarter GDP, and reassurance from the Chinese authorities that an 'appropriately loose' monetary policy would be maintained.

Since a rising stock market is by definition self-justifying, it determines that the interpretation to be placed on data and news items is a favourable one, an outcome that served to bolster the belief of investors that we were in the early stages of a new bull market that would pick up steam as the economy recovered. However, given that the jobless claims number is commonly subject to a revision of 10% and more, taking a 0.8% drop as evidence that the US jobs market was "stabilising" seemed to many observers as very much an act of faith on the part of investors. Similarly, the continuation of a loose monetary policy in China could prove a mixed blessing when it came at the risk of the potential for long-term disaster if the Chinese banking system was as overstretched as many believed.

Too close to the sun?

In the event such reservations were of little concern to investors in London, who pushed the FTSE100 over 4700 at one point on the first trading day of August in response to bumper first half profits from **Barclays**, a confident statement from **HSBC**, and a surge in the manufacturing sector's Purchasing Managers' Index (PMI) from 47.4 to 50.8, the first time it had crossed the 50-level that separates expansion from contraction since March 2008. Since the PMI is regarded as a reliable indicator of economic growth, the reading was widely taken as pointing to the economy growing again in the second half of the year, and sterling reacted by gaining 3 cents against the dollar to $1.69. The 74 point advance in the FTSE100 to 4682 was led by the banks and the miners, the latter boosted by a further dramatic rise in industrial metal prices, with copper adding 9% to just short of $6000 a tonne on continuing aggressive stockpiling by China. On Wall Street, the Dow plussed 99 points to 9270 while the NASDAQ and the S&P500 topped the 2000 and 1000 marks respectively for the first time since early October 2008, responding to encouraging data from the manufacturing sector and **Ford's** first monthly sales increase in two years.

By this time even the most ardent bulls would have been happy to see markets taking a breather. After all, the news coming from the economic front was not all that good but in most cases just not quite as bad as expected, and there was a growing belief that when recovery did take place, investors would be faced with the unfamiliar landscape of a "new normal" of changed industrial priorities and consumer habits. But it was still a surprise that the first hint of a setback for a London market that had been on a winning streak since early March should derive from a change of heart at the Bank of England and the decision to add another £50 billion to its quantitative easing programme. Only weeks earlier, emerging "green shoots" had fostered the impression that even the last £25 billion in the original programme would not have to be disbursed. To now throw £50 billion into the pot was widely interpreted as a frank admission by the Bank that the recovery was not going according to plan as a result of the recession being deeper than previously thought, and more firepower was needed to bring down bond yields and long-term interest rates. Sterling at once dropped from $1.69 to $1.67 and the 10-year gilt yield from 3.86 to 3.62 per cent. Less predictable, because it was seemingly less logical, was a surge in the FTSE100, taking it to a new closing high for the year. Second thoughts after critical press comment the next day saw the advance reversed, but a bounding Wall Street, on much better than expected job numbers leading to a fall in the unemployment percentage from 9.5% to 9.4%, helped the index to another new peak for the year at 4731, up 41 points, supported by the FTSE250, up 39 to 8416.

Quo vadis?

Views on where the economy and the stock market were heading were now broadly divided into two camps. The bulls were confident that they would follow the normal pattern of the post-War years and recover in tandem, citing the unprecedented government-sponsored stimulus programmes that had led to the newfound stability of the banking system and the green shoots sprouting in the industrial landscape, all to be supported by continuing growth in China. Stock markets everywhere rising by some 50% over the past five months validated this view, it was argued.

The contras disagreed, believing that this time things really were different. **Pimco**, the American bond dealer, for example, stressed the worrying and uncertain implications arising from the imbalance between the amount of private credit and national output in the wake of securitisation, which had increased hugely the measure of available credit. That it had done so by simply monetising existing debt, and a lot of it not very sound either, had gone against the natural order of things by blurring the distinction between credit and debt, and instead of serving to expand national growth, the process had sparked a global financial crisis of unprecedented proportions. Now that a great part of that debt had been transferred from the private sector to the public sector, the prospects for a vigorous economic recovery were jeopardised by governments' need to repair their finances, primarily by cutting future spending rather than raising taxes, given their inhibiting effect on private sector growth. Furthermore, these budgetary problems were greatly aggravated by the ever-rising costs of pensions and healthcare for ageing populations in all the so-called rich nations. Of course, such problems did not weigh so heavily, if at all, on the governments of China and the other emerging giants, but in the interests of maintaining political stability, they could well do so in the future and curb their headlong growth.

Liquidity rules

These reservations of the bears were of more concern to economists than to investors, the latter being keener to read and believe the apparent message conveyed by rising stock markets that we were 'squarely in the recovery trade', to quote a JP Morgan analyst. Nevertheless, a number of commentators were ready to point out that there was nothing exceptional about 50% quick-fire rallies and that while they were good for traders, all too often they turned out badly for long-term investors. Notably, the long decline of Japan's Nikkei Dow from its peak of 38915 in 1989 was punctuated by more than one such rally, but even after another since 9th March, it still stood at just 10585 on 11th August 2009. One writer was prepared to attribute the dramatic rise in markets to the action of the world's central banks in creating more money than depressed economies required to overcome the financial crisis. This surplus or excess liquidity arose from a largely unforeseen contraction in economic activity, which then had left it free to feed into riskier assets like stocks and commodities, a process capable of generating yet another asset-price inflation bubble. The writer's conclusion was that there was no point in governments instituting a market-based economy and applauding its ability to self-correct, and then when things got uncomfortable politically, stepping in to halt the corrective process.

Perhaps more worrying, and not just for the bulls but for everyone, were the opinions of veteran Wall Street analyst, Robert Prechter, noted for having issued a major "sell" recommendation just days ahead of the October 1987 market crash. He was ready to see the present rally carry on a little longer but remained convinced that the next wave down was going to be larger than any experienced so far and that it would penetrate the March lows. He had forecast that Ben Bernanke's rescue of the financials and the Obama administration's stimulus measures would lead to the "relief rally" that began in March, but believed that deflationary forces were so firmly in place that they would snuff out the recovery that everyone seemed to expect. Instead there would be a credit implosion that would see widespread asset price devaluation as excessive debt was eventually purged from the system. Cash and cash equivalents were his investments of choice.

If few market analysts shared the Prechter vision, more than one was prepared to admit that the latest statements from the Federal Reserve and the Bank of England indicating their apparent resolve to keep interest rates at zero for much longer than expected, suggested that neither institution regarded recovery as in the bag. As for the argument over whether the greater danger posed by current policies would involve the release of inflationary or deflationary forces, the contemporaneous announcements of figures showing that US consumer prices fell 2.1% in July, marking the sharpest annual drop since 1949, and that UK inflation was heading for a fall of more than 1% below the Bank of England's 2% target, made it clear that the authorities remained hostages to fortune. Then, considering that the continuing rise in unemployment, sluggish income growth, lower housing wealth, high levels of household debt and tighter credit must inevitably lead to a fall in consumer confidence and a reduction in spending, it became all too obvious that liquidity would not necessarily translate into demand. Taking all this in the context of the largest margin of excess industrial capacity around the world since 1945, and a deflationary outcome began to look at least as likely as an inflationary one.

Growth picks up

However, there were many more analysts who believed that the unprecedented monetary and fiscal stimulus indulged in from pole to pole was certain to work, and if the Fed's stated conviction that the recession was 'leveling out', did not quite fit the bill, then the surprise return to growth of France and Germany in the second quarter more than made up for it. Japan then joined the party with a reported 0.9% pick-up in GDP over the same period, trumping the Eurozone pair's 0.3%, and moving into positive territory ahead of the US. Such apparently encouraging data was not enough for some sceptical analysts who were reluctant to see this trio of reports as evidence of a synchronised global recovery but rather a result of imports falling more than exports were rising in unstable trading conditions. As such, they thought, the numbers were positive only for headline GDP but not for much else.

A surprise drop in the leading US consumer confidence indicator and disappointing retail sales revived doubts about the ability of household spending to do enough to stabilise US corporate revenues and led to a sharp fall in markets in the second half of August. Anxiety was further heightened by a near 20% slide in the Shanghai Composite index over the month on rumours that the authorities were planning to rein in bank lending in an effort to curb excessive speculation, but another run of good US housing and manufacturing numbers quickly dispelled the gloom and markets were up and running again as September dawned. A flurry of M&A activity, headlined by **Kraft's** £10.2 billion hostile bid for **Cadbury**, and **Deutsche Telekom's** and **France Telecom's** plan to merge their UK operations, was seen as demonstrating the attractions of UK equities for overseas buyers at a time when sterling was exceptionally weak against the dollar and the euro, and investors were only too willing to chase the FTSE100 through the 5000 level again on 9th September for the first time in almost a year.

Something for everyone

Wall Street was equally happy to resume its advance, with investor sentiment boosted by the Fed chairman's repeated statements that the US economy was 'nearing recovery' and the recession was 'very likely over'. They were reinforced by a sharp rebound in consumer confidence readings and retail sales figures between July and August widely taken as confirming that the economy was 'coming back online'. Official pronouncements, however, on both sides of the Atlantic were more muted, seeming to be more in agreement with Warren Buffett's judgement that the US economy had 'hit a plateau at the bottom' than with the stock market's eager anticipation of a bounding recovery. Mervyn King at the Bank of England was also keen to stress that the level of activity was the element to be watched.

Nevertheless, investors were ready to give the economy the benefit of the doubt, and by the end of the third week of September, the FTSE100 had topped 5170 and the Eurofirst 300 had breached the 1000 level for the first time in over a year, while on Wall Street the indices were at record levels for 2009 with the Dow at 9829, the S&P500 at 1071 and the NASDAQ at 2146. The fact that the dollar was at a five-month low on a trade-weighted basis was widely taken as evidence that risk-taking was back in fashion, but if this was indeed the case, some commentators thought it strange that bond yields were at historic lows and gold was over $1000. The explanation appeared to be that capital markets were "alight with liquidity" and thus capable of providing funds for anything investors wanted to buy. Reports that trading in the London markets was dominated by small investors at levels not seen since the peak of the dotcom boom of 1999/2000 appeared to support this view, confirming the fears of analysts who were convinced that markets were discounting a degree of economic recovery that simply was not going to happen. The IMF then added weight to this belief by pointing out that banking crises have a history of leaving 'lasting scars' on economies in the form of losses in capital, employment and productivity resulting in steep drops in output that do not rebound for 'at least seven years'. One such 'scar' appeared to be the reluctance of banks to follow the urging of the authorities to extend loans to the private sector, a situation that had seen a 10% year-on-year drop in US consumer credit outstanding in July, in effect negating the whole aim of the stimulus package.

Liquid fuel

By the final week of September, the dramatic surge that had carried stock markets everywhere up by around 50% seemed to be losing momentum. Initial enthusiasm derived from the Fed's announcement that economic activity had 'picked up' soon faded as investors considered the implications of a joint statement from the Fed and leading central banks to the effect that some of the emergency operations to provide dollar liquidity would be scaled back from October. The news opened up the whole question of the exit strategy from the greatest economic stimulus in history, sparking fears that a premature withdrawal would pull the rug from under the market rally. In the event, the pause in markets proved to be short-lived as investors interpreted reports from the G20 meeting in Pittsburgh as affirming that these unconventional policies would remain in place and interest rate normalisation be delayed until a durable economic recovery was in place. Thus the surprise drop in US durable goods orders in August was taken as a bull point, in that it boosted the prospect of quantitative easing continuing as a policy measure and ensuring a flow of low-cost funding for buyers of equities and bonds. After all, with cash deposits returning a fraction of 1%, yields of over 3% on equities and government bonds appeared irresistible and the past six months had demonstrated very clearly that share prices could go up as well as down. A number of commentators were prepared to see the stock market as in bubble territory but still behaving relatively rationally in that it was supported by cheap credit and government money and was still by no means overvalued historically. As such they thought the rally had further to run and with corporations benefiting too from low borrowing costs, earnings would pick up and be seen to justify the advance in share prices.

More sceptical observers believed that a market that saw bad news as good news in the hope that it would be kept indefinitely on a life support system of doubtful efficacy, was one divorced from reality and investors were playing a dangerous game. Such thoughts took the shine off the rally in the last days of the third quarter but a flurry of M&A activity on Wall Street managed to maintain popular expectations that the final quarter would see more of the same.

A tough act to follow

October is a notoriously difficult month for stock markets and true to form these expectations took a knock on the first day of the new quarter as the latest run of US economic data called into question the prospect of an early recovery. An unexpected turn for the worse in the jobs market, and manufacturing numbers failing to meet estimates, was not the sort of news needed to support the rally. The Dow plunged over 200 points and markets everywhere followed their lead. Over the next two days the FTSE100 shed 143 points to 4988 and Asian markets, already off their best, continued to fall, with Japan's Nikkei Dow sliding below the 10000 mark and the Hong Kong index losing 579 points to 20375. This abrupt reversal in the direction markets had been taking for the past seven months now caused commentators to focus on all the points the bears had made over the same period. Top of the list was the failure of consumers to consume and the likelihood of that state persisting given continuing job losses and sharply diminished credit growth

Such a significant gap in the economy could not be filled for very long by government incentive schemes involving handouts, subsidies and an ultra-accommodative monetary policy. The precipitous drop in US car sales in September from the August peak of the "cash-for-clunkers" programme, seemed to present clear evidence of what was likely to happen when stimuli were withdrawn – as they would have to be to avoid ever-expanding government deficits. If such arguments were convincing enough to give investors cause to pause in their buying spree, they were not enough to do so for more than a couple of days and by the end of the first week in October markets were heading back towards their September peaks. "Excess liquidity" was clearly the name of the game, and in the words of one prominent US commentator, 'If they print enough money, stocks can go anywhere they want to'.

Breaking the circle

The sight of practically every asset class rising again in mid-September had led to markets being described as 'behaving weirdly', but the three-figure gains by the Dow and the FTSE100 in reaction to the news that the Australian central bank had become the first of those in the G20 to raise interest rates and begin gradually lessening the stimulus provided by monetary policy, suggested that "schizophrenic" was another suitable description. After all, if markets had been rising on a tide of cheap and plentiful money and in the expectation that it would continue to flow, then the first sign of a turnaround might have been expected to trigger a fall. Instead, the rate rise was interpreted as evidence that a global recovery was well underway, while still taking into account the fact that with a strong and stable banking sector, and a steady demand for its ample natural resources from China, Australia was far better placed than its fellow G20 members. The widely accepted view was that rates would remain on hold in the US and the other leading economies until recovery was assured and Australia would remain the odd man out for a long time to come.

As for exit strategies, tomorrow was another day. The Bank of England now apparently confirmed this view by keeping rates at record lows at its regular monthly meeting and the European Central Bank did the same, both content to adopt a "wait and see" approach to the effect of such exceptional stimulus measures on their economies. However, the prospect of a nascent recovery accompanied by near-zero interest rates for the foreseeable future proved far too attractive for investors to wait and see, and at the start of the third week in October they drove the FTSE100 and the major Eurozone indices to new highs for the year.

The London market also appeared to draw encouragement from Shadow Chancellor George Osborne's promise of tough action to reduce the budget deficit if the Conservatives won the next election. The prospect of £100 billion of fiscal tightening, split between £80 billion of spending cuts and £20 billion of tax rises, might not have been expected to register as a bull point for the stock market; but, according to the influential Centre for Economic and Business Research (CEBR), its implementation would involve 'an exciting policy mix' of a severe fiscal freeze, offset by interest rates kept at a low level until 2014. Then, just to help things along, the trade deficit for August fell to £2.3 billion from £2.6 billion the month before, thanks to sterling's "helpful" weakness in rebalancing the economy towards export-led growth.

10,000? Yes, we can!

In the US, investors anticipated a bumper third quarter earnings season by driving the Dow and the S&P500 to new peaks for the year, encouraged by a surprise profit from aluminium giant, Alcoa, in place of an expected loss. Earlier expressions of concern about the implications of a falling dollar in the context of the huge twin deficits had become muted as White House rhetoric about maintaining 'a strong dollar' was now replaced with talk about the need to rebalance the world economy away from is dependence on US consumption. A weaker dollar was going to be as helpful to the US economy as weaker sterling was to the UK economy. One commentator forecast that the Dow would top 10,000 by the end of the week and it managed to do so well ahead of schedule on 15th October, boosted by the better than expected results accompanied by an upbeat forecast from **Intel** and a six-fold increase in quarterly profits from **JPMorgan**. To no one's surprise, **Goldman Sachs** revealed better than forecast third quarter earnings, but they were below the high end whispered figure; and then **Bank of America** and **Citigroup** reminded investors that the banking sector still had its problems, as they both reported falls in earnings arising from mounting credit losses. The shares of all three fell back, causing the Dow to slip below the 10,000 mark once more, a decline abetted by a 4% drop in **GE's** shares after an overall revenue fall of some 20% in the third quarter, reflecting weakness in both the consumer and business sectors in which it operated.

However, the brief drop in the Dow and the other indices was a case of *reculer pour mieux sauter* and a renewed surge took them all to new peaks for 2009 on the first day of the following week. Sentiment was boosted by a dramatic jump in the profits from

Apple as a result of booming iPod and Macintosh computer sales, and the shares topped $200 to record a new all-time high. **Texas Instruments'** results also beat expectations and industrial bellwether **Caterpillar** surprised on the upside by stating its belief that the worst of the recession was behind us and raising guidance for the coming year. Results from **Coca-Cola** and **Dupont** were received with less enthusiasm since they clearly demonstrated that rising earnings owed more to cost-cutting than to revenue gains. This more critical interpretation of headline earnings figures was seemingly justified by **Sun Microsystems'** announcement of 3000 job losses in the wake of the merger with **Oracle**, and a flattening out of the hoped for uptrend in housing starts evident in the September figures.

Bears in retreat

The bears had been forced to take a back seat in recent weeks as the world's stock markets continued with the rally that had taken off in March. They were ready to admit that "you can't fight the tape" but still insisted that a cyclical bear market had begun in March 2000 and that two bull runs since then, namely the one beginning in March 2003 and the other in March this year, were no more than rallies within the context of a major downtrend that had still to run its course. They remained convinced that politically-inspired cheap money policies had fuelled both liquidity-driven rallies, but at the same time massive damage had already been done to the financial structures of all the major economies. They agreed with the Bank of International Settlements (BIS) that the current financial crisis was 'unlike any other; and that the transfer of an unsupportable burden of debt from the private sector to the public sector was a political fix that would lead to even greater problems down the line. There were limits to how much debt the public sector could carry without smothering the economy, and overburdened as it now was, the debt would have to be reduced to manageable proportions. The process of doing so would necessarily involve severe cuts in public spending, tax rises and a policy switch from infinite accommodation to finite restraint, which weakened economies would find hard to bear.

Looking for the exit

However, the idea that investors should pay more attention to market action than to economic forecasts gained credence from the reaction to the news that the UK third quarter GDP had fallen by 0.4% instead of rising by a widely expected 0.2%, when the *FT* headline, 'Data dash hopes for end of recession', was greeted by a near 100 point surge by the FTSE100 to 5299. The close turned out to be a more modest 5242 as the gain shrank to 35 points. The conclusion that most commentators were prepared to draw from this apparently contradictory market action was that if the UK economy was lagging in the recovery stakes, monetary policy would remain loose, weaker sterling was giving it a competitive edge over its Eurozone rivals and it would soon catch up.

Meanwhile, UK equities presented a buying opportunity. This view appeared to have a lot going for it until the penultimate day of the month, when the US authorities reported a surprise 3.7% rise in third quarter GDP. The immediate reaction was a near 200 point jump in the Dow, taking it back almost to the 10,000 level. The move was accompanied by headlines in the popular press greeting the exit of the world's largest economy from the recession and pointing out the benefits to the rest of the world that would stem from this event. Thus it was a considerable surprise that on the last day of October, markets should go into sharp reverse. The explanation for this apparently anomalous reaction was precisely the opposite to the one attributed to the rise in the UK market, namely that the end of the recession would hasten the ending of the ultra-accommodative money conditions to which markets had become so accustomed.

This argument appeared to have enough substance to overrule the one put forward by unrepentant bulls that doubts about the sustainability of the recovery would delay the implementation of exit strategies 'for the foreseeable future' (in the words of one prominent analyst). Moreover, such a timescale seemed curiously at odds with the decision of Norway in the same week to raise interest rates, Australia to take them up another notch, and for Japan to announce that it would stop buying corporate bonds and commercial paper at the end of the year.

Banks on the rack

At the beginning of the first week in November, it looked as if the bears had got it right at last. The Dow had fallen back almost 400 points from its peak of 10,119 touched two weeks earlier, and the FTSE100 had dipped below 5000 intraday. Neither index had been helped by its bank constituents. In the US, small and medium business lender **CIT's** efforts to avoid bankruptcy with a $3 billion loan facility had not succeeded and its entry into Chapter 11 meant wipe-out for common and preferred stock holders and the loss of $2.3 billion of TARP funding. Allied with the Fed's rescue of 115 regional banks, the news cast a shadow over the whole banking sector, with **Bank of America** losing over 7% and **Citigroup** 5%.

In London, banks were in the headlines again following the competition rulings of the European Commission forcing the break-up of **Lloyds** and **RBS**. In order to join the government-funded asset protection scheme for some £280 billion of toxic loans, **RBS** was in line to receive another £25.5 billion, raising the public's stake to 84%, in return for disposing of some 300 branches countrywide and its insurance arm comprising Churchill, Direct Line and Green Flag, along with a US commodity trading operation. **Lloyds** managed to avoid joining the costly asset protection scheme by setting up a £13.5 billion rights issue (in which the government would maintain its stake at 43% by contributing £5.8 billion) and raising £7.5 billion in a convertible bond, but still had to dispose of its online business and a swathe of branches, notably those of building society Cheltenham & Gloucester and TSB Scotland, enabling them to revert to a "socially useful" role as institutions serving the local community. Dutch bank **ING** was the subject of similar treatment, but given all the banks' key role in providing credit and their need to raise capital, it was doubtful that changes of such scale would ever have been instituted at national level.

Some commentators expressed the hope that the European Commission would push for a more decisive break-up of the investment banking "casino" element from the retail and commercial "utility" activities of many other banks, a measure that bankers were already lobbying strenuously to avoid. Still, the rulings made it clear that banking in the Eurozone would never be the same again, and share prices fell across the sector, in spite of the fact that "the foxes were still in charge of the chicken coop".

Everyone a winner

But such worries were of no concern to investors, who could fairly argue on the basis of recent performance that equities presented a unique "win, win" buying opportunity. After all, if the recovery was really on track, then corporate profits would rise, albeit from a low base, and share prices would go up. If the recovery faltered, then government-sponsored stimuli would remain in place and a continuing flow of easy money would find its way into equities. This thesis appeared to be fully validated in the first seven days of November, as the FTSE100 topped 5200 again in response to another £25 billion dose of quantitative easing, and the Dow regained 10,000 plus territory once more on the news that the unemployment rate had jumped from 9.8% to 10.2% in October.

The latest G20 gathering promptly pledged continuing support for fragile economies and markets extended their gains with sentiment further boosted by M&A activity on the US domestic front and **Kraft** returning with a hostile bid for **Cadbury**. Confidence in the world automobile industry was also lifted by a surprise $1 billion profit in the third quarter from **Ford**, and by **GM** pulling out of the deal to sell Opel/Vauxhall. Warren Buffett now provided the bulls yet more encouragement by making what he called an 'all-in wager on the economic future of the US' by buying up the rest of the **Burlington Northern Santa Fe** railroad to take his holding up to 100%.

Time runs...

By now the bears were down but certainly not out, as they continued to question the wisdom of trying to deal with a crisis arising out of an overabundance of cheap money by flooding the system with even more and even cheaper money. The result, they insisted, was the creation of yet another asset bubble, as investors chased anything and everything if it would give them a yield. A dollar weakened by the prospect of near-zero interest rates until well into 2010 provided the perfect vehicle for an expanding "carry trade" and one with a de facto government guarantee to limit the risk-taking involved.

Such a situation looked too good to be true and according to the bears, that's exactly what it was – you could not print your way to prosperity. The basis of their argument was that huge government deficits resulting from stimulus measures presented the same problems at the national level as such debts would at a corporate or personal level, namely how to finance them. If the stimulus worked and economies revived, rising profits would lead to rising taxes and reducing deficits would facilitate government bond sales. On the other hand, if worries about the prospect of tax rises caused consumers to restrain their spending, producers would curtail their investment plans and deficits would continue to rise, making funding even more difficult. So far central banks had used much of the money created to buy their own government's bonds – in effect funding the deficit in-house – but such a process could not continue indefinitely. At some point governments would have to stand on their own two feet, and delay in reaching this objective could be seen by markets as a sign that the greatest stimulus measures in financial history were on course to fail.

For the moment, the jury was still out but the bears were convinced that asset buyers had become too addicted to cheap money and would soon have problems with both likely outcomes. A strong V-shaped recovery would see a return to a "normal" interest rate regime, prompting them to run for cover, while a weak flatline recovery that could no longer be reinvigorated by further stimulus would also remove support for asset prices, leaving them facing losses.

Yellow brick road

But, as usual, investors cared little for such worries, and by mid-November, with the FTSE100 at 5382, the Dow at 10,406 and the S&P500 at 1109, the road to hell envisaged by the Czech president at the G20 meeting in March appeared to be morphing into the yellow brick road. However, given that gold was the ultimate safe haven investment, its parallel rise seemed paradoxical, suggesting that no one really knew where the road was going and it was perhaps too soon to dismiss the concerns of the Czech president. Falling bond yields also indicated that a considerable section of the investment community was not prepared to make the same 'all-in-wager' on the equity market as Warren Buffett had effectively proclaimed at the time of his purchase of Burlington Northern.

Nevertheless, equity buyers everywhere were seemingly content to keep right on to the end of the road, emboldened by further statements from the Fed about interest rates remaining low for 'an extended period', allied with the raising of growth prospects for 2010 as the US economy recovered 'at a gradual pace'. Economic and corporate news continued to be mixed, but the odd intraday scare occasioned by a not-so-good news item was calmed by the end of the day in the absence of any real selling pressure, and investors seemed to have every reason to look forward to the traditional December advance.

Who pays the piper?

Common sense and history tell us that there is never a good day to release bad news. Thus the shock request from Dubai's government-owned holding company, Dubai World, for a debt repayment standstill timed over Thanksgiving when Wall Street was closed and at the start of the four-day festival of Eid when markets in the Gulf were also closed, failed to prevent the steepest sell-offs around the world, since March. The event raised the prospect of sovereign debt defaults not only in emerging market countries with big deficits but among many others in the developed world similarly over-indebted as a result of bailing out the private sector with largesse from the public purse. Dubai's announcement was given more point by coming just two days after the long delayed revelation from the Bank of England that it had covertly lent £62 billion to **RBS** and **HBOS** at the height of the financial crisis in October 2008 to prevent their imminent collapse.

The markets concluded that, in solving one problem, central banks had created another, by elevating the threat of default in the corporate sector to a national level; causing the cost of insuring against sovereign default in emerging nations to rise steeply, and at the same time triggering a sharp increase in risk aversion across the board. Equities, commodities and emerging market currencies were sold off as investors bought into so-called safe haven assets, government bonds, the dollar and the Japanese yen.

Wall Street was closed but the FTSE plunged 170 points to 5194 and the Eurofirst 300 suffered its biggest fall in seven months, losing 33 points to 988. Asian markets were also badly hit. In Hong Kong, the index dived over 1000 points to 21134 and the Shanghai Composite lost 175 to 3096, while in Japan, the Nikkei Dow recorded its fifth successive weekly fall, losing 301 to 9081. Worries over exposure to the Dubai fallout made sure that banks headed the list of fallers, but popular expectations that oil-rich Abu Dhabi would stand by its prodigal neighbour trimmed losses in markets everywhere.

Bond yields rise

The failure of even the Dubai government to stand by its own enterprise and the reluctance of Abu Dhabi to offer unequivocal support led to continuing sharp losses in the Gulf markets, but those in the rest of the world rebounded with investors apparently convinced that all we had seen was "a little local difficulty" with no chance of derailing the global recovery. The December rally appeared to be back on track and, by the end of the second week, the Dow had topped 10500 again, the FTSE100 had crossed the 5300 level once more, and most Asian and other emerging markets were hitting new highs for the year, all encouraged by a surprise fall in the US unemployment rate from 10.2% to 10%. Sentiment on Wall Street received a further boost as banks queued up to repay their TARP loans to the government; $45 billion from **Bank of America**, $20 billion from **Citigroup**, and $25 billion from **Well Fargo**.

However, the Dubai crisis had focused investors' attention on the problems that could stem from escalating government deficits and their concerns were highlighted only days later when ratings agency Fitch downgraded Greece's credit status to triple-B with a 'negative' outlook, and Standard & Poor's revised its outlook on Spain from 'stable' to 'negative'. Related bond yields rose sharply but concerns were not confined to the fiscally weaker countries in the European Union and those in the US and the UK also recorded significant rises.

Twenty years on

The UK gilt market's reaction to the Chancellor's pre-budget report pointed out very clearly the difficulties that would arise if governments failed to spell out how they planned to reduce their yawning budget deficits. Promises of higher taxes on the rich, accompanied by assurances of maintained spending on health and education with no detail of targeted cuts elsewhere, saw a jump in the 10-year gilt yield from 3.66% to 3.86%. By contrast, the Irish budget unveiled on the same day, which was uncompromisingly tough, slashing welfare expenditure and public sector pay, was well received by the country's gilt market and yields actually fell slightly.

The lesson was that since sovereign states were now the leveraged institutions in need of rescue, self-help was the only answer, and political expediency had to take a back seat. Policy drift was no longer a viable option, but the UK example showed that at least one government was unwilling to come up with a radical deficit reduction strategy when an election was in the offing, and the prospect arose of situations developing on the pattern of that which followed the bursting of the Japanese bubble twenty years ago.

Thus, as gaping holes in corporate balance sheets took years to fill, large and persistent government borrowing would support the economy, supplementing a dominant and state-cosseted but still dysfunctional banking system failing to fulfil its primary role of credit provision. The fact that Japan remained a faltering low-growth economy still looking for government stimulus to keep it going did not suggest a happy outcome for the policies endorsed by the G20 nations in 2009, nor indeed for their stock markets if the course of Japan's Nikkei Dow from its peak in December 1989 was anything to go by.

Banking on recovery

Despite the parading of such misgivings by many serious commentators, investors appeared to have bought into the global recovery story and were determined not to let anyone or anything spoil their festive mood. The Bank of England tried to do so with a timely reminder in its latest Financial Stability Report that the banks remained vulnerable to a reversal in their so-recently improved fortunes. After all, The Bank insisted, their first half profits surge had been underpinned by the government's sustained support for the banking system and unprecedented monetary policy measures, and priority had to be given to the strengthening of balance sheets 'opportunistically while profits are buoyant' instead of paying out dividends and bonuses. Bank shares took the news badly, dragging the FTSE100 down 102 points to 5217. No help was forthcoming from Wall Street, where banks were also in the firing line when Citigroup looked like having problems in repaying its $20 billion TARP loan through a stock offering after investors jibbed at the $3.25 subscription price. The Dow dived 132 points to 10,308 while the S&P500 lost 13 to 1096.

In the event, this despondent mood proved short-lived and at the beginning of Christmas week markets were back on a roll. Sovereign debt default fears were allayed to some extent by Abu Dhabi stepping in with a $10 billion loan for Dubai World and by confident statements in European circles that Greece would find support from Germany and not be allowed to endanger Eurozone solidarity. **Citigroup** managed to get enough stock away at a lower price and repaid the $20 billion bailout money, and on the same day **Wells Fargo** completed its $25 billion payback on schedule.

Economic data on both sides of the Atlantic remained mixed and disappointing on balance, but markets everywhere still ended the year at close to new highs, setting the seal on one of the best years on record. However, this was also the tenth anniversary of the market peaks of 1999, and the dramatic gains of 2009 no longer looked so impressive over a 10-year timescale. Thus the FTSE100's 22% rebound in 2009 had to be viewed in the context of a 22% fall over the decade. Similarly, the S&P 500's 23.4% advance had to be qualified by a decline of 24% since 1999, and the NASDAQ Composite's 44% gain still left it barely half its 2000 high point.

Eastern promise

By contrast, emerging markets had proved themselves to be not only the star performers of 2009 but also of the decade. China's Shanghai Composite was up 80% on the year and 140% over the decade, while India's BSE Sensex was up 81% and 250% over the same periods. Brazil's BOVESPA topped both with gains of 80% and 300%, and Russia's Micex had surged eightfold since 1999, all their economies benefiting from China's insatiable demand for commodities, especially oil and metals, to pursue its massive programme of industrialisation. This striking superiority in performance of developing over developed markets clearly influenced the views of market forecasters, who were practically unanimous in looking for more of the same in the year ahead. They saw a big question mark hanging over the latter's exit strategy from the greatest financial stimulus in history and its likely impact on a still fragile recovery process, while among the BRICs growth appeared assured.

Forecasts for the FTSE100 were remarkably muted and a *Sunday Times* poll of "expert" opinion came up with an average of 5187, with a minority of bears looking for a revisit of the March lows, influenced by the absence of a convincing deficit reduction strategy and the possibility of an indecisive election outcome leading to a run on the pound, rising bond yields and the loss of the country's triple-A rating. The other end of the spectrum was favoured by analysts mesmerised by near-zero interest rates and who continued to see equities as the only game in town. The FTSE250 substantially outperformed the FTSE100, rising by 35% on the year, largely owing to the sharp recovery of its many cyclical constituents, which at the beginning of the year had been priced at virtually break-up valuations. However, forecasters were united in agreeing that 2010 would be the year when the multinational big-cap defensives like pharmaceuticals, tobaccos, beverages and utilities would come into their own. They also pointed out that the return of the commodities boom meant that the high proportion of miners in the index would provide a further boost.

At the same time, more than one commentator noted that rising commodity prices might be good for the FTSE100 but were not good for the UK economy, and also reflected a worrying dependence on the fortunes of China, which as the world's number three economy was being relied upon to provide the impetus for global recovery. Their concern was that China's double-digit growth had been fuelled by huge increases in bank lending, inflationary pressures were already evident, and that the authorities were already hinting at lending curbs. If China's boom proved unsustainable, then the outlook for 2010 could take a dramatic turn for the worse. Some writers were also tempted to see in China today an uncomfortable parallel with Japan when it was riding high in the late eighties, with booming share and property prices making it the wonder of the age. Today Japan remains the odd man out in Asian markets, down 44% over the decade, but its 19% gain in 2009 had revived the spirits of its many fans who had grown old waiting for a turnaround and were now encouraged to believe that their ship would come in one fine day in 2010. But whatever would happen, it was unlikely that a popular trick question in the City in the late 1980s will ever make the rounds again. Which are the three biggest stock markets in the world? Everyone got the first two right with New York and Tokyo but were wrong when they named London as the third. The answer was Osaka, Japan's second city. Sic transit...

Gold still had its devoted band of supporters even after a decade-long 280% rise and one of 25% over the year. Investment demand had now overtaken industrial and jewellery demand as the principle driver of the price and while less reliable given its speculative element, it could well continue while government printing presses were running and effectively debasing all paper currencies.

Geopolitical upsets seemed to have had little impact on stock markets in 2009, but they were not going away and the potential for more serious effects clearly exists. Given the instability in the Middle East, the world's principal oil-producing region, resulting from the invasion and occupation of Afghanistan and Iraq, the near disintegration of nuclear-armed Pakistan, and internal strife in Iran, there was every prospect of such factors having a greater impact in the year ahead.

Leads and Lags

The bears had been taken completely by surprise by the blistering market rally that had begun in March, but while still convinced that it would end in tears, some of them were prepared to admit that at such times it was demonstrably more important to listen to what the market was saying about itself then to what others were saying about the market. And what the market had been saying since March was that things were not necessarily going to turn out as badly as the bears believed. There were leads and lags in the market as well as in the economy and even if the bears turn out to be right in the end, the time frame up to that by no means certain outcome could be extensive. Thus if investing for the long term is no longer such a good idea, as suggested by the performance of the indices over the past decade, then a high performance, short-term rally was not one to be missed. Changing times required changing strategies. We were all traders now.

APPENDIX A
Graphs of key financial indices

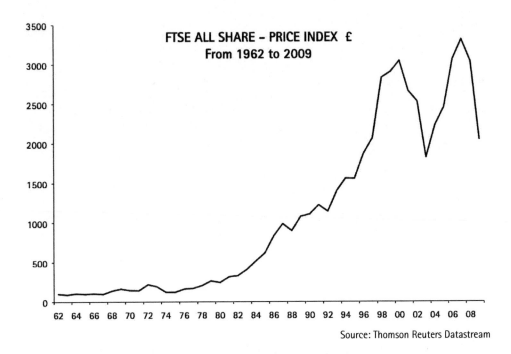

FTSE ALL SHARE – PRICE INDEX £
From 1962 to 2009

Source: Thomson Reuters Datastream

S&P 500 COMPOSITE – PRICEINDEX U$
From 1963 to 2009

Source: Thomson Reuters Datastream

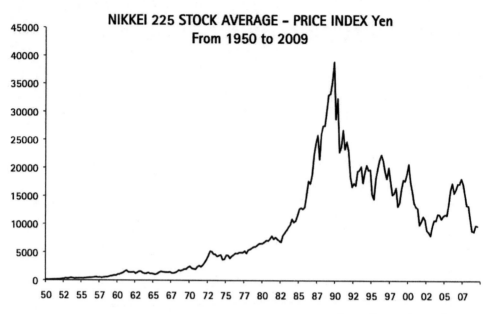

NIKKEI 225 STOCK AVERAGE – PRICE INDEX Yen
From 1950 to 2009

Source: Thomson Reuters Datastream

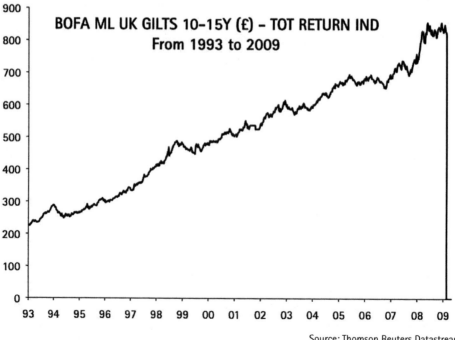

BOFA ML UK GILTS 10–15Y (£) – TOT RETURN IND
From 1993 to 2009

Source: Thomson Reuters Datastream

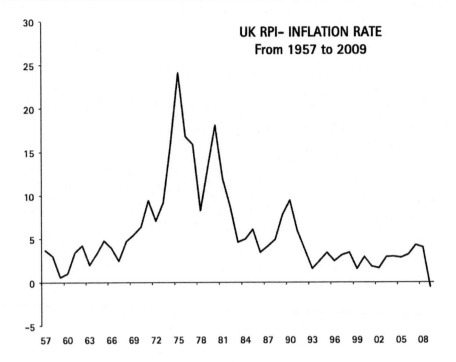

Source: Thomson Reuters Datastream

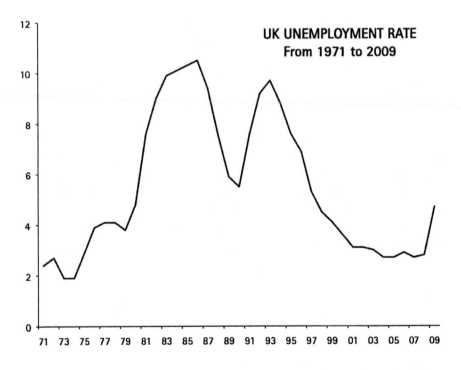

Source: Thomson Reuters Datastream

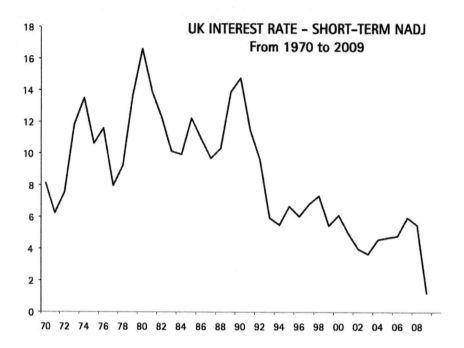

Source: Thomson Reuters Datastream

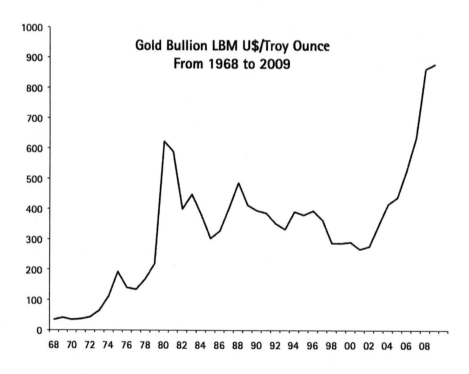

Source: Thomson Reuters Datastream

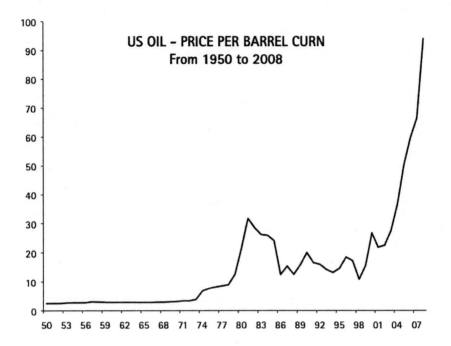

Source: Thomson Reuters Datastream

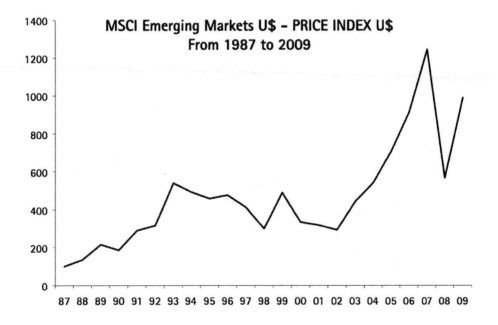

Source: Thomson Reuters Datastream

APPENDIX B
Governments since 1945

Government	Prime Ministers	Chancellors of the Exchequer
LABOUR		
July 1945 – March 1950	Clement Atlee	Hugh Dalton
March 1950 – October 1951		Sir Stafford Cripps
		Hugh Gaitskell
CONSERVATIVE		
October 1951 – April 1955	Sir Winston Churchill	R. A. Butler
April 1955 – January 1957	Sir Anthony Eden	Harold Macmillan
January 1957 – October 1964	Harold Macmillan	Peter Thorneycroft
	Lord Alec Douglas-Home	D. Heathcote-Amory
		Selwyn Lloyd
		Reginald Maudling
LABOUR		
October 1964 – March 1966	Harold Wilson	Jim Callaghan
March 1966 – June 1970		Roy Jenkins
CONSERVATIVE		
June 1970 – February 1974	Edward Heath	Iain Macleod
		Anthony Barber
LABOUR		
February 1974 – May 1979	Harold Wilson	Denis Healey
	Jim Callaghan	
CONSERVATIVE		
May 1979 – June 1983	Margaret Thatcher	Sir Geoffrey Howe
June 1983 – June 1987	John Major	Nigel Lawson
June 1987 – April 1993		John Major
April 1992 – May 1997		Kenneth Clarke
NEW LABOUR		
May 1997 – June 2007	Tony Blair	Gordon Brown
June 2007 – May 2010	Gordon Brown	Alistair Darling
CONSERVATIVE/LIBERAL DEMOCRAT COALITION		
May 2010 –	David Cameron	George Osborne

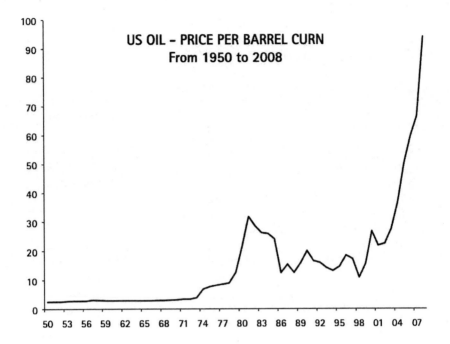

US OIL – PRICE PER BARREL CURN
From 1950 to 2008

Source: Thomson Reuters Datastream

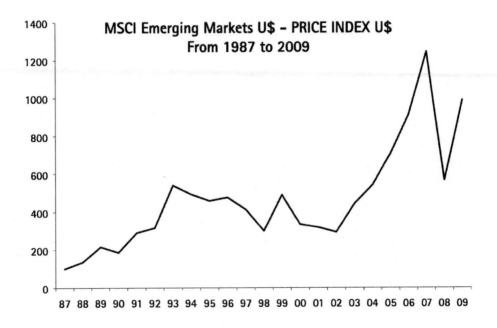

MSCI Emerging Markets U$ – PRICE INDEX U$
From 1987 to 2009

Source: Thomson Reuters Datastream

APPENDIX B
Governments since 1945

Government	Prime Ministers	Chancellors of the Exchequer
LABOUR		
July 1945 – March 1950	Clement Atlee	Hugh Dalton
March 1950 – October 1951		Sir Stafford Cripps
		Hugh Gaitskell
CONSERVATIVE		
October 1951 – April 1955	Sir Winston Churchill	R. A. Butler
April 1955 – January 1957	Sir Anthony Eden	Harold Macmillan
January 1957 – October 1964	Harold Macmillan	Peter Thorneycroft
	Lord Alec Douglas-Home	D. Heathcote-Amory
		Selwyn Lloyd
		Reginald Maudling
LABOUR		
October 1964 – March 1966	Harold Wilson	Jim Callaghan
March 1966 – June 1970		Roy Jenkins
CONSERVATIVE		
June 1970 – February 1974	Edward Heath	Iain Macleod
		Anthony Barber
LABOUR		
February 1974 – May 1979	Harold Wilson	Denis Healey
	Jim Callaghan	
CONSERVATIVE		
May 1979 – June 1983	Margaret Thatcher	Sir Geoffrey Howe
June 1983 – June 1987	John Major	Nigel Lawson
June 1987 – April 1993		John Major
April 1992 – May 1997		Kenneth Clarke
NEW LABOUR		
May 1997 – June 2007	Tony Blair	Gordon Brown
June 2007 – May 2010	Gordon Brown	Alistair Darling
CONSERVATIVE/LIBERAL DEMOCRAT COALITION		
May 2010 –	David Cameron	George Osborne

INDEX